INTRODUCTION TO **SECURITY OF CYBER-PHYSICAL SYSTEMS**

INTRODUCTION TO **SECURITY OF CYBER-PHYSICAL SYSTEMS**

JEEVA JOSE
VIJO MATHEW

KHANNA BOOK PUBLISHING CO. (P) LTD.
PUBLISHER OF ENGINEERING AND COMPUTER BOOKS
4C/4344, Ansari Road, Darya Ganj, New Delhi-110002
Phone : 011-23244447-48 Mobile: +91-99109 09320
E-mail : contact@khannabooks.com; Website : www.khannabooks.com

Dear Readers,

To prevent the piracy, this book is secured with HIGH SECURITY HOLOGRAM on the front title cover. In case you don't find the hologram on the front cover title, please write us to at contact@khannabooks.com or whatsapp us at +91-99109 09320 and avail special gift voucher for yourself.

Specimen of Hologram on front Cover title:

Moreover, there is a SPECIAL DISCOUNT COUPON for you with EVERY HOLOGRAM.

How to avail this SPECIAL DISCOUNT:

Step 1: Scratch the hologram

Step 2: Under the scratch area, your "coupon code" is available

Step 3: Logon to www.khannabooks.com

Step 4: Use your "coupon code" in the shopping cart and get your copy at a special discount

Step 5: Enjoy your reading!

Price : ₹ 299.00

ISBN: 978-93-5538-058-6

INTRODUCTION TO SECURITY OF CYBER-PHYSICAL SYSTEMS

by Jeeva Jose, Vijo Mathew

First Edition: 2022

Published by:

Khanna Book Publishing Co. (P) Ltd.

Visit us at: **www.khannabooks.com**

Write us at: **contact@khannabooks.com**

CIN: U22110DL1998PTC095547

To view complete list of books, Please scan the QR Code:

Printed in India.

PREFACE

A cyber-physical system or intelligent system is a computer system in which a mechanism is controlled or monitored by computer-based algorithms. Cyber-physical systems are normally connected to each other and in turn connected to the virtual world of global digital networks. They are created at the intersection of networks, cybernetic computing and physical processes. Examples of cyber physical system include smart grid, autonomous automobile systems, medical monitoring, industrial control systems, robotics systems, and automatic pilot avionics. Internet of Things is about connecting objects and machines to the internet and eventually to each other; while cyber physical systems are integration of computation, networking and physical process.

The security is a common factor in each layer of cyber-physical system. To understand the security of cyber-physical systems, the security and privacy in information systems as well as its technologies and tools need to be studied in general. The progression of this book is arranged to meet this requirement and to align with AICTE syllabus of IoT. The below figure will illustrate this relationship.

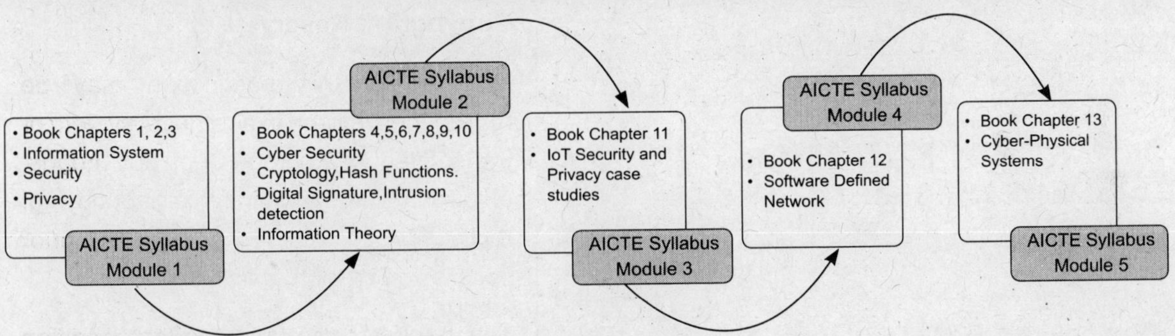

The cyber-physical systems may or may not be connected to internet. After going through this book, the student will have a good knowledge to apply the basics and security issues related to cyber-physical systems.

–Authors

CONTENTS

CHAPTER 1

Information System

CONTENTS

1.1 INTRODUCTION

In this chapter, we are discussing on the basic concept of information system and its components.

1.2 INFORMATION SYSTEM

Information System (IS) refers to a collection of many pieces of equipment involved in the collection, processing, storage, and dissemination of information. Hardware, software, computer network connections, information, system users, are all part of an IS. Information systems are the combination of people, information technology and business processes to accomplish a business objective. Personal computers, smartphones, databases, and networks are few examples of information systems components.

Information system can be used for a broad variety of purposes, from managing supply chains to interacting with digital marketplaces. Enterprises and corporations use information systems to interact with their suppliers and customer base, perform their operations, manage their organization, and carry out their marketing campaigns. Individuals also rely on information systems to interact with peers and friends through social networks, carrying out everyday activities such as banking and shopping, or simply looking for knowledge and information.

1.3 INFORMATION SYSTEM TRIANGLE

Every information system (IS) has people, processes, and information technology. In fact, many IS professionals add most of their value working with people and processes. They manage the programmers but typically avoid programming themselves. We can represent an information system as a triangle with people, processes, and information technology on the three vertices. This is referred as information systems triangle.

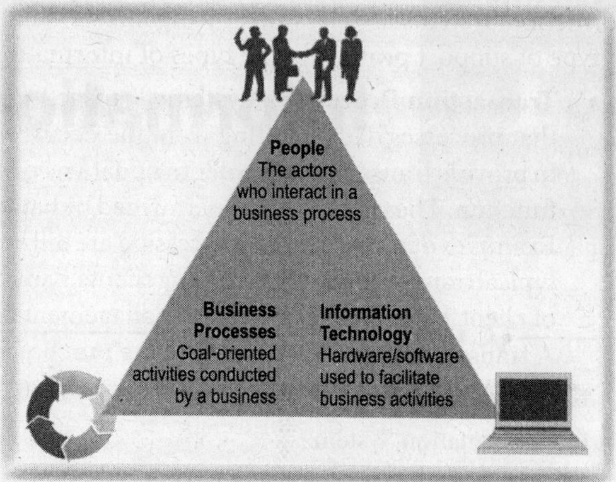

Figure. 1.1: Information System Triangle

The three parts of the information systems triangle must interact smoothly each other to realize business objectives. The job of the information system professional is to ensure that a balance is maintained and enhanced for the good of all the actors and the business as a whole. An information system is a combination of hardware, software as well as telecommunication networks that people build to collect, create and distribute useful data. Information system defines the flow of information within the system. The objective of an information system is to provide appropriate information to the user. This is attained by gathering the data, processing of the data and communication of the information to the user of the system.

1.4 DIMENSIONS OF INFORMATION SYSTEM

The information system in the earlier days were based on paper reports, telephonic information, personnel reporting to which slowly fax and e-mail got added. Basically, this was based on manual operations. Presently, information systems are based on computer systems like ERP, accounting packages, computer control systems, SCADA etc. This has reduced the human dependency and manual errors. This increased speed and reliability. Now the information system is moving to IoT. This system takes the data through embedded sensors, process and analyze the data in intelligent systems and provide required inputs for actions to actuators. The human intervention is required only for the critical decisions and actions.

The information system can be looked from organizational, management and technology dimensions. IoT comes into picture when looking from technological dimensions.

- **Organizational dimension:** Information system are part of organization. Information system will have the standard operating procedure and culture of an organization embedded within them. This involves functional specialties, business processes, culture and political interest groups.
- **Management dimension:** Managers perceive business challenges in the environment. Information systems supply tools and information needed by the managers to allocate, coordinate and monitor their work, make decision, create new products and services and make long range strategic decision.
- **Technology dimension:** Management uses technology to carry out their functions. It consists of computer hardware, software, data management technology, networking and telecom technology. It is one of the many tools managers use to cope with the change.

1.5 TYPES OF INFORMATION SYSTEM

Information Systems are classified by organizational levels, mode of data, processing, system objectives and type of support provided. The types of information systems are

- **Transaction Processing System:** Transaction Processing System (TPS) are information system that processes data resulting from the occurrences of business transactions. Their objectives are to provide transaction in order to update records and generate reports i.e to perform store keeping function. The transaction is performed by batching processing and online transaction processing. Examples of transactional processing are bill system, payroll system, stock control system etc. The typical transactions include billing clients, bank deposits, new hire data, inventory counts, or a record of client-customer relationship management data.

  A transaction encompasses all of the purchases, sales and services, along with any daily business transactions or activities required to operate a company. Quantities and the types of transactions performed vary, depending on the industry and size/scope of the company. A transaction processing system ensures that all of the contractual, transactional, and customer relationship data is stored in a safe location and accessible to everyone who needs it. It also assists in the processing of sales order entries, payroll, shipping, sales management, or other routine transactions needed to maintain operations. By utilizing, transactional processing system, organizations can have a high level of reliability and accuracy in their user/customer data while minimizing the potential for human error.

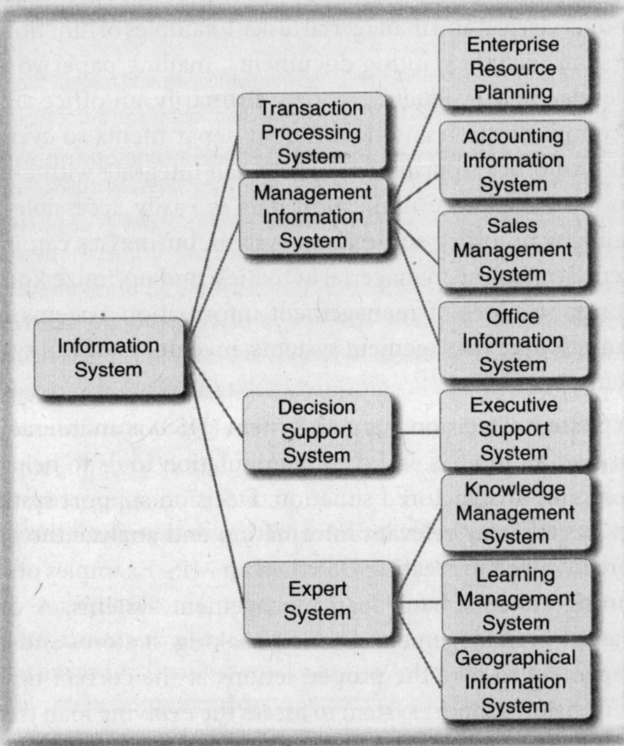

Figure 1.2: Types of Information Systems

- **Management Information System:** A Management Information System (MIS) uses various transaction data from a transactional processing system to help middle management optimize planning and decision-making. It retrieves transaction processing system (TPS) information, aggregates it, and generates reports to help those at the management level know important details of a situation. Summaries and comparisons are utilized to allow senior managers to optimize the decision-making process to achieve better results. Most of the report formats encompass summaries of annual sales data, performance data, or historical records. This provides a secure and systemized way for managers to meet their targets and oversee business units. Many different types of report are produced in MIS. Some of the reports are a summary report, on-demand report, ad-hoc reports and an exception report. Examples of management information system are:
    - **Enterprise Resource Planning:** Enterprise Resource Planning (ERP) provides organization-wide integration of important business activities, handles the allocation of resources to optimize efficiency.
    - **Accounting Information System:** This system manages all of the accounting information in an organization, including payroll to streamline human resource tasks.
    - **Sales Management System:** An information system that manages and monitors all of the sales and marketing data in an organization to streamline each step of the sales process.
    - **Office Information System:** This system is a network of various tools, technologies, and people required to conduct clerical and managerial tasks. Examples of functions performed by an office information system include printing documents, mailing paperwork, mailing, maintaining a company calendar, and producing reports. Primarily, an office automation system assists in enhancing communication among different departments so everyone can collaborate to complete a task. An office information system can integrate with e-mail or word processing applications to ensure all communication data is easily accessible and in one centralized location. By utilizing an office automation system, businesses can improve communication between workers, streamline managerial activities, and optimize knowledge management.

      Some other common types of management information systems include process control systems, human resource management systems, inventory control systems, and management reporting systems.

- **Decision Support System:** Decision Support System (DSS) is an interactive information system that provides information, models and data manipulation tools to help in making the decision in a semi-structured and unstructured situation. Decision support system comprises tools and techniques to help in gathering relevant information and analyze the options and alternatives, the end user is more involved in creating DSS than an MIS. Examples of decision support system are financial planning systems, bank loan management systems. A decision support system processes data to assist in management decision-making. It stores and gathers the information required for management to take the proper actions at the correct time. For example, a bank manager can use a decision support system to assess the evolving loan trends to determine which yearly loan targets to meet. Decision models are programmed into the information system to analyze and summarize large quantities of information and put it into a visual that makes it understandable. As a decision support system is interactive, management can easily add or delete data and ask important questions. This provides the evidence required for mid-management to make the right choices that will ensure that the company meets its targets.

- **Executive Support System:** Executive support is a decision support system used by executive leaders and owners to optimize decision-making. An expert system helps enterprise leaders find answers to non-routine questions so they can make choices that improve the company's outlook and performance. Unlike a decision support system, an executive support system provides better telecommunication functionality and a bigger computing functionality. Graphics software is integrated within an executive support system to display data about tax regulations, new competitive startups, internal compliance issues, and other relevant executive information. This allows leaders to track internal performance, monitor the competition, and pinpoint growth opportunities.

- **Expert System:** Expert systems include expertise in order to aid managers in diagnosing problems or in problem-solving. These systems are based on the principles of artificial intelligence research. Experts systems is a knowledge-based information system. Knowledge base and software modules are the components of an expert system. These modules perform inference on the knowledge and offer answers to a user's question

- **Knowledge Management System:** A knowledge management system stores and extracts information to help users enhance their knowledge and optimize collaboration efforts to complete tasks. Examples of documents found in a knowledge management system include employee training materials, company policies, and procedures, or answers to customer questions. This system is used by employees, customers, management, and other various stakeholders involved with the organization. It ensures that technical abilities are integrated throughout the company while providing visuals to help employees make sense of the data they see. This information system also provides intuitive access to external information required by workers who need outside knowledge to complete their roles. For example, a knowledge management system may hold competitor data that helps a sales team member to optimize his/her strategy when pitching to a customer. As the system shares expertise and provides answers to essential questions, using one can improve communication among team members and assist everyone in meeting performance goals.

- **Learning Management System:** A learning management system is a software application for the administration, documentation, tracking, reporting, automation and delivery of educational courses, training programs, or learning and development programs. The learning management system concept emerged directly from e-learning.

- **Geographical Information System:** Geographical Information System (GIS) is an information system that captures, stores, analyzes, manages and presents data linked to geography. It is a combination of cartography, statistics and database technologies and can be integrated into any enterprise applications. GIS is used in geography, remote sensing, archaeology land surveying, urban planning and many more.

1.6 COMPONENTS OF INFORMATION SYSTEM

The components of an Information System from technology dimension are shown in figure

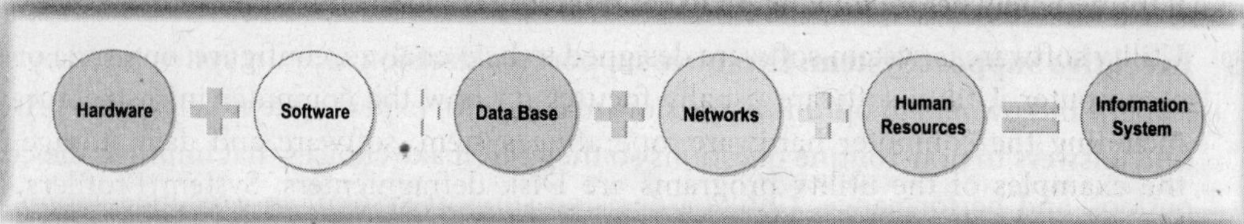

Figure 1.3: Information System Components

1.6.1 Information System Hardware

Information system hardware is the physical equipment used for input, output, processing and communication. This includes the computers, media devices, peripherals, smart phones, modems, antennas, cables, etc. The type of hardware to use depends on the type and size of the organization.

1.6.2 Information System Software

These are programs used to control and coordinate the hardware components. It is also used for analyzing and processing of the data. The information system software is classified into three types.

- **System software:** This is the software designed to provide a platform for other software. This can be operating system, language processor or utility software.
  - An operating system is a software which performs all the basic tasks like file management, memory management, process management, handling input and output, and controlling peripheral devices such as disk drives and printers. Examples of operating software are macOS, Linux, Android and Microsoft Windows.
  - The language processor is a special translator system used to turn a program written in a high-level language, which we call "source code", into machine code, which we call "object program" or "object code". Compiler, Assembler and Interpreter are the examples of language processor. The language processor that reads the complete source program written in high level language as a whole in one go and translates it into an equivalent program in machine language is called as a Compiler. The Assembler is used to translate the program written in Assembly language into machine code. The source program is a input of assembler that contains assembly language instructions. The output generated by assembler is the

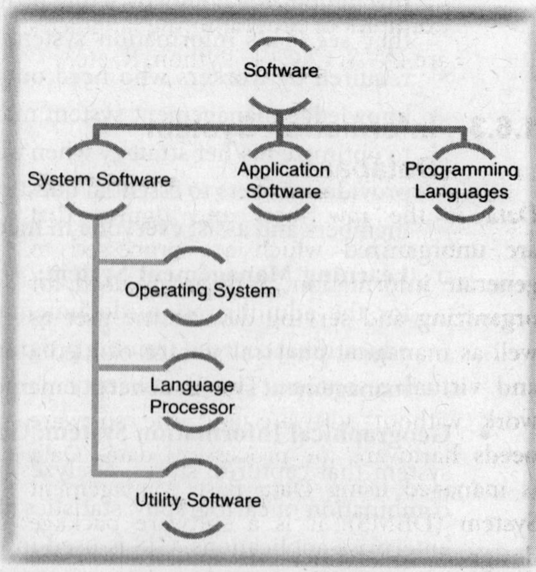

Figure 1.4: Types of Softwares

object code or machine code understandable by the computer. The translation of single statement of source program into machine code is done by language processor and executes it immediately before moving on to the next line is called an interpreter.

- Utility software is system software designed to help analyze, configure, optimize or maintain a computer. Utility software usually focuses on how the computer infrastructure operates including the computer hardware, operating system, software and data storage. Some of the examples of the utility programs are Disk defragmenters, System Profilers, Network Managers, Application Launchers, Antivirus software, Backup software, Disk repair software, Disk Cleaners, Registry Cleaners, Disk Space analyser, file manager, File Compression and Data Security.

- **Applications software:** This is capable of dealing with user inputs and helps the user to complete the task. It is also called end-user programs or only an app. It resides above system software. First user deal with system software after that he/she deals with application software. The end user uses applications software for a specific purpose. It programmed for simple as well as complex tasks. It can either be installed or access online. It can be a single program or a group of small programs that is referred as an application suite. The application software includes word processors, graphics software, database software, spreadsheet software, presentation software, web browsers, enterprise software, CAD/CAM software, email software etc.
- **Programming Languages:** This is the third category of computer software which is used by the programmers to write their programs, scripts, and instructions which can be executed by a computer. The other name of the programming language is computer language. The programming language can be considered as a brick which can be used to construct computer programs and operating system. The examples of programming languages are JAVA, C, C++, Python, R, etc.

1.6.3 Information System Database

Data is the raw facts and figures that are unorganized which are processed to generate information. Software is used for organizing and serving data to the user as well as managing physical storage of media and virtual resources. The hardware can't work without software and the software needs hardware for processing data. Data is managed using Data Base Management System (DBMS). It is a software package designed to define, manipulate, retrieve and manage data in a database. A DBMS

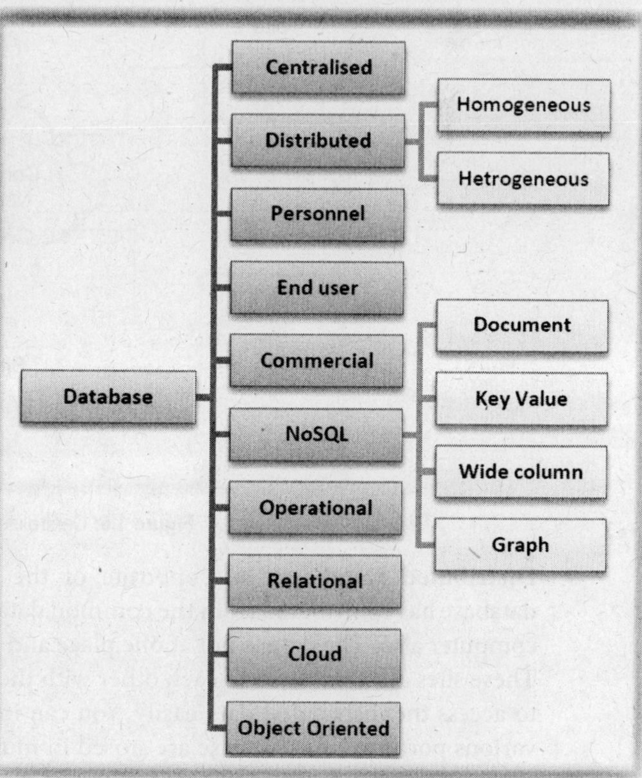

Figure 1.5: Classification of Database

generally manipulates the data itself, the data format, field names, record structure and file structure. It also defines rules to validate and manipulate this data. Database software is used for efficient access of required data, and to manage knowledge bases.

Depending upon the usage requirements and the types of databases that are available in the market, the database is categorized as centralized database, distributed database, personal database, end-user database, commercial database, NoSQL database, operational database, relational database, cloud database, object-oriented database, graph database.

Let us explain each type of database

- **Centralised Database:** A centralized database is a database that is located, stored, and maintained in a single location. This location is most often a central computer or database system like a PC, server or a mainframe computer. The data is stored at a centralized location and the users from different locations can access this data. This type of database contains application procedures that help the users to access the data even from a remote location. Various kinds of authentication procedures are applied for the verification and validation of end users. A registration number is provided by the application procedures which keeps a track and record data usage.

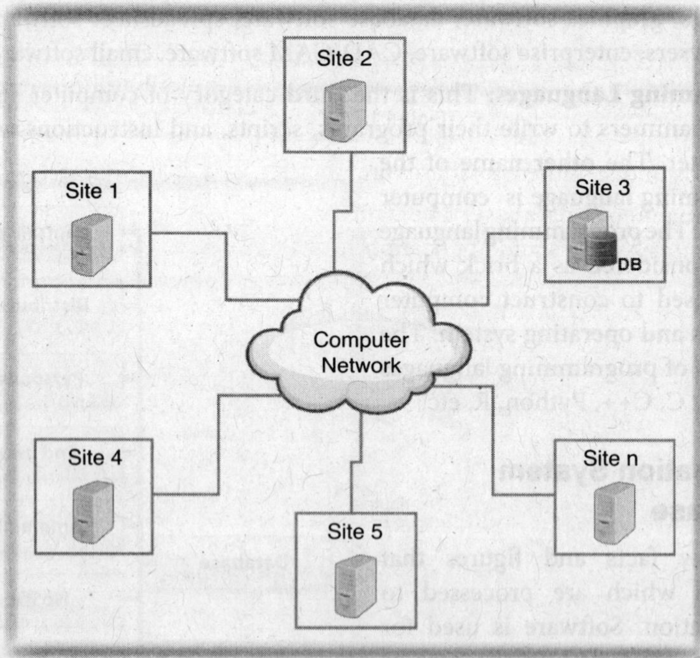

Figure 1.6: Centralized Database

- **Distributed Database:** Just opposite of the centralized database concept, the distributed database has contributed from the common database as well as the information captured by local computer also. The data is not at one place and is distributed at various sites of an organization. These sites are connected to each other with the help of communication links which helps them to access the distributed data easily. You can imagine a distributed database as a one in which various portions of a database are stored in multiple different physical locations along with the application procedures which are replicated and distributed among various points in a network.

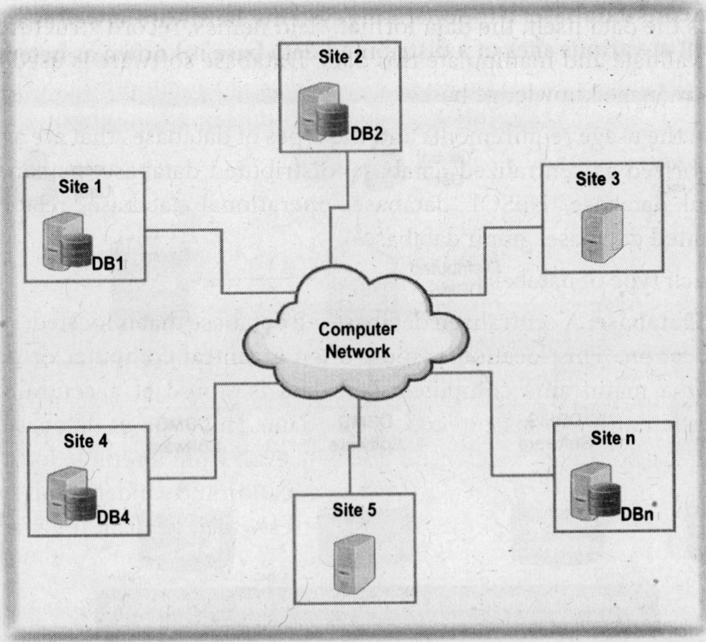

Figure 1.7: Distributed Database

The two kinds of distributed databases are homogenous and heterogeneous.

- **Homogeneous database:** The databases which have same type of hardware, runs on same operating systems and application procedures are known as homogeneous distributed data base.

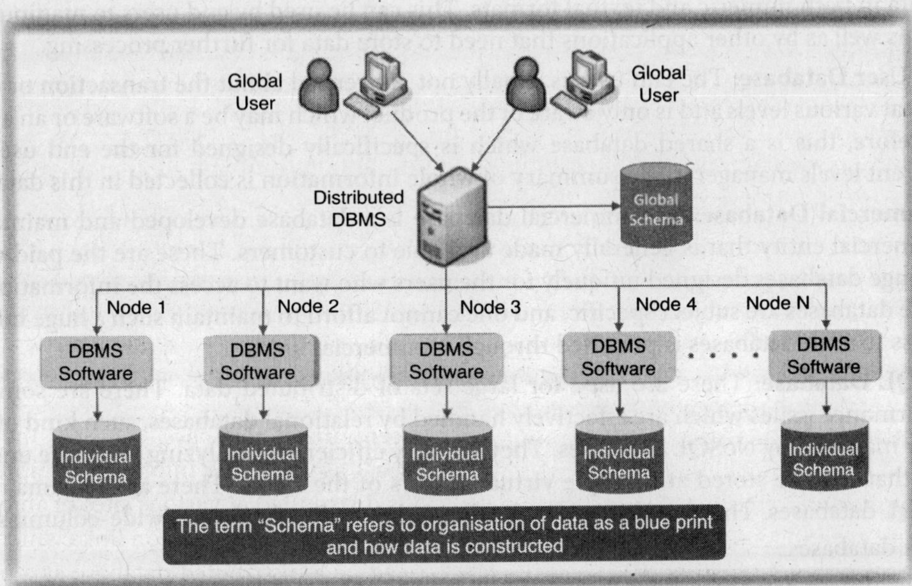

Figure 1.8: Homogeneous Distributed Database

- **Heterogeneous database:** If the operating systems, hardware as well as application procedures are different at various sites of a distributed data base is known as heterogeneous.

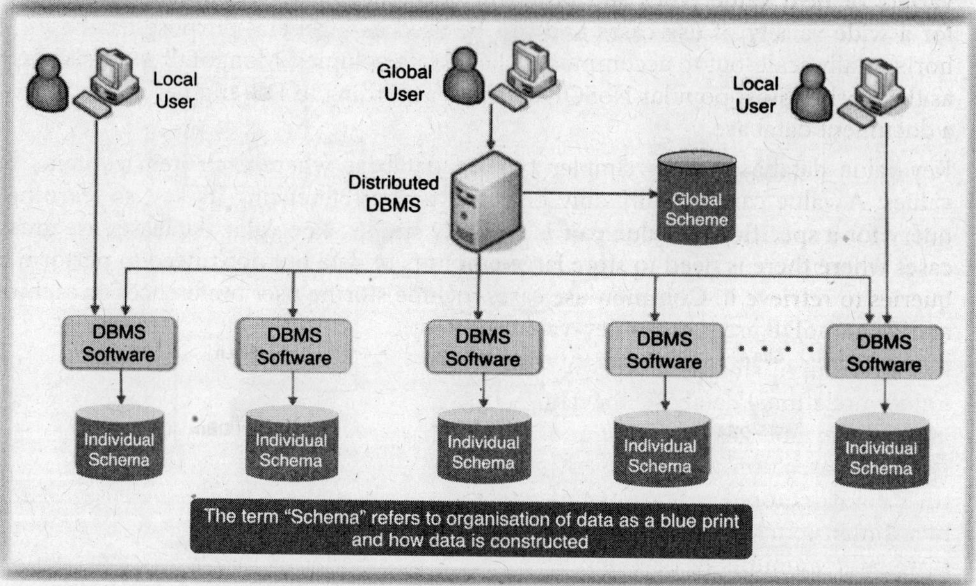

Figure 1.9: Heterogeneous Distributed Database

- **Personal Database:** This is the database in which data is collected and stored on personal computers which is small and easily manageable. The data is generally used by the same department of an organization and is accessed by a small group of people. Personal database management systems are tools specifically designed to store, retrieve, and manage large amounts of data in both numeric and textual formats. This can be used by end users to manipulate lists of data as well as by other applications that need to store data for further processing.
- **End User Database:** The end user is usually not concerned about the transaction or operations done at various levels and is only aware of the product which may be a software or an application. Therefore, this is a shared database which is specifically designed for the end user, just like different levels managers. The summary of whole information is collected in this database.
- **Commercial Database:** A commercial database is a database developed and maintained by a commercial entity that is generally made available to customers. These are the paid versions of the huge databases designed uniquely for the users who want to access the information for help. These databases are subject specific, and one cannot afford to maintain such a huge information. Access to such databases is provided through commercial links.
- **NoSQL Database:** These are used for large sets of distributed data. There are some big data performance issues which are effectively handled by relational databases, such kind of issues are easily managed by NoSQL databases. They are very efficient in analyzing large size unstructured data that may be stored at multiple virtual servers of the cloud. There are four major types of NoSQL databases. They are document databases, key-value databases, wide-column stores, and graph databases.
  - Document databases store data in documents similar to JavaScript Object Notation (JSON) objects. Each document contains pairs of fields and values. The values can typically be a

variety of types including things like strings, numbers, booleans, arrays, or objects, and their structures typically align with objects developers are working with in code. Because of their variety of field value types and powerful query languages, document databases are great for a wide variety of use cases and can be used as a general-purpose database. They can horizontally scale-out to accommodate large data volumes. MongoDB is consistently ranked as the world's most popular NoSQL database according to DB-engines and is an example of a document database.

- Key-value databases are a simpler type of database where each item contains keys and values. A value can typically only be retrieved by referencing its key, so learning how to query for a specific key-value pair is typically simple. Key-value databases are great for use cases where there is need to store large amounts of data but don't need to perform complex queries to retrieve it. Common use cases include storing user preferences or caching. Redis and DynamoDB are popular key-value databases.
- A wide-column store is a type of NoSQL database. It uses tables, rows, and columns, but unlike a relational database, the names and format of the columns can vary from row to row in the same table. A wide-column store can be interpreted as a two-dimensional key–value store. Wide-column stores provide a lot of flexibility over relational databases because each row is not required to have the same columns. Many consider wide-column stores to be two-dimensional key-value databases. Wide-column stores are great for when you need to store large amounts of data and you can predict what your query patterns will be. Wide-column stores are commonly used for storing Internet of Things data and user profile data. Cassandra and HBase are two of the most popular wide-column stores.
- Graph databases store data in nodes and edges. Nodes typically store information about people, places, and things while edges store information about the relationships between the nodes. Graph databases excel in use cases where you need to traverse relationships to look for patterns such as social networks, fraud detection, and recommendation engines. Neo4j and Janus Graph are examples of graph databases. The graph is a collection of nodes and edges where each node is used to represent an entity and each edge describes the relationship between entities. Graph databases are basically used for analyzing interconnections. For example, companies might use a graph database to mine data about customers from social media.

- **Operational Database:** An operational database is a database that creates or updates large amounts of data in real time. This is also called transactional data base. This can be based on any number of database technologies that support the availability levels, speed, concurrency, data integrity and recoverability required. Information related to operations of an enterprise is stored inside this database. Functional lines like marketing, employee relations, customer service etc. require such kind of databases.
- **Relational Databases:** A relational database uses a structure that allows us to identify and access data in relation to another piece of data in the database. Often, data in a relational database is organized into tables. These databases are categorized by a set of tables where data gets fit into a pre-defined category. The table consists of rows and columns where the column has an entry for data for a specific category and rows contains instance for that data defined according to the category. The Structured Query Language (SQL) is the standard user and application program interface for a relational database. There are various simple operations that can be applied over the table which makes these databases easier to extend, join two databases with a common relation and modify all existing applications.

- **Cloud Databases:** Now a days, data has been specifically getting stored over clouds also known as a virtual environment, either in a hybrid cloud, public or private cloud. A cloud database is a database that has been optimized or built for such a virtualized environment. There are various benefits of a cloud database, some of which have the ability to pay for storage capacity and bandwidth on a per-user basis, and they provide scalability on demand, along with high availability. A cloud database also gives enterprises the opportunity to support business applications in a software-as-a-service deployment.
- **Object-Oriented Databases:** An object-oriented database is a collection of object-oriented programming and relational database. There are various items which are created using object-oriented programming languages like C++, Java etc. which can be stored in relational databases. Object-oriented databases are well-suited for those items. An object-oriented database is organized around objects rather than actions, and data rather than logic. For example, a multimedia record in a relational database can be a definable data object, as opposed to an alphanumeric value.

1.6.4 Information System Network

Information system network refers to the telecommunication networks like the intranet, extranet and the internet. These resources facilitate the flow of information in the organization. Networks consists of both the physicals devises such as networks cards, routers, hubs, cables etc and software such as operating systems, web servers, data servers and application servers.

1.6.4.1 Components of Information System Network

The information system network components are shown in figure 1.10

- **Terminals:** This is for accessing the network. A terminal is a device which ends a telecommunications link and is the point at which a signal enters or leaves a network. Examples of terminal equipment include telephones, fax machines, computer terminals, printers etc.
- **Processors:** This process information which are interconnected by the network. A network processor is a specialized CPU programmed to handle the tasks of upper layer network protocols at high speed. The network processors are programmable and usually perform header parsing, pattern matching, bit field manipulation, table look-ups, packet modification and data movement.
- **Communications links:** This forms a channel or media through which information is send from a device to a receiving device. Link is a communication channel that connects two or more devices for the purpose of data transmission. The link may be a dedicated physical link or a virtual circuit that uses one or more physical links or shares a physical link with other telecommunications links.

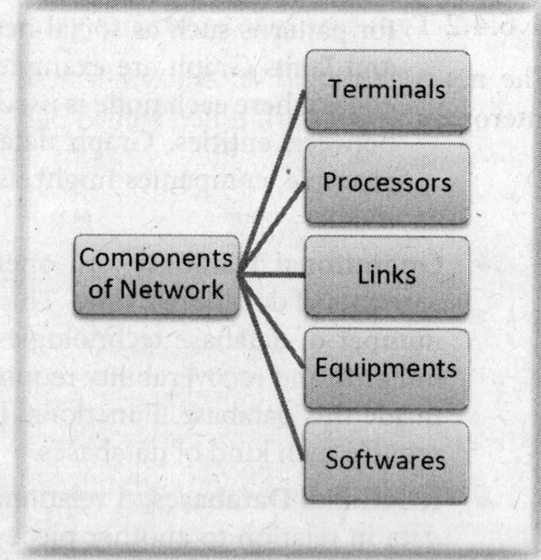

Figure 1.10: Components of Information System Network

- **Communication equipments:** Communications equipment refers to hardware used mainly for telecommunications such as user end devices, multiplexers, base transceiver stations etc. It encompasses different types of communication technologies including telephones, radios, computers, mobiles etc.
- **Telecommunications softwares:** This controls message transmission over the network. Telecommunication software is a vital component of all telecommunications network. Telecommunication software middleware can help diverts networks communicate with each other. For example, MS explorer. The telecommunication software package provides a variety of communication support services like
  - **Access control:** This function establishes the connection between terminal and computer in a network. The software works with a communication processor (such as a modem) to connect and disconnect communication links and establish communication parameter.
  - **Transmission control:** This function allows computers and terminals to send or receive commands, message data, and program.
  - **Network management:** This function manages communication in a telecommunication network.
  - **Error control:** This function involves the detection and correction of transmission errors. Errors are usually caused by distortion in the communication channel, such as line noise and power surges.
  - **Security management:** This function protects a communication network from unauthorized access. Network operating system or other security program restricts access to data files and other computing resources in LANs and other types of networks.

1.6.4.2 Types of Information System Networks

The network can be wired, wireless, terrestrial or aerial. These networks exist together to form an interoperable network called hybrid network.

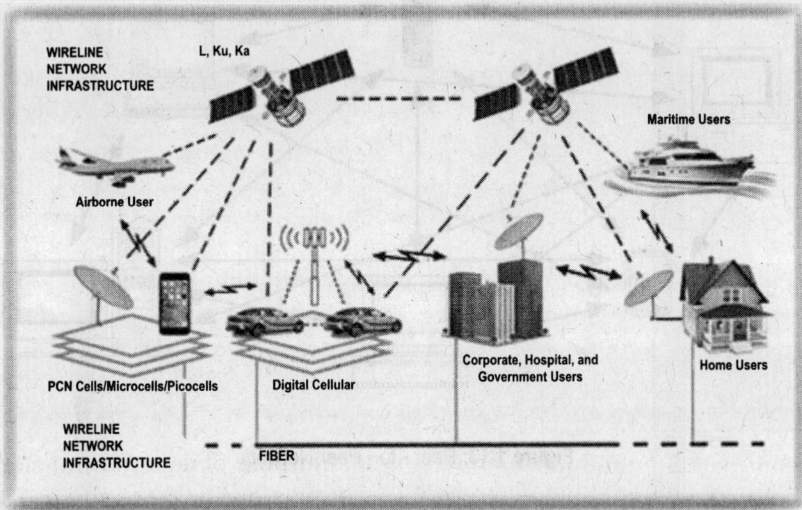

Figure 1.11: Hybrid Network with Wired, Wireless, Satellite and Terrestrial Network

All the networks that we are discussing find its application in Internet of Things. IoT networks can be distinguished from the point of view of their geographical scope. They are:

- **Nano Network:** This is a network of very small devices that perform very simple tasks such as sensing, computing, storing, and actuation. Such systems are applied in biomedical, military and other nano technologies.
- **Near-Field Communication:** Near-Field Communication (NFC) is a low-speed network to connect electronic devices at a distance within 4 cm from each other. The applications of this is in contactless payment systems, access control cards, ticketing etc.

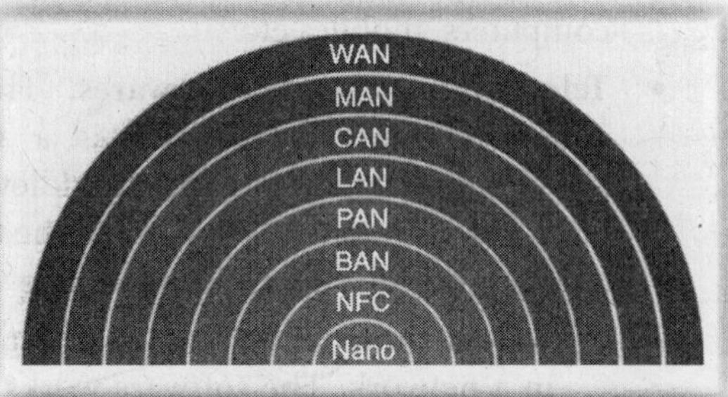

Figure 1.12: Types of Networks

- **Body Area Network:** Body Area Network (BAN) is a network to connect wearable computing devices that are worn either fixed on the body or near the body in different positions, or embedded inside the body.
- **Personal Area Network:** Personnel Area Network (PAN) is a network to link up devices within a radius of roughly one or a couple of rooms.
- **Local Area Network:** Local Area Network (LAN) is a network covering the area of one building. LAN is a privately owned network that interconnects within a building or on a campus site that includes several buildings. There are two principal LAN designs.
  - ❑ **Peer-to-peer:** In this type of network, peripherals are located at terminals and system administration is largely left up to the users

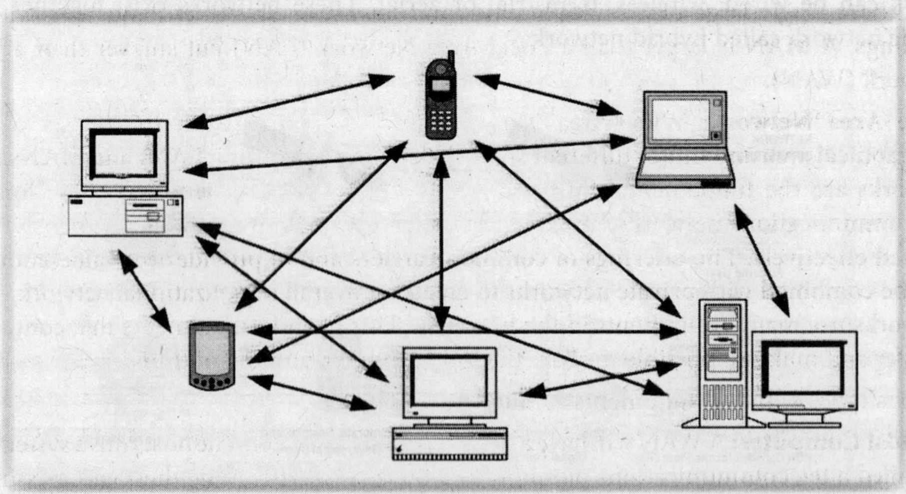

Figure 1.13: Peer - to - Peer Network

  - ❑ **Server-based:** In this type of network, shared resources are placed in dedicated server that manages a given resource on behalf of user workstations, sharing the resources such as file server, printer server, gateway, optical disk server etc. Most of the servers are dedicated to their task, using them as workstations will degrade the performance of the net.

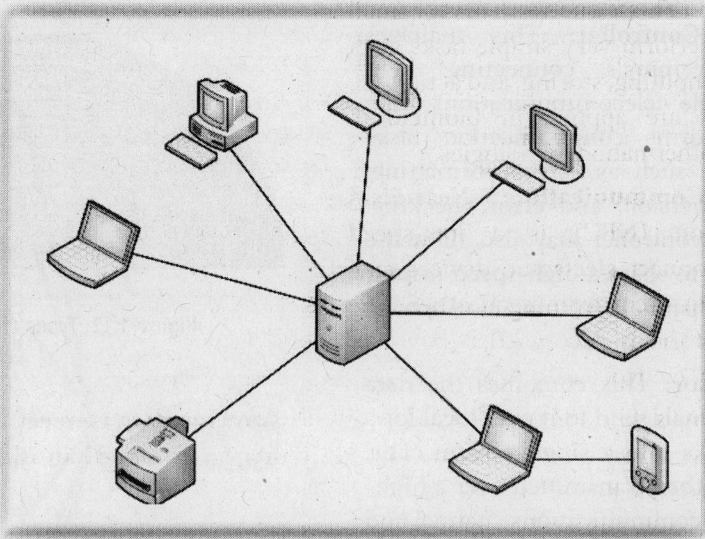

Figure 1.14: Server Based Network

- **Campus/Corporate Area Network:** Campus/Corporate Area Network (CAN) is a network that unites smaller local area networks within a limited geographical area such as enterprise, university etc.
- **Metropolitan Area Network:** Metropolitan Area Network (MAN) is a big network for a certain metropolitan area. This network that connects computers within a metropolitan area, which could be a single large city, multiple cities and towns, or any given large area with multiple buildings. A MAN is larger than a Local Area Network (LAN) but smaller than a Wide Area Network (WAN).
- **Wide Area Network:** Wide Area Network (WAN) is a network that exists over a large geographical area and unites different smaller networks, including LANs and MANs. Wide area networks are the fundamental infrastructure of organizational network. These long-distance telecommunications networks employ a variety of equipments so that the expensive links may be used effectively. The offerings of common carriers and of providers of value-added services may be combined with private networks to create an overall organizational network. Wide Area Networks use many equipments in the network. This include equipments that control message transfer and makes it possible to share the links among a number of transfers.

  Various types of these equipments are discussed below.

  - **Host Computer:** A WAN will have a powerful host computer. The host runs a system program, called a telecommunications monitor, which processes incoming messages, passing them to the appropriate application programs, and accepts outgoing messages from the applications in order to transmit them into the network.
  - **Front-End Processor:** This relieves the host computer from most of the tasks involved in network control. Under the control of its own software, the front-end processor accepts

messages coming from the network and routes outgoing messages to their destinations. It performs the necessary code conversions, encrypts and decrypts secure messages, and performs error checking so that the host deals with clean messages.

- **Cluster Controller:** This manages several terminals, connecting them to a single telecommunications link, and performs communication tasks for them, such as screen formatting, code conversion, and error checking. A cluster controller may also allow the terminals to share a high-speed printer and may handle electronic mail among the cluster terminals.
- **Multiplexor:** This combines the data that terminals send to it over local low-speed links into a single stream. This stream is then transmitted over a high-speed telecommunications channel and is split by another multiplexor on the opposite end of the channel.
- **Concentrator:** This combines transmission from several slower terminals that operate in a burst mode into a single transmission stream that requires a link of lower speed than the sum of the speeds of all the terminals combined. A concentrator stores messages from terminals and forwards them when warranted.

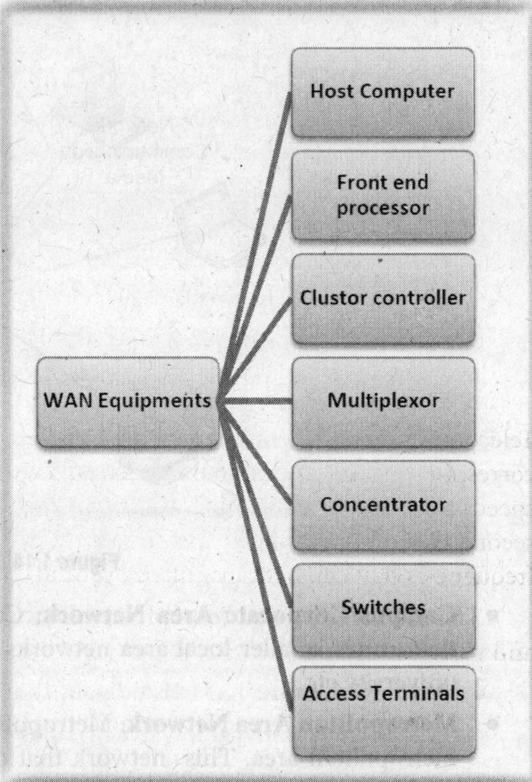

Figure 1.15: Wide Area Network Equipments

- **Switches:** Switches establishes connections between nodes that need to communicate.
- **Access Terminals:** These include a variety of dumb terminals, with no processing capacity as well as intelligent terminals with processing capacity, such as personal computers.

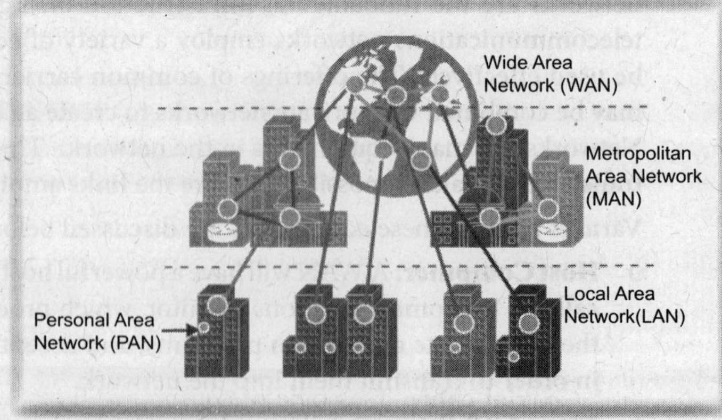

Figure 1.16: PAN, LAN, MAN and WAN Relationship

1.6.4.3 Network Communication Media

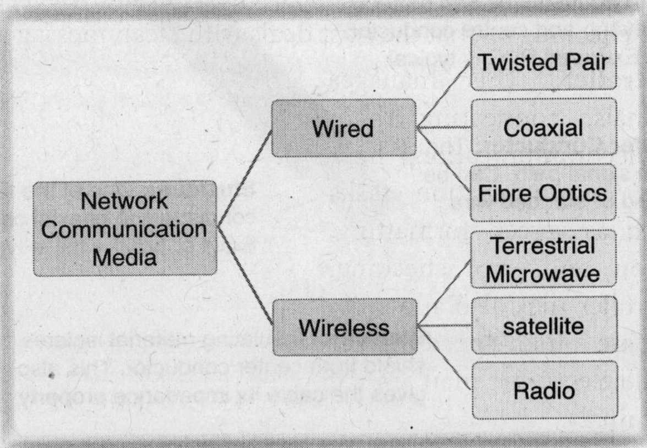

Figure 1.17: Various Communication Medias

Telecommunications links may be implemented with various communication media, with a corresponding variety of characteristics. The main feature of a medium is its potential transmission speed, also known as channel capacity, which for data transmission purposes is expressed in bits per second (bps). An alternative measure of transmission channel capacity is bandwidth - the range of signal frequencies that can be transmitted over the channel.

The media employed to implement communication networks can be generally classified as wired and wireless.

- **Wired medium:** The twisted pair, coaxial and fiber optics comes under wired medium.
  - **Twisted pair cable:** This is a communications medium consisting of a pair of wires. The wires will be normally copper based, insulated and twisted.

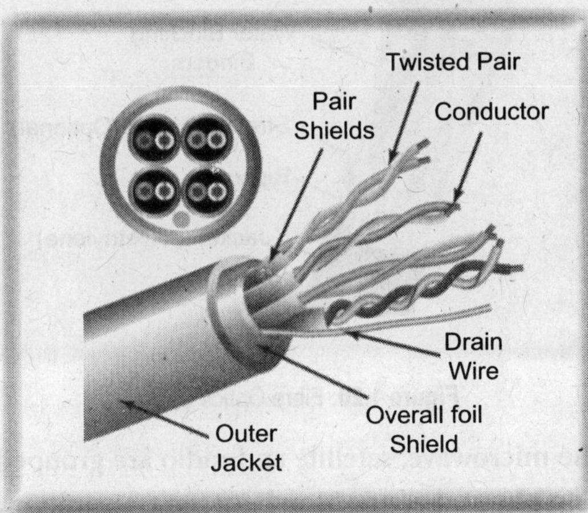

Figure 1.18: Twisted Pair Cable

  - **Coaxial cable:** This type of communications medium consists of a relatively thick central conductor shielded by several layers of insulation and the second conductor just under the cable's shell.

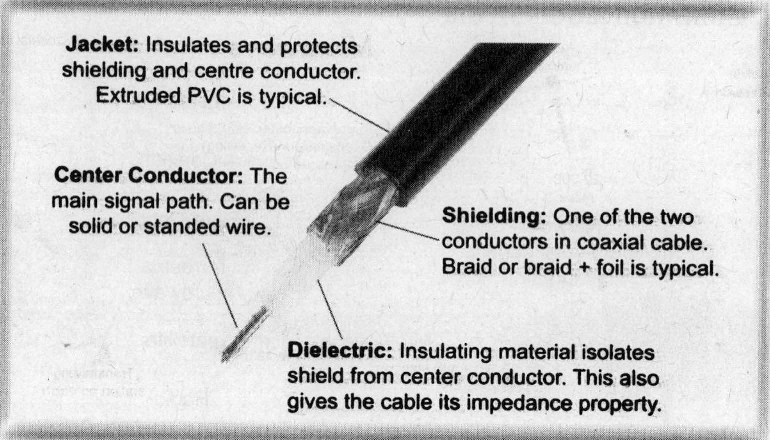

Figure 1.19: Coaxial Cable

- **Fiber Optics Cable:** This is a high-capacity communications medium that consists of many strands of pure flexible glass rods with a data carrying core in the middle, surrounded by a reflective coating and a protective sheath.

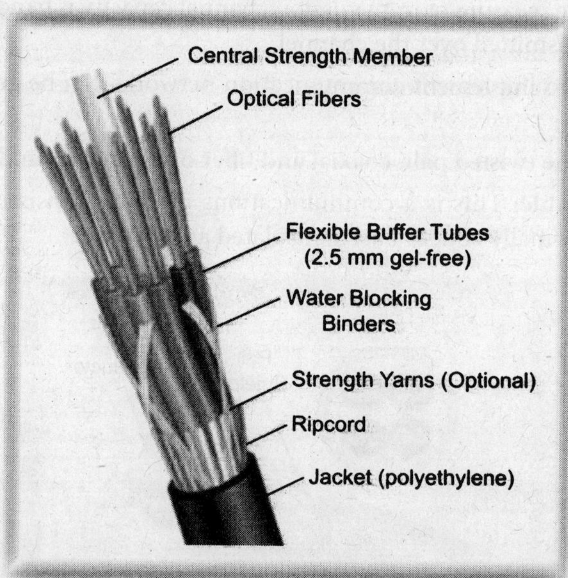

Figure 1.20: Fibre Optics Cable

- **Wireless medium:** The microwave, satellite and radio are grouped under wireless medium. In this medium, there is no physical connection between transmitter and receiver.
  - **Terrestrial Microwave Transmission:** This is long-distance telecommunications by means of microwave signals travelling on the surface of the earth. The towers are located at point of sight of the other tower.

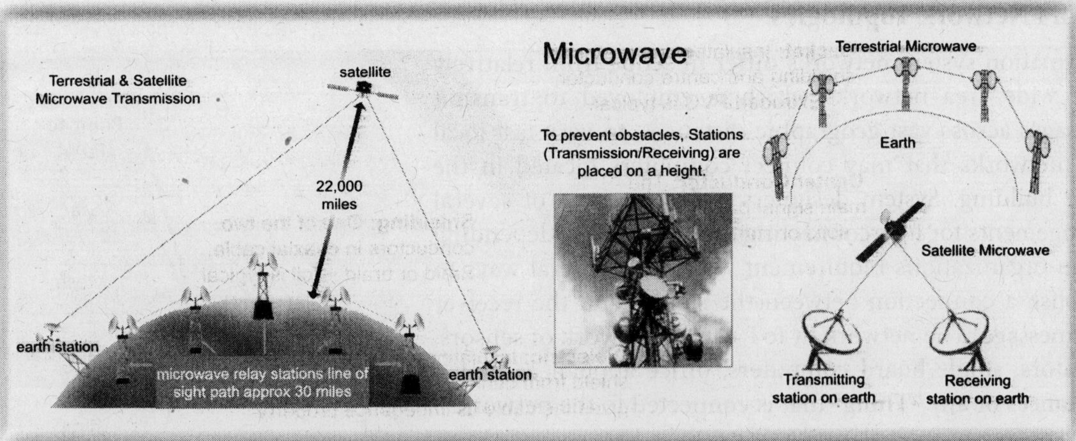

Figure 1.21: Terrestrial and Satellite Microwave Transmission

- **Satellite Microwave Transmission:** In this form of microwave transmission, the signal is transmitted by an earth station to a satellite which rebroadcasts the signal to the receiving station.
- **Radio Transmission:** This is a wireless communications technology that transmits voice or data over the air using a lower frequency band than microwaves. The waves from the transmitters are send to atmosphere. It gets reflected at the ionosphere and returns to the earth and will be received by receiving stations or radios at a different location.

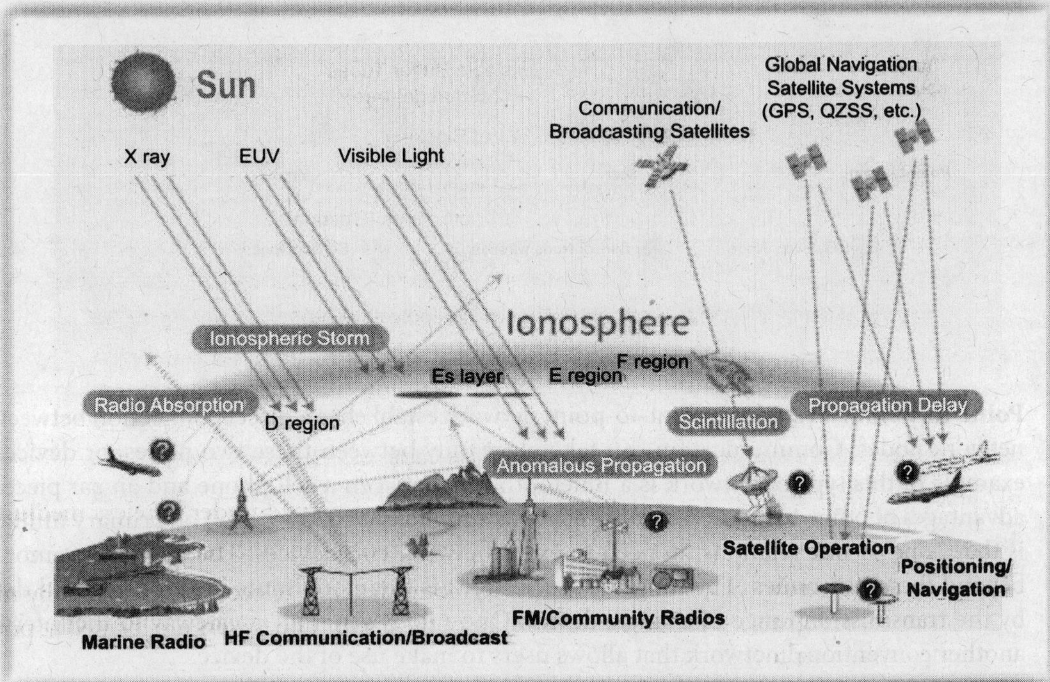

Figure 1.22: Radio Transmission and Reception

1.6.4.4 Network Topologies

Information system networks differ in scope from relatively slow wide area networks which is employed to transmit messages across vast geographic distances, to very fast local area networks that may connect computers located in the same building. System designers will select one of several arrangements for interconnecting network nodes, depending on an organization's requirement. There are several ways to establish a connection between the sender and the receiver of a message. The network in IoT can be network of sensors, actuators, single board computers, office appliances, home appliances or any "Thing" that is connected to the network.

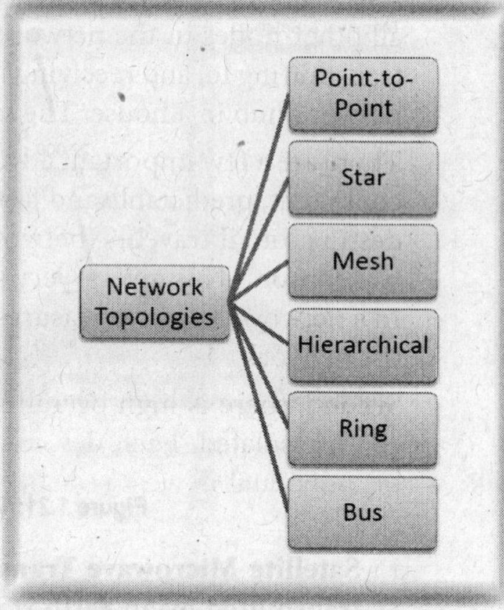

Figure 1.23: Various Network Topologies

The purpose of network is to provide a connection between nodes that need to communicate. The arrangement of nodes and links in a network is called a topology. A variety of arrangements are possible, each with its own advantages and drawbacks. Network topology has to fit the structure of the organizational unit that will use the network, and this topology should also be adapted to the unit's communication traffic patterns and to the methods that the databases will be stored in order to facilitate access to them. The following network topologies are the most widely used in Internet of Things (IoT).

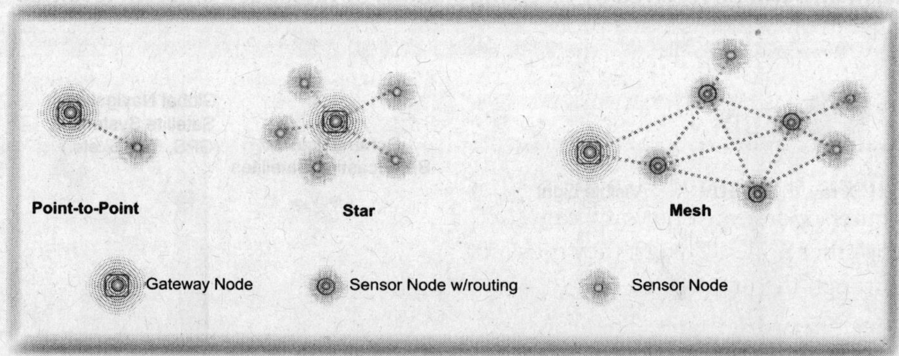

Figure 1.24 : Point-to-Point, Star and Mesh Network Topologies

- **Point-to-Point Network:** A point-to-point network establishes a direct connection between two network nodes. Communication can take place only between these two nodes, or devices. An example of this type of network is a Bluetooth link between a cell phone and an ear piece. The advantages of point-to-point networking are its simplicity and low cost. The primary limitations is that one-to-one relationship need to exists between two devices. The network cannot scale beyond these two nodes. The range of the network is therefore limited to one hop and defined by the transmission range of a single device. One side is generally a gateway to the internet or another conventional network that allows users to make use of the device.

- **Star Network:** A star network consists of one central hub (gateway node), to which all other sensor nodes in the network are linked. This central hub acts as a common connection point for all other nodes in the network. All peripheral nodes may thus communicate with all others by transmitting to, and receiving from, the central hub only. An example of this topology is the WiFi network hub in a house. The hub is generally also the link to the outside world.

  There are a few important advantages to a star topology. First, the performance of the network is consistent, predictable and fast. In a star network, a data packet travels only one hop to reach its destination, if traveling between the hub and a sensor or at most two hops, if traveling between two sensors. This gives a very low and predicable network latency. Latency is a measure of delay. In a network, latency measures the time that it takes for some data to get to its destination across the network.

  Second, there is high overall network reliability due to the ease with which faults and devices can be isolated. Each device utilizes its own, single link to the hub. This makes the isolation of individual devices straightforward and makes it easy to detect faults and to remove failing network components.

  The disadvantages of this network type are similar to the point-to-point network. The range is limited to the transmission range of a single device. Additionally, there is no ability to route around radio frequency (RF) obstacles if there is a network interference or interruption.

  Finally, in a star networking, if there is a failure in gateway, complete network will be failed. In a star network, the hub acts as the gateway, providing access to the shared database and software. All communications between the nodes must go through this central node. The star network is rather easy to manage and expand, since in both cases it is largely the single central node that is affected in an expansion of a processing capacity. The central node is a focus of vulnerability. It may be overloaded or it may fail, disabling the entire network.

- **Mesh Network:** A mesh network consists of three types of nodes. They are
  - **Gateway node:** As in a star network, provided so data can reach the outside world
  - **Simple sensors/router nodes:** These nodes are with repeater/routing capability. Sensor/router nodes must not only capture and disseminate their own data, but also serve as relays for other nodes. That is, they must collaborate with neighboring nodes to propagate the data through the network.
  - **Mesh network nodes:** These are deployed such that every node is within transmission range of at least one other sensor/router node. Data packets pass through multiple sensor/routers nodes to reach the gateway node.

  This networking topology is used for many applications requiring a long range and broad area coverage. Applications include building automation, energy management, industrial automation, and asset management, to name a few. Because the network range is not limited to the transmission range of a single device, the network range can be very broad, covering large areas, such as a building or campus. Mesh networks can scale up to thousands of nodes, providing a high density of coverage with a broad assortment of sensors and actuating devices. The flexibility of network layout allows coverage in environments facing high radio frequency challenges, such as high RF interference or RF obstacles. Intermittent network interruptions are mitigated by self-healing and packet retransmission capabilities that together provide a high degree of network resilience.

The primary disadvantage is that mesh networks are, by their nature, more complex than point-to-point or star network topologies. A sight survey is typically done followed by installation and commissioning of the network. Also, there is higher network latency in mesh networked due to multiple networks hops typical from the sensor to gateway.

- **Hierarchical Network:** This topology matches the organizational structure of many firms and are frequently used in WANs. The user nodes may be, in turn, interconnected using one of the LAN topologies. Failure of the host does not disable divisional processing, which is a fail-safe feature. Cost-effectiveness leads some downsizing firms to move away from hierarchical networks to client/server computing.

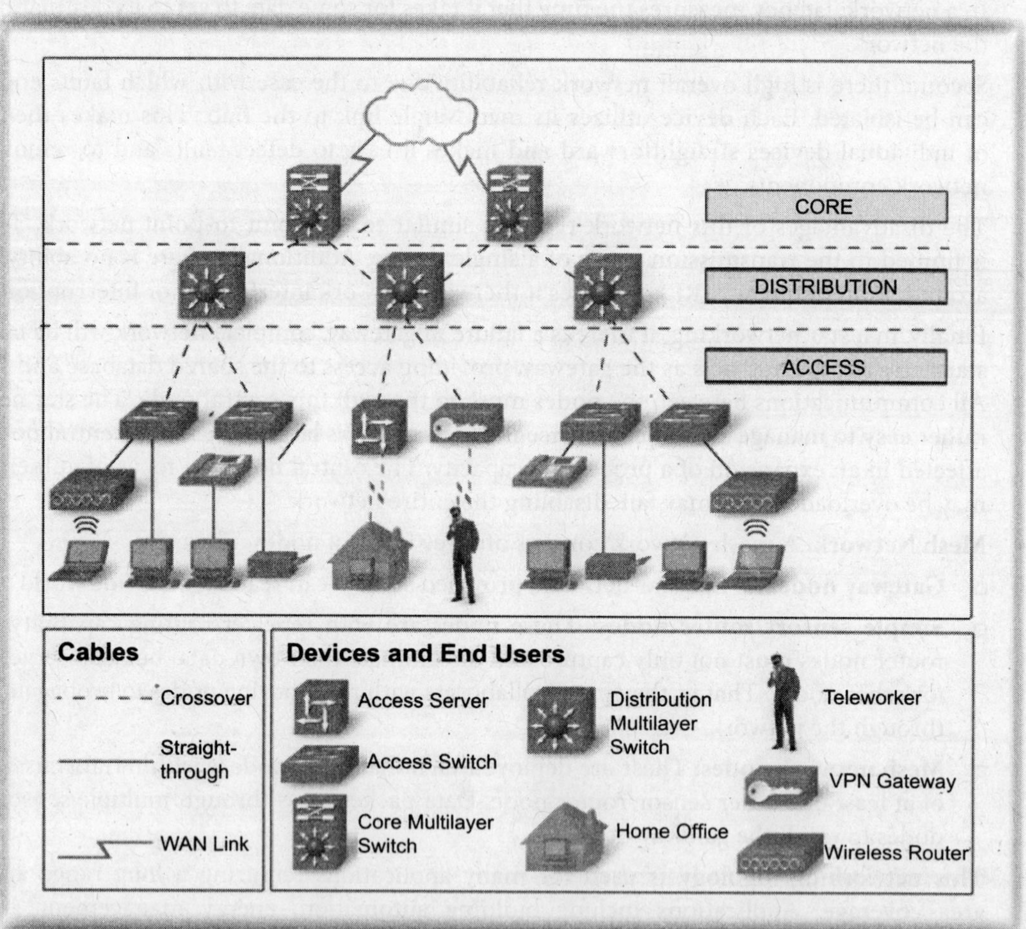

Figure 1.25: Hierarchical Network

- **Ring Network:** Each node in a ring network is connected to two of its neighbors. The nodes are usually close to one another. This topology is frequently used in LANs. When one node sends a message to another, the message passes through each intermediate node, which restores the signal, as signals deteriorate in transmission. If a node fails, the ring is out of service, unless the ring contains two channels transmitting in opposite directions.

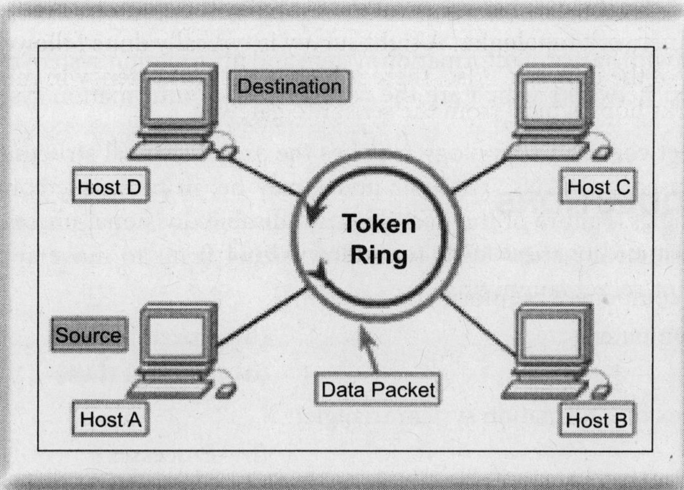

Figure 1.26: Ring Network

- **Bus Network:** The nodes on a bus network are connected to a common link such as coaxial cable. This arrangement is used in LANs. A failing device does not affect the rest of the network. Failure of the bus itself is required to bring the network down.

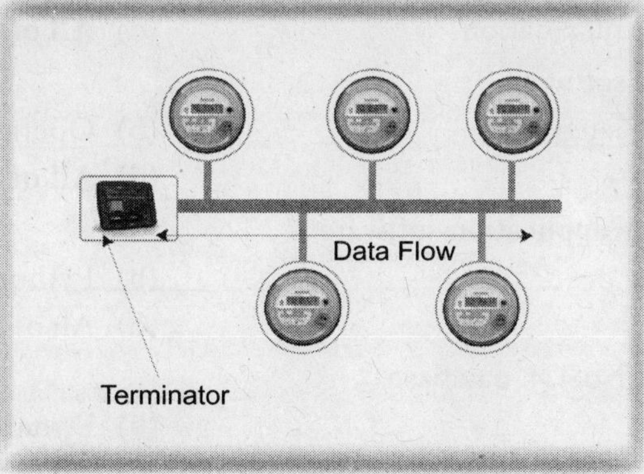

Figure 1.27: Bus Network

1.6.5 Information System Human Resources

This component is associated with the manpower required to run and manage the system. People are the end user of the information system. The main purpose of the information system is to benefit the end user. The end user can be accountants, engineers, salespersons, customers, clerks, or managers etc. People are developing and operating information systems. People imagine information systems, people develop information systems, people support information systems, and people use information systems. They include systems analysts, computer operators, programmers, computer engineer, database administer, help-desk/support analyst, Trainer, clerical IS personnel, chief information officer, functional manager, ERP manager, project manager and information security offer.

1.7 SUMMARY

We started this chapter with basics of information system and information system triangle. The hardware, software, data base and networks which are the components of information systems are explained in detail.

1.8 OBJECTIVE QUESTIONS

The answer of the multiple-choice questions is marked in bold.

1. Which is not a component of information system?
   (a) Personal computers (b) smartphones
   (c) databases (d) **None of these**
2. Which is a vertex of information system triangle?
   (a) People (b) Processes
   (c) Information technology (d) **All of these**
3. IoT comes into picture when looking from .... dimensions.
   (a) Management (b) Organisational
   (c) **Technological** (d) All of these
4. .... is a type of Information System.
   (a) Decision support (b) Expert system
   (c) Management Information (d) **All of these**
5. .... is a software.
   (a) Programming language (b) Operating system
   (c) System software (d) **All of these**
6. .... is an application software.
   (a) **Web browser** (b) Python
   (c) Java (d) All of these
7. .... is a NoSQL database.
   (a) **MongoDB** (b) DynamoDB
   (c) Neo4j (d) All of these
8. .... is component of telecommunication network.
   (a) Software (b) Processor
   (c) Terminal (d) **All of these**
9. .... is a network type based on their geographical scope.
   (a) NFC (b) PAN
   (c) BAN (d) **All of these**
10. Which of below is a wireless communication media?
    (a) Fiber Optics (b) **Microwave**
    (c) Coaxial (d) None of these

1.9 REVIEW QUESTIONS

1. Explain information system triangle.
2. Discuss three dimensions of information system.
3. Explain different types of information system.
4. Explain the components of information system.
5. Discuss on different types of IoT networks.
6. Explain different WAN equipments.
7. Explain different IoT network topologies.
8. Discuss various types of communication media.
9. Discuss various data bases.
10. Explain different types of software.

1.10 ABBREVIATIONS AND SYMBOLS

Abbreviations	Full Form	Description
BAN	Body Area Network	BAN is a wireless network of wearable computing devices. This is also known as wireless body area network (WBAN) or a body sensor network (BSN) or a medical body area network (MBAN)
CAD	Computer Aided Design	CAD is the use of computers to aid in the creation, modification, analysis, or optimization of a design.
CAM	Computer Aided Manufacturing	CAM is the use of software and computer-controlled machinery to automate a manufacturing process.
CAN	Campus Area Network/Corporate Area Network	CAN is a computer network made up of an interconnection of local area networks within a limited geographical area.
CPU	Central Processing Unit	CPU is the portion of a computer that retrieves and executes instructions.
DBMS	Data Base Management System	DBMS is a software system that uses a standard method to store and organize data.
DSS	Decision Support System	DSS is a computerized program used to support decisions, judgments, and courses of action in an organization or a business.
ERP	Enterprise Resource Planning	ERP is a process used by companies to manage and integrate the important parts of their businesses.
GIS	Geographical Information System	GIS is a computer system for capturing, storing, checking, and displaying data related to positions on earth's surface.
IS	Information System	IS is a formal, sociotechnical, organizational system designed to collect, process, store, and distribute information.

JSON	Java Script Object Notation	JSON is an open standard file format and data interchange format that uses human readable text to store and transmit data objects consisting of attribute value pairs and arrays.
LAN	Local Area Network	LAN is a computer network that interconnects computers within a limited area such as a residence, school, laboratory, university campus or office building.
MAN	Metropolitan Area Network	MAN is a computer network that connects computers within a metropolitan area, which could be a single large city, multiple cities and towns, or any given large area with multiple buildings.
MIS	Management Information System	MIS is an information system used for decision-making, and for the coordination, control, analysis, and visualization of information in an organization.
MS	Microsoft	MS is a multinational technology company which produces computer software, consumer electronics, personal computers, and related services.
NFC	Near Field Communication	NFC is a contact-less communication technology based on a radio frequency field using a base frequency of 13.56 MHz.
PAN	Personal Area Network	PAN is a computer network that enables communication between computer devices near a person.
RF	Radio Frequency	RF is the oscillation rate of an alternating electric current or voltage or of a magnetic, electromagnetic field or mechanical system in the frequency range from around 20 kHz to around 300 GHz.
SCADA	Supervisory Control And Data Acquisition	SCADA is a control system architecture comprising computers, networked data communications and graphical user interfaces for high-level process supervisory management.
SQL	Structured Query Language	SQL is a programming language designed to get information out of and put it into a relational database.
TPS	Transaction Processing System	TPS is a type of information system that collects, stores, modifies and retrieves the data transactions of an enterprise.
WAN	Wide Area Network	WAN is a large computer network that connects groups of computers over large distances

1.11 LIST OF FIGURES AND TABLES

The details of figures and tables used in this chapter is as below.

CHAPTER

2

Information System Security

CONTENTS

2.1 INTRODUCTION

In this chapter, we will discuss on basics of information system security and control. Various types of security issues related to information systems and tools to ensure security are discussed. Towards end of the chapter, data security considerations, security policies and mobile security are explained.

2.2 SECURITY

Security means safety as well as the measures taken to be safe or protected. Security is the freedom from potential harm caused by others. The security can be related to personnel, national, industrial, residential, financial etc. Each type of security threats is different and the measures to be taken for that is also different.

2.3 INFORMATION SYSTEM SECURITY

Security in information system, is the defense of digital information and information technology assets against internal or external, malicious and accidental threats. This defense includes detection, prevention and correction to threats through the use of security policies, software tools and information technology services. Hardware, as well as software are covered under this category and is the superset covering cyber security and network security.

Cyber security is the application of technologies, processes and controls to protect systems, networks, programs, devices and data from cyber-attacks. It aims to reduce the risk of cyber-attacks and protect against the unauthorized exploitation of systems, networks and technologies.

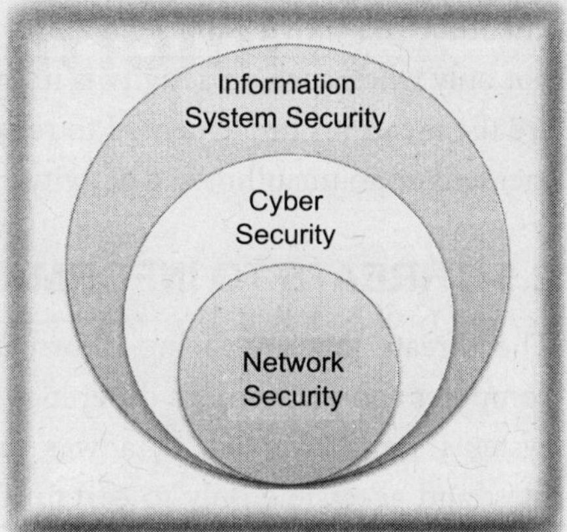

Figure 2.1: Subsets of Information System Security

Network security is the process of taking physical and software preventative measures to protect the underlying networking infrastructure from unauthorized access, misuse, malfunction, modification, destruction, or improper disclosure, thereby creating a secure platform. This security refers to networks that are not connected to internet.

In present technology age, information systems security is one of the biggest challenges facing by society. Information systems have become an integral part of everyday life in the home, businesses, government and organizations. Information systems have changed the way that people live their lives, conduct business and even run the government. Many current problems are threatening the reliability and security of information systems. Along with new techniques and technology for fixing these problems, users of information systems must also protect themselves. There are certain ways that users of information systems can protect themselves against all of the current problems.

2.4 INFORMATION SECURITY CONTROL

Security controls are safeguards to avoid, detect, counteract, or minimize security risks to physical property, information, computer systems, or other assets. In the field of information security, such controls protect the confidentiality, integrity and availability of information. There are three primary areas or classifications of security controls. These controls include

- **Security Management:** Security management is the identification of an organization's assets like people, buildings, machines, systems and information assets, followed by the development, documentation, and implementation of policies and procedures for protecting them. This also includes the processes development for the organizational structure and technology to protect an organization's IT assets against internal and external threats. Information system security management is also known as administrative security control.
- **Operational Security:** Operational security is a security and risk management process that prevents sensitive information from getting into the wrong hands. This maintain the security and integrity of ID system facilities, data centers, and equipment are important to protect data. Operational information system security control is also known as technical security control.
- **Physical Security:** Physical security control is the implementation of security measures in a defined structure used to deter or prevent unauthorized access to sensitive material.

These three controls are grouped under preventive, detective and corrective control functions. Preventive controls are security mechanisms, tools, or practices that can deter or mitigate undesired actions or events. Detective controls include security measures implemented by an organization to detect unauthorized activity and send alerts to the concerned individuals. Detective security controls function not only when such an activity is in progress, but also after it has occurred. Corrective security controls are the measures implemented to restore the systems or resources to their previous state after a security incident or an unauthorized activity.

2.5 THREATS TO INFORMATION SYSTEM

The threats that are facing information systems have either occurred through computer crime or computer abuse. There is a difference between computer crime and computer abuse. Before information systems were invented, data was protected more because most information was stored in paper files, and accessible only to certain departments of a business with less users. With the evolution of information systems, large amounts of data can be stored in electronic form rather than in paper files. Since more users can access the data electronically, the data in turn, is more susceptible to the threat of computer crime and computer abuse. Insecure telecommunication networks also contribute highly to the security issues of information systems. Other threats to information systems are hardware failure, fire, software failure, electrical problems, personnel actions, user errors, and telecommunication problems.

Computer crime is the commitment of criminal activity using computer as an instrument or target. This includes financial frauds, human trafficking, online harassment, child pornography, intellectual property violation, stealing identities, or violating privacy. This is also called cybercrime when internet is also used for the criminal activity. Computer abuse refers to a broad category of activities wherein a computer is used to improperly or illegally cause harm to somebody else or their property. Cyber bullying, hacking, identity theft, and even using official computer for personal business are all examples of computer abuse. Computer crime occurs when a person uses a computer to commit an illegal act, while computer abuse is when a person uses a computer to commit an unethical but not always illegal act.

2.6 LAYERED SECURITY

Layered security is an approach that uses several components to protect the operations with multiple levels of security measure. The purpose of a layered security approach is to make sure that every individual defense component has a backup to counter any flaws or gaps in other defenses of security. This security is implemented in overlapping layers that ensure the three elements needed to secure assets like prevention, detection, and correction.

2.6.1 Seven Layer Information System Security

The seven-layer information system security is shown in the figure.

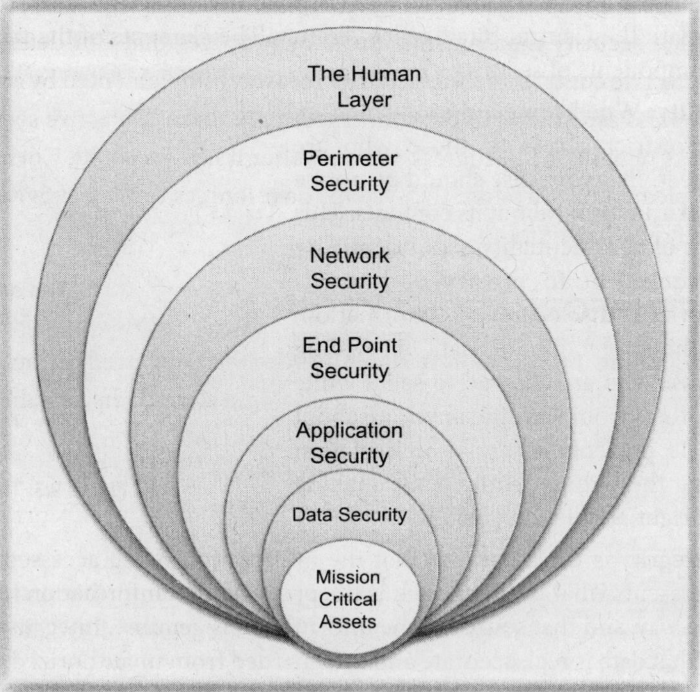

Figure 2.2: Information System Security Layers

- Mission Critical Assets – This is the information system asset that need to protect.
- Data Security – Data security controls protect the storage and transfer of data.
- Application Security – Applications security controls protect access to an application, an application's access to your mission critical assets, and the internal security of the application.
- Endpoint Security – Endpoint security controls protect the connection between devices and the network.
- Network Security – Network security controls protect an organization's network and prevent unauthorized access of the network.
- Perimeter Security – Perimeter security controls include both the physical and digital security methodologies that protect the business overall.
- The Human Layer – Humans are the weakest link in any cybersecurity posture. Human security controls include phishing simulations and access management controls that protect mission critical assets from a wide variety of human threats, including cyber criminals, malicious insiders, and negligent users.

2.7 SECURITY TRIAD

The security triad is actually a security model that has been developed to help people think about various parts of information technology security. The three main components of security triad are Confidentiality, Integrity and Availability (CIA). Each component represents a fundamental objective of information security. This model is also referred to as the AIC (Availability, Integrity, and Confidentiality) triad to avoid the confusion with the Central Intelligence Agency. The elements of the triad are considered the three most crucial components of security.

- **Confidentiality:** When protecting information, we want to restrict access to those who are allowed to see it. Everyone else should be not be allowed to learn anything about its contents. This is the essence of confidentiality. Confidentiality is roughly equivalent to privacy and avoids the unauthorized disclosure of information. It involves the protection of data, providing access for those who are allowed to see it while disallowing others from learning anything about its content. It prevents essential information from reaching the wrong people while making sure that the right people can get it.

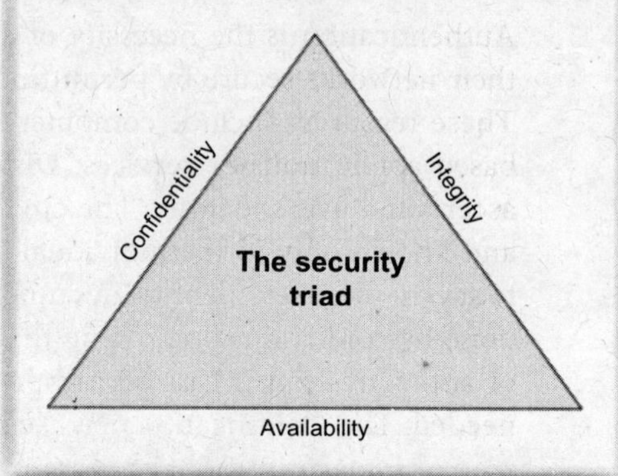

Figure 2.3: The Security Triad

- **Integrity:** Integrity is the assurance that the information being accessed has not been altered and truly represents what is intended. It is the property that information has not be altered in an unauthorized way, and that source of the information is genuine. Integrity refers to the methods for ensuring that data is real, accurate and safeguarded from unauthorized user modification. An example of this would be when a hacker is hired to go into the university's system and change a grade. Integrity can also be lost unintentionally, such as when a computer power surge corrupts a file or someone authorized to make a change accidentally deletes a file or enters incorrect information.
- **Availability:** Information availability is the third part of the CIA triad. Availability means that information can be accessed and modified by anyone authorized to do so in an appropriate timeframe. Depending on the type of information, appropriate timeframe can mean different things. For example, a stock trader needs information to be available immediately, while a sales person may be happy to get sales numbers for the day in a report the next morning. Companies such as Amazon.com will require their servers to be available twenty-four hours a day, seven days a week. Other companies may not suffer if their web servers are down for a few minutes once in a while.

2.8 TOOLS FOR INFORMATION SYSTEM SECURITY

In order to ensure the confidentiality, integrity and availability of information, organizations can choose from a variety of tools. Each of these tools can be utilized as part of an overall information security policy. These tools are not exclusive, some tools for confidentiality are suitable for integrity and availability and vice versa.

2.8.1 Confidentiality Tools

The popular confidentiality tools are shown in the figure and we will discuss on each of that.

- **Authentication:** An authentication is a process that ensures and confirms a user's identity or role that someone has. It is usually based on a combination of something the person has (like a smart card or a radio key for storing secret keys), something the person knows (like a password), or something the person is (like a human with a fingerprint). Tools for authentication are used to ensure that the person accessing the information is the correct person.

Authentication is the necessity of every organization because it enables organizations to keep their networks secure by permitting only authenticated users to access its protected resources. These resources include computer systems, networks, databases, websites and other network-based applications or services. Different systems may require different types of credentials to ascertain a user's identity. The credential often takes the form of a password, which is a secret and known only to the individual and the system. The most common form of authentication today is the user identity document (ID) and password. In this case, the authentication is done by confirming something that the user knows like their ID and password. But this form of authentication is easy to compromise and stronger forms of authentication are sometimes needed. The identification of a user through the use of a physical characteristic, such as an eye-scan or fingerprint is called biometrics.

Good password policies must be put in place in order to ensure that passwords cannot be compromised. Some of the more common policies that organizations should put in place are encouraging for complex passwords, changing of passwords regularly, and train users not to give away passwords.

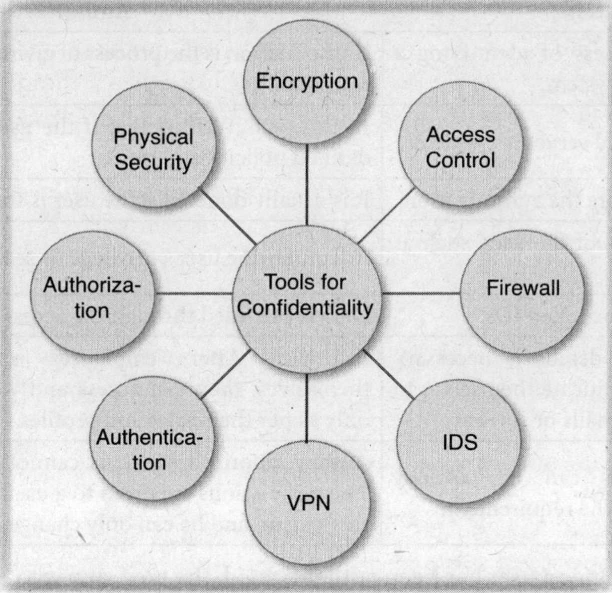

Figure 2.4: Confidentiality Tools for Information System Security

- **Authorization:** Authorization is a security mechanism which gives permission to do or have something. It is used to determine a person or system is allowed access to resources, based on an access control policy, including computer programs, files, services, data and application features. It is normally preceded by authentication for user identity verification. System administrators are typically assigned permission levels covering all system and user resources. During authorization, a system verifies an authenticated user's access rules and either grants or refuses resource access.

- **Difference between authentication and authorization:** Authentication confirms that users are who they say they are. Authorization gives those users permission to access a resource.

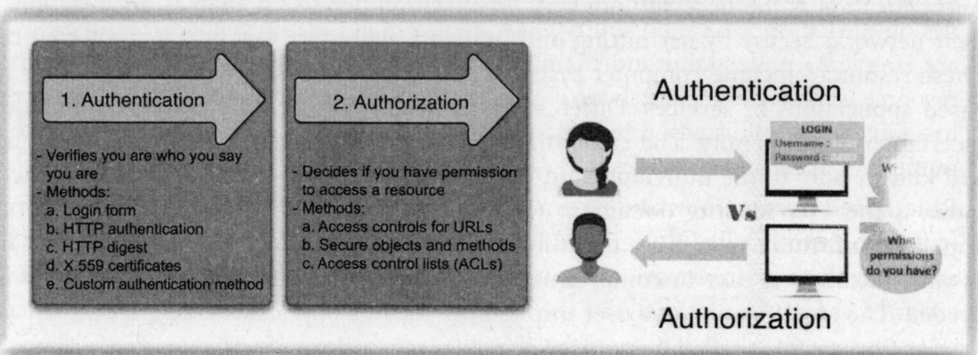

Figure 2.5: Explanation of Authentication and Authorization

Table 2.1: Displays the comparison between authentication and authorization

Table 2.1: Comparison of Authentication and Authorization

Authentication	Authorization
Authentication is the process of identifying a user to provide access to a system.	Authorization is the process of giving permission to access the resources.
In this, the user or client and server are verified.	In this, it is verified that if the user is allowed through the defined policies and rules.
It is usually performed before the authorization.	It is usually done once the user is successfully authenticated.
It requires the login details of the user, such as user name & password, etc.	It requires the user's privilege or security level.
Data is provided through the token IDs.	Data is provided through the access tokens.
Example: Entering Login details is necessary for the employees to authenticate themselves to access the organizational emails or software.	Example: After employees successfully authenticate themselves, they can access and work on certain functions only as per their roles and profiles.
Authentication credentials can be partially changed by the user as per the requirement.	Authorization permissions cannot be changed by the user. The permissions are given to a user by the owner/manager of the system, and he can only change it.

- **Access Control:** Once a user has been authenticated, the next step is to ensure that they can only access the information resources that are appropriate. This is done through the use of access control. Access control defines rules and policies to determine which all users are authorized to read, modify, add, and, or delete information. In access control systems, users need to present credentials before they can be granted access such as a person's name or a computer's serial number. In physical systems, these credentials may come in many forms, but credentials that can't be transferred provide the most security. We will discuss on two popular access control models.

- **Access Control List:** For each information resource that an organization wishes to manage, a list of users who have the ability to take specific actions can be created. This is an Access Control List (ACL). For each user, specific capabilities are assigned, such as read, write, delete, or add. Only users with those capabilities are allowed to perform those functions. If a user is not on the list, they have no ability to even know that the information resource exists. ACLs are simple to understand and maintain. The primary drawback is that each information resource is managed separately, so if a security administrator wanted to add or remove a user to a large set of information resources, it would be quite difficult. The maintenance of large number of users and resources is very difficult.
- **Role-Based Access Control:** The drawbacks of access control list led to an improved method of access control, called Role-Based Access Control (RBAC). Instead of giving specific users access rights to an information resource, users are assigned to roles and then those roles are assigned the access. This allows the administrators to manage users and roles separately, simplifying administration and, by extension, improving security.

- **Encryption:** Many times, an organization needs to transmit information over the Internet or transfer it on external media such as a CD or flash drive. In these cases, even with proper authentication and access control, it is possible for an unauthorized person to get access to the data. Encryption is a process of encoding data upon its transmission or storage so that only authorized individuals can read it. This encoding is accomplished by a computer program, which encodes the plain text that needs to be transmitted; then the recipient receives the cipher text and decodes it. This process is called decryption.
- **Firewalls:** Another method that an organization should use to increase security on its network is a firewall. A firewall can exist as hardware, software or both. A hardware firewall is a device that is connected to the network and filters the packets based on a set of rules. A software firewall runs on the operating system and intercepts packets as they arrive to a computer. A firewall protects all company servers and computers by stopping packets from outside the organization's network that do not meet a strict set of criteria. A firewall may also be configured to restrict the flow of packets leaving the organization. This may be done to eliminate the possibility of employees watching YouTube videos or using Facebook from a company computer. Some organizations may choose to implement multiple firewalls as part of their network security configuration, creating one or more sections of their network that are partially secured.
- **Intrusion Detection Systems:** Another device that can be placed on the network for security purposes is an Intrusion Detection System (IDS). An intrusion detection system does not add any additional security; instead, it provides the functionality to identify if the network is being attacked. An IDS can be configured to watch for specific types of activities and then alert security personnel if that activity occurs. An intrusion detection system also can log various types of traffic on the network for analysis later.
- **Virtual Private Networks:** Virtual Private Network (VPN) is the easiest and most effective way for people to protect their Internet traffic and keep their identities private online. VPN, is an encrypted connection over the Internet from a device to a network. The encrypted connection helps ensure that sensitive data is safely transmitted. It prevents unauthorized people from eavesdropping on the traffic and allows the user to conduct work remotely. When connected

to a secure VPN server, the Internet traffic goes through an encrypted tunnel that nobody can see into, including hackers, governments, and internet service provider. When using VPN, it can hide the Internet Protocol (IP) address and physical location while encrypting your internet traffic so that no one can know the activity doing online. VPN allows a user who is outside of the organization network to take a detour around the firewall and access the internal network from the outside. This feature helps employees to work remotely.

- **Physical Security:** Physical security describes measures designed to deny the unauthorized access of IT assets like facilities, equipment, personnel, resources and other properties from damage. It protects these assets from physical threats including theft, vandalism, fire and natural disasters. An organization can implement the best authentication scheme in the world, develop the best access control, and install firewalls and intrusion prevention, but its security cannot be complete without implementation of physical security. Physical security is the protection of the actual hardware and networking components that store and transmit information resources. To implement physical security, an organization must identify all of the vulnerable resources and take measures to ensure that these resources cannot be physically tampered with or stolen. Few of the physical security measures are as below.

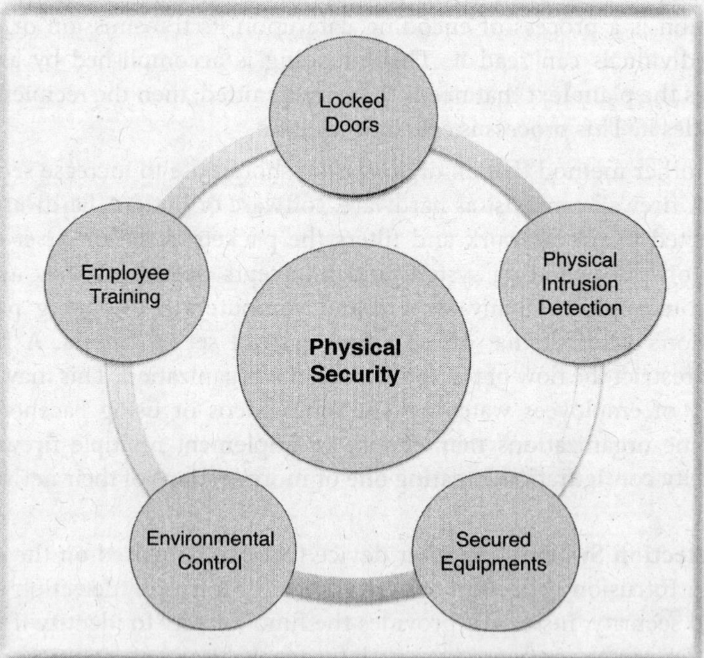

Figure 2.6: Physical Security Methods

- **Locked Doors:** All the security in the world is useless if an intruder can simply walk in and physically remove a computing device. High-value information assets should be secured in a location with controlled access.
- **Physical Intrusion Detection:** High-value information assets should be monitored the using of security cameras to detect unauthorized access to the physical locations where they exist.

The vibration sensors or sound sensors-based security systems can be implemented in areas which require high security. The intrusion detection can be made efficient by employing manual security personnel.

- **Secured Equipment:** Devices should be locked down to prevent them from being stolen. One employee's hard drive could contain all of your customer information, so it is essential that it be secured. The access to the equipment physical location can be controlled by access controls integrated with biometric identification systems. The equipment can be in individually secured by password protection as well as with bio metric supported access control.
- **Environmental Control:** An organization's servers and other high-value equipment should always be kept in a room that is controlled for temperature, humidity, and airflow. The risk of a server failure rises when these factors go out of a specified range.
- **Employee Training:** One of the most common ways thieves steal corporate information is by stealing employee's laptops while employees are out of office premises. Employees should be trained to secure their equipment whenever they are away from the office.

2.8.2 Integrity Tools

- **Checksums:** A checksum is a numerical value used to verify the integrity of a file or a data transfer. In other words, it is the computation of a function that maps the contents of a file to a numerical value. They are typically used to compare two sets of data to make sure that they are the same. A checksum function depends on the entire contents of a file. It is designed in a way that even a small change to the input file such as flipping a single bit is likely to results in different output value.
- **Data Correcting Codes:** It is a method for storing data in such a way that small changes can be easily detected and automatically corrected.

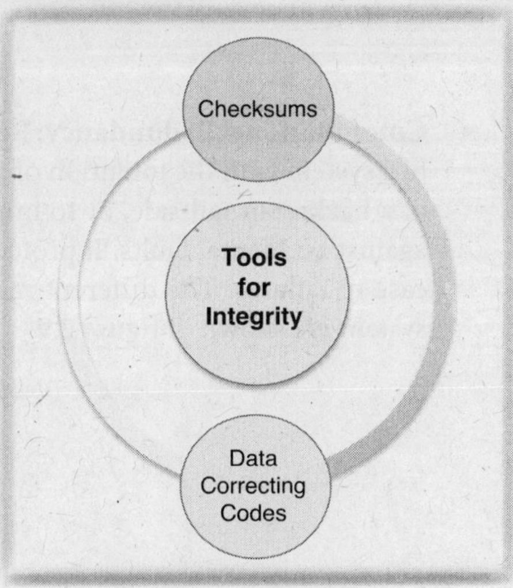

Figure 2.7: Integrity Tools

2.8.3 Availability Tools

- **Physical Protections:** Physical safeguard means to keep information available even in the event of physical challenges. It ensures sensitive information and critical information technology are housed in secure areas. Physical protections are important for maintaining the confidentiality also.

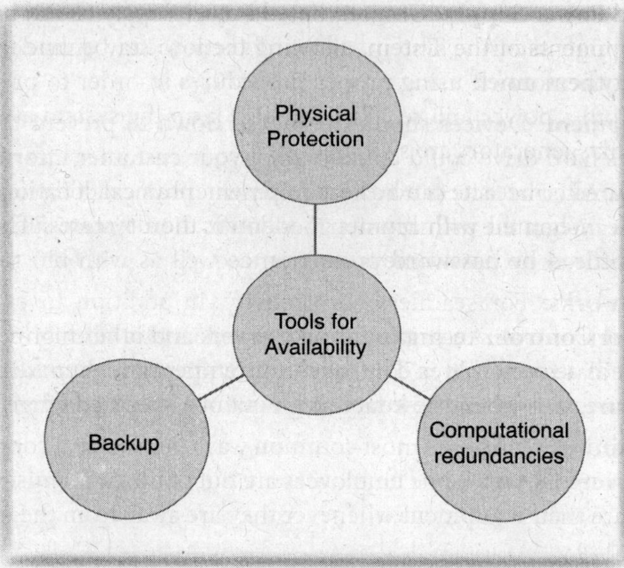

Figure 2.8: Availability Tools

- **Computational Redundancy:** Redundancy is the duplication of critical components or functions of a system with the intention of increasing reliability of the system. This is normally in the form of a backup or fail-safe, or to improve actual system performance. It is applied as fault tolerant against accidental faults. It protects computers and storage devices that serve as fallbacks in the case of failures. The different methods of redundancies which are common in an information system are shown in figure 2.9.

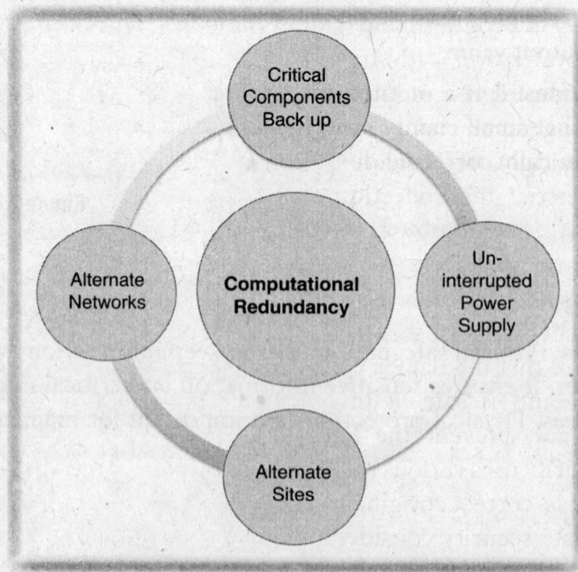

Figure 2.9: Methods of Computational Redundancy

- **Uninterrupted Power Supply:** Uninterrupted Power Supply (UPS) provides battery backup to critical components of the system, allowing them to stay online longer and allowing the IT staff to shut them down using proper procedures in order to prevent the data loss that might occur from a power failure. This will also keep the system available till the alternate arrangements like generators are switched-on.
- **Alternate Sites:** Alternate site can be kept ready where an exact replica of their critical data is always available. When the primary site goes down, the alternate site is immediately brought online so that little or no downtime is experienced.
- **Alternate Networks:** For seamless connectivity, in addition to existing communication network, network of other technologies like mobile, optic fiber or copper wire can be kept ready for immediate switch over. The service provider shall be more than one. They shall be in parallel operation or should be kept ready to switch over immediately on failure of existing operator's network.
- **Critical Components Backup:** The backup is required for the computer system hardware, software and network. A comprehensive backup plan for the entire organization is important for availability. Not only should the data on the servers be backed up, but individual computers used throughout the organization should also be backed up. A good backup plan should consist of several components. This includes a full understanding of the organizational information resources, details of information that the organization actually have and where is it stored. Some data may be stored on the organization's servers, other data on users' hard drives, some in the cloud, and some on third-party sites. An organization should make a full inventory of all of the information that needs to be backed up and determine the best way to back it up.

2.9 DATA SECURITY CONSIDERATIONS

Data security is the protection of programs and data in computers and communication systems against unauthorized access, modification, destruction, disclosure or transfer whether accidental or intentional by building physical arrangements and software controls. This refers to the right of individuals or organizations to deny or restrict the collection and use of information about unauthorized access. Data security requires system managers to reduce unauthorized access to the systems by building physical arrangements and software checks. Data security uses various methods to make sure that the data is correct, original, kept confidentially and is safe. It includes ensuring the integrity, privacy, prevent the loss or destruction of data. Data security uses various methods to make sure that the data is correct, original, kept confidentially and is safe. Data security consideration involves the protection of data against unauthorized access, modification, destruction, loss, disclosure or

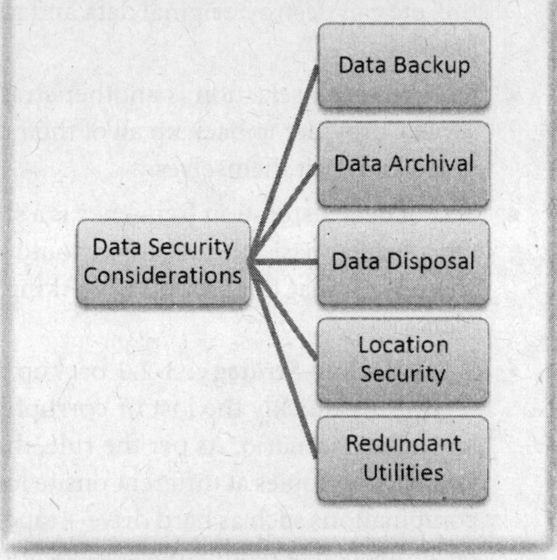

Figure 2.10: Main Data Security Considerations

transfer whether accidental or intentional. Some of the important data security considerations are data backups, archival, disposal, location security and redundant utilities

2.9.1 Data Backup

Backing up data and files is one of the most important areas in the information technology world. It is now essential for all the computer users, system administrators, information security officers and businesses to backup their critical data, in order to protect it from loss or corruption. However, storing the data in one backup location is not sufficient to safeguard the important data and files. Data backup refers to save additional copies of our data in separate physical or cloud locations from data files in storage. It is essential for us to keep securely, store, and backup our data on a regular basis. Securing of the data will help us to prevent from accidental or malicious damage/modification to data, theft of valuable information, breach of confidentiality agreements and privacy laws. Data security prevents premature release of data which can create intellectual property right claims, and ensures that data is released after checking for authenticity and accuracy. Keeping reliable and regular backups of our data protects against the risk of damage or loss due to power failure, hardware failure, software or media faults, viruses or hacking, or even human errors.

Data backup is the process of making copies of data files to use in the event when the original files are lost. It is also used to make copies for historical records or to meet the requirements of a data retention policy. As information has become a strategic asset, whole industry has sprung up around the technologies necessary for implementing a proper backup strategy. Below strategies are important for data backup.

- The frequency of data backup in an organization is based on their strategy. The frequency of backups will be based on how important the data is to the company as well as the ability of the company to replace any data that is lost. Critical data should be backed up more frequently while less critical data could be backed up in comparatively long-time gaps.
- Data backup storage location is a strategic decision of the organization. If all of the backup data is stored in the same facility as the original copies of the data, then events, such as an earthquake, fire, etc can destroy original data and the backup so it is essential to back up the data in an offsite location.
- Storage entity selection is another strategic decision of backup. A company can contract with a service provider to back up all of their data or they can purchase large amounts of online storage space and do it themselves.
- Test of data restoration frequency is a strategic decision related to data backup of an organization. On a regular basis, the backups should be put to the test by having some of the data restored. This will ensure that the process is working and will give the organization confidence in the backup plan.
- **3-2-1 Backup Strategy:** 3-2-1 backup strategy is to protect the data and increase the chances of recovering quickly the lost or corrupted data. The 3-2-1 backup rule is to keep the data safe in any failure scenario. As per the rule, three copies of the primary data is to be made. Of this, save two backup copies at different onsite locations in different storage media like NAS, SAN etc with combinations such as hard drive + tape backup or DVD + flash drive. The third backup copy will be at offsite like remote physical location, cloud, FTP, etc.

Storing one backup copy offsite strengthens data security while having another backup copy onsite helps faster and simpler recovery in case of failure. As cloud-based backup companies evolved, mostly the offsite backup has become the cloud.

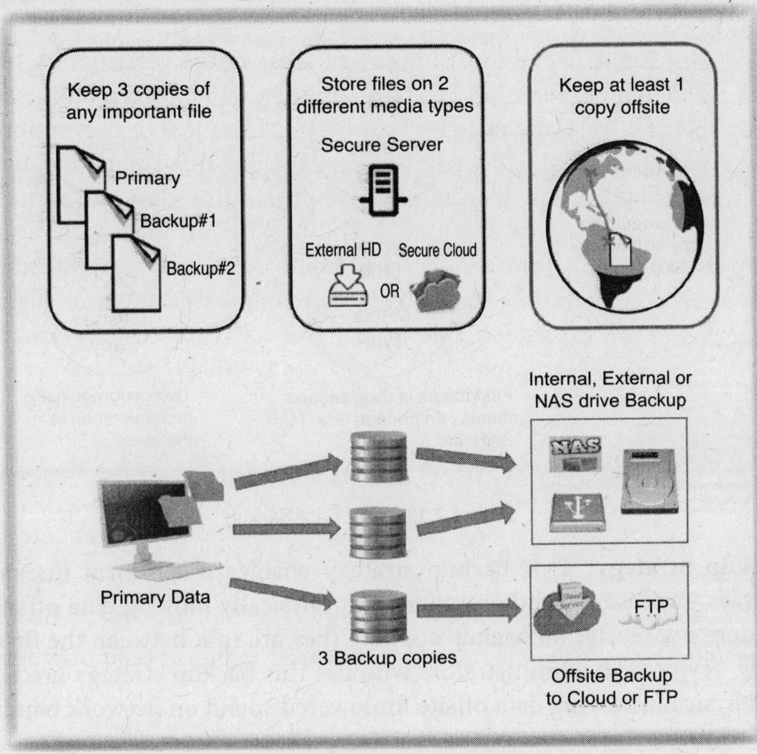

Figure 2.11: :3-2-1 Data Backup

- **3-1-2 Backup Strategy:**

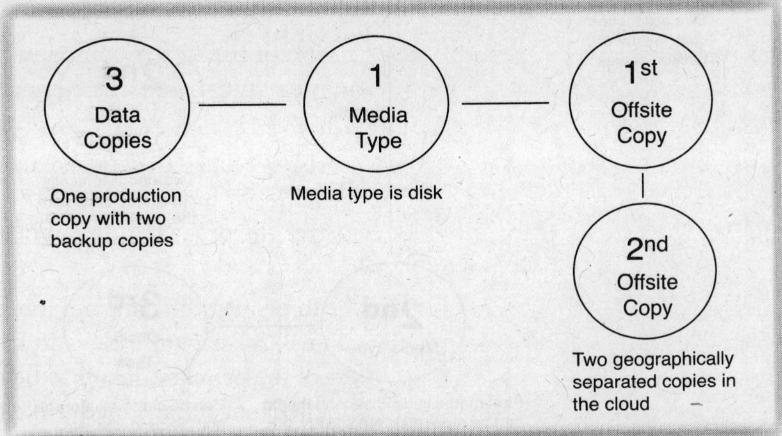

Figure 2.12: 3-1-2 Data Backup

- **3-2-2 Backup Strategy:** 3-2-2 backup strategy provides mix of local and cloud-based protection. In this backup strategy, we can achieve continuity through the use of both the cloud and a local second media type. The cloud provides both continuity and extended retention. The local second media provides another copy of what we have in the cloud in a 3-2-2 backup strategy.

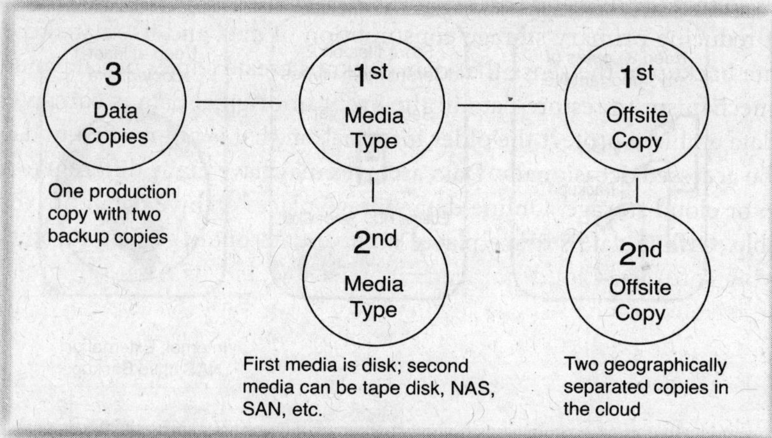

Figure 2.13: 3-2-2 Data Backup

- **3-2-3 Backup Strategy:** This backup strategy enables to perform disaster recovery in two different ways – with the cloud and then with physically moving data offsite. In this approach, the cloud does not receive all backup copies – they are split between the first and second media type locally. Typical IT administrators who use this backup strategy are trading off increased labor like physically moving data offsite for lowered spend on network bandwidth.

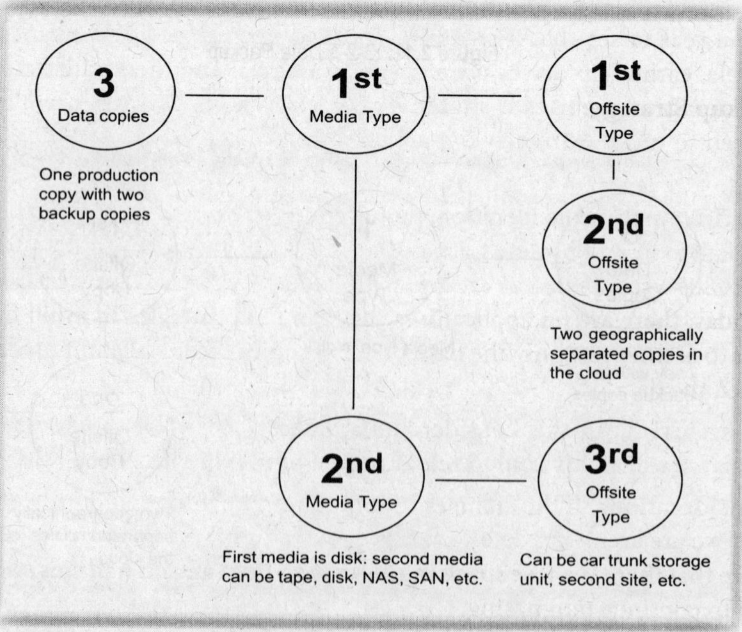

Figure 2.14: 3-2-3 Data Backup

2.9.2 Data Archival

Data archiving is the process of keeping the data at a secure place for long-term storage. The data might be stored in safe locations so that it can be used whenever it is required. The archive data is still essential to the organization and may be needed for future reference. Also, data archives are indexed and have search capabilities so that the files and parts of files can be easily located and retrieved. The data archival serve as a way of reducing primary storage consumption of data and its related costs. Data archival is different from data backup in the sense that data backups create copies of data and this will be used as a data recovery mechanism to restore data in the event of original data is corrupted or destroyed. On the other hand, data archives protect the older information that is not needed in day-to-day operations but may have to be accessed occasionally. Data archives may have many different forms. It can be stored as online, offline, or cloud storage. Online data storage places archive data onto disk systems where it is readily accessible. Offline data storage places archive data onto the tape or other removable media using data archiving software. Cloud storage is inexpensive, but its costs can grow over time as more data is added to the cloud archive. The following considerations will help us to improve the long-term usefulness of archives. The medium and device used for storing the archive data are carefully decided based on the utility. Below are the considerations for data archiving.

- **Storage medium:** The first thing is to what storage medium we use for archives. The archived data will be stored for long periods of time, so we must need to choose the type of media that will be lost as long as our retention policy dictates.
- **Storage device:** This consideration takes into account about the storage device we are using for our archives which will be accessible in a few years. There is no way to predict which types of storage devices will stand the best. So, it is essential to try to pick those devices that have the best chance of being supported over the long term.
- **Revisiting old archives:** The archive policies and the storage mechanisms that are in use today for archiving data would change over time. The archived data has to be reviewed at least once a year to see that if anything needs to be migrated into a different storage medium. For example, earlier zip drives were used for archival and then transferred all archives to CD. Later the storage of archives is shifted to DVD. Since DVD drives can also read CDs, so there was no need to move extremely old archives from CD to DVD. Presently, archiving is moving to cloud.
- **Data usability:** In this consideration, we have seen one major problem in the real world in which archived data is in an obsolete format. For example, document files that had been archived in the early 1980s were created by an application known as PFS Write which was supported till late 90s but today, there are no applications that can read that file. To avoid this situation, it might be helpful to archive not only the data but also copies the installation media for the applications that created the data.
- **Selective archiving:** In this consideration, we have to decide about what should be archived. That means we will archive only a selective part of data because not all data is equally important.
- **Space considerations:** If the archives become huge, we must plan for the long-term retention of all data. If we are archiving data to removable media, capacity planning might be simple which makes sure that there is a free space in the vault to hold all and it makes sure that there is a room in budget to continue purchasing.

- **Online vs. offline storage:** In this consideration, we have to decide whether to store the archives on a dedicated archive online server or offline which is a removable media. Both methods of archival have advantages and disadvantages. Storing of data online keeps the data easily accessible. But keeping data online may be vulnerable to theft, tampering, corruption, etc. Offline storage enables us to store an unlimited amount of data, but it is not readily accessible.

2.9.3 Data Disposal

Data destruction or disposal of data is the method of destroying data which is stored on tapes, hard disks and other electronic media so that it is completely unreadable, unusable and inaccessible for unauthorized purposes. The organization retains records of data as long as they are needed. When it is no longer required, appropriately destroys them or disposes of that data in some way. The managed process of data disposal avoids the unnecessary storage costs incurred by using office or server space in maintaining records which is no longer needed by the organization. The following are the considerations for the secure disposal of data.

- **Eliminate access:** In this consideration, we have to ensure that eliminating access account does not have any rights to re-access the disposed of data again.
- **Destroy the Data:** In this consideration, we should understand that removal of data from storage media will be safe. Even reformatting or repartitioning a drive to "erase" the data that it stores is not good enough. Presently many tools are available which can help us to delete files more securely. To encrypt the data on the drive before performing any deletion can help us to make data more difficult to recover later.
- **Destroy the device:** In the most cases, storage media need to be physically destroyed to ensure that our sensitive data is not leaked to whoever gets the drives next. To do this, there are experts who can effectively make any data on our drives unrecoverable.
- **Keep the record of which systems have been decommissioned:** In this, we have to make sure that the storage media has been fully decommissioned securely and they do not consist of something misplaced or overlooked. It is best, if storage media that have not been fully decommissioned are kept in a specific location, while decommissioned equipment placed somewhere else so that it will help us to avoid making mistakes.
- **Keep careful records:** In this consideration, it is necessary to keep the record of whoever is responsible for decommissioning a storage media. If more than one person is assigned for such responsibility, he should sign off after the completion of the decommissioning process. So that, if something happened wrong, we know whom to talk to find out what happened and how bad the mistake is.
- **Eliminate potential clues:** In this consideration, we have to clear the configuration settings from networking equipment. We do this because it can provide crucial clues to a security cracker to break into network and the systems that reside on it.
- **Keep system secure until disposal of data:** In this consideration, we should have to make clear guidelines about who should have access to the equipment in need of secure disposal. It will be better to ensure that nobody should have access authentication to it before disposal of data won't get his or her hands on it.

2.9.4 Location Security

Organizations face a daunting task in deciding where to locate their business-critical data. Since the amount of data is enormous it is stored across different devices in multiple locations from on-premises to cloud. Knowing the location of the data center helps in planning the location security to protect the data. Companies usually locate their data hubs several miles outside the city. They need to look carefully into the location restrictions. For example, the warehouse located in a disaster-prone area poses a huge risk of data compromise during a calamity.

2.9.5 Redundant utilities

The data center has critical data and facilities required to keep the business up and running. To restrict unwanted intruders from entering the data center's perimeter, strong security barriers must be set up. These barriers can be two-factor authentication, access control, or leveraging CCTV surveillance. But no matter how complex the security is there will always be some data loss. This can be due to various reasons like employee negligence or malicious activity. Hence duplication of critical components of the system becomes necessary. This increases the reliability of the system, improves performance, and provides a fail-safe backup.

2.10 SECURITY POLICIES

Besides the technical controls listed above, organizations also need to implement security policies as a form of administrative control. In fact, these policies should really be a starting point in developing an overall security plan. A good information-security policy lays out the guidelines for employee use of the information resources of the company and provides the company recourse in the case that an employee violates a policy.

A good policy can be "a formal, brief, and high-level statement or plan that embraces an organization's general beliefs, goals, objectives, and acceptable procedures for a specified subject area." Policies require compliance; failure to comply with a policy will result in disciplinary action. A policy does not lay out the specific technical details, instead it focuses on the desired results. A security policy should be based on the guiding principles of confidentiality, integrity, and availability.

A good example of a security policy that many will be familiar with is a web use policy. A web use policy lays out the responsibilities of company employees as they use company resources to access the Internet.

A security policy should also address any governmental or industry regulations that apply to the organization. For example, if the organization is a university, it must be aware of the Family Educational Rights and Privacy Act (FERPA), which restricts who has access to student information. Health care organizations are obligated to follow several regulations, such as the Health Insurance Portability and Accountability Act (HIPAA).

2.11 MOBILE SECURITY

As the use of mobile devices such as smartphones and tablets increase, organizations must be ready to address the unique security concerns that the use of these devices bring. One of the first questions an organization must consider is whether to allow mobile devices in the workplace at all. Many employees already have these devices, so organizations should decide whether they should allow employees to bring their own devices and use them as part of their employment activities or should they provide the devices to the employees. Creating a BYOD (Bring Your Own Device) policy allows employees to integrate themselves more fully into their job and can bring higher employee satisfaction and productivity. In many cases, it may be virtually impossible to prevent employees from having their own smartphones or tablets in the workplace. If the organization provides the devices to its employees, it gains more control over use of the devices, but it also exposes itself to the possibility of an administrative and cost burden.

Mobile devices can pose many unique security challenges to an organization. Probably one of the biggest concerns is theft of intellectual property. For an employee with malicious intent, it would be a very simple process to connect a mobile device either to a computer via the USB port or wirelessly to the corporate network, and download confidential data. It would also be easy to secretly take a high-quality picture using a built-in camera. When an employee does have permission to access and save company data on his or her device, a different security threat emerges: that device now becomes a target for thieves. Theft of mobile devices including laptops is one of the primary methods that data thieves use.

Security of mobile devices will start with a good policy regarding their use. Organizations should consider developing a mobile device policy that addresses the use of the camera, use of voice recording, application purchases, encryption at rest, Wi-Fi auto connect settings, Bluetooth settings, VPN use, password settings, lost or stolen device reporting, and backup.

Besides policies, there are several different tools that an organization can use to mitigate some of these risks. For example, if a device is stolen or lost, geolocation software can help the organization to find it. In some cases, it may even make sense to install remote data-removal software, which will remove data from a device if it becomes a security risk. Below are few of the considerations for mobile security.

- **Usability:** When looking to secure information resources, organizations must balance the need for security with users' need to effectively access and use these resources. If a system's security measures make it difficult to use, then users will find ways to overcome that, which may make the system more vulnerable than it would have been without the security measures. For example, If the organization requires an extremely long password with several special characters, an employee may resort to writing it down and putting it in a drawer since it will be impossible to memorize.
- **Train Workforce:** Organizations can use a security awareness training program to educate their employees about the importance of data security. Organizations begin by creating a team to create a strategic plan for the security awareness training program. The team should include executive management as well as initiative leaders. The team can develop programs to educate the organization's work force. This training should consist of digital security best practices and phishing testing.
- **Embrace a Data-Centric Security Strategy:** Mobile communications, Internet of Things (IoT) and the cloud have dissolved the traditional boundaries of the network. As such, organizations need to now approach network security from a more holistic and strategic viewpoint. Organizations need to specifically embrace a data-centric approach through which they develop a strategic understanding of what data they have and how valuable that data is to their business

operations. Once they have an idea of what data they have, organizations should protect their data by doing encryption the right way. Organizations should develop a robust data backup strategy and test that strategy and their backups often.

- **Implement Multi-Factor Authentication:** Many are quick to change the login credentials following the public disclosure of a data breach. But by then, it could be too late. Acknowledging that threat, organizations should take additional steps to protect their users' accounts against compromise. They can do so by following controlled use of administrative privileges and using Multi-Factor Authentication (MFA) for all administrative account access. They should also encourage users to implement MFA across their personal web accounts.
- **Set Strict Permissions for the Cloud:** As organisations increasingly migrate their workloads to the cloud, organizations need to lock down their cloud-based data. In many of those incidents, a misconfiguration was responsible for exposing the personal information of millions of customers. Security personnel should subsequently audit those accounts and their levels of access to ensure the principle of least privilege. They should not necessarily apply default permissions to their cloud-based data.
- **Exercise Vigilance for Patch Management:** Organizations can strengthen the security of their data by patching vulnerabilities through which malicious actors could gain access to their network assets. They can do this by formulating a patch management program through which they test patches before they deploy them on their production systems. Organizations' engagement with a security fix doesn't end after they've implemented it. They need to follow up a patch's deployment by scanning their system to confirm that the vulnerability is no longer present. This step will reveal if the patch has addressed the vulnerable components and if organizations need to take additional measures to remediate the vulnerability.

2.12 SUMMARY

In this chapter, we have explained information system security, control and threats followed by security layers and security triad. The tools for confidentiality, integrity and availability are discussed. The chapter concludes with discussion on data security considerations, security policies as well as mobile security.

2.13 OBJECTIVE QUESTIONS

The answer of the multiple-choice questions is marked in **bold**.

1. Which is a subset of information security system?

(a) Network security (b) Cyber security
(c) **All of these** (d) None of these

2. .... is a classification of security control.

(a) Security management (b) Operational security
(c) Physical security control (d) **All of these**

3. .... is an example of computer abuse.

(a) Cyber bullying (b) Identity theft
(c) **All of these** (d) None of these

4. Which is not a layer in seven layer information system security?
   (a) **Cyber security** (b) Perimeter security
   (c) Application security (d) Data security
5. Which is not a component of security triad?
   (a) Confidentiality (b) **Trust**
   (c) Integrity (d) Availability
6. .... is not a tool for information system confidentiality.
   (a) VPN (b) IDS
   (c) Firewall (d) **Check sums**
7. Which is the tool common for confidentiality and availability?
   (a) **Physical protection** (b) Backup
   (c) Encryption (d) All of these
8. Which of the below is a data security consideration?
   (a) Redundant utility (b) Location security
   (c) Data Backup (d) **All of these**
9. Which is a consideration for data archiving?
   (a) Storage medium (b) Storage device
   (c) Selective archiving (d) **All of these**
10. .... is a consideration for data disposal.
    (a) Eliminate access (b) Destroy data
    (c) Destroy device (d) **All of these**

2.14 REVIEW QUESTIONS

1. Explain on information system security.
2. Discuss about information system security control.
3. Explain the threats to information system.
4. Explain seven-layer information system security.
5. Discuss the security triad.
6. Discuss about the confidentiality tools for information system security.
7. Differentiate between authentication and authorization.
8. Explain various physical security methods in information system.
9. Write short note on information system integrity tools.
10. Explain various availability tools using in information system.
11. Discuss various methods of computational redundancy.
12. Explain on main data security considerations.

13. Explain various data backup strategy.
14. Explain on data archiving
15. Explain about data disposal.
16. Discuss on different mobile security considerations.
17. Explain the security policies of information system.

2.15 ABBREVIATIONS AND SYMBOLS

Abbreviations	Full Form	Description
ACL	Access Control List	ACL is a set of rules that is usually used to filter network traffic.
BYOD	Bring Your Own Device	This is an organizational policy that encourages, employees to access enterprise data and systems using personal devices.
CCTV	Closed-Circuit Television.	CCTV also known as video surveillance, is the use of video cameras to transmit a signal to a specific place, on a limited set of monitors.
CD	Compact Disk	CD is a digital optical disc data storage format that was co-developed by Philips and Sony to store and play digital audio recordings.
CIA	Confidentiality Integrity and Availability	CIA is the cornerstone of any organization's security infrastructure and they should function as goals and objectives for every security program.
DVD	Digital Versatile Disc	DVD is a type of optical media used for storing digital data.
FERPA	Family Educational Rights and Privacy Act	This US legislation gives students the right to inspect, correct, amend and control the disclosure of information in education records.
FTP	File Transfer Protocol	FTP is a set of rules that computers follow for the transferring of files from one system to another over the Internet.
HIPAA	Health Insurance Portability and Accountability Act	HIPAA is a national standard to protect individuals' electronic personal health information that is created, received, used, or maintained by an entity.
HTTP	Hypertext Transfer Protocol	HTTP is an application-layer protocol for transmitting hypermedia documents such as HTML.
ID	Identity Document	ID a document used to verify a person's identity.
IDS	Intrusion Detection System	IDS is a device or software application that monitors a network or system for malicious activity or policy violations.

Abbreviations	Full Form	Description
IPS	Intrusion Prevention System	IPS is a form of network security that works to detect and prevent identified threats.
IT	Information Technology	IT is everything that use computers for like communications networks, safeguarding data, administering databases or doing a range of other work to computing efficiency and security.
MFA	Multi-Factor Authentication	MFA is used to ensure that digital users are who they say they are by requiring that they provide at least two pieces of evidence to prove their identity.
NAS	Network Attached Storage	NAS is a data storage device that connects to and is accessed through a network, instead of connecting directly to a computer.
RBAC	Role Based Access Control	RBAC is a mechanism that restricts system access by the role which determines permissions the system grants to the user. This is also known as role-based security.
SAN	Storage Area Network	SAN is a specialized, high speed network that provides block level network access to storage.
UPS	Uninterruptible Power Supply	UPS provides backup power when your regular power source fails or voltage drops to an unacceptable level. This is also known as battery backup.
VPN	Virtual Private Network	VPN connection disguises the data traffic online and protects it from external access.

2.16 LIST OF FIGURES AND TABLES

The details of figures and tables used in this chapter is as below.

CHAPTER

3 Privacy in Information System

CONTENTS

3.1 INTRODUCTION

In this chapter, we will discuss on privacy, its importance, challenges and laws that are related to information system. The actions required for information privacy and the tools as well as solutions required for that are discussed. Privacy is the right to be let alone, or freedom from interference or intrusion. Privacy is a human right, essential to autonomy and the protection of human dignity, serving as the foundation upon which many other human rights are built. Privacy enables us to create barriers and manage boundaries to protect ourselves from unwarranted interference in our lives, which allows us to negotiate who we are and how we want to interact with the world around us. Privacy helps us to establish boundaries for limiting who has access to our bodies, places and things, as well as our communications and our information.

3.2 INFORMATION PRIVACY

Privacy of information in an information system usually relates to personal data stored on computer systems or transmission through the network. With the advancement of the digital age, personal information vulnerabilities have increased. The need to maintain information privacy is applicable to collected personal information, such as medical records, financial data, criminal records, political records, business related information or website data. Information privacy is also known as data privacy. Information privacy is considered an important aspect of information sharing. Information privacy may be applied in numerous technical and legal ways to ensure that information is available only to those with authorized access.

3.3 IMPORTANCE OF PRIVACY

The privacy is important due to below reasons.

- **Limit on Power:** Privacy is a limit on government power, as well as the power of private organizations. The more someone knows about us, the more power they can have over us. Personal data is used to make very important decisions in our lives. Personal data can be used to affect our reputations and it can be used to influence our decisions and shape our behavior. It can be used as a tool to exercise control over us. If personnel data reach in the wrong hands, it can be used to cause us great harm.
- **Respect for Individuals:** Privacy is about respecting individuals. If a person has a reasonable desire to keep something private, it is disrespectful to ignore that person's wishes without a compelling reason to do so. The desire for privacy can conflict with important values, so privacy may not always win out in the balance. Sometimes people's desires for privacy are just brushed aside because of a view that the harm in doing so is trivial. Even if this doesn't cause major injury, it demonstrates a lack of respect for that person.
- **Reputation Management:** Privacy enables people to manage their reputations. How we are judged by others affects our opportunities, friendships, and overall well-being. Although we can't have complete control over our reputations, we must have some ability to protect our reputations from being unfairly harmed. Protecting reputation depends on protecting against not only falsehoods but also certain truths. Knowing private details about people's lives doesn't necessarily lead to more accurate judgment about people. People judge badly, they judge in haste, they judge out of context, they judge without hearing the whole story, and they judge with hypocrisy. Privacy helps people to protect themselves from these troublesome judgments.
- **Maintaining Appropriate Social Boundaries:** People establish boundaries from others in society. These boundaries are both physical and informational. We need places of solitude to retreat to, places where we are free of the gaze of others in order to relax and feel at ease. We also establish informational boundaries and we have an elaborate set of these boundaries for the many different relationships that we have. Privacy helps people to manage these boundaries. Breaches of these boundaries can create awkward social situations and damage our relationships. Privacy is also helpful to reduce the social friction that we encounter in life. Most people don't want everybody to know everything about them. Sometimes we don't want to or have to know everything about other people.
- **Trust:** In relationships, whether personal, professional, governmental, or commercial, we depend upon trusting the other party. Breaches of confidentiality are breaches of that trust. In professional relationships such as our relationships with doctors and lawyers, this trust is key to maintaining open and honest in the relationship. Likewise, we trust other people whom we interact with as well as the companies we do business with. When trust is breached in one relationship, that could make us more reluctant to trust in other relationships.
- **Control Over One's Life:** Personal data is essential to so many decisions made about us, from whether we get a loan, a license or a job to our personal and professional reputations. Personal data is used to determine whether we are investigated by the government, or searched at the airport, or denied the ability to fly. Indeed, personal data affects nearly everything, including

what messages and content we see on the Internet. Without having knowledge of what data is being used, how it is being used, the ability to correct and amend it, we are virtually helpless in today's world. Moreover, we are helpless without the ability to have a say in how our data is used or the ability to object and have legitimate grievances be heard when data uses can harm us. One of the hallmarks of freedom is having autonomy and control over our lives, and we can't have that if so many important decisions about us are being made in secret without our awareness or participation.

- **Freedom of Thought and Speech:** Privacy is key to freedom of thought. A watchful eye over everything we read or watch can make us un-comfortable from exploring ideas outside the mainstream. Privacy is also key to protecting speaking unpopular messages. We may want to criticize people we know to others but do not want to share that criticism with the world. A person might want to explore ideas that their family, friends or colleague's dislike.
- **Freedom of Social and Political Activities:** Privacy helps to protect our ability to associate with other people and engage in political activity. A key component of freedom of political association is the ability to do so with privacy if one chooses. We protect privacy at the ballot because of the concern that failing to do so would make people un comfortable invoting their true conscience. Privacy of the associations and activities that lead up to going to the voting booth matters as well, because this is how we form and discuss our political beliefs. The watchful eye can disrupt and unduly influence these activities.
- **Freedom to Change:** Many people are not static. They change and grow throughout their lives. There is a great value in the ability to have a second chance, to correct and move beyond a mistake for to reinvent oneself. Privacy nurtures this ability. It allows people to grow and mature without being chained with all the foolish things they might have done in the past. Certainly, not all misdeeds should be shielded, but some should be, because we want to encourage and facilitate growth and improvement.
- **Need to Explain or Justify:** An important reason why privacy matters is not having to explain or justify oneself. We may do a lot of things which, if judged from by others who lack complete knowledge or understanding, may seem odd or embarrassing or worse. It can be a heavy burden, if we constantly have to wonder how everything we do will be perceived by others and have to be at the ready to explain.

3.4 IMPORTANCE OF INFORMATION PRIVACY

Information or data is one of the most important assets a company has. With the rise of the data economy, companies find enormous value in collecting, sharing and using data. Companies such as Google, Facebook, and Amazon have all built empires on the top of data economy. Transparency in how businesses request consent, abide by their privacy policies, and manage the data that they've collected is vital to building trust and accountability with customers and partners who expect privacy. Many companies have learned the importance of privacy the hard way, through highly publicized privacy fails. To safely exist in one's space and freely express one's opinions behind closed doors is critical to living in a democratic society. Information privacy of different data types are explained below.

- **Internet or Online Privacy:** All personal data shared over the Internet is subject to privacy issues. Most websites publish a privacy policy that details the website's intended use of collected online and/or offline collected data.

- **Financial Privacy:** Financial information is particularly sensitive, as it may easily use to commit online and/or offline fraud.
- **Medical Privacy:** All medical records are subject to stringent laws that address user access privileges. By law, security and authentication systems are often required for individuals that process and store medical records.

3.5 CHALLENGES IN INFORMATION PRIVACY

Information privacy is a branch of data security concerned with the handling of data with consent, notice, and regulatory obligations. Information privacy is also known as data privacy. Practical information privacy concerns are often revolving around on methods of data sharing with third parties as well as methods of data collection, storage and meeting regulatory restrictions.

The main challenges in information privacy are

- **Embedding Data Privacy:** Many businesses only have data privacy included onto their IT security or disaster recovery plan but that's not good enough because data privacy touches on so many parts of business. It needs to be baked into the data strategy and staff training. Ensure to collaborate with and get buy-in from all departments. Make sure to choose tools that support current privacy policies.
- **Proliferating Devices:** Data privacy becomes harder to handle when adding IoT, bring-your-own-device IT policies and proliferation of Internet connected tablets, phones and watches. When adding more devices into the work place, more data need to manage. The organization must be able to manage compliance and data privacy from any source, different operating systems and multiple apps. To manage this, ensure that the right data governance procedures is in place.
- **Increasing Maintenance Costs:** Keeping systems secure and preventing data privacy issues at the enterprise level can be expensive. The costs of data breach are more significant. Automating the processes is the solution for this issue. It helps in reducing the number of data silos, eliminating points of friction and manual processing, reducing the risk of human error, more opportunities for de-duplication, improved governance and control which will lower costs.
- **Difficulty in Access Control:** Data privacy breaches are often caused by poorly managed access control within organizations. People and processes matter as much as technology. Humans are the weakest link in the chain of privacy and security. It is harder to manage user access and secure sensitive data manually. To remedy this, there is a need for an effective data architecture and strong data governance processes.
- **Visibility into all data:** If the organization isn't aware of the location, nature, and sensitivity of data that they are holding, they cannot keep the right information private. Many organizations do not have visibility to its all data. Usage of tools to discover and classify the data is essential for getting visibility into all organizational data. This will ensure capability to treat data uniquely and protect the sensitive data from any privacy issues.
- **Bad Data Culture:** Huge data is increasingly a risk rather than an asset. Earlier many organizations and IT leaders believed that more data is always better. That's no longer automatically true. Keeping data for its own sake broadens the attack surface for data theft and increases the risk of breaching many data privacy laws. Forward-thinking IT teams need to balance the value of collecting, storing and processing large volumes of data against the pressing requirements for

privacy, security and compliance. Instead, build a great data culture that understands the value of data and data privacy.

- **Ever-increasing scale of data:** As cloud storage and computation costs come down, businesses are now having huge data. As the quantity of data grows, the challenge of managing these data is high. With hundreds of systems and millions of data records, there is a need for solution to protect privacy of data.
- **Regulations and Documentation:** With many internal and external regulations to follow in various organizations, it is difficult to keep track of the level of data privacy required for different datasets. By building processes, data modeling and automating as much as possible, the complexities for handling different regulations and efforts on keeping data privacy can be reduced.

3.6 INFORMATION PRIVACY LAWS AND ACTS

Lawmakers have recognized the importance of having data privacy regulation and the need to hold organizations responsible for end-user data. Organizations are now required to determine what data privacy acts and laws affect their users. For instance, organizations must know where the data originated, what personally identifiable information it might contain and usage methodology.

Information privacy, data privacy or data protection laws provide a legal framework on how to obtain, use and store data of persons. The various laws around the world describe the rights of persons to control who is using its data. Let's take a closer look at how the most recent data privacy regulations impact users and organizations. There are laws related to privacy protection in many countries. This includes usually the right to get details on data stored location, purpose of using and to request the deletion. We shall discuss some of these laws.

The European Union has the General Data Protection Regulation (GDPR). This is a regulation on data protection and privacy in the European Union (EU) and the European Economic Area (EEA). It also addresses the transfer of personal data outside the EU and EEA areas. GDPR is considered as the most wide-ranging and comprehensive data privacy legislation. The law grants citizens a number of rights, including the right to data portability which allows people to move their data between platforms and the right not to be subject to decisions based on automated data processing. Example of this is the use of an algorithm to reject applicants for jobs or loans. The practical implications of rules are incredibly complex.

France's data protection law dates back to 1978 with the enactment of Law 78-17 on information technologies, data files and civil liberties. In such cases data may be kept for a maximum of one year. Violations of the 1978 law may result in criminal, civil, or administrative proceedings. In 2017, the French ministry of justice introduced the French data protection bill. The bill amends the current French data protection act 1978, in light of the GDPR and the law enforcement directive.

GDPR is sometimes referred to as DSGVO in Germany. The European Union's General Data Protection Regulations, which came into effect in 2018, has been put in place to deal with privacy concerns about the massive volumes of personal data that are being collected, processed, and retained across many use cases.

In the United Kingdom, the data protection act implemented in 1984 and in 1998 implemented the EU directive on the protection of personal data. In 2016, GDPR superseded previous protection acts and in 2018, data protection act was updated as the data protection law in the UK. It is a national law which complements the GDPR.

In Switzerland, the right to privacy is guaranteed in article 13 of the Swiss federal constitution. Switzerland is in European continent, but is not a member of the European Union or of the European Economic Area. The Swiss Federal Data Protection Act (DPA) and the Swiss Federal Data Protection Ordinance (DPO) entered into force in 1993 which is amended in 2008. Unlike the data protection legislation of many other countries, the DPA protects both personal data pertaining to persons and legal entities.

In Canada, the Personal Information Protection and Electronic Documents Act (PIPEDA) came into effect in 2001. The PIPEDA brought Canada into compliance with EU data protection law.

Right to privacy is a fundamental right in India. Information Technology Act 2000 stand for the purpose of information system privacy.

In the Philippines, The Data Privacy Act of 2012 mandated the creation of the national privacy commission that would monitor and maintain policies that involve information privacy and personal data protection in the country. Modeled after the EU data protection directive and the Asia-Pacific Economic Cooperation (APEC) privacy framework, the independent body would ensure compliance of the country with international standards set for data protection. The law requires government and private organizations composed of at least 250 employees or those which have access to the personal and identifiable information of at least 1000 people to appoint a data protection officer that would assist in regulating the management of personal information in such entities.

Brazil's General Personal Data Protection Law popularly known as LGPD came into existence in 2020. The law's primary aim is to unify forty different Brazilian laws that regulate the processing of personal data. The bill has 65 articles and has many similarities to the GDPR.

The United States is notable for not having adopted a comprehensive information privacy law, but rather having adopted limited sectoral laws in some areas like the California Consumer Privacy Act (CCPA). This is the right to know about the personal information a business collects about them and how it is used and shared. In USA, data privacy is not highly regulated. Even if the data was collected without permission, the person entering the data is deemed to own the right to store and use it, except to any extent regulated by laws and rules such as the federal Communications Act's provisions, regulating use of customer proprietary network information (CPNI). Few U.S. federal laws with provisions which tend to promote information flow efficiencies are Health Insurance Portability and Accountability Act of 1996 (HIPAA), Children's Online Privacy Protection Act (COPPA), and the Fair and Accurate Credit Transactions Act (FACTA).

The HIPAA is a data privacy regulation that was put in place to safeguard patient personal health information. In December 2000, the U.S. department of health and human services issued the privacy rule to carry out HIPAA's mandate to safeguard the privacy of individually identifiable health information.

The GLBA (Gramm-Leach-Bliley Act) is also known as the Financial Modernization Act of 1999. It is a United States federal law that requires financial institutions to explain how they share and protect their customers' private information. The GLBA requires financial institutions to safeguard consumer financial data.

The Fair Credit Reporting Act (FCRA) allows individuals to opt out of unwanted credit offers. The FCRA has been effective in preventing the proliferation of specious so-called private credit guides. It provides consumers the ability to view, correct, contest, and limit the uses of credit reports. This also protects the credit agency from the charge of negligent release in the case of misrepresentation by the requester. Credit agencies must ask the requester the purpose of a requested information release, but need to make no effort to verify the truth of the requester's assertions. It prevents creditors or their agents from disclosing the fact that an individual is in debt to a third party, although it allows creditors and their agents to attempt to obtain information about a debtor's location.

Children's Online Privacy Protection Act (COPPA), aims to protect the privacy of children under thirteen. This law stipulates that companies must ask for parents' permission to collect data on children, and specifies the way that this data can then be held and processed.

The table 1.1 consolidates the information privacy laws available in various regions and countries.

Table 3.1: Regions and Information Privacy Laws

Region	Laws
Brazil	LGPD
Canada	Personal Information Protection and Electronic Documents Act
European Union	General Data Protection Regulation
France	French Data Protection Bill
Germany	DSGVO
India	Information Technology Act
Philippines	Data Privacy Act
Switzerland	Swiss Federal Data Protection Act
United Kingdom	Data Protection Act
United States of America	CCPA, HIPAA, COPPA, FACTA, FCRA

3.7 ACTIONS FOR INFORMATION PRIVACY

Information privacy can be focused on a business or individual. The important actions required to ensure the privacy in a business focused environment are

- Integrate training on data privacy in the general training program and it should be part of the onboarding process for new staff.
- Use tools recommended for information system privacy.
- Monitor network for any suspicious activity to detect a possible attack.
- Implement the zero-trust model. Zero trust security is an IT security model that requires strict identity verification for every person and device trying to access resources on a private network, regardless of whether they are sitting within or outside of the network perimeter.
- Use multi-factor authentication for additional layers of security.
- All IoT devices need to be updated with the latest security software.
- Back up data should be made mandatory.

3.8 PLANNING STEPS FOR INFORMATION PRIVACY

The five major steps that organizations should take to keep nonpublic information privacy is discussed below. This will also outline how organizations can establish and enforce information-security policies that will help them to comply with these privacy regulations.

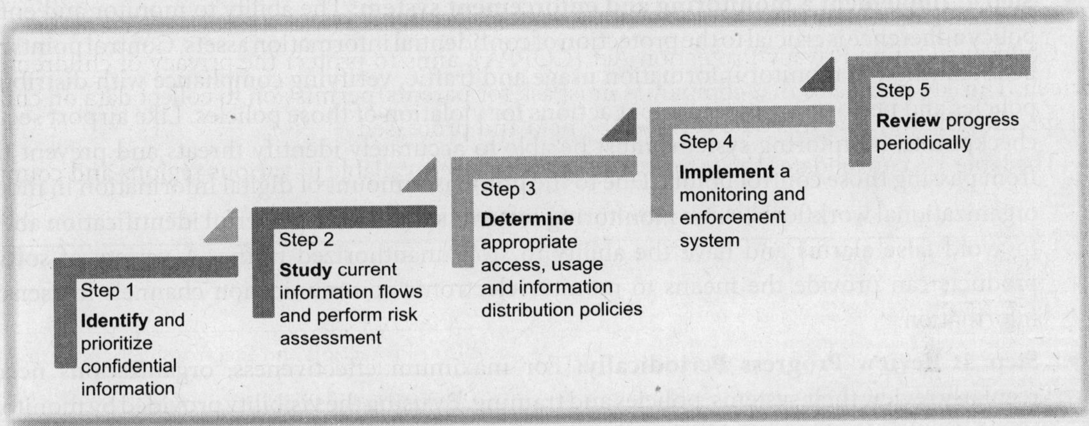

Figure 3.1: Information Privacy Planning Steps

- **Step 1: Identify and Prioritize Confidential Information:** The vast majority of organizations don't know how to start protecting confidential information. By categorizing types of information by value and confidentiality, companies can prioritize what data to secure first. Customer information systems or employee record systems are the easiest places to start because only a few specific systems typically own the ability to update that information. Social security numbers, account numbers, personal identification numbers, credit card numbers and other types of structured information are finite areas that need to be protected. Securing unstructured information such as contracts, financial releases and customer correspondence is an important next step that should be rolled out on a departmental basis.
- **Step 2: Study Current Information Flows and Perform Risk Assessment:** It's essential to understand current workflows, both procedurally and in practice to see how confidential information flows around an organization. Identifying the major business processes that involve confidential information is a straight forward exercise, but determining the risk of leakage requires a more in-depth examination. Organizations need to ask questions themselves like: Which participants touch information assets? How are assets created, modified, processed or distributed by these participants? What is the chain of events? Is there a gap between stated policies/procedures and actual behavior? By analyzing information flows with these questions in mind, organizations can quickly identify vulnerabilities in their handling of sensitive information.
- **Step 3: Determine Appropriate Access, Usage and Information-Distribution Policies:** Based on the risk assessment, an organization can quickly craft distribution policies for various types of confidential information. These policies govern exactly who can access, use or receive which type of content and when, as well as oversee enforcement actions for violations of those policies.

Different types of distribution policies typically emerge for customer information, executive communications, intellectual property and employee records. Once these distribution policies are defined, it's essential to implement monitoring and enforcement points along communication paths.

- **Step 4: Implement a monitoring and enforcement system:** The ability to monitor and enforce policy adherence is crucial to the protection of confidential information assets. Control points must be established to monitor information usage and traffic, verifying compliance with distribution policies and performing enforcement actions for violation of those policies. Like airport security checkpoints, monitoring systems must be able to accurately identify threats and prevent them from passing those control points. Due to the immense amount of digital information in modern organizational workflows, these monitoring systems should have powerful identification abilities to avoid false alarms and have the ability to stop unauthorized traffic. A variety of software products can provide the means to monitor electronic communication channels for sensitive information.
- **Step 5: Review Progress Periodically:** For maximum effectiveness, organizations need to regularly review their systems, policies and training. By using the visibility provided by monitoring systems, organizations can improve employee training, expand deployment and systematically eliminate vulnerabilities. In addition, systems should be reviewed extensively in the event of a breach to analyze system failures and to flag suspicious activity. External audits can also prove useful in checking for vulnerabilities and threats. Companies often implement security systems but either fail to review incident reports that arise or to extend coverage beyond the parameters of the initial implementation. Through regular system benchmarking, organizations can protect confidential information. This can extend security to different communication channels such as e-mail, web posts, instant messaging, peer-to-peer etc. and can expand protection to additional departments or functions. Protecting confidential information assets throughout an enterprise is a journey rather than a one-time event. It fundamentally requires a systematic way to identify sensitive data; understand current business processes; craft appropriate access, usage and distribution policies and monitor outgoing and internal communications. It is very important to understand the potential costs as well as the un welcome consequences for not establishing a system to secure nonpublic information.

3.9 TOOLS AND SOLUTIONS FOR INFORMATION SYSTEM PRIVACY

A tool is a hardware or program used for software development, system maintenance, security, or making any process convenient in an information system is known as a tool. Few of the tools for ensuring information system privacy are discussed below.

- **Tracker Blocker:** A tracker is a script in the code of websites designed to gather data points about the visitor while interacting with the site. Sometimes they are placed purposefully by the site the person is visiting, while other times a tracker may be from a website that was never visited. A tracking blocker is software or browser settings which limit programmatic trackers from capturing and recording a user's online activity.
- **Ad Blocker:** Ad blocking or ad filtering is a software capability for blocking or altering online

advertising in a web browser or an application. This may be done using browser extensions or other methods. Technically speaking, ad blockers do not block advertisements. They block web requests that download content into the browser. In other words, ad blockers stop ads from downloading on your browser, allowing web pages to load faster and offering a better browser experience.

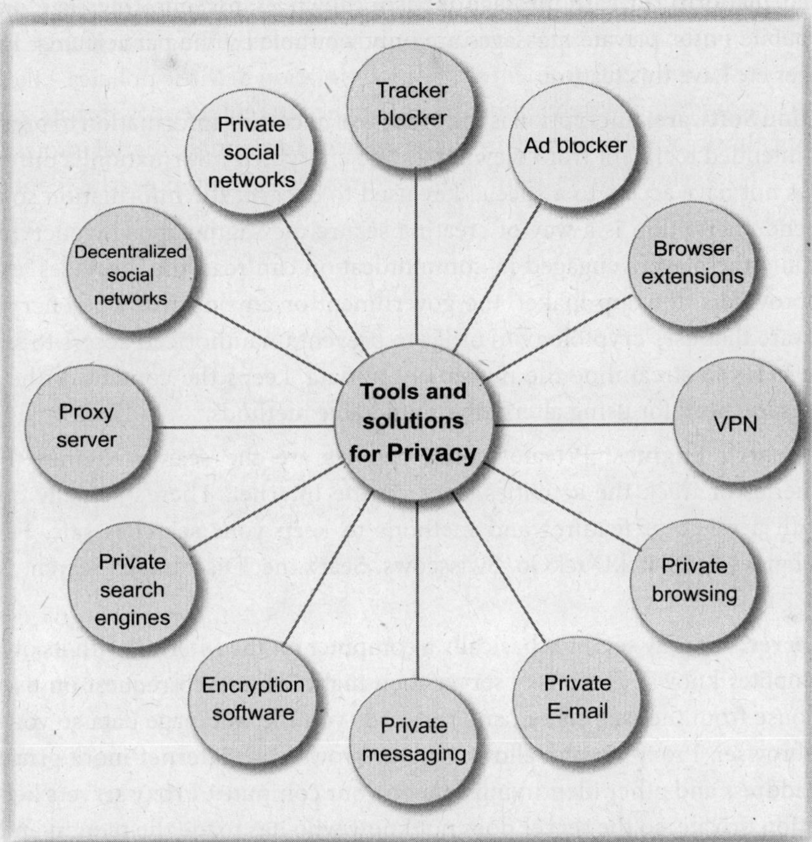

Figure 3.2: Tools and Solutions for Information System Privacy

- **Browser Extensions:** Most web browsers allow to install extensions, also called "add-ons." Extensions are small applications that add features to the browser, and enhance or modify the way web pages are displayed. These extensions won't block every kind of snooping, but they will vastly reduce the exposure to most of the efforts to track user's Internet activity.
- **Virtual Private Networks:** A Virtual Private Network (VPN) gives online privacy and anonymity by creating a private network from a public internet connection. VPNs mask the Internet Protocol (IP) address so the online actions are virtually untraceable.
- **Private Browsing:** Private browsing is a feature that major web browsers offer to help keep the temporary browsing data private. When using a private browser, such as incognito mode, the browsing history, search records, and cookies are not retained.

- **Private E-mail:** A private email is an email system that's offered via a private server for better functionality, privacy and security. Most public email providers like Google, Yahoo, Hotmail etc. use their own servers to host your emails. With private E-mail server, the organization will get control over who can run, use and manage your email system.
- **Private Messaging:** A private message is a private communication channel between users on any given platform. Private message is also known as personal message or direct message. Unlike public posts, private messages are only viewable by the participants. Facebook, Twitter, Messenger etc have this feature.
- **Encryption Software:** Encryption is the process of encoding information to prevent anyone other than its intended recipient from viewing it. The encrypted information is unreadable to anyone who does not have access to a special key used to decrypt the information so that it's readable. End-to-end encryption is a way of creating secure messaging apps by encrypting information so that only the players engaged in communication can read the messages, excluding Internet service providers, the app maker, the government or anyone else. File encryption software is the software that uses cryptology in order to prevent unauthorized access to sensitive data. The software helps to streamline the movement of data, keeps the content of the files secure, and eliminates the need for using alternative vulnerable methods.
- **Private Search Engines:** Private search engines are the search engines that do not store user's queries or track the activities steps on the Internet. There's actually quite a number of them with a range of features and methods to keep your searches safe. Few of the private search engines are DuckDuckGo, Swisscows, Searx.me, Disconnect Search, MetaGer, Qwant, Yase etc.
- **Proxy Server:** A proxy server is basically a computer on the Internet with its own IP address that your computer knows. The proxy server then makes your web request on user behalf, collects the response from the web server, and forwards you the web page data so you can see the page in your browser. Proxy servers allow users to browse the Internet more privately by changing your IP address and other identifying data on your computer. Proxy servers keep user's personal information private, so the server does not know who has made the request and thus keeps your browsing activities and browsing history private.
- **Decentralized Social Networks:** In a decentralized social networking framework, a user does not need to join any particular social networking service such as Facebook, Twitter. Instead, the user chooses a server which user trusts to host the data.
- **Private Social Networks:** When an information gets posted online, it is no longer private, and may end up falling into wrong hands. Even if we have put in place the highest possible security measures, some of our friends, colleagues and companies that interact with on social media, can end up leaking our personal information. A private social network is an online social space that allows users to choose exactly who they connect with and who has access to the things they share. This will increase the privacy. Few of the private social networks are Everyme, 23Snaps, Notabli, Nextdoor, Yammer, Couple, Path, FamilyWall etc.

3.10 INFORMATION PRIVACY VS. INFORMATION SECURITY

Organizations commonly believe that keeping sensitive information secure from hackers means they're automatically compliant with information privacy regulations but this is not reality. Information security and information privacy are often used interchangeably, but there are distinct differences.

Information security is protecting data from internal and external attackers. Information privacy is governing how data is collected, shared and used. Consider a scenario where actions are taken to secure Personally Identifiable Information (PII). The data is encrypted, access is restricted, and multiple overlapping monitoring systems are in place. However, if that PII was collected without proper consent, it could be violating a data privacy regulation even though the data is secure.

Data protection is the force behind our right to privacy. Despite recent advances in data privacy legislation and practice, consumer's privacy is regularly invaded or compromised by companies and governments. While data protection can be ensured without data privacy but data privacy cannot be ensured without data protection.

Ensuring data privacy means that the company should not collect all of the customer's personal data whether it is with passive location tracking, applications secretly absorbing personal address book or websites recording every keystroke. Instead, employees should be regularly trained on data protection so they understand the processes and procedures necessary to ensure proper collection, sharing and use of sensitive data as part of a data security portfolio.

Information privacy also includes the regulations required for companies to protect data. As more data protection regulation grows worldwide, global privacy requirements and demands will also expand and change. The table 3.2 shows a comparison of information security and information privacy.

Table 3.2: Comparison of Information Security and Information Privacy

Variables	Information Security	Information Privacy
Foundation	Is a process	Is a right
Purpose	Protection of business information	Protection of personal information
Features that should be ensured	Confidentiality, integrity and availability	Non linkability, Non traceability, Non observability and anonymity
Responsibility of	Chief Information Security Officer (CISO)	Personal Data Protection Delegate (PDPD)/Chief Privacy Officer (CPO)
Focus on	Data centric	Person centric
Good practices	Series ISO 27000, NIST and ENISA Documents	ISO/IEC 29100 Information Technology – Security Techniques –Privacy framework
Report	Independent	Independent

3.11 SUMMARY

In this chapter, we have discussed importance of privacy, information privacy and its challenges. The various laws and acts in information privacy are investigated. Towards the end, the actions, planning steps, tools and solutions required explained and close by comparing information privacy and information security.

3.12 OBJECTIVE QUESTIONS

The answer of the multiple-choice questions is marked in **bold**.

1. .... is an information privacy law of Brazil
   (a) **LGPD** (b) DSGVO
   (c) FCRA (d) CCPA
2. Which is the privacy law of India?
   (a) **IT Act** (b) COPPA
   (c) GDPR (d) CCPA
3. Which is the first step in planning information privacy?
   (a) **Identify** (b) Study
   (c) Determine (d) Implement
4. Which is the tool for privacy?
   (a) Ad blocker (b) VPN
   (c) Encryption software (d) **All of these**
5. Which one is common to information security and information privacy?
   (a) Process (b) Confidentiality
   (c) Anonymity (d) **Independent**

3.13 REVIEW QUESTIONS

1. Discuss the importance of privacy.
2. Explain the importance of information privacy.
3. Explain the challenges in information privacy.
4. Discuss on various information privacy laws and acts.
5. Discuss the actions required for information privacy in business environment.
6. Discuss the planning steps for information privacy.
7. Discuss on various tools and solutions for information system privacy.
8. Differentiate information privacy and information security.

3.14 ABBREVIATIONS AND SYMBOLS

Abbreviations	Full Form	Description
APEC	Asia Pacific Economic Co-operation	APEC is an inter-governmental forum for the geographic area surrounding the Pacific Ocean that promotes free trade throughout the Asia-Pacific region.
CCPA	California Consumer Privacy Act	CCPA provides privacy rights and consumer protection for residents of California, United States.
CISO	Chief Information Security Officer	CISO is the senior-level executive within an organization responsible for establishing and maintaining the enterprise vision, strategy, and program to ensure information assets and technologies are adequately protected.
COPPA	Children's Online Privacy Protection Act	COPPA imposes certain requirements on operators of websites or online services directed to children under 13 years of age.
CPNI	Customer Proprietary Network Information	CPNI is confidential information about a customer's purchase and use of telecommunications services, such as where, when, and with whom a call takes place.
CPO	Chief Privacy Officer	CPO is a senior level executive with primary responsibility is to manage risk related to information privacy laws and compliance regulations.
DSGVO	Datenschutz-Grundverordnung	This is same as GDPR
EEA	European Economic Area	EEA consists of the countries of European Union (EU) and three countries of the European Free Trade Association (EFTA)
ENISA	European Network and Information Security Agency	ENISA is a European Union agency dedicated to preventing and addressing network security and information security problems.
EU	European Union	EU is a political and economic union of countries that are located in Europe.
FACTA	Fair and Accurate Credit Transactions Act	FACTA is an amendment to FCRA which is to protect consumers from identity theft.
FCRA	Fair Credit Reporting Act	FCRA is a US law which regulates the collection of consumers' credit information and access to their credit reports.
GDPR	General Data Protection Regulation	GDPR is a regulation on data protection and privacy in the European Union and the European Economic Area. It also addresses the transfer of personal data outside their areas.

Abbreviations	Full Form	Description
GLBA	Gramm-Leach-Bliley Act	GLBA requires financial products or services providing organisations to explain their information sharing practices to their customers and to safeguard sensitive data.
HIPAA	Health Insurance Portability and Accountability Act	HIPAA is a US law that provides national standards to protect sensitive patient health information from being disclosed without the patient's consent or knowledge.
IEC	International Electrotechnical Commission	IEC standards such as ISO/IEC 27001 and IEC 62443, together with testing and certification are important tools in cyber security.
ISO	International Organization for Standardization	ISO is an international standard setting body composed of representatives from various national standards organizations.
LGPD	Lei Geral de Proteção de Dados Pessoais	This is general personal data protection law in Brazil
NIST	National Institute of Standards and Technology	NIST cyber security frame work is a guidance on how both internal and external stakeholders of organizations can manage and reduce cyber security risk.
PII	Personally Identifiable Information	PII is any data that could potentially be used to identify a particular person.
PIPEDA	Personal Information Protection and Electronic Documents Act	PIPEDA is a Canadian law relating to data privacy. It governs how private sector organizations collect, use and disclose personal information in the course of commercial activities.
UK	United Kingdom	UK is an island nation in Europe formed by merging England, Scotland, Wales and Northern Ireland.

3.15 LIST OF FIGURES AND TABLES

The details of figures and tables used in this chapter is as below.

Figure / Table	Description
Figure 3.1	Information Privacy Planning Steps
Figure 3.2	Tools and Solutions for Information System Privacy
Table 3.1	Regions and Information Privacy Laws
Table 3.2	Comparison of Information Security and Information Privacy

CHAPTER

4 Cyber Security

CONTENTS

4.1 INTRODUCTION

The importance, history and objectives of cyber security is explained in this chapter. The various types of cyber-attacks and the attackers are analyzed. This is followed by cyber security principles, challenges and risk analysis are explained in this session.

4.2 CYBER SECURITY

Cybersecurity is primarily about people, processes, and technologies working together to encompass the full range of threat reduction, vulnerability reduction, deterrence, international engagement, incident response, resiliency, and recovery policies and activities, including computer network operations, information assurance, law enforcement, etc. It is the protection of Internet-connected systems, including hardware, software, and data from cyber-attacks. It is made up of two words one is cyber and other is security. Cyber is related to the technology which contains systems, network and programs or data. Whereas security related to the protection which includes systems security, network security and application and information security. It is the body of technologies, processes, and practices designed to protect networks, devices, programs, and data from attack, theft, damage, modification or unauthorized access. It may also be referred to as information technology security. We can also define cyber security as the set of principles and practices designed to protect our computing resources and online information against threats. Due to the heavy dependency on computers in a modern industry that store and transmit an abundance of confidential and essential information about the people, cyber security is a critical function of many businesses.

4.3 IMPORTANCE OF CYBER SECURITY

We live in a digital era which understands that our private information is more vulnerable than ever before. We all live in a world which is networked together, from internet banking to government infrastructure, where data is stored on computers and other devices. A portion of that data can be sensitive information, whether that be intellectual property, financial data, personal information, or other types of data for which unauthorized access or exposure could have negative consequences.

Cyber-attack is now an international concern and has given many concerns that hacks and other security attacks could endanger the global economy. Organizations transmit sensitive data across networks and to other devices in the course of doing businesses, and cyber security describes to protect that information and the systems used to process or store it. As the volume of cyber-attacks grows, companies and organizations, especially those that deal information related to national security, health, or financial records, need to take steps to protect.

4.4 HISTORY OF CYBER SECURITY

The most important feature of a computer virus is its ability to self-replicate. Every self-replicating program can be called as a virus. The idea of self-replicating programs can be traced back as early as 1949, when the mathematician John von Neumann imagined as a future possibility of specialized computers that could build copies of themselves and pass on their programming to their decedents.

In 1969, Leonard Kleinrock, professor of University of California, Los Angeles and his student Charley Kline, sent the first electronic message from the university's SDS Sigma 7 host computer to Bill Duvall who was a programmer at the Stanford Research Institute. This is a well-known story and a moment in the history of a digital world. The sent message was the word "login." The system crashed after they typed the first two letters "lo." Since then, there is a belief that they typed the beginning message "lo and behold." Lo and behold or lo is used to emphasize a surprising event that is about to be mentioned. Actually "login" was the intended message. Those two letters "lo" of message changed the way we communicate with one another.

In 1970's, Bob Thomas who was a researcher for BBN Technologies in Cambridge, Massachusetts created the first computer virus. He realized that it is possible for a computer program to move across a network, leaving a small series of signs wherever it went. He created an experimental program and named that "creeper" and designed it to travel between Tenex terminals on the early Arpanet, printing the message "I'm the creeper, catch me if you can!"

The American computer programmer named Ray Tomlinson who was the inventor of email was also working for BBN Technologies at that time. He liked the idea of creeper. He created a program which can follow and delete the transmitting creeper program. He named the program "reaper", the first antivirus software which would find copies of the "creeper" and delete it.

After invention of creeper and reaper, cyber-crimes became more powerful. As computer software and hardware developed, security breaches also increase. With every new development, came an aspect of vulnerability or a way for hackers to overcome methods of protection. In 1986, the Russians were the first who implement the cyber power as a weapon. Marcus Hess, a German citizen, hacked into 400 military computers, including processors at the Pentagon. He intended to sell secrets to the KGB, but an American astronomer, Clifford Stoll caught him before that could happen.

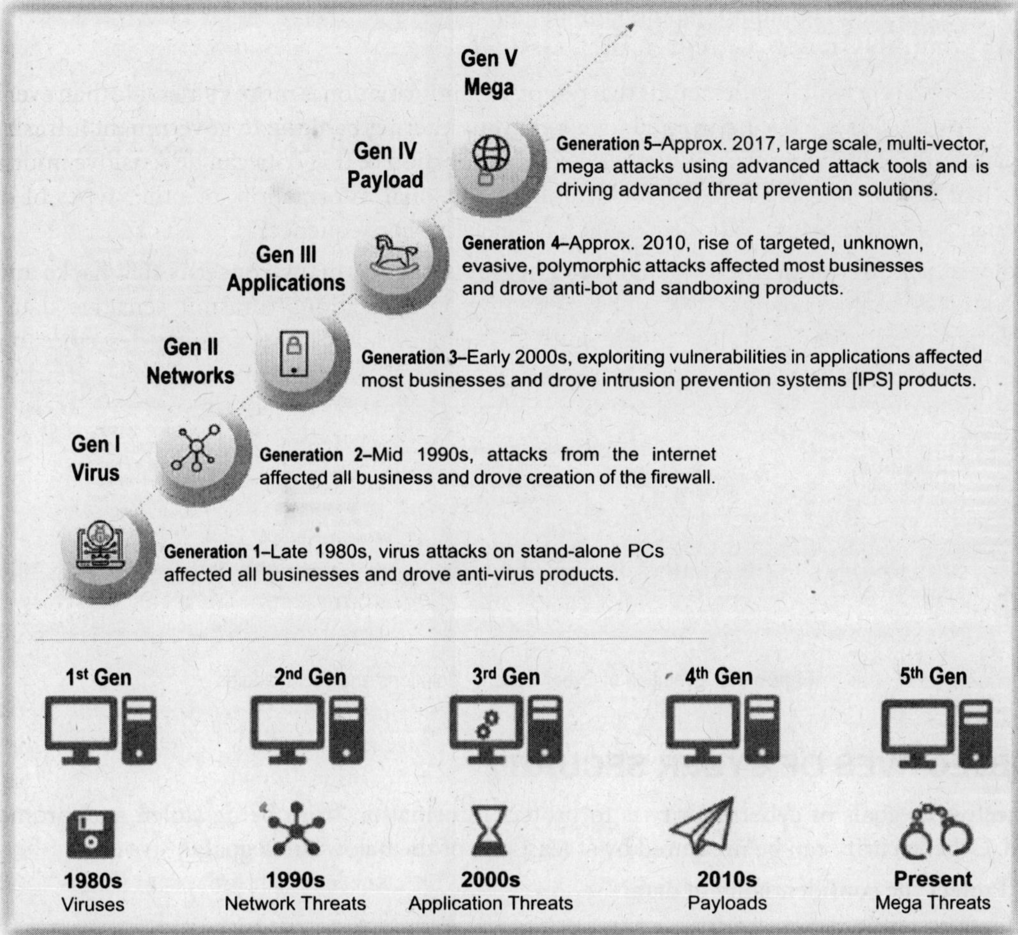

Figure 4.1: Evolution of Cyber Threats

In 1988, an American computer scientist, Robert Morris, wanted to check the size of the Internet. He wrote a program for testing the size of the Internet. This program went through networks, invaded Unix terminals, and copied itself. The program became the first famous network virus and named as Moris worm or Internet worm. The Morris worm could be infected a computer multiple times, and each additional process would slow the machine down, eventually to the point of being damaged. Robert Morris was charged under the Computer Fraud and Abuse Act. The act itself led to the founding of the Computer Emergency Response Team. This is a non-profit research centre for issues that could endanger the Internet.

Nowadays, viruses are deadlier, more invasive, and harder to control. We have already experienced cyber incidents on a massive scale and are enough to prove that cyber security is a necessity for corporations and small businesses alike. The figure 4.1 explains on the generations in the evolution of cyber threats.

For each type of cyber threats, the security solutions are developed. The figure 4.2 shows the security solutions and the latest technologies using for those solutions.

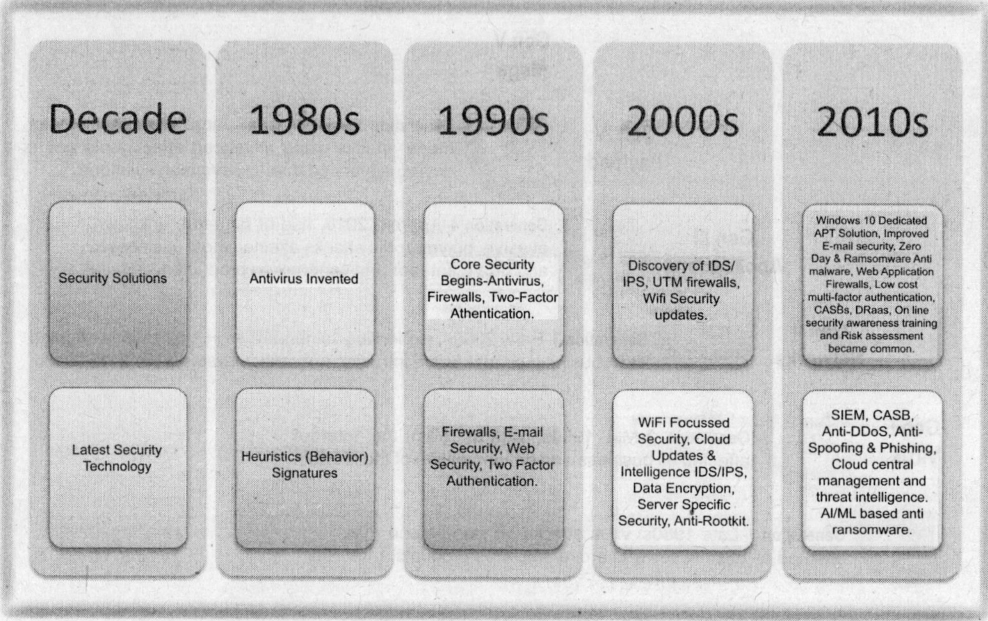

Figure 4.2: Evolution of Cyber Security Solutions and Technologies

4.5 OBJECTIVES OF CYBER SECURITY

The objective or goals of cybersecurity is to protect information from being stolen, compromised or attacked. Cybersecurity can be measured by at least one of the below three goals

- Protect the confidentiality of data.
- Preserve the integrity of data.
- Promote the availability of data for authorized users.

These goals form the confidentiality, integrity, availability (CIA) triad, the basis of all security programs. The CIA triad is a security model that is designed to guide policies for information security within the premises of an organization.

4.6 CYBER ATTACKS

A cyber-attack is an exploitation of computer systems and networks. It uses malicious code to alter computer code, logic or data and lead to cybercrimes, such as information and identity theft. We are living in a digital era. Now a days, most of the people use computer and Internet. Due to the dependency on digital things, the illegal computer activity is growing and changing like any type of crime. The evolution of the cyber-attack methods are displayed in figure 4.3.

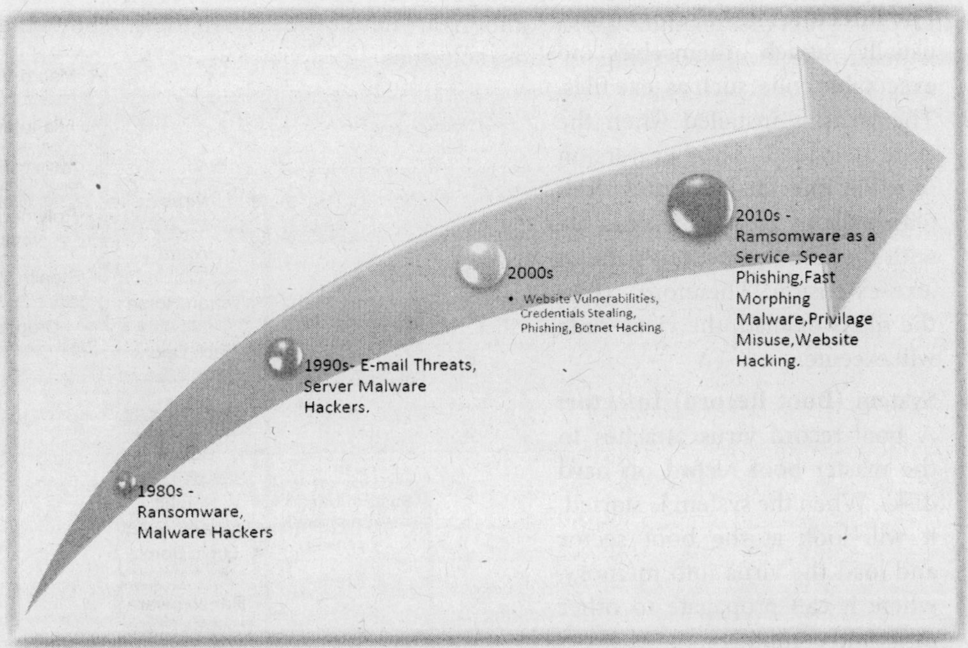

Figure 4.3: Evolution of Cyber Attack Methods

There are different types of cyber-attacks. All attack types can be divided into either passive or active. Passive attacks, have the purpose to intercept the sensitive data without causing any destruction to the operation of the entire system. Passive attack aims to achieve data or scan open ports and vulnerabilities of the network. Whereas active attacks, are aimed at causing direct damage or to gain the control of the system or infrastructure. The cyber-attacks can be generally classified based on system-based attack and web-based attack. The classification based on this into various categories is shown in figure 4.4.

4.6.1 System-Based Cyber Attacks

System-based cyber-attack is by exploitation of computer systems and networks. These are the attacks which are intended to compromise a computer or a computer network. Some of the important system-based attacks are as follows:

- **Virus:** It is a type of malicious software program that spread throughout the computer files without the knowledge of a user. It is a self-replicating malicious computer program that replicates by inserting copies of itself into other computer programs when executed. It can also execute instructions that cause harm to the system. Various types of viruses are as below.
  - **Macro Virus:** These viruses infect applications such as Microsoft Word or Excel. Macro viruses attach to an application's initialization sequence. When the application is opened, the virus executes instructions before transferring control to the application. The virus replicates itself and attaches to other code in the computer system.

- **File Infector:** File infector viruses usually attach themselves to executable code, such as .exe files. The virus is installed when the code is loaded. Another version of a file infector associates itself with a file by creating a virus file with the same name, but with an .exe extension. Therefore, when the file is opened, the virus code will execute.
- **System (Boot-Record) Infector:** A boot-record virus attaches to the master boot record on hard disks. When the system is started, it will look at the boot sector and load the virus into memory, where it can propagate to other disks and computers.
- **Polymorphic Virus:** These viruses conceal themselves through varying cycles of encryption and decryption. The encrypted virus and an associated mutation engine are initially decrypted by a decryption program. The virus proceeds to infect an area of code. The mutation engine then develops a new decryption routine and the virus encrypts the mutation engine and a copy of the virus with an algorithm corresponding to the new decryption routine. The encrypted package of mutation engine and virus is attached to new code, and the process repeats. Such viruses are difficult to detect but have a high level of entropy because of the many modifications of their source code. Anti-virus software or free tools like Process Hacker can use this feature to detect them.

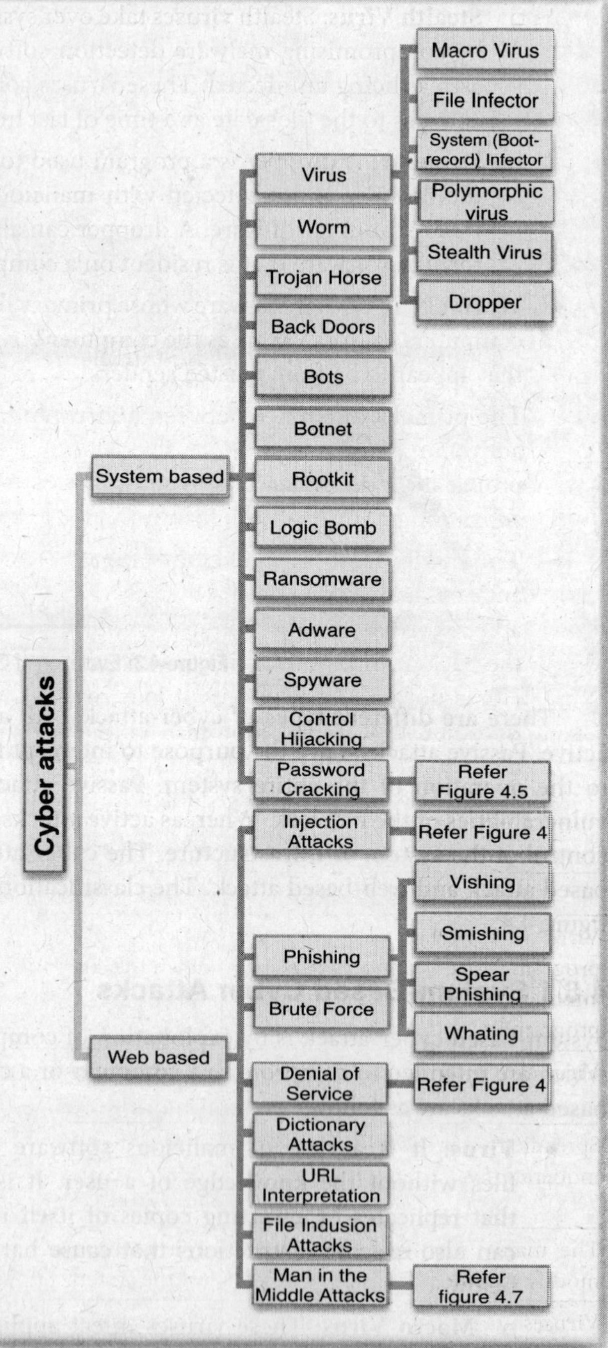

Figure 4.4: Cyber-Attack Categories

- **Stealth Virus:** Stealth viruses take over system functions to conceal themselves. They do this by compromising malware detection software so that the software will report an infected area as being uninfected. These viruses conceal any increase in the size of an infected file or changes to the file's date and time of last modification.
- **Dropper:** A dropper is a program used to install viruses on computers. In many instances, the dropper is not infected with malicious code and, therefore might not be detected by virus-scanning software. A dropper can also connect to the Internet and download updates to virus software that is resident on a compromised system.

- **Worm:** It is a type of malware whose primary function is to replicate itself to spread to uninfected computers. It works same as the computer virus. Worms often originate from email attachments that appear to be from trusted senders.

  The primary difference between a virus and a worm is that viruses must be triggered by the activation of their host. Worms are stand-alone malicious programs that can self-replicate and propagate independently as soon as they have breached the system. Worms do not require activation or any human intervention to execute or spread their code.

- **Trojan Horse:** It is a malicious program that occurs unexpected changes to computer setting and unusual activity, even when the computer is idle. It misleads the user of its true intent. It appears to be a normal application but when opened/executed some malicious code will run in the background. A user has to execute Trojans for spreading and damaging the system. Trojan Horse does not replicate itself like virus and worms. It is a hidden piece of code which steal the important information of user. For example, Trojan horse software observe the e-mail ID and password while entering in web browser for logging. Difference between Virus, Worms and Trojan horse is given in the table 4.1.

Table 4.1: Comparison between Virus, Worms and Trojan Horse

Virus	Worm	Trojan Horse
Virus is a software or computer program that connect itself to another software or computer program to harm computer system.	Worms replicate itself to cause slow down the computer system.	Trojan Horse will not replicate itself but will capture some important information about a computer system or a computer network.
Virus can't be controlled by remote.	Worms can be controlled by remote.	Trojan horse can also be controlled by remote.
Spreading rate of viruses are moderate.	Spreading rate of worms are faster than virus and Trojan horse.	Spreading rate of Trojan horse is slow in comparison to virus and worms.
The main objective of virus is to modify the information.	The main objective of worms is to eat the system resources.	The main objective of Trojan horse is to steal the information.
Viruses are executed via executable files.	Worms are executed via weaknesses in system.	Trojan horse executes through a program and interprets as utility software.

- **Backdoors:** It is a method that bypasses the normal authentication process. A developer may create a backdoor so that an application or operating system can be accessed for troubleshooting or for other purposes.

- **Bots:** A bot (short form for "robot") is an automated process that interacts with other network services. Some bots program run automatically, while others only execute commands when they receive specific input. Bot attack use automated web requests to manipulate, defraud, or disrupt a website, application, API, or end-users. Common examples of bot's program are the crawler, chatroom bots and malicious bots.
- **Botnet:** A botnet attack is a large-scale cyber attack carried out by malware-infected devices which are controlled remotely. It turns compromised devices into 'zombie bots' for a botnet controller. Botnet attacks are similar to having a threat actor working within the network.A threat actor or malicious actor is either a person or a group of people that take part in an action that is intended to cause harm to the cyber space including computers, devices, systems, or networks.
- **Rootkits:** Rootkit is a type of malware designed to give hackers access to and control over a target device. Although most rootkits affect the software and the operating system, some can also infect computer's hardware and firmware.
- **Logic Bomb:** A logic bomb is a type of malicious software that is added to an application and is triggered by a specific occurrence, such as a logical condition or a specific date and time.
- **Ransomware:** Ransomware is a type of malware that blocks access to the victim's data and threatens to publish or delete it unless a ransom is paid. While some simple computer ransomware can lock the system in a way that is not difficult for a knowledgeable person to reverse, more advanced malware uses a technique called cryptoviral extortion, which encrypts the victim's files in a way that makes them nearly impossible to recover without the decryption key.
- **Adware:** Adware is a software application used by companies for marketing purposes. Advertising banners are displayed by adwares while any program is running. Adware can be automatically downloaded to the system while browsing any website and can be viewed through pop-up windows or through a bar that appears on the computer screen automatically.
- **Spyware:** Spyware is a type of program that is installed to collect information about users, their computers or their browsing habits. It tracks everything you do without your knowledge and sends the data to a remote user. It also can download and install other malicious programs from the Internet. Spyware works like adware but is usually a separate program that is installed unknowingly when user install another freeware application.
- **Control Hijacking:** By this, intruder aims to take control of entire system by launching control hijacking attack. The methods for this are buffer overflow, integer overflow and format string attack. Buffer overflow is a phenomenon when a program is writing data outside of the given buffer, often it is the consequence of the wrong processing of input data. Integer overflow is an error occurred due to the inability to represent the numeric value within given storage space. Format string is an intrusion during which the input string is executed as a command.
- **Password Cracking:** Password cracking is the process of using an application program to identify an unknown or

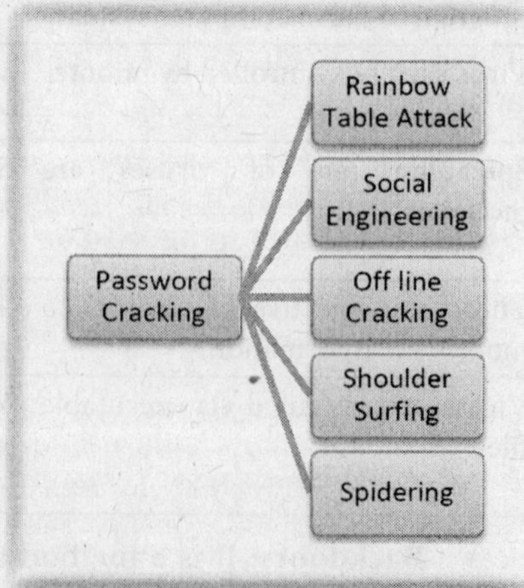

Figure 4.5: Methods of Password Cracking

forgotten password to a computer or network resource. It can also be used to help a threat actor obtain unauthorized access to resources.

- **Rainbow Table Attack:** A rainbow table attack is a type of hacking wherein the perpetrator tries to use a rainbow hash table to crack the passwords stored in a database system. A rainbow table is a hash function used in cryptography for storing important data such as passwords in a database. Sensitive data are hashed two or more times with the same or with different keys in order to avoid rainbow table attacks.
- **Social Engineering:** This refers to the process of tricking users make believe that the hacker is a legitimate agent. A common tactic is for hackers to call a victim and pose as technical support, asking for things like network access passwords in order to provide assistance. Another example of social engineering would be that the hacker contacts the target on a social networking site and starts a conversation with the target. Gradually the hacker gains the trust of the target and then uses that trust to get access to sensitive information like password or bank account details.
- **Offline Cracking:** Offline password cracking is an attempt to recover one or more passwords from a password storage file that has been recovered from a target system. Typically, this would be the Security Account Manager (SAM) file on Windows, or the shadow file on Linux.
- **Shoulder Surfing:** Shoulder surfing is the act of watching somebody as they reveal private information. Shoulder surfing can be used to steal any type of information. It's most often used to find out passwords, payment details, and PINs. But it can also be used to steal personal information for the purposes of identity theft.
- **Spidering:** Spidering refers to the process of hackers getting to know their targets intimately in order to acquire credentials based on their activity. The process is very similar to techniques used in phishing and social engineering attacks. This involves amount of work on the part of the hacker and it is generally more successful. For example, if the target is a large company, hackers may attempt to source internal documentation, such as handbooks for new starters, in order to get a sense of the sort of platforms and security the target uses. The documents often have guide lines on how to access certain services, or notes on office Wi-Fi usage.

4.6.2 Web-based Cyber Attacks

These are the attacks which occur on a website or web applications. Some of the important web-based attacks are as follows

- **Injection Attacks:** It is the attack in which some data will be injected into a web application to manipulate the application and fetch the required information. Various types of injection attacks are shown in figure 4.6.

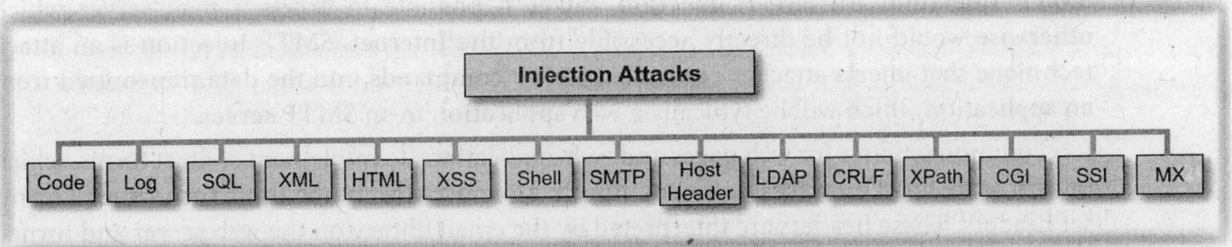

Figure 4.6: Injection Attacks Classification

- **Code Injection:** Code injection attack, also called Remote Code Execution (RCE), occurs when an attacker exploits an input validation flaw in software to introduce and execute malicious code. Code is injected in the language of the targeted application and executed by the server-side interpreter. Code injection attacks typically exploit an application vulnerability that allows the processing of invalid data. This type of attack exploits poor handling of untrusted data, and these types of attacks are usually made possible due to a lack of proper input/output data validation.
- **Log Injection:** logging is a technique to maintain or collect application specific data into a log file to monitor how the application is doing in running state. Every event is stored into a log file for future reference, especially in the time of debugging a bug. Log injection, also known as log forgery, describes a vulnerability arising from any scenario in which un-trusted input is allowed to pollute or compromise the integrity of application or system log files.
- **SQL Injection:** A SQL (Structured Query Language) injection attack is when a third party is able to use SQL commands to interfere with back-end databases that is not intended to be displayed. This is also known as SQLI.
- **XML Injection:** XML injection manipulates or compromises the logic of an XML application or service. The injection of unintended XML content and/or structures into an XML message can alter the intended logic of an application, and XML Injection can cause the insertion of malicious content into resulting messages/documents.
- **HTML Injection:** Hypertext Markup Language (HTML) injection is a technique used to take advantage of non-validated input to modify a web page presented by a web application to its users. Attackers take advantage of the fact that the content of a web page is often related to a previous interaction with users. When applications fail to validate user data, an attacker can send HTML formatted text to modify site content that gets presented to other users. A specifically crafted query can lead to inclusion in the web page of attacker controlled HTML elements which will change the way the application content gets exposed to the web.
- **Cross Site Scripting:** Cross Site Scripting (XSS) is a security vulnerability that allows an attacker to inject javascript code. Often HTML injection and XSS injection go hand in hand.
- **Shell Injection:** Shell injection is a cyber-attack that involves executing arbitrary commands on a host operating system (OS). Attacker injects the commands by exploiting an application vulnerability, such as insufficient input validation. This is also known as operating system command injection. The web security vulnerability that allows an attacker to execute arbitrary operating system commands on the server that is running an application and fully compromise the application and all its data.
- **SMTP Injection:** An SMTP injection makes it possible to access a mail server which otherwise would not be directly accessible from the Internet. SMTP Injection is an attack technique that injects attacker-controlled SMTP commands into the data transmitted from an application which will be typically a web application to an SMTP server.

  It is common practice for web pages and web applications to implement contact forms, which in turn send email messages to the intended recipients. Most of the time, such contact forms set headers. These headers are interpreted by the email library on the web server and turned into resulting SMTP commands, which are then processed by the SMTP server. User input is often not validated before being sent to the email library. In such cases, the contact form might be vulnerable to email header injection. This is referred to as SMTP header injection or simply email injection. A malicious user may be able to introduce additional headers into the message, thereby instructing the mail server to behave differently than intended. Email injection is not directly dangerous to the owner of the web server, but a vulnerable contact form may be used for sending spam or for phishing. This makes it a serious application security vulnerability.

- **Host Header Injection:** Host header injection, is a web attack where the attacker provides a false host header to the web application. It is common practice for the same web server to host several websites or web applications on the same IP address. The host header specifies which website or web application should process an incoming HTTP request. The web server uses the value of this header to dispatch the request to the specified website or web application. Each web application hosted on the same IP address is commonly referred to as a virtual host. if the Host header was malformed in some way, this could lead to issues when routing incoming requests to the intended application.
- **LDAP Injection:** LDAP (Lightweight Directory Access Protocol) is a common software protocol designed to enable anyone on a network to find resources such as other individuals, files, and devices. Directory services such as LDAP are useful for intranets. It can also be used to store usernames and passwords as part of a single sign-on (SSO) system. SSO is an authentication method that enables users to securely authenticate with multiple applications and websites by using just one set of credentials. LDAP injection is a vulnerability in which queries are constructed from untrusted input without prior validation or sanitization. LDAP uses queries constructed from predicates that involve the use of special characters (e.g., brackets, asterisks, ampersands, or quotes). Metacharacters such as these control the meaning of the query; thereby, affecting the type and number of objects retrieved from the underlying directory. If an attacker can submit input containing these control characters, they can alter the query and change the intended behavior.
- **CRLF Injection:** CRLF injection is a software application coding vulnerability that occurs when an attacker injects a CRLF character sequence where it is not expected. CRLF is the acronym used to refer to Carriage Return (\r) Line Feed (\n). As one might notice from the symbols in the brackets, "Carriage Return" refers to the end of a line, and "Line Feed" refers to the new line. Hence, both CR and LF are used to denote the ending point of a line. When a user requests content on a website, the server returns the website content along with the HTTP headers. The headers and the contents are separated by a defined combination of CR and LF. It is because of CRLF that a server knows where a new header begins or ends. A CRLF injection vulnerability is a type of server-side injection which occurs when an attacker inserts the CRLF characters in an input field to deceive the server by making it think that an object has terminated and a new one has begun. This happens when the web application doesn't sanitize user input for CRLF characters. When CRLF injection is used to split an HTTP response header, it is referred to as HTTP Response Splitting.
- **XPath Injection:** XML Path (XPath) is a query language used to uniquely identify or address parts of an XML document. An XPath expression can be used to search through an XML document, and extract information from any part of the document, such as an element or attribute. Its syntax is always implementation independent, which means the attack may be automated. Similar to SQL injection, XPath injection attacks occur when a web site uses user-

supplied information to construct an XPath query for XML data. By sending intentionally malformed information into the web site, an attacker can find out how the XML data is structured, or access data that they may not normally have access to. They may even be able to elevate their privileges on the web site if the XML data is being used for authentication such as an XML based user file.

- **CGI Injection:** Common Gateway Interface (CGI), is a standard protocol used primarily by the web server to produce dynamic web pages. Attackers take the advantage of CGI scripts to perform an attack by sending illegitimate inputs to the web server.
- **SSI Injection:** SSI injection (Server-side Include) is a server-side exploit that lets an attacker send code into an application to be executed later, locally, by the web server. With an SSI injection attack, the attacker can access sensitive information such as password files, and execute shell commands.
- **MX Injection:** MX injection is an injection technique that is similar to other injection techniques like SQL injection, XPath injection, SSI injection and many more. An application that has a mail server that is not accessible directly to the Internet is vulnerable to this attack.

- **Phishing:** Phishing is a type of attack which attempts to steal sensitive information like user login credentials and credit card number. It occurs when an attacker is masquerading as a trustworthy entity in electronic communication. The three types of phishing are vishing, spear phishing and whaling.
  - **Vishing:** Vishing is short for "voice phishing," which involves defrauding people over the phone, enticing them to divulge sensitive information. Vishing refers to phishing attacks that involve the use of voice calls, using either conventional phone systems or Voice over Internet Procotol (VoIP) systems.
  - **Smishing:** Smishing (sometimes stylized as SMiShing) refers to phishing attacks that involve the use of messages sent using SMS (Short Message Service). False text messages are received by would-be victims, who in turn either reply directly or visit a phishing web site. As this is implemented through SMS, the name of the attack is "SMiShing."
  - **Spear Phishing:** Spear phishing is the act of sending and emails to specific and well-researched targets while purporting to be a trusted sender. The aim is to either infect devices with malware or convince victims to hand over information or money.
  - **Whaling:** Whaling is a highly targeted phishing attack which are aimed at senior executives, masquerading as a legitimate email. Whaling is digitally enabled fraud through social engineering, designed to encourage victims to perform a secondary action, such as initiating a wire transfer of funds.
- **Brute Force:** It is a type of attack which uses a trial-and-error method. This attack generates a large number of guesses and validates them to obtain actual data like user password and personal identification number. This attack may be used by criminals to crack encrypted data to test an organization's network security.
- **Denial of Service:** Denial of Service (DoS) is an attack which is meant to make a server or network resource unavailable to the users. It accomplishes this by flooding the target with traffic or sending it information that triggers a crash. It uses the single system and single Internet connection to attack a server. Denial of service attacks operates in three methods such as volume-based attacks,

Protocol attacks and application layer attacks. The goal of volume based attack is to saturate the bandwidth of the attacked site. This includes UDP floods, ICMP floods, and other spoofed-packet floods. The attacker's goal is to saturate the bandwidth of the attacked site, and magnitude is measured in bits per second (bps). Protocol attack consumes actual server resources which is measured in a packet. This includes SYN floods, fragmented packet attacks, Ping of Death, Smurf DDoS etc. This type of attack consumes actual server resources, or those of intermediate communication equipment, such as firewalls and load balancers. This is measured in packets per second (pps). Application layer attacker's goal is to crash the web server and is measured in request per second. Includes low-and-slow attacks, GET/POST floods, attacks that target Apache, Windows or OpenBSD vulnerabilities and more. Comprised of seemingly legitimate and innocent requests, the goal of these attacks is to crash the web server. The magnitude is measured in requests per second (rps). The figure 4.7 shows various types of DoS attacks.

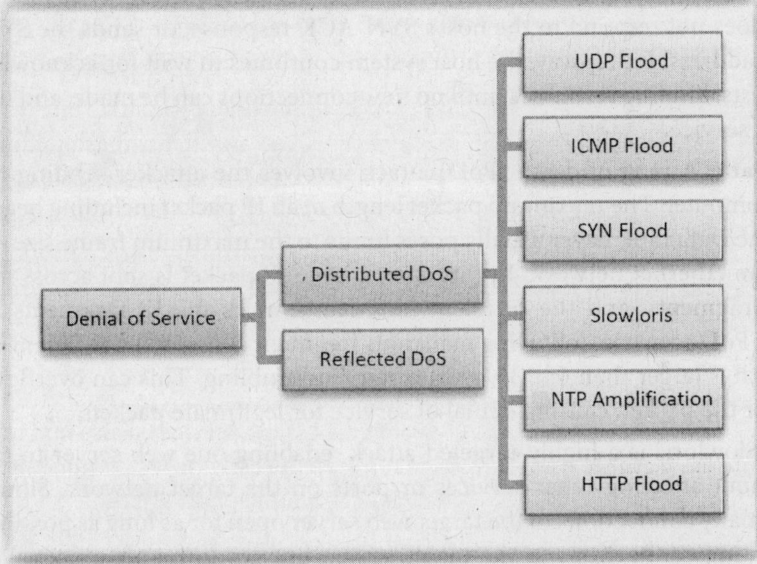

Figure 4.7: Types of DoS Attacks

- **Distributed Denial of Service:** A distributed denial-of-service (DDoS) attack is a malicious attempt to disrupt the normal traffic of a targeted server, service or network by overwhelming the target or its surrounding infrastructure with a flood of Internet traffic. DDoS attacks are launched from multiple connected devices that are distributed across the Internet. These multi-person, multi-device barrages are generally harder to deflect, mostly due to the sheer volume of devices involved.
- **Reflected Denial of Service:** A reflection amplification attack is a technique that allows attackers to both magnify the amount of malicious traffic they can generate and obscure the sources of the attack traffic. This type of distributed denial-of-service (DDoS) attack overwhelms the target, causing disruption or outage of systems and services.

The common DDoS attacks are described below.

1. **UDP Flood:** A UDP flood, is DDoS attack that floods a target with User Datagram Protocol

(UDP) packets. The goal of the attack is to flood random ports on a remote host. This causes the host to repeatedly check for the application listening at that port, and when no application is found reply with an Internet Control Message Protocol (ICMP) 'Destination Unreachable' packet. This process will weaken host resources and ultimately lead to inaccessibility.

2. **ICMP Flood:** Similar in principle to the UDP flood attack, an ICMP flood overwhelms the target resource with ICMP Echo Request (ping) packets, generally sending packets as fast as possible without waiting for replies. This type of attack can consume both outgoing and incoming bandwidth. The victim's servers will often attempt to respond with ICMP Echo Reply packets, resulting in significant overall system slowdown. This is also known as pink flood.
3. **SYN Flood:** SYN flood DDoS attack exploits a known weakness in the TCP connection sequence (the "three-way handshake"), wherein a SYN request to initiate a TCP connection with a host must be answered by a SYN-ACK response from that host, and then confirmed by an ACK response from the requester. In a SYN flood scenario, the requester sends multiple SYN requests, but either does not respond to the host's SYN-ACK response, or sends the SYN requests from a spoofed IP address. Either way, the host system continues to wait for acknowledgement for each of the requests, binding resources until no new connections can be made, and ultimately resulting in denial of service.
4. **Ping of Death:** A ping of death (PoD) attack involves the attacker sending multiple malicious pings to a computer. The maximum packet length of an IP packet including header is 65,535 bytes. However, the Data Link Layer usually poses limits to the maximum frame size – for example 1500 bytes over an ethernet network. In this case, a large IP packet is split across multiple IP packets known as fragments, and the recipient host reassembles the IP fragments into the complete packet. In a PoD scenario, following malicious fragment content, the recipient ends up with an IP packet which is larger than 65,535 bytes when reassembling. This can overflow memory buffers allocated for the packet, causing denial of service for legitimate packets.
5. **Slowloris:** Slowloris is a highly-targeted attack, enabling one web server to take down another server, without affecting other services or ports on the target network. Slowloris does this by holding as many connections to the target web server open for as long as possible. It accomplishes this by creating connections to the target server, but sending only a partial request. Slowloris constantly sends more HTTP headers, but never completes a request. The targeted server keeps each of these false connections open. This eventually overflows the maximum concurrent connection pool, and leads to denial of additional connections from legitimate clients.
6. **NTP Amplification:** In NTP amplification attacks, the perpetrator exploits publically-accessible Network Time Protocol (NTP) servers to overwhelm a targeted server with User Datagram Protocol (UDP) traffic. The attack is defined as an amplification assault because the query-to-response ratio in such scenarios is anywhere between 1:20 and 1:200 or more. This means that any attacker who obtains a list of open NTP servers can easily generate a devastating high-bandwidth, high-volume DDoS attack.
7. **HTTP Flood:** In an HTTP flood DDoS attack, the attacker exploits seemingly-legitimate HTTP GET or POST requests to attack a web server or application. HTTP floods do not use malformed packets, spoofing or reflection techniques, and require less bandwidth than other attacks to bring down the targeted site or server. The attack is most effective when it forces the server or application to allocate the maximum resources possible in response to every single request.

- **Dictionary Attacks:** A dictionary attack is a systematic method of guessing a password by trying many common words and their simple variations. Attackers use extensive lists of the most commonly used passwords, popular pet names, fictional characters, or literally just words from a dictionary hence the name dictionary attack.
- **URL Interpretation:** It is a type of attack where we can change the certain parts of a URL, and one can make a web server to deliver web pages for which he is not authorized to browse.
- **File Inclusion Attacks:** It is a type of attack that allows an attacker to access unauthorized or essential files which is available on the web server or to execute malicious files on the web server by making use of the include functionality.
- **Man-In-The-Middle Attack:** Man-In-The-Middle (MITM) attackis a form of cyber-attack where a user is introduced with some kind of meeting between the two parties by a malicious individual, manipulates both parties and achieves access to the data that the two people were trying to deliver to each other. There are several reasons and strategies for hackers to use a MITM attack. Usually, they steal credit card numbers or user login details. They also spy on private meetings, which may include corporate secrets or other useful information. The feature that almost every attack has, in general, is that the attacker pretends to be somebody user trustor a webpage. If an attacker puts himself between a client and a webpage, a Man-in-the-Middle attack occurs. This form of assault comes in many different ways. For example, In order to intercept financial login credentials, a fraudulent banking website can be used. Between the user and the real bank webpage, the fake site lies "in the middle."

  In figure 4.8, we can see that the intruder positioned himself in between the client and server to intercept the confidential data or manipulate the incorrect information of them.

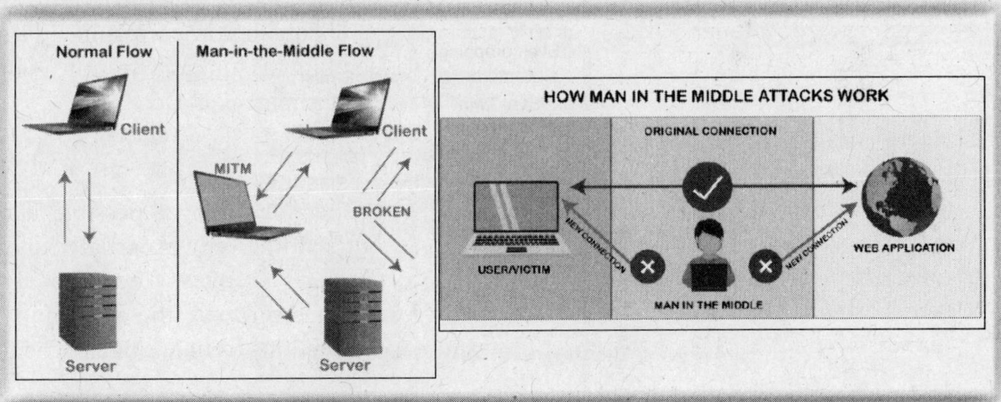

Figure 4.8: Working of MITM Attack

The figure 4.9 illustrate an example of MITM cyber-attack in a bank. To obtain access to banking, the attacker is trying to imitate both sides of the discussion. This instance is accurate for the client and the server discussions and also person-to-person discussions. Shown in this instance, the attacker retrieves a public key and can modulate his own passwords to manipulate the audience to accept that they are safely communicating with each other at either end.

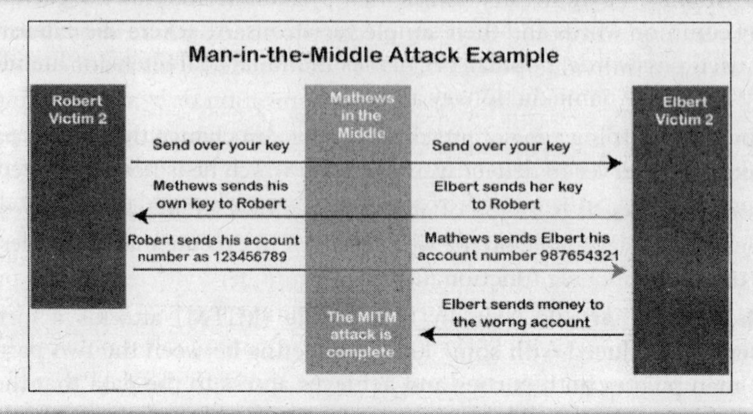

Figure 4.9: MITM Attack Example

Various types of MITM attacks are shown in figure 4.10. We will explain each one of these MITM attacks.

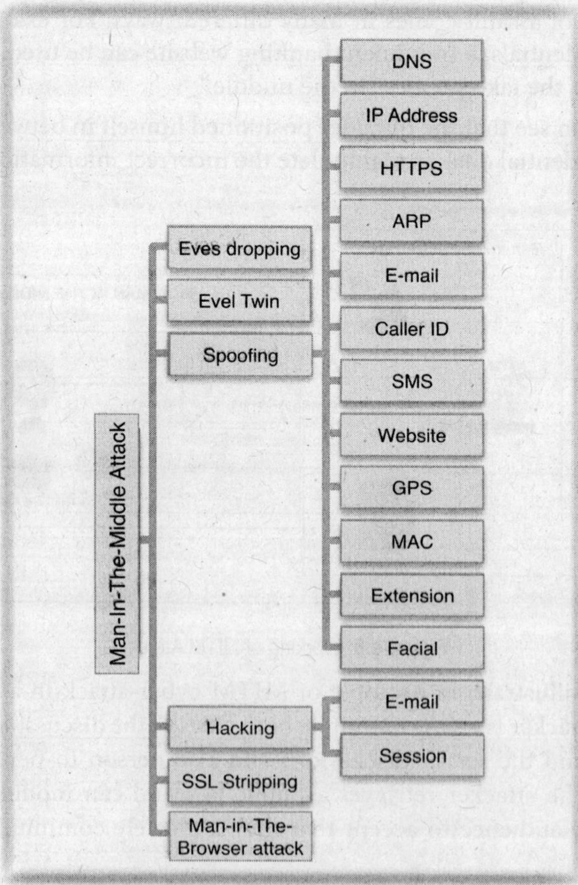

Figure 4.10: Types of Man-In-The-Middle Attack

- **Eaves Dropping:** Eavesdrop is defined as to listen secretly to the private conversation of other people. Eavesdropping is as an electronic attack where digital communications are intercepted by an individual whom they are not intended. This is done in two main ways such as directly listening to digital or analog communication or by data sniffing. Direct listening is the process of tapping wires, capturing RF cable leakage, optical fiber tapping using special equipments etc and know about the conversation. It is also called wiretapping applied to the computer networks. Sniffing is the process of monitoring and capturing all the data passing through a given network using sniffing tools.
- **Evil Twin Attack:** An attacker can set up a fraudulent wireless access point known as an evil twin that mimics the characteristics including the SSID(Service Set Identifier) of a legitimate Access Point (AP). SSID is the name of your wireless network.Users may connect automatically to the evil twin or do so thinking the fraudulent AP is part of a trusted WiFi network. This type of attack is known as "Evil Twin" attack.

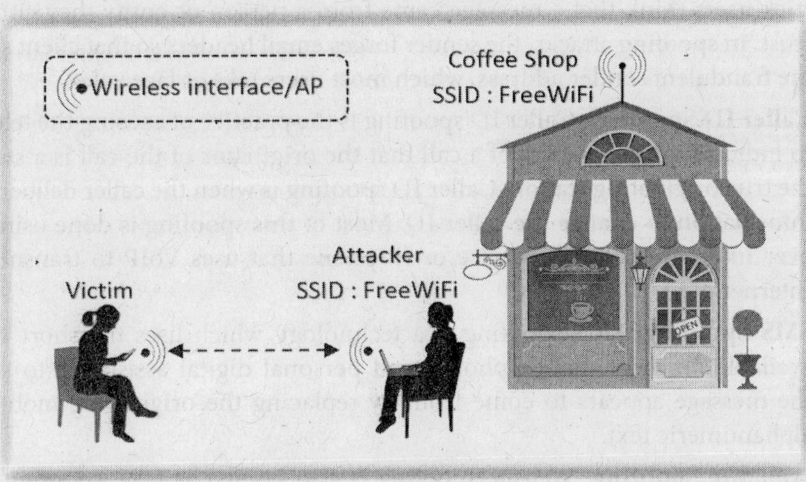

Figure 4.11: Evil Twin Attack

- **Spoofing:** Spoofing is the act of disguising a communication from an unknown source as being from a known, trusted source.
  - **DNS Spoofing:** Domain Name Server (DNS) spoofing is an attack in which altered DNS records are used to redirect online traffic to a fraudulent website that resembles its intended destination. It is a type of computer security hacking whereby a data is introduced into a DNS resolver's cache causing the name server to return an incorrect IP address, diverting traffic to the attackers computer or any other computer. The DNS spoofing attacks can go on for a long period of time without being detected and can cause serious security issues. In this attack, user is forced to navigate to a fake website disguised to look like a real one, with the intention of diverting traffic or stealing credentials of the users.
  - **IP Spoofing:** As we know, devices connected to the same network contains individual IP address. Each device is equipped with its IP address in several enterprise internal web networks. In IP spoofing, the attackers imitate an approved console's IP address. For a

network, it appears just as the system is authorized. It might be causing a network to be exploited by unauthorized access. They may stay quiet and track the actions or a Denial of Service (DoS) attack may also be released.

- **HTTPS Spoofing:** Duplicating an HTTPS webpage is not currently possible. A theoretical approach for circumventing HTTPS, however, has been illustrated by cybersecurity experts. The attacker creates an authoritative address. It uses letters of international alphabets rather than standard scripts. This acts as phishing emails with unusual characters that you might have used. Rolex may be written Rólex, for example.
- **ARP Spoofing:** ARP (Address Resolution Protocol) request is sent out by a client, and an attacker produces a fraudulent response. The attacker is like a computer modem in this situation, which enables the attacker to access the traffic flow. Usually, this is restricted to local area networks (LAN) that use the ARP protocol.
- **E-mail Spoofing:** Email spoofing is a technique used in spam and phishing attacks to trick users think that a message came from a person or entity they either know or can trust. In spoofing attacks, the sender forges email headers so that client software displays the fraudulent sender address, which most users take at face value.
- **Caller ID Spoofing:** Caller ID spoofing is the practice of causing the telephone network to indicate to the receiver of a call that the originator of the call is a station other than the true originating station. Caller ID spoofing is when the caller deliberately sends false information to change the caller ID. Most of this spoofing is done using a VoIP (Voice over Internet Protocol) service or IP phone that uses VoIP to transmit calls over the Internet.
- **SMS Spoofing:** SMS spoofing is a technology which uses the short message service, available on most mobile phones and personal digital assistants, to set from who in the message appears to come from by replacing the originating mobile number with alphanumeric text.
- **Web Site Spoofing:** Website spoofing is also known as URL spoofing. The scammers make a fraudulent website that resembles the legitimate one. The spoofed website will have a familiar login page, stolen logos and similar branding, and even a spoofed URL that appears correct at first glance. Hackers build these websites to steal user's login details and potentially drop malware onto the computer. Often, website spoofing takes place in conjunction with email spoofing. For example, scammers might send you an email containing a link to the fake website.
- **GPS Spoofing:** A GPS spoofing attack attempts to deceive a GPS receiver by broadcasting fake GPS signals, structured to resemble a set of normal GPS signals, or by rebroadcasting genuine signals captured elsewhere or at a different time.
- **MAC Spoofing:** MAC spoofing is a technique for changing a factory-assigned Media Access Control (MAC) address of a network interface on a networked device. The MAC address that is hard-coded on a network interface controller (NIC) cannot be changed. Essentially, MAC spoofing entails changing a computer's identity, for any reason.
- **Extension Spoofing:** Extension spoofing attack hides the extension of an attachment, tricking victims into downloading executables that install malware.

- **Facial Spoofing:** Facial spoof attack is a process in which a fraudulent user can subvert or attack a face recognition system by masquerading as registered user and thereby gaining illegitimate access and advantages.
- **Biometric Spoofing:** In biometric spoofing, the fraudster might use spoofing attacks to impersonate someone in order to defeat biometric authentication mechanism. For example, to spoof a facial biometric algorithm, they might attempt to use a non-live image such as a video or photograph to impersonate a targeted victim.

- **Hacking:** Hacking is an attempt to exploit a computer system or a private network by taking unauthorized access or control over computer network security systems for some illicit purpose.
  - **E-mail Hacking:** An attacker exploits the email system of a user in a such a kind of cybersecurity intrusion. The intruder also watches quietly, collecting data and eavesdropping on the discussion via email. The Attackers may have a scan pattern that searches for targeted keywords, such as "financial" or "hidden democratic policies." Through social engineering, email hacking operates perfectly. To imitate an online friend, the attackers might use relevant data from some kind of hijacked email address. Spear-phishing can also be used to trick a user into downloading malicious apps.
  - **Session Hacking:** It is a security attack on a user session over a protected network. Web applications create cookies to store the state and user sessions. By stealing the cookies, an attacker can have access to all of the user data. Usually, this form of MITM attack is often used to hack social media platforms. The webpage contains a "session browser cookie" on the victim's machine for most social media platforms. If the person steps off, this cookie is disproved. But when the session is running, the cookie offers identity, exposure, and monitoring data. A session hijack happens when a configuration cookie is stolen by an intruder. Unless the victim's account is hacked with malware or application attackers, it can arise. It can occur if a user exploits an XSS cross-scripting intrusion, in which the hacker injects malicious script into a site that is commonly visited.

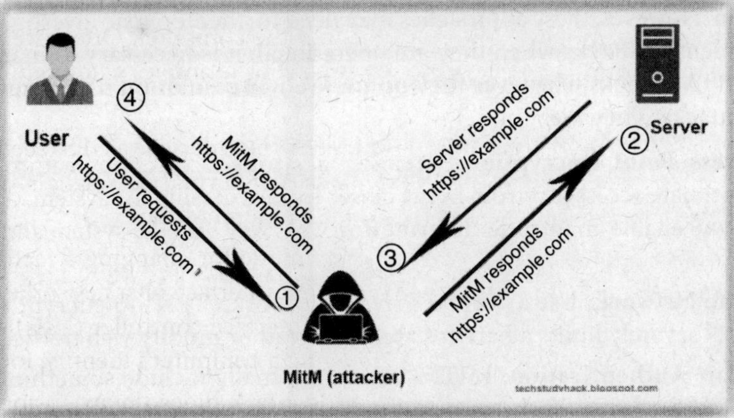

Figure 4.12: SSL Stripping Attack

- **SSL Stripping:** Secure HTTPS is formed by merging SSL (Secure Socket Layer) with HTTP. SSL stripping is a technique by which a website is downgraded from HTTPS application protocol to HTTP. By this action, it will become insecure and exposes to eavesdropping and data manipulation. Hence it is also known as SSL downgrading. In other words, the attack is used to circumvent the security which is enforced by SSL certificates on https sites.
- **Man-In-The-Browser Attack:** A Man-In-The-Browser (MITB) Attack is a type of Man-In-The-Middle (MITM) Attack specifically involving a browser infected with some type of proxy malware. This malware allows an attacker to intercept or modify information sent from a user's browser to a server, and works regardless of the existence of a two or three step authentication system for a web application. The attacker is able to insert himself into the communications channel between two trusting parties by compromising a web browser used by one of the parties, for the purpose of eavesdropping, data theft and/or session tampering.

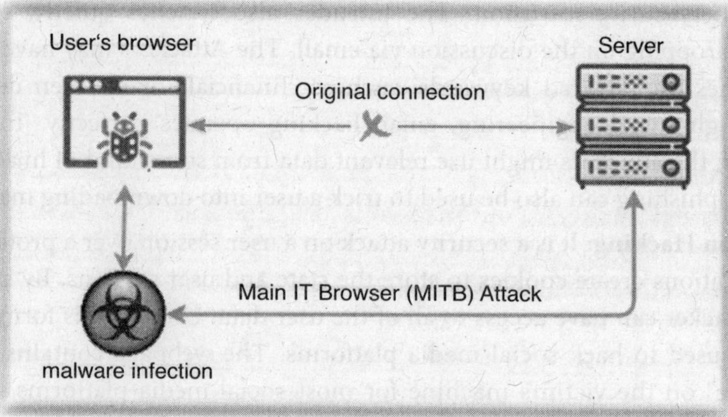

Figure 4.13: MITB Attack

Detection of Man-In-The-Middle attack is very important. It is harder to identify a MITM attack without taking the appropriate measures. This assault will theoretically proceed unchecked till we consciously evaluate whether our interactions have been monitored. Usually, the main technique for identifying potential attacks is searching for adequate page authorization and introducing some kind of temper authentication. However, these approaches may need further forensic investigation after-the-fact. Instead of trying to identify attacks when they are operational, it is necessary to manage precautionary measures to avoid MITM attacks whenever they occur. We will discuss on some prevention techniques to avoid the MITM attacks. They are:

1. **Wireless Access Point Encryption:** Creating a strong protection feature on access points eliminates legitimate access just from being closer from accessing the system. A vulnerable system of protection will enable an intruder to brute-force his way into the system and start attacking the MITM.
2. **Virtual Private Network:** Use a Virtual Private Network (VPN) to encrypt the web traffic. An encrypted VPN severely limits a hacker's ability to read or modify web traffic.
3. **Public Key Pair Authentication:** MITM attacks normally include something or another being spoofed. In different layers of the protocol stack, public key pair authentication such as RSA is used to ensure that the objects user communicate with that are essentially the objects user want to communicate with.

4. **Strong Network User Credentials:** Ensure that the email login credentials are strong and modified regularly. This is applicable to login credentials for Wi-Fi and password of router. When a hacker detects the wireless router login details, they can switch the fraudulent servers to the DNS servers. Or, at worst, hack the modem with harmful malware.
5. **Communication Security:** Communication security help the users to protect from unauthorized messages and provides secure data encryption. Enabling two-factor authentication is the most powerful way to avoid account hacking. It implies that user have to give another protection factor, in addition to the login credentials. An example of two-factor authentication is a login credential along with a text to user e-mail or an SMS to the phone number.
6. **Be Vigilant on security lapses:** Use proper hygiene for network protection on all platforms, such as smartphone applications. Since phishing emails are the most popular attack tool, cautious on spam email. Analyze the references cautiously before opening. Mount plug-ins for the browser from trusted sources. Reduce the chance of exploits by logging out inactive accounts.
7. **Avoid using public Wi-Fi:** It can be hard to identify MITM attacks as they are occurring. The easiest way to remain secure is to avoid using free public Wi-Fi.

4.7 CYBER ATTACKERS

In computer and computer networks, an attacker is the individual or organization who performs the malicious activities to destroy, expose, alter, disable, steal, gain unauthorized access to or make unauthorized use of an asset. As the Internet access becomes more pervasive across the world, and each of us spends more time on the web, there is also an attacker grows as well. Attackers use all tools and techniques they would try and attack us to get unauthorized access. There are four types of attackers which are described below.

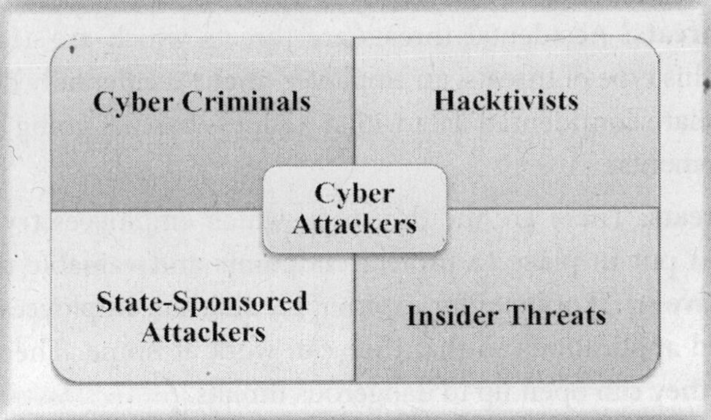

Figure 4.14: Types of Cyber Attackers

- **Cyber Criminals:** Cyber criminals are individual or group of people who use technology to commit cybercrime with the intention of stealing sensitive company information or personal data and generating profits. In today's, world they are the most prominent and most active type of attacker. Cyber criminals use computers in below three broad ways to do cyber-crimes.
  - Select computer as their target- In this, they attack other people's computers to do cybercrime, such as spreading viruses, data theft, identity theft, etc.

- Uses the computer as their weapon- In this, they use the computer to do conventional crime such as spam, fraud, illegal gambling, etc.
- Uses the computer as their accessory- In this, they use the computer to steal data illegally.

- **Hacktivists:** Hacktivists are individuals or groups of hackers who carry out malicious activity to promote a political agenda, religious belief, or social ideology. Hacktivism is a digital disobedience. It's hacking for a cause. Hacktivists are not like cyber criminals who hack computer networks to steal data for the cash. They are individuals or groups of hackers who work together and see themselves as fighting injustice.
- **State-Sponsored Attacker:** State-sponsored attackers have particular objectives aligned with either the political, commercial or military interests of their country of origin. These types of attackers are not in a hurry. The government organizations have highly skilled hackers and specialize in detecting vulnerabilities and exploiting these before the holes are patched. It is very challenging to defeat these attackers due to the vast resources at their disposal.
- **Insider Threats:** The insider threat is a threat to an organization's security or data that comes from within. These types of threats are usually occurred from employees or former employees. They may also arise from third parties, including contractors, temporary workers, suppliers or customers. Insider threats can be categorized below.
  - **Malicious Threats:** Malicious threats are attempts by an insider to access and potentially harm an organization's data, systems or IT infrastructure. These insider threats are often attributed to dissatisfied employees or ex-employees who believe that the organization was doing something wrong with them in some way, and they feel justified in seeking revenge. Insiders may also become threats when they are influenced by malicious outsiders, either through financial incentives or extortion.
  - **Accidental Threats:** Accidental threats are threats which are accidently done by insider employees. In this type of threats, an employee might accidentally delete an important file or inadvertently share confidential data with a business partner going beyond company's policy or legal requirements.
  - **Negligent Threats:** These are the threats in which employees try to avoid the policies of an organization put in place to protect endpoints and valuable data. For example, if the organization have strict policies for external file sharing, employees might try to share work on public cloud applications so that they can work at home. There is nothing wrong with these acts, but they can open up to dangerous threats.

4.8 CYBER SECURITY PRINCIPLES

These guiding principles have been developed to respond to cyber security challenge by providing a consistent approach to help, inform, educate, and protect Internet Service Providers (ISP) and customers from online crimes. These guiding principles are aspirational, developed and delivered as a partnership between Government and ISPs. They recognize that ISPs have different sets of customers, offer different levels of support and services to protect those customers from cyber threats. Some of the essential cyber security principles are described Figure 4.15.

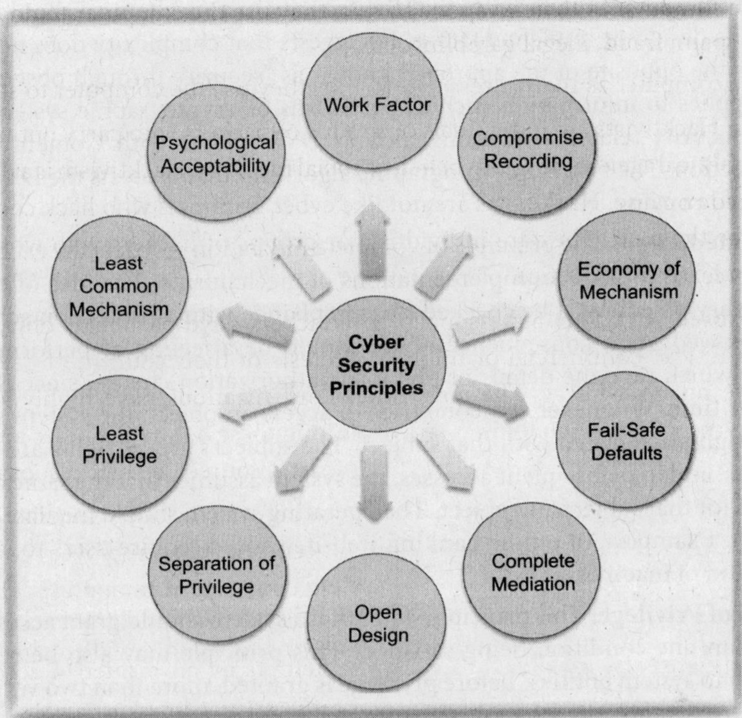

Figure 4.15: Cyber Security Principles

- **Economy of Mechanism:** This principle states that security mechanisms should be as simple and small as possible. The economy of mechanism principle simplifies the design and implementation of security mechanisms. If the design and implementation are simple and small, fewer possibilities exist for errors. The checking and testing process is less complicated so that fewer components need to be tested. Interfaces between security modules are the suspect area which should be as simple as possible. Interface modules often make implicit assumptions about input or output parameters or the current system state. If any of these assumptions are wrong, the module's actions may produce unexpected results. Simple security framework facilitates its understanding by developers as well as users and enables the efficient development and verification of enforcement methods for it.
- **Fail-Safe Defaults:** The fail-safe defaults principle states that the default configuration of a system should have a conservative protection scheme. This principle also restricts how privileges are initialized when a subject or object is created. Example: If we add a new user to an operating system, the default group of the user should have fewer access rights to files and services.
- **Least Privilege:** This principle states that a user should only have those privileges that need to complete his task. Its primary function is to control the assignment of rights granted to the user, not the identity of the user. If the head of the organization demands root access to a UNIX system from the system administer, the right should not be given unless that person has a task that requires such level of access. If possible, the elevated rights of a user identity should be removed as soon as those rights are no longer needed.

- **Open Design:** This principle states that the security of a mechanism should not depend on the secrecy of its design or implementation. It suggests that complexity does not add security. This principle is the opposite of the approach known as "security through obscurity." This principle not only applies to information such as passwords or cryptographic systems but also to other computer security related operations such as DVD player with Content Scrambling System (CSS) protection. The CSS is a cryptographic algorithm that protects the DVD movie disks from unauthorized copying.
- **Complete Mediation:** The principle of complete mediation restricts the caching of information, which often leads to simpler implementations of mechanisms. The idea of this principle is that access to every object must be checked for compliance with a protection scheme to ensure that they are allowed. As a consequence, there should be a feeling of performance improvement techniques which save the details of previous authorization checks, since the permissions can change over time. Whenever someone tries to access an object, the system should authenticate the access rights associated with that subject. The subject's access rights are verified once at the initial access, and for subsequent accesses, the system assumes that the same access rights should be accepted for that subject and object. The operating system should mediate all and every access to an object. Example: An online banking website should require users to sign-in again after a certain period of inactivity.
- **Separation of Privilege:** This principle states that a system should grant access permission based on more than one condition being satisfied. This principle may also be restrictive because it limits access to system entities. Before privilege is granted, more than two verifications should be performed. An example is the requirement to change to root. In this case, two conditions need to meet such as the user must know the root password and the user must be in the right group.
- **Least Common Mechanism:** This principle states that in systems with multiple users, the mechanisms allowing resources shared by more than one user should be minimized as much as possible. This principle may also be restrictive because it limits the sharing of resources. For example; If there is a need to access a file or application by more than one user, then these users should use separate channels to access these resources. This helps to prevent from unforeseen consequences that could cause security problems.
- **Psychological Acceptability:** This principle states that a security mechanism should not make the resource more complicated to access if the security mechanisms were not present. The psychological acceptability principle recognizes the human element in computer security. If security-related software or computer systems are too complicated to configure, maintain or operate, the user will not employ the necessary security mechanisms. For example, if a password is matched during a password change process, the password changing program should state why it was denied rather than giving a cryptic error message. At the same time, applications should not impart unnecessary information that may lead to a compromise in security. An example of this is that when we enter a wrong password, the system should only tell us that the user id or password is incorrect. It should not tell us that only the password was wrong as this gives the attacker information.
- **Work Factor:** This principle states that the cost of circumventing a security mechanism should be compared with the resources of a potential attacker when designing a security scheme. In some cases, the cost of circumventing ("known as work factor") can be easily calculated. In other words, the work factor is a common cryptographic measure which is used to determine the

strength of a given cipher. It does not map directly to cybersecurity, but the overall concept does apply. Example: Suppose the number of experiments needed to try all possible four character passwords is 331776. If the potential attacker must try each experimental password at a terminal, one might consider a four-character password to be satisfactory. On the other hand, if the potential attacker could use an astronomical computer capable of trying a million passwords per second, a four-letter password would be a minor barrier for a potential intruder.

- **Compromise Recording:** The compromise recording principle states that sometimes it is more desirable to record the details of intrusion that to adopt a more sophisticated measure to prevent it. Example: The servers in an office network may keep logs for all accesses to files, all emails sent and received, and all browsing sessions on the web. Another example is that Internet connected surveillance cameras are a typical example of a compromise recording system that can be placed to protect a building.

4.9 CYBER SECURITY CHALLENGES

Today cyber security is the main component of the country's overall national security and economic security strategies. In India, there are so many challenges related to cyber security. With the increase of the cyber-attacks, every organization needs a security analyst who makes sure that their system is secured. These security analysts face many challenges related to cyber security such as securing confidential data of government organizations, securing the private organization servers, etc. The recent important cyber security challenges are described below.

- **Ransomware Evolution:** Ransomware is a type of malware in which the data on a victim's computer is locked, and payment is demanded before the ransomed data is unlocked. After successful payment, access rights returned to the victim. Ransomware is the bane of cybersecurity, data professionals, IT, and executives. Ransomware attacks are growing day by day in the areas of cybercrime. IT professionals and business leaders need to have a powerful recovery strategy against the malware attacks to protect their organization. It involves proper planning to recover corporate as well as customers' data and application as well as reporting any breaches against the Notifiable Data Breaches scheme. Today's DRaaS (Disaster Recovery as a Service) solutions are the best defense against the ransomware attacks. With DRaaS solutions method, we can automatically back up our files, easily identify which backup is clean, and launch a fail-over with the press of a button when malicious attacks corrupt our data.

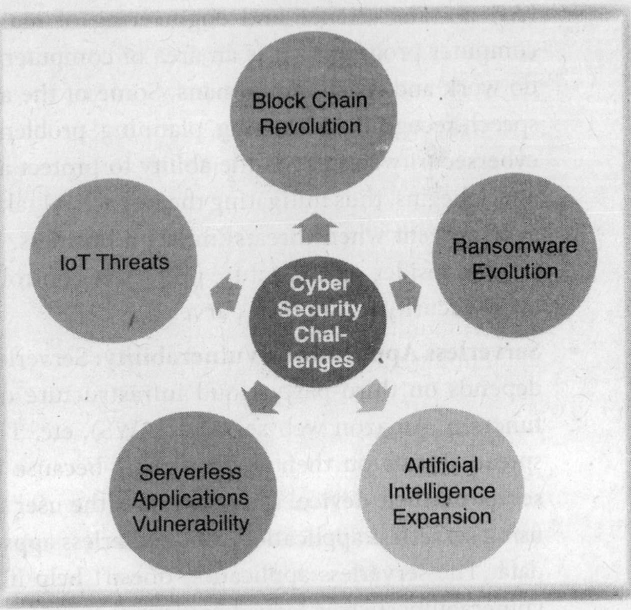

Figure 4.16: Cyber Security Challenges

- **Blockchain Revolution:** Blockchain technology is the most important invention in computing era. It is the first time in human history that we have a genuinely native digital medium for peer-to-peer value exchange. The blockchain is a technology that enables cryptocurrencies like bitcoin. The blockchain is a vast global platform that allows two or more parties to do a transaction or do business without needing a third party for establishing trust. It is difficult to predict what blockchain systems will offer in regards to cybersecurity. The professionals in cyber security can make some educated guesses regarding blockchain. As the application and utility of blockchain in a cyber security context emerges, there will be a healthy tension but also complementary integrations with traditional, proven, cyber security approaches.
- **Internet of Things Threats:** Internet of Things (IoT) is a system of interrelated physical devices which can be accessible through the Internet. The connected physical devices have a unique identifier (UID) and have the ability to transfer data over a network without any requirements of the human-to-human or human-to-computer interaction. The firmware and software which is running on IoT devices make consumer and businesses highly susceptible to cyber-attacks. When IoT things were designed, it is not considered in mind about the cybersecurity and for commercial purposes. Every organization needs to work with cybersecurity professionals to ensure the security of their password policies, session handling, user verification, multifactor authentication, and security protocols to help in managing the risk.
- **Artificial Intelligence Expansion:** According to John McCarthy, father of Artificial Intelligence (AI) is "The science and engineering of making intelligent machines, especially intelligent computer programs." It is an area of computer science which creates intelligent machines that do work and react like humans. Some of the activities related to artificial intelligence include speech recognition, learning, planning, problem-solving, etc. The key benefits with AI into our cybersecurity strategy is the ability to protect and defend an environment when the malicious attack begins, thus mitigating the impact. AI take immediate action against the malicious attacks at a moment when threats impact a business. IT business leaders and cyber security strategy teams consider AI as a future protective control that will allow our business to stay ahead of the cyber security technology curve.
- **Serverless Applications Vulnerability:** Serverless architecture and apps is an application which depends on third-party cloud infrastructure or on a back-end service such as google cloud function, Amazon web services (AWS), etc. The serverless apps invite the cyber attackers to spread threats on their system easily because the users access the application locally or off-server on their device. Therefore, it is the user responsibility for the security precautions while using serverless application. The serverless apps do nothing to keep the attackers away from our data. The serverless application doesn't help if an attacker gains access to our data through a vulnerability such as leaked credentials, a compromised insider or by any other means. We can run software with the application which provides best chance to defeat the cyber criminals. The serverless applications are typically small in size. It helps developers to launch their applications quickly and easily. They don't need to worry about the underlying infrastructure. The web-services and data processing tools are examples of the most common serverless applications.

4.10 CYBER SECURITY RISK ANALYSIS

Risk analysis refers to the review of risks associated with the particular action or event. The risk analysis is applied to information technology, projects, security issues and any other event where risks may be analyzed based on a quantitative and qualitative basis. Risks are part of every IT project and business organizations. The analysis of risk should be occurred on a regular basis and be updated to identify new potential threats. The strategic risk analysis helps to minimize the future risk probability and damage. The reasons for enterprises and organizations for doing risk analysis are

- To anticipates and reduce the effect of harmful results occurred from adverse events.
- To plan for technology or equipment failure or loss from adverse events, both natural and human-caused.
- To evaluate whether the potential risks of a project are balanced in the decision process when evaluating to move forward with the project.
- To identify the impact of and prepare for changes in the enterprise environment.

Every organization needs to understand about the risks associated with their information systems to effectively and efficiently protect their IT assets. Risk analysis can help an organization to improve their security in below explained ways.

- Concerning financial and organizational impacts, it identifies, rate and compares the overall impact of risks related to the organization.
- It helps to identify gaps in information security and determine the next steps to eliminate the risks of security.
- It can also enhance the communication and decision-making processes related to information security.
- It improves security policies and procedures as well as develop cost-effective methods for implementing information security policies and procedures.
- It increases employee awareness about risks and security measures during the risk analysis process and understands the financial impacts of potential security risks.

The basic steps followed by a risk analysis process are as below

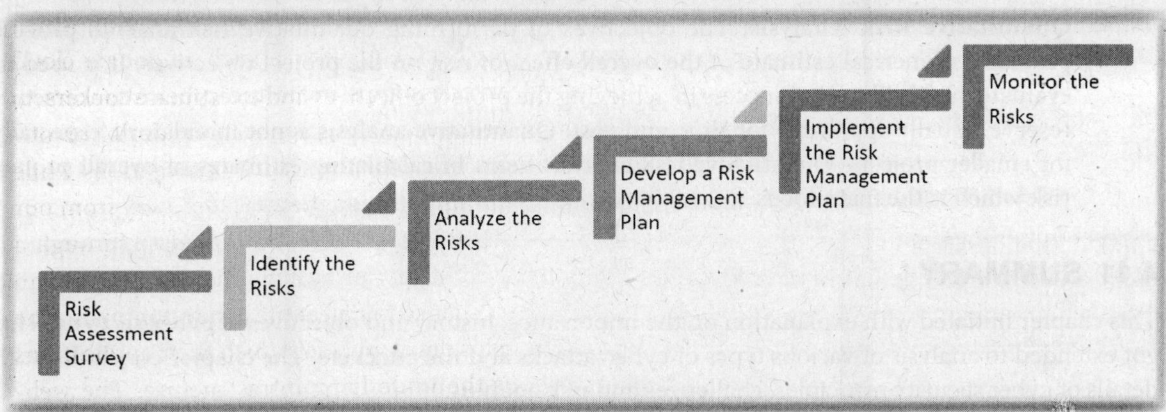

Figure 4.17: Steps in Risk Analysis Process

Risk assessment survey: Conducting a risk assessment survey is the first step. This is for getting the inputs from management and department heads to the risk assessment process. The risk assessment survey refers to begin documenting the specific risks or threats within each department.

Identify the risks: This step is used to evaluate an IT system or other aspects of an organization to identify the risk related to software, hardware, data, and IT employees. It identifies the possible adverse events that could occur in an organization such as human error, flood, fire or earthquake.

Analyze the risks: Once the risks are evaluated and identified, the risk analysis process should analyze each risk that will occur, as well as determine the consequences linked with each risk. It also determines how they might affect the objectives of an IT project.

Develop a risk management plan: After analysis of the risk that provides an idea about which assets are valuable and which threats will probably affect the IT assets negatively, there is a need to develop a plan for risk management. This is to come up with control recommendations that can be used to mitigate, transfer, accept or avoid the risk.

Implement the risk management plan: The primary goal of this step is to implement the measures to remove or reduce the analyses risks. We can remove or reduce the risk from starting with the highest priority and resolve or at least mitigate each risk so that it is no longer a threat.

Monitor the risks: This step is responsible for monitoring the security risk on a regular basis for identifying, treating and managing risks that should be an essential part of any risk analysis process.

4.10.1 Types of Risk Analysis

The different types of risk analysis are qualitative risk analysis and quantitative risk analysis.

- **Qualitative Risk Analysis:** The qualitative risk analysis process is a project management technique that prioritizes risk on the project by assigning the probability and impact number. Probability is something a risk event will occur whereas impact is the significance of the consequences of a risk event. The objective of qualitative risk analysis is to assess and evaluate the characteristics of individually identified risk and then prioritize them based on the agreed-upon characteristics. The assessing individual risk evaluates the probability that each risk will occur and effect on the project objectives. The categorizing risks will help in filtering them out. Qualitative analysis is used to determine the risk exposure of the project by multiplying the probability and impact.
- **Quantitative Risk Analysis:** The objectives of performing quantitative risk analysis process provide a numerical estimate of the overall effect of risk on the project objectives. It is used to evaluate the likelihood of success in achieving the project objectives and to estimate contingency reserve, usually applicable for time and cost. Quantitative analysis is not mandatory, especially for smaller projects. Quantitative risk analysis helps in calculating estimates of overall project risk which is the main focus.

4.11 SUMMARY

This chapter initiated with explanation on the importance, history and objectives of cyber security. This got extended to analysis of various types of cyber-attacks and the attackers. The chapter concludes with details of cyber security principles, challenges and risk analysis.

4.12 OBJECTIVE QUESTIONS

The answer of the multiple-choice questions is marked in **bold**.

1. Who is the creator of creeper virus?
   (a) **Bob Thomas** (b) Ray Tomlinson (c) Robert Morris (d) None of these
2. Who is the inventor of reaper anti-virus?
   (a) Bob Thomas (b) **Ray Tomlinson** (c) Robert Morris (d) None of these
3. .... is a system based cyber-attack.
   (a) **Virus** (b) DoS (c) MITM (d) Phishing
4. .... Is a web based cyber-attack.
   (a) Virus (b) Worms (c) Trojan Horse (d) **Phishing**
5. .... cannot be controlled remote.
   (a) **Virus** (b) Worms (c) Trojan Horse (d) All of these
6. .... Is not a MITM attack.
   (a) DNS spoofing (b) E-mail hacking
   (c) Session hacking (d) **Back door attacks**
7. .... is a cyber attacker.
   (a) Cyber criminal (b) Hackvists (c) **All of these** (d) None of these
8. Which is a cyber security principle?
   (a) east privilege (b) Open design
   (c) Complete mediation (d) **All of these**
9. Which one is a cyber security challenge?
   (a) Block chain revolution (b) IoT
   (c) AI expansion (d) **All of these**
10. .... is the first step in risk analysis process.
    (a) **Risk assessment** (b) Risk identification
    (c) Risk analysis (d) Risk monitoring

4.12 REVIEW QUESTIONS

1. Explain cyber security and its importance.
2. Discuss about the history and evolution of cyber threats.
3. Discuss about the objectives of cyber security.
4. Explain on the evolution of cyber-attack methods.
5. Explain different types of system based cyber-attacks.
6. Explain various types of web based cyber-attacks.
7. Discuss the various types of Man-In-The-Middle cyber-attacks.
8. Compare Virus, Worms and Trojan horse.
9. Explain the working of Man-In-The-Middle cyber-attacks.

10. Discuss the prevention techniques to avoid MITM attacks.
11. Explain different types of cyber attackers.
12. Discuss various types of threat to information security within the organisation.
13. Explain the principles of cyber security.
14. Discuss the various cyber security challenges.
15. Explain the reasons for conducting risk analysis by organisations.
16. Explain the methods in which security of an organisation can be improved by doing risk analysis.
17. Explain the steps in risk analysis process.
18. Discuss different types of risk analysis.

4.15 ABBREVIATIONS AND SYMBOLS

Abbreviations	Full Form	Description
API	Application Programming Interface	API is a software connection between computers or between computer programs.
ARP	Address Resolution Protocol	ARP is a communication protocol used for discovering the link layer address, such as a MAC address, associated with a given Internet layer address, typically an IPv4 address.
AWS	Amazon Web Services	Amazon Web Services is a subsidiary of Amazon providing on-demand cloud computing platforms and APIs to individuals, companies, and governments, on a metered pay-as-you-go basis.
BDR	Backup and Disaster Recovery	BDR is a combination of data backup and disaster recovery solutions that work cohesively to ensure business continuity.
CASB	Cloud Access Security Broker	CASB is an on-premises or cloud-based security policy enforcement point that is placed between cloud service consumers and cloud service providers to combine and interject enterprise security policies as cloud-based resources are accessed.
CSS	Content Scrambling System	CSS is a Digital Rights Management (DRM), encryption system that encrypts data on commercial DVDs to prevent users from copying the disc's data to a computer file or another disc.
DNS	Domain Name System	DNS is a hierarchical and decentralized naming system for computers, services, or other resources connected to the Internet or a private network.
DoS	Denial-of-Service	DoS is an attack meant to shut down a machine or network, making it inaccessible to its intended users.
DRaaS	Disaster Recovery as a Service	DRaaS is a cloud computing service model that allows an organization to back up its data and IT infrastructure in a third party cloud computing environment and provide services through a SaaS solution, to regain access and functionality to IT infrastructure after a disaster.

Abbreviations	Full Form	Description
HTTPS	Hyper Text Transfer Protocol Secure	HTTP Secure, is a combination of the Hypertext Transfer Protocol with the SSL/TLS (Transport Layer Security).
ICMP	Internet Control Message Protocol	ICMP is a network layer protocol used by network devices to diagnose network communication issues. This is mainly used to determine whether or not data is reaching its intended destination in a timely manner.
IDS	Intrusion Detection System	IDS is a device or software application that monitors a network for malicious activity or policy violations.
IP	Internet Protocol	IP is a set of rules for routing and addressing packets of data so that they can travel across networks and arrive at the correct destination.
IPS	Intrusion Prevention System	IPS is a network security/threat prevention technology that examines network traffic flows to detect and prevent vulnerability exploits.
ISP	Internet Service Provider	ISP is a company that provides access to the Internet.
KGB	Komitet Gosudarstvennoy Bezopasnosti (Committee for State Security)	KGB is the Soviet Russia foreign intelligence and domestic security agency of the Soviet Union.
ML	Machine Learning	ML is the study of computer algorithms that improve automatically through experience and by the use of data. This is part of Artificial Intelligence (AI).
SaaS	Software as a Service	SaaS is a software licensing and delivery model in which software is licensed on a subscription basis and is centrally hosted. It is also known as On-Demand Software.
SMB	Small and Midsize Businesses	SMB are businesses whose annual business value is below certain limits. This is also known as Small and Medium Sized Enterprise SME or MSME.
SMS	Short Message Service	SMS is a text messaging service component of most telephone, Internet, and mobile device systems.
SQL	Structured Query Language	SQL is a domain-specific language used in programming and designed for managing data held in a relational database management system, or for stream processing in a relational data stream management system.
SSID	Service Set IDentifier	This is the unique name that identifies a wireless network. It is in the packet header when a data packet is transmitted. The devices on the Wi-Fi network use this identifier for communications via the network.
SSL	Secure Sockets Layer	SSL is Netscape's protocol for creating an encrypted connection between a web server and a web browser.

Abbreviations	Full Form	Description
UDP	User Datagram Protocol	UDP is a communications protocol that is primarily used to establish low-latency and loss-tolerating connections between applications on the internet. UDP speeds up transmissions by enabling the transfer of data before an agreement is provided by the receiving party.
URL	Uniform Resource Locator	URL is commonly known as web address. This is a reference to a web resource that specifies its location on a computer network and a mechanism for retrieving it.
UTM	Unified Threat Management	UTM is an approach to information security where a single hardware or software installation provides multiple security functions. This contrasts with the traditional method of having point solutions for each security function.
WAF	Web Application Firewall	WAF helps protect web applications by filtering and monitoring HTTP traffic between a web application and the Internet.
XML	Extensible Markup Language	XML is a markup language that defines a set of rules for encoding documents in a format that is both human-readable and machine-readable.
XSS	Cross Site Scripting	XSS is a common attack vector that injects malicious code into a vulnerable web application.

4.16 LIST OF FIGURES AND TABLES

The details of figures and tables used in this chapter is as below.

CHAPTER 5

Policy, Standards, Certifications and Cyber Laws

CONTENTS

5.1 INTRODUCTION

In this chapter, we will be able to understand about security policy, cyber security policies, standards, certifications and cyber laws.

5.2 SECURITY POLICIES

Security policies are a formal set of rules which is issued by an organization to ensure that the user who are authorized to access organisation's technology and information assets comply with rules and guidelines related to the security of information. It is a written document in the organization which is responsible for how to protect the organizations from threats and how to handles them when they will occur. A security policy is also considered to be a "living document" which means that the document is never finished, but it is continuously updated as requirements of the technology and employee changes.

5.2.1 Need for Security Policies

- **Increases Efficiency:** The best thing about having a policy is being able to increase the level of consistency which saves time, money and resources. The policy should inform about individual duties, and tell what can be done and they cannot do.
- **Upholds Discipline and Accountability:** When any human mistake occurs and system security is compromised, then the security policy will back up any disciplinary action and also support a case in a court of law.
- **Educate Employees on Security Literacy:** A well-written security policy can also be seen as an educational document which informs the readers about their importance of responsibility in

protecting the organization's sensitive data. It involves in choosing the right passwords as well as providing guidelines for file transfers and data storage which increases employee's overall awareness of security and how it can be strengthened.

5.3 CYBER SECURITY POLICIES

The security policy used in information system is called cyber security policy. The different types of cyber security policies are organizational policy, system-specific policy and issue-specific policy. Some of the issue-specific policies are virus and spyware protection policy, firewall policy, intrusion prevention policy, live update policy, application and device control policy, exceptions policy and host integrity policy.

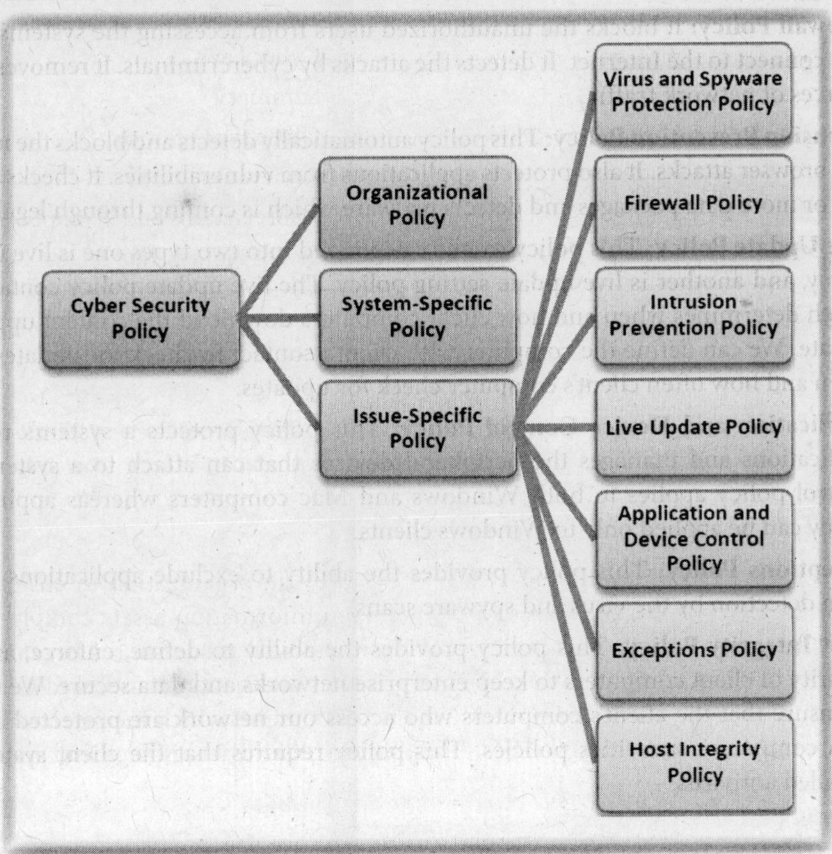

Figure 5.1: Types of Cyber Security Policy

- **Organizational policy:** An organizational security policy is a set of rules or procedures that is imposed by an organization on its operations to protect its sensitive data. The organizational security policy is also called master security policy. This will provide information security direction for the organization which include information security objectives, information on how to meet contractual, legal or regulatory requirements of business and contain a commitment to continually improve information security management system.

- **System-Specific Policy:** A System-specific policy is concerned with a specific or individual computer system. System-specific security policies are written documents that provide standards or procedures for configuring and maintaining information systems such as time-sheet and expense account systems or information technology equipment such as network firewall devices.
- **Issue-Specific Policy:** An Issue-specific policy is concerned with a certain functional aspect that may require more attention. Most types of security policies are automatically created during the installation. We can also customize policies to suit our specific environment. Issue-specific policies are also called customized policies. Few types of issue-specific cyber security policies are
  - **Virus and Spyware Protection Policy:** It helps to detect, removes, and repairs the side effects of viruses and security risks by using signatures. It helps to detect the applications that exhibit suspicious behaviour.
  - **Firewall Policy:** It blocks the unauthorized users from accessing the systems and networks that connect to the Internet. It detects the attacks by cybercriminals. It removes the unwanted sources of network traffic.
  - **Intrusion Prevention Policy:** This policy automatically detects and blocks the network attacks and browser attacks. It also protects applications from vulnerabilities. It checks the contents of one or more data packages and detects malware which is coming through legal ways.
  - **Live Update Policy:** This policy can be categorized into two types one is live update content policy, and another is live update setting policy. The live update policy contains the setting which determines when and how client computers download the content updates from live update. We can define the computer with client's contact to check for updates and schedule when and how often client's computer check for updates.
  - **Application and Device Control Policy:** This policy protects a system's resources from applications and manages the peripheral devices that can attach to a system. The device control policy applies to both Windows and Mac computers whereas application control policy can be applied only to Windows clients.
  - **Exceptions Policy:** This policy provides the ability to exclude applications and processes from detection by the virus and spyware scans.
  - **Host Integrity Policy:** This policy provides the ability to define, enforce, and restore the security of client computers to keep enterprise networks and data secure. We use this policy to ensure that the client's computers who access our network are protected and compliant with companies securities policies. This policy requires that the client system must have installed antivirus.

5.4 CYBER SECURITY STANDARDS

A standard is a technical document designed to be used as a rule, guideline or definition. It is a consensus-built, repeatable way of doing something. Standards are created by bringing together all interested parties such as manufacturers, developers, consumers and regulators of a particular product, process or service. All parties benefit from standardization through increased safety and quality as well as lower transaction costs and prices.

To make cybersecurity measures explicit, the written norms are required. These norms are known as cybersecurity standards. A security standard is a published specification that establishes a common language, and contains a technical specification or other precise criteria and is designed to be used consistently, as a rule, a guideline, or a definition." The goal of security standards is to improve the security of information technology systems, networks, and critical infrastructures. The well-written cybersecurity standards enable consistency among product developers and serve as a reliable standard for purchasing security products.

Information security standards are generally provided for all organizations regardless of their size or the industry and sector in which they operate. This section includes information about each standard that is usually recognized as an essential component of any cybersecurity strategy.

International Organization for Standardization (ISO) standards provide a world-class specification for products, services and computers, to ensure quality, safety and efficiency. They are instrumental in facilitating international trade. ISO is an independent, non-governmental international organization. Today, it has a membership of 162 national standards bodies and 784 technical committees and subcommittees to take care of standards development. ISO has published over 22336 international standards and its related documents which covers almost every industry, from information technology, to food safety, to agriculture and healthcare.

ISO 27000 Series is the family of information security standards which is developed by the International Organization for Standardization and the International Electrotechnical Commission (IEC) to provide a globally recognized framework for best information security management. It helps the organization to keep their information assets secure such as employee details, financial information, and intellectual property. The need of ISO 27000 series arises because of the risk of cyber-attacks which the organization face. The cyber-attacks are growing day by day making hackers a constant threat to any industry that uses technology. The ISO 27000 series can be categorized into many types. The below table shows details of that.

Table 5.1: ISO 27000 Series

Standard	Description
ISO 27001	This standard allows us to prove the clients and stakeholders of any organization to managing the best security of their confidential data and information. This standard involves a process-based approach for establishing, implementing, operating, monitoring, maintaining, and improving information security management system.
ISO 27000	This standard provides an explanation of terminologies used in ISO 27001.
ISO 27002	This standard provides guidelines for organizational information security standards and information security management practices. It includes the selection, implementation, operating and management of controls taking into consideration the organization's information security risk environments.
ISO 27005	This standard supports the general concepts specified in 27001. It is designed to provide the guidelines for implementation of information security based on a risk management approach. To completely understand the ISO/IEC 27005, the knowledge of the concepts, models, processes, and terminologies described in ISO/IEC 27001 and ISO/IEC 27002 is required. This standard is capable for all kind of organizations such as non-government organization, government agencies, and commercial enterprises.
ISO 27032	It is the international Standard which focuses explicitly on cybersecurity. This Standard includes guidelines for protecting the information beyond the borders of an organization such as in collaborations, partnerships or other information sharing arrangements with clients and suppliers.

5.5 CYBER SECURITY CERTIFICATION

Certification is the formal attestation or confirmation of certain characteristics of an object, person, or organization. This confirmation is often, but not always, provided by some form of external review, education, assessment, or audit.

A certification in cyber security will lead to professional job. At some point in professional life, IT security certification from a renowned third-party organization may be necessary. Cyber security certifications are available in different shapes and subjects such as forensic, intrusion to ethical hacking. They are typically administrated by independent accredited organizations such as CompTIA, EC-Council, GIAC, ISACA and (ISC)^2. The certification program is divided into three categories in these accredited organizations. The basic entry-level certification is meant to educate in foundation principles, best practices, important tools, latest technologies, etc. The intermediate and expert-level certifications presume that the person have extensive job experience and a detailed grasp of the subject matter. The cybersecurity certification can be expensive and time-consuming. This certification leads to promotion as well as better job prospects. Some of the popular certifications in information security are given in the table.

Table 5.2: Information System Security Certifications

Certification	Description	Logo
CISSP	Certified Information System Security Professional is a high-level certification that is focused on security policy and management. It is the most frequently acquired certification in the business by the individuals. It is one of the top-paying IT security certifications.	CISSP
CISA	Certified Information System Auditor has been designed for the professionals who audit, control, monitor and assess information technology and business systems.	CISA
CISM	Certified Information Security Manager has been geared towards people in managerial positions such as the CIO of IT security.	CISM
GCIH	GIAC Certified Incident Handler is for the incident handlers responsible for detecting, responding to and resolving computer security incidents.	GCIH
CEH	Certified Ethical Hacker has been discussed among white hat hackers and penetration testers.	CEH Certified Ethical Hacker
OSCP	Offensive Security Certified Professional has been designed for the penetration testers and includes a rigorous 24-hour certification exam.	OSCP

5.6 CYBER LAWS

Cyber laws help to reduce or prevent people from cybercriminal activities on a large scale with the help of protecting information access from unauthorized people, freedom of speech related to the use of the Internet, privacy, communications, email, websites, intellectual property, hardware and software, such as data storage devices. Internet traffic is increasing rapidly day by day, that has led to a higher percentage of legal issues worldwide. Because cyber laws are different according to the country and jurisdiction, legal actions ranges from fines to imprisonment, and enforcement is challenging. Cyberlaw offers legal protections for people who are using the Internet as well as running an online business. It is most important for Internet users to know about the local area and cyber law of their country by which they could know what activities are legal or not on the network. Also, they can prevent themselves from unauthorized activities.

Cyber laws are formed to punish people who perform any illegal activities online. It is important to punish related persons for illegal of issues such as online harassment, attacking another website or individual, data theft, disrupting the online workflow of any enterprise and other illegal activities. If anyone breaks a cyber law, the action would be taken against that person on the basis of the type of cyberlaw he broke, where he lives, and where he broke the law. It is most important to punish the criminals or to bring them to behind bars, as most of the cybercrimes cross the limit of crime that cannot be considered as a common crime.

Cyber laws deal with multiple activities and areas that occur online and serve several purposes. Some laws are formed to describe the policies for using the Internet and the computer in an organization, and some are formed to offer people security from unauthorized users and malicious activities. There are various broad categories that come under cyber laws. Some of them are as follows.

- **Fraud:** Cyber laws are formed to prevent financial crimes such as identity theft, credit card theft and other that occurring online. A person may face criminal charges if he commits any type of identity theft. These laws have explained strict policies to prosecute and defend against allegations of using the Internet.
- **Copy Right Issues:** The Internet is the source that contains different types of data, which can be accessed anytime, anywhere. But there is no authority for anyone to copy the content of any other person. The strict rules are defined in the cyber laws if anyone goes against copyright that protects the creative work of individuals and companies.
- **Scam/Treachery:** There are different frauds and scams available on the Internet that can be personally harmful to any company or an individual. Cyber laws offer many ways to protect people and prevent any identity theft and financial crimes that happen online.
- **Online Insults and Character Degradation:** There are multiple online social media platforms that are the best resources to share your mind with anyone freely. But there are some rules in cyber laws if you speak and defame someone online. Cyber laws address and deal with many issues, such as racism, online insults, gender targets etc. to protect a person's reputation.
- **Online Harassment and Stalking:** Harassment is a big issue in cyberspace, which is a violation of both criminal laws and civil. In cyber laws, there are some hard laws defined to prohibit these kinds of crimes.
- **Data Protection:** People using the Internet depends on cyber laws and policies to protect their personal information. Companies or organizations are also relying on cyber laws to protect the data of their users as well as maintain the confidentiality of their data.

- **Contracts and Employment Law:** When you are visiting a website, you click a button that gives a message to ask you to agree for terms and conditions; if you agree with it, that ensures you have used cyber law. For every website, there are terms and conditions available that are associated with privacy concerns.
- **Trade Secrets:** There are many organizations that are doing online businesses, which are often relying on cyber laws to protect their trade secrets. For example, online search engines like Google spend much time to develop the algorithms that generate a search result. They also spend lots of time developing other features such as intelligent assistance, flight search services, etc. Cyber laws help these organizations to perform legal action by describing necessary legal laws for protecting their trade secrets.

5.7 SUMMARY

The cyber security policies, standards, information system certifications and the cyber laws are discussed and explained in this session.

5.8 OBJECTIVE QUESTIONS

The answer of the multiple-choice questions is marked in **bold**.

1. Which one is a benefit of security policy?
   (a) Increase efficiency (b) Uphold discipline
   (c) Improve security literacy (d) **All of these**
2. Which is not an issue-specific policy?
   (a) Fire wall (b) Intrusion prevention
   (c) Exceptions (d) **Organizational**
3. Which is not a cyber security certification?
   (a) CISSP (b) CISA
   (c) CISM (d) **ISO**
4. Which is a category in cyber laws?
   (a) Copy right (b) Financial fraud
   (c) Harassment (d) **All of these**

5.9 REVIEW QUESTIONS

1. Explain the need for a security policy.
2. Discuss on different types of cyber security policy.
3. Discuss few types of issue-specific cyber security policies.
4. Discuss on various cyber security standards.
5. Explain various information system security certifications.
6. Discuss on various categories that come under cyber laws.

5.10 ABBREVIATIONS AND SYMBOLS

Abbreviations	Full Form	Description
$(ISC)^2$	International Information System Security Certification Consortium	$(ISC)^2$ is a non-profit organization which specializes in training and certifications for cyber security professionals.
CompTIA	Computing Technology Industry Association	CompTIA is an American non-profit trade association, issuing professional certifications for the information technology industry.
EC-Council	The International Council of Electronic Commerce Consultants	EC-Council is an American organization that offers cybersecurity certification, education, training, and services in various cybersecurity skills.
GIAC	Global Information Assurance Certification	GIAC is an information security certification entity that specializes in technical and practical certification as well as new research in the form of its GIAC gold program.
IEC	International Electrotechnical Commission	IEC is an international standards organization that prepares and publishes international standards for all electrical, electronic and related technologies.
ISACA	Information Systems Audit and Control Association	ISACA is an international professional association focused on IT governance.
ISO	International Organization for Standardization	ISO is an international standard-setting body composed of representatives from various national standards organizations.

5.11 LIST OF FIGURES AND TABLES

The details of figures and tables used in this chapter is as below.

Figure / Table	Description
Figure 5.1	Types of Cyber Security Policy
Table 5.1	ISO 27000 Series
Table 5.2	Information System Security Certifications

CHAPTER

6

Cyber Security Technologies and Tools

CONTENTS

6.1 INTRODUCTION

In this chapter, we are discussing on different cyber security technologies, the cyber security vulnerability assessment and the various cyber security tools.

6.2 CYBER SECURITY TECHNOLOGIES

With the rapid growth in the Internet, cybersecurity has become a major concern to organizations throughout the world. The fact that the information and tools & technologies needed to penetrate the security of corporate organization networks are widely available has increased the security concern. Security technologies aims to keep the attacker out and if that fails, the defenses have failed. Every organization who uses Internet require security technologies to cover the control functions such as deterrent, preventive, detective, corrective and recovery. Table 6.1 shows the security control functions, types and technological solutions to maintain the security.

Table 6.1: Types of Security Controls and Functions

Security Controls	Control Functions				
	Deterrent	**Preventive**	**Detective**	**Corrective**	**Recovery**
Physical (Operational)	• Warning Signs	• Door locks • Fences • Gates and Badging system	• Surveillance Cameras • CCTV	• Fire Suppression System • Repair Physical Damage • Re-issue access cards	• Disaster Recovery Site
Technical	• Acceptable use Banners	• Fire walls • Intrusion Prevention System (IPS) • Multi-Factor Authentication (MFA) • Anti-virus	• Security Information and Event Management (SIEM) • Intrusion Detection System (IDS) • Honeypots	• Vulnerability Patches • Re-boot a System • Quarantine a Virus	• Back up Media
Administrative (Management)	• Policies and Procedures	• Separation of Duties • Data Classification • Hiring and Termination Policies	• Periodic Access Rights Reviews • Audit Logs and Unauthorized Changes	• Employee Discipline Actions • Implement Business Continuity Plan • Have an incident response Plan	• Disaster Recovery Plan

Deterrent controls are mechanisms such as policies, procedures, standards, guidelines, laws, and regulations that are used to guide the execution of security within an organization. Deterrent controls are utilized to promote compliance with external controls, such as regulatory compliance.

Preventive controls are designed to be implemented prior to a threat event and reduce and/or avoid the likelihood and potential impact of a successful threat event. Examples of preventative controls include encryption, firewalls, and physical barriers.

Detective controls attempt to detect undesirable acts that have occurred. They provide evidence after-the-fact that a loss or error has occurred, but do not prevent them from occurring.

Corrective controls include any measures taken to repair damage or restore resources and capabilities to their prior state following an unauthorized or unwanted activity.

Recovery controls are designed to recover a system and returned to normal operation following an incident. This is more cost-effective than attempting for at total prevention. Examples of recovery controls include system restoration, backups, rebooting, key escrow, insurance, redundant equipment, fault-tolerant systems, failovers, and contingency plans.

Most security is based on three types of things like something we have, something we know or something we are. This is shown in figure 6.1.

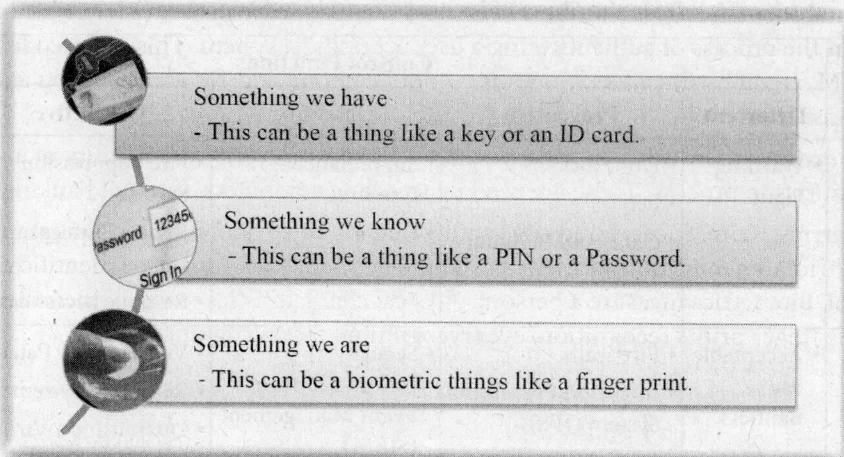

Figure 6.1: Common Things of Security

- **Key:** A key can be a physical mechanical device, electronic USB security key, an electronic access card, mobile phone etc to open a mechanical or electronic lock or system.

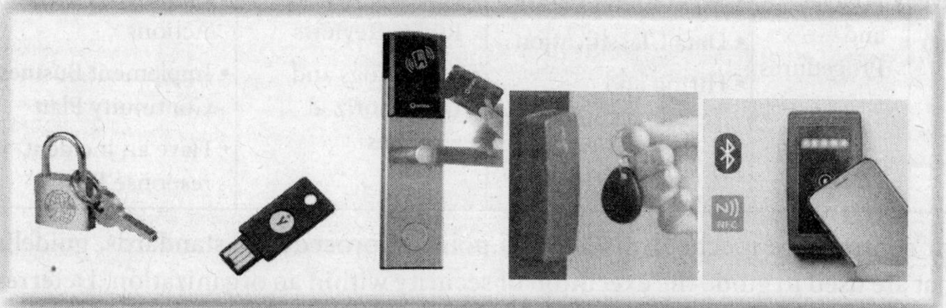

Figure 6.2: Different Types of Keys

- **Identity Document:** Identity Document (ID) is a document issued by government, institutions, employers etc with details and photo of the person to whom it is issued. The examples of IDs are PAN card, passport, Aadhar, electoral card etc. Some ID cards issued by institutions work also as electronic access key.

Figure 6.3: Different Identity Documents

- **Personal Identification Number:** Personal Identification Number (PIN), is a numeric passcode used in the process of authenticating a user accessing a system. This is the code that is required by ATM, credit card readers, computers, mobile phones etc. for identification and authorization for transaction.
- **Password:** A password is a string of characters used to verify the identity of a user during the authentication process. These are used in accessing computers, Internet banking etc.
- **Biometrics:** Biometrics are body measurements and calculations related to human characteristics. Biometric authentication is used in computer science as a form of identification and access control. Biometrics measure a person's physical characteristics to verify their identity. These can include finger prints recognition, eyes recognition, face recognition etc.

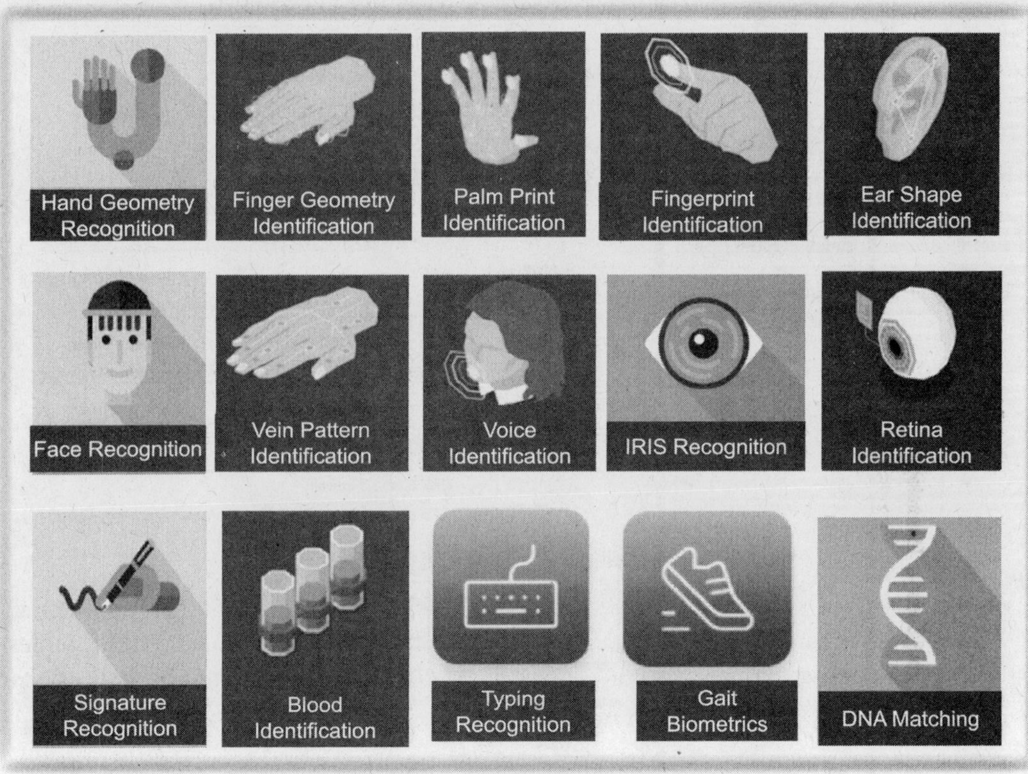

Figure 6.4: Types of Biometric Authentications

6.3 CLASSIFICATION OF CYBER SECURITY TECHNOLOGIES

The figure 6.5 provides a general classification overview of cyber security technologies.

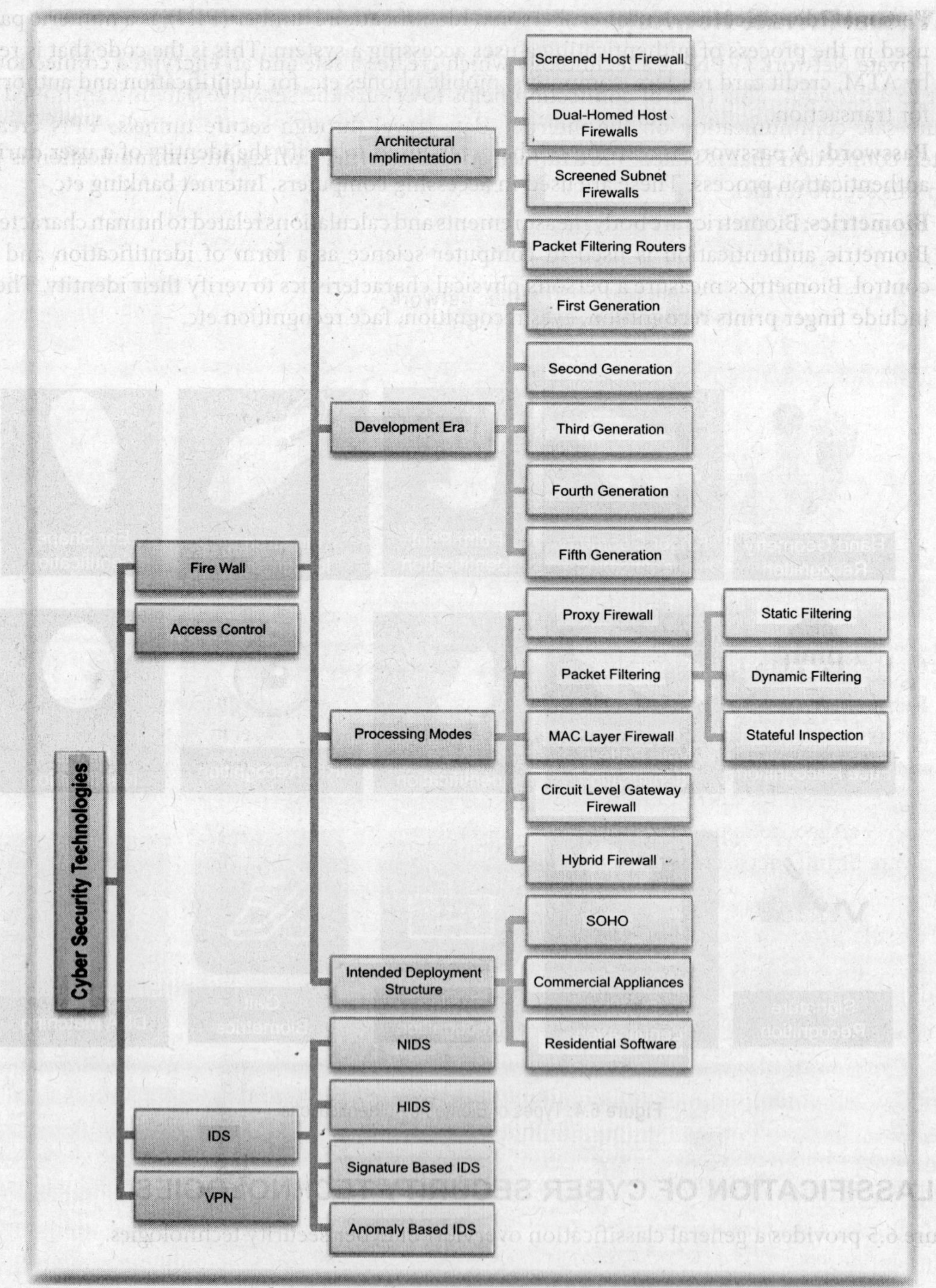

Figure 6.5: Cybersecurity Technologies Classification

Some of the important security technologies used in the cybersecurity are described below.

6.3.1 Virtual Private Network

Virtual Private Network (VPN) is a technology which creates a safe and an encrypted connection from Internet to a network. This type of connection helps to ensure the sensitive data is transmitted safely. To ensure safe communication on the internet, data travel through secure tunnels. VPN creates an encrypted connection that is called VPN tunnel, and all internet traffic and communication is passed through this secure tunnel.

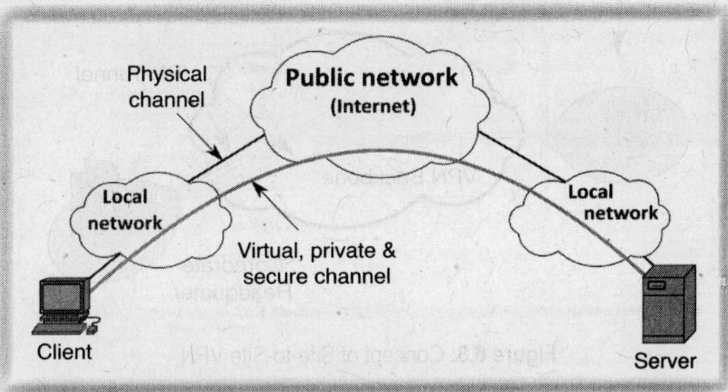

Figure 6.6: Concept of Virtual Private Network

Virtual private network is basically of two types.

- **Remote Access VPN:** This permits a user to connect to a private network and access all its services and resources remotely. The connection between the user and the private network occurs through the Internet and the connection is secure and private. Remote access VPN is useful for both home users and business users both. Home users of VPN, primarily use VPN services to bypass regional restrictions on the internet and access blocked websites. Users aware of Internet security also use VPN services to enhance their Internet security and privacy.

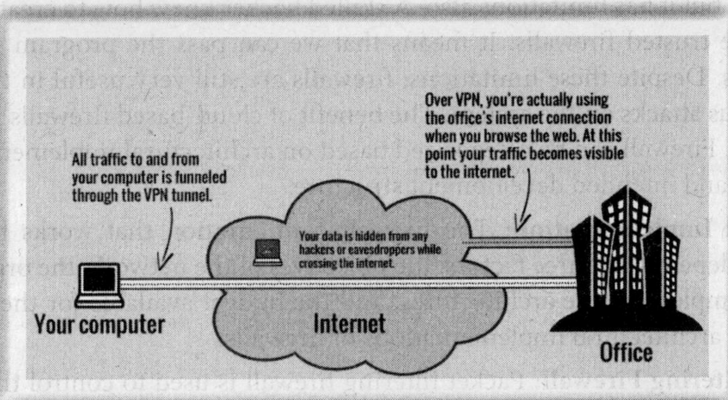

Figure 6.7: Working of Remote Access VPN

- **Site-to-Site VPN:** A site-to-site virtual private network (VPN) is a connection between two or more networks, such as a corporate network and a branch office network. Many organizations use site-to-site VPNs to leverage an Internet connection for private traffic. This is also called as router-to-router VPN.

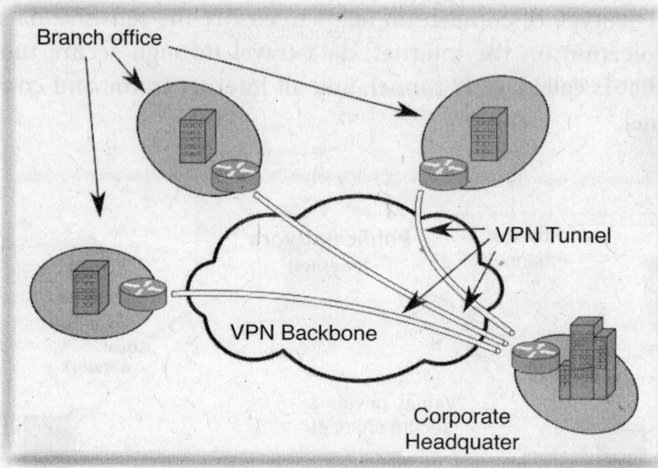

Figure 6.8: Concept of Site-to-Site VPN

6.3.2 Firewall

Firewall is a network security system that monitors and controls incoming and outgoing network traffic based on predetermined security rules. A firewall typically establishes a barrier between a trusted network and an untrusted network, such as the Internet. Its job is to prevent unauthorized access to or from a private network. All messages are entering or leaving the intranet pass through the firewall. The firewall examines each message and blocks those messages that do not meet the specified security criteria. It can be implemented as hardware, software, or a combination of both. A hardware firewall is physical device between user network and gateway. A software firewall is internal program on the computer and works through port numbers and applications. Cloud-based firewalls are also available as a service (FaaS). The firewall is very useful, but it has limitations also. A skilled hacker knew how to create data and programs that are believing like trusted firewalls. It means that we can pass the program through the firewall without any problems. Despite these limitations, firewalls are still very useful in the protection of less sophisticated malicious attacks on the system. The benefit of cloud-based firewalls is that they can grow with the organization. Firewall can be categorized based on architectural implementation, development era, processing mode and intended development structure.

- **Architectural Implementation:** The firewall configuration that works best for a particular organization depends on three factors: the objectives of the network, the organization's ability to develop and implement the architectures, and the budget available for the function. There are four common architectural implementations of firewalls.
    - **Packet-Filtering Firewall:** Packet filtering firewall is used to control the network access by monitoring the outgoing and incoming packets. It allows them to pass or halt based on the source and destination IP addresses, protocols and ports. During communication, a node transmits a packet. This packet is filtered and matched with the predefined rules and policies. Once it is matched,the packet is considered as secure and verified. This will be accepted otherwise will block it.

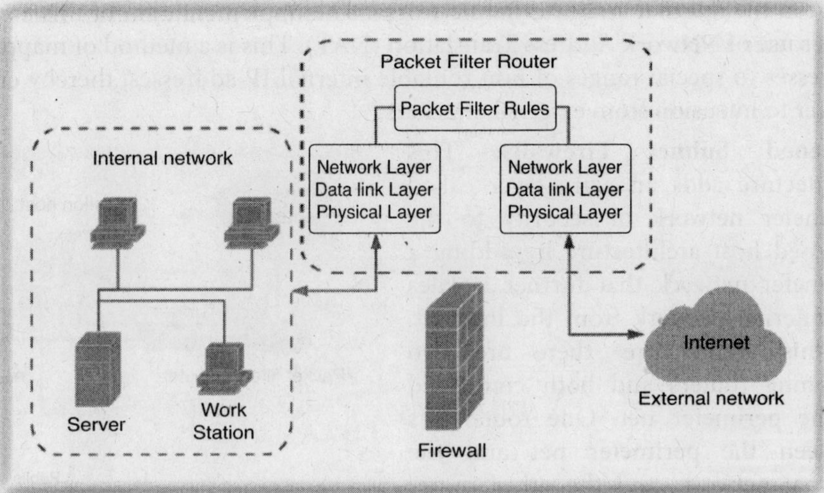

Figure 6.9: Principle of Packet Filter Firewall

- **Screened Host Firewalls:** This firewall architecture combines the packet-filtering router with a separate and dedicated firewall. The application gateway needs only one network interface. It is allowing the router to pre-screen packets to minimize the network traffic and load on the internal proxy. The packet-filtering router filters dangerous protocols from reaching the application gateway and site systems. This is also known as bastion host firewall. A bastion is a structure projecting outward from the wall of a fort, most commonly angular in shape and positioned at the corners of the fort to get better view of the battle field and to use weapons against attackers. A bastion host is a special-purpose computer on a network specifically designed and configured to withstand attacks. It is also known as the 'jump box' that acts like a proxy server and allows the client machines to connect to the remote server.

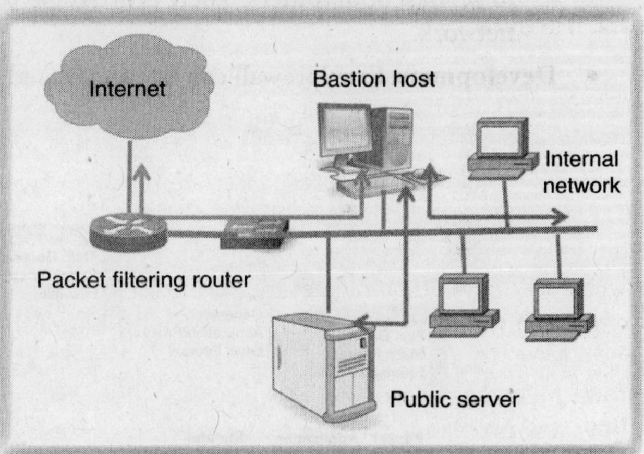

Figure 6.10: Screened Host Firewall (Single homed bastion host)

- **Dual-Homed Host Firewalls:** A dual-homed host or dual-homed gateway is a system fitted with two network interfaces that is located between an untrusted network like the Internet and trusted network such as a corporate network to provide secure access. Dual-homed host firewall's architecture is built around the dual-homed host computer, a computer that has at least two Network Interface Controllers (NIC). One of this is to be connected with the external network and other is connected to the internal network which provides an additional layer of protection. With these NICs, all traffic must go through the firewall in order to move between the internal and external networks. The implementation of this architecture often makes use of Network Address Translation (NAT). This is a method of mapping assigned IP addresses to special ranges of non routable internal IP addresses, thereby creating another barrier to intrusion from external attackers.

- **Screened Subnet Firewalls:** This architecture adds an extra layer called perimeter network of security to the screened host architecture by adding a perimeter network that further isolates the internal network from the Internet. In this architecture, there are two screening routers and both connected to the perimeter net. One router sits between the perimeter net and the internal network, and the other router sits between the perimeter net and the external network. To break into the internal network, an attacker would have to get past both routers. There is no single vulnerable point that will compromise the internal network.

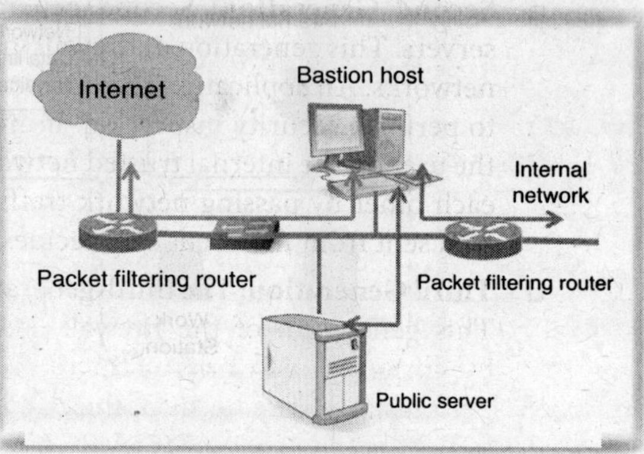

Figure 6.11: Screened Subnet Firewalls

- **Development Era:** Firewall can be categorized on the basis of its generation from first to fifth.

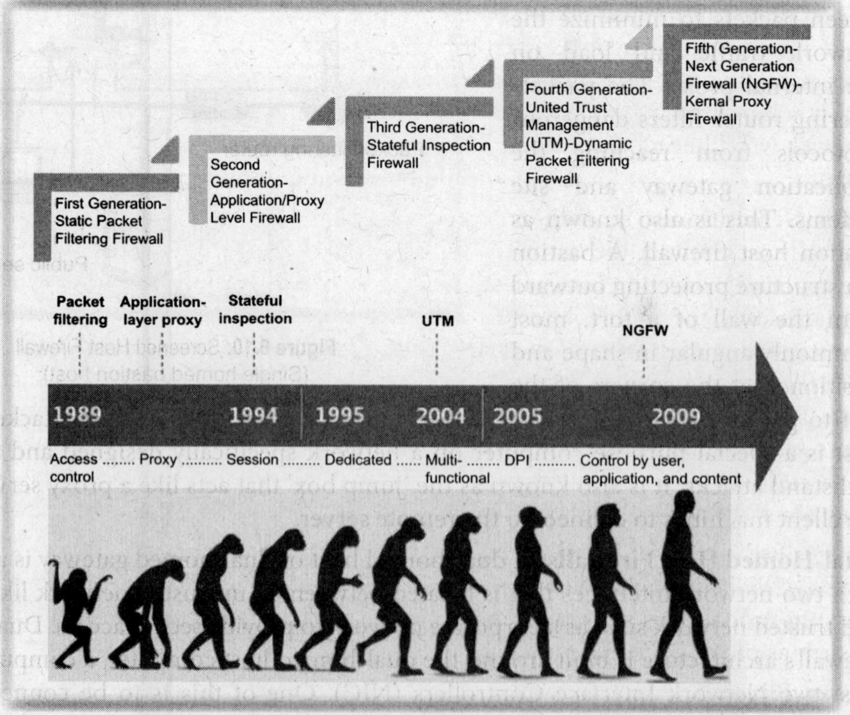

Figure 6.12: Development of Firewall Technologies

- **First Generation:** The first-generation firewall comes with static packet filtering firewall. A static packet filter is the simplest and least expensive forms of firewall protection. In this generation, each packet entering and leaving the network is checked and will be either passed or rejected depends on the user-defined rules.
- **Second Generation:** Second generation firewall comes with application level or proxy servers. This generation of firewall increases the security level between trusted and untrusted networks. An application level firewall uses software to intercept connections for each IP and to perform security inspection. It involves proxy services which act as an interface between the user on the internal trusted network and the Internet. Each computer communicates with each other by passing network traffic through the proxy program. This program evaluates data sent from the client and decides which to move on and which to drop.
- **Third Generation:** The third-generation firewall comes with the stateful inspection firewalls. This generation of the firewall has evolved to meet the major requirements demanded by corporate networks of increased security while minimizing the impact on network performance. The needs of the third-generation firewalls will be even more demanding due to the growing support for VPNs, wireless communication, and enhanced virus protection. The most challenging element of this evolution is maintaining the firewall's simplicity, its maintainability and security without compromising flexibility.
- **Fourth Generation:** The fourth-generation firewall comes with dynamic packet filtering firewall. This firewall monitors the state of active connections, and on the basis of this information, it determines which network packets are allowed to pass through the firewall. By recording session information such as IP addresses and port numbers, a dynamic packet filter can implement a much tighter security posture than a static packet filter. The united trust management (UTM) firewall evolved during this generation. This is a security system for the real-time network protection. It is the evolution of the traditional firewall into a comprehensive network security solution. A UTM uses technologies such as network firewall, web filtering, gateway antivirus, IPS, anti-spam, VPN, etc. to protect networks from threats.
- **Fifth Generation:** The fifth-generation firewall comes with kernel proxy firewall. This firewall works under the kernel of Windows NT Executive. This firewall proxy operates at the application layer. In this, when a packet arrives, a new virtual stack table is created which contains only the protocol proxies needed to examine the specific packet. These packets investigated at each layer of the stack, which involves evaluating the data link header along with the network header, transport header, session layer information, and application layer data. This firewall works faster than all the application-level firewalls because all evaluation takes place at the kernel layer and not at the higher layers of the operating system. This generation is known as next generation fire wall (NGFW). It uses the concepts of the traditional firewall along with newer technologies such as network firewall, IPS, deep packet inspection (DPI), sand boxing, application control, URL filtering, advanced malware protection, network profiling, identity policy, VPN, etc.

- **Processing mode:** This categorization is based on the mode of processing and there are five types such as proxy, packet, circuit level gateway, MAC and hybrid.
  - **Proxy Firewall:** Proxy firewall is also known as application gateway which is normally installed on a dedicated computer to provide network security. This proxy firewall acts as an intermediary between the requester and the protected device. This proxy firewall filters

incoming node traffic to certain specifications which means that, only transmitted network application data is filtered. Such network applications include FTP, Telnet, Real Time Streaming Protocol (RTSP), BitTorrent, etc.

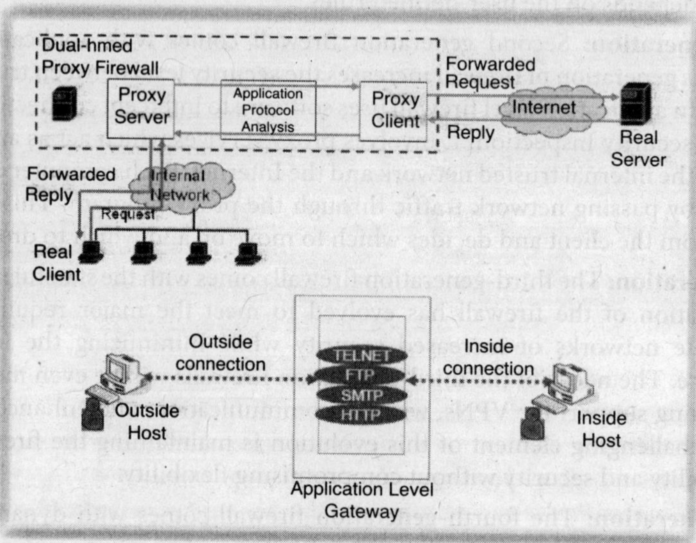

Figure 6.13: Proxy Firewall

- **Packet Filtering Firewall:** Packet filtering firewalls examine header information of data packets that come into a network. This firewall installed on TCP/IP network will determine whether to forward it to the next network connection or drop a packet based on the rules programmed in the firewall. It scans network data packets looking for a violation of the rules of the firewall's database. Most firewall often based on a combination of Internet Protocol (IP) source and destination address, direction (inbound or outbound), Transmission Control Protocol (TCP) or User Datagram Protocol (UDP) source and destination port requests. Packet filtering firewalls can be categorized into three types as below.

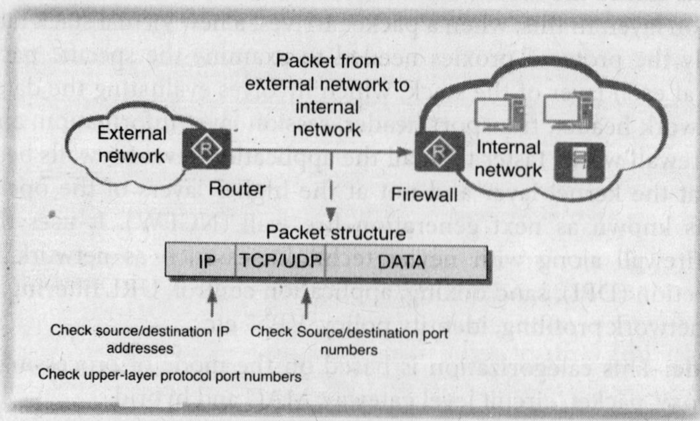

Figure 6.14: Packet Filtering Firewall Model

1. **Static Packet Filtering Firewall:** The system administrator set a rule for the firewall. These filtering rules will govern how the firewall decides which packets are allowed and which are denied.

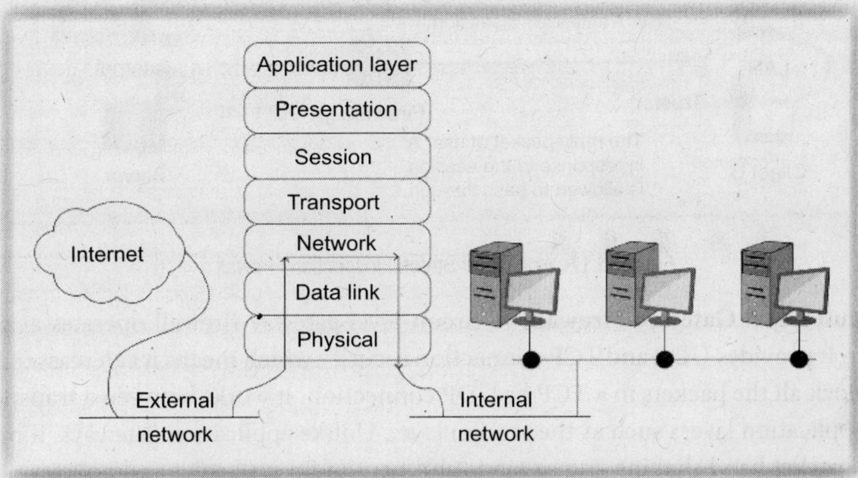

Figure 6.15: Static Packet Filtering Firewall Model

2. **Dynamic Packet Filtering Firewall:** It allows the firewall to set some rules for itself, such as dropping packets from an address that is sending many bad packets.

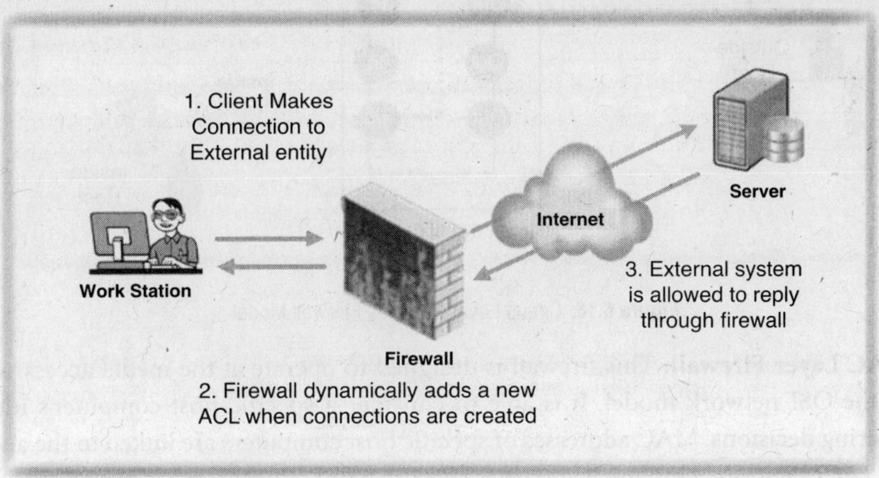

Figure 6.16: Working of Dynamic Packet Filtering Firewall

3. **Stateful Inspection Firewall:** Stateful inspection firewall monitors communications packets over a period of time and examines both incoming and outgoing packets. Outgoing packets that request specific types of incoming packets are tracked and only those incoming packets constituting a proper response are allowed through the firewall.

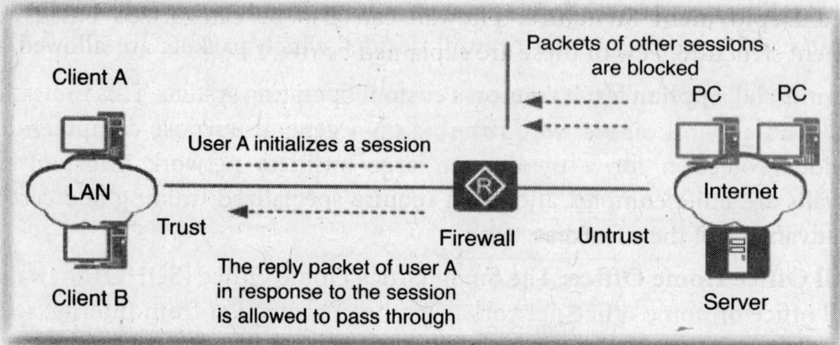

Figure 6.17: Working of Stateful Inspection Firewall

- **Circuit Level Gateway Firewall:** A circuit-level gateway firewall operates at the transport layer. It provides UDP and TCP connection security which means it can reassemble, examine or block all the packets in a TCP or UDP connection. It works between a transport layer and an application layers such as the session layer. Unlike application gateways, it monitors TCP data packet hand shaking and session fulfilment of firewall rules and policies. It can also act as a VPN over the Internet by doing encryption from firewall to firewall.

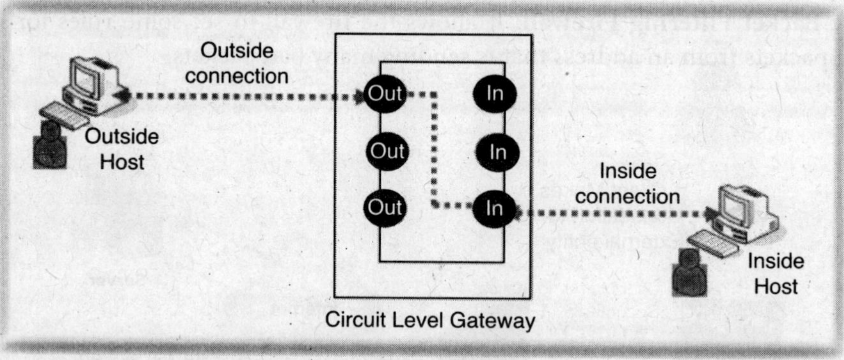

Figure 6.18: Circuit Level Gateway Firewall Model

- **MAC Layer Firewall:** This firewall is designed to operate at the media access control layer of the OSI network model. It is able to consider a specific host computer's identity in its filtering decisions. MAC addresses of specific host computers are linked to the access control list (ACL) entries. This entry identifies specific types of packets that can be sent to each host and all other traffic is blocked. It will also check the MAC address of a requester to determine whether the device being used are able to make the connection is authorized to access the data or not.
- **Hybrid Firewall:** It is a type of firewalls which combine features of other four types of firewalls. This can be a combination of packet filtering firewall and proxy firewall or of packet filtering firewall and circuit gateway firewall.

- **Intended Deployment Structure:** Firewall can also be categorized based on the intended deployment structure. Few of these are explained below.
  - **Commercial Appliances:** It runs on a custom operating system. This firewall system consists of firewall application software running on a general-purpose computer. It is designed to provide protection for a medium-to-large business network. Most of the commercial firewalls are quite complex and often require specialized training and certification to take full advantage of their features.
  - **Small Office Home Office:** The Small Office Home Office (SOHO) firewall is designed for small office or home office networks who need protection from Internet security threats. A firewall for a SOHO is the first line of defense and plays an essential role in an overall security strategy. SOHO firewall has limited resources so that the firewall product they implement must be relatively easy to use and maintain, and be cost-effective. This firewall connects a user's local area network or a specific computer system to the Internet.
  - **Residential Software:** Residential-grade firewall software is installed directly on a user's system. Some of these applications combine firewall services with other protections such as antivirus or intrusion detection.

6.3.3 Access Control

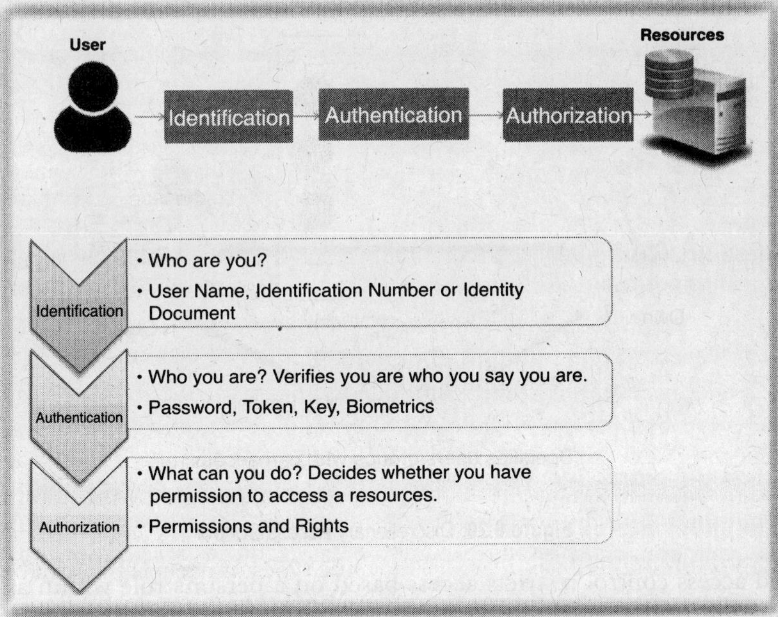

Figure 6.19: Elements of Access Control

Access control is a process of selecting restrictive access to a system. It is a concept in security to minimize the risk of unauthorized access to the business or organization. In this, users are granted access permission with certain privileges to a system and resources. Here, users must provide the credentials to be granted access to a system. These credentials come in many forms such as password, keycard, the biometric reading, etc. Access control ensures security technology and access control policies to protect confidential information like customer data. The access control can be physical access control or logical access control. In case of physical access control, the access control limits access to buildings, rooms, campuses, and physical IT assets physically. The logical access control limits connection to computer networks, system files, and data. The more secure method for access control involves two factor authentication. The first factor is that a user who desires access to a system must show credential and the second factor could be an access code, password, and a biometric reading.

The three elements of access control are identification, authentication and authorization.

Identification: For access control to be effective, it must provide some way to identify an individual.

Authentication: This is a process which verifies that someone claims to be granted access.

Authorization: This provides input that whether a user should be allowed to gain access to a system or deny it.

The main types of access control systems are discretionary access control, role-based access control, mandatory access control, rule-based access control.

- Discretionary access control is a model of access control based on access being determined by the owner of the resource. The owner of the resource can decide who does and does not have access, and exactly what access they are allowed to have.

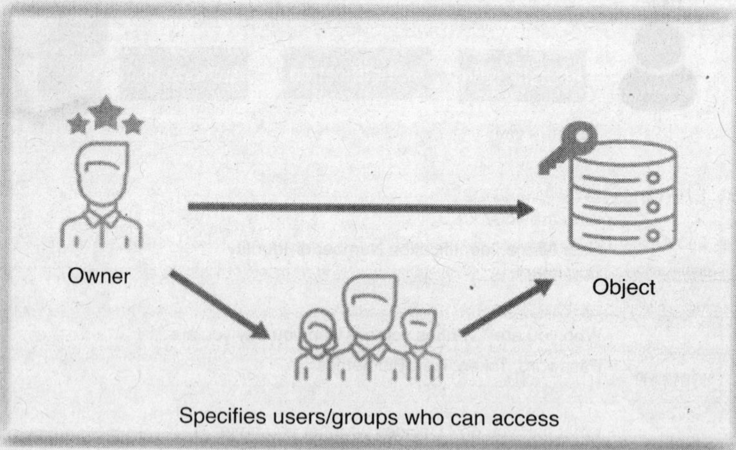

Figure 6.20: Discretionary Access Control

- Role-based access control restricts access based on a person's role within an organization and has become one of the main criteria for access. Users can be grouped into roles based on their responsibilities within an organization as this generally determines their system access needs. Access is then granted to each user based on the access requirements established for each role. If strict access requirements are set out for each role, access management will be easy to manage.
- Mandatory access control is a security strategy that restricts the ability of individual resource owners to grant or deny access to resource objects in a file system.

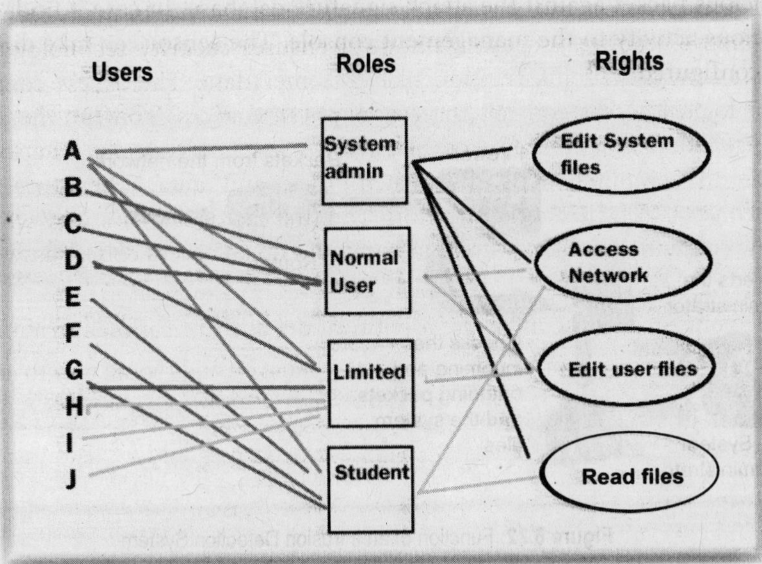

Figure 6.21: Role Based Access Control

- In rule-based access control, rules will be parameters, such as allowing access only from certain IP addresses, denying access from certain IP addresses, or something more specific. In a more specific instance, access from a specific IP address may be allowed unless it comes through a certain port such as the port used for FTP access. These types of controls prevent cybercriminals from accessing the information even if they do find a way in to the network. This can also be implemented on a file or system level, restricting data access to business hours only.

6.3.4 Intrusion Detection System

An intrusion detection system (IDS) is a combination of hardware and software application that monitors a network for malicious activity or policy violations. Protection is becoming a vital necessity as Internet services such as online banking and e-commerce keep growing. The IDS acquires and analyses information on malicious activities and reports them to the system administrator and can also be stored in a Security Information and Event Management System (SIEM). While an organization makes its information system available to harmless Internet users, at the same time the information is available to the malicious users as well. The malicious users use different techniques like password cracking, sniffing unencrypted or clear text traffic etc. to exploit the system vulnerabilities and compromise critical systems. Therefore, there needs to be some kind of security to the organization's private resources from the Internet as well as from inside users. Different organizations across the world deploy firewalls to protect their private network from the public network. The business requires some kind of access to be granted on the internal systems to Internet users.

The components of an IDS are management console, data base and sensors. Management console is the management and reporting console. Sensors are agents that monitor hosts or networks on a real time basis. An intrusion detection system has a database of attack signatures. The attack signatures are patterns of different types of previously detected attacks. If the sensors detect any malicious activity, it matches the malicious packet against the attack signature database. In case it finds a match, the sensor reports the malicious activity to the management console. The sensor can take different actions based on how they are configured.

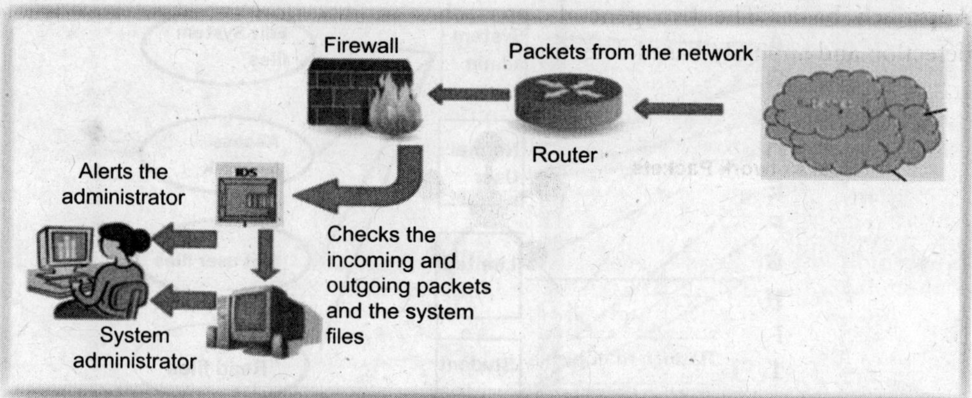

Figure 6.22: Function of an Intrusion Detection System

Intrusion detection systems are used to detect anomalies with the aim of catching hackers before they do real damage to a network. They can be either network- or host-based. A host-based intrusion detection system is installed on the client computer, while a network-based intrusion detection system resides on the network. Intrusion detection systems work by either looking for signatures of known attacks or deviations from normal activity. These deviations or anomalies are pushed up the stack and examined at the protocol and application layer. An IDS may be implemented as a software application running on customer hardware or as a network security appliance. Cloud-based intrusion detection systems are also available to protect data and systems in cloud deployments.

6.3.4.1 Types of Intrusion Detection Systems

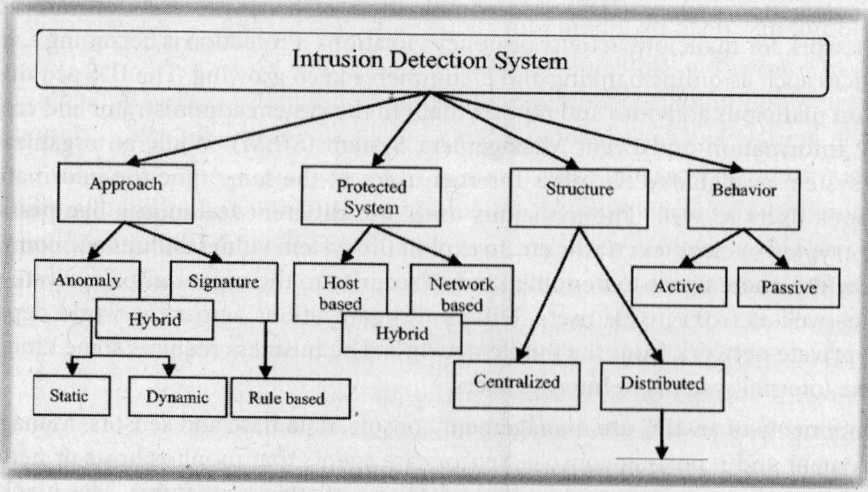

Figure 6.23: Intrusion Detection System Classification

Intrusion detection systems are generally categorized based on approach, protected system, structure and behavior. The other classification of intrusion detection system are protocol based, application protocol based and hybrid.

- **Approach basis:** The two general approaches to intrusion detection are signature-based detection and anomaly-based detection.

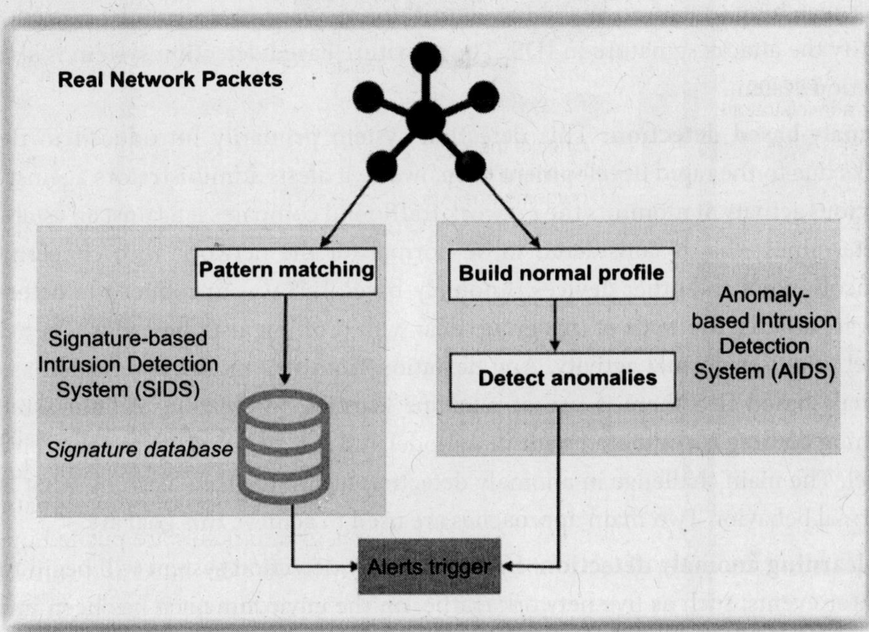

Figure 6.24: Working of Sigrfature Based and Anomaly Based Intrusion Detection System

- **Signature-Based Intrusion Detection System:** It is a detection system which refers to the detection of an attack by looking for the specific patterns, such as byte sequences in network traffic, or known malicious instruction sequences used by malware. This IDS originates from anti-virus software which can easily detect known attacks. In this terminology, it is impossible to detect new attacks, for which no pattern is available. Methods of the misuse detection group operate with priori prepared patterns, called signatures, of known attacks that are used to detect intrusions by pattern matching. Almost any intrusion can be described in terms of its indications and signs. This is the basic principle used by misuse detection systems. Initially, patterns which are also known as signatures of all known attacks must be described in some abstract form and has to be given to IDS. This patterns are used later by IDS to identify an intrusion. Signature-based IDS detects the attacks on the basis of the specific patterns such as number of bytes or number of 1's or number of 0's in the network traffic. It also detects on the basis of the already known malicious instruction sequence that is used by the malware. Signature-based IDS can easily detect the attacks whose pattern (signature) already exists in system but it is quite difficult to detect the new malware attacks as their pattern (signature) is not known.

Here IDS compare all incoming or outgoing activity against all known threats in its knowledge base and raise an alarm if any activity matches information in the knowledge base. The process for actually comparing a signature with an attack include simple string matching which involves looking for unique key words in network traffic to identify attacks – to more complex approaches such as rule-based matching which defines the behavior of an attack as a signature. Various string-matching or pattern-matching algorithms are used to inspect the content of packets and identify the attacks signature in IDS. The signature based detection system is also called misuse detection system.

- **Anomaly-based detection:** This detection system primarily introduced to detect unknown attacks due to the rapid development of malware. It alerts administrators against the potentially malicious activity. It monitors the network traffic and compares it against an established baseline. It determines what is considered to be normal for the network with concern to bandwidth, protocols, ports and other devices. Anomaly-based IDS was introduced to detect the unknown malware attacks. Methods of this group deal with profiling user behavior. They define a certain model of a user normal activity. Any deviation from this model is regarded as anomalous. In anomaly-based IDS there is use of machine learning to create a trustful activity model and anything coming is compared with that model and it is declared suspicious if it is not found in model. The main challenge in anomaly detection technique is in learning what is considered as a normal behavior. Two main approaches are used to achieve this goal are

  Self-learning anomaly detection: In this anomaly detection system will begin to automatically monitor events, such as live network traffic, on the environment it has been implemented and attempt to build information on what is considered authorized normal behavior.

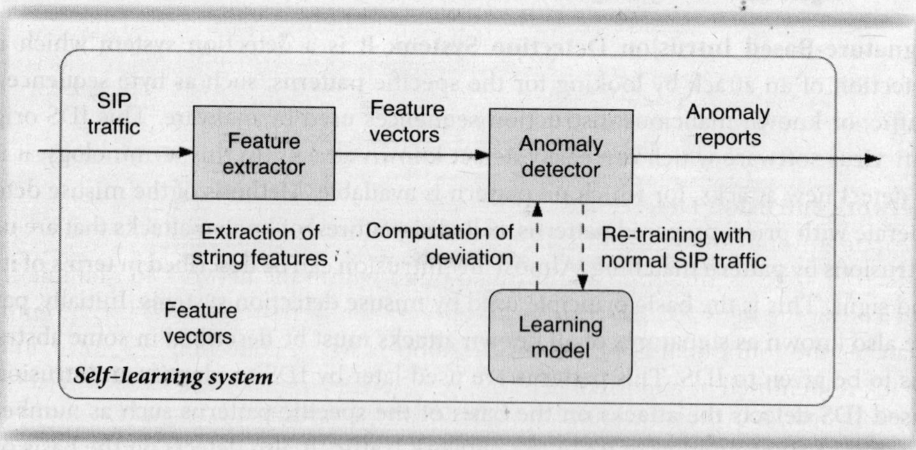

Figure 6.25: Working of Self-Learning Anomaly Detection

The Session Initiation Protocol (SIP) is a signaling protocol that enables the Voice over Internet Protocol (VoIP) by defining the messages sent between endpoints and managing the actual elements of a call. SIP supports voice calls, video conferencing, instant messaging and media distribution.

Programmed anomaly detection: In this IDS must manually learn what is considered normal behavior by having a user or some form of function by teaching the system through input of information. This may involve feeding the system a network traffic data set which contains normal network traffic.

- **Protected System Based:** The Network Intrusion Detection System (NIDS) and Host Intrusion Detection System (HIDS) comes under this category.

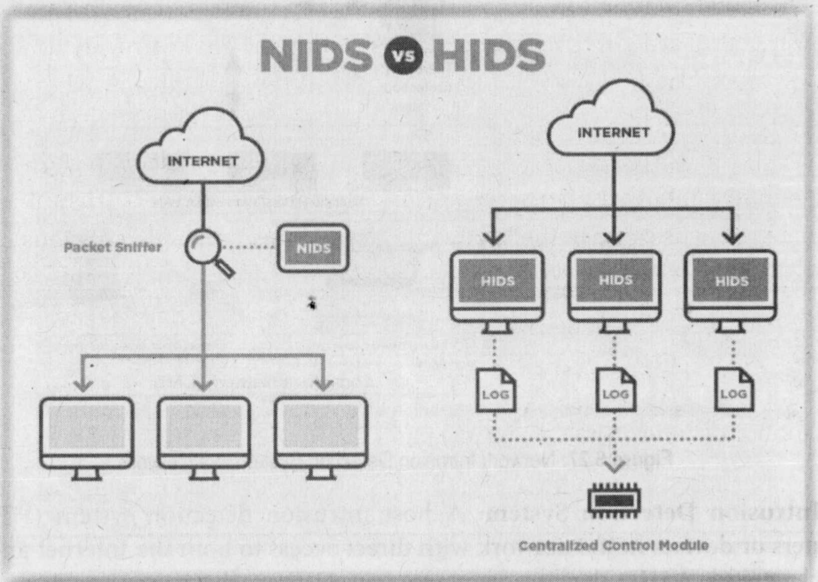

Figure 6.26: NIDS and HIDS Difference in System

- **Network Intrusion Detection System:** Network Intrusion Detection System (NIDS) monitors the inbound and outbound traffic to and from all the devices over the network. Network intrusion detection systems are set up at a planned point within the network to examine traffic from all devices on the network. It performs an observation of passing traffic on the entire subnet and matches the traffic that is passed on the subnets to the collection of known attacks. Once an attack is identified or abnormal behavior is observed, the alert can be sent to the administrator. An example of NIDS is installing it on the subnet where firewalls are located in order to see if someone is trying crack the firewall.

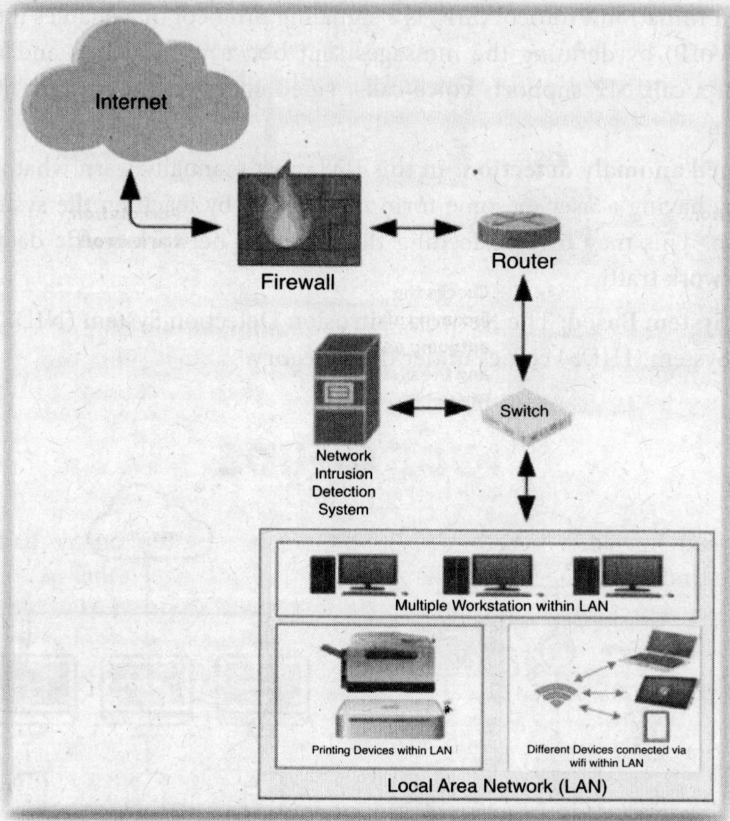

Figure 6.27: Network Intrusion Detection System in a Network

- **Host Intrusion Detection System:** A host intrusion detection system (HIDS) runs on all computers or devices in the network with direct access to both the Internet and the enterprise's internal network. A HIDS has an advantage over a NIDS in that it may be able to detect anomalous network packets that originate from inside the organization or malicious traffic that a NIDS has failed to detect. A HIDS may also be able to identify malicious traffic that originates from the host itself, such as when the host has been infected with malware and is attempting to spread to other systems. A HIDS monitors the incoming and outgoing packets from the device only and will alert the administrator if suspicious or malicious activity is detected. It takes a snapshot of existing system files and compares it with the previous snapshot. If the analytical system files were edited or deleted, an alert is sent to the administrator to investigate. HIDS usage can be seen on mission critical machines, which are not expected to change their layout. Unlike NIDS which monitors the entire network, HIDS monitors system data and looks for malicious activity on an individual host. A HIDS analyzes the change management in the operating system files, logs, as well as software and many more.

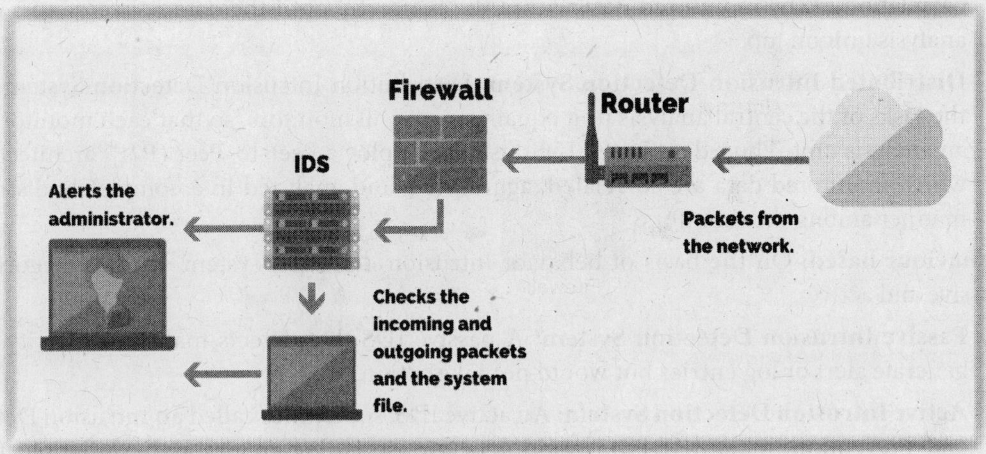

Figure 6.28: Host Intrusion Detection System

- **Structure based:** Intrusion detection system can be divided based on the structure as centralized, decentralized and distributed. The structural differences between them are shown in the figure. "A" in the figure represents analysis unit and "M" represents monitoring points.

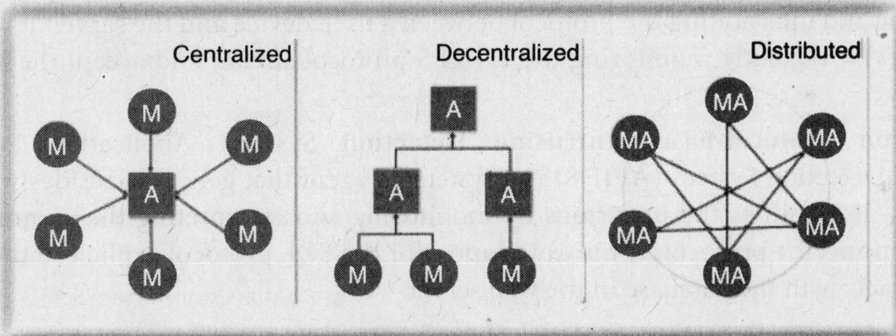

Figure 6.29: Structure Based Classification of Intrusion Detection System

- **Centralized Intrusion Detection System:** The Centralized Intrusion Detection System (CIDS) consist of several monitors that monitor the behavior of their respective host or the network traffic passing by. These monitors share their data with a central analysis unit; these data can be either alerts as a result of a local detection or extracted data from the local network traffic. Hence, the analysis unit is either applying alert correlation algorithms on top of received alerts or standard detection algorithms on top of received network traffic data. Centralized IDS do not scale with the increasing size of the system that needs to be protected. Moreover, the central analysis unit represents a performance bottleneck and a single point of failure.
- **Decentralized Intrusion Detection System:** Decentralized Intrusion Detection System (DIDS) usually employ a hierarchical structure of monitoring points or multiple self-contained IDS deployments. Through this structure, they overcome the performance bottleneck of centralized intrusion detection systems because they employ preprocessing and

correlation of the monitored data within the hierarchy until the data converge to a central analysis unit on top.

- **Distributed Intrusion Detection System:** Distribution Intrusion Detection System shares the tasks of the central analysis unit equally among all monitors, so that each monitor is also an analysis unit. Thus, distributed IDSs usually employ a Peer-to-Peer (P2P) architecture, in which monitored data are correlated, aggregated, and analyzed in a completely distributed manner among the monitors.

- **Behaviour based:** On the basis of behavior intrusion detection system can be categorized as passive and active
    - **Passive Intrusion Detection System:** A passive IDS that detects malicious activity would generate alert or log entries but would not take action.
    - **Active Intrusion Detection System:** An active IDS, sometimes called an Intrusion Detection and Prevention System (IDPS), would generate alerts, log entries and configured to take actions, like blocking IP addresses or shutting down access to restricted resources.

In addition to above, the intrusion detection system can be categorized as protocol-based IDS and application protocol-based IDS.

- **Protocol-based Intrusion Detection System:** Protocol-based intrusion detection system (PIDS) comprises of a system or agent that would consistently resides at the front end of a server, controlling and interpreting the protocol between a user/device and the server. It will secure the web server by regularly monitoring the HTTPS protocol stream and accept the related HTTP protocol.
- **Application Protocol-based Intrusion Detection System:** Application Protocol-based Intrusion Detection System (APIDS) is a system or agent that generally resides within a group of servers. It identifies the intrusions by monitoring and interpreting the communication on application specific protocols. This would monitor the SQL protocol explicit to the middleware as it transacts with the database in the web server.
- **Hybrid Intrusion Detection System:** Hybrid intrusion detection system is made by the combination of two or more approaches of the intrusion detection system. In the hybrid intrusion detection system, host agent or system data is combined with network information to develop a complete view of the network system. Hybrid intrusion detection system is more effective in comparison to the other intrusion detection systems.

6.3.5 Comparison of IDS with Firewalls

IDS and firewall both are related to the network security and works complimentary. Firewalls restrict access between networks to prevent intrusion. A firewall does a job of filtering the incoming traffic from the Internet. IDS alerts the system administrator in the case when someone tries to break in the firewall security and tries to have access on any network in the trusted side. An intrusion detection system can be compared with a burglar alarm. The lock system in a car protects the car from theft but if somebody breaks the lock system and tries to steal the car, it is the burglar alarm that detects that the lock has been broken and alerts the owner by raising an alarm. The intrusion detection system, in a similar way complements the firewall security. Firewalls do the job of filtering incoming traffic from the Internet; however, there are ways to circumvent the firewall. For example, external users can connect to the intranet by dialing in through a modem installed in the private network of the organization. This kind of access would not be seen by the firewall. Therefore, an intrusion detection system is a security system that monitors computer systems and network traffic and analyzes that traffic for possible hostile attacks originating from outside the organization and also for system misuse or attacks originating from inside the organization.

6.3.6 Intrusion Prevention System

The functions of the Intrusion Prevention System (IPS) are shown in the figure

An Intrusion Detection System (IDS) is a system that monitors network traffic for suspicious activity and alerts when such activity is discovered. An Intrusion Prevention System (IPS), monitors network packets for potentially damaging network traffic similar to an IDS, but has the primary goal of preventing threats once detected. An IPS is similar to an intrusion detection system but differs in that an IPS can be configured to block potential threats. Like intrusion detection systems, IPS can be used to monitor, log and report activities, but they can also be configured to stop threats without the involvement of a system administrator. An IDS simply warns of suspicious activity taking place, but it doesn't prevent it.

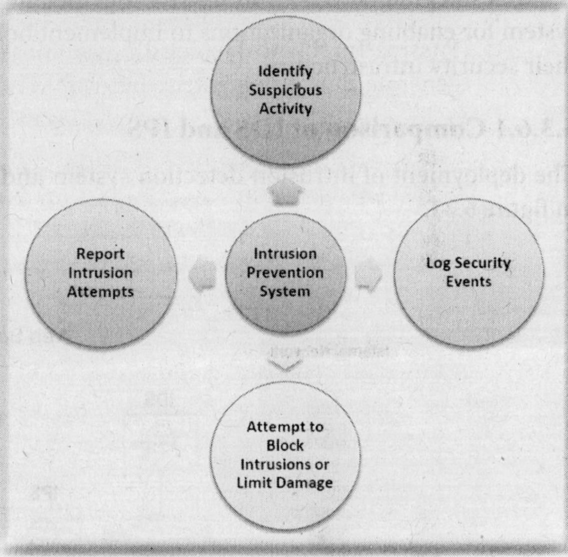

Figure 6.30: Functions of Intrusion Prevention System

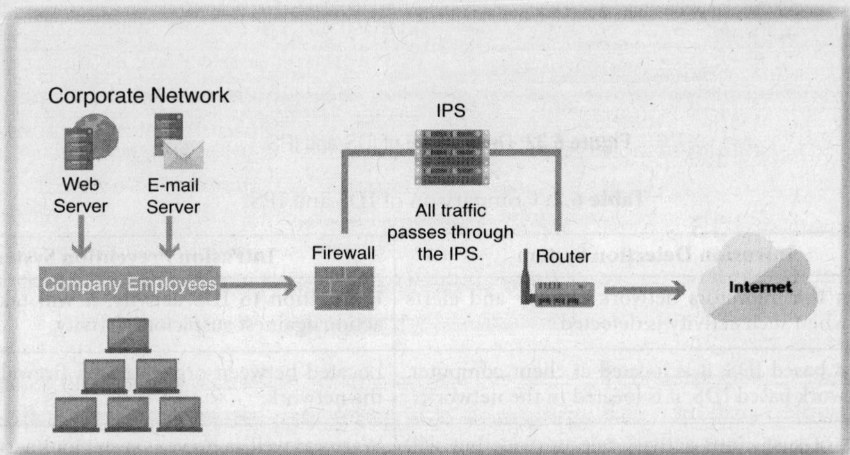

Figure 6.31: Network Intrusion Prevention System

An IPS is typically located between an organization's firewall and the rest of its network and may have the ability to stop any suspected traffic from getting to the rest of the network. Intrusion prevention systems execute responses to active attacks in real time and can actively catch intruders that firewalls or antivirus software may miss. However, organizations should be careful with IPS because they can also be prone to false positives. An IPS false positive is likely to be more serious than an IDS false positive because the IPS prevents the legitimate traffic from getting through, whereas the IDS simply flags it as potentially malicious. It has become a necessity for most organizations to have either an IDS or an IPS or both as part of their Security Information and Event Management (SIEM) framework. Several vendors integrate an IDS and an IPS together in one product known as unified threat management system for enabling organizations to implement both simultaneously alongside firewalls and systems in their security infrastructure.

6.3.6.1 Comparison of IDS and IPS

The deployment of intrusion detection system and intrusion prevention system in a network is shown in figure 6.32.

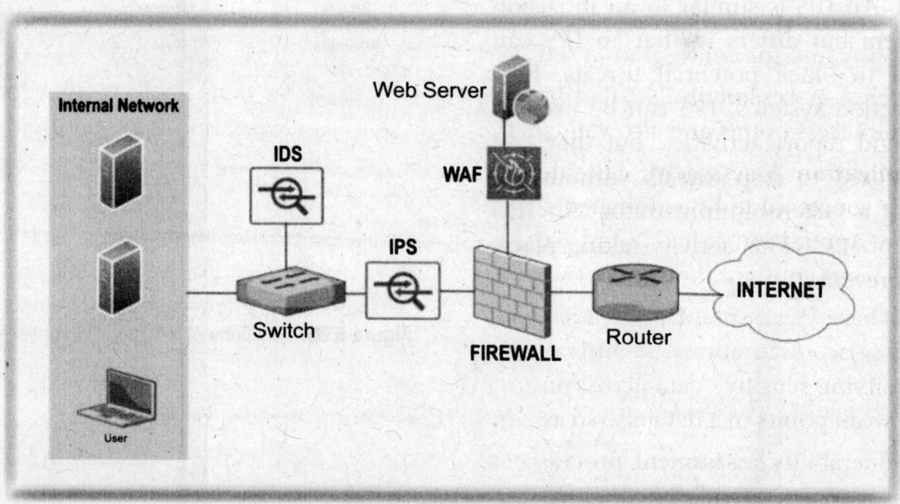

Figure 6.32: Deployment of IDS and IPS

Table 6.2: Comparison of IDS and IPS

Criteria	Intrusion Detection System	Intrusion Prevention System
Function	System that monitors network activity and alerts users when such activity is detected.	In addition to IDS activity, it will take preventive action againest suspicious activity.
Location	In host based IDS, it is located at client computer. In network based IDS, it is located in the network.	Located between organisation's firewall and rest of the network.
Use	Warns of suspicious activity taking place but will not prevent it.	Warns as well as prevent suspicious activity.
False Positive	Even if IDS labels legitimate traffic as malicious, it will not block from entering the network .	If IPS, labels legitimate traffic as malicious, it will block in from entering the network and will impact the organisation functions.

6.4 CYBER SECURITY VULNERABILITY ASSESSMENT

A vulnerability assessment refers to the process of defining, identifying, classifying, and prioritizing vulnerabilities that are specific to computer systems, applications, digital assets, and network infrastructures. vulnerability assessment informs organizations on the weaknesses present in their environment and provides direction on how to reduce the risk those weaknesses cause. It provides a thorough, inclusive assessment of hardware and software assets, identifying vulnerabilities and providing an intuitive risk score. These processes typically rely on vulnerability scanners to get the job done. It evaluates if the system is susceptible to any known vulnerabilities, assigns severity levels to those vulnerabilities, and recommends remediation or mitigation, if and whenever needed. Five types of cyber security vulnerability assessment are

- **Network Assessment:** The assessment of policies and practices to prevent unauthorized access to private or public networks and network-accessible resources. Network-based scans helps to identify possible network security attacks and vulnerable systems on wireless networks
- **Host Assessment:** The assessment of critical servers, which may be vulnerable to attacks if not adequately tested or not generated from a tested machine image. Host-based scans helps to locate and identify vulnerabilities in servers, workstations, or other network hosts, and provide greater visibility into the configuration settings and patch history of scanned systems
- **Wireless Assessment:** This is the assessment of an organization's Wi-Fi network, to identify rogue access points and also validate that a company's network is securely configured.
- **Application Assessment:** The identifying of security vulnerabilities in web applications and their source code by automated scans on the front-end or static/dynamic analysis of source code. Application scans, to test websites in order to detect known software vulnerabilities and erroneous configurations in network or web applications
- **Database Assessment:** The assessment of databases or big data systems for vulnerabilities and misconfigurations, identifying rogue databases or insecure dev/test environments, and classifying sensitive data across an organization's infrastructure. Database scans are to identify the weak points in a database so as to prevent malicious attacks

The vulnerability assessment process consists of four steps such as vulnerability identification, analysis, risk assessment and remediation.

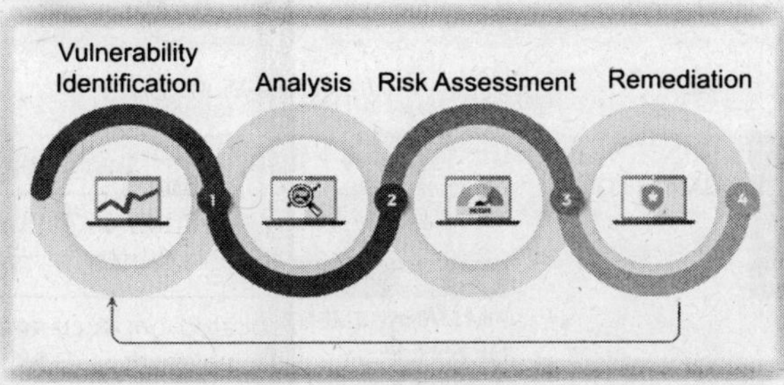

Figure 6.33: Vulnerability Assessment Process

- **Identification:** This step is also known as testing. The objective of this step is to draft a comprehensive list of an application's vulnerabilities. Security analysts test the security health of applications, servers or other systems by scanning them with automated tools, or testing and evaluating them manually. Analysts also rely on vulnerability databases, vendor vulnerability announcements, asset management systems and threat intelligence feeds to identify security weaknesses.

- **Analysis:** The objective of this step is to identify the source and root cause of the vulnerabilities identified in step one. It involves the identification of system components responsible for each vulnerability, and the root cause of the vulnerability. For example, the root cause of a vulnerability could be an old version of an open-source library. This provides a clear path for remediation which is upgrading the library.
- **Risk Assessment:** The objective of this step is the prioritizing of vulnerabilities. It involves security analysts assigning a rank or severity score to each vulnerability, based on such factors as - Which systems are affected? What data is at risk? Which business functions are at risk? Ease of attack or compromise, severity of an attack and potential damage as a result of the vulnerability.
- **Remediation:** The objective of this step is the closing of security gaps. It's typically a joint effort by security staff, development and operations teams, who determine the most effective path for remediation or mitigation of each vulnerability. Specific remediation steps might include - introduction of new security procedures, measures or tools, the updating of operational or configuration changes, development and implementation of a vulnerability patch.

Cyber security vulnerability assessment cannot be a one-off activity. To be effective, organizations must operationalize this process and repeat it at regular intervals. It is also critical to foster cooperation between security, operation and development teams which is a process known as DevSecOps.

6.5 FILE INTEGRITY MONITORING

File Integrity Monitoring (FIM) refers to an IT security process and technology that tests and checks operating system (OS), database, and application software files to determine whether or not they have been tampered with or corrupted. FIM is a type of change auditing, verifies and validates these files by comparing the latest versions of them to a known, trusted "baseline." If FIM detects that file have been altered, updated, or compromised, It will generate alerts to ensure further investigation and if necessary, remediation, takes place. File integrity monitoring encompasses both reactive (forensic) auditing as well as proactive, rules-based active monitoring. FIM works by detecting changes to files and

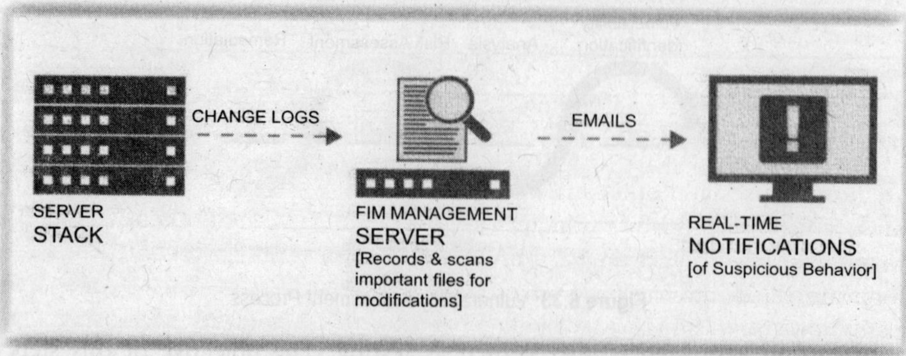

Figure 6.34: File Integrity Monitoring Working

configurations. When initially installing FIM, it creates a baseline to determine the status quo, which is stored in a database as cryptographic hashes that cannot be edited, deleted, or altered. A file integrity checker calculates a hash value, usually MD5 or SHA-1, of important files and stores them in a database. The checker can then be used to calculate and compare the current hash values of these files against those in the database. The difference between IDS and FIM is that intrusion detection system cannot detect encrypted traffic but file integrity monitoring can do that.

6.6 CYBER SECURITY TOOLS

Protecting our IT environment is very critical. Every organization needs to take cybersecurity very seriously. There are numbers of hacking attacks which are affecting businesses of all sizes. Hackers, malware, viruses are some of the real security threats in the virtual world. It is essential that every company is aware of the dangerous security attacks and it is necessary to keep themselves secure. There are many different aspects of the cyber defense that need to be considered. Here are six essential tools and services that every organization needs to consider to ensure their cybersecurity is as strong as possible. They are described below.

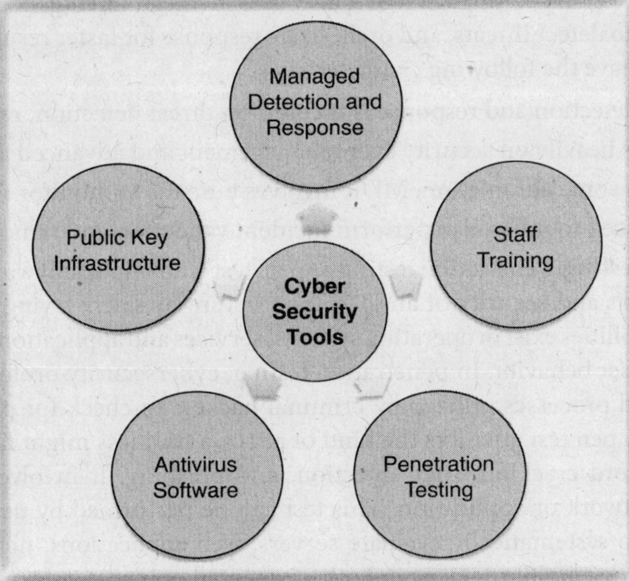

Figure 6.35: Cyber Security Tools

- **Antivirus Software:** Antivirus software is a program which is designed to prevent, detect, and remove viruses and other malware attacks on the individual computer, networks, and IT systems. It also protects our computers and networks from variety of threats and viruses such as trojan horses, worms, keyloggers, browser hijackers, rootkits, spyware, botnets, adware, and ransomware. Most antivirus program comes with an auto-update feature, enabling the system to check for new viruses and threats regularly. It provides some additional services such as scanning emails to ensure that they are free from malicious attachments and web links.

- **Public Key Infrastructure:** Public Key Infrastructure (PKI) tool supports the distribution and identification of public encryption keys. It enables users and computer systems to securely exchange data over the Internet and verify the identity of the other party. We can also exchange sensitive information without PKI, but in that case, there would be no assurance of the authentication of the other party. People associate PKI with SSL or TLS. It is the technology which encrypts the server communication and is responsible for HTTPS and padlock that we can see in our browser address bar. PKI can also be used to enable Multi-Factor Authentication (MFA) and access control. PKJ can create compliant trusted digital signatures, encrypt email communications and authenticate the sender's identity. It can digitally sign and protect the code, which will build identity and trust into IoT ecosystems.
- **Managed Detection and Response:** Today's cybercriminals and hackers use more advanced techniques and software to breach organization security So, there is a necessity for every business to be used more powerful forms of defenses of cybersecurity. Managed Detection and Response (MDR) is an advanced security service that provides threat hunting, threat intelligence, security monitoring, incident analysis, and incident response. It is a service that arises from the need for organizations who has a lack of resources to be more aware of risks and improve their ability to detect and respond to threats. MDR also uses artificial intelligence and machine learning to investigate, auto detect threats, and orchestrate response for faster result. The managed detection and response have the following characteristics.
  - Managed detection and response is focused on threat detection, rather than compliance.
  - MDR relies heavily on security event management and advanced analytics.
  - Alona with some automation, MDR involves humans to monitor network.
  - MDR service providers also perform incident validation and remote response.
- **Penetration Testing:** Penetration testing or pen-test is an important way to evaluate our business's security systems and security of an IT infrastructure by safely trying to exploit vulnerabilities. These vulnerabilities exist in operating systems, services and application, improper configurations or risky end-user behavior. In penetration testing, cybersecurity professionals will use the same techniques and processes utilized by criminal hackers to check for potential threats and areas of weakness. A pen test attempts the kind of attack a business might face from criminal hackers such as password cracking, code injection, and phishing. It involves a simulated real-world attack on a network or application. This test can be performed by using manual or automated technologies to systematically evaluate servers, web applications, network devices, endpoints, wireless networks, mobile devices and other potential points of vulnerabilities. Once the pen test has successfully taken place, the testers will present us with their findings threats and can help by recommending potential changes to our system.

  Vulnerability assessment look for known vulnerabilities in systems and report potential exposures. Penetration tests are intended to exploit weaknesses in the architecture of IT network and determine the degree to which a malicious attacker can gain unauthorized access to the assets.
- **Staff Training:** Staff training will create knowledgeable employees who understand the cybersecurity which is one of the strongest forms of defense against cyber-attacks. Presently many training tools are available that can educate company's staff about the best cybersecurity practices. Every business can organize these training tools to educate their employee who can

understand their role in cybersecurity. Cyber-criminals continue to expand their techniques and level of sophistication to breach businesses security, which has made it essential for organizations to invest in training tools. Failing to do this, can leave the organization in a position where hackers can easily target their security system. So, the expense of the investment on training will provide a reward for the business organization with long-term security and protection.

6.7 SUMMARY

We initiated this session with discussions of various cyber security technologies. Followed by this, we explained cyber security vulnerability assessment and scanning along with file integrity monitors. The discussion is completed with the details of various cyber security tools.

6.8 OBJECTIVE QUESTIONS

The answer of the multiple-choice questions is marked in **bold**.

1. .... is not a operational security control.
   (a) CCTV (b) Door locks (c) Warning sings (d) **IDS**
2. Below is an example of something you have.
   (a) PIN (b) Password (c) **ID card** (d) Finger print
3. .... is not biometrics.
   (a) Retina recognition (b) DNA matching
   (c) Signature recognition (d) **Password**
4. Static packet filtering firewall works in .... layer.
   (a) Physical (b) Data link (c) **Network** (d) Transport
5. .... is also known as application gateway.
   (a) **Proxy firewall** (b) Stateful inspection firewall
   (c) Dynamic packet filtering firewall (d) Static packet filtering firewall
6. The first firewall is of .... type.
   (a) **Static packet filtering** (b) Proxy firewall
   (c) Stateful Inspection firewall (d) None of these
7. Permissions and access is provided by ....
   (a) Identification (b) Authentication
   (c) **Authorization** (d) None of these
8. .... is an access control.
   (a) Discretionary (b) Role based (c) Mandatory (d) **All of these**
9. IDS located in computers of the network are called ....
   (a) NIDS (b) **HIDS** (c) All of these (d) None of these
10. .... IDS has only one analysis unit.
    (a) **Centralized** (b) Decentralized (c) Distributed (d) All of these

11. Which is the most effective IDS?
    (a) NIDS (b) HIDS
    (c) **Hybrid** (d) Protocol based
12. .... is a common function of IDS and IPS.
    (a) Monitor (b) Log (c) Prevent (d) **a and b**
13. .... is a step in cyber security vulnerability.
    (a) Analysis (b) Risk assessment (c) Remediation (d) **All of these**
14. .... can detect encrypted traffic.
    (a) IDS (b) NIDS (c) **FIM** (d) All of these
15. .... exploit weakness in architecture of IT network.
    (a) Vulnerability assessment (b) **Penetration test**
    (c) All of these (d) None of these

6.9 REVIEW QUESTIONS

1. Explain on security control.
2. Explain the control functions in a security system.
3. Discuss the common three" Things" of security.
4. Discuss about firewall in cyber system.
5. Discuss about access control in cyber system.
6. Explain on intrusion detection system.
7. Discuss on virtual private network.
8. Explain on the development of firewall.
9. Explain on three elements of access control.
10. Discuss on main types of access control systems.
11. Explain on various intrusion detection systems categorized on basis of approach.
12. Explain on various intrusion detection systems categorized on basis of protected system.
13. Explain on various intrusion detection systems categorized on basis of structure.
14. Explain on various intrusion detection systems categorized on basis of behavior.
15. Compare intrusion detection system and firewall.
16. Explain the functions of intrusion prevention system.
17. Explain different types of vulnerability assessment.
18. Compare intrusion detection system and intrusion prevention system.
19. Explain vulnerability assessment process.
20. Explain file integrity monitoring and compare with IDS.
21. Discuss on various cyber security tools.

6.10 ABBREVIATIONS AND SYMBOLS

Abbreviations	Full Form	Description
ACL	Access Control List	ACL is a table that tells a computer operating system which access rights each user has to a particular system object, such as a file directory or individual file.
APIDS	Application Protocol Based Intrusion Detection System	APIDS is an intrusion detection system that focuses its monitoring and analysis on a specific application protocol or protocols in use by the computing system.
ATM	Automatic Teller Machine	ATM is an electronic banking outlet that allows customers to complete basic transactions without the aid of a bank employee.
FIM	File Integrity Monitoring	FIM is an internal control or process that performs the act of validating the integrity of operating system and application software files using a verification method between the current file state and a known, good baseline.
FTP	File Transfer Protocol	FTP is a communications protocol used to send files from computer to computer with one of them acting as the server, providing the two have an Internet connection.
HIDS	Host based Intrusion Detection System	HIDS monitor processes and applications running on devices such as servers and workstations.
HTTP	Hypertext Transfer Protocol	HTTP is an application-layer protocol for transmitting hypermedia documents, such as HTML.
ID	Identity Document	An identity document is any document that may be used to prove a person's identity.
IDPS	Intrusion Detection and Prevention System	IDPS monitors to mitigate attacks and block new threats.
IDS	Intrusion Detection System	IDS is a device or software application that monitors a network or systems for malicious activity or policy violations.
IP	Internet Protocol	IP is a set of rules that dictate how data should be delivered over the Internet.
IPS	Intrusion Prevention System	IPS is a network security/threat prevention technology that examines network traffic flows to detect and prevent vulnerability exploits.
MAC	Message Authentication Code	MAC is a security code that need to be provided by the user of a computer to access accounts or portals.
MD5	Message Digest algorithm 5	MD5 hashing algorithm is a one-way cryptographic function that accepts a message of any length as input and returns as output a fixed-length digest value to be used for authenticating the original message.
MDR	Managed Detection and Response	MDR is an advanced managed security service that provides threat intelligence, threat hunting, security monitoring, incident analysis, and incident response.

Abbreviations	Full Form	Description
MFA	Multi Factor Authentication	MFA is an electronic authentication method in which a user is granted access to a website or application only after successfully presenting two or more pieces of evidence to an authentication mechanism.
NAT	Network Address Translation	NAT is the process where a network device, usually a firewall, assigns a public address to a computer or group of computers inside a private network.
NIC	Network Interface Controller	NIC is a computer hardware component that connects a computer to a computer network.
NIDS	Network based Intrusion Detection System	NIDS detects malicious traffic on a network.
PAN	Permanent Account Number	PAN is a ten-character alphanumeric identifier, issued by the Indian income tax department for identification of personnel.
PIDS	Protocol based Intrusion Detection System	PIDS is an intrusion detection system which is typically installed on a web server, and is used in the monitoring and analysis of the protocol in use by the computing system.
PIN	Personnel Identification Number	PIN is a numeric passcode used in the process of authenticating a user accessing a system.
PKI	Public Key Infrastructure	PKI is a set of roles, policies, hardware, software and procedures needed to create, manage, distribute, use, store and revoke digital certificates and manage public-key encryption.
RTSP	Real Time Streaming Protocol	RTSP is a protocol which provides framework for real time media data transfer at the application level.
SHA-1	Secure Hash Algorithm 1	SHA-1 is a cryptographic hash function which takes an input and produces a 160-bit hash value. This hash value is known as a message digest.
SIEM	Security Information and Event Management	SIEM works by collecting log and event data generated by an organizations applications, security devices and host systems and bringing it together into a single centralized platform.
SIP	Session Initiation Protocol	SIP is a signaling protocol used for initiating, maintaining, and terminating real-time sessions that include voice, video and messaging applications.
SMTP	Simple Mail Transfer Protocol	SMTP is a set of communication guidelines that allow software to transmit an electronic mail over the Internet.
SOHO	Small Office Home Office	SOHO refers to a small business that is often run out of small office spaces, homes or even virtually.
SQL	Structured Query Language	SQL is a standardized programming language used to manage relational databases and perform various operations on the data in them.
SSL	Secure Sockets Layer	SSL and its successor TLS are protocols for establishing authenticated and encrypted links between networked computers.

Abbreviations	Full Form	Description
TCP	Transmission Control Protocol	TCP is an Internet protocol that connects a server and a client.
TELNET	Teletype Network	TELNET is a protocol that provides a command line interface for communication with a remote device or server, sometimes employed for remote management but also for initial device setup like network hardware.
TLS	Transport Layer Security	TLS is a security protocol to facilitate privacy and data security for communications over the Internet. A primary use of TLS for encrypting communication between web applications and servers such as web browsers loading a website.
UDP	User Datagram Protocol	UDP is a communications protocol that facilitates the exchange of messages between computing devices in a network. It's an alternative to the transmission control protocol (TCP).
USB	Universal Serial Bus	USB is an industry standard that establishes specifications for cables and connectors and protocols for connection, communication and power supply between computers, peripherals and other computers.
VoIP	Voice over Internet Protocol	VoIP is a technology that allows to make voice calls using an Internet connection instead of phone line. This is also called IP telephony.
VPN	Virtual Private Network	VPN is an encrypted connection over the Internet from a device to a network.

6.11 LIST OF FIGURES AND TABLES

The details of figures and tables used in this chapter is as below.

CHAPTER 7

Cryptology

CONTENTS

7.1 INTRODUCTION

We will discuss on cryptology and its various classifications in this chapter. Various ciphers will be also explained. The drawbacks and concerns of cryptology is analyzed followed by explanation on quantum cryptology and future of cryptology.

7.2 CRYPTOLOGY

Cryptology, is the science concerned with data communication and storage in secure as well as in secret form. Cryptology can be considered as the study of cryptosystems. A cryptosystem is a pair of algorithm that take a key and convert plaintext to ciphertext and back. Plaintext is what we want to protect which is the input to an encryption algorithm. Ciphertext is the unreadable output of an encryption algorithm. Cryptology can be divided into two branches cryptography and cryptanalysis.

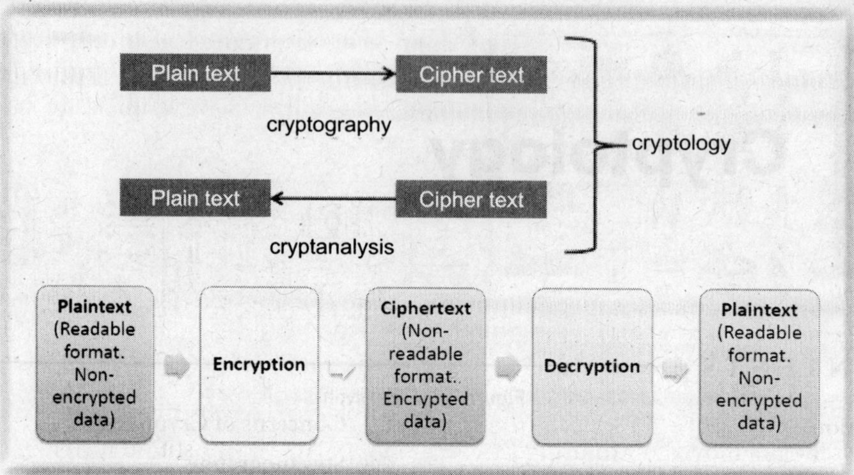

Figure 7.1: Cryptology Process

The art of cryptology is considered to be born along with the art of writing. As civilizations evolved, human beings got organized into tribes, groups, and kingdoms. This led to the emergence of ideas such as power, battles, supremacy, and politics. These ideas further fueled the natural need of people to communicate secretly with selective recipient which in turn ensured the continuous evolution of cryptology. The historical mile stones in cryptology after discovery of manuscripts can be seen in below figure. During the period from 4000 BC to 100 BC, the cryptology was non-formal. By the introduction of caesar code, the era of formal cryptology started.

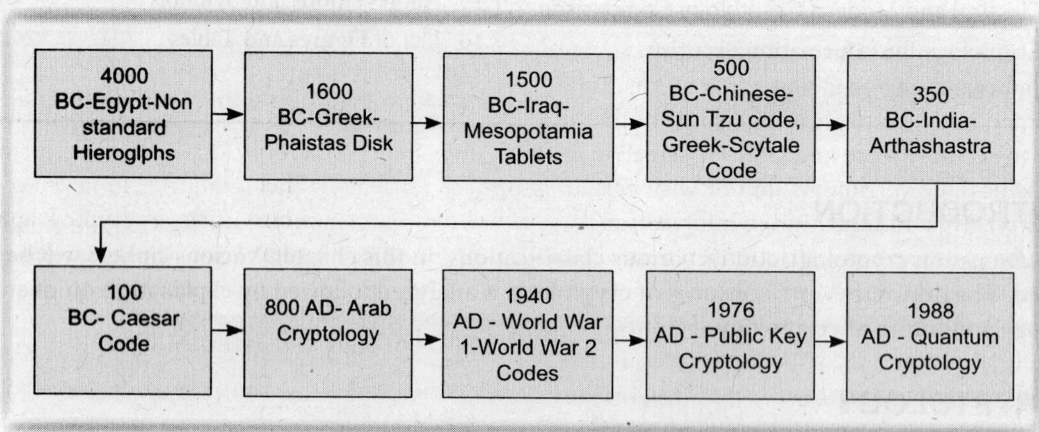

Figure 7.2: Miles Stones in Cryptology

The first known evidence of cryptology can be traced to the use of 'hieroglyph'. Some 4000 years ago, the Egyptians used to communicate by messages written in hieroglyph. This code was the secret known only to the scribes who used to transmit messages on behalf of the kings. These consisted of complex pictograms, the full meaning of which was only known to an elite few.

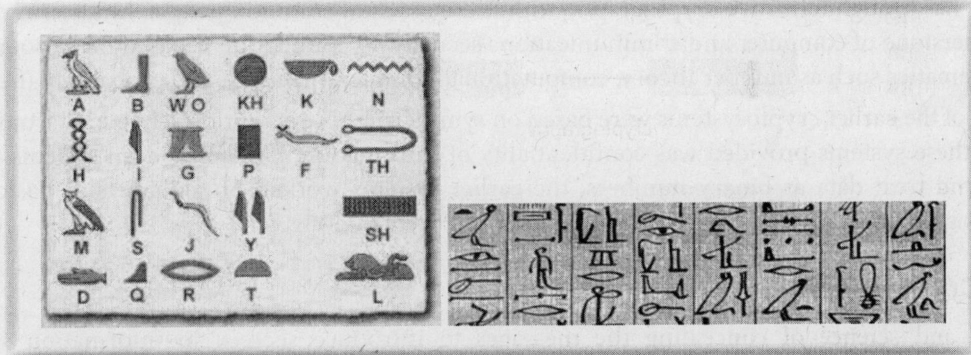

Figure 7.3: Hieroglyph

Later, the scholars moved on to using simple mono-alphabetic substitution ciphers. This involved replacing alphabets of message with other alphabets with some secret rule. This rule became a key to retrieve the message back from the garbled message. The first known use of a modern cipher was by Julius Caesar (100 BC to 44 BC), who did not trust his messengers when communicating with his governors and officers. The earlier Roman method of cryptography, popularly known as the caesar shift cipher, relies on shifting the letters of a message by an agreed number, the recipient of this message would then shift the letters back by the same number and obtain the original message.

It is during and after the European renaissance, various Italian and papal states led the rapid proliferation of cryptology techniques. Various analysis and techniques were researched in this era to break the secret codes. Improved coding techniques such as vigenere coding came into existence in the 15th century. Only after the 19th century, cryptography evolved from the adhoc approaches to encryption to the more sophisticated art and science of information security. In the early 20th century, the invention of mechanical and electromechanical machines, such as the Enigma rotor machine, provided more advanced and efficient means of coding the information. In recent times, cryptography has turned into a battleground of some of the world's best mathematicians and computer scientists. The ability to securely store and transfer sensitive information has proved a critical factor in success in war and business. Governments do not wish certain entities in and out of their countries to have access to ways to receive and send hidden information that may be a threat to national interests, cryptography has been subject to various restrictions in many countries, ranging from limitations of the usage and export of software to the public dissemination of mathematical concepts that could be used to develop cryptosystems. The Internet has allowed the spread of powerful programs and the underlying techniques of cryptology, so many of the most advanced cryptosystems and ideas are now in the public domain.

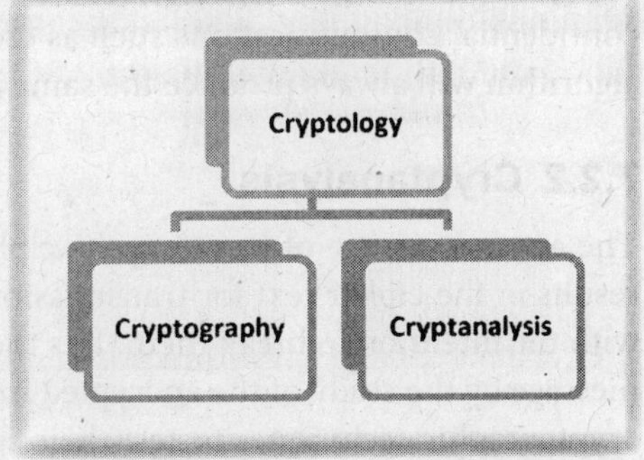

Figure 7.4: Cryptology Classification

During the period of World War II, cryptology became excessively mathematical. With the advances taking place in this field, government organizations, military units, and some corporate houses started adopting the applications of cryptology. They used cryptology to guard their secrets from others. The development of computers and the

Internet has brought effective cryptography within the reach of common people. Modern cryptology is the cornerstone of computer and communications security. Its foundation is based on various concepts of mathematics such as number theory, computational-complexity theory, and probability theory.

All of the earlier cryptosystems were based on symmetric key encryption scheme. The only security service these systems provided was confidentiality of information. Unlike modern systems which are digital and treat data as binary numbers, the earlier systems worked on alphabets as basic element. Cryptology is generally classified as cryptography and cryptanalysis.

7.2.1 Cryptography

The art and science of concealing the messages to introduce secrecy in information security is recognized as cryptography. It is the science of encryption algorithms and their use. This is a technique of securing information and communications through use of codes so that only those people for whom the information is intended can understand it and process it. Thus, preventing unauthorized access to information. The prefix "crypt" means "hidden" or "vault" and the suffix "graphy" stands for "writing." Cryptography is the process where an ordinary plain text is converted to cipher text which is the text made such that intended receiver of the text can only decode it and hence this process is known as encryption. The process of conversion of cipher text to plain text this is known as decryption.

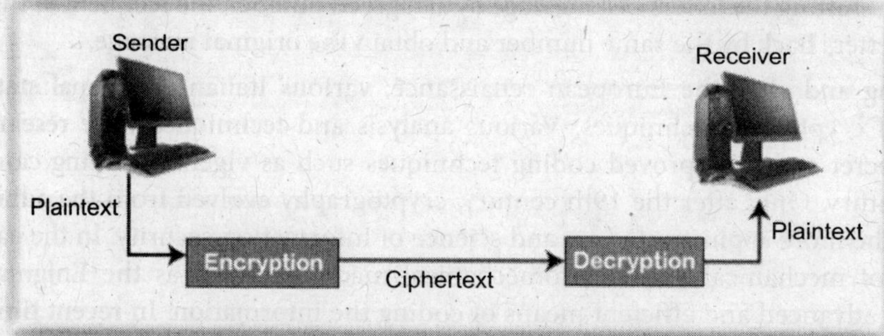

Figure 7.5: Encryption and Decryption Process

In computer science, cryptography refers to secure information and communication techniques derived from mathematical concepts and a set of rule-based calculations called algorithms, to transform messages in ways that are hard to interpret. These deterministic algorithms are used for cryptographic key generation, digital signing, verification to protect data privacy, web browsing on the Internet, and confidential communications such as credit card transactions and email. Deterministic algorithm is an algorithm will always produce the same output with particular input.

7.2.2 Cryptanalysis

The art and science of breaking the cipher text is known as cryptanalysis. The cryptographic process results in the cipher text for transmission or storage. It involves the study of cryptographic mechanism with the intention to break them. It is the science of deriving encryption keys or otherwise decrypting a message by the study of the encrypted message. Cryptanalysis is also used during the design of the new cryptographic techniques to test their security strengths. Cryptanalysis is the decryption and analysis of codes, ciphers or encrypted text. Cryptanalysis uses mathematical formulas to search for algorithm vulnerabilities and break into cryptography or information security systems. Cryptanalysis is the study of ciphertext, ciphers and cryptosystems with the aim of understanding how they work and finding improved techniques for defeating or weakening them.

7.3 CIPHER

In cryptology, a cipher is an algorithm for performing encryption or decryption with a series of well-defined steps that can be followed as a procedure. It is also known as encipherment. Encipher or encode

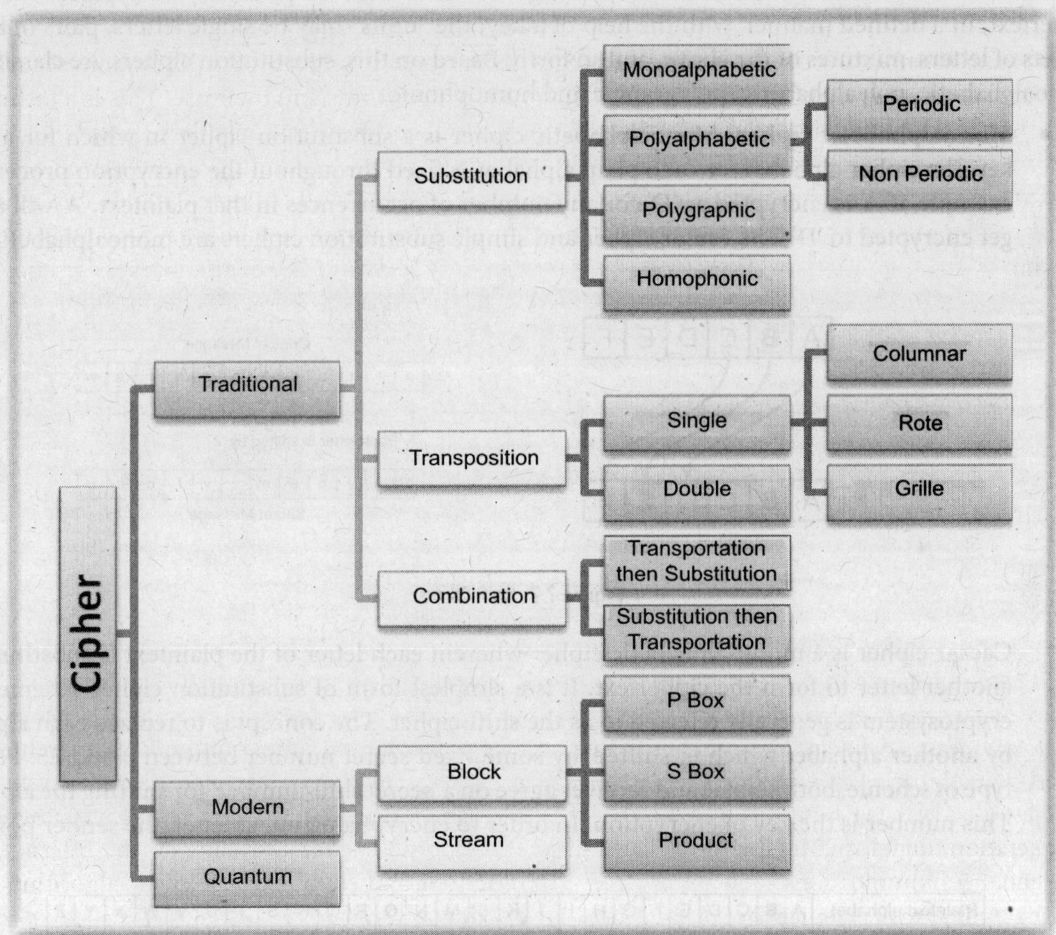

Figure 7.6: Classification of Cipher

is the process of converting information into cipher or code. Ciphers are also known as encryption algorithms which are systems for encrypting and decrypting data. A cipher converts the original message, called plaintext, into ciphertext using a key that determine how it is done. The figure shows the classification of cipher.

7.3.1 Traditional Ciphers

In cryptography, a traditional cipher is a type of cipher that was used historically but for the most part, has fallen into disuse. In contrast to modern cryptographic algorithms, most traditional ciphers can be computed and solved by hand. This is also called classical cipher. Traditional ciphers are grouped as substitution cipher, transposition cipher and combination cipher.

7.3.1.1 Substitution Cipher

A substitution cipher is a method of encrypting in which units of plaintext are replaced with the ciphertext, in a defined manner, with the help of a key; the "units" may be single letters, pairs of letters, triplets of letters, mixtures of the above, and so forth. Based on this, substitution ciphers are classified as monoalphabetic, polyalphabetic, polygraphic and homophonic.

- **Monoalphabetic cipher:** Monoalphabetic cipher is a substitution cipher in which for a given key, the cipher alphabet for each plain alphabet is fixed throughout the encryption process. For example, if 'A' is encrypted as 'D', for any number of occurrences in that plaintext, 'A' will always get encrypted to 'D'. The caesar cipher and simple substitution ciphers are monoalphabetic.

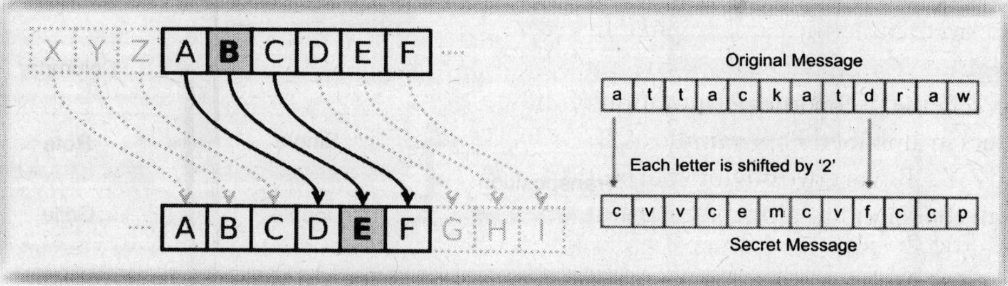

Figure 7.7: Shift Cipher

Caesar cipher is a mono-alphabetic cipher wherein each letter of the plaintext is substituted by another letter to form the ciphertext. It is a simplest form of substitution cipher scheme. This cryptosystem is generally referred to as the shift cipher. The concept is to replace each alphabet by another alphabet which is 'shifted' by some fixed secret number between 0 and 25. For this type of scheme, both sender and receiver agree on a 'secret shift number' for shifting the alphabet. This number is the key of encryption. In order to encrypt a plaintext letter, the sender positions

Plaintext alphabet	A	**B**	C	D	E	F	G	H	I	J	**K**	L	M	N	**O**	P	Q	R	S	T	U	V	W	X	Y	Z
Ciphertext alphabet	D	**E**	F	G	H	I	J	K	L	M	**N**	O	P	Q	**R**	S	T	U	V	W	X	Y	Z	A	B	C

Figure 7.8: Encryption Process of Shift Cipher

the sliding ruler underneath the first set of plaintext letters and slides it to left by the number of positions of the secret shift. The plaintext letter is then encrypted to the ciphertext letter on the sliding ruler underneath. The result of this process is shown in the figure 7.8 for an agreed shift of three positions. In this case, the plaintext 'BOOK' is encrypted to the ciphertext 'ERRN'. Here is the ciphertext alphabet for the secret shift is 3.

On receiving the ciphertext, the receiver who also knows the secret shift, positions his sliding ruler underneath the ciphertext alphabet and slides it to right by the agreed shift number, 3 in this case. He then replaces the ciphertext letter by the plaintext letter on the sliding ruler underneath. Hence the ciphertext 'ERRN' is decrypted to 'book'. To decrypt a message encoded with a shift of 3, generate the plaintext alphabet using a shift of '3' as shown below.

Ciphertext alphabet	A	B	C	D	E	F	G	H	I	J	K	L	M	N	O	P	Q	R	S	T	U	V	W	X	Y	Z
Plaintext alphabet	X	Y	Z	A	B	C	D	E	F	G	H	I	J	K	L	M	N	O	P	Q	R	S	T	U	V	W

Figure 7.9: Decryption Process of Shift Cipher

Caesar cipher is not a secure cryptosystem because there are only 26 possible keys to try out. An attacker can carry out an exhaustive key search with available limited computing resources.

Simple substitution cipher is an improvement to the caesar cipher. Instead of shifting the alphabets by some number, this scheme uses some permutation of the letters in alphabet. For example, A.B ... Y.Z and Z.Y ... B.A are two obvious permutation of all the letters in alphabet. Permutation is nothing but a jumbled up set of alphabets. With 26 letters in alphabet, the possible permutations are 26! (Factorial of 26) which is equal to 4x1026. The sender and the receiver may choose any one of these possible permutation as a ciphertext alphabet. This permutation is the secret key of the scheme. Write the alphabets A, B, C, ..., Z in the natural order. The sender and the receiver decide on a randomly selected permutation of the letters of the alphabet. Underneath the natural order alphabets, write out the chosen permutation of the letters of the alphabet. For encryption, sender replaces each plaintext letters by substituting the permutation letter that is directly beneath it in the table. This process is shown in the following figure. In this example, the chosen permutation is K,D, G, ..., O. The plaintext 'book' is encrypted to 'DJJA'. Here is a jumbled ciphertext alphabet, where the order of the ciphertext letters is a key.

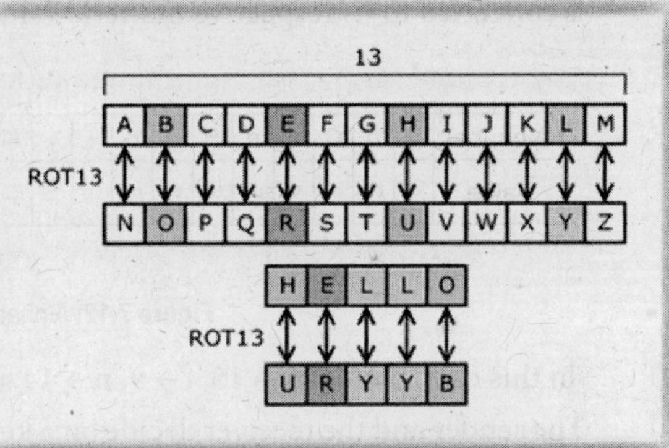

Figure 7.10: Simple Substitution Cipher

Plaintext alphabet	A	B	C	D	E	F	G	H	I	J	K	L	M	N	O	P	Q	R	S	T	U	V	W	X	Y	Z
Ciphertext alphabet	K	D	G	F	N	S	L	V	B	W	A	H	E	X	J	M	Q	C	P	Z	R	T	Y	I	U	O

Figure 7.11: Encryption Process of Simple Substitution Cipher

On receiving the ciphertext, the receiver, who also knows the randomly chosen permutation, replaces each ciphertext letter on the bottom row with the corresponding plaintext letter in the top row. The ciphertext 'DJJA' is decrypted to 'book'. The possible number of keys is large (26!) and even the modern computing systems are not yet powerful enough to comfortably launch a brute force attack to break the system.

- **Polyalphabetic Cipher:** Polyalphabetic cipher is a substitution cipher in which the cipher alphabet for the plain alphabet may be different at different places during the encryption process. The two types of polyalphabetic ciphers are periodic and non-periodic.

  A periodic polyalphabetic cipher with period "d" encrypts a plaintext message into ciphertext by replacing each plaintext letter with a letter from one of "d" substitution alphabets. The "d" alphabets are typically selected from a sequence of related alphabets that is repeated as often as necessary to encrypt the message. In case of non-periodic, key stream period "d" is longer than the plain text message. The examples of polyalphabetic ciphers are vigenere cipher, auto-key, one time pad and rotor cipher.

  Vigenere cipher uses a text string (word) as a key, which is then used for doing a number of shifts on the plaintext. For example, let's assume the secret key is 'point'. Each alphabet of the key is converted to its respective numeric value.

Alphabet	a	b	**C**	d	e	**F**	g	h	I	j	**K**	l	m	n	o	p	q	r	s	**T**	u	v	w	x	y	z
value	1	2	3	4	5	6	7	8	9	10	11	12	13	14	14	16	17	18	19	20	21	22	23	24	25	26

Figure 7.12: Alphabet to Value Conversion

In this case, p → 16, o → 15, i → 9, n → 14, and t → 20. Thus, the key is '16 15 9 14 20'.

The sender and the receiver decide on a key. Say 'point' is the key. Numeric representation of this key is '16 15 9 14 20'. The sender wants to encrypt the message 'book is good'. Write the message and below to that write the numeric representation of key repeatedly till the message is covered. The key must be less than or equal to the size of the message.

Message	b	o	o	k	i	s	g	o	o	d
Key value	16	15	9	14	20	16	15	9	14	20

Figure 7.13: Key Value Creation

The ciphertext is created by adding the corresponding numeric key value and the alphabet value. In the case of 'b', the numeric key value is 16 and alphabet value is 2. The addition of this gives 18 and the corresponding alphabet to this value is 'r' which will be the ciphertext. Here, each plaintext character has been shifted by a different amount and that amount is determined by the key.

Message	b	o	o	k	i	s	g	o	o	d
Key value	16	15	9	14	20	16	15	9	14	20
Alphabet value	2	14	14	11	9	19	7	14	14	4
Total value-shift	18	29	23	25	29	35	23	23	28	24
Cipher text	r	c	w	y	c	i	w	w	b	x

Figure 7.14: Vigenere Cipher Creation for Encryption

For decryption, the receiver uses the same key and shifts received ciphertext in reverse order to obtain the plaintext. Vigenere cipher was designed by tweaking the standard caesar cipher to reduce the effectiveness of cryptanalysis on the ciphertext and make a cryptosystem more robust. It is significantly more secure than a regular caesar cipher. In the history, it was regularly used for protecting sensitive political and military information. It was referred to as the unbreakable cipher due to the difficulty it posed to the cryptanalysis.

One-time pad (OTP) cipher is vigenere cipher with perfect secrecy. The circumstances are the length of the keyword is same as the length of the plaintext, the keyword is a randomly generated string of alphabets and the keyword is used only once. One-time pad is an encryption system that is unbreakable provided certain conditions are met. The conditions that make a one-time pad impossible to crack are also ones that make the technique impractical for many modern applications. Plaintext is paired with a random secret key is also called a one-time pad.

In rotor cipher, the primary component is a set of rotors, also termed wheels or drums, which are rotating disks with an array of electrical contacts on either side. The wiring between the contacts implements a fixed substitution of letters, replacing them in some complex fashion. On its own, this would offer little security; however, after encrypting each letter, the rotors advance positions, changing the substitution. By this means, a rotor machine produces a complex polyalphabetic substitution cipher, which changes with every key press.

The autokey cipher is about changing plaintext letters based on secret key letters. Each letter of the message is shifted along some alphabet positions. The number of positions is equal to the place in the alphabet of the current key letter. Unlike in other similar ciphers, after using all of secret key letters, the algorithm doesn't go back to its first letter but starts to take plaintext letters as new key letters. As this avoid repetition of the same secret key letters, the cipher is resistant to attacks based on dividing ciphertext into parts corresponding to subsequent secret key characters. However, its weakness is that all key characters create words and sentences which in addition are the same as in plain text.

- **Polygraphic Cipher:** Polygraphic substitution divide the plaintext into groups of letters. Then, they replace each group of letters by one of the predefined letters, numbers, graphic symbols, or by another group of characters. Polygraphic substitution ciphers were invented as an improvement of simple substitution ciphers. They were very popular during the renaissance and they were used in Europe for many centuries. The playfair cipher, hill cipher, two-square cipher and four-square cipher are examples of polygraphic cipher.

Playfair cipher technique encrypts pairs of letters, instead of single letters as in the simple substitution cipher. The playfair is significantly harder to break since the frequency analysis used for simple substitution ciphers does not work with it. In playfair cipher, initially a key table is created. The key table is a 5×5 grid of alphabets that acts as the key for encrypting the plaintext. Each of the 25 alphabets must be unique and one letter of the alphabet (usually J) is omitted from the table as we need only 25 alphabets instead of 26. If the plaintext contains J, then it is replaced by I. The sender and the receiver deicide on a particular key, say 'book'. In a key table, the first characters (going left to right) in the table is the phrase, excluding the duplicate letters. Here 'o' is duplicate. The rest of the table will be filled with the remaining letters of the alphabet, in natural order. The key table works out to be as in figure 7.15.

B	**O**	**K**	A	C
D	E	F	G	H
I	L	M	N	P
Q	R	S	T	U
V	W	X	Y	Z

Figure 7.15: Key Table Creation in Playfair Cipher

Let us encrypt with the secret message "hide money". This message is split into pairs of two letters. If there is an odd number of letters, a Z is added to the last letter. It will be written as – HI DE MO NE YZ. The rules of encryption are

- If both the letters are in the same column, take the letter below each one (going back to the top if at the bottom)
- If both letters are in the same row, take the letter to the right of each one (going back to the left if at the farthest right)
- If neither of the preceding two rules are true, form a rectangle with the two letters and take the letters on the horizontal opposite corner of the rectangle.

B	**O**	**K**	A	C
D	E	F	G	**H**
I	L	M	N	P
Q	R	S	T	U
V	W	X	Y	Z

As per the third rule HI of secret message will be encrypted as PD

B	**O**	**K**	A	C
D	**E**	F	G	H
I	L	M	N	P
Q	R	S	T	U
V	W	X	Y	Z

As per second rule, DE of secret message will be encrypted as EF

B	**O**	**K**	A	C
D	**E**	F	G	H
I	**L**	**M**	N	P
Q	R	S	T	U
V	W	X	Y	Z

As per third rule MO of secret message will be encrypted as LK

B	**O**	**K**	A	C
D	**E**	F	G	H
I	L	M	**N**	P
Q	R	S	T	U
V	W	X	Y	Z

As per third rule NE of secret message will be encrypted as GL

B	**O**	**K**	A	C
D	E	F	G	H
I	L	M	N	P
Q	R	S	T	U
V	W	X	**Y**	**Z**

As per second rule YZ of secret message will be encrypted as ZV

B	O	K	A	C
D	E	F	G	H
I	L	M	N	P
Q	R	S	T	U
V	W	X	Y	Z

Figure 7.16: Encryption Process in Playfair Cipher

Using these rules, the result of the encryption of 'hide money' with the key of 'book' would be – PD EF LK GL ZV. Decrypting the playfair cipher is as simple as doing the same process in reverse. Receiver has the same key and can create the same key table, and then decrypt any messages made using that key. This is a substitution cipher and is difficult to break compared to the simple substitution cipher. As in case of substitution cipher, cryptanalysis is possible on the playfair cipher as well, however it would be against 625 possible pairs of letters (25×25 alphabets) instead of 26 different possible alphabets. The playfair cipher was used mainly to protect important, yet non-critical secrets, as it is quick to use and requires no special equipment.

Hill cipher represents a polygraphic substitution cipher that follows a uniform substitution across multiple levels of blocks. Polygraphic substitution cipher defines that hill cipher can work seamlessly with two-letter blocks, three-letter blocks, or any multiple-sized blocks for building a uniform cipher. Hill cipher is based on a particular mathematical topic of linear algebra and the sophisticated use of matrices in general, as well as rules for modulo arithmetic. Most of the problems and solutions for Hill ciphers are of mathematical nature, which also makes it easy to withhold or hide letters precisely.

Two-square cipher (or double square cipher) encryption uses two squared grid/checkboard placed side to side (horizontal variant), or one above the other (vertical variant), sometimes generated with a key word (deranged alphabet). The Two-square cipher, also called double Playfair, is a manual symmetric encryption technique. It was developed to ease the cumbersome nature of the large encryption/decryption matrix used in the four-square cipher while still being slightly stronger than the (single-square) playfair cipher. The technique encrypts pairs of letters (digraphs), and thus falls into a category of ciphers known as polygraphic substitution ciphers. This adds significant strength to the encryption when compared with monographic substitution ciphers which operate on single characters. The use of digraphs makes the two-square technique less susceptible to frequency analysis attacks, as the analysis must be done on 676 possible digraphs rather than just 26 for monographic substitution. The frequency analysis of digraphs is possible, but considerably more difficult - and it generally requires a much larger ciphertext in order to be useful. The two-square cipher comes in two varieties - horizontal and vertical. The vertical two-square uses two 5 by 5 matrices one above the other. The horizontal two-square has the two 5 by 5 matrices side by side. Each of the 5 by 5 matrices contains the letters of the alphabet (usually omitting "Q" or putting both "I" and "J" in the same location to reduce the alphabet to fit). The alphabets in both squares are generally mixed alphabets, each based on some keyword or phrase.

Four-square cipher encryption is made, with four square grids (possibly generated from a keyword) themselves positioned in a square. The four-square cipher is a manual symmetric encryption technique which utilizes four 5×5 matrices of letters arranged in a square. Each of these 5×5 squares contain all of the letters of the alphabet, though leaving out the letter Q to bring it down to fit in 25 characters. The plaintext is split into pairs of two letters and then encrypted using a method similar to the playfair cipher.

- **Homophonic Cipher:** The homophonic substitution cipher is a substitution cipher in which single plaintext letters can be replaced by any of several different ciphertext letters. As we allow more and more possible alternatives for each letter, the resulting cipher can become very secure. The homophonic substitution cipher is a substitution cipher in which single plaintext letters can be replaced by any of several different ciphertext letters. They are generally much more difficult to break than standard substitution ciphers. The number of characters each letter is replaced by is part of the key, e.g. the letter 'E' might be replaced by any of 5 different symbols, while the letter 'Q' may only be substituted by 1 symbol. The easiest way to break standard substitution ciphers is to look at the letter frequencies, the letter 'E' is usually the most common letter in english, so the most common ciphertext letter will probably be 'E'. If we allow the letter 'E' to be replaced by any of 3 different characters, then we can no longer just take the most common letter, since the letter count of 'E' is spread over several characters. As we allow more and more possible alternatives for each letter, the resulting cipher can become very secure.

7.3.1.2 Transposition Cipher

This is a type of cipher where the order of the alphabets in the plaintext is rearranged to create the ciphertext. The actual plaintext alphabets are not replaced. The transposition cipher is of single type or double type.

An example is a 'single columnar transposition', cipher where the plaintext is written horizontally with a certain alphabet width. Then the ciphertext is read vertically as shown. For example, the plaintext is "golden statue is in eleventh cave" and the secret random key chosen is "five". We arrange this text horizontally in table with number of column equal to key value. The resulting text is shown in Figure 7.17.

g	o	l	d	e
n	s	t	a	t
u	e	i	s	i
n	e	l	e	v
e	n	t	h	c
a	v	e		

Figure 7.17: Transposition Cipher

The ciphertext is obtained by reading column vertically downward from first to last column. The ciphertext is 'gnuneaoseenvltiltedasehetivc'. To decrypt, the receiver prepares similar table. The number of columns is equal to key number. The number of rows is obtained by dividing number of total ciphertext alphabets by key value and rounding of the quotient to next integer value. The receiver then writes the received ciphertext vertically down and from left to right column. To obtain the text, he reads horizontally left to right and from top to bottom row. Examples of transposition ciphers are rail fence cipher, scytale, route cipher, myszkowski transposition, disrupted transposition, columnar, grilles route.

7.3.1.3 Combination Ciphers

The combination ciphers use substitution cipher and transposition ciphers together. In some, application, transposition cipher is followed by substitution and in the others vice versa.

7.3.2 Modern Ciphers

Modern ciphers manipulates traditional characters, i.e., letters and digits directly. It operates on binary bit sequences. It is mainly based on 'security through obscurity'. The techniques employed for coding were kept secret and only the parties involved in communication knew about them. Block ciphers and stream ciphers comes under the classification of modern ciphers.

7.3.2.1 Block Cipher

In this scheme, the plain binary text is processed in blocks (groups) of bits at a time; i.e. a block of plaintext bits is selected, a series of operations is performed on this block to generate a block of ciphertext bits.

Figure 7.18: Block Cipher Encryption

The number of bits in a block is fixed. A block cipher takes a block of plaintext bits and generates a block of ciphertext bits, generally of same size. The size of block is fixed in the given scheme. The choice of block size does not directly affect to the strength of encryption scheme. The strength of cipher depends up on the key length. Though any size of block is acceptable, few aspects are to be borne in mind while selecting a size of a block. Avoid very small block size. If a block size is m bits. Then the possible plaintext bits combinations are then 2m. If the attacker discovers the plain text blocks corresponding to some previously sent ciphertext blocks, then the attacker can launch a type of 'dictionary attack' by building up a dictionary of plaintext/ciphertext pairs sent using that encryption key. A larger block size makes attack harder as the dictionary needs to be larger. With very large block size, the cipher becomes inefficient to operate. Such plaintexts will need to be padded before being encrypted. A preferred block size is a multiple of 8 as it is easy for implementation as most computer processor handle data in multiple of 8 bits. Block ciphers process blocks are of fixed sizes (say 64 bits). The length of plaintexts is mostly not a multiple of the block size. For example, a 150-bit plaintext provides two blocks of 64 bits each with third block of balance 22 bits. The last block of bits needs to be padded up with redundant information so that the length of the final block equal to block size of the scheme. In our example, the remaining 22 bits need to have additional 42 redundant bits added to provide a complete block. The process of adding bits to the last block is referred to as padding. Too much padding makes the system inefficient. Also, padding may make the system insecure, if the padding is done with same bits always.

The block cipher is of three types, they are P-Box, S-Box and Product Cipher. The S-boxes and P-boxes are used to make the relation between the plaintext and the ciphertext difficult to understand.

- **Permutation Box Cipher:** Permutation Box (P-Box) is a tool that changes the order of the input bits and they appear in the output. In this case, the key is order transmission of input bits in output bits.

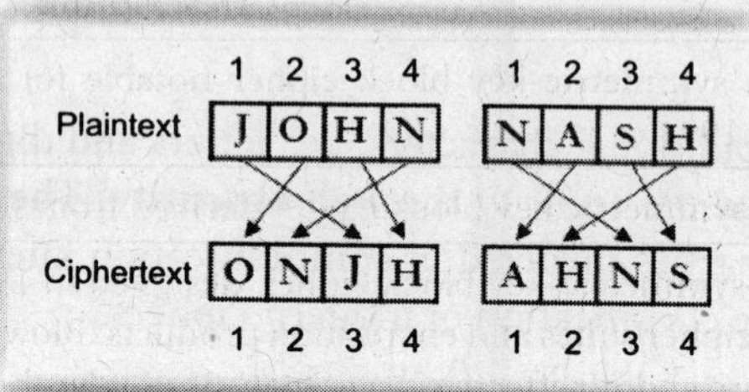

Figure 7.19: Permutation Box Cipher

Permutation box is following three types.

Table 7.1: Types of Permutation Box Cipher

Type of P-Box Cipher	Description
Straight permutation	The input size is equal to the output size. The bits are transposed without change.
Compression permutation	The input size is larger than the output size. The bits are compressed in this permutation.
Expansion permutation	The input size is smaller than the output size. The bits are expanded in this permutation.

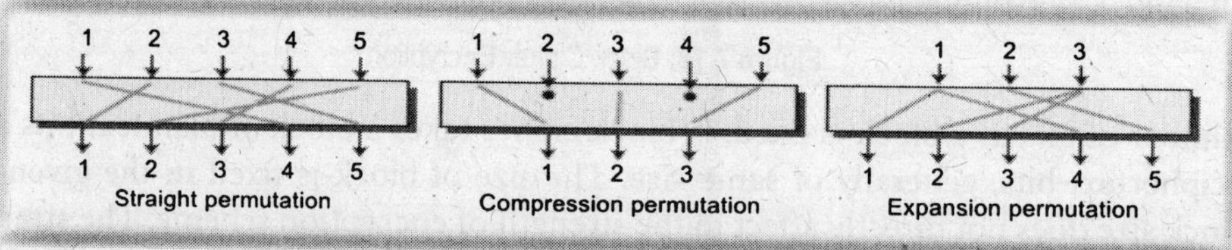

Figure 7.20: Types of Permutation Box Cipher

- **Substitution Box Cipher:** Substitution-Box (S-Box) is a basic component of symmetric-key algorithms. In block ciphers, the S-Boxes are used to make the relation between the key and the ciphertext difficult to understand.
- **Product Cipher:** A product cipher combines two or more transformations in a manner intending that the resulting cipher is more secure than the individual components. The product cipher combines a sequence of permutation (P-box), substitution (S-box) in modular form. The figure 7.21 represents permutation box cipher modules and S1 to S12 substitution box cipher modules.

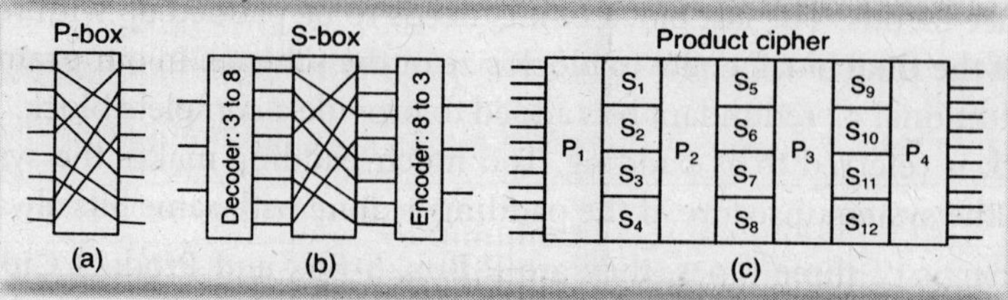

Figure 7.21: Representation of P-box, S-box and Product Cipher

The most popular block ciphers are shown in table 7.2.

Table 7.2: Popular Block Ciphers

Block Cipher	Description
Rivest Cipher 5 (RC5)	This is a symmetric-key block cipher notable for its simplicity. Designed by Ronald Rivest in 1994.
Rivest Cipher 6 (RC6)	This is a symmetric key block cipher derived from RC5.
Blowfish	This is a symmetric-key block cipher, designed in 1993 by Bruce Schneier and included in many cipher suites and encryption products. Blowfish provides a good encryption rate in software and no effective cryptanalysis of it has been found to date. It uses longer key lengths (128-bit, 192-bit, 256-bit) to prevent cyber-attacks.
Two Fish Cipher	This scheme of block cipher uses block size of 128 bits and a key of variable length. It is based on the earlier block cipher blowfish with a block size of 64 bits.
Serpent Cipher	This is a block cipher with a block size of 128 bits and key lengths of 128, 192, or 256 bits. It is a slower but has more secure design than other block ciphers.

7.3.2.2 Stream Ciphers

In this scheme, the plaintext is processed one bit at a time i.e. one bit of plaintext is taken, and a series of operations is performed on it to generate one bit of ciphertext. Technically, stream ciphers are block ciphers with a block size of one bit.

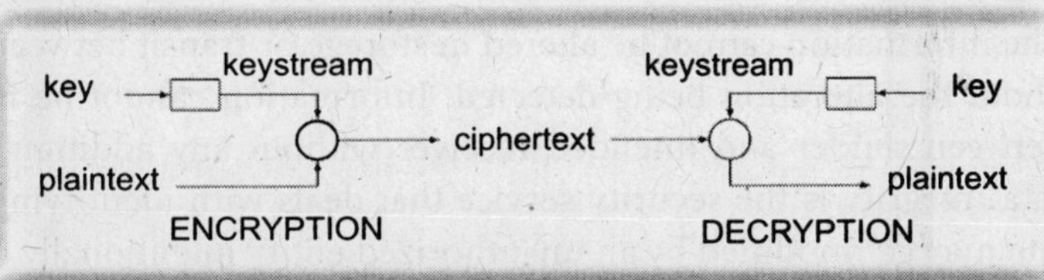

Figure 7.22: Stream Cipher Encryption and Decryption

The most popular stream cipher is Rivest Cipher 4 (RC4). It is remarkable for its simplicity and speed in software but multiple vulnerabilities have been discovered in RC4, rendering it insecure. It is especially vulnerable when the beginning of the output keystream is not discarded, or when non random or related keys are used. It was designed by Ron Rivest, Matt Robshaw, Ray Sidney, and Yiqun Lisa Yin so sometimes RC is expanded as "Ron's Code".

7.4 CLASSICAL AND MODERN CRYPTOLOGY COMPARISON

There are three major characteristics that separate classical cryptology from modern cryptology.

Table 7.3: Comparison of Classical and Modern Cryptology

Classical Cryptology	Modern Cryptology
It manipulates traditional characters, i.e., letters and digits directly.	It operates on binary bit sequences.

Classical Cryptology	Modern Cryptology
It is mainly based on 'security through obscurity'. The techniques employed for coding were kept secret and only the parties involved in communication knew about them.	It relies on publicly known mathematical algorithms for coding the information. Secrecy is obtained through a secrete key which is used as the seed for the algorithms. The computational difficulty of algorithms, absence of secret key, etc., make it impossible for an attacker to obtain the original information even if he knows the algorithm used for coding.
It requires the entire cryptosystem for communicating confidentially.	Modern cryptography requires parties interested in secure communication to possess the secret key only.

7.5 CRYPTOLOGY FOR INFORMATION SECURITY

Cryptology includes techniques to hide information in storage or transit. In today's computer-centric world, it is most often associated with scrambling plaintext into ciphertext (encryption), then back again (decryption). Individuals who practice this field are known as cryptologist. Modern cryptology concerns itself with the following objectives.

- **Confidentiality:** Information can only be accessed by the person for whom it is intended and no other person can access it. The information cannot be understood by anyone for whom it was not intended. Confidentiality is the fundamental security service provided by cryptology. It is sometimes referred to as privacy or secrecy. Confidentiality can be achieved through numerous means starting from physical securing to the use of mathematical algorithms for data encryption.
- **Integrity:** The information cannot be altered in storage or transit between sender and intended receiver without the alteration being detected. Information cannot be modified in storage or transition between sender and intended receiver without any addition to information being detected. Data Integrity is the security service that deals with identifying any alteration to the data. The data may get modified by an unauthorized entity intentionally or accidently. Integrity service confirms that whether data is intact or not since it was last created, transmitted, or stored by an authorized user. Data integrity cannot prevent the alteration of data, but provides a means for detecting whether data has been manipulated in an unauthorized manner.
- **Non-repudiation:** To repudiate means to deny. Non-repudiation is the assurance that someone cannot deny something. Typically, non-repudiation refers to the ability to ensure that a party to a contract or a communication cannot deny the authenticity of their signature on a document or the sending of a message that they originated. The creator/sender of information cannot deny his or her intention to send information at later stage. It is a security service that ensures that an entity cannot refuse the ownership of a previous commitment or an action to a recipient or third party. Non-repudiation is a property that is most desirable in situations where there are chances of a dispute over the exchange of data.
- **Authentication:** Authenticity refers to the characteristic of a communication, document, or any data that ensures the quality of being genuine or corrupted. The major role of authentication is to confirm that a user is genuine, one who he / she claims to be. Controls such as bio metrics, smart cards, and digital certificates ensure the authenticity of data, transactions, communications, or documents. Authentication is the act of proving an assertion, such as

the identity of a computer system user. In contrast with identification, the act of indicating a person or thing's identity, authentication is the process of verifying that identity. The sender and receiver can confirm each other's identity and the origin/destination. Authentication provides the identification of the originator. It confirms to the receiver that the data received has been sent only by an identified and verified sender. Authentication service has two variants. Message authentication identifies the originator of the message without any regard router or system that has sent the message. Entity authentication is assurance that data has been received from a specific entity, say a particular website. Apart from the originator, authentication may also provide assurance about other parameters related to data such as the date and time of creation/ transmission.

- **Availability:** An objective indicating that data or system is at disposal of license users once require. Availability is the assurance that the systems responsible for delivering, storing, and processing information are accessible when required by authorized users. Availability means data is accessible by licensed users. If an attacker isn't able to compromise the primary components of data security, they'll try and execute attacks like denial of service that will bring down the server, creating the web site unavailable to legitimate users because of lack of availability. Measures to maintain data availability can include redundant systems' disk arrays and clustered Machines, anti-virus software to stop malware from destroying networks, and distributed denial-of-service (DDoS) prevention systems.

7.6 DRAWBACKS OF CRYPTOLOGY

Apart from the explained objectives of information security, there are issues that affect the effective use of information.

- A strongly encrypted, authentic, and digitally signed information can be difficult to access even for a legitimate user at a crucial time of decision-making.
- The network or the computer system can be attacked and rendered non-functional by an intruder.
- Availability which is one of the fundamental aspects of information security, cannot be ensured through the use of cryptology. Other methods are needed to guard against the threats such as denial of service or complete breakdown of information system.
- Another fundamental need of information security of authentication also cannot be realized through the use of cryptology. Administrative controls and procedures are required to be exercised for the same.
- Cryptology does not guard against the vulnerabilities and threats that emerge from the poor design of systems, protocols, and procedures. These need to be fixed through proper design and setting up of a defensive infrastructure.
- Cryptology comes at cost. The cost is in terms of time and money. Addition of cryptology techniques in the information processing leads to delay. The use of public key cryptology requires setting up and maintenance of public key infrastructure requiring the handsome financial budget.
- The security of cryptology technique is based on the computational difficulty of mathematical problems. Any breakthrough in solving such mathematical problems or increasing the computing power can render a cryptographic technique vulnerable.

7.7 CONCERNS OF CRYPTOLOGY

Attackers can bypass cryptography, hack into computers that are responsible for data encryption and decryption, and exploit weak implementations, such as the use of default keys. However, cryptography makes it harder for attackers to access messages and data protected by encryption algorithms. Growing concerns about the processing power of quantum computing to break current cryptography encryption standards led the National Institute of Standards and Technology (NIST) to put out a call for papers among the mathematical and science community for new public key cryptography standards. Unlike today's computer systems, quantum computing uses quantum bits (qubits) that can represent both 0s and 1s, and therefore perform two calculations at once. While a large-scale quantum computer may not be built in the next decade, the existing infrastructure requires standardization of publicly known and understood algorithms that offer a secure approach.

7.8 STEGANOGRAPHY

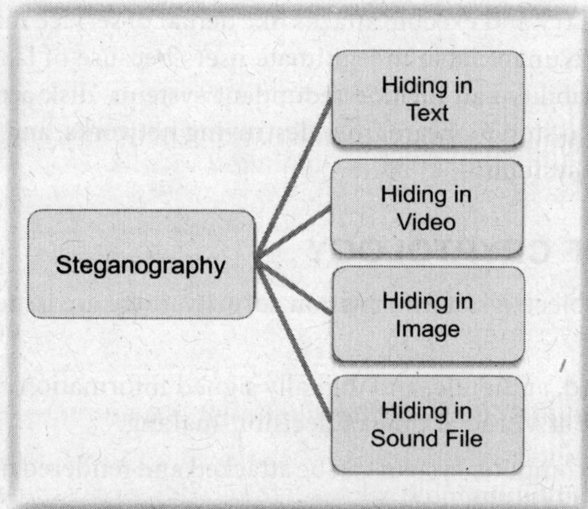

Figure 7.23: Methods of Steganography

Steganography is similar but adds another dimension to cryptography. Steganography is the technique of hiding secret data within an ordinary, non-secret, file or message in order to avoid detection. The secret data is then extracted at its destination. The use of steganography can be combined with encryption as an extra step for hiding or protecting data. In this method, people not only want to protect the secrecy of an information by concealing it, but they also want to make sure any unauthorized person gets no evidence that the information even exists. For example, invisible watermarking. In steganography, an unintended recipient or an intruder is unaware of the fact that observed data contains hidden information. In cryptography, an intruder is normally aware that data is being communicated, because they can see the coded/scrambled message.

7.9 QUANTUM CRYPTOLOGY

Quantum cryptology or Quantum Key Distribution (QKD) uses a series of photons (light particles) to transmit data from one location to another over a fiber optic cable. The photons travel to a receiver, which uses two beam splitters (horizontal/vertical and diagonal) to "read" the polarization of each photon. Quantum communication systems offer the promise of virtually unbreakable encryption. It revolutionizes secure communication by providing security based on fundamental laws of physics instead of mathematical algorithms or computing technologies used today.

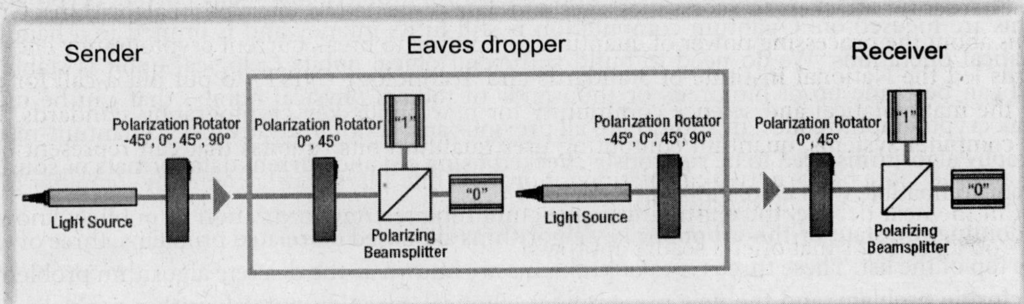

Figure 7.24: Quantum Cryptology Concept

Following are the advantages of quantum cryptology

- It revolutionizes secure communication by providing security based on fundamental laws of physics instead of mathematical algorithms or computing technologies used today.
- It is virtually not hackable.
- It is simple to use.
- Less resources are needed in order to maintain it.
- It is used to detect eavesdropping in QKD (Quantum Key Distribution). This is due to the fact that it is not possible to copy the data encoded in quantum state. If someone tries to read such encoded data then quantum state changes the existing state.
- The performance of such cryptography systems is continuously improved. This results into its quick adoption in encrypting most valuable secrets of the government and industries.

The disadvantages of quantum cryptology are explained below.

- The worldwide implementation of this can take up lots of jobs and hence unemployment will increase.
- While traveling through the channel (optical fibre or air), there is possibility of change in polarization of photon due to various causes.
- Quantum cryptography lacks many vital features such as digital signature, certified mail etc.
- Need of dedicated channel is a must between source and destinations which implies high cost. It is impossible to send keys to two or more different locations using a quantum channel as multiplexing is against quantum's principles. This demands separate channels between source and many destinations. This is major disadvantage of quantum communication through optical channel.
- The largest distance supported by QKD is about 250 KM at a speed of 16 bps through guided medium.

Due to recent developments in the field of quantum computers, the search to build and apply quantum-resistant cryptographic algorithms brings classical cryptography to the next level. Using those machines, many of today's most popular cryptosystems can be cracked by the Shor Algorithm. This is an algorithm that uses quantum computation to equate the prime number phases expressed as sine waves to factor large integers, effectively solving the discreet logarithm problem that many current cryptographic algorithms are focused on. Quantum computation is still in its infancy and is limited to a handful of mathematical operations. We do need to build sufficient logical qubits (a logical qubit is stable over time and can be made up of hundreds or thousands of today's physical qubits) that can be used to fully break cryptographic codes. In addition to all previous and continuing advances, quantum-resistant cryptography algorithms need to be rigorously checked using old and current data formats or sources to make them compatible with all platforms.

Predominantly, state-of-the-art public key algorithms are based on related problems, three of which are at the top of the list. These three types of problems are known as the discrete algorithm problem, the entire factoring problem, and the new pre-eminent elliptical curve discrete algorithm problem. These three groups can be broken by Shor's quantum PC approximation. This is a concern as these equations are commonly used to ensure the protected sharing of confidential information across the Internet, the development of digital signatures and security of other links over unsafe networks.

7.9.1 Quantum and Modern Cryptology Comparison

By modern cryptology, we mean the presently using cryptology techniques. In present cryptology, the original text is transformed into ciphertext which is then transmitted across a channel controlled by a data string called a key. The receiver will be able to get the original information and decrypt to the original text only if he is in possession of this key. Present cryptology comes with two main techniques like symmetric and asymmetric. These techniques face a threat from quantum algorithms. For example, the Shor algorithm is capable of breaking asymmetric cryptology techniques. Another quantum algorithm known as the Grover algorithm is capable of attacking symmetric cryptology. Quantum cryptology, on the other hand, offers safe key exchanges based on the principle of quantum mechanics.

The security of present cryptology is threatened by weak random key generators, advances in CPU power, new attack mechanisms, and the development of quantum computers. With regard to quantum computers, present encryption is useless. The data encrypted today can be intercepted and stored for decryption by quantum computers in the future.

Quantum cryptology offers the advantages of 'unconditional security' and sniffing detection. These characteristics can help in solving cyberspace security problems for the future Internet and applications such as the IoT.

Table 7.4: Modern Cryptology and Quantum Cryptology Comparison

Criteria	Modern Cryptology	Quantum Cryptology
Based on	Mathematical computation	Quantum mechanics
Usage	widely	sophisticated
Digital signature	Present	Absent.
Bit rate	Depends on computational power.	Average bit rate is 1 MBPS.

Criteria	Modern Cryptology	Quantum Cryptology
Bit storage	2n, n-bit strings.	One, n-bit string.
Communication range	Millions of miles.	Maximum 10 miles.
Tested /Deployed	Deployed and tested.	In initial stages, not tested fully.
Communication medium	Independent.	Dependent.
Expenditure	Less.	High.

7.10 POST QUANTUM CRYPTOLOGY

In view of the inherited shortcomings and major disadvantages involved in the implementation of an effective and smooth Quantum Key Distribution (QKD), the quest for a classic, non-quantum cryptology algorithm that will operate in current real-time infrastructures is an increasingly growing field of study. These quantum robust algorithms are called Post-Quantum Cryptology (PQC) algorithms and are assumed to remain stable after the availability of functional large-scale quantum computing machines.

- **Hash-Based Signatures:** Hash-based signature schemes are public key signatures that are based on the one-wayness of cryptographic hash functions. A hash-based signature scheme initializes from a One-Time Signature (OTS), i.e., a signature scheme where each key pair only needs to be used to sign a message with.
- **Code-Based Signatures:** Code-based cryptology is an upcoming contender for the diversification of today's public-key cryptosystems, most of which rely on the complexities of either the factorization or the discrete logarithm problem. Code-based cryptology, unlike public-key algorithms, is based on the problem of decoding unknown error-correcting codes. There are two simple code-based crypto systems named after Robert McEliece and Harald Niederreiter, their inventors. Compared to traditional cryptosystems, such as RSA, both share the issue of having massive key lengths, which make their implementation impossible on embedded devices with very limited resources. The input message is converted into a code-word for plain text encryption by either adding random errors to the message or encoding a message in the error sequence. By deleting the errors or retrieving the original input message from the errors, decryption restores plain-text. It is, therefore, important to conceal the algebraic structure of the text, essentially cloaking it as an anonymous generic code. An adversary understanding the particular code used will be able to decrypt the message.
- **Multivariate Cryptology:** The challenge of solving non-linear equation structures over finite fields is the foundation of multivariate cryptology schemes. Seeking a solution for such structures is called a NP-complete or NP-hard problem. NP is the set of problems where we can confirm a given solution in polynomial time. These may or may not be the same set. NP Complete is the set of problems that can be confirmed in polynomial time, but there is no known way to solve them in polynomial time. The same basic architecture is used for all Multivariate Public-Key Cryptosystems (MPKC), as they all depend on the use of multivariate polynomials over a finite field. The polynomial equations are of degree two in most cases, resulting in multivariate quadratic polynomials, which are still credited with being solved as NP-hard

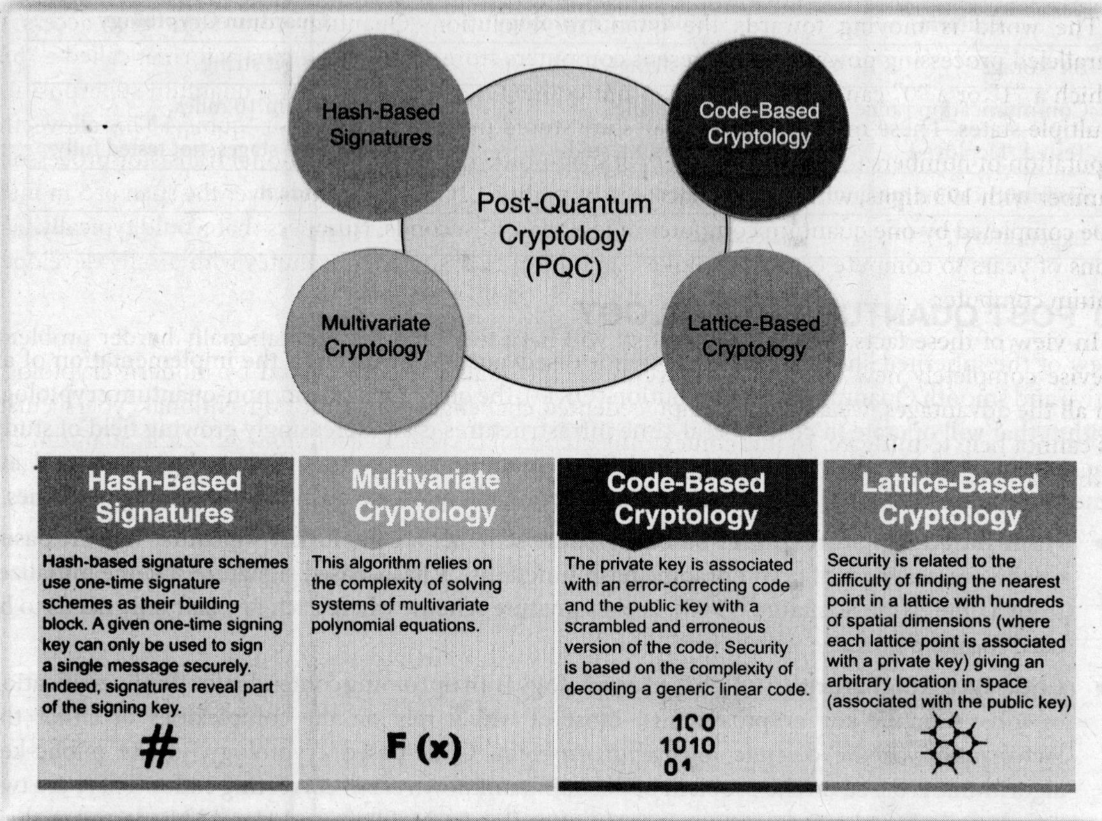

Figure 7.25: Types and Implementation of Post-Quantum Cryptology

- **Lattice-Based Cryptology:** Miklos Ajtai first demonstrated Lattice-based algorithms, with the suggestion of designing stable cryptographic algorithms based on the hard lattice problem (NP). A lattice-based public-key encryption scheme was adopted, but a scheme that was sufficiently robust and proven stable was not presented until 2005, when Oded Regev proposed his scheme. This method uses both lattices and a generalization of the problem of parity learning. A lattice, given in n-dimensional vector space, is a particular arrangement of points with a periodic structure and is used in a variety of fields. Lattice-based cryptographic algorithms are mostly based on either the problem with the nearest vector or the problem with the shortest vector. In most lattice-based cryptographic algorithms, the cryptographic builders used are very time efficient and simple, while still providing security proofs based on the worst-case hardness.

7.11 FUTURE OF CRYPTOLOGY

Organizations currently rely on public key encryption, digital signatures and key exchanges to protect business commerce, communications, identity and data. These cryptographic schemes are underpinned by a set of vetted algorithms, and the level of protection is based on the strength of the underlying math and difficulty of calculation.

The world is moving towards the quantum revolution. Quantum computers give access to unparalleled processing power. While present computers store data using a binary format called a "bit" in which a "1" or a "0" can be stored; a quantum computer stores data using a quantum superposition of multiple states. These multiple valued states are stored in "quantum bits" or "qubits". This allows the computation of numbers to be several orders of magnitude faster than traditional transistor processors. A number with 193 digits, which can be factored by eighty 2.2GHz computers over the span of 5 months can be completed by one quantum computer in less than 17 seconds. Numbers that would typically take billions of years to compute could only take a matter of hours or even minutes with a fully developed quantum computer.

In view of these facts, modern cryptology will have to look for computationally harder problems or devise completely new techniques of archiving the goals presently served by modern cryptology. With all the advantages, we are facing unprecedented challenges which the conventional cybersecurity tools cannot help to mitigate. In this context, the quantum cryptology techniques, like the quantum key distribution methods can prove to be beneficial.

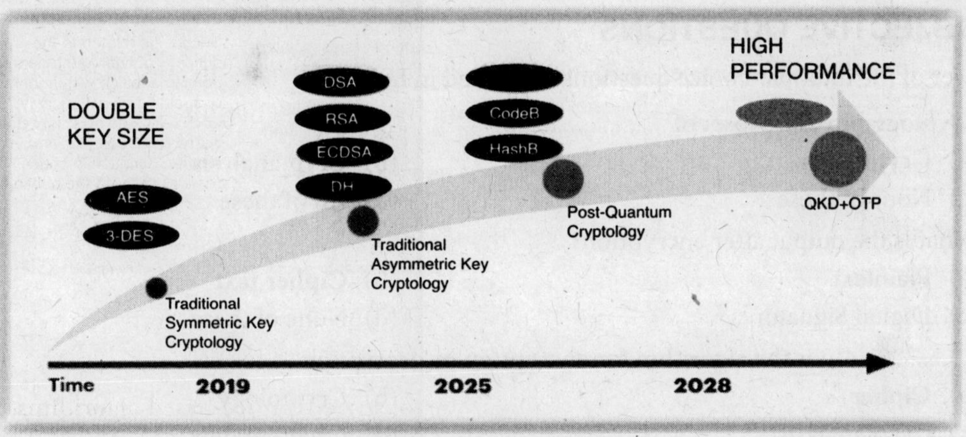

Figure 7.26: Development of Cryptology

Quantum cryptology is different from other symmetric and asymmetric cryptology techniques as instead of mathematics, it relies more on the concepts of physics as a key aspect of its security model. This type of cryptology uses photons (particles/waves of light) and their intrinsic properties to develop an unbreakable cryptosystem. It works by sending photons across an optical link, ensuring high security from hacking. Quantum cryptology uses a series of photons to transmit data over an optical fiber channel. The key is determined by comparing the measurements of the properties of a fraction of these photons. In quantum cryptology, the sender transmits photons through a polarizer using one of the four possible polarizations and bit designations — vertical (one bit), horizontal (zero bit), 45 degrees right (one bit), or 45 degrees left (Zero bit). On the receiver's side, one of the two available beam splitters, horizontal/vertical or diagonal, is used to understand the polarization of each received photon. This continues till the whole stream of photons is received at the other end. The receiver informs the sender about sequence-wise which beam splitter was used to receive the photon. The sender compares this information with the sequence of polarizers used to send the key. The photons read using the wrong beam splitter are discarded, and the resulting sequence of bits becomes the key. What makes this cryptology method highly unsusceptible to hacking or eavesdropping is the state of the photon changes if it is read in transmission, and this change is detected at the endpoints.

A One-Time Password (OTP) is an automatically generated numeric or alphanumeric string of characters that authenticates the user for a single transaction or login session. An OTP is more secure than a static password, especially a user-created password, which can be weak and/or reused across multiple accounts. The future cryptology will be based on the combination of quantum key distribution and one-time password.

7.12 SUMMARY

The chapter initiated with description of cryptology, cryptography and cryptanalysis. The different types of classical ciphers and modern ciphers were discussed in detail. The cryptology for information security is explained followed by drawbacks and concerns in cryptology. The chapter concludes with discussion on quantum cryptology and the future of cryptology.

7.13 OBJECTIVE QUESTIONS

The answer of the multiple-choice questions is marked in **bold**.

1. Cryptography is a subset of ....
   (a) **Cryptology** (b) Cryptanalysis
   (c) None of these (d) All of these
2. What is the output after encryption?
   (a) Plaintext (b) **Cipher text**
   (c) Digital Signature (d) None of these
3. .... is the algorithm for encryption or decryption.
   (a) **Cipher** (b) Cryptology
   (c) Cryptanalysis (d) Cryptography
4. .... is not a traditional cipher.
   (a) **Block** (b) Substitution (c) Transposition (d) Combination
5. .... is a mono-alphabetic cipher.
   (a) **Caesar** (b) Vigenere
   (c) Auto-key (d) One-Time Pad
6. .... is a polygraphic cipher.
   (a) Playfair (b) Hill (c) Two-Square (d) **All of these**
7. .... is a block cipher.
   (a) RC5 (b) RC6 (c) Blowfish (d) **All of these**
8. .... is a stream cipher.
   (a) **RC4** (b) RC5 (c) RC6 (d) All of these
9. .... is the technique of hiding secret data within a file.
   (a) **Steganography** (b) Cryptography
   (c) Cryptology (d) None of these

10. Digital signature is present in ....
    (a) **Modern cryptology** (b) Quantum cryptology
    (c) All of these (d) None of these
11. .... is a post quantum cryptology.
    (a) Code based (b) Multivariate
    (c) Lattice based (d) **All of these**
12. Future cryptology will be based on ....
    (a) OTP (b) QKD
    (c) **QKD+OTP** (d) None of these

7.14 REVIEW QUESTIONS

1. Explain cryptology.
2. Discuss on the development of cryptology.
3. Explain cryptography and cryptanalysis.
4. Discuss on substitution ciphers and its types.
5. Explain various transposition ciphers.
6. Describe combination ciphers.
7. Discuss on various modern ciphers.
8. Explain quantum cipher.
9. Compare classical and modern cryptology.
10. Explain the contribution of cryptology for information security.
11. Discuss the drawbacks and concerns of cryptology.
12. Explain steganography.
13. Discuss quantum cryptology with advantages and disadvantages.
14. Compare quantum and modern cryptology.
15. Discuss future of cryptology.

7.15 ABBREVIATIONS AND SYMBOLS

Abbreviations	Full Form	Description
AES	Advanced Encryption Standard	AES is a symmetric encryption algorithm.
BC	Before Christ	BC refers to the period of time before the birth of Christ
CPU	Central Processing Unit	CPU is the electronic circuitry that executes instructions comprising a computer program.
DES	Data Encryption Standard	DES is a symmetric cryptographic algorithm.
DH	Diffie–Hellman	DH algorithm is a key-exchange protocol that enables two parties communicating over public channel to establish a mutual secret without it being transmitted over the Internet. DH enables the two to use a public key to encrypt and decrypt their conversation or data using symmetric cryptography.

Abbreviations	Full Form	Description
DSA	Digital Signature Algorithm	DSA refers to a standard for digital signatures. It was introduced in 1991 by the National Institute of Standards and Technology (NIST) as a better method of creating digital signatures.
ECC	Elliptic Curve Cryptography	ECC is a key-based technique for encrypting data. ECC focuses on pairs of public and private keys for decryption and encryption of web traffic.
ECDSA	Elliptic Curve Digital Signature Algorithm	ECDSA is a variant of the Digital Signature Algorithm (DSA) which uses elliptic curve cryptography.
OTP	One-Time Pad	OTP is an encryption technique that cannot be cracked, but requires the use of a single-use pre-shared key that is no smaller than the message being sent. In this technique, a plaintext is paired with a random secret key (one-time pad).
QKD	Quantum Key Distribution	Quantum key distribution is a secure communication method which implements a cryptographic protocol involving components of quantum mechanics.
RSA	Rivest, Shamir, Adleman	They are the inventors of public-key encryption technology, which is a public-key cryptosystem for secure data transmission.

7.16 LIST OF FIGURES AND TABLES

The details of figures and tables used in this chapter are as below.

CHAPTER

8 Cryptosystem

CONTENTS

8.1 INTRODUCTION

We will be discussing on cryptosystems and its various types in this chapter. The different possibilities of cryptosystem attacks are also explained.

8.2 CRYPTOSYSTEM

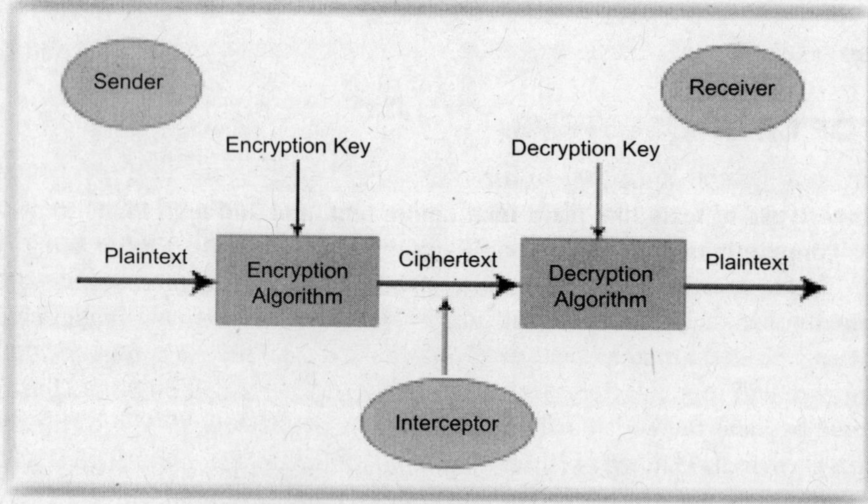

Figure 8.1: Cryptosystem Components

Cryptosystems use a set of procedures known as cryptographic algorithms, or ciphers, to encrypt and decrypt messages to secure communications among computer systems, devices such as smartphones, and applications. A cipher suite uses one algorithm for encryption, another algorithm for message authentication, and another for key exchange. This process, embedded in protocols and written in software that runs on operating systems and networked computer systems, involves public and private key generation for data encryption/decryption, digital signing and verification for message authentication, and key exchange. The cryptosystem is also called cipher system. The various components of a basic cryptosystem are as follows

- **Plaintext:** It is the data to be protected during transmission.
- **Encryption Algorithm:** It is a mathematical process that produces a ciphertext for any given plaintext and encryption key. It is a cryptographic algorithm that takes plaintext and an encryption key as input and produces a ciphertext.
- **Ciphertext:** It is the scrambled version of the plaintext produced by the encryption algorithm using a specific the encryption key. The ciphertext is not guarded. It flows on public channel. It can be intercepted or compromised by anyone who has access to the communication channel.
- **Decryption Algorithm:** It is a mathematical process, that produces a unique plaintext for any given ciphertext and decryption key. It is a cryptographic algorithm that takes a ciphertext and a decryption key as input, and outputs a plaintext. The decryption algorithm essentially reverses the encryption algorithm and is thus closely related to it.
- **Encryption Key:** It is a value that is known to the sender. The sender inputs the encryption key into the encryption algorithm along with the plaintext in order to compute the ciphertext.
- **Decryption Key:** It is a value that is known to the receiver. The decryption key is related to the encryption key, but is not always identical to it. The receiver inputs the decryption key into the decryption algorithm along with the ciphertext in order to compute the plaintext. For a given cryptosystem, a collection of all possible decryption keys is called a key space. An interceptor (an attacker) is an unauthorized entity who attempts to determine the plaintext. He can see the ciphertext and may know the decryption algorithm. He should not know the decryption key.

8.3 TYPES OF CRYPTOSYSTEMS

A cryptosystem is a system consisting of an encryption algorithm, a decryption algorithm, and well-defined three types of texts like plain text, cipher text, and key text. Plaintext is the text in a language that is commonly understood among a larger group of people. Cipher text is the text in a secret language. This is known as cryptogram also. A key text is a string of characters used within an encryption algorithm for altering data so that it appears random. For a given key text the encryption algorithm will map a plaintext to a uniquely determined ciphertext. For the corresponding key text, the decryption algorithm will map the ciphertext to the uniquely determined plaintext. The cryptosystem may be performed by hand methods ("hand cipher"), by machine methods ("machine cipher"), or by software. Cryptosystem is also known as cipher system. Based on modern cryptology, cryptosystems can be classified as asymmetric key, symmetric key and keyless (Hash functions).

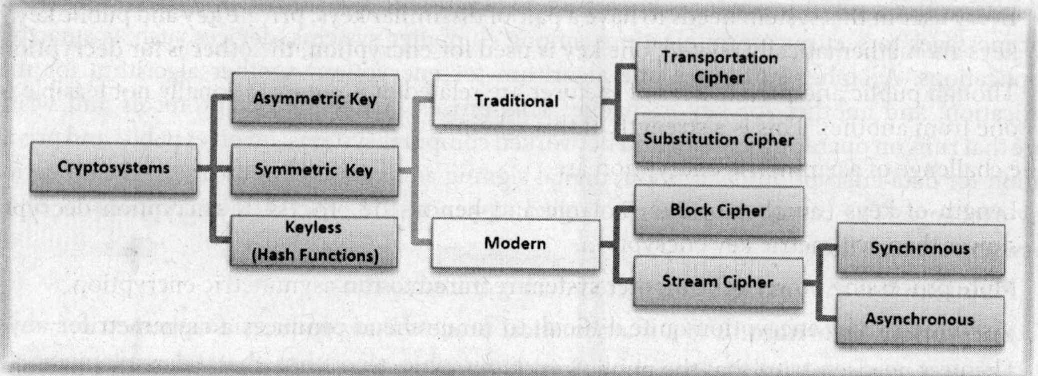

Figure 8.2: Classification of Cryptosystems

8.3.1 Asymmetric Key

Asymmetric key cryptosystem was invented in the 20th century to come over the necessity of pre-shared secret key between communicating persons. In this cryptosystem, different keys are used for encrypting and decrypting the information and hence the name asymmetric key encryption. This is also known as public key encryption. Though the keys are different, they are mathematically related and hence, retrieving the plaintext by decrypting ciphertext is feasible.

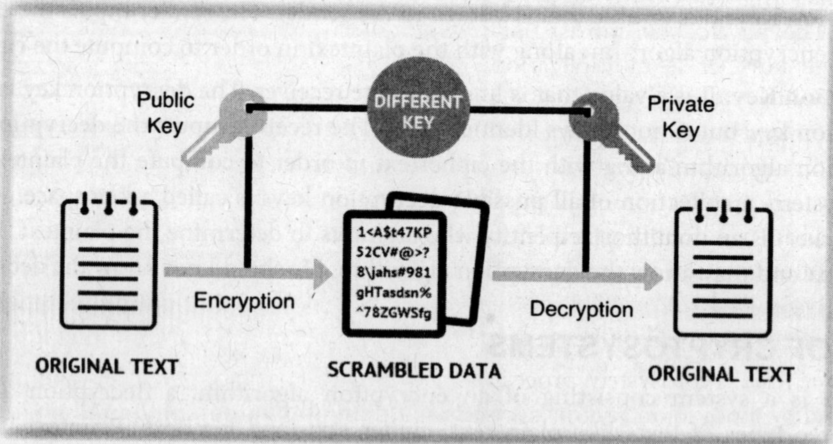

Figure 8.3: Asymmetric Key Cryptosystem

Asymmetric-key cryptosystem algorithms use a pair of keys, a public key associated with the sender for encrypting messages and a private key that only the originator knows for decrypting that information. Public key and private key are different. Even if the public key is known by everyone the intended receiver can only decode it because he alone knows the private key. It requires to put the public key in public repository and the private key as a well-guarded secret. Hence, this scheme of encryption is also called public key encryption. Features of this asymmetric cryptosystem are

- Every user in this system needs to have a pair of dissimilar keys, private key and public key. These keys are mathematically related, one key is used for encryption, the other is for decryption.
- Though public and private keys of the user are related, it is computationally not feasible to find one from another. This is a strength of this scheme.

The challenge of asymmetric encryption are

- Length of keys (number of bits) is large and hence, the process of encryption-decryption is slower than symmetric key encryption.
- More processing power of computer system required to run asymmetric encryption.
- Asymmetric key encryption quite difficult to comprehend compared to symmetric.
- The user needs to trust that the public key that is using in communications with a person really is the public key of that person and has not been spoofed by a malicious third party.

The cryptosystems are known based on the cipher used in that. The commonly known asymmetric cryptosystems are shown in figure 8.4. Few of these asymmetric cryptosystems are explained below.

- **RSA Cryptosystem:** RSA is one of the oldest asymmetric cryptosystem algorithms that is used for secure data transmission. The acronym RSA comes from the surnames of Rivest, Shamir, and Adleman,. who publicly described this algorithm in 1977. This is widely used in Internet. The idea of RSA is based on the fact that it is difficult to factorize a large integer. The public key consists of two numbers where one number is multiplication of two large prime numbers. Private key is also derived from the same two prime numbers. If somebody can factorize the large number, the private key is compromised. Therefore, encryption strength totally lies on the key size and if we double or triple the key size, the strength of encryption increases exponentially. RSA keys are typically 1024 or 2048 bits long and seems to be an impossible task to break that, but experts believe that 1024 bit keys could be broken in the near future.

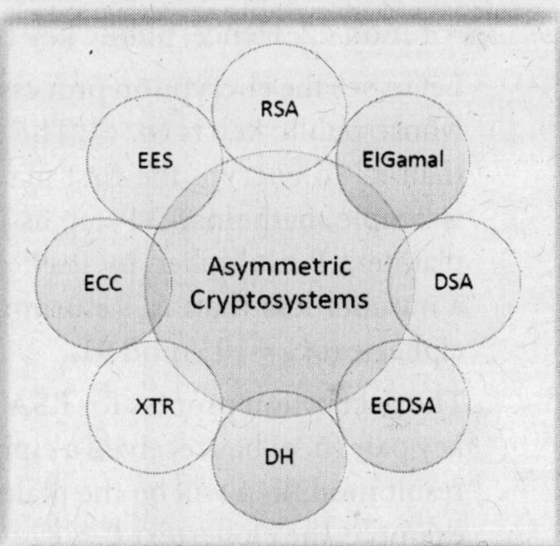

Figure 8.4: Types of Asymmetric Cryptosystems

We will see RSA cryptosystem process. First is the generation of public key and private key. This is followed by encryption and decryption algorithms. The process followed in the generation of keys is described below.

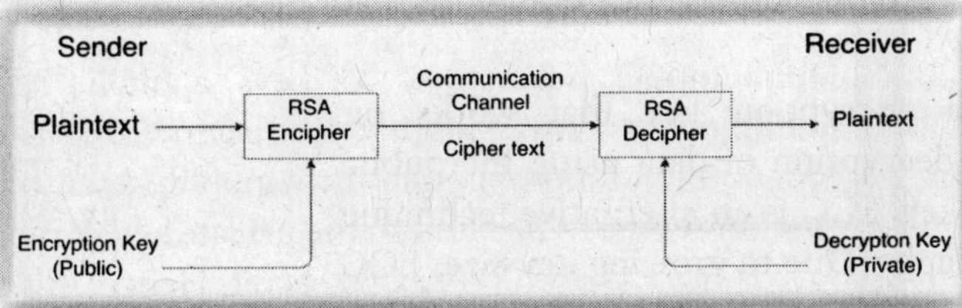

Figure 8.5: RSA Cryptosystem

Generate the RSA modulus – Select two large primes, p and q. Calculate n = p*q. Find derived Number (e). Number e must be greater than 1 and less than (p – 1) (q – 1). There must be no common factor for e and (p – 1)(q – 1) except for 1.

Generate public key – The pair of numbers (n, e) form the RSA public key and is made public.

Generate private key – Unique private key number d is calculated from p, q, and e. Number d is the inverse of e modulo (p – 1)(q – 1). This means that d is the number less than (p – 1) (q – 1) such that when multiplied by e, it is equal to 1 modulo (p - 1)(q - 1). This relationship is written mathematically as ed = 1 mod (p – 1) (q – 1). The Extended Euclidean Algorithm takes p, q, and e as input and gives d as output.

An example of generating RSA key pair is given below. Let two primes be p = 7 and q = 13. Thus, modulus n = pq = 7 × 13 = 91. Select e = 5, which is a valid choice since there is no number that is common factor of 5 and (p – 1)(q – 1) = 6 × 12 = 72, except for 1. The pair of numbers (n, e) = (91, 5) forms the public key and can be made available to anyone whom we wish to be able to send us encrypted messages. Input p = 7, q = 13, and e = 5 to the Extended Euclidean Algorithm. The output will be d = 29. Check that the d calculated is correct by computing de = 29 × 5 = 145 = 1 mod 72. Hence, public key is (91, 5) and private keys is (91, 29).

Let us see the encryption process. Suppose the sender wish to send some text message to someone whose public key is (n, e). The sender then represents the plaintext as a series of numbers less than n. To encrypt the first plaintext P, which is a number modulo n. The encryption process is simple mathematical step as C = Pe mod n. In other words, the ciphertext C is equal to the plaintext P multiplied by itself e times and then reduced modulo n. This means that C is also a number less than n. Returning to our key generation example with plaintext P = 10, we get ciphertext C = 105 mod 91.

The decryption process for RSA is also very straightforward. Suppose that the receiver of public-key pair (n, e) has received a ciphertext C. Receiver raises C to the power of his private key d. The result modulo n will be the plaintext P. Plaintext = Cd mod n. Returning again to our numerical example, the ciphertext C = 82 would get decrypted to number 10 using private key 29 Plaintext = 8229 mod 91 = 10.

- **Elliptic Curve Cryptosystem:** Elliptic-Curve Cryptosystem (ECC) is an approach to public-key cryptology based on the algebraic structure of elliptic curves over finite fields. ECC, was introduced independently by two mathematicians named Neal Koblitz and Victor S. Miller in 1985. As the name implies, ECC is based on mathematical equations that describe ellipses.

  ECC is a data encryption key that works on encryption and decryption of data using the public key and private key. ECC is an alternative technique of RSA cryptography. Due to growing key size, ECC came into focus which has a smaller key size with enhanced security performance. ECC works with public key cryptographic systems and generates keys

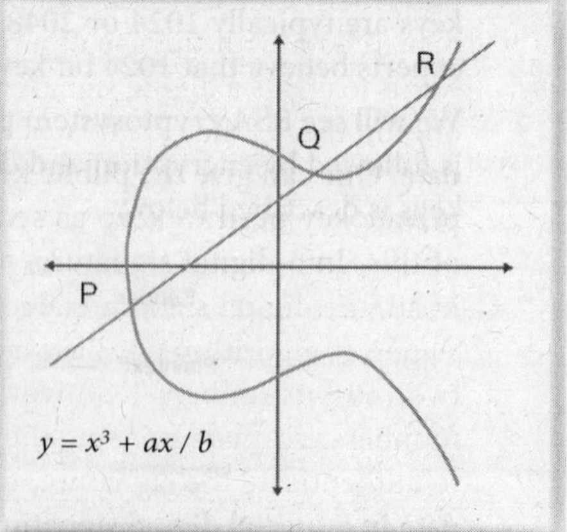

Figure 8.6: Elliptic Curve for ECC

that are difficult to crack for hackers. ECC works on $y^2=x^3 + ax + b$ equation. ECC has smaller key sizes starting from 160, 224, 256, 384, and 521-bit sizes.

ECC allows smaller keys compared to non-EC cryptography to provide equivalent security. ECC is based on sets of numbers that are associated with mathematical objects called elliptic curves. It is believed that the discrete logarithm problem is much harder when applied to points on an elliptic curve. Also, an equivalent security level can be obtained with shorter keys if we use elliptic curve-based variants. The shorter keys result in two benefits such as ease of key management and efficient computation. These benefits make elliptic-curve-based variants of encryption scheme highly attractive for application where computing resources are constrained.

- **ElGamal Cryptosystem:** ElGamal cryptosystem is based on the discrete logarithm problem having the difficulty of finding discrete logarithm in a cyclic group. The table provides a brief comparison between RSA and ElGamal schemes.

Table 8.1: RSA and ElGamal Comparison

Criteria	RSA	ElGamal
Number of variables using	Two	Three
Encryption Speed	Fast	Slow
Encryption Speed	Slow	Fast
Key length for a particular security level	Long	Short
Popularity	High	Low

- **Digital Signature Algorithm Cryptosystem:** Digital Signature Algorithm (DSA) is adopted as a Federal Information Processing Standard for digital signatures by NIST in FIPS 186-4. The procedure followed when using DSA is not as simple as using a private and public key at the start and end of the transmission, respectively. It generates two digital signatures by applying complex and unique mathematical functions. Digital signatures work on the principle of two mutually authenticating cryptographic keys. Signatures are based on public/private key pairs. With a public-key algorithm like RSA, one can create a mathematically linked private key and public key. One can sign a digital message with his private key. A person can encrypt signature related data with the use of a private key. The private key should always be with a person who wants to create a digital signature. Both the public and the private key can always be derived from one another as they are related mathematically. Signer's public key is the only way to decrypt this data. One can give the public key to anyone who needs verification of the signer's signature. The private key need to keep as secret as one can generate signature on a document with the help of this. In a digital signature, validly is only assured by public and private keys. On the other hand, the digital signature algorithm does not use a private key to encrypt data. Also, a digital signature algorithm does use a public key to decrypt this data. To create a digital signature with two 160-bit numbers, DSA works on the principle of a unique mathematical function. These two numbers are made by using the private key and the message digest. As the public key is not used to authenticate the signature, the verification process is complex. Both keys are used to secure data in a special digital signature algorithm for further security assurance. Now, a hash function

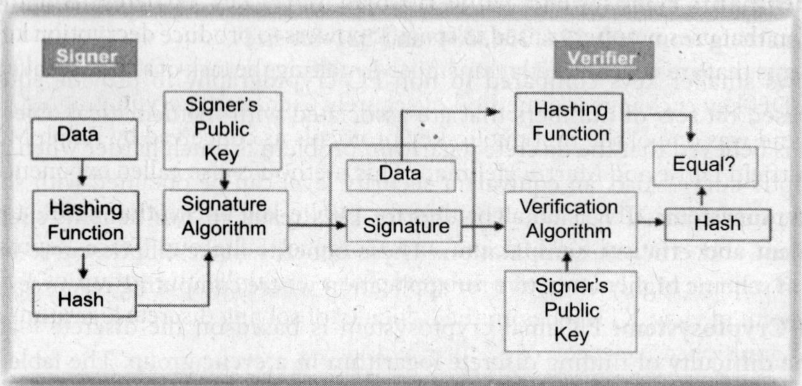

Figure 8.7: Digital Signature Algorithm process

is used to create a message digest. The generated message digest, along with the DSA algorithm, is what gives the digital signature. This signature is then sent along with the message. At the receiving end, the same hash function is used to authenticate the source and the data.

- **Elliptic Curve Digital Signature Algorithm Cryptosystem:** Elliptic Curve Digital Signature Algorithm (ECDSA) is a Digital Signature Algorithm (DSA) which uses keys derived from Elliptic Curve Cryptography (ECC). This is mainly used by Bitcoin. ECDSA functionally provides the same outcome as other DSAs, but ECDSA is based on the more efficient ECC. ECDSA requires smaller keys to provide equivalent security and is therefore more efficient.

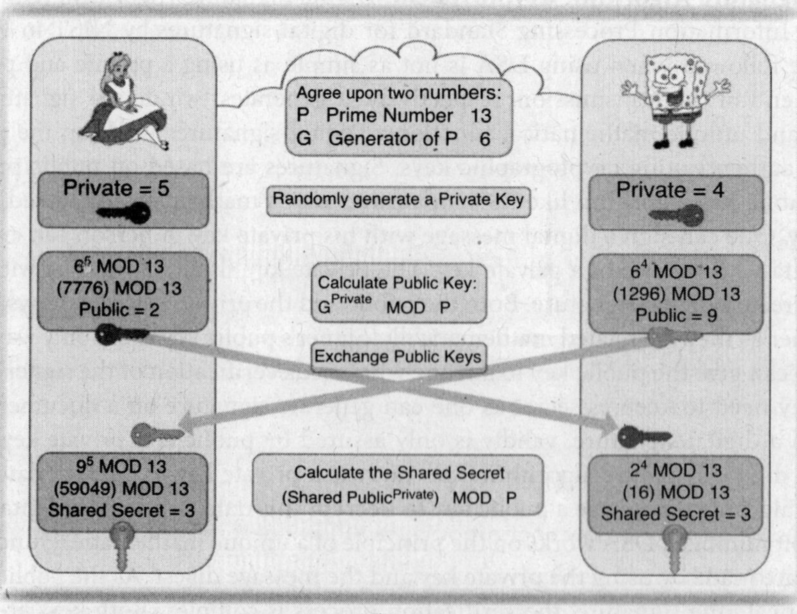

Figure 8.8: Steps of the Diffie-Hellman exchange between Sender and Receiver

- **Diffie-Hellman Cryptosystem:** Diffie-Hellman (DH) key exchange is a method of digital encryption that uses numbers raised to specific powers to produce decryption keys on the basis of components that are never directly transmitted, making the task of a code breaker mathematically difficult. DH key exchange is a method of securely exchanging cryptographic keys over a public channel and was one of the first public-key protocols as conceived by Ralph Merkle and named after Whitfield Diffie and Martin Hellman. This method is also called exponential key exchange.
- **XTR Cryptosystem:** XTR is an algorithm for public-key encryption. XTR stands for 'ECSTR', which is an abbreviation for Efficient and Compact Subgroup Trace Representation. It is a method to represent elements of a subgroup of a multiplicative group of a finite field. From security point of view, XTR relies on the difficulty of solving discrete logarithm related problems in the full multiplicative group of a finite field.
- **EES Cryptosystem:** Escrowed Encryption Standard (EES) is a voluntary alternative to the original federal encryption standard used to safeguard unclassified information.

8.3.2 Symmetric Cryptosystem

This cryptosystem is also referred to as secret key as well as single key cryptosystem. Prior to 1970, all cryptosystems employed symmetric key encryption. Even today, its relevance is very high and it is being used extensively in many cryptosystems. It is very unlikely that this encryption will fade away, as it has certain advantages over asymmetric key encryption.

It has an encryption system where the sender and receiver of message use a single common key to encrypt and decrypt messages. These systems are faster and simpler but the problem is that sender and receiver have to exchange key in a secure manner. The features of symmetric key cryptosystem are as follows.

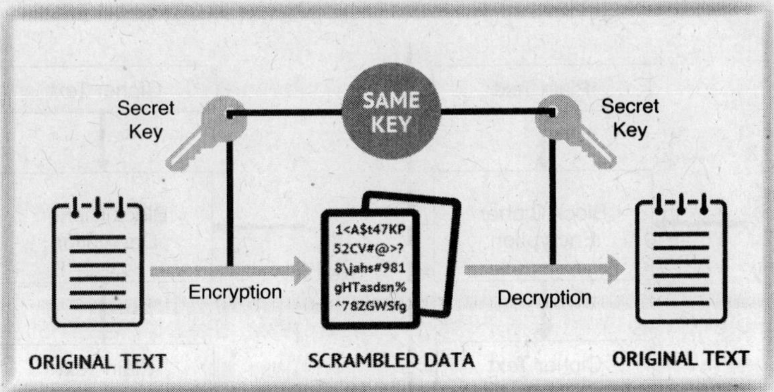

Figure 8.9: Symmetric Cryptosystem

- Persons using symmetric key encryption must share a common key to exchange information.
- Keys need to be changed regularly to prevent any attack on the system.
- Length of key in this encryption is smaller and hence, process of encryption-decryption is faster than asymmetric key encryption.

- Processing power of computer system required to run symmetric algorithm is less.

The challenge of symmetric key cryptosystem is mentioned below.

- Before communication, both the sender and the receiver need to agree on a secret symmetric key. It requires a secure key establishment mechanism in place.
- A robust mechanism is required to exchange the key between the communicating parties. As keys are required to be exchanged regularly, this mechanism becomes expensive and cumbersome.
- As the sender and the receiver use the same symmetric key, there is an implicit requirement that the sender and the receiver 'trust' each other like informing the sender, if receiver has lost the key to avoid reaching that in wrong hands.

The symmetric cryptosystem can be generally classified as traditional and modern. The transportation and substitution cryptosystems are considered as traditional while the block cipher and stream cipher are considered as modern.

- **Transposition Cryptosystem:** In transposition cryptosystem, encryption is by which the positions held by units of plaintext are shifted according to a regular system, so that the ciphertext constitutes a permutation of the plaintext.
- **Substitution Cryptosystem:** In substitution cryptosystem, encryption and decryption will be with substitution cipher.
- **Block Cipher Cryptosystem:** Block ciphers cryptosystem encrypt or decrypt a group of plaintext symbols as one block. This method applies a deterministic algorithm along with a symmetric key to encrypt a block of text, rather than encrypting one bit at a time.

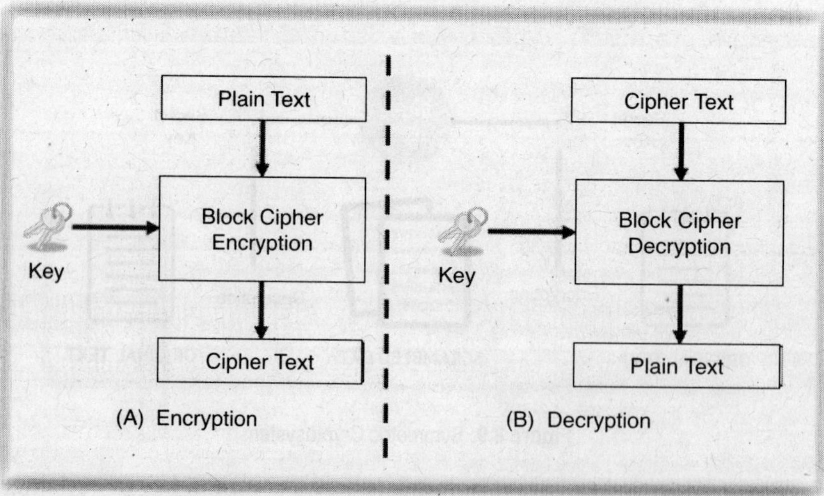

Figure 8.10: Block Cipher Encryption and Decryption

- **Stream Cipher Cryptosystem:** Stream cipher cryptosystem convert one symbol of plaintext directly into a symbol of ciphertext. A stream cipher is a symmetric key cipher where plaintext digits are combined with a pseudorandom cipher digit stream (keystream). In a stream cipher, each plaintext digit is encrypted one at a time with the corresponding digit of the keystream, to give a digit of the ciphertext stream.

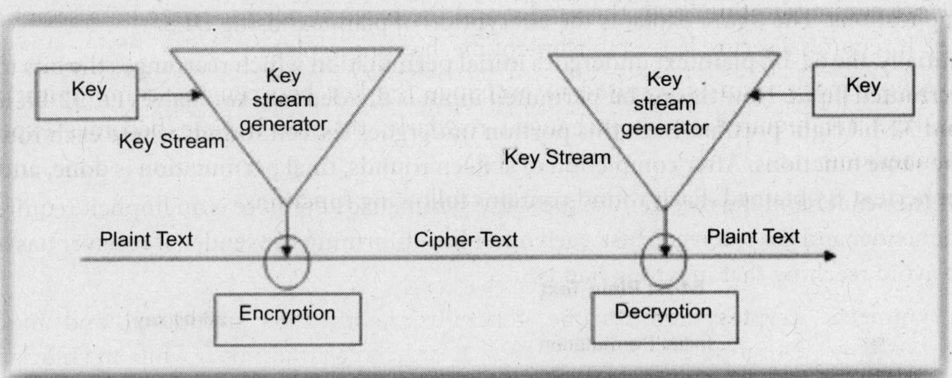

Figure 8.11: Stream Cipher Cryptosystem

Stream ciphers are classified as synchronous and asynchronous

- **Synchronous Stream Cipher Cryptosystem:** A synchronous stream cipher is a stream cipher, in which the keystream is generated independently of the plaintext and of the ciphertext. The keystream is usually produced by a pseudorandom generator, parameterized by a key, which is the secret key of the whole scheme.
- **Asynchronous Stream Cipher Cryptosystem:** In asynchronous, the keystream depends on the secret key of the scheme, but also of a fixed number. This is also called self-synchronous stream cipher.

The different types of symmetric cryptosystem based on the ciphers used are shown in the figure.

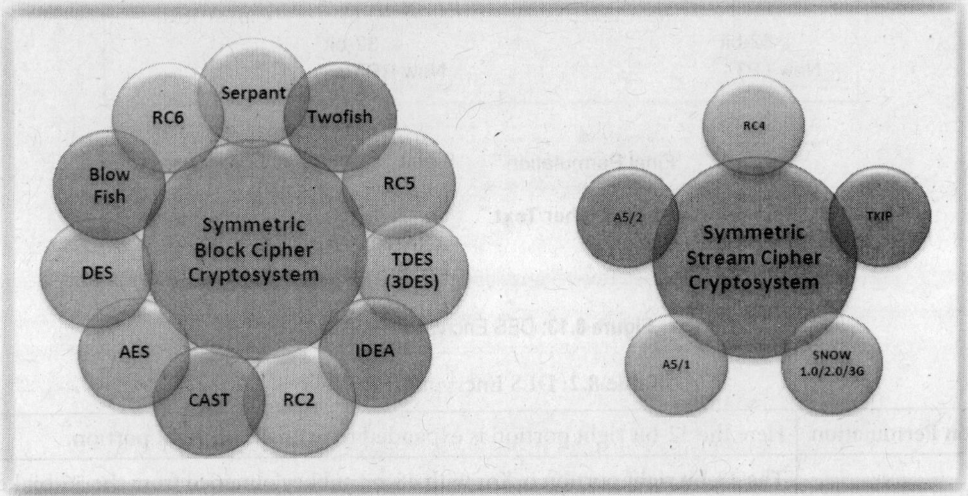

Figure 8.12: Various Symmetric Cryptosystems

- **Data Encryption Standard:** The Data Encryption Standard (DES) algorithm is a symmetric-key block cipher created in the early 1970s by an IBM team and adopted by the National Institute of Standards and Technology (NIST). Its short key length of 56 bits makes it insecure for applications. The figure explains the encryption of plaintext using DES.

  Initially, the 64-bit plaintext undergoes initial permutation which rearranges the bits to get 64-bit permuted input. Now this 64 bit permuted input is divided into two halves i.e. 32-bit left portion and 32-bit right portion. Both this portion undergoes sixteen rounds where each round follows the same functions. After completion of sixteen rounds, final permutation is done, and the 64-bit ciphertext is obtained. Each round contains following functions.

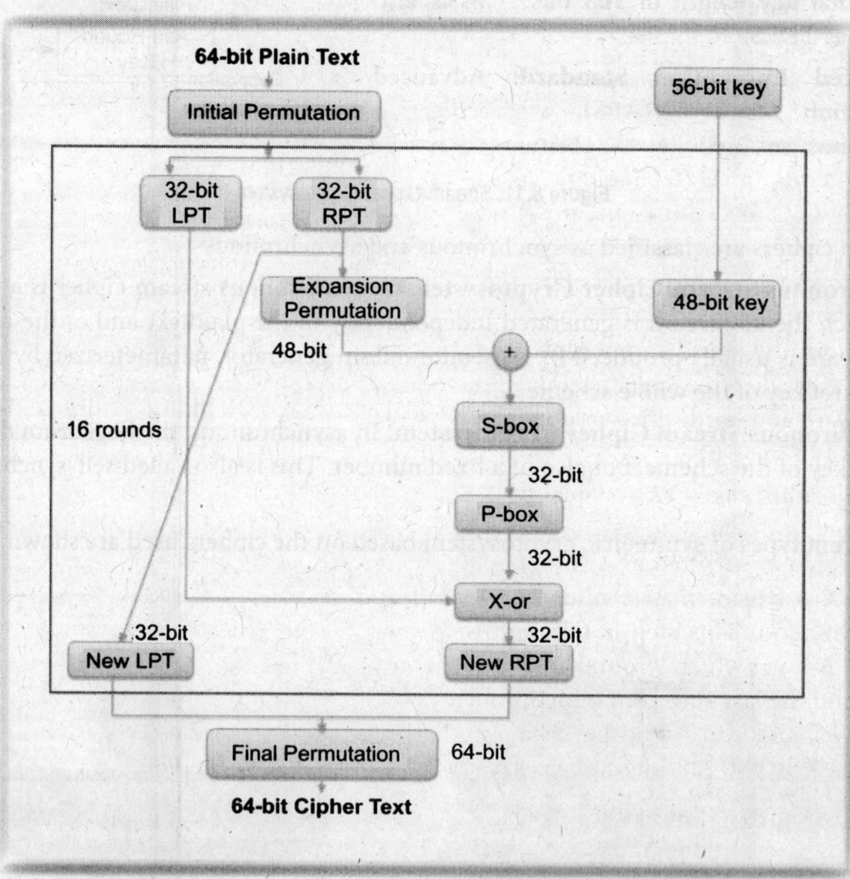

Figure 8.13: DES Encryption Process

Table 8.2: DES Encryption Process

Expansion Permutation	Here the 32-bit right portion is expanded to form 48-bit right portion.
Xor	The 48-bit right portion is Xor with 48-bit subkey obtained from the 56-bit key, which results in the 48-bit output.
S-box	The 48-bit output obtained by Xor step is reduced to 32-bit again.

Expansion Permutation	Here the 32-bit right portion is expanded to form 48-bit right portion.
P-box	Here the 32-bit result obtained from S-box is again permuted, which result in 32-bit permuted output.

- **Triple Data Encryption Standard:** Triple Data Encryption Standard (3DES), is a symmetric-key block cipher which applies the DES cipher algorithm three times to each data block. Part of what 3DES does is to protect against brute force attacks. The original DES symmetric encryption algorithm specified the use of 56-bit keys. In 1999, to protect against practical brute force attacks, 3DES adopted the use of three distinct DES keys, for a total key length of 168 bits. This is also known as TDES.
- **Advanced Encryption Standard:** Advanced Encryption Standard (AES), a specification established in 2001 by the National Institute of Standards and Technology as a Federal Information Processing Standard (FIPS 197), to protect sensitive information. AES is a symmetric block cipher to protect classified information. AES is implemented in software and hardware throughout the world to encrypt sensitive data. AES is a royalty-free specification implemented in software and hardware worldwide. AES is the successor to the DES.

  AES algorithm takes 128-bit plaintext and 128-bit secret key which together forms a 128-bit block which is depicted as 4 X 4 square matrix. This 4 X 4 square matrix undergoes an initial transformation. This step is followed by the 10 rounds. Among which 9 round contain following stages and the last 10th round involves sub bytes, shift rows, and add round keys stages only and provides 16 bytes (128-bit) ciphertext.

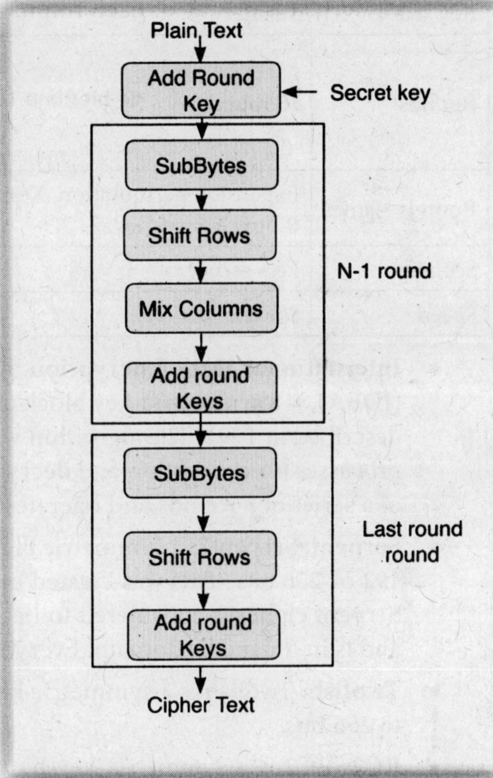

Figure 8.14: Advanced Encryption Standard Process

Table 8.3: Advanced Encryption Standard Process

Sub bytes	It uses S-box by which it performs byte by byte substitution of the entire block (matrix).
Shift rows	Rows of the matrix are shifted.
Mix columns	Columns are of the matrix are shuffled from right to left.
Add round keys	Here, the Xor of the current block and the expanded key is performed.

The table 8.4 compares various parameters of DES and AES

Table 8.4: DES comparison with AES

Parameters	DES	AES
Basic	Data block is divided into two halves.	Data block is processed as a single matrix.
Principle	Works on feistel cipher structure.	Works on substitution and permutation principle.
Plaintext	Plain text is of 64 bits	Plain text can be of 128,192, or 256 bits
Key size	Smaller	Larger
Rounds	16 rounds	10 rounds for 128-bit algorithm 12 rounds for 192-bit algorithm 14 rounds for 256-bit algorithm
Rounds Names	Expansion permutation, Xor, S-box, P-box, Xor and swap.	Sub bytes, shift rows, mix columns, add round keys.
Security	Less secure.	More secure.
Speed	Slower	Faster

- **International Data Encryption Algorithm:** The International Data Encryption Algorithm (IDEA), is a symmetric-key block cipher designed by James Massey and Xuejia Lai and was first described in 1991. The algorithm was intended as a replacement for the DES. IDEA uses similar processes for encryption and decryption, with some inverted ordering of round keys. It consists of a series of 8 rounds and operates on 64-bit blocks using a 128-bit key.
- **Serpent:** Serpent is a symmetric block cipher with block length of 128 bits and key length of 128, 192 or 256 bits. This was created in 1998 by Ross Anderson, Eli Biham and Lars Knudsen. The Serpent cipher is considered to be stronger but also slower than AES. It has not been patented and is in the public domain. Everybody can use it in their software without any limitations.
- **Twofish:** Twofish is a symmetric key block cipher with a block size of 128 bits and key sizes up to 256 bits.
- **RC2:** RC2 is a symmetric-key block cipher designed by Ron Rivest in 1987. "RC" stands for "Ron's Code" or "Rivest Cipher". Other ciphers designed by Rivest are RC4, RC5 and RC6. It is faster than DES and is designed as a "drop-in" replacement for DES. RC2 block size is 8 bytes. This means that the input data is first divided into blocks of 8 bytes and then each of them is processed separately. Each data block is treated as four words, each word has 2 bytes. The array of four words is presented as R[0] R[1] R[2] R[3]. Both encryption and decryption take this array as input and modify the four words. The output is returned in the same array.
- **RC5:** RC5 is a symmetric key block encryption algorithm designed by Ron Rivest in 1994. It is notable for being simple, fast. The fastness is due to the reason that, it uses only basic computer operations like XOR, shift, etc. RC5 is a block cipher and addresses two word blocks at a time.

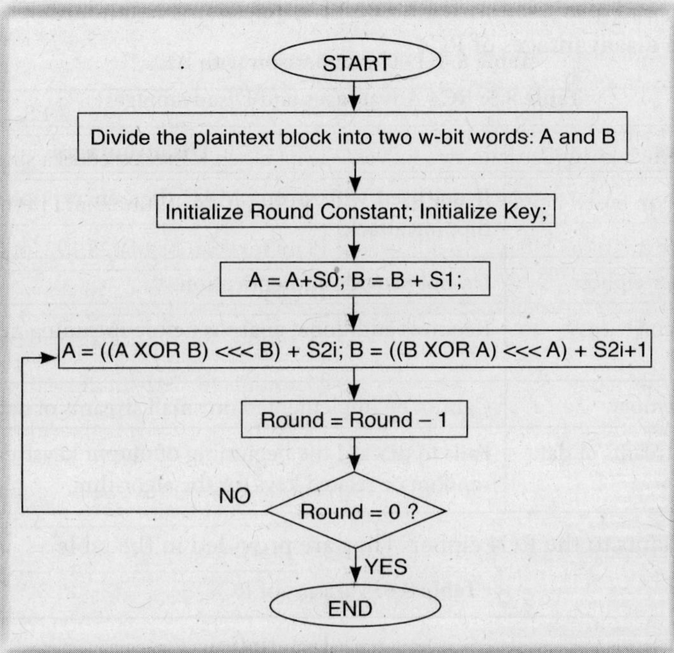

Figure 8.15: Flow Chart for RC5 Encryption Algorithm

- **RC6:** RC6 is a fast block cipher. It was developed based on RC5 and does its job quicker than RC5 due to more registers. RC6 uses integer multiplication in its algorithmic computation. RC6 is also rotation-dependent on every word bit, as opposed to the insignificant bits with RC5. It is derived from RC5, and is a symmetric key block cipher. This is patented by RSA Security. It uses a block size of 128 bits and has keys sizes of 128, 192, 256 bits and up to 2040-bits.
- **CAST:** The CAST encryption algorithm belongs to a class of private key block ciphers which are composed of substitution boxes (S-boxes) with fewer input bits than output bits. CAST-256 (or CAST6) is a symmetric-key block cipher published in 1998. It is an extension of an earlier cipher, CAST-128 (CAST5). Both were designed according to the "CAST" design methodology invented by Carlisle Adams and Stafford Tavares. Howard Heys and Michael Wiener also contributed to the design.
- **Blowfish:** Blowfish is a symmetric-key block cipher, designed in 1993 by Bruce Schneier and included in many cipher suites and encryption products. Blowfish provides a good encryption rate in software.

The various commonly using cryptosystems with stream cipher is as below

- **RC4:** RC4 is a symmetric synchronous stream cipher. It was invented by Ron Rivest in 1987 for RSA security. It is a stream cipher and operate on a stream of data byte by byte. RC4 stream cipher is one of the most widely used stream ciphers because of its simplicity and speed of operation. It is a variable key-size stream cipher with byte-oriented operations. It uses either 64 bit or 128-bit key sizes. It is generally used in applications such as Secure Socket Layer (SSL), Transport Layer

Security (TSL), and also used in IEEE 802.11 wireless LAN standard. The table brings out the advantages and disadvantages of RC4.

Table 8.5: RC4 Advantages and Disadvantages

Advantages	Disadvantages
Simple to use.	If not used with strong MAC then encryption is vulnerable to a bit-flipping attack.
Fast as compared to other ciphers.	Do not provide authentication.
Strong in coding and easy to implement.	Requires additional analysis before including new systems.
Do not require more memory.	Cannot be implemented on small streams of data.
Implemented on large streams of data.	Fails to discard the beginning of output keystream or fails to use non-random or related keys for the algorithm.

There are four variants to the RC4 cipher. They are provided in the table.

Table 8.6: Variants of RC4

RC4 Variant	Description
Spritz	Spritz is used to create cryptographic hash functions and deterministic random bit generator.
RC4A	This is a variant that was proposed to be faster and stronger than the average RC4 cipher. RC4A was found to have not truly random numbers used in its cipher.
VMPC	Variably Modified Permutation Composition (VMPC) is a version of RC4 that was found to have not truly random numbers used in its cipher, like RC4A.
RC4A+	RC4A+ is an advanced version of RC4A that is longer and more complex than RC4 and RC4A, but is stronger as a result of its complexity as well.

- **TKIP:** TKIP (Temporal Key Integrity Protocol) is a stream cipher symmetric cryptosystem. It provides per-packet key mixing a message integrity and re-keying mechanism.
- **A5/1:** This is a stream cipher used to provide over-the-air communication privacy in the GSM cellular telephone standard. It was initially kept secret, but became public knowledge through leaks and reverse engineering.
- **A5/2:** This is a stream cipher used to provide voice privacy in the GSM cellular telephone protocol. It was designed in 1993 as a replacement for A5/1, to allow the GSM standard to be exported to countries with restrictions on the import of products with cryptographic security features. The cipher is based on a combination of four linear feedback shift registers with irregular clocking and a non-linear combiner.
- **SNOW 1.0/2.0/3G:** These are synchronous stream ciphers developed by Thomas Johansson and Patrik Ekdahl of Lund University. This is the cryptosystem using in 4G LTE mobile network.

A comparison of basic key properties of symmetric and asymmetric cryptosystems is provided in the table.

Table 8.7: Symmetric and Asymmetric Cryptosystem Comparison

Criteria	Symmetric encryption	Asymmetric encryption
Relation between keys	Same	Different, but mathematically related
Encryption key	Symmetric	Public
Decryption key	Symmetric	Private

Due to the advantages and disadvantage of both the systems, symmetric key and asymmetric key cryptosystems are often used together in a practical information security system.

8.3.3 Hash Functions Cryptosystem

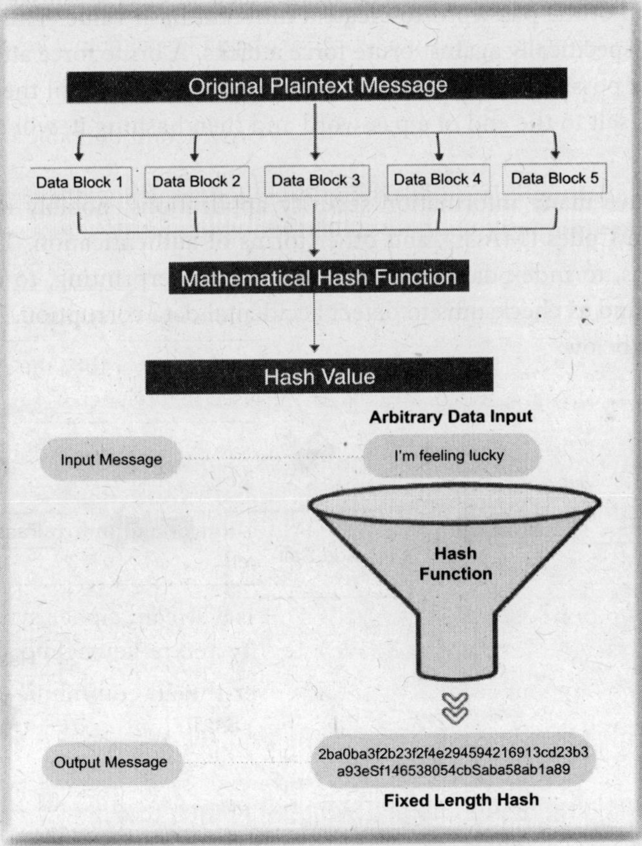

Figure 8.16: Working of Hash Function

A hash function is a mathematical function that converts a numerical input value into another compressed numerical value. A deterministic algorithm with a particular input, will always produce the same output, with the underlying machine always passing through the same sequence of states. The hashing algorithm takes the infinite arbitrary input of bits, applies calculations to them and gives a final output of a finite number of bits. The primary idea lies in using a deterministic algorithm that can take in one input and generate a fixed length string every time. Consequently, the same input will always give the same output. Values returned by a hash function are called hash values.

One way hash function is a mathematical function that generates a fingerprint of the input, but there is no way to get back to the original input. If the input is the same then the hash is always the same. If it changes even by one character, the output hash will be completely different. A hash can be used to verify that input A is identical to input B but cannot be used to get the input back from the output like other mathematical encryptions. A one-way hash function has many names such as compression function, contraction function, message digest, digital fingerprint, cryptographic checksum, message integrity check, hash value and manipulation detection code. This is central to modern cryptography.

Salting is a concept that typically pertains to password hashing. Essentially, it's a unique value that can be added to the end of the password to create a different hash value. This adds a layer of security to the hashing process, specifically against brute force attacks. A brute force attack is where a computer or botnet attempt every possible combination of letters and numbers until the password is found. The idea is that by adding a salt to the end of a password and then hashing it, will complicate the password cracking process.

Hash functions have many information-security applications, notably in digital signatures like Message Authentication Codes (MACs), and other forms of authentication. They can also be used as ordinary hash functions, to index data in hash tables, for fingerprinting, to detect duplicate data or uniquely identify files, and as checksums to detect accidental data corruption. The applications of hash functions are explained below.

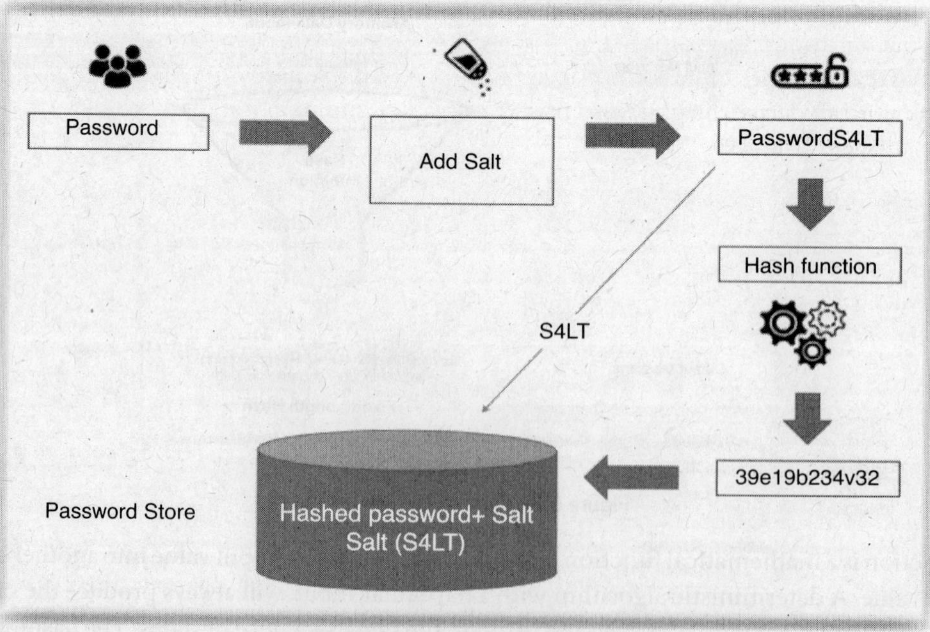

Figure 8.17: Salting in Hashing

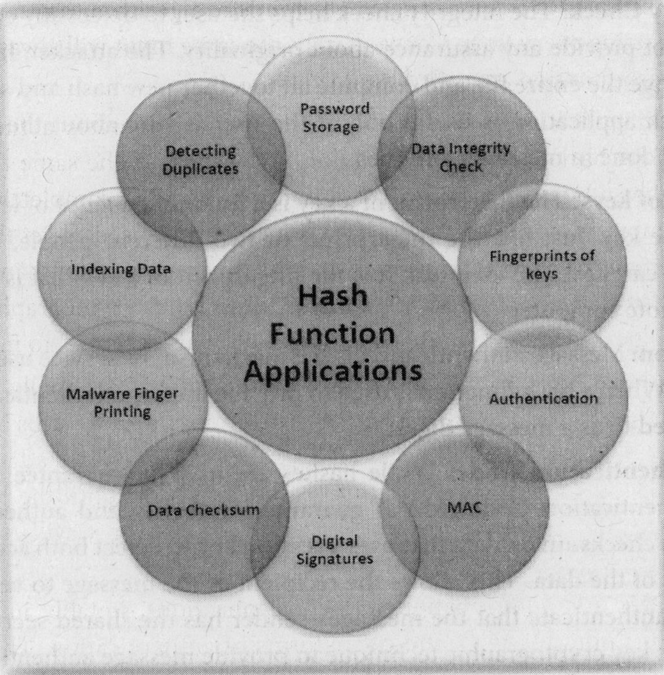

Figure 8.18: Hash Function Applications

- **Password Storage:** Hash functions provide protection to password storage. Hashing a password is quick and easy to store. Instead of storing the user's password as plain text, which is open for anyone to read, it is stored as a hash which is impossible for a human to read. An intruder can only see the hashes of passwords, even if he accessed the password. He can neither logon using hash nor can derive the password from hash value since hash function possesses the property of pre-image resistance.

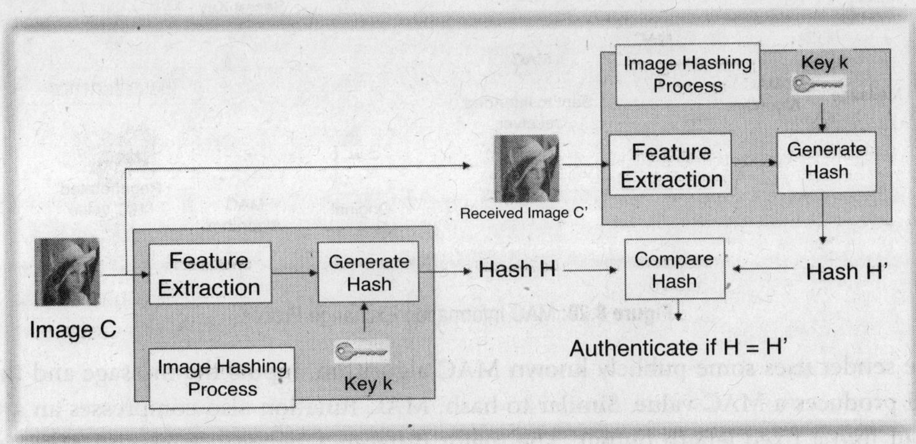

Figure 8.19: Hash Function for Image Authentication

- **Data Integrity Check:** The integrity check helps the user to detect any changes made to original file. It does not provide any assurance about originality. The attacker, instead of modifying file data, can change the entire file and compute all together new hash and send to the receiver. The integrity check application is useful only if the user is sure about the originality of file. This checks can be done in messages and files.
- **Fingerprints of keys:** The fingerprint of a key is a unique sequence of letters and numbers used to identify the key. Just like the fingerprints of two different people, the fingerprints of two different keys can never be identical. It is the fingerprint of a key that is verified when trying to login to a remote computer.
- **Authentication:** Message authentication is the mechanism or service used to verify the integrity of a message. When a hash function is used to provide message authentication, the hash function value is referred to as a message digest.
- **Message Authentication Code:** While hashes are used to guarantee the integrity of data, a Message Authentication Code (MAC) guarantees integrity and authentication. A MAC is a cryptographic checksum on data that uses a session key to detect both accidental and intentional modifications of the data. This allows the recipient of the message to verify the integrity of the message and authenticate that the message's sender has the shared secret key. MAC algorithm is a symmetric key cryptographic technique to provide message authentication. For establishing MAC process, the sender and receiver share a symmetric key. Essentially, a MAC is an encrypted checksum generated on the underlying message that is sent along with a message to ensure message authentication. The process of using MAC for authentication is shown in the figure.

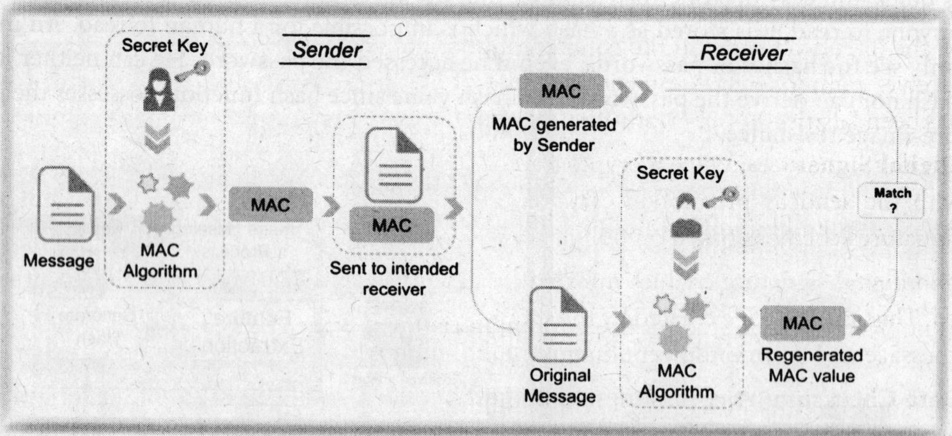

Figure 8.20: MAC Information Exchange Process

The sender uses some publicly known MAC algorithm, inputs the message and the secret key and produces a MAC value. Similar to hash, MAC function also compresses an arbitrary long input into a fixed length output. The major difference between hash and MAC is that MAC uses secret key during the compression. The sender forwards the message along with the MAC.

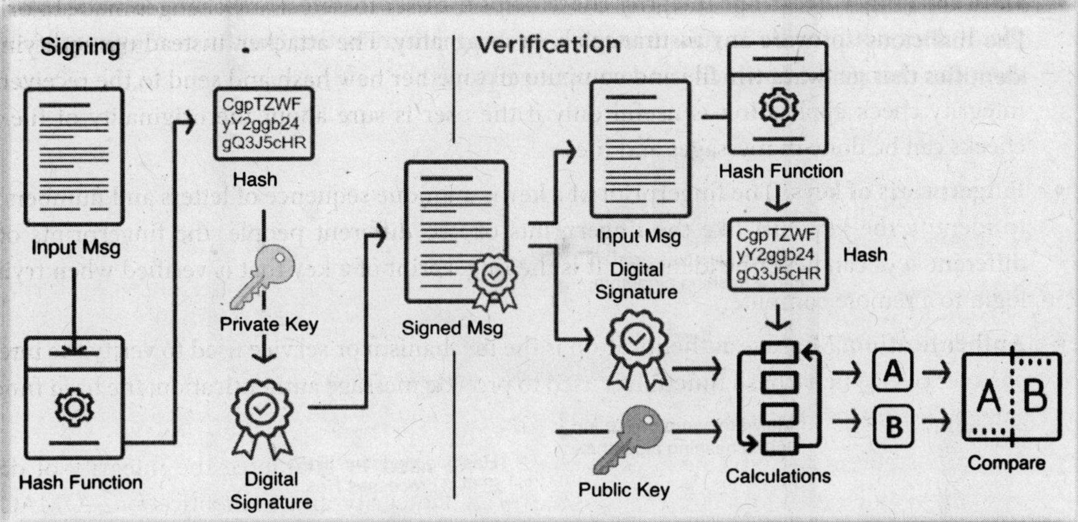

Figure 8.21: Working of Digital Signature Using Hash Function

Here, we assume that the message is sent in the clear, as we are concerned of providing message origin authentication, not confidentiality. If confidentiality is required then the message needs encryption. On receipt of the message and the MAC, the receiver feeds the received message and the shared secret key into the MAC algorithm and re-computes the MAC value. The receiver now checks equality of freshly computed MAC with the MAC received from the sender. If they match, then the receiver accepts the message and assures himself that the message has been sent by the intended sender. If the computed MAC does not match the MAC sent by the sender, the receiver cannot determine whether it is the message that has been altered or it is the origin that has been falsified. As a bottom-line, a receiver safely assumes that the message is not the genuine.

- **Digital Signatures:** Once a cryptographic hash is created for a message, the hash is encrypted with the sender's private key. This encrypted hash is called a digital signature. The digital signature scheme is based on public key cryptography.

A valid digital signature enables information integrity using hash function and ensure message is not altered. Thus the message created by the sender is authenticated as well as sender cannot deny having sent the message and ensure non-repudiation.

- **Data Checksum:** A checksum is a value that represents the number of bits in a transmission message and is used to detect high-level errors within data transmissions. Prior to transmission, every piece of data or file can be assigned a checksum value after running a cryptographic hash function. The term checksum is also known as hash sum or hash value. Checksums work by giving the party on the receiving end information about the transmission to make sure that the full range of data is fully delivered. If the checksum value calculated by the end user is different from the original checksum value of the file, it can alert all parties in the transmission that the file was corrupted or tampered by a third party.

- **Malware Finger Printing:** Hashing is a common method used to uniquely identify malware. The malicious software is run through a hashing program that produces a unique hash that identifies that malware which is a sort of fingerprint.

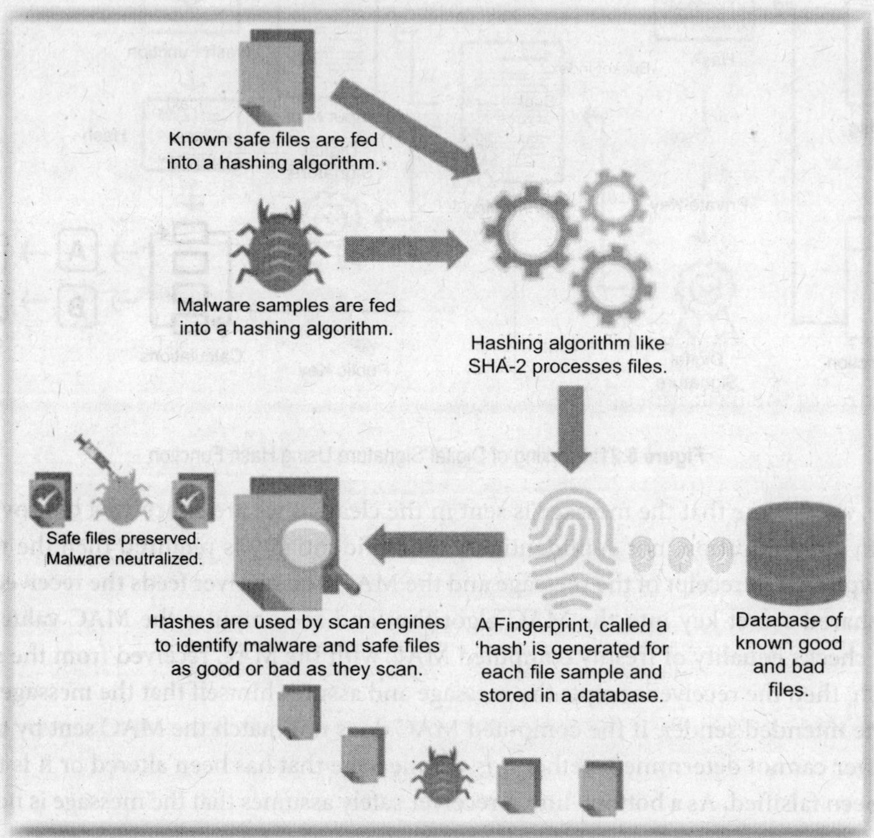

Figure 8.22: Malware Scanner with Hashing to Identify Good and Bad Files

- **Indexing Data:** A hash table uses a hash function to compute an index, also called a hash code, into an array of buckets or slots, from which the desired value can be found. During lookup, the key is hashed and the resulting hash indicates where the corresponding value is stored. Hashing is an effective technique to calculate the direct location of a data record on the disk without using index structure.

  In the figure 8.23, hash is a function that maps a search key to an index between [0 .. B-1]. B is the size of the hash table. Bucket is a location in the bucket array. By hashing technique, different search keys can be hashed into the same hash bucket.

- **Detecting Duplicates:** If we have a good hash function which is collision resistant, which refers to have a minimal probability of collisions, we can use it to find duplicate records. As we know that the hash function generates a unique hash to each record, we can cross reference all the hashes to find such duplicates. This method applies to files too.

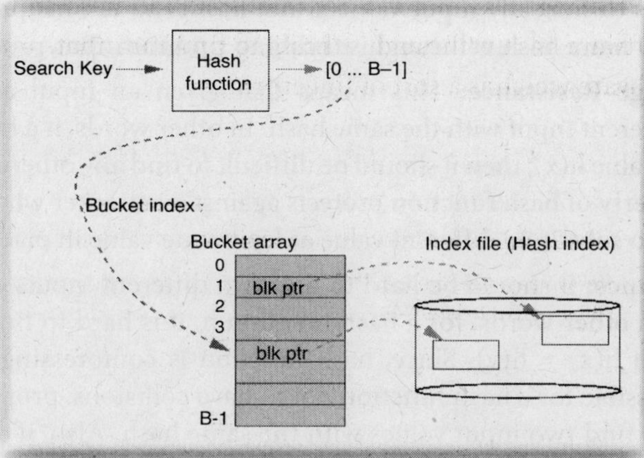

Figure 8.23: Hashing as Indexing Technique to Find Records on Disk

The features of the hash function are explained below.

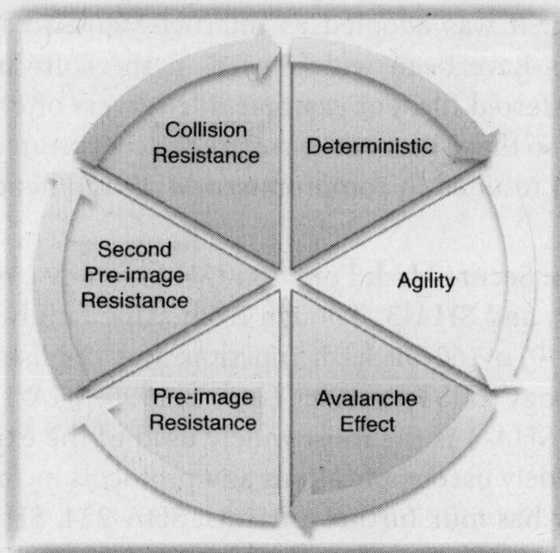

Figure 8.24: Features of Hash Function

- **Deterministic:** Each hash value is unique, and the code remains constant regardless of the number of times of running the same data through the hashing algorithm.
- **Avalanche Effect:** This is the feature of providing fixed length output. The hash code output will always remain the same as long as the data does not get changed. However, a slight change in the input data will give different output data. Hash function coverts data of arbitrary length to a fixed length called hash value. This process is referred to as hashing the data. In general, the hash is much smaller than the input data, hence hash functions are sometimes called compression functions. Since a hash is a smaller representation of a larger data, it is also referred to as a digest. Hash function with n bit output is referred to as an n-bit hash function.
- **Pre-Image Resistance:** This property means that it should be computationally hard to reverse a hash function. In other words, if a hash function h produced a hash value z, then it should be

a difficult process to find any input value x that hashes to z. This property protects against an attacker who only has a hash value and is trying to find the input.

- **Second Pre-Image Resistance:** This means that given an input and its hash, it should be hard to find a different input with the same hash. In other words, if a hash function h for an input x produces hash value h(x), then it should be difficult to find any other input value y such that h(y) = h(x). This property of hash function protects against an attacker who has an input value and its hash, and wants to substitute different value as legitimate value in place of original input value.
- **Collision Resistance:** It should be hard to find two different inputs of any length that result in the same hash. In other words, for a hash function h, it is hard to find any two different inputs x and y such that h(x) = h(y). Since, hash function is compressing function with fixed hash length, it is impossible for a hash function not to have collisions. property makes it very difficult for an attacker to find two input values with the same hash. Also, if a hash function is collision resistant then it is second pre-image resistant. This property is also referred to as collision free hash function.

Let us discuss on some popular hash functions

- **Message Digest:** The Message Digest (MD) family comprises of hash functions MD2, MD4, MD5 and MD6. It was adopted as Internet Standard RFC 1321. It is a 128-bit hash function. MD5 digests have been widely used in the software world to provide assurance about integrity of transferred file. For example, file servers often provide a pre-computed MD5 checksum for the files, so that a user can compare the checksum of the downloaded file to it. The collision attack in 2004 resulted in compromised MD5 and hence it is no longer recommended for use.
- **Secure Hash Function:** Secure Hash Function (SHA) family comprise of four SHA algorithms; SHA-0, SHA-1, SHA-2, and SHA-3. Though from same family, they are structurally different. The first version SHA-0, a 160-bit hash function, was published by the National Institute of Standards and Technology (NIST) in 1993. Later in 1995, SHA-1 was designed to correct alleged weaknesses of SHA-0. SHA-1 is the most widely used of the existing SHA hash functions. It is employed in several widely used applications and protocols including Secure Socket Layer (SSL) security. SHA-2 family has four further variants, SHA-224, SHA-256, SHA-384, and SHA-512 depending up on number of bits in their hash value. Though SHA-2 is a strong hash function. NIST chose the Keccak algorithm as the new SHA-3 standard. Keccak offers many benefits, such as efficient performance and good resistance for attacks.

The table compares various criteria in message digest and secure hash function.

Table 8.8: Comparison of MD5 and SHA

Criteria	Message Digest 5	SHA
Security	Less Secure	More Secure
Message Digest Length	128 Bits	160 Bits
Attacks required to find out original message	2^128 bit operations	2^160 bit operations
Attacks to try and find two messages producing the same MD	2^ 64 bit operations	2^80 bit operations
Speed	Faster – 64 iterations	Slower- 80 iterations

- **RIPEMD:** The RIPEMD is an acronym for RACE Integrity Primitives Evaluation Message Digest. This set of hash functions was designed by open research community and generally known as a family of European hash functions. RIPEMD is a family of cryptographic hash functions developed in 1992 and 1996. The five members in the family of RIPEMD are RIPEMD-128, RIPEMD-160, RIPEMD-256, and RIPEMD-320, of which RIPEMD-160 is the most common. The 256 and 320-bit versions reduce the chance of accidental collision, but do not have higher levels of security as compared to RIPEMD-128 and RIPEMD-160 respectively.
- **Whirlpool:** Whirlpool is a cryptographic hash function published in 2000 and revised in 2001 and 2003. It is a block cipher hash function and designed after square block cipher. It takes less than 2^256 bits length input and convert it in 512-bit hash. It is derived from the modified version of Advanced Encryption Standard (AES). One of the designers was Vincent Rijmen, a co-creator of the AES. Three versions of whirlpool have been released namely whirlpool-0, whirlpool-T and whirlpool.
- **BLAKE 2:** BLAKE is a cryptographic hash function based on Dan Bernstein's ChaCha stream cipher, but a permuted copy of the input block, XORed with round constants, is added before each ChaCha round. BLAKE2 hash function is faster than MD5, SHA-1, SHA-2, and SHA-3, and is secure as the latest standard SHA-3. It has been adopted by many projects due to its high speed, security, and simplicity. BLAKE2 comes in two flavors such as BLAKE2b and BLAKE2s. BLAKE2b (or just BLAKE2) is optimized for 64-bit platforms including NEON-enabled ARMs and produces digests of any size between 1 and 64 bytes. BLAKE2s is optimized for 8- to 32-bit platforms and produces digests of any size beteen 1 and 32 bytes.

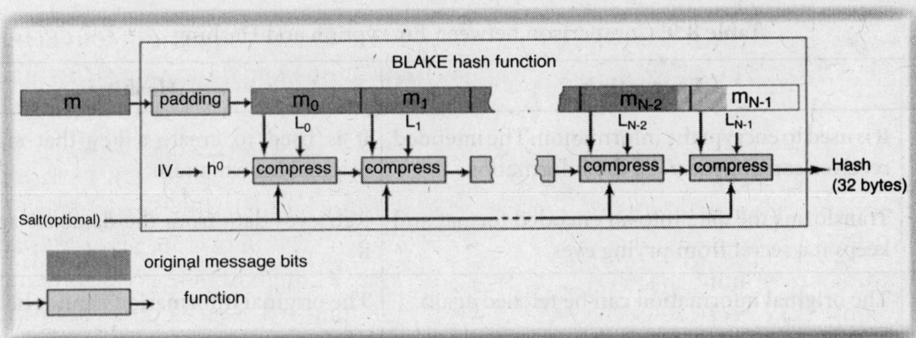

Figure 8.25: Blake Hash Function Working

- **Tiger:** Tiger is a cryptographic iterated hash function that processes 512-bit blocks and produces a 192-bit hash value. It was proposed by Anderson and Biham in 1996. They show that a collision can be found for Tiger reduced to 19 rounds with a complexity of about 262 evaluations of the compression function.

Let us compare between encryption and hashing. Encryption is a process of converting plaintext into an encoded message that is in an unreadable format. An encrypted message can be decrypted with a key. Modern encryption works on a public key and private key for encryption and decryption purposes.

Hashing converts plaintext into a hash key with the use of a hash function. The hash keys reside in a database and compare whether the original information is matched or not. The table compares various criteria of encryption and hashing.

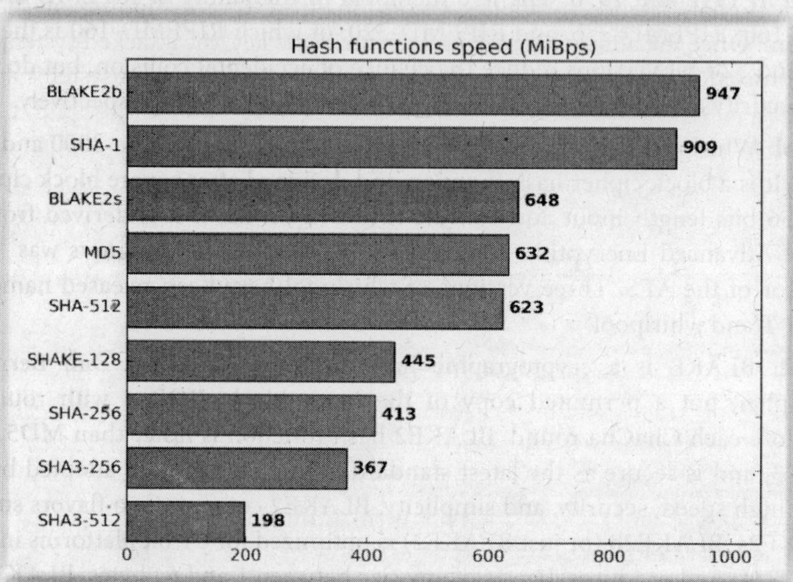

Figure 8.26: Speed Comparison of Hash Functions

Table 8.9: Comparison between Encryption and Hashing

Criteria	Encryption	Hashing
Application	It is used to encrypt the information. The intended receiver can only decrypt the information.	It is used to create a key that signifies the original information.
Function	Transforms the data into an encoded format and keeps it a secret from prying eyes.	Retrieves data from the database and indexes it.
Original Information	The original information can be fetched again.	The original information cannot be recovered.
Security	Less secure.	More secure.
Key	Always creates a new key for each data.	Sometimes creates the same key for new information.
Size	The size of encrypted information will be increased with the growth in the information.	The size of hashed information remains the same even the length of the information is increased.
Type	Encryption is a two-way function (encryption and decryption)	Hashing is a single way function that changes information into an irretrievable digest.

8.4 CRYPTOSYSTEMS ATTACKS

The basic intention of an attacker is to break a cryptosystem and to find the plaintext from the ciphertext. To obtain the plaintext, the attacker only needs to find out the secret decryption key, as the algorithm is already in public domain. Hence, he applies maximum effort towards finding out the secret key used in the cryptosystem. Once the attacker is able to determine the key, the attacked system is considered as broken or compromised. Based on the methodology used, attacks on cryptosystems are categorized as follows.

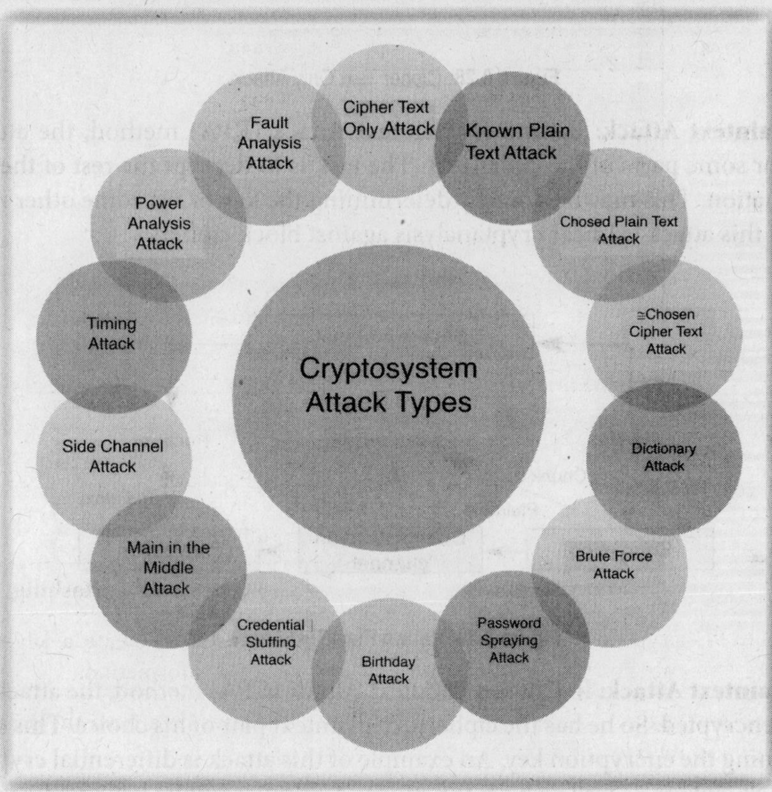

Figure 8.27: Various Types of Cryptosystem Attacks

- **Ciphertext Only Attacks:** In ciphertext only attacks (COA) method, the attacker has access to a set of ciphertext(s). He does not have access to corresponding plaintext. COA is said to be successful when the corresponding plaintext can be determined from a given set of ciphertext. Occasionally, the encryption key can be determined from this attack. Modern cryptosystems are guarded against ciphertext-only attacks.

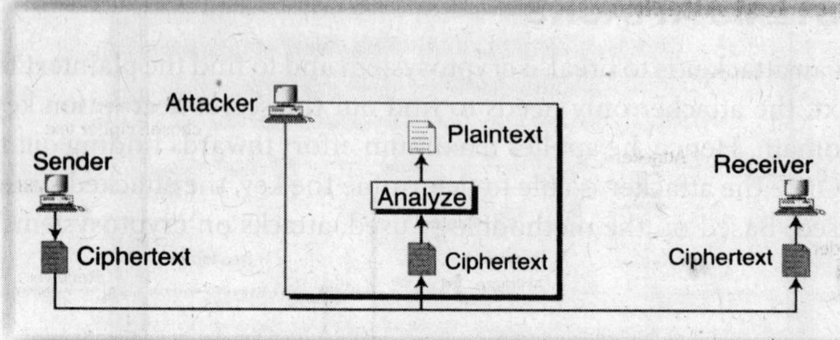

Figure 8.28: Cipher Text Only Attack

- **Known Plaintext Attack:** In Known Plaintext Attack (KPA) method, the attacker knows the plaintext for some parts of the ciphertext. The task is to decrypt the rest of the ciphertext using this information. This may be done by determining the key or via some other method. The best example of this attack is linear cryptanalysis against block ciphers.

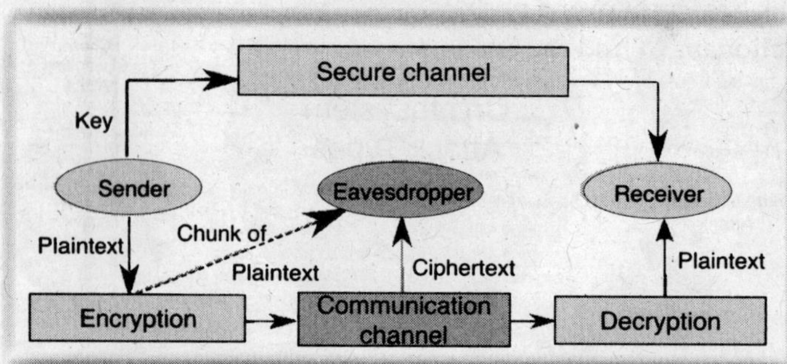

Figure 8.29: Known Plain Text Attack

- **Chosen Plaintext Attack:** In Chosen Plaintext Attack (CPA) method, the attacker has the text of his choice encrypted. So he has the ciphertext-plaintext pair of his choice. This simplifies his task of determining the encryption key. An example of this attack is differential cryptanalysis applied against block ciphers as well as hash functions. A popular public key cryptosystem, RSA is also vulnerable to chosen-plaintext attacks.

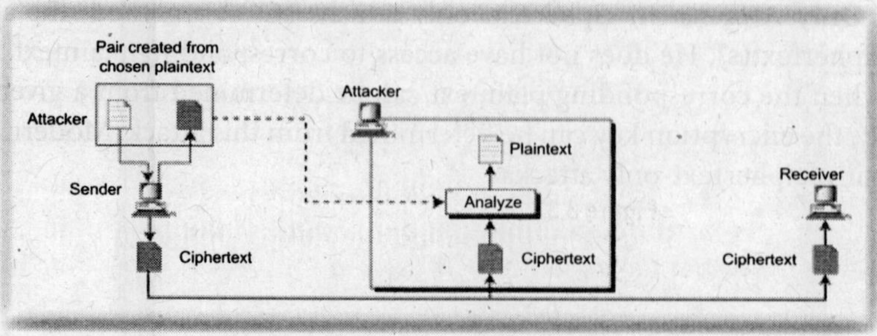

Figure 8.30: Chosen Plain Text Attack

- **Chosen Cipher Text Attack:**

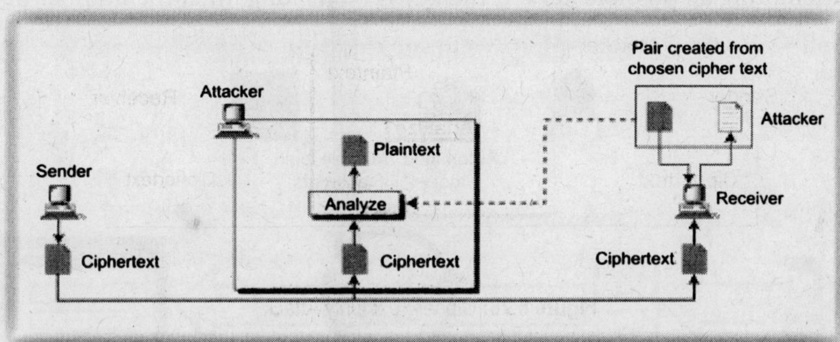

Figure 8.31: Chosen Cipher Text Attack

- **Dictionary Attack:** This attack has many variants, all of which involve compiling a 'dictionary'. In simplest method of this attack, attacker builds a dictionary of ciphertexts and corresponding plaintexts that he has learnt over a period of time. In future, when an attacker gets the ciphertext, he refers the dictionary to find the corresponding plaintext.

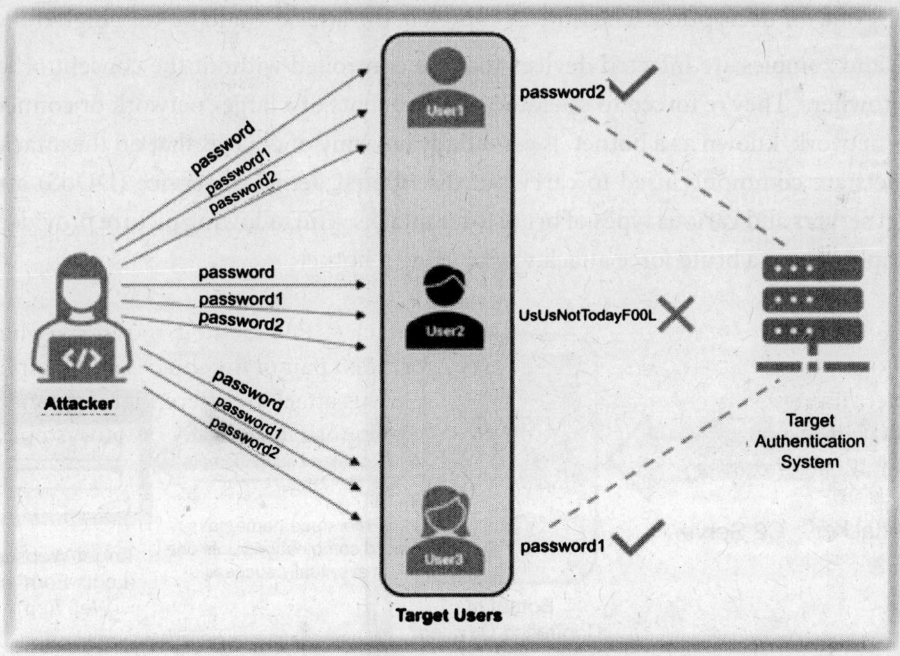

Figure 8.32: Working of Dictionary Attack

- **Brute Force Attack:** In Brute Force Attack (BFA) method, the attacker tries to determine the key by attempting all possible keys. If the key is 8 bits long, then the number of possible keys is

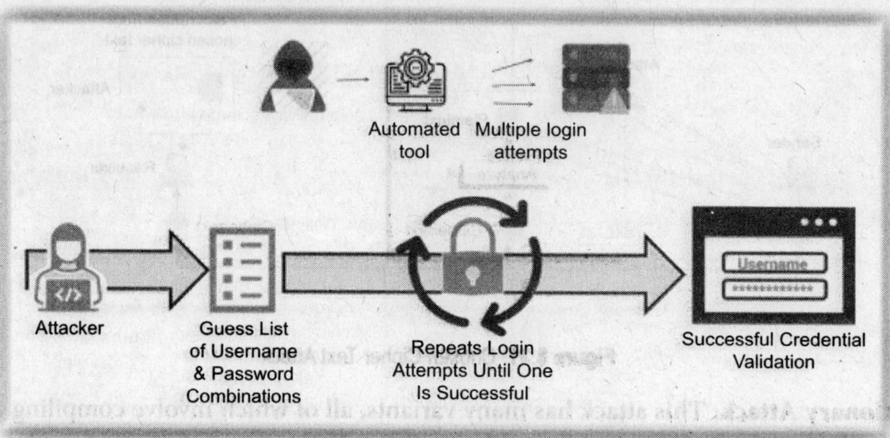

Figure 8.33: Working of Brute Force Attack

$2^8 = 256$. The attacker knows the ciphertext and the algorithm, now he attempts all the 256 keys one by one for decryption. The time to complete the attack would be very high if the key is long.

Bots and zombies are infected devices that are controlled without the consent or knowledge of their owners. They're forced to operate as components of a larger network or connected devices. This network, known as a botnet, is essentially an army of devices that do the attacker's bidding. Botnets are commonly used to carry out distributed denial of service (DDoS) attacks against target servers and various types of brute force attacks. The following picture provides a simplified example of how a brute force attack works using a botnet.

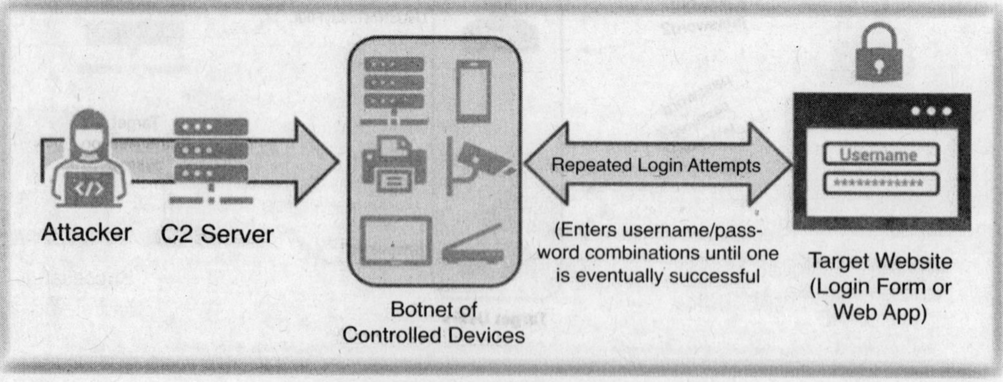

Figure 8.34: Working of Botnet Brute Force Attack

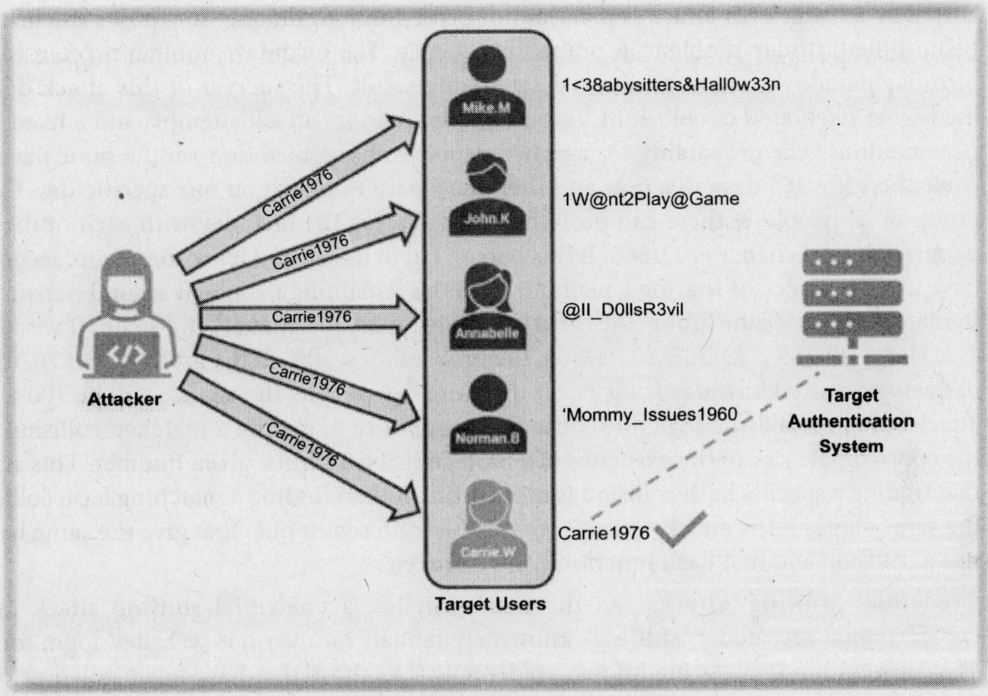

Figure 8.35: Working of Password Spraying Attack

- **Password Spraying attack:** This is also known as brute force attack. Here the attacker takes an approach that's basically the opposite of the simple technique of brute force attack. A password spraying attack involves an attacker using a targeted list of common secrets (passwords) while guessing a large list of potential usernames. Basically, they "spray" the pre-determined list of passwords while rotating through their massive list of usernames to see what sticks.

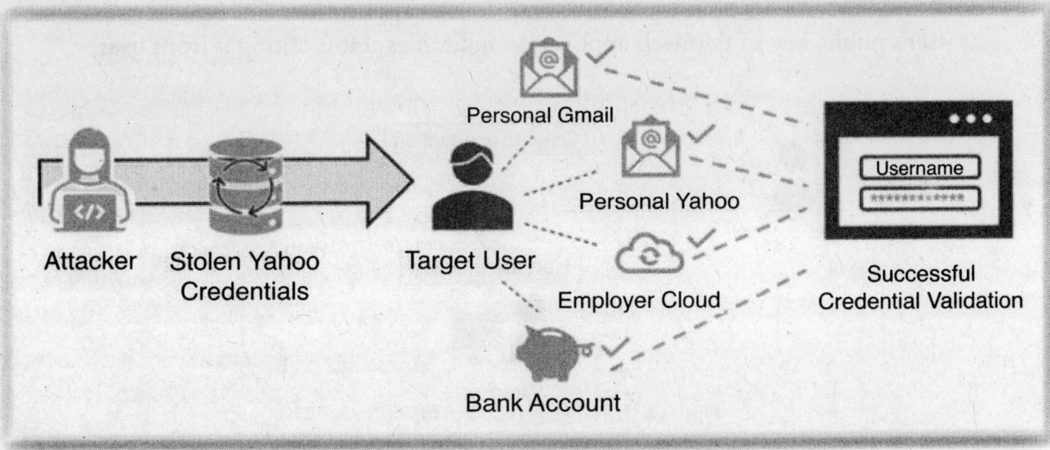

Figure 8.36: Working of Credential Stuffing Attacks

- **Birthday Attack:** This attack is a variant of brute-force technique. It exploits the mathematics behind the birthday problem in probability theory. The birthday problem is often called 'The birthday paradox' since it produces a surprising result. The success of this attack depends on the higher likelihood of collisions found between random attack attempts and a fixed degree of permutations. The probability for any two people to have birthday on the same day is 1/365 , since there are 365 days in a year and their days have to match on one specific day. Consider a group of 23 people. If there can be 1 chance of sharing the birthday with each of the 22 other people, the total chance is 22/365. If this person fail to match and leave the group, second person have 21/365 chance of sharing a birthday with the remaining people. If second person also fails to match and leaves the group, the third person has a 20/365 chance, and so on. If we add 22/365 + 21/365 + 20/365 + 19/365 … + 1/365, the probability is 50%. If the group size is 70, the chance of having a shared birthday is 99.9%. If there are 366 people, the chance will be 100%.Birthday attacks use probabilistic logic to reduce the complexity in getting a matched collision and find the approximate risk of the existence of a hash collision within a given number. This also means that finding a specific hash collision is more difficult than finding a matching hash collision with the same values.If the attacker is able to find two different inputs that give the same hash value, it is a collision and that hash function will be broken.
- **Credential Stuffing Attacks:** As the name implies, a credential stuffing attack involves a cybercriminal repeatedly "stuffing" known credentials into various websites' login form fields. This process involves testing known credentials (i.e., those that have been stolen or otherwise compromised) on multiple websites. The attacker will eventually get one or more of the target websites where someone has an account that uses those credentials.
- **Man In The Middle Attack:** The targets of Man In The Middle Attack (MITM) attack are mostly public key cryptosystems where key exchange is involved before communication takes place. User wants to communicate to web application, hence requests public key of B. An attacker intercepts this request and sends his public key instead. Thus, whatever user sends to web application, the attacker is able to read. In order to maintain communication, the attacker re-encrypts the data after reading with his public key and sends to web application. The attacker sends his public key as user's public key so that web application takes it as if it is taking it from user.

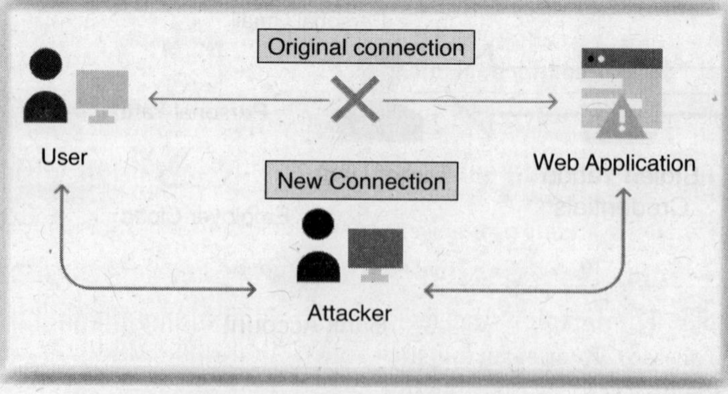

Figure 8.37: Man In The Middle Attack

- **Side Channel Attack:** Side Channel Attack (SCA) is not against any particular type of cryptosystem or algorithm. Instead, it is launched to exploit the weakness in physical implementation of the cryptosystem.

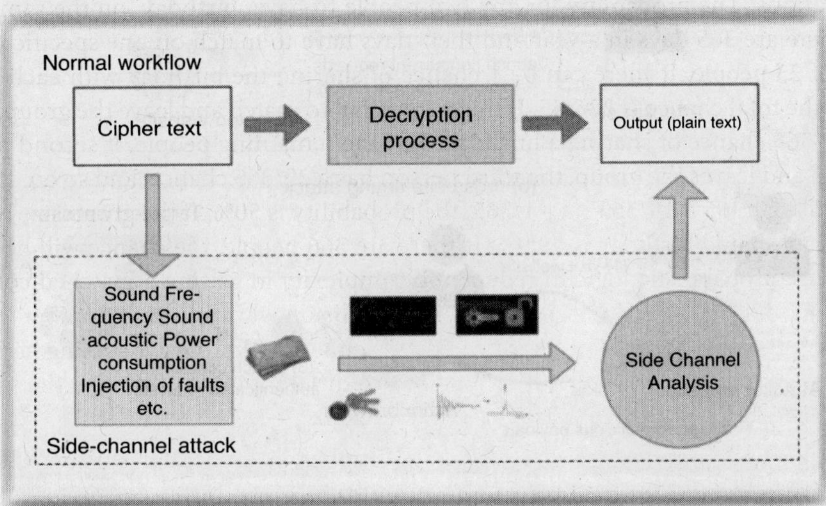

Figure 8.38: Side Channel Attack

The different types of side channel attacks and their counter measures are provided in below table.

Table 8.10: Types of Side Channel Attacks

Side Channel Attack Types		Explanation	Counter Measures
Timing Attack		Analyze the time taken by the device in different computations	Constant time techniques, Injection noise, Determinism, Partitioning time & hardware, Auditing
Electromagnetic Attack		Analyze electromagnetic field of the device to obtain secret information	Circuit redesign, Electromagnetic shielding, Creating secure zone
Fault Analysis Attack		Analyze faulty outputs to get confidential information	Restart the process again on getting faulty output
Power Analysis Attack	Simple Power Analysis	Analyze the power traces on the inputs given	Hiding, Masking
	Differential Power Analysis	Involves statistical analysis of large number of power traces	Hiding, Blinding, Masking, Noise insertion, Temporal de synchronization and algorithmic measures

- **Timing Attacks:** They exploit the fact that different computations take different times to compute on processor. By measuring such timings, it is be possible to know about a particular computation the processor is carrying out. For example, if the encryption takes a longer time, it indicates that the secret key is long.

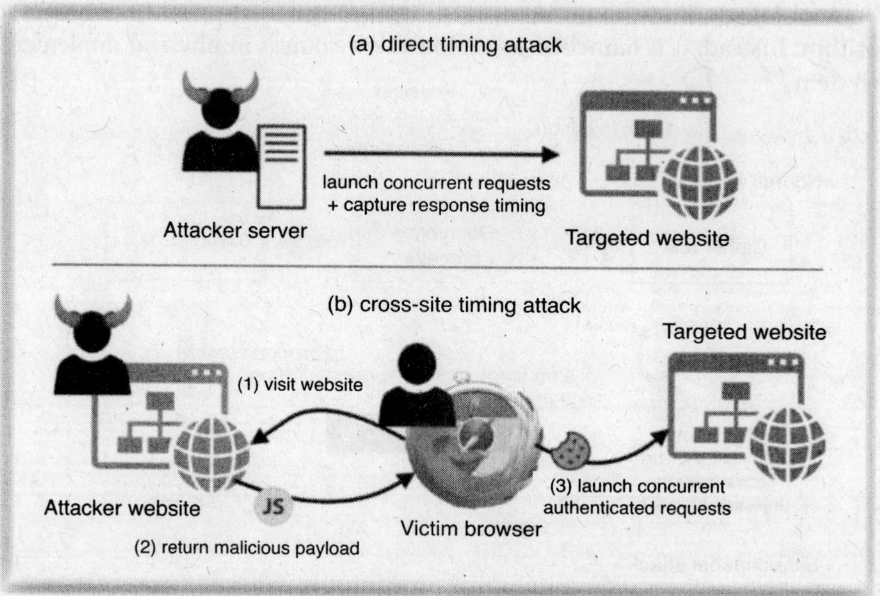

Figure 8.39: Timing Attack

- **Power Analysis Attacks:** These attacks are similar to timing attacks except that the amount of power consumption is used to obtain information about the nature of the underlying computations. Power analysis attacks allow the extraction of secret information from smart cards. Smart cards are used in many applications including banking, mobile communications, pay TV, and electronic signatures. In all these applications, the security of the smart cards is of crucial importance.

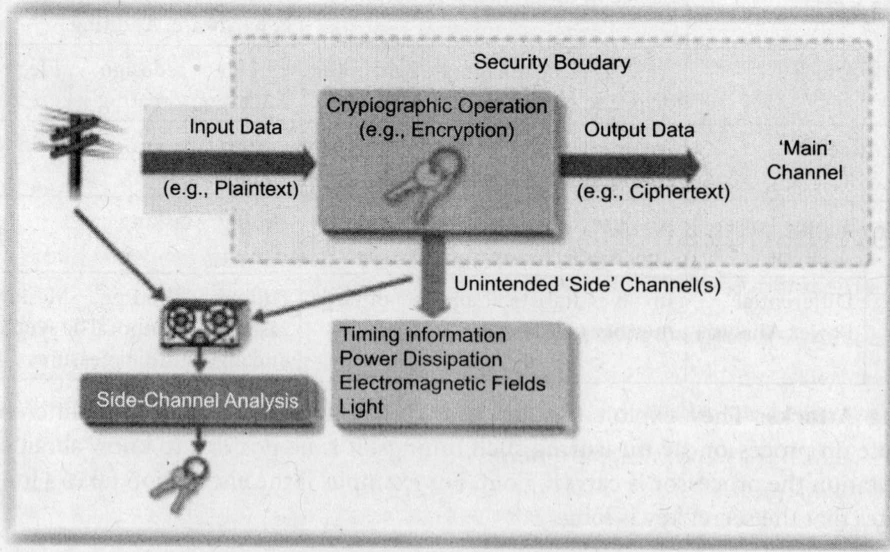

Figure 8.40: Power Analysis based Side Channel Attack

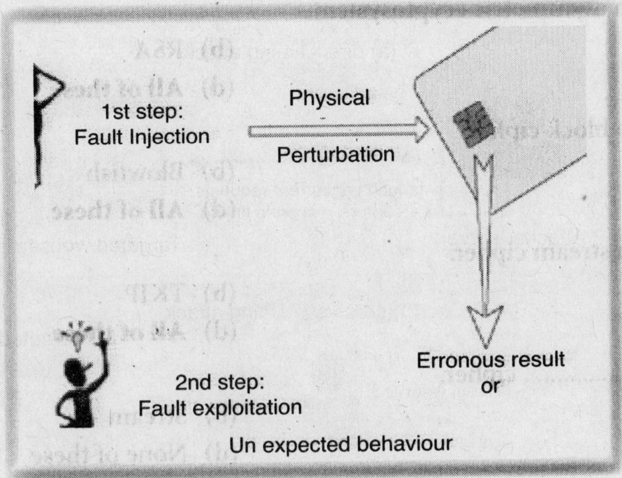

Figure 8.41: Fault Analysis Attack

- **Fault Analysis Attacks:** Fault analysis attack is a type of active side-channel attack in the field of cryptography, specifically cryptanalysis. The principle is to induce faults to unexpected environmental conditions of cryptographic implementations, to reveal their internal states. In these attacks, errors are induced in the cryptosystem and the attacker studies the resulting output for useful information. A fault attack is an attack on a physical electronic device (e.g., smartcard, HSM, USB token) which consists in stressing the device an external means (e.g., voltage, light) in order to generates errors in such a way that these errors lead to a security failure of the system (key recovery, ePurse balance increase etc.). This is also known as Differential Fault Analysis attack (DFA).

8.5 SUMMARY

The discussion in this chapter initiated with introduction of cryptosystem and its components. Types of cryptosystems such as symmetric, asymmetric and hash function working are explained in detail along with its applications. Popular cryptosystems based on various ciphers are explained. The chapter concludes discussion on cyber system attacks with detailed explanation of each type.

8.6 OBJECTIVE QUESTIONS

The answer of the multiple-choice questions is marked in **bold**.

1. .... is not a cryptosystem component.
   (a) Plaintext (b) Encryption key
   (c) Encryption algorithm (d) **Sender**

2. .... is a keyless cryptosystem.
   (a) Asymmetric (b) Symmetric
   (c) **Hash** (d) All of these

3. .... is a asymmetric cryptosystem.
   (a) ECC
   (b) RSA
   (c) DSA
   (d) **All of these**
4. .... is a block cipher.
   (a) RC6
   (b) Blowfish
   (c) AES
   (d) **All of these**
5. .... is a stream cipher.
   (a) RC4
   (b) TKIP
   (c) SNOW
   (d) **All of these**
6. Serpent is a .... cipher.
   (a) **Block**
   (b) Stream
   (c) Hash
   (d) None of these
7. .... is an application of hash function.
   (a) Data checksum
   (b) MAC
   (c) Digital signature
   (d) **All of these**
8. .... is a feature of hash function.
   (a) Deterministic
   (b) Agility
   (c) Avalanch effect
   (d) **All of these**
9. .... is a hash function.
   (a) MD
   (b) SHA
   (c) RIPEMD
   (d) **All of these**
10. .... is a cryptosystem attack.
   (a) Fault analysis
   (b) Dictionary
   (c) Birthday
   (d) **All of these**

8.7 REVIEW QUESTIONS

1. Explain various components of a cryptosystem.
2. Discuss asymmetric key cryptosystem.
3. Discuss symmetric key cryptosystem.
4. Discuss the features and challenges of symmetric key cryptosystem.
5. Explain keyless (Hash function) cryptosystem.
6. Discuss various types of asymmetric cryptosystems.
7. Explain various symmetric block cipher cryptosystems.
8. Explain various symmetric stream cipher cryptosystems.
9. Compare various parameters of DES and AES.

10. Explain the advantages and disadvantages of RC4.
11. Explain four variants of RC4.
12. Compare symmetric and asymmetric encryption.
13. Discuss hash function cryptosystem.
14. Explain various applications of hash functions.
15. Explain working of digital signature using hash function.
16. Discuss the features of hash function.
17. Compare MD and SHA.
18. Compare encryption and hashing.
19. Discuss various types of cryptosystem attacks.
20. Discuss various types of side channel attacks and the counter measures.

8.8 ABBREVIATIONS AND SYMBOLS

Abbreviations	Full Form	Description
RSA	Rivest–Shamir–Adleman	RSA is a public-key cryptosystem that is widely used for secure data transmission.
ECC	Elliptic Curve Cryptography	ECC is a key-based technique for encrypting data. It focuses on pairs of public and private keys for decryption and encryption of web traffic.
DSA	Digital Signature Algorithm	DSA is used for digital signature and its verification.
ECDSA	Elliptic Curve Digital Signature Algorithm	ECDSA is a Digital Signature Algorithm (DSA) which uses keys derived from elliptic curve cryptography.
DH	Diffie–Hellman	DH algorithm is a key-exchange protocol that enables two parties communicating over public channel to establish a mutual secret without it being transmitted over the Internet.
XTR	XTR stands for 'ECSTR', which is an abbreviation for Efficient and Compact Subgroup Trace Representation.	XTR is an algorithm for public-key encryption. It is a method that makes use of traces to represent and calculate powers of elements of a subgroup of a finite field.
EES	Escrowed Encryption Standard	EES defines a US Government family of cryptographic processors, popularly known as "Clipper" chips, intended to protect unclassified government and private-sector communications and data.
NIST	National Institute of Standards and Technology	NIST is a physical sciences laboratory and non-regulatory agency of the United States Department of Commerce. Its mission is to promote American innovation and industrial competitiveness.

Abbreviations	Full Form	Description
FIPS	Federal Information Processing Standards	It is a set of US government standards that define how certain things are used in the government.
RC	Rivest's Cipher or Ron's code	RC algorithms are a set of symmetric-key encryption algorithms.
DES	Data Encryption Standard	DES is a symmetric-key algorithm for the encryption of digital data.
AES	Advanced Encryption Standard	AES is a specification for the encryption of electronic data established by the U.S. National Institute of Standards and Technology.
IDEA	International Data Encryption Algorithm	IDEA was originally called Improved Proposed Encryption Standard (IPES), is a symmetric-key block cipher
TDES	Triple Data Encryption Standards	Triple DES, 3DES or TDES, is the Triple Data Encryption Algorithm (TDEA or Triple DEA), is a symmetric-key block cipher, which applies the DES cipher algorithm three times to each data block.
TKIP	Temporal Key Integrity Protocol	TKIP is an encryption protocol included as part of the IEEE 802.11i standard for wireless LAN.
TSL	Transport Layer Security	TLS, is a security protocol for encrypting the communication between web applications and servers, such as web browsers loading a website.
IEEE	Institute of Electrical and Electronics Engineers	IEEE is a professional association for electronic engineering and electrical engineering.
VMPC	Variably Modified Permutation Composition	The Key Scheduling Algorithm (KSA) of the VMPC Stream Cipher transforms a cryptographic key of length from 128 to 512 bits.
MAC	Message Authentication Code	MAC is a cryptographic checksum on data that uses a session key to detect both accidental and intentional modifications of the data.
MD	Message-Digest	MD refers to a short string or hash value of fixed length that is computed from the longer variable-length message being hashed by the algorithm.
SHA	Secure Hash Algorithm	SHA, are a family of cryptographic functions designed to keep data secured. It works by transforming the data using a hash function.
RIPEMD	RACE Integrity Primitives Evaluation Message Digest	RIPEMD Family designates a family of five different hash functions: RIPEMD, RIPEMD-128, RIPEMD-160, RIPEMD-256 and RIPEMD-320.

8.9 LIST OF FIGURES AND TABLES

The details of figures and tables used in this chapter is as below.

CHAPTER 9

Digital Signature and E-mail Security

CONTENTS

9.1 SIGNATURES

Signature is proof that the matter mentioned in the document has been considered, reviewed and accepted. There are four types of signatures.

- **Wet Signature:** It is any physical mark on documents created by a person. In most cases it will be the person's name written in a unique style with ink in paper document or contract. Placing thumb impression on document using ink is another method of wet signature.
- **Click Wrap Signature:** This is used for mostly online purchases, where a simple tick in a box is an acceptance of the terms and conditions contained mentioned in the website.
- **Electronic Signature:** Electronic Signature (e-Signature) is a digital version of a wet signature, where many countries have defined the legality and description of uses for e-signatures.

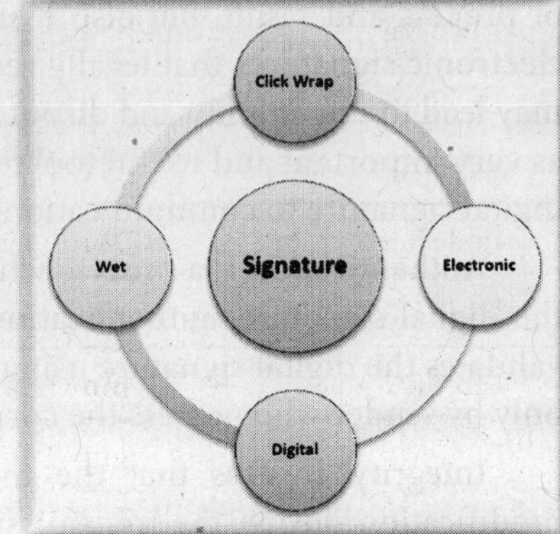

Figure 9.1: Signature Types

- **Digital Signature:** It is an authentication mechanism that enables a code to be attached as a signature. It is required for certain specific agreements, and issued through a certification agency. The comparison of digital and electronic signature is provided in the table.

Table 9.1: Comparison of Digital and Electronic Signature

Criteria	Digital Signature	Electronic Signature
Usage	To secure a document	To verify a document
Authorization	Authorized and regulated by certification authorities	Usually not authorized
Security	More security features	Less security features
Types	Based on Adobe and Microsoft	Include verbal, electronic ticks or scanned signatures.
Verification	Can be verified	Cannot be verified.
Authenticity	Highly authentic	Less authentic
Application	Concerned about securing the document	Shows intent to sign the contract

9.2 DIGITAL SIGNATURE

A digital signature is a mathematical technique which validates the authenticity and integrity of a message, software or digital documents. It allows us to verify the author's name, date and time of signatures, and authenticate the message contents. The digital signature offers far more inherent security and intended to solve the problem of tampering and impersonation (Intentionally copy another person's characteristics) in digital communications.

The computer-based business information authentication interrelates both technology and the law. It also calls for cooperation between the people of different professional backgrounds and areas of expertise. The digital signatures are different from other electronic signatures not only in terms of process and result, but also it makes digital signatures more serviceable for legal purposes. Some electronic signatures that legally recognizable as signatures may not be secure as digital signatures and may lead to uncertainty and disputes. The digital signature using public key cryptography is considered as very important and useful tool to achieve information security. The important reasons to implement digital signature to communication are authentication, integrity and non-repudiation.

Authentication is a process which verifies the identity of a user who wants to access the system. In the digital signature, authentication helps to authenticate the sources of messages. When the verifier validates the digital signature using public key of a sender, he is assured that signature has been created only by sender who possess the corresponding secret private key and no one else.

Integrity ensures that the message is real, accurate and safeguards from unauthorized user modification during the transmission. In case an attacker has access to the data and modifies it, the digital signature verification at receiver end fails. The hash of modified data and the output provided by the verification algorithm will not match. Hence, receiver can safely deny the message assuming that data integrity has been breached.

Non-repudiation means assurance of something that cannot be denied. It ensures that someone is responsible to a contract or communication and cannot later deny the authenticity of their signature on a document or in a file or a message that they originated. Since it is assumed that only the signer has the knowledge of the signature key, he can only create unique signature on a given data. Thus, the receiver can present data and the digital signature to a third party as evidence if any dispute arises in the future.

By adding public-key encryption to digital signature scheme, we can create a cryptosystem that can provide the four essential elements of security namely privacy, authentication, integrity and non-repudiation A digital signature consists of below algorithms.

- **Key generation algorithm:** The key generation algorithm selects private key randomly from a set of possible private keys. This algorithm provides the private key and its corresponding public key. Digital signature is an electronic signature, which assure that the message was sent by a particular sender. While performing digital transactions authenticity and integrity should be assured, otherwise, the data can be altered or someone can also act as if he was the sender and expect a reply.
- **Signing algorithm:** A signing algorithm produces a signature for the document. To create a digital signature, signing algorithms like email programs create a one-way hash of the electronic data which is to be signed. The signing algorithm then encrypts the hash value using the private key (signature key). This encrypted hash along with other information like the hashing algorithm is the digital signature. This digital signature is added with the data and sent to the verifier. The reason for encrypting the hash instead of the entire message or document is that a hash function converts any input into a much shorter fixed-length value. This saves time as instead of signing a long message a shorter hash value has to be signed.
- **Signature verifying algorithm:** A signature verifying algorithm either accepts or rejects the document's authenticity. Verifier receives digital signature along with the data. It then uses verification algorithm to process on the digital signature and the public key (verification key) and generates some value. It also applies the same hash function on the received data and generates a hash value. Then the hash value and the output of the verification algorithm are compared. If they both are equal, then the digital signature is valid else it is invalid.

The working of digital signatures is explained in figure 9.2.

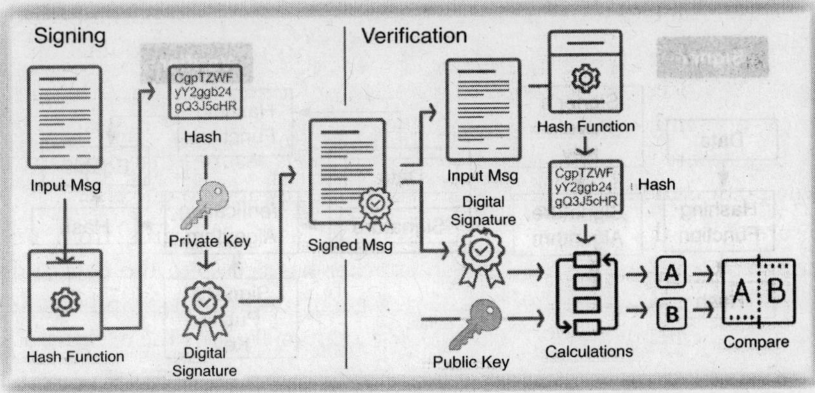

Figure 9.2: Working of Digital Signature

Digital signatures are created and verified by using public key cryptology, also known as asymmetric cryptology. By the use of a public key algorithm, two keys that are mathematically linked can be generated, one is a private key and another is a public key. The user who is creating the digital signature uses their own private key to encrypt the signature-related document. There is only one way to decrypt that document is with the use of signer's public key. This technology requires all the parties to trust that the individual who creates the signature has been able to keep their private key secret. If someone has accessed the signer's private key, there is a possibility that they could create fraudulent signatures in the name of the private key holder. The steps which are followed in creating a digital signature are explained in figure 9.3.

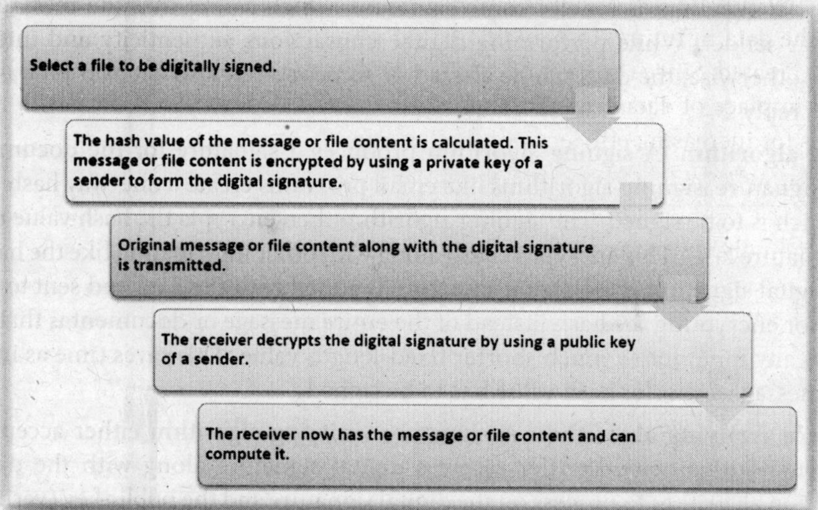

Figure 9.3: Steps of Creating Digital Signature

The digital signature scheme is based on public key cryptography. The model of digital signature scheme is presented in the Figure.

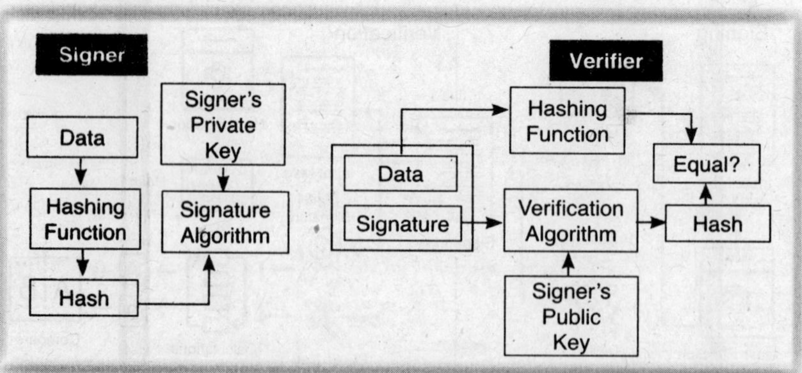

Figure 9.4: Model Digital Signature

Each person adopting this model will have a public-private key pair. Generally, the key pairs used for encryption or decryption and signing or verifying are different. The private key used for signing is referred to as the signature key and the public key as the verification key. Signer feeds data to the hash function and generates hash of data. Hash value and signature key are then fed to the signature algorithm which produces the digital signature on given hash. Signature is added to the data and then both are sent to the verifier. Verifier feeds the digital signature and the verification key into the verification algorithm. The verification algorithm gives some value as output. Verifier also runs same hash function on received data to generate hash value. For verification, this hash value and output of verification algorithm are compared. Based on the comparison result, verifier decides whether the digital signature is valid. Since digital signature is created by 'private' key of signer and no one else can have this key; the signer cannot repudiate signing the data in future. Instead of signing data directly by signing algorithm, usually a hash of data is created. Since the hash of data is a unique representation of data, it is sufficient to sign the hash in place of data. The most important reason of using hash instead of data directly for signing is for increasing efficiency of the scheme.

Let us assume RSA is used as the signing algorithm. The encryption or signing process using RSA involves modular exponentiation. Signing large data through modular exponentiation is computationally expensive and time consuming. The hash of the data is a relatively small digest of the data, hence signing a hash is more efficient than signing the entire data.

In many digital communications, it is desirable to exchange an encrypted messages than plaintext to achieve confidentiality. In public key encryption scheme, a public encryption key of sender is available in open domain, and hence anyone can spoof his identity and send any encrypted message to the receiver. This makes it essential for users employing public key cryptography for encryption to seek digital signatures along with encrypted data to be assured of message authentication and non-repudiation. This can be archived by combining digital signatures with encryption scheme. Let us briefly discuss how to achieve this requirement. There are two possibilities, sign-then-encrypt or encrypt-then-sign. The crypto system based on sign-then-encrypt can be exploited by receiver to spoof identity of sender and can send that data to third party. Hence, this method is not preferred. The process of encrypt-then-sign is more reliable and widely adopted. This is presented in the figure 9.5.

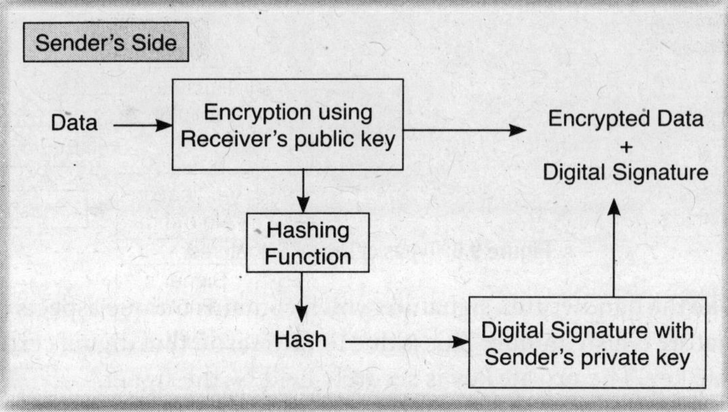

Figure 9.5: Encryption with Digital Signature

The receiver after receiving the encrypted data and signature on it, first verifies the signature using sender's public key. After ensuring the validity of the signature, he then retrieves the data through decryption using his private key. The most distinct feature of Public Key Infrastructure (PKI) is that it uses a pair of keys to achieve the underlying security service. The key pair comprises of private key and public key. Since the public keys are in open domain, they are likely to be abused. It is, thus, necessary to establish and maintain some kind of trusted infrastructure to manage these keys. Different document processing platform supports different types of digital signature which are described below.

- **Certified Signature:** Digital signature certificates are electronic format of physical certificates. The certified digital signature documents display a unique blue ribbon across the top of the document. The certified signature contains the name of the document signer and the certificate issuer which indicate the authorship and authenticity of the document. The benefits of certified digital signature are
  - **Trust worthy:** A digital signature certificate contains both a public and a private key. Once the document is signed and sent to the other recipient, a hashed version of that document is created.
  - **Secure:** If the document is altered at a later date, then then it won't match the hash in the digital signature. This makes a certified digital signature more secure than just using an electronic signature.

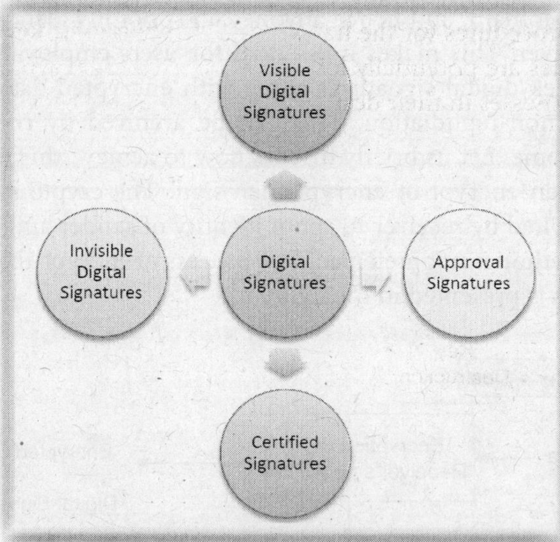

Figure 9.6: Types of Digital Signatures

  - **Unique:** Like the handwritten signature which contains unique aspects of the signer, certified digital signature is also unique. This is due to the reason that digital certificate is with a public and a private key. The private key is securely held by the signer.
  - **Easier to validate:** A certified digital signature makes it easier to prove that you sent the document, and that no one else tampered with it after it's been sent. And if need to legally prove that a document hasn't been altered in any way, a certified digital signature can help on that.

- **Approval Signatures:** The approval digital signatures on a document can be used in the organization's business workflow. They help to optimize the organization's approval procedure. The procedure involves capturing approvals made by us and other individuals and embedding them within the PDF document. The approval signatures include details such as an image of our physical signature, location, date, and official seal.
- **Visible Digital Signature:** A visible digital signature includes a metadata that holds a visible signature appearance when viewing the document, showing that it has been signed. The visible digital signature allows a user to sign a single document digitally. This signature appears on a document in the same way as signatures are signed on a physical document.
- **Invisible Digital Signature:** The invisible digital signatures carry a visual indication of a blue ribbon within a document in the taskbar. We can use invisible digital signatures when we do not have or do not want to display our signature but need to provide the authenticity of the document, its integrity, and its origin.

Key management refers to the secure administration of cryptographic keys. Key management deals with entire key lifecycle is represented in the figure 9.7. In cryptography, a key is a string of characters used within an encryption algorithm for altering data so that it appears random. Like a physical key, it locks (encrypts) data so that only someone with the right key can unlock (decrypt) it. Cryptographic keys are pieces of data. The security of any cryptosystem depends upon how securely its keys are managed. Without secure procedures for the handling of cryptographic keys, the benefits of the use of strong cryptographic schemes are potentially lost. It is observed that cryptographic schemes are rarely compromised through weaknesses in their design. However, they are often compromised through poor key management.

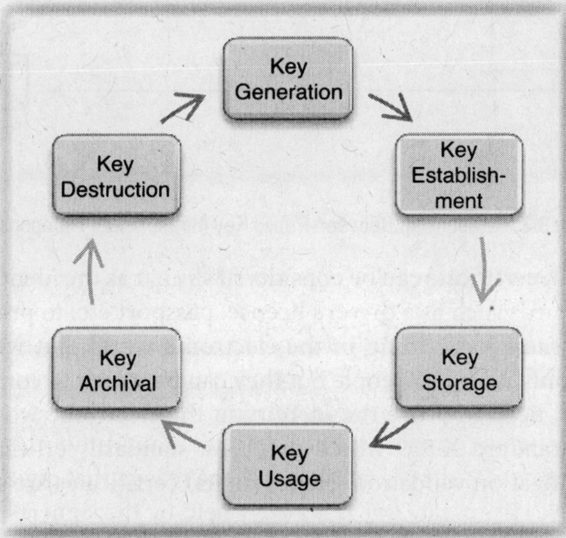

Figure 9.7 Key Management Life Cycle

The two requirements of key management for public key cryptography are secrecy of private keys and assurance of public keys. Secrecy of private key means that throughout the key lifecycle, secret keys must remain secret from all parties except those who are owner and are authorized to use them. In public key cryptography, the public keys are in open domain and seen as public pieces of data. By default, there are no assurances of whether a public key is correct, with whom it can be associated, or what it can be used for. Thus, key management of public keys needs to focus much more explicitly on assurance of purpose of public keys. The most crucial requirement of 'assurance of public key' can be achieved through the PKI, a key management system for supporting public-key cryptography.

9.3 PUBLIC KEY INFRASTRUCTURE

Public Key Infrastructure (PKI) provides assurance of public key. It provides the identification of public keys and their distribution. PKI comprises of the components such as public key certificate which is commonly referred to as digital certificate, private key tokens, certification authority, registration authority, certificate management system.

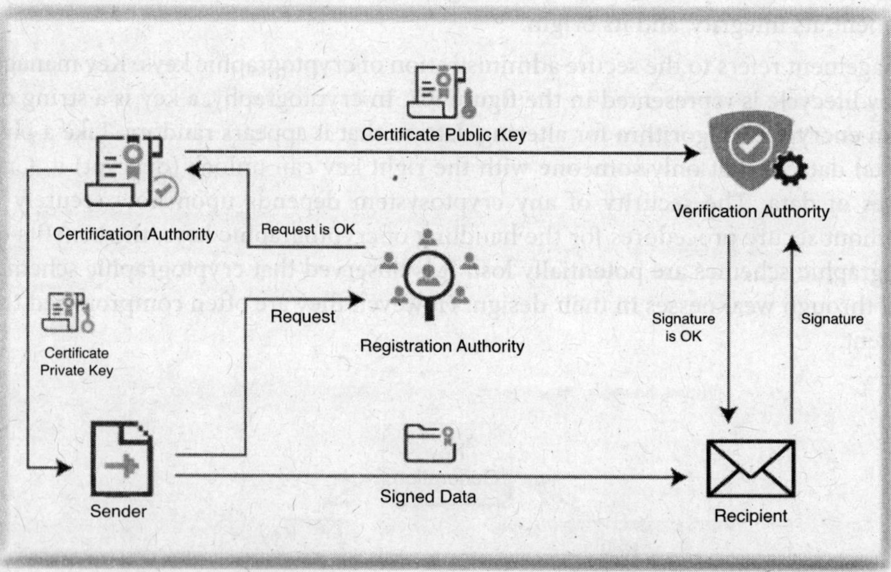

Figure 9.8: Relationship Between Public Key Infrastructure Components

- **Digital Certificate:** A certificate can be considered similar as the identity card issued to a person. People use identity cards such as a driver's license, passport etc. to prove their identity. A digital certificate does the same basic thing in the electronic world, but with one difference. Digital Certificates are not only issued to people but they can be issued to computers, software packages or anything else that need to prove the identity in the electronic world. Digital certificates are based on the ITU standard X.509 which defines a standard certificate format for public key certificates and certification validation. Hence digital certificates are sometimes also referred to as X.509 certificates.

  Public key pertaining to the user client is stored in digital certificates by the Certification Authority (CA) along with other relevant information such as client information, expiration date, usage, issuer etc. CA digitally signs this entire information and includes digital signature in the certificate. Anyone who needs the assurance about the public key and associated information of client, he carries out the signature validation process using CA's public key. Successful validation assures that the public key given in the certificate belongs to the person whose details are given in the certificate. The process of obtaining digital certificate by a person or entity is presented in the following illustration.

The certifying authority accepts the application from a client to certify his public key. The CA, after verifying identity of client, issues a digital certificate to that client.

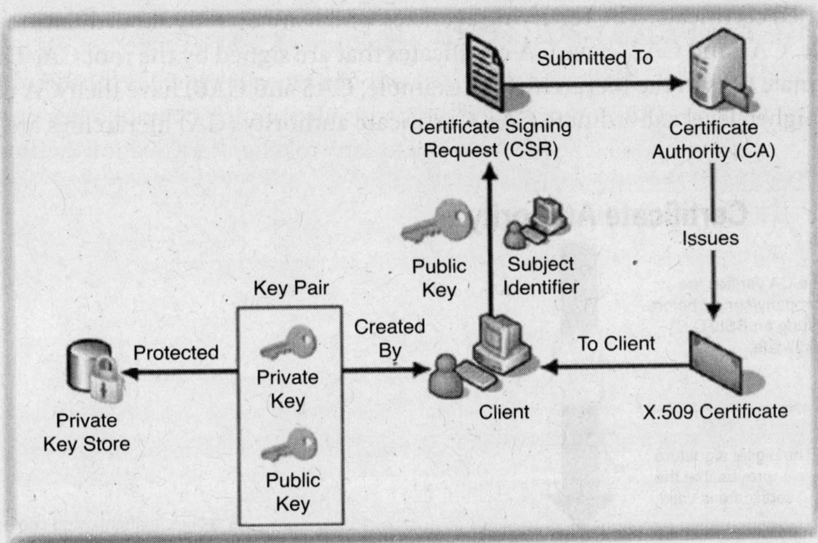

Figure 9.9: Digital Certificate Obtaining Process

- **Certifying Authority:** The Certifying Authority (CA) issues certificate to a client and assist other users to verify the certificate. The CA takes responsibility for identifying correctly the identity of the client asking for a certificate to be issued, and ensures that the information contained within the certificate is correct and digitally signs it. The key functions of a CA are as follows.
  - **Generating key pairs:** They may generate a key pair independently or jointly with the client.
  - **Issuing digital certificates:** They issues a certificate after client provides the credentials to confirm his identity. The certifying agency then signs the certificate to prevent modification of the details contained in the certificate.
  - **Publishing Certificates:** Certifying authority need to publish certificates so that users can find them. There are two ways of achieving this. One is to publish certificates which is the equivalent to an electronic telephone directory. The other is to send certificate to those people who might need it by one means or another.
  - **Verifying Certificates:** The certifying authority makes its public key available in environment to assist verification of his signature on clients' digital certificate.
  - **Revocation of Certificates:** At times, certifying authority revokes the certificate issued due to some reason such as compromise of private key by user or loss of trust in the client. After revocation, certifying authority maintains the list of all revoked certificate that is available to the environment.

With vast networks and requirements of global communications, it is practically not feasible to have only one trusted certifying authority from whom all users obtain their certificates. Moreover, availability of only one certifying authority may lead to difficulties if they are compromised. In such case, the hierarchical certification model allows public key certificates to be used in environments where two communicating parties do not have trust relationships with the same agency. The root CA is at the top of the hierarchy and the root CA's certificate is a self-signed certificate. The certifying agencies which are directly subordinate to the root CA (For example, CA1 and CA2) have CA certificates that are signed by the root CA. The CAs under the subordinate CAs in the hierarchy (For example, CA5 and CA6) have their CA certificates signed by the higher-level subordinate CAs. Certificate authority (CA) hierarchies are reflected in

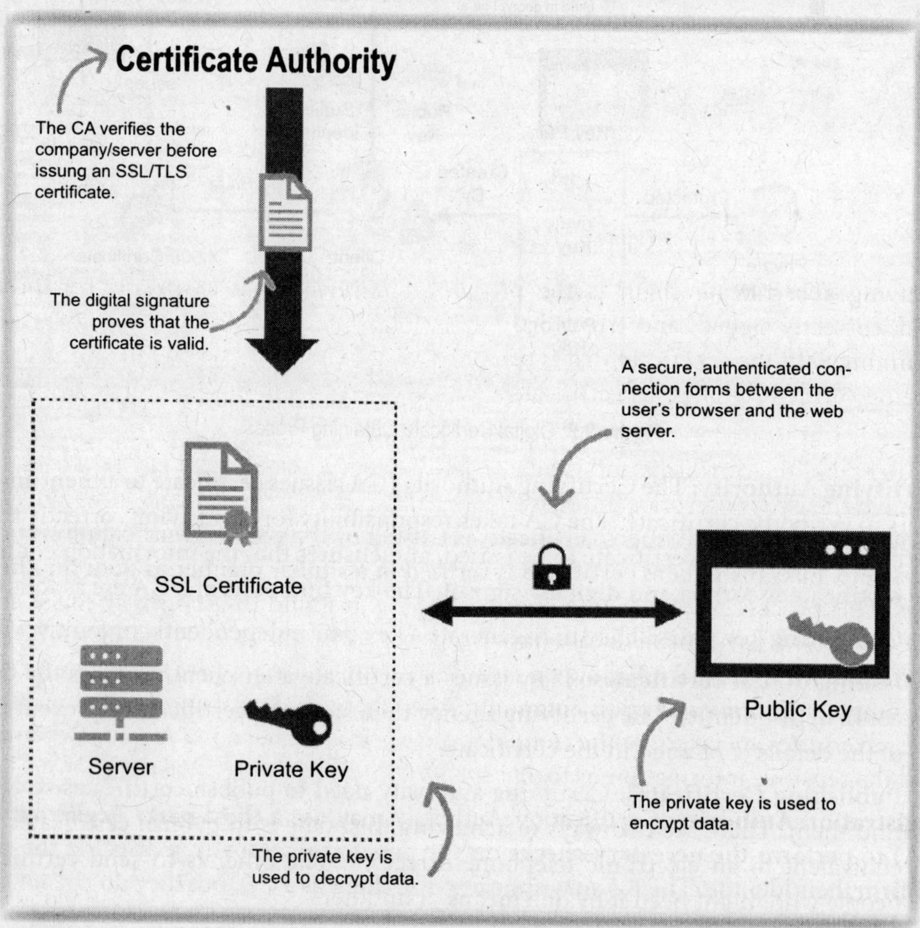

Figure 9.10: Functions of Certifying Authority

certificate chains. A certificate chain traces a path of certificates from a branch in the hierarchy to the root of the hierarchy. The following illustration shows a CA hierarchy with a certificate chain.

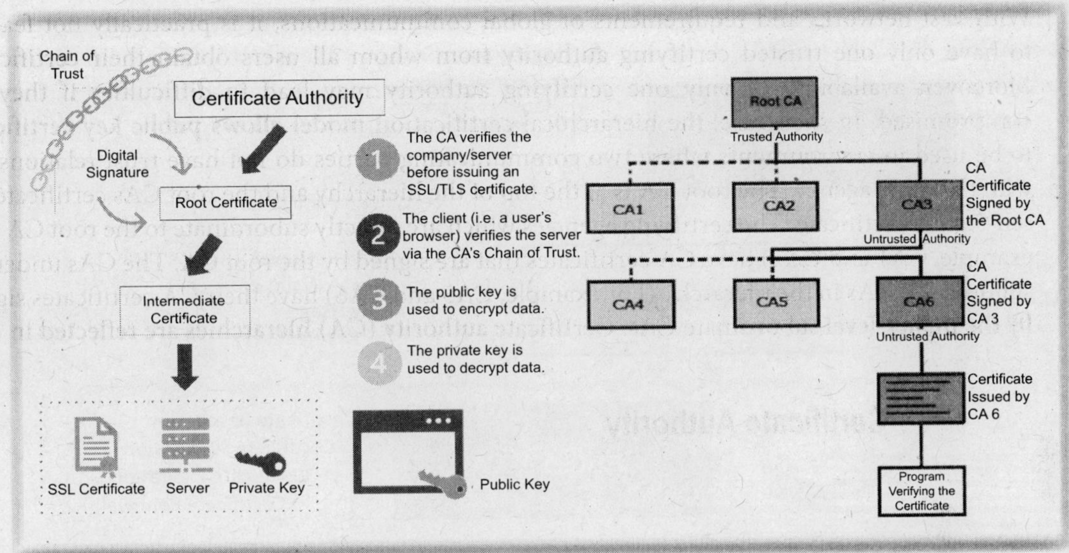

Figure 9.11: Certification Authority Hierarchy

Verifying a certificate chain is the process of ensuring that a specific certificate chain is valid, correctly signed, and trustworthy. The following procedure verifies a certificate chain, beginning with the certificate that is presented for authentication – A client whose authenticity is being verified supplies his certificate, generally along with the chain of certificates up to root CA.

Verifier takes the certificate and validates by using public key of issuer. The issuer's public key is found in the issuer's certificate which is in the chain next to client's certificate. Now if the higher CA who has signed the issuer's certificate, is trusted by the verifier, verification is successful and stops here. Else, the issuer's certificate is verified in a similar manner as done for client in above steps. This process continues till either trusted CA is found in between or else it continues till root CA. Now a days, the networks have gone global and information has taken the digital form of bits and bytes. Critical information now gets stored, processed and transmitted in digital form on computer systems and open communication channels. Since information plays such a vital role, adversaries are targeting the computer systems and open communication channels to either steal the sensitive information or to disrupt the critical information system.

- **Registration Authority:** Certification Authority may use a third-party Registration Authority (RA) to perform the necessary checks on the person or company requesting the certificate to confirm their identity. The RA may appear to the client as a CA, but they do not actually sign the certificate that is issued.
- **Certificate Management System:** Certificate Management System (CMS) is the management system through which certificates are published, suspended, renewed, or revoked. Certificate management systems do not normally delete certificates because it may be necessary to prove their status at a point of time for legal reasons. A CA along with associated RA runs certificate management systems to track their responsibilities and liabilities.

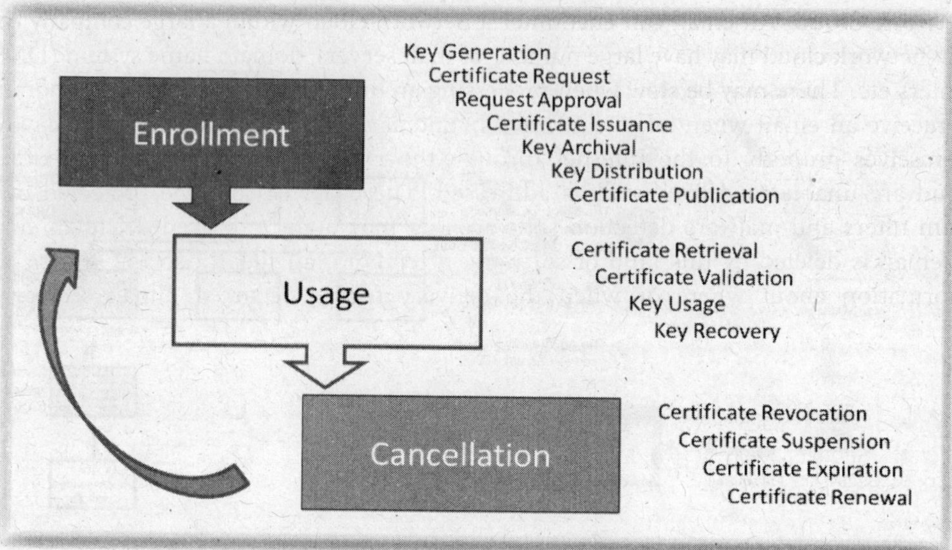

Figure 9.12: Certificate Management System

- **Private Key Tokens:** While the public key of a client is stored on the certificate, the associated secret private key can be stored on the key owner's computer. This method is generally not adopted. If an attacker gains access to the computer, he can easily gain access to private key. For this reason, a private key is stored on secure removable storage token access to which is protected through a password.

  Different vendors often use different and sometimes proprietary storage formats for storing keys. For example, Entrust corporation uses the proprietary .epf format, while Verisign, GlobalSign, and Baltimore use the standard p12 format.

9.4 ELECTRONIC MAIL

Electronic mail (e-mail) is a method of exchanging messages between people using electronic devices. Email is electronic of letter. The working of E-mail is explained in the figure.

A. **Sender creates and sends an email:** The originating sender creates an email in the Mail User Agent (MUA) and clicks 'Send'. The MUA is the application that sender uses to compose and read email, such as Eudora, Outlook, etc.

B. **Sender's MDA/MTA routes the email:** The sender's MUA transfers the email to a Mail Delivery Agent (MDA) or Mail Transfer Agent (MTA).The main function of the MTA is forwarding the incoming message to the proper end-user or destination. Microsoft Exchange and UNIX sendmail are the best examples of MTAs. MDA is a computer program that receives email from a MTA, then sorts and delivers the email to the recipient's mailbox. Frequently, the sender's MTA also handles the responsibilities of an MDA. Most common MTAs do this, including sendmail and qmail. The MDA/MTA accepts the email, then routes it to local mailboxes or forwards it if it isn't locally addressed. In the figure, an MDA forwards the email to an MTA and it enters the first of a series of "network clouds," labeled as a "company network" cloud.

C. **Network Cloud:** An email can encounter a network cloud within a large company or Internet. The network cloud may have large number of mail servers, domain name system (DNS) servers, routers etc. These may be slow when processing an unusually heavy load or temporarily unable to receive an email when taken down for maintenance. Sometimes it may not have identified themselves properly to the Internet through the DNS so that other MTAs in the network cloud are unable to deliver mail as addressed. These devices may be protected by firewalls, spam filters and malware detection software that may bounce or even delete an email. When an email is deleted by this kind of software, it tends to fail silently, so the sender is given no information about where or when the delivery failure occurred. Email service providers

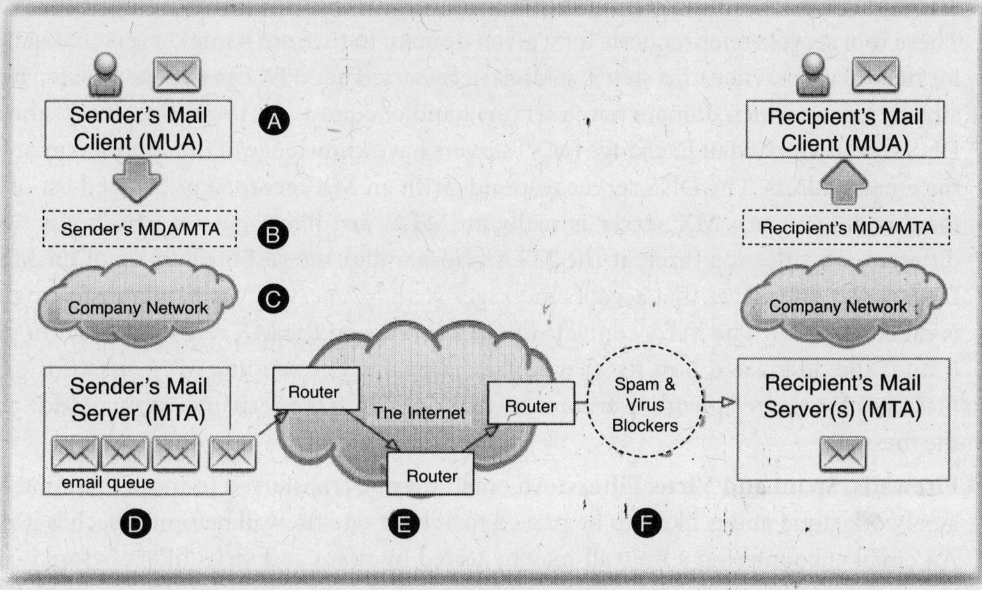

Figure 9.13: Working of E-Mail

and other companies that process a large volume of email often have their own, private network clouds. These organizations commonly have multiple mail servers, and route all email through a central gateway server (i.e., mail hub) that redistributes mail to whichever MTA is available. Email on these secondary MTAs must usually wait for the primary MTA (i.e., the designated host for that domain) to become available, at which time the secondary mail server will transfer its messages to the primary MTA.

D. **Email Queue:** The email in the diagram is addressed to someone at another company, so it enters an email queue with other outgoing email messages. If there is a high volume of mail in the queue, the message will be delayed until the MTA processes the messages ahead of it.

E. **MTA to MTA Transfer:** When transferring an email, the sending MTA handles all aspects of mail delivery until the message has been either accepted or rejected by the receiving MTA. As the email clears the queue, it enters the Internet network cloud, where it is routed along a host-to-host chain of servers. Each MTA in the Internet network cloud needs to "stop and ask directions" from the DNS in order to identify the next MTA in the delivery chain. The exact route depends partly on server availability and mostly on which MTA can be found to accept email for the domain specified in the address. Most email takes a path that is dependent on server availability, so a pair of messages originating from the same host and addressed to the same receiving host could take different paths. These days, it's mostly spammers that specify any part of the path, deliberately routing their message through a series of relay servers in an attempt to obscure the true origin of the message. To find the recipient's IP address and mailbox, the MTA must drill down through the DNS, which consists of a set of servers distributed across the Internet. Beginning with the root nameservers at the top-level domain (.tld), then domain nameservers that handle requests for domains within that .tld, and eventually to nameservers that know about the local domain. There are thirteen root servers serving the top-level domains (e.g., .org, .com, .edu, .gov, .net, etc.). These root servers refer requests for a given domain to the root name servers that handle requests for that tld. In practice, this step is seldom necessary. The MTA can bypass this step because it has already knows which domain name servers handle requests for these .tlds. It asks the appropriate DNS server which Mail Exchange (MX) servers have knowledge of the subdomain or local host in the email address. The DNS server responds with an MX record: a prioritized list of MX servers for this domain. An MX server is really an MTA, just like a person who holds two jobs with different job titles (or three, if the MTA also handles the responsibilities of an MDA). To the DNS server, the server that accepts messages is an MX server. When is transferring messages, it is called an MTA. The MTA contacts the MX servers on the MX record in order of priority until it finds the designated host for that address domain. The sending MTA asks if the host accepts messages for the recipient's username at that domain (i.e.,username@domain.tld) and transfers the message.

F. **Firewalls, Spam and Virus Filters:** An email may be transferred to more than one MTA within a network cloud and is likely to be passed to at least one firewall before it reaches it's destination. An email encountering a firewall may be tested by spam and virus filters before it is allowed to pass inside the firewall. These filters test to see if the message qualifies as spam or malware. If the message contains malware, the file is usually quarantined and the sender is notified. If the message is identified as spam, it will probably be deleted without notifying the sender. Spam is difficult to detect because it can assume so many different forms. When an email from a list or other automated source seems to have vanished somewhere in the network cloud, the culprit is usually a spam filter at the receiver's ISP or company.

9.5 SECURITY IN E-MAIL

To protect customer accounts and data from attackers, email service providers have email protection measures in place. These steps involve email servers with robust frameworks for password and authentication, secure emails (both inbox and in transit), firewalls for web applications and spam detection tools.

As a platform for delivering viruses, spam, and phishing attacks, e-mail is prominent with attackers. To manipulate users into disclosing personal information, they use misleading texts, culminating in identity fraud. They tempt users to register files or click URLs on the user's computer that allow maliciously (like email malware). For threats, anyone wants to penetrate network architecture and hack sensitive customer information, email is often a key entry point. The characteristics of E-mail security are often flexible. It's not like, all reliable email services are confidential and protected indeed. Some of the most common features of e-mail service providers are mentioned-below.

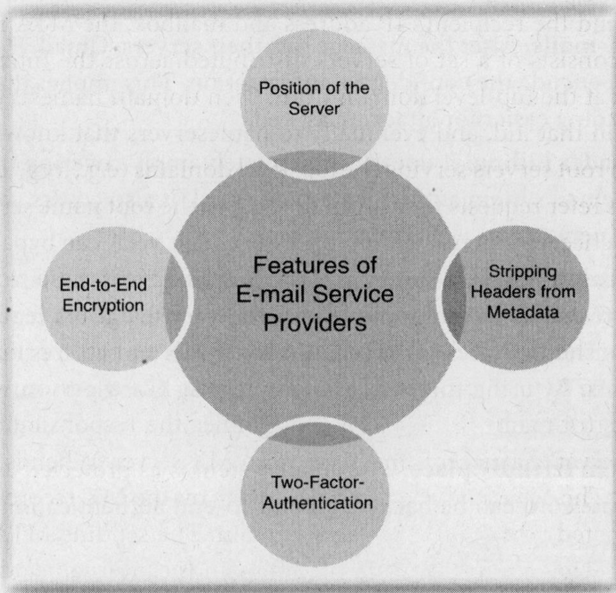

Figure 9.14: Features of E-mail Service Providers

- **End-to-end encryption:** This is a method of secure communication that prevents third parties from accessing data while it's transferred from one end. No email service can call itself secure without end-to-end encryption. The message is only encoded till it hits Gmail or Yahoo mail when using a standard service. If end-to-end encryption is used, the text can only be read by the sender and the receiver.
- **Two-Factor-Authentication:** Two-factor-authentication (2FA) gives great protection and protects the accounts in case anyone learns the password. Two-factor authentication, sometimes referred to as two-step verification or dual-factor authentication, is a security process in which users provide two different authentication factors to verify themselves. The first factor is a password and the second commonly includes a code sent to smartphone, or biometrics using fingerprint, face, or retina.
- **Stripping Headers from Metadata:** Metadata is "data about data" and the header in files such as HTML, WAV, MP3, text, etc contain a header, which defines the data within the file. For the sake of the sender and recipient confidentiality, protected email providers wipe out the header's metadata.
- **Position of the Server:** Many nations are not private information friendly. Some even have regulations for data protection that enable your personal information to be retained for a certain

time. The Five Eyes alliance is an intelligence-sharing arrangement between five English-speaking democracies such as the US, UK, Canada, Australia and New Zealand. They exchange intelligence information and are among the hardest locations for a safe email provider to enroll.

The benefits of using a protected email service is evident. Below are the considerations for selecting the suitable e-mail.

- **Protect the E-mails:** After the message hits their servers, Gmail, Hotmail, and other popular services don't encode the confidential information. This implies that they can translate them and make reading easier for attackers as well.
- **Metadata header hiding:** It doesn't immediately imply covering the headers with metadata if your daily email system authenticates your mail. It also covers your email account, laptop, browser, and network, as well as the receiver.
- **Do not be a commodity:** If the email is good and free to use, there may be some possibilities that user is treated as a commodity. However, very few users realize that service providers like Gmail constantly searches the mailbox for words and utilizes them to display customized advertisements. By using this way, you are helping Google to earn money from user's data with the help of Gmail.
- **Save e-mails in friendly place:** The email system is as protected as the passwords that have selected. If password can be hacked, all end-to-end authentication and logs regulations can be hacked.

9.6 SECURE E-MAIL SERVICE

End-to-end encryption is the distinguishing characteristic of encrypted messaging. It implies that there is no option for the mail service provider or a third party to decode the message. This can be done only by the receiver. As G-mail, Yahoo mail are not end to end encrypted, the messages can be read by any standard email service provider such as google and making them simpler for attackers to get. For protection, Pretty Good Privacy (PGP) and Secure/Multipurpose Internet Mail Extension (S/MIME) are the most prominent options. PGP incorporates symmetrical and asymmetrical protection, whereas S/MIME provide the certificates that must be approved by the certification authority at the regional or public level. We will discuss some different types of encryption levels that are used to secure email communication.

- **Transport-level Encryption:** Transport Layer Security (TLS) is a type of encryption protocol used to provide communication security over a network. Websites use TLS to secure all communications between their servers and web browsers. TLS cryptographic protocol that provides end-to-end security of data sent between applications over the Internet. Transport-level authentication guarantees that email moves securely across the network. Transport layer security, is counterpart of Secured Socket Layer (SSL) which is not in common application now. It is configured for encrypting emails (IMAP, SMTP) as well as other protocols, like HTTP (Hyper-Text Transfer Protocol) or FTP (File Transfer Protocol), on top of TCP (Transmission Control Protocol).

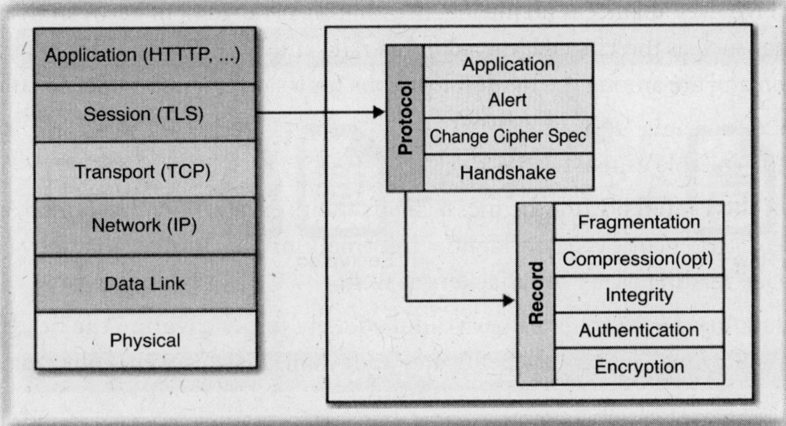

Figure 9.15: Transport Level Encryption

- **End-to-End Encryption:** End-to-End Encryption (E2EE) is a method of secure communication that prevents third parties from accessing data while it's transferred from one end system or device to another. In E2EE, the data is encrypted on the sender's system or device, and only the intended recipient can decrypt it. E2EE means that the text can be decrypted neither by the email service provider nor any other third party. Only the sender and the receiver having the public and private keys can unlock it. User encode the text with the public key of the partner. Now, this can only be decoded with the private key of the partner. Before it hits the partner, the encoded data passes via servers. User utilizes the private key to decode the message in exchange.

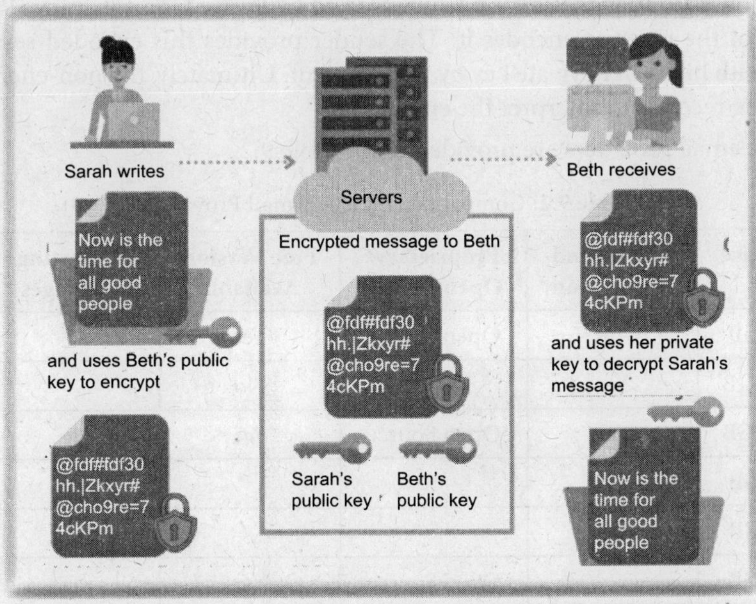

Figure 9.16: End-To-End Encryption Example

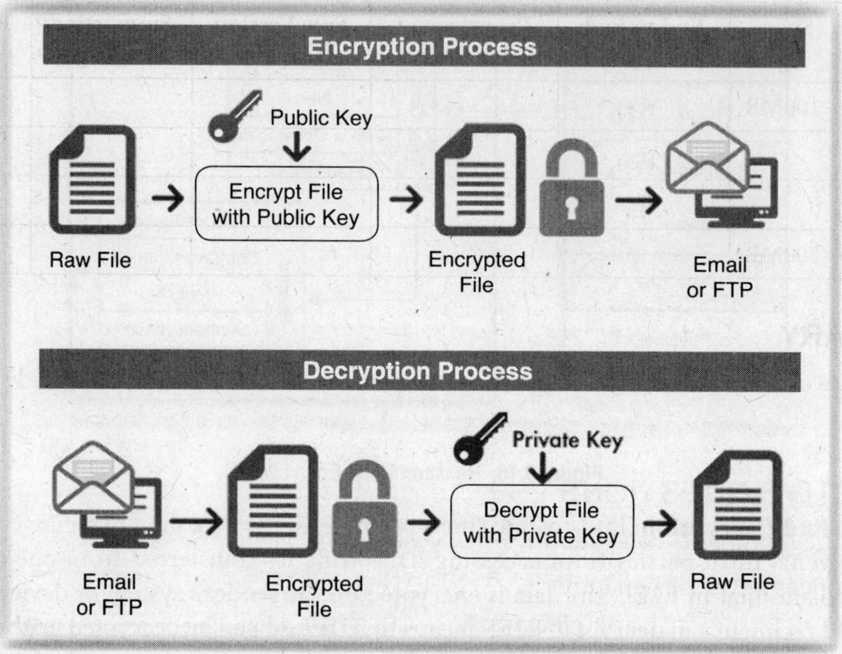

Figure 9.17: PGP Email Cryptology Process

- **PGP Email Cryptology:** In this, there is no need for users to share private keys. PGP email authentication incorporates a hashing algorithm, symmetric encryption and public-key authentication. Just after the session key is created by Pretty Good Privacy (PGP) protocol, the shared key of the receiver encodes it. The sender provides this encoded session key and it is decrypted with his or her private key by the recipient. Ultimately, the non-encrypted session key is used by the receiver to interpret the email.

A list of safe email providers are provided in the table 9.2.

Table 9.2: Comparison of Safe E-mail Providers

Service Provider	Space	End to End Encryption	Proprietary/ Open Source	Free Version Available	Supporting Languages	PGP	IMAP
Tutanota	1GB	Yes	Open Source	Yes	20	No	No
Hush Mail	10GB	Yes		No		Yes	Yes
Proton Mail	20GB	Yes	Open Source	Yes	20		
CounterMail	4GB	Yes				Yes	
Zoho Mail	5GB	Yes					
Posteo	2GB		Open Source				
StartMail	10GB	Yes				Yes	Yes

Service Provider	Space	End to End Encryption	Proprietary/ Open Source	Free Version Available	Supporting Languages	PGP	IMAP
TorGuard	100MB	Yes				Yes	
Mailbox		Yes					
Librem Mail		Yes					
Mailfence	500MB						

9.7 SUMMARY

In this chapter, we discussed on digital signatures, public key infrastructure, E-mail and security related to that.

9.8 OBJECTIVE QUESTIONS

The answer of the multiple-choice questions is marked in **bold**.

1. Which one is a type of signature?
   (a) wet (b) Clickwrap (c) Digital (d) **All of these**
2. Digital signature consists of .... algorithm.
   (a) Key generation (b) Signing (c) Verifying (d) **All of these**
3. .... is a type of digital signature.
   (a) Approval (b) Certified (c) Visible (d) **All of these**
4. .... is a process in key management.
   (a) Archival (b) Establishment (c) Generation (d) **All of these**
5. .... is a component of public key infrastructure.
   (a) Certification Authority (b) Registration Authority
   (c) Digital Certificate (d) **All of these**
6. .... is not a secure e-mail service provider.
   (a) Tutanota (b) Hush (c) **G-mail** (d) Proton

9.9 REVIEW QUESTIONS

1. Discuss various types of signatures.
2. Explain digital signature.

3. Explain various types of digital signatures.
4. Explain digital certificate obtaining process.
5. Discuss on key management.
6. Explain public key infrastructure.
7. Explain the working of e-mail.
8. Discuss security in e-mail.

9. Discuss on various secure e-mail service providers.
10. Explain the features of e-mail service providers.

9.10 ABBREVIATIONS AND SYMBOLS

Abbreviations	Full Form	Description
PKI	Public Key Infrastructure	PKI is a set of roles, policies, hardware, software and procedures needed to create, manage, distribute, use, store and revoke digital certificates and manage public-key encryption.
MUA	Mail User Agent	MUA also referred to as an email client, is a computer application that allows to send and retrieve email. MUAs can be software applications, such as Outlook Express and Lotus notes, or they can be webmail services such as those provided by Yahoo!, Microsoft Outlook.com, and Gmail.
MDA	Mail Delivery Agent	A Mail Delivery Agent (MDA) is a computer program that receives email from a Mail Transfer Agent (MTA); then sorts and delivers the email to the recipient's mailbox. The recipient accesses the email in their mailbox using a Mail User Agent (MUA).
MTA	Mail Transfer Agent	MTA is also known as message transfer agent or mail relay is software that transfers electronic mail messages from one computer to another using SMTP. The terms mail server, mail exchanger and MX host are also used in some contexts.
MX	Mail Exchange	ME is the software that provides the back end to an integrated system for email, calendaring, messaging, and tasks.
ISP	Internet Service Provider	ISP refers to a company that provides access to the Internet to customers.
S/MIME	Secure/Multipurpose internet Mail Extensions	S/MIME is a widely accepted protocol for sending digitally signed and encrypted messages.
PGP	Pretty Good Privacy	PGP is an encryption program that provides cryptographic privacy and authentication for data communication.

9.11 LIST OF FIGURES AND TABLES

The details of figures and tables used in this chapter is as below.

Figure / Table	Description
Figure 9.1	Signature Types
Figure 9.2	Working of Digital Signature
Figure 9.3	Steps of Creating Digital Signature
Figure 9.4	Model Digital Signature

CHAPTER

10

Information Theory

CONTENTS

10.1 INTRODUCTION

In this chapter, we are discussing on information theory and its physical relevance as well as applications.

10.2 INFORMATION THEORY

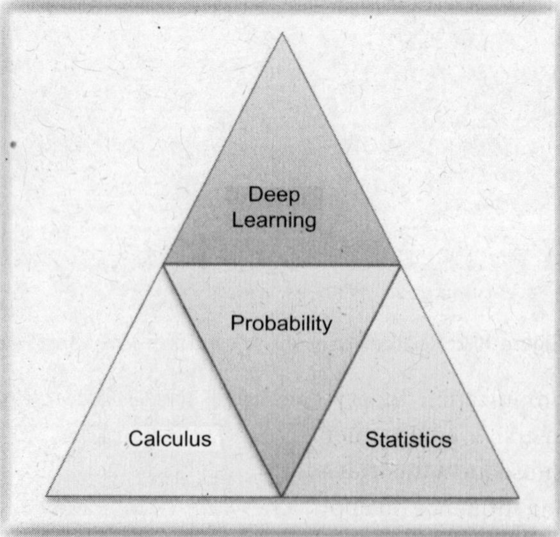

Figure 10.1: Building Blocks of Information Theory

Information theory is the mathematical treatment of the concepts, parameters and rules governing the transmission of messages through communication systems. Information theory was created to find practical ways to make better, more efficient codes and find the limits on how fast computers could process digital signals. Information theory is an important field that has made significant contribution to deep learning and artificial intelligence. Information theory can be seen as a sophisticated amalgamation of basic building blocks of deep learning, calculus, probability and statistics.

Deep learning can be considered as a subset of machine learning. It is a field that is based on learning and improving on its own by examining computer algorithms. While machine learning uses simpler concepts, deep learning works with artificial neural networks, which are designed to imitate how humans think and learn. Calculus is the study of how things change. It provides a framework for modeling systems in which there is change, and a way to arrive at the predictions of such models. A probability is a number that reflects the chance or likelihood of a particular event will occur. Probabilities can be expressed as proportions that range from 0 to 1, and they can also be expressed as percentages ranging from 0% to 100%. Statistics is the discipline that concerns the collection, organization, analysis, interpretation, and presentation of data.

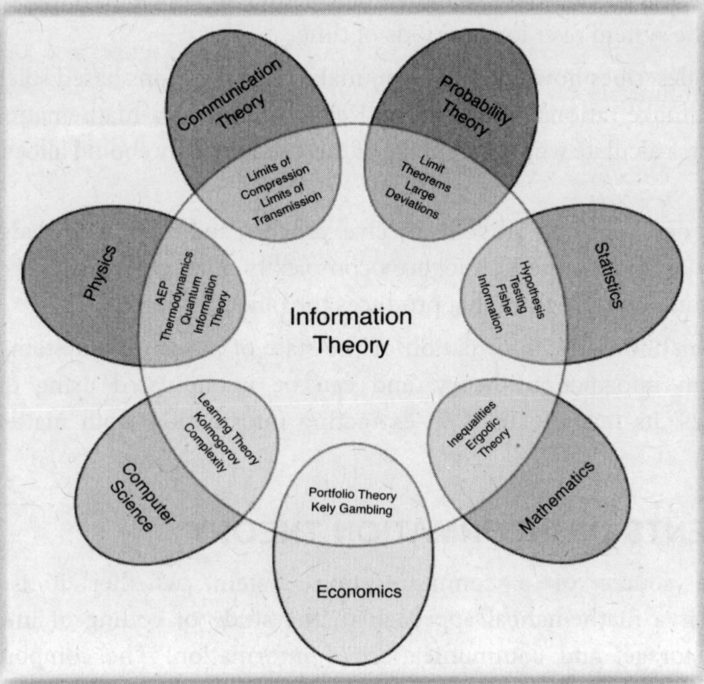

Figure 10.2: Relationship of Information Theory with Other Fields.

The elements in communication theory may be a basis for designing interactive systems, such as virtual reality and immersive environments and video-games. Communication theory has also contributed to developing subsequent theories and approaches, such as the "bidirectional communication theory", and has had a strong influence on approaches such as interactive design and human factors.

The compression theory says that if D is the tolerable amount of distortion, then R(D) is the best possible compression rate. When the compression is loss less, there is no distortion and D=0. The best possible compression rate is R (0).

Probability theory, is the branch of mathematics concerned with the analysis of random phenomena. In probability theory, the theory of large deviations concerns the asymptotic behavior of remote tails of sequences of probability distributions. Large deviations theory formalizes the practical ideas of concentration of measures and widely generalizes the assumption of convergence of probability measures. Roughly speaking, large deviations theory concerns itself with the exponential decline of the probability measures of certain kinds of extreme or tail events.

Fisher information tells us how much information about an unknown parameter we can get from a sample. Fisher information is used to construct hypothesis tests and confidence intervals using maximum likelihood estimators.

Ergodic theory is a branch of mathematics that studies statistical properties of deterministic dynamical systems. The ergodic theorem, when applied to a mechanical system such as one might meet in statistical mechanics or in celestial mechanics, allows one to conclude remarkable results about the average behavior of the system over long periods of time.

Portfolio theory describes how investors who make their decisions based solely on expected return and volatility should make rational choices. The Kelly criterion is a mathematical formula that helps investors and gamblers calculate what percentage of their money they should allocate to each investment or bet.

Learning theory describes how students receive, process, and retain knowledge during learning. In algorithmic information theory, the Kolmogorov complexity of an object, such as a piece of text, is the length of a shortest computer program that produces the object as output.

Quantum information is the information of the state of a quantum system. It is the basic entity of study in quantum information theory, and can be manipulated using quantum information processing techniques. Its main focus is in extracting information from matter at the microscopic scale.

10.3 COMPONENTS OF INFORMATION THEORY

Information is the source of a communication system, whether it is analog or digital. Information theory is a mathematical approach to the study of coding of information along with the quantification, storage, and communication of information. The components of information theory are entropy, data compression, channel capacity, rate distortion, network information theory, and hypothesis testing.

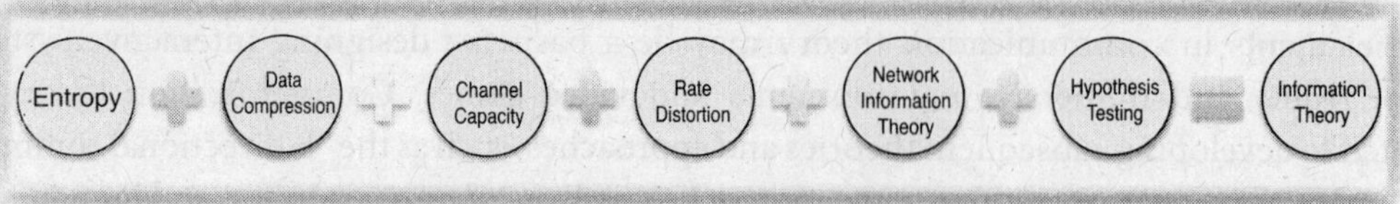

Figure 10.3: Information Theory Components

The primary goal of information theory is to quantify how much information is in data. The most important metric in information theory is called entropy. Entropy of a random variable is the average level of "information", "surprise", or "uncertainty" inherent in the variable's possible outcomes. Entropy quantifies the amount of uncertainty or surprise involved in the value of a random variable or the outcome of a random process. Entropy provides a measure of the average amount of information needed to represent an event drawn from a probability distribution for a random variable. In data communications, the term entropy refers to the relative degree of randomness. The higher the entropy, the more frequent are signaling errors. Entropy is directly proportional to the maximum attainable data speed in bits per second. Entropy is also directly proportional to noise and bandwidth. The concept of entropy in information theory describes with how much randomness or uncertainty are there is in a signal or random event. An alternative way to look at this is to talk about how much information is carried by the signal. Information is an ordered symbol of sequences to interpret its meaning. Basic idea is quantification and communication of information in the form of an Entropy. Entropy is a scientific concept, as well as a measurable physical property that is most commonly associated with a state of disorder, randomness, or uncertainty. Entropy describes the degree of uncertainty of a random variable which can take multiple states. It is the expected value of self-information from values of a discrete random variable and is also considered as the weighted average of self-information for various outputs. It is directly related to the minimum expected number of binary questions needed to identify the random variable. Larger the entropy, more questions we'll have to ask, more uncertainty around identity of a random variable. It gives the lower bound on number of bits required for encoding symbols drawn from any distribution P. Lower or higher values of entropy depend on the likelihood of outcome being certain or not. Differential entropy is an entropy for continuous distribution of a random variable x. In decision tree, information theory is used to decide the best split at each level to minimize entropy. Entropy can be defined as a measure of the average information content per source symbol.

$$H = -\sum_{i} p_i \log_b p_i$$

Where pi is the probability of the occurrence of character number i from a given stream of characters and *b* is the base of the algorithm used. Hence, this is also called as Shannon's entropy.

Data compression may be viewed as a branch of information theory in which the primary objective is to minimize the amount of data to be transmitted.

Channel capacity, is defined to be the maximum rate at which information can be transmitted through a channel. The fundamental theorem of information theory says that at any rate below channel capacity, an error control code can be designed whose probability of error is arbitrarily small.

Rate distortion theory is a major branch of information theory which provides the theoretical foundations for lossy data compression. It addresses the problem of determining the minimal number of bits per symbol, that should be communicated over a channel, so that the input signal can be approximately reconstructed at the output signal without exceeding an expected distortion.

Network information theory considers the information carrying capacity of a network. We have a system with multiple senders and receivers containing many new elements in the communication problems such as interference, cooperation and feedback. It involves the fundamental limits of communication and information theory in networks with multiple senders and receivers and optimal coding techniques and protocols which achieve these limits.

Hypothesis testing is an act in statistics whereby an analyst tests an assumption regarding a population parameter. The purpose of hypothesis testing is to determine whether there is enough statistical evidence in favor of a certain belief, or hypothesis, about a parameter. Information theory is widely using for hypothesis testing in statistics

10.4 SELF-INFORMATION

Within the context of information theory, self-information is defined as the amount of information that knowledge about the outcome of a certain event, adds to someone's overall knowledge. The amount of self-information is expressed in the unit of information: a bit. It is defined as a measure of information associated to a single value of discrete random variable. It is also called as the reciprocal of occurrence of an event. Let's better understand it with an example. "Sun rises in the east" - This is a highly certain event and has highest occurrence. So, the amount of information obtained in this case is zero or less. "It is going to rain in the desert tomorrow" - This is highly uncertain event and occurrence is low compared to the first message. So, this gives us more information compared to the previous one.

Self-information is expressed in a unit of information, for example bits, nats/shannons, or hartleys (also known as digits, dits, bans), depending on the base of the logarithm used in its definition.

Self-information I is given by: $I(X(i)) = \log(1/p(Xi))$

where, $X(i)$ has $x1, x2, \ldots$ as a set of random events, $P(X(i))$ is Probability of occurrence of an event, & $I(X(i))$ is the amount of information obtained from the occurrences of above events. From above formula, we can conclude that the information content only depends on probability $p(Xi)$ and not on actual value.

10.4.1 Development of Information Theory

Globally, interest in the concept of information grew after the creation of the telegraph. In 1844 the American inventor Samuel F.B. Morse built a telegraph communication. Morse encountered many electrical problems when he sent signals through buried transmission lines, but he encountered fewer problems when the lines were suspended on poles. This attracted the attention of many distinguished physicists. In a similar manner, the invention of the telephone in 1875 by Alexander Graham Bell and its subsequent proliferation attracted further scientific investigations, to the problems associated with transmitting signals over wires. Much of their work was done using Fourier analysis. This is a method of defining periodic waveforms in terms of trigonometric functions. This type of mathematical analysis that attempts to identify patterns or cycles in a time series data set which has already been normalized. In particular, it seeks to simplify complex or noisy data by decomposing it into a series of trigonometric or exponential functions, such as sine waves. In all of these cases the analysis was dedicated to solving the practical engineering problems of communication systems.

The formal study of information theory started in 1924, when Harry Nyquist, a researcher at Bell Laboratories, published a paper entitled "Certain Factors Affecting Telegraph Speed." He realized that noiseless communication channels have maximum data transmission rates, and he derived a formula for calculating these rates. In 1928, Nyquist's colleague R.V.L. Hartley, whose paper "Transmission of Information" established the first mathematical foundations for information theory.

The real birth of modern information theory initiated with the publication of Claude Shannon's "A Mathematical Theory of Communication" in the Bell System Technical Journal in 1948. A key step in Shannon's work was his realization that, in order to have a theory, communication signals must be treated in isolation from the meaning of the messages that they transmit. This view is in sharp contrast with the common conception of information, in which meaning has an essential role. Shannon also realized that the amount of knowledge conveyed by a signal is not directly related to the size of the message. Shannon realized that a useful theory of information would first have to concentrate on the problems associated with sending and receiving messages, and it would have to leave questions involving any intrinsic meaning of a message known as the semantic problem for later investigators. If the technical problem could not be solved—that is, if a message could not be transmitted correctly, then the semantic problem was not likely ever to be solved satisfactorily. Solving the technical problem was therefore the first step in developing a reliable communication system.

The practical stimuli for Shannon's work were the problems faced in BELL laboratories for creating a reliable telephone system. A key question that had to be answered in the early days of telecommunication was, how to transmit the maximum number of telephone conversations over existing cables. Prior to Shannon's work, the factors for achieving maximum utilization were not clearly understood. Shannon's work defined communication channels and showed how to assign a capacity to them, not only in the theoretical sense where no interference, or noise, was present but also in practical cases where real channels were subjected to real noise. Shannon produced a formula that showed how the bandwidth of a channel which is, its theoretical signal capacity and its signal-to-noise ratio which is a measure of interference affected its capacity to carry signals. In doing so he was able to suggest strategies for maximizing the capacity of a given channel and showed the limits of what was possible with a given technology. This was of great utility to engineers, who could focus thereafter on individual cases and understand the specific trade-offs involved.

Shannon also made a discovery that, even in the presence of noise, it is always possible to transmit signals arbitrarily close to the theoretical channel capacity. This discovery inspired engineers to look for practical techniques to improve performance in signal transmissions that were far from optimal. Shannon's work clearly distinguished between gains that could be realized by adopting a different encoding scheme from gains that could be realized only by altering the communication system itself. Before Shannon, engineers lacked a systematic way of analyzing and solving such problems. Shannon's work thus presented many key ideas that have guided engineers and scientists ever since. Though information theory does not always make clear exactly how to achieve specific results, people now know which questions are worth asking and can focus on areas that will yield the highest return. They also know which sorts of questions are difficult to answer and the areas in which there is not likely to be a large return for the amount of effort expended.

Since 1940s, the principles of classical information theory have been applied to many fields. The applications of information theory surveys achievements not only in such areas of telecommunications as data compression and error correction but also in the separate disciplines of physiology, linguistics, and physics.

Information theory is chiefly of interest to communication engineers, though some of the concepts have been adopted and used in such fields as psychology and linguistics. Information theory overlaps heavily with communication theory, but it is more oriented toward the fundamental limitations on the processing and communication of information and less oriented toward the detailed operation of particular devices. Information theory was created to find practical ways to make better, more efficient codes and find the limits on how fast computers could process digital signals. Every piece of digital information is the result of codes that have been examined and improved using Shannon's equation. The central paradigm of classic information theory is the engineering problem of the transmission of information over a noisy channel. Concepts, methods and results from coding theory and information theory are widely used in cryptography and cryptanalysis.

The information carried by a message depends on its probability. If there is one possible symbol, then there is no information to be gained since the outcome is not in question. More generally, if one symbol from a set has a probability of unity, then no information is conveyed. Information is the source of a communication system, whether it is analog or digital. Information theory is a mathematical approach to the study of coding of information along with the quantification, storage, and communication of information.

10.5 APPLICATIONS OF INFORMATION THEORY

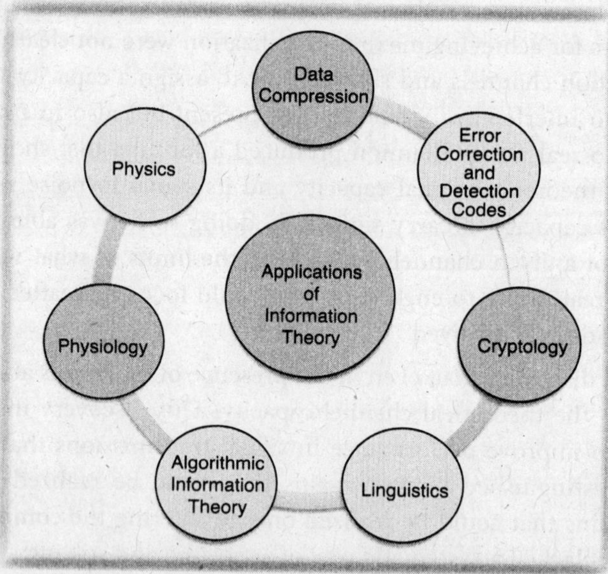

Figure 10.4: Applications of Information Theory

- **Data Compression:** Applications of fundamental topics of information theory include lossless data compression (e.g. ZIP files), lossy data compression (e.g. MP3s and JPEGs) and channel coding (e.g. for DSL). Shannon's concept of entropy which is a measure of the maximum possible efficiency of any encoding scheme. This can be used to determine the maximum theoretical compression for a given message alphabet. In particular, if the entropy is less than the average length of an encoding, compression is possible. The table shows the relative frequencies of letters in representative sample english text.

Table 10.1: Relative Frequencies of Characters in English Text

Character	Relative frequency (probability)	Character	Relative frequency (probability)	Character	Relative frequency (probability)
(space)	0.1859	H	0.0467	P	0.0152
E	0.1031	L	0.0321	G	0.0152
T	0.0796	D	0.0317	B	0.0127
A	0.0642	U	0.0228	V	0.0083
O	0.0632	C	0.0218	K	0.0049
I	0.0575	F	0.0208	X	0.0013
N	0.0574	M	0.0198	Q	0.0008
S	0.0514	W	0.0175	J	0.0008
R	0.0484	Y	0.0164	Z	0.0005

The table assumes that all letters have been capitalized and ignores all other characters except for spaces. The letter frequencies depend upon the particular text sample. Calculating the entropy of this distribution using Shannon's formula gives 4.08 bits per character. Normally 8 bits per character is used in the most common coding standard, Shannon's theory shows that there exists an encoding that is roughly twice as efficient as the normal one for this simplified message alphabet. These results, however, apply only to large samples and assume that the source of the character stream transmits characters in a random fashion based on the probabilities in the table. Real text does not perfectly fit this model; parts of it tend to be highly nonrandom and repetitive. Thus, the theoretical results do not immediately translate into practice.

In 1977–78 the Israelis Jacob Ziv and Abraham Lempel published two papers that showed how compression can be done dynamically. The basic idea is to store blocks of text in a dictionary and, when a block of text reappears, to record which block was repeated rather than recording the text itself. Although there are technical issues related to the size of the dictionary and the updating of its entries, this dynamic approach to compression has proved very useful, in part because the compression algorithm adapts to optimize the encoding based upon the particular text. Many computer programs use compression techniques based on these ideas. In practice, most text files compress by about 50 percent which is approximately 4 bits per character. This is the number suggested by the entropy calculation.

- **Error Correcting and Detecting Codes:** In telecommunication, information theory and coding theory, forward error correction (FEC) or channel coding is a technique used for controlling errors in data transmission over unreliable or noisy communication channels.

  Shannon's work in the area of discrete, noisy communication pointed out the possibility of constructing error-correcting codes. Error-correcting codes add extra bits to help correct errors and thus operate in the opposite direction from compression. Error-detecting codes, on the other hand, indicate that an error has occurred but do not automatically correct the error. Frequently the error is corrected by an automatic request to retransmit the message. Because error-correcting codes typically demand more extra bits than error-detecting codes. In some cases, it is more efficient to use an error-detecting code simply to indicate what has to be retransmitted.

Deciding between error-correcting and error-detecting codes requires a good understanding of the nature of the errors that are likely to occur under the circumstances in which the message is being sent. Transmissions to and from space vehicles generally use error-correcting codes because of the difficulties in getting retransmission. Because of the long distances and low power available in transmitting from space vehicles, it is easy to see that the utmost skill and art must be employed to build communication systems that operate at the limits imposed by Shannon's results.

A common type of error-detecting code is the parity code, which adds one bit to a block of bits so that the ones in the block always add up to either an odd or even number. For example, an odd parity code might replace the two-bit code words 00, 01, 10, and 11 with the three-bit words 001, 010, 100, and 111. Any single transformation of a 0 to a 1 or a 1 to a 0 would change the parity of the block and make the error detectable. In practice, adding a parity bit to a two-bit code is not very efficient, but for longer codes adding a parity bit is reasonable. For instance, computer and fax modems often communicate by sending eight-bit blocks, with one of the bits reserved as a parity bit. Because parity codes are simple to implement, they are also often used to check the integrity of computer equipment.

As noted earlier, designing practical error-correcting codes is not easy, and Shannon's work does not provide direct guidance in this area. Nevertheless, knowing the physical characteristics of the channel, such as bandwidth and signal-to-noise ratio, gives valuable knowledge about maximum data transmission capabilities.

- **Cryptology:** Cryptology is the science of secure communication. Information theory has several applications in cryptography. First, it allows to prove the unconditional security of cryptographic systems. Second, it allows to prove impossibility and lower bound results on the achievability of unconditional security.

  Shannon's analysis of communication codes led him to apply the mathematical tools of information theory to cryptography in "Communication Theory of Secrecy Systems" in 1949. He began his analysis by noting that simple transposition ciphers such as those obtained by permuting the letters in the alphabet that do not affect the entropy because they merely relabel the characters in his formula without changing their associated probabilities.

  Cryptographic systems employ special information called a key to help encrypt and decrypt messages. Sometimes different keys are used for the encoding and decoding, while in other instances the same key is used for both processes. Shannon made the general observation: "the amount of uncertainty we can introduce into the solution cannot be greater than the key uncertainty." This means, among other things, that random keys should be selected to make the encryption more secure. While Shannon's work did not lead to new practical encryption schemes, he did supply a framework for understanding the essential features of any such system.

- **Linguistics:** While information theory has been most helpful in the design of more efficient telecommunication systems, it has also motivated linguistic studies of the relative frequencies of words, the length of words, and the speed of reading. The best-known formula for studying relative word frequencies was proposed by the American linguist George Zipf in 1932. Zipf's Law states that the relative frequency of a word is inversely proportional to its rank. That is, the second most frequent word is used only half as often as the most frequent word, and the 100th most frequent word is used only one hundredth as often as the most frequent word. Consistent with the encoding ideas, the most frequently used words tend to be the shortest. It is uncertain how much of this phenomenon is due to a "principle of least effort," but using the shortest sequences for the most common words certainly promotes greater communication efficiency.

Information theory provides a means for measuring redundancy or efficiency of symbolic representation within a given language. For example, if English letters occurred with equal regularity ignoring the distinction between uppercase and lowercase letters, the expected entropy of an average sample of English text would be log2(26), which is approximately 4.7. The table of relative frequencies of characters in English text shows an entropy of 4.08, which is not really a good value for English because it overstates the probability of combinations. Scientists have studied sequences of eight characters in English and come up with a figure of about 2.35 for the average entropy of English. Because this is only half the 4.7 value, it is said that English has a relative entropy of 50 percent and a redundancy of 50 percent.

A redundancy of 50 percent means that roughly half the letters in a sentence could be omitted and the message still can be reconstructed. The question of redundancy is of great interest to crossword puzzle creators. For example, if redundancy was 0 percent, so that every sequence of characters was a word, then there would be no difficulty in constructing a crossword puzzle because any character sequence that the designer wanted to use would be acceptable. As redundancy increases, the difficulty of creating a crossword puzzle also increases. Shannon showed that a redundancy of 50 percent is the upper limit for constructing two-dimensional crossword puzzles and that 33 percent is the upper limit for constructing three-dimensional crossword puzzles. Shannon also observed that when longer sequences, such as paragraphs, chapters, and whole books, are considered, the entropy decreases and English becomes even more predictable. He considered longer sequences and concluded that the entropy of English is approximately one bit per character. This indicates that in longer text nearly all of the message can be guessed from just a 20 to 25 percent random sample.

Various studies have attempted to come up with an information processing rate for human beings. Some studies have concentrated on the problem of determining a reading rate. Such studies have shown that the reading rate seems to be independent of language. That is, people process about the same number of bits whether they are reading English or Chinese even though Chinese characters require more bits for their representation than English letters. There exist about 10,000 common Chinese characters, compared with 26 English letters contain more information. Thus, on balance, reading rates are comparable.

- **Algorithmic Information Theory:** Algorithmic information theory (AIT) is the information theory of individual objects, using computer science, and concerns itself with the relationship between computation, information, and randomness. In the 1960s the American mathematician Gregory Chaitin, the Russian mathematician Andrey Kolmogorov, and the American engineer Raymond Solomonoff began to formulate and publish an objective measure of the intrinsic complexity of a message. Chaitin, a research scientist at IBM, developed the largest body of work and polished the ideas into a formal theory known as Algorithmic Information Theory. This comes from defining the complexity of a message as the length of the shortest algorithm, or step-by-step procedure, for its reproduction.

- **Physiology:** Almost as soon as Shannon's papers on the mathematical theory of communication were published in the 1940s, people began to consider the question of how messages are handled inside human beings. After all, the nervous system is, above all else, a channel for the transmission of information, and the brain is, among other things, an information processing and messaging center. Because nerve signals generally consist of pulses of electrical energy, the nervous system appears to be an example of discrete communication over a noisy channel. Thus, both physiology and information theory are involved in studying the nervous system.

  Many researchers expected that the human brain would show a tremendous information processing capability. Interestingly, when researchers sought to measure information processing capabilities during "intelligent" or "conscious" activities, such as reading or piano playing, they came up with a maximum capability of less than 50 bits per second. For example, a typical reading rate of 300 words per minute works out to about 5 words per second. Assuming an average of 5 characters per word and roughly 2 bits per character yields the aforementioned rate of 50 bits per second. The exact number depends on various assumptions and could vary depending on the individual and the task being performed. It is known, that the senses gather some 11 million bits per second from the environment.

  The table 10.2 shows how much information is processed by each of the five senses. This table immediately directs attention to the problem of determining what is happening to all this data. In other words, the human body sends 11 million bits per second to the brain for processing, yet the conscious mind seems to be able to process only 50 bits per second.

  Table 10.2: Information Transmission Rates of the Senses

Sensory system	Bits per second
Eyes	10000K
Skin	1000K
Ears	100K
Smell	100K
Taste	1K

  It appears that a tremendous amount of compression is taking place if 11 million bits are being reduced to less than 50. Note that the discrepancy between the amount of information being transmitted and the amount of information being processed is so large that any inaccuracy in the measurements is insignificant.

  Two more problems suggest themselves when thinking about this immense amount of compression. First is the problem of determining how long it takes to do the compression, and second is the problem of determining where the processing power is found for doing this much compression.

The solution to the first problem is suggested by the approximately half-second delay between the instant that the senses receive a stimulus and the instant that the mind is conscious of a sensation. To compensate for this delay, the body has a reflex system that can respond in less than one-tenth of second, before the mind is conscious of the stimulus. This half-second delay seems to be the time required for processing and compressing sensory input.

The solution to the second problem is suggested by the approximately 100 billion cells of the brain, each with connections to thousands of other brain cells. Equipped with this many processors, the brain might be capable of executing as many as 100 billion operations per second, a truly impressive number.

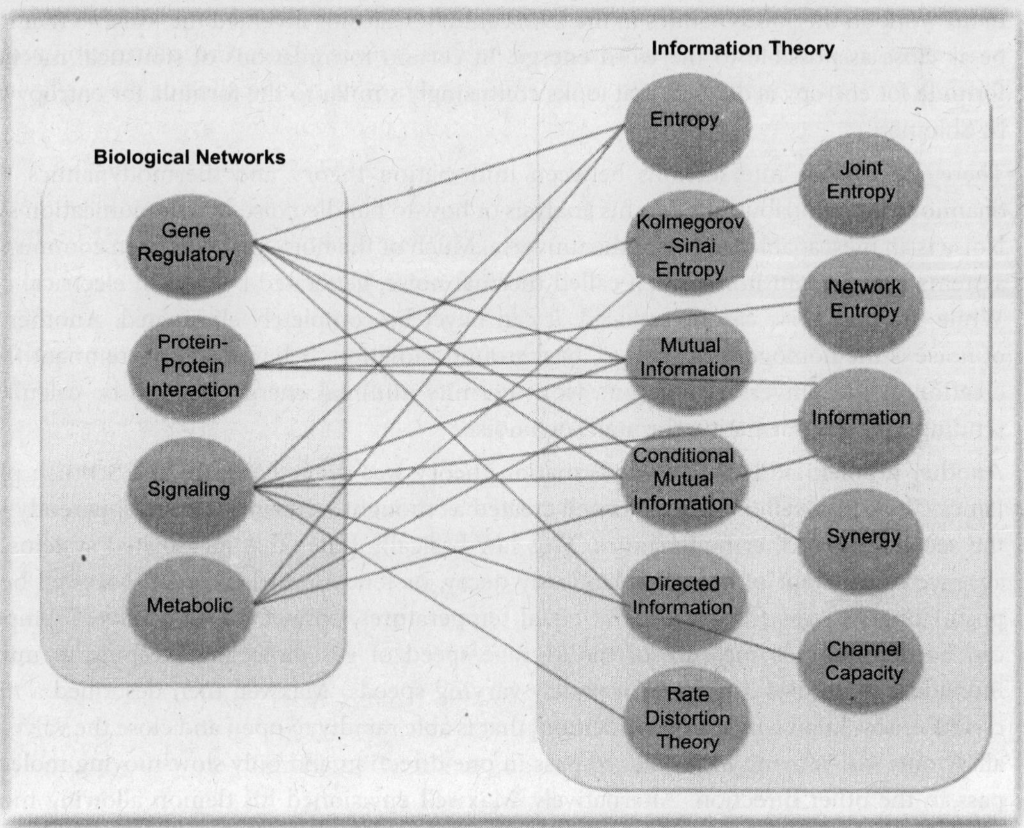

Figure 10.5: Information Theory in System Biology

It is often assumed that consciousness is the dominant feature of the brain. The brief observations above suggest a rather different picture. It now appears that the vast majority of processing is accomplished outside conscious notice and that most of the body's activities take place outside direct conscious control. This suggests that practice and habit are important because they train circuits in the brain to carry out some actions "automatically," without conscious interference. Even such a "simple" activity as walking is best done without interference from consciousness, which does not have enough information processing capability to keep up with the demands of this task.

The brain also seems to have separate mechanisms for short-term and long-term memory. Based on psychologist George Miller's paper "The Magical Number Seven, Plus or Minus Two: Some Limits on Our Capacity for Processing Information" (1956), it appears that short-term memory can only store between five and nine pieces of information to which it has been exposed only briefly. Note that this does not mean between five and nine bits, but rather five to nine chunks of information. Obviously, long-term memory has a greater capacity, but it is not clear exactly how the brain stores information or what limits may exist. Some scientists hope that information theory may yet afford further insights into how the brain functions.

- **Physics:** The term entropy was originally introduced by the German physicist Rudolf Clausius in his work on thermodynamics in the 19th century. Clausius invented the word so that it would be as close as possible to the word energy. In certain formulations of statistical mechanics a formula for entropy is derived that looks confusingly similar to the formula for entropy derived by Shannon.

  There are various intersections between information theory and thermodynamics. One of Shannon's key contributions was his analysis of how to handle noise in communication systems. Noise is an inescapable feature of the universe. Much of the noise that occurs in communication systems is a random noise, often called thermal noise, generated by heat in electrical circuits. While thermal noise can be reduced, it can never be completely eliminated. Another source of noise is the homogeneous cosmic background radiation, believed to be a remnant from the creation of the universe. Shannon's work permits minimal energy costs to be calculated for sending a bit of information through such noise.

  Another problem addressed by information theory was dreamed up by the Scottish physicist James Clerk Maxwell in 1871. Maxwell created a "thought experiment" that apparently violates the second law of thermodynamics. This law basically states that all isolated systems, in the absence of an input of energy, relentlessly decay, or tend toward disorder. Maxwell began by postulating two gas-filled vessels at equal temperatures, connected by a valve. (Temperature can be defined as a measure of the average speed of gas molecules, keeping in mind that individual molecules can travel at widely varying speeds) Maxwell then described a mythical creature, now known as Maxwell's demon, that is able rapidly to open and close the valve so as to allow only fast-moving molecules to pass in one direction and only slow-moving molecules to pass in the other direction. Alternatively, Maxwell envisioned his demon allowing molecules to pass through in only one direction. In either case, a "hot" and a "cold" vessel or a "full" and "empty" vessel, the apparent result is two vessels that, with no input of energy from an external source, constitute a more orderly isolated system—thus violating the second law of thermodynamics.

  Information theory allows one exorcism of Maxwell's demon to be performed. In particular, it shows that the demon needs information in order to select molecules for the two different vessels but that the transmission of information requires energy. Once the energy requirement for collecting information is included in the calculations, it can be seen that there is no violation of the second law of thermodynamics.

10.6 TYPES OF COMMUNICATION

In information theory, the communication is divided into four types. This is shown in figure

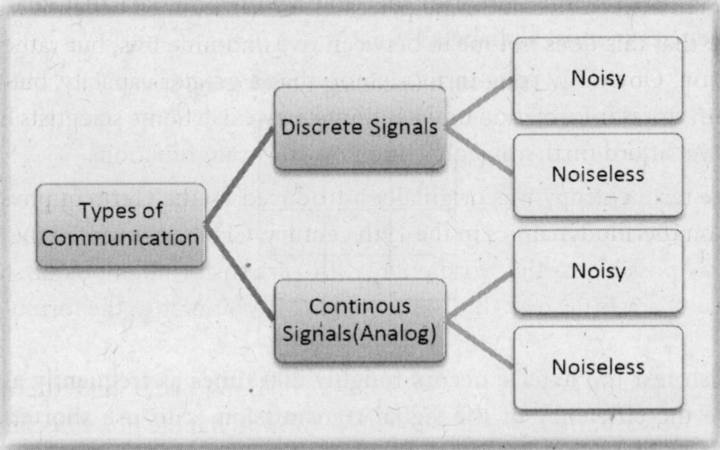

Figure 10.6: Types of Communication

10.6.1 Discrete Signals

Discrete signals can represent only a finite number of different, recognizable states. English alphabet is a discrete communication system. It consists of a finite set of characters, such as uppercase and lowercase letters, and various punctuation marks. Signal components in any discrete communication system will be referred to as characters. Messages are composed by stringing these individual characters together appropriately.

For noiseless communications, the decoder at the receiving end receives exactly the characters sent by the encoder. However, these transmitted characters are typically not in the original message's alphabet. For example, in morse code appropriately spaced short and long electrical pulses, light flashes, or sounds are used to transmit the message. Similarly, many forms of digital communication use a signal alphabet consisting of just two characters, sometimes called bits. These characters are generally denoted by 0 and 1, but in practice they might be different electrical or optical levels. A key question in discrete, noiseless communication is deciding how to most efficiently convert messages into the signal alphabet. The concepts involved will be illustrated by the following simplified example.

The message alphabet will be called M and will consist of the four characters A, B, C, and D. The signal alphabet will be called S and will consist of the characters 0 and 1. Furthermore, it will be assumed that the signal channel can transmit 10 characters from S each second. This rate is called the channel capacity. Subject to these constraints, the goal is to maximize the transmission rate of characters from M.

The first question is how to convert characters between M and S. One straight forward way is shown in the table encoding 1 of M using S. Using this conversion, the message ABC would be transmitted using the sequence 000110. The conversion from M to S is referred to as encoding. This type of encoding is not meant to disguise the message but simply to adapt it to the nature of the communication system. Because each character from M is represented by two characters from S and because the channel capacity is 10 characters from S each second, this communication scheme can transmit five characters from M each second. However, the scheme shown in the table ignores the fact that characters are used with widely varying frequencies in most alphabets.

Table 10.3: Encoding 1 of M using S

M	→	S
A		0
B		1
C		10
D		11

In typical English text the letter e occurs roughly 200 times as frequently as the letter z. Hence, one way to improve the efficiency of the signal transmission is to use shorter codes for the more frequent characters—an idea employed in the design of morse code. For example, let it be assumed that generally one-half of the characters in the messages that we wish to send are the letter A, one-quarter are the letter B, one-eighth are the letter C, and one-eighth are the letter D. The table Encoding 2 of M using S summarizes this information and shows an alternative encoding for the alphabet M. Now the message ABC would be transmitted using the sequence 010110, which is also six characters long. To see that this second encoding is better, on average, than the first one requires a longer typical message. For instance, suppose that 120 characters from M are transmitted with the frequency distribution shown in the table.

Table 10.4: Encoding 2 of M using S

Frequency	M	→	S
50%	A		0
25%	B		10
12.50%	C		110
12.50%	D		111

The results are summarized in the table comparison of two encodings from M to S. This table shows that the second encoding uses 30 fewer characters from S than the first encoding. Recall that the first encoding, limited by the channel capacity of 10 characters per second, would transmit five characters from M per second, irrespective of the message. Working under the same limitations, the second encoding would transmit all 120 characters from M in 21 seconds (210 characters from S at 10 characters per second) which yields an average rate of about 5.7 characters per second. Note that this improvement is for a typical message (one that contains the expected frequency of A's and B's). For a typical message—in this case, one with unusually many C's and D's—this encoding might actually take longer to transmit than the first encoding.

Table 10.5: Comparison of Two Encodings from M to S

Character	Number of cases	Length of encoding 1	Length of encoding 2
A	60	120	60
B	30	60	60
C	15	30	45
D	15	30	45
Totals	120	240	210

A natural question to ask at this point is whether the above scheme is really the best possible encoding or whether something better can be devised. Shannon was able to answer this question using a quantity called "entropy". A brief review of some practical issues in decoding and encoding messages are discussed below.

To be useful, each encoding must have a unique decoding. Consider the encoding shown in the table A less useful encoding. While every message can be encoded using this scheme, some will have duplicate encodings. For example, both the message AA and the message C will have the encoding 00. Thus, when the decoder receives 00, it will have no obvious way of telling whether AA or C was the intended message. For this reason, the encoding shown in this table would have to be characterized as "less useful."

Table 10.6: A Less Useful Encoding

M	→	S
A		0
B		1
C		0
D		11

Encodings that produce a different signal for each distinct message are called "uniquely decipherable." Most real applications require uniquely decipherable codes.

Another useful property is ease of decoding. For example, using the first encoding scheme, a received signal can be divided into groups of two characters and then decoded using the table Encoding 1 of M using S. Thus, to decode the signal 11010111001010, first divide it into 11 01 01 11 00 10 10, which indicates that DBBDACC was the original message.

Table 10.7: Decoding a Message Encoded with Encoding 2

Decoded so far	Remainder of signal string
	1001100111010
A	1001100111010
A B	1100111010
A B A	1100111010
A B A C	111010

Decoded so far	Remainder of signal string
A B A C A	111010
A B A C A D	10
A B A C A D A	10
A B A C A D A B	

The scheme shown in the table encoding 2 of M using S must be decrypted using a different technique because strings of different length are used to represent characters from M. The technique here is to read one digit at a time until a matching character is found in this table. For example, suppose that the string 01001100111010 is received. Reading this string from the left, the first 0 matches the character A. Thus, the string 1001100111010 now remains. Because 1, the next digit, does not match any entry in the table, the next digit must now be added. This two-digit combination, 10, matches the character B.

The table decoding a message encoded with encoding 2 shows each unique stage of decoding this string. While the second encoding might appear to be complicated to decode, it is logically simple and easy to automate. The same technique can also be used to decode the first encoding.

The table an impractical encoding, on the other hand, shows a code that involves some complications in its decoding. The encoding here has the virtue of being uniquely decipherable, but to understand what makes it "impractical," consider the following strings: 011111111111111 and 01111111111111. The first is an encoding of CDDDD and the second of BDDDD. Unfortunately, to decide whether the first character is a B or a C requires viewing the entire string and then working back. Having to wait for the entire signal to arrive before any part of the message can be decoded can lead to significant delays.

Table 10.8: An Impractical Encoding

M	→	S
A		0
B		1
C		11
D		111

In contrast, the encodings in both the table encoding 1 of M using S and the table encoding 2 of M using S allow messages to be decoded as the signal is received, or "on the fly." The table 10.9 compares the first two encodings.

Table 10.9: Another Comparison of Encodings from M to S

Character	Number of cases	Length of encoding 1	Length of encoding 2
A	30	60	30
B	30	60	60
C	30	60	90
D	30	60	90
Totals	120	240	270

Encodings that can be decoded on the fly are called prefix codes or instantaneous codes. Prefix codes are always uniquely decipherable, and they are generally preferable to non-prefix codes for communication because of their simplicity. Additionally, it has been shown that there must always exist a prefix code whose transmission rate is as good as that of any uniquely decipherable code, and, when the probability distribution of characters in the message is known, further improvements in the transmission rate can be achieved by the use of variable-length codes, such as the encoding used in the table 10.4 Huffman codes, invented by D.A. Huffman in 1952, produce the minimum average code length among all uniquely decipherable variable-length codes for a given symbol set and a given probability distribution.

Shannon's concept of entropy can now be taken up. Recall that the table 10.5 showed that the second encoding scheme would transmit an average of 5.7 characters from M per second. But suppose that, instead of the distribution of characters shown in the table, a long series of A were transmitted. as each A is represented by just a single character from S, this would result in the maximum transmission rate, for the given channel capacity, of 10 characters per second from M. On the other hand, transmitting a long series of Ds would result in a transmission rate of only 3.3 characters from M per second because each D must be represented by 3 characters from S. The average transmission rate of 5.7 is obtained by taking a weighted average of the lengths of each character code and dividing the channel speed by this average length. The formula for average length is given by:

Average Length = $.5 \times 1 + .25 \times 2 + .125 \times 3 + .125 \times 3 = 1.75$, where the length of each symbol's code is multiplied by its probability, or relative frequency. For instance, since the letter B makes up 25 percent of an average message, its relative frequency is .25. That figure is multiplied by 2, the number of characters that encode B in the signal alphabet. When the channel speed of 10 characters per second is divided by the average length computed above, the result is 10/1.75, or approximately 5.7 characters from M per second.

The average length formula can be generalized as Average Length = p_1 Length(c_1) + p_2 Length(c_2) + ... + p_k Length(c_k), where p_i is the probability of the ith character (here called c_i) and Length(c_i) represents the length of the encoding for c_i. Note that this equation can be used to compare the transmission efficiency of existing encodings, but it cannot be used to discover the best possible encoding. Shannon, was able to find a quantity that provide a theoretical limit for the efficiency of any possible encoding, based solely upon the average distribution of characters in the message alphabet. This is the quantity that he called entropy, and it is represented by H in the formula $H = p_1 \log_s(1/p_1) + p_2 \log_s(1/p_2) + \ldots\ldots + p_k \log_s(1/p_k)$. There are several things worth noting about this equation. First is the presence of the symbol $\log_s$. Here the subscript s represents the number of elements in the signal alphabet S; $\log_s$, therefore, may be thought of as calculating an "optimal length" for a given distribution. Second, note that the reciprocals of the probabilities ($1/p_1$, $1/p_2$, ...) are used rather than the probabilities themselves (p_1, p_2, ...). Before explaining this equation in more detail, the following discovery of Shannon makes explicit the relationship between H and the Average Length H ≤ Average Length. Thus, the entropy for a given message alphabet determines the limit on average encoding efficiency (as measured by message length). Because the signal alphabet, S, has only two symbols (0 and 1), a very small table of values of $\log_2$, as shown in below table will suffice for illustration.

Some values of log2					
n	log2(n)	n	log2(n)	n	log2(n)
1.0	0.000	4.0	2.000	7.0	2.807
1.5	0.585	4.5	2.170	7.5	2.907
2.0	1.000	5.0	2.322	8.0	3.000
2.5	1.322	5.5	2.459	8.5	3.087
3.0	1.585	6.0	2.585	9.0	3.170
3.5	1.807	6.5	2.700	9.5	3.248

With these preliminaries established, it is now possible to decide whether the encodings introduced earlier are truly optimal. In the first distribution as shown in the table 10.3, all characters have a probability of 0.25. In this case, the entropy is given by

.25 log2 (1/.25) + .25 log2 (1/.25) + .25 log2 (1/.25) + .25 log2 (1/.25), which is equal to 4 × .25 × 2 = 2. Recall that the average length for the first encoding is also 2; hence, this encoding is optimal and cannot be improved.

For the second distribution as shown in the table 10.4, the entropy is

.5 log2(1/.5) + .25 log2(1/.25) + .125 log2(1/.125) + .125 log2(1/.125), which is equal to .5 + .5 + .375 + .375 = 1.75. Recall that this is equal to the average length of the second encoding for this distribution of characters. Once again, an optimal encoding has been found.

The two examples considered might suggest that it is always easy to find an optimal code. Therefore, it may be worth looking at a counter example. Suppose that the probabilities for the characters in M are altered as shown in the table 10.10. For the distribution given in this table,

$$H = .4 \log2(2.5) + 3 \times .2 \log2(5) = 1.922.$$

In this case, however, all simple encodings for M—those that substitute a string of characters from S for each character in M—have an average length ≥ 2. Thus, the bound computed using entropy cannot be attained with simple encodings. Shannon illustrated a technique for improving the performance of codes at the cost of complicating the encoding and decoding. The basic idea is to encode blocks of characters taken from M. For example, consider how often pairs of the characters shown in this table occur, assuming that the characters appear independently of each other. The probability for each pair is obtained by multiplying together the probabilities of the individual characters that make up the pair, as shown in the table 10.10. The pair AA would occur on the average 16 percent of the time (.16 = .4 × .4).

Table 10.10: Altered Probabilities for M

Character	Probability
A	0.4
B	0.2
C	0.2
D	0.2

The 16 possible pairs of A, B, C, and D, together with their probabilities, and a possible encoding, are shown in the table 10.11. As can be verified, the encoding given in this table is a prefix code. The average length of the encoding in this table is 3.92 characters of S for every 2 characters of M, or 1.96 characters of S for every character of M. This is better than the 2.0 obtained earlier, although still not equal to the entropy. Because the entropy is not exactly equal to any fraction, no code exists whose average length is exactly equal to the entropy. But Shannon did show that more complex codes can always be created whose average length is as close to the entropy limit as desired at the cost of being increasingly complex and difficult to utilize.

Table 10.11: Probabilities of Pairs of Characters from M

Pair	Probability	Encoding	Pair	Probability	Encoding	Pair	Probability	Encoding	Pair	Probability	Encoding
AA	0.16	0	BA	0.08	110	CA	0.08	1000	DA	0.08	111
AB	0.08	101	BB	0.04	1011	CB	0.04	1110	DB	0.04	1010
AC	0.08	11	BC	0.04	1001	CC	0.04	1101	DC	0.04	1001
AD	0.08	10	BD	0.04	1111	CD	0.04	1100	DD	0.04	1000

Summarizing, the average character distribution in the message alphabet determines a limit, known as Shannon's entropy, on the best average (that is, the shortest) attainable encoding scheme. The theoretical best encoding scheme can be attained only in special circumstances. Finally, an encoding scheme can be found as close to the theoretical best as desired, although its use may be impractical because of the necessary increase in its complexity.

In the discussion, it is assumed unrealistically that all messages are transmitted without error. In the real world, however, transmission errors are unavoidable especially given the presence in any communication channel of noise, which is the sum total of random signals that interfere with the communication signal. In order to take the inevitable transmission errors of the real world into account, some adjustment in encoding schemes is necessary. The figure 10.7 shows a simple model of transmission in the presence of noise, the binary symmetric channel. Binary indicates that this channel transmits only.

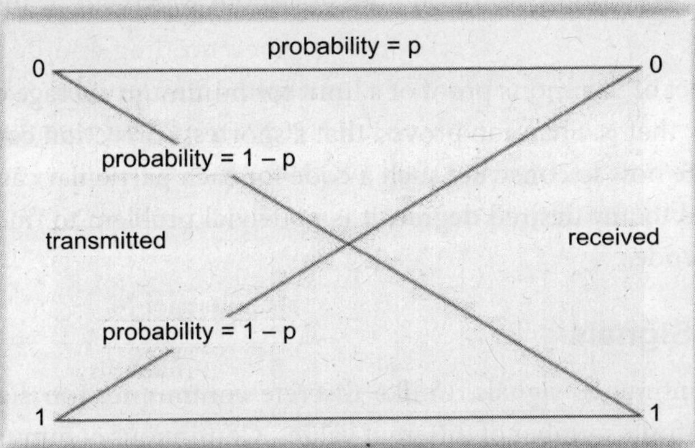

Figure 10.7: The Binary Symmetric Channel

two distinct characters, generally interpreted as 0 and 1, while symmetric indicates that errors are equally probable regardless of which character is transmitted. The probability that a character is transmitted without error is labeled p; hence, the probability of error is 1 – p

This type of channel transmits only two distinct characters, generally interpreted as 0 and 1, hence the designation binary. The probability of correctly receiving either character is the same, namely, p, which accounts for the designation symmetric.

Consider what happens as zeros and ones, hereafter referred to as bits, emerge from the receiving end of the channel. Ideally, there would be a means of determining which bits were received correctly. In that case, it is possible to imagine two printouts:

10110101010010011001010011101101000010100101—Signal

00000000000010000000010000000001000000011001—Errors

Signal is the message as received, while each 1 in errors indicates a mistake in the corresponding signal bit. (Errors itself is assumed to be error-free.) Shannon showed that the best method for transmitting error corrections requires an average length of E = p log2(1/p) + (1 – p) log2(1/(1 – p)) bits per error correction symbol. Thus, for every bit transmitted at least E bits have to be reserved for error corrections. A reasonable measure for the effectiveness of a binary symmetric channel at conveying information can be established by taking its raw throughput of bits and subtracting the number of bits necessary to transmit error corrections. The limit on the efficiency of a binary symmetric channel with noise can now be given as a percentage by the formula 100 × (1 – E). Some examples follow.

Suppose that p = 1/2, meaning that each bit is received correctly only half the time. In this case E = 1, so the effectiveness of the channel is 0 percent. In other words, no information is being transmitted. In effect, the error rate is so high that there is no way to tell whether any symbol is correct—one could just as well flip a coin for each bit at the receiving end. On the other hand, if the probability of correctly receiving a character is .99, E is roughly .081, so the effectiveness of the channel is roughly 92 percent. That is, a 1 percent error rate results in the net loss of about 8 percent of the channel's transmission capacity.

One interesting aspect of Shannon's proof of a limit for minimum average error correction length is that it is nonconstructive; that is, Shannon proved that a shortest correction code must always exist, but his proof does not indicate how to construct such a code for each particular case. While Shannon's limit can always be approached to any desired degree, it is no trivial problem to find effective codes that are also easy and quick to decode.

10.6.2 Continuous Signals

Communication with continuous signals, unlike discrete communication signals, deals with signals that have potentially an infinite number of different values. Continuous communication is closely related to discrete communication (in the sense that any continuous signal can be approximated by a discrete signal), although the cannot understand easily due to sophisticated mathematics involved.

The most important mathematical tool in the analysis of continuous signals is Fourier analysis, which can be used to model a signal as a sum of simpler sine waves. Fourier analysis is a method of defining periodic waveforms in terms of trigonometric functions. The figure 10.8 indicates how the first few stages might appear. It shows a square wave, which has points of discontinuity ("jumps"), being modeled by a sum of sine waves. The curves to the right of the square wave show what are called the harmonics of the square wave. Above the line of harmonics are curves obtained by the addition of each successive harmonic. These curves can be seen to resemble the square wave more closely with each addition. If the entire infinite set of harmonics were added together, the square wave would be reconstructed almost exactly. Fourier analysis is useful because most communication circuits are linear, which essentially means that the whole is equal to the sum of the parts. Thus, a signal can be studied by separating, or decomposing, it into its simpler harmonics.

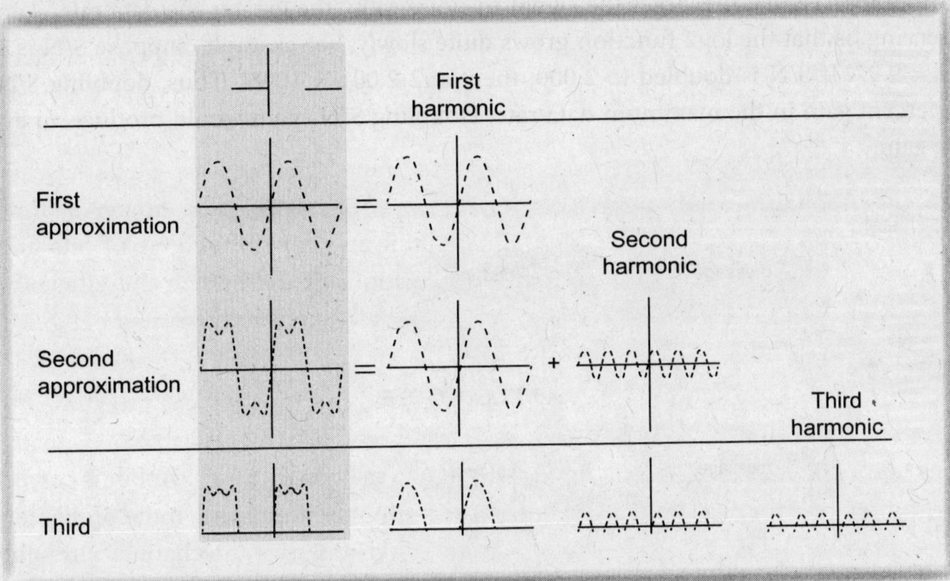

Figure 10.8: Fourier Analysis of Signal

Using Fourier analysis, a step function is modeled, or decomposed, as the sum of various sine functions. This example demonstrates how even an obviously discontinuous and piecewise linear graph (a step function) can be reproduced to any desired level of accuracy by combining enough sine functions, each of which is continuous and nonlinear.

A signal is said to be bandwidth-limited if it can be represented by a finite number of harmonics. Engineers limit the bandwidth of signals to enable multiple signals to share the same channel with minimal interference. A key result that pertains to bandwidth-limited signals is Nyquist's sampling theorem, which states that a signal of bandwidth B can be reconstructed by taking 2B samples every second. In 1924, Harry Nyquist derived the following formula for the maximum data rate that can be achieved in a noiseless channel:

Maximum Data Rate = 2 B log2 V bits per second,

where B is the bandwidth of the channel and V is the number of discrete signal levels used in the channel. For example, to send only zeros and ones requires two signal levels. It is possible to envision any number of signal levels, but in practice the difference between signal levels must be smaller, for a fixed bandwidth, as the number of levels increases. As the differences between signal levels decrease, the effect of noise in the channel becomes more pronounced.

Every channel has some sort of noise, which can be thought of as a random signal that contends with the message signal. If the noise is too great, it can obscure the message. Part of Shannon's seminal contribution to information theory was showing how noise affects the message capacity of a channel. Shannon derived the formula Maximum Data Rate = B log2(1 + S/N) bits per second, where B is the bandwidth of the channel, and the quantity S/N is the signal-to-noise ratio, which is often given in decibels (dB). Observe that the larger the signal-to-noise ratio, the greater the data rate. Another point worth observing, is that the log2 function grows quite slowly. For example, suppose S/N is 1,000, then log2 1,001 = 9.97. If S/N is doubled to 2,000, then log2 2,001 = 10.97. Thus, doubling S/N produces only a 10 percent gain in the maximum data rate. Doubling S/N again would produce an even smaller percentage gain.

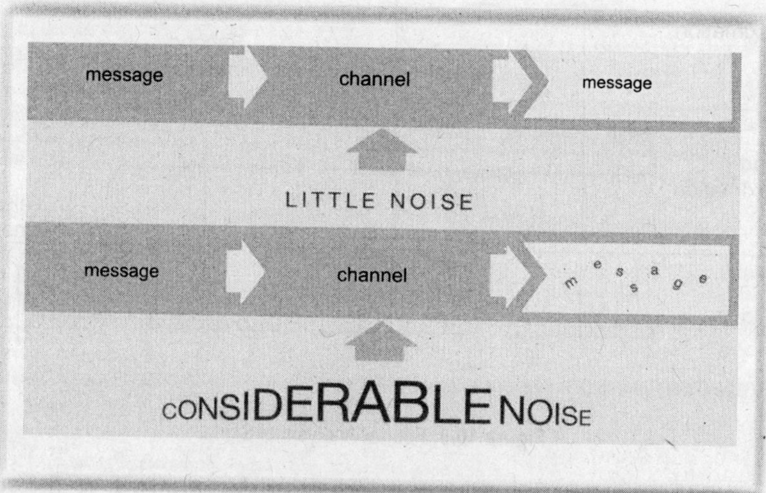

Figure 10.9: Communication Noise

In electronics and information theory, noise refers to those random, unpredictable, and undesirable signals, or changes in signals, that mask the desired information content.

Kullback- Leibler (KL) Divergence is the measure of distance between two probability distributions P and Q over the same random variable x. KL divergence distribution can be used in supervised learning when modeling data to a particular distribution. Cross entropy, which is derived from KL divergence is used to define the loss function and for optimization in machine learning.

10.7 SUMMARY

We have discussed on information theory components, its development, applications and relationship with other fields. The chapter concludes with discussion on types of communications related to information theory.

10.8 OBJECTIVE QUESTIONS

The answer of the multiple-choice questions is marked in bold.

1. .... is a component of information theory.

(a) Entropy (b) Data Compression
(c) Channel Capacity (d) **All of these**

2. .... is an application of information theory.

(a) Cryptology (b) Lingustics
(c) Physiology (d) **All of these**

3. Which one is a building block of information theory?

(a) Deep Learning (b) Probability
(c) Stastistics (d) **All of these**

10.9 REVIEW QUESTIONS

1. Discuss components of information theory.
2. Discuss applications of information theory.
3. Explain self-information.
4. Explain entropy.

10.10 ABBREVIATIONS AND SYMBOLS

Abbreviations	Full Form	Description
MP3	Moving Picture Experts Group Audio Layer 3	MP3 is a digital audio compression technique that compresses an audio file (such as CDA (Compact Disk Audio), WAV (Waveform Audio File), or AU(Audio) to about one-fifth of its original size.
JPEG	Joint Photographic Experts Group	PEG or JPEG is a commonly used method of lossy compression for digital images, particularly for those images produced by digital photography.
DSL	Digital Subscriber Line	DSL connects user to the internet through a dedicated pair of copper wires within your telephone lines and the use of a modem.

Abbreviations	Full Form	Description
FEC	Forward Error Correction	FEC is an error correction technique to detect and correct a limited number of errors in transmitted data without the need for retransmission.

10.11 LIST OF FIGURES AND TABLES

The details of figures and tables used in this chapter is as below.

CHAPTER 11

IoT Security and Privacy Case Study

CONTENTS

11.1 INTRODUCTION

In this chapter, we are discussing on the case studies in IoT security and privacy.

11.2 INTERNET OF THINGS

The Internet of Things (IoT) is the interconnection of endpoints of devices which can be uniquely addressed and identified with an Internet Protocol (IP) address. With the IoT, devices can be connected to the Internet, sense, gather, receive and send data and communicate with each other and applications through IP technologies, platforms and connectivity solutions.

11.3 IOT SECURITY AND PRIVACY

IoT security is the act of securing IoT devices and the networks they are connected to. All hardware, software and connectivity need to be secure for IoT to work effectively. Without security, any connected object from refrigerators to manufacturing bots can be hacked. Once hackers gain control, they can take the device's functionality and steal the user's digital data. IoT privacy is the special consideration required to protect the information of individuals from exposure in the IoT environment, in which almost any physical or logical entity or device can be given a unique identifier and the ability to communicate autonomously over the Internet or similar network.

Security is about the safeguarding of data, whereas privacy is about the safeguarding of user identity. Security refers to protection against the unauthorized access of data. The figure gives a quick view of related areas of security and privacy in an IoT for data protection.

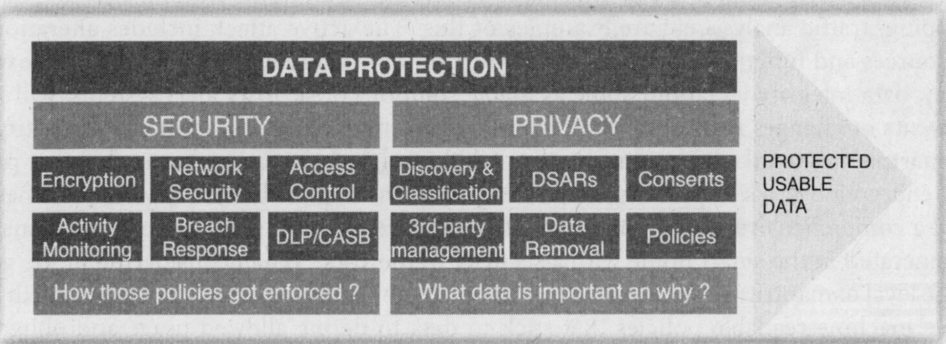

Figure 11.1: Data Security and Privacy in IoT

Data Loss Prevention (DLP) is the practice of detecting and preventing data breaches, exfiltration, or unwanted destruction of sensitive data. Organizations use DLP to protect and secure their data and comply with regulations.Data exfiltration is a technique used by malicious actors to target, copy, and transfer sensitive data.

A Cloud Access Security Broker (CASB) is cloud-hosted or on-premises software or hardware that act as an intermediary between users and cloud service providers.

A Data Subject Access Request (DSAR) is the demand by individual data provider to data controlling organization asking details of their personal information that has been collected, stored and how it is being used.

The table 11.1 compares various aspects of security and privacy.

Table 11.1: Comparison of Security and Privacy

Criteria	Security	Privacy
Definition	Refers to protection against unauthorized access	It is the ability to protect personally identifiable information
Function	Provides protection for all types of data and information including the ones that are stored electronically	Protects sensitive information related to individuals and organizations
Relationship	Can be achieved without privacy	Cannot be achieved without security
Focus	Focuses on all sorts of information assets that an organization collects	Focuses on personal information such as names, addresses, social security numbers, log in credentials, financial accounts, information etc.
Actions	Implements security protocols to provide confidentiality, integrity and availability of information assets.	Protects privacy rights with respect to processing of personal data.

We will discuss on a case study of security and privacy related to an IoT implemented smart home.

11.4 CASE STUDY 1 - SECURITY AND PRIVACY IN SMART HOME

Security and privacy in the smart homes have several challenges, in terms of access control, data integrity, confidentiality, and availability. Attacks may occur as passive or active. The passive attack attempt may be to learn or make use of information from the smart home without affecting its resources. Eavesdropping, traffic analysis etc are examples of this. The active attack includes alteration of smart home's resources and functioning, as well as introduction of fraudulent information. The examples are DoS, replay, data integrity violation. Some available solutions of security alert systems, will respond to unusual events or changes within the smart home environment and will immediately notify the users on their smartphones to take counter measures. A light weight key management scheme is proposed to cope with encryption tasks in presence of power-constrained smart home's devices. The need is more robust and a comprehensive system that is able to couple an efficient management and transmission of the data generated in the smart home with a security framework. When considering in the general IoT context, the level of maturity of solutions in the enforcement by means of sticky policies is still low. Sticky policies are machine-readable policies that stick to data to define allowed usage and obligations as it travels across multiple parties, enabling users to improve control over their personal information. Sticky policy shall be used to monitor the data flow. The growing diffusion of smart home applications of IoT raise serious concerns of security and privacy. Data is usually exchanged by wireless communications and remotely transmitted to the home owners which are increasing the risk of violation and leakage of information. Hence, the access to the smart homes resources by unauthorized entities must be prevented by proper policies.

The system presented in the case study is called Net worked Smart Object (NOS). Each NOS has been conceived following the IoT general purpose approach. NOS is able to handle every kind of information in a dynamic way. It is a matter of fact that often users are not fully aware of the constraints applied to their information or are not aware of the level of consent that has been granted by themselves for the use of the data. Such limitations must be overcome by designing efficient solutions to support users in their decisions and to automatically protect sensitive or private data. A real data-set, obtained from existing smart homes, is used in order to show the behavior of NOS's enforcement system, effectiveness and potentialities. The smart home scenario is very relevant with respect to security and privacy issues in the IoT. Such information can reveal people's habits and movements during the day, thus allowing malicious people to attack the inhabitants. Therefore, it is fundamental to guarantee adequate levels of security and privacy in the smart home domain.

The solution is based on NOS middleware. A network of NOSs is responsible for the storage and the processing of the information in a distributed manner. The goal is minimizing latency, providing support for user mobility and improving the resilience of the whole system avoiding points of failure. NOSs are also able to evaluate, by means of well-defined automatic algorithms, the security and data quality of the information transmitted in order to satisfy user requirements, while providing a lightweight and secure information exchange process, based on an authenticated publish and subscribe mechanism that use Message Queue Telemetry Transport (MQTT). NOSs essentially handle two main entities such as nodes and users. The nodes are heterogeneous devices such as RFID, NFC, actuators, sensors, etc. which generate data for the IoT platform and transmit them to NOSs through protocols that depend on the specific interacting devices such as HTTP, CoAP, and so on.

The users are who interact with the IoT system through services making use of such IoT-generated data, accessing them by means of mobile devices connected to the Internet through Wi-Fi, 3G or Bluetooth. Since different data types and formats are received, NOSs initially put them in the raw data storage unit. In such a collection data is periodically processed, in a batch way, by the data normalization and analyzers units, in order to obtain a uniform representation and to add metadata on security aspects such as level of confidentiality, integrity, privacy and robustness of the authentication mechanism and data quality ones like level of accuracy, precision, timeliness and completeness. Then, data is put in normalized data collection. Therefore, data, once received by NOS, are temporarily stored, processed, and, finally, shared with users.

The nodes, may decide, in an early registration phase, to agree with NOSs on a specific encryption mechanism for exchanging information in a secure way (i.e., registered sources), or may decide to transmit the data in clear (i.e., non-registered sources) whereas, users must register themselves to NOSs in order to establish proper credentials for accessing to resources and for future communications.

A sticky policy-based enforcement framework has been integrated in the NOS platform presented. Policies are expressed by means of a flexible and interoperable specification language, based on JSON syntax. Due to its flexibility and effectiveness, Attribute Based Access Control (ABAC) has been chosen as access control model. ABAC is a logical access control model that is distinguishable because it controls access to objects by evaluating rules against the attributes of the entities (subject and object) actions and the environment relevant to a request. In such a solution, NOSs own no policies/credentials, while a trust authority is responsible for their management. The registered owners/sources of the data send them in an encrypted way along with the associated sticky policy then each NOS can contact the trust authority in order to obtain the access decision related to the current sticky policy. Finally, decryption keys for accessing the data themselves are released to eligible requestors, in a secure way. ABAC scheme is used since both requestors' credentials and related specific attributes are used to grant or not the access to the IoT platform and to the IoT resources. Note that such attributes have to match those eventually included in the sticky policy. For each incoming data, the following information are gathered.

S. No.	Type	Description
1	Kind of data source	Describes the kind of node
2	Communication mode	The way in which the data are collected (e.g., discrete or streaming communication)
3	Data schema	Which represents the type (e.g., number, text) and the format of the received data
4	Data itself	Data

Moreover, a sticky policy containing the following information is also associated (i) the owner of the data (*e.g.*, in the form of a unique identifier) (ii) one or more purposes for which the data can be used (e.g., statistical or analytical purpose, sharing in social networks, private use within organizations, etc.) (iii) a timestamp that points out the validity (i.e., the lifetime) of the data within the IoT/smart home system (iv) one or more constraints which represent the rules to be applied to data. After reception, a topic is assigned to each data; access to topics is regulated on demand by NOSs through proper requests to the trust authority, by means of the associated sticky policy. When a user/device is notified of a new published data, it has to demonstrate to its own the correct attributes, compliant with the purpose, the validity, and the constraints contained in the sticky policy. Otherwise, the received data cannot be decrypted.

The framework, presented is evaluated in the smart home scenario and aims to demonstrate its feasibility for improving the reliability of a smart home system, while maintaining its efficiency. The proposed approach aims to prevent and counteract most of the passive and active attacks. More in detail, simulated attacks concerns: data integrity violation attempts, false access requests injection, and eavesdropping. Note that attacks such as DoS or DDoS cannot be counteracted by the proposed mechanism, but an effective solution will be available.

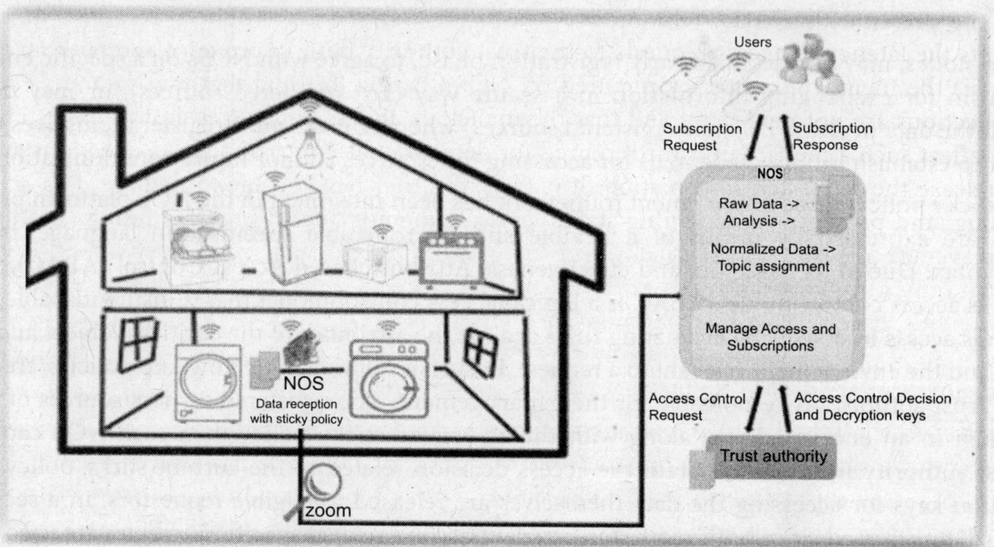

Figure 11.2: NOS Components and Interactions in the Smart Home

In the validation setup, data from real-world smart homes test-bed are used. Details about the real deployments are available. In this experiment, the behavior of a set of nodes that send to a NOS the data gathered from smart homes is emulated by means of a laptop. A WiFi network is adopted to allow the communication between the laptop and the Raspberry Pi, where NOS is deployed. The same Wi-Fi connection is also used for information exchange with the MQTT broker and with the trust authority module, implemented as separate components. The goal of the proposed validation is to analyze the performance of the system in presence of a huge amount of data in real-time and in presence of malicious entities, by simulating: (i) the association of the data acquired by the smart homes with the sticky policies, as defined; (ii) the access requests to data both by authorized and unauthorized/malicious users. The considered data gathering period is one month from the various smart meters, installed into the seven smart homes. Information collected include the electricity consumption of room's lights, washer, dryer, dishwasher, fridge, freezer, microwave, duct heater, furnace and so on. Data fetch rate from data sources to the NOS corresponds to one minute. Three kinds of users are considered in the experiment.

(i) The owners of the various smart homes, who wants to know the actual conditions of their home as well as to remotely control appliances. They have administration rights, and can grant access permissions to other people;

(ii) The inhabitants of the smart homes, who have no administration rights like children, babysitters, housekeepers etc.

(iii) The intruders who have no access permissions granted and want to get information about the habits of the home-dwellers and/or compromise the correct behaviour of the smart home for malicious purpose.

Access requests as well as malicious attacks by the aforementioned kinds of users are randomly simulated for a group of smart homes at a variable rate interval. In case of violation attempt, in order to gain access to the resources, the intruder must (i) know the credentials distributed by authorized users (ii) go up to the decryption keys (iii) satisfy the defined sticky policy. The failed access attempts can cause delays in the system's responses to valid requests, thus revealing the presence of an attack.

In the presented scenario, relevant metrics to be analyzed are (i) query response times, which represents the latency of access requests to the trust authority both in presence and without malicious attacks (ii) the memory occupancy required on NOS , taking in mind that raw data and normalized data collections are not persistent, and that the malicious attacks considered in this case study do not directly affect such a metric (iii) time required for detecting false access requests injections and decide to not release the requested information. It is observed that NOS is able to manage data acquisition, processing, and provision maintaining stable levels of memory occupancy on average of 19 MB and delay on average of 6 ms without attacks, and 10 ms in presence of attacks. Such an aspect represents an important indicator of the scalability and efficiency of the solution. In presence of malicious attacks and access violation attempts, the smart home's resources are protected and the delay is maintained under an acceptable threshold. Furthermore, the time required by NOS and trust authority for discarding bad data access requests is very promising on average of 2.5 ms.

A sticky policy-based enforcement framework, which has been integrated into the NOS distributed and cross domain IoT middleware, has been adopted within a smart home scenario. As demonstrated by means of a real-world case study, the designed solution provides advantages in terms of resilience, latency, and storage requirements, also in presence of malicious attacks, which represent critical aspects in the actual smart home applications.

11.5 CASE STUDY – SMART POWER GRID NETWORK SECURITY & PRIVACY

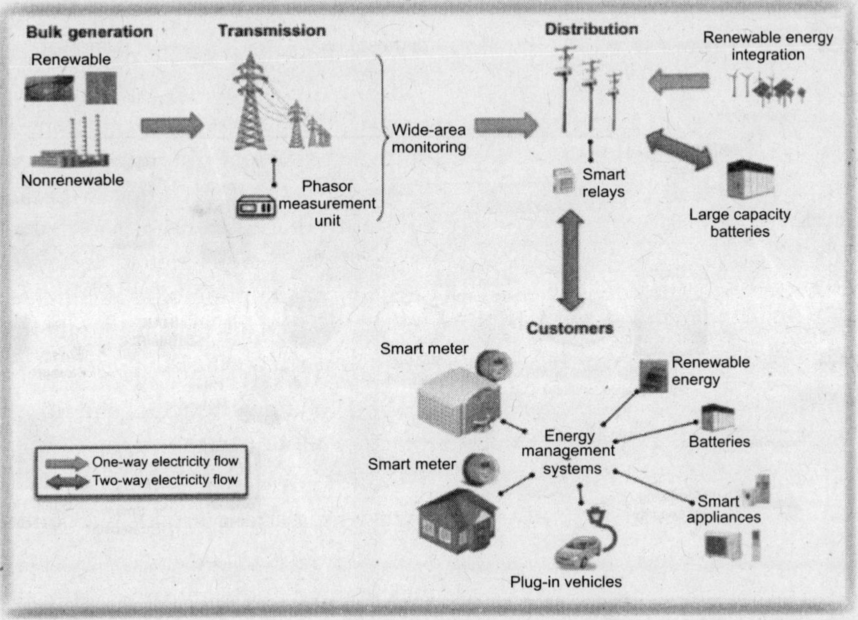

Figure 11.3: Electrical Power Smart Grid

Smart grid is an evolving electrical power system framework with Information and Communication Technology (ICT) driven power equipment and a massively layered structure. The new generation sensors, smart meters and electronic devices are integral components of smart grid. However, the upcoming deployment of smart devices at different layers followed by their integration with communication networks may introduce cyber threats. The figure shows the smart electrical power grid. The generation of electricity is integrating more renewable energy sources. The transmission system is being automated and phasor measurement units are being deployed to provide wide-area measurements. The distribution of electricity is also being automated with smart devices such as smart relays and will incorporate the integration of renewable energy, energy storage, and electricity produced by consumers will be used for the demand in local microgrids. Finally, the consumer premises will have smart meters and energy management systems to coordinate electricity consumption among smart appliances.

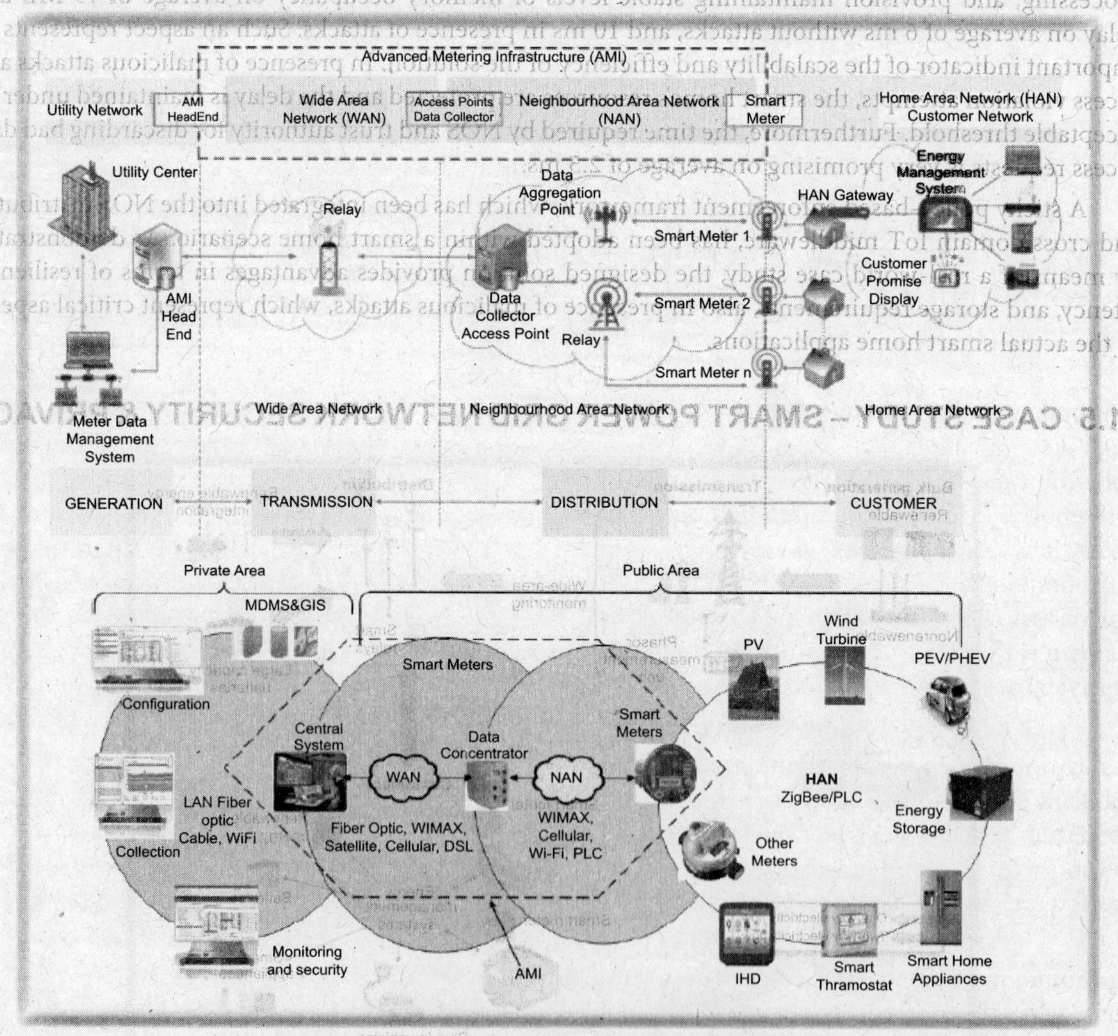

Figure 11.4: Advanced Metering Infrastructure

A smart grid consists of four segments such as Generation, Transmission, Distribution, and Consumption. Each of these segments, relies on complex control signaling. The generation control signals consist of three branches. (1) Automatic Voltage Regulator, where generator exciter control is used to improve power system stability by controlling the amount of reactive power being absorbed or injected into the system. (2) Governor control is the primary frequency control mechanism that detects disturbances and accordingly alters settings to change the power output from a generator. (3) Automatic Generation Control (AGC) is a secondary frequency control loop that fine tunes the system frequency to its nominal value. The Transmission control signals consist of two branches. (1) Estimation system which calculates system variables, such as voltage, magnitude, and phase angle, by projecting faulty

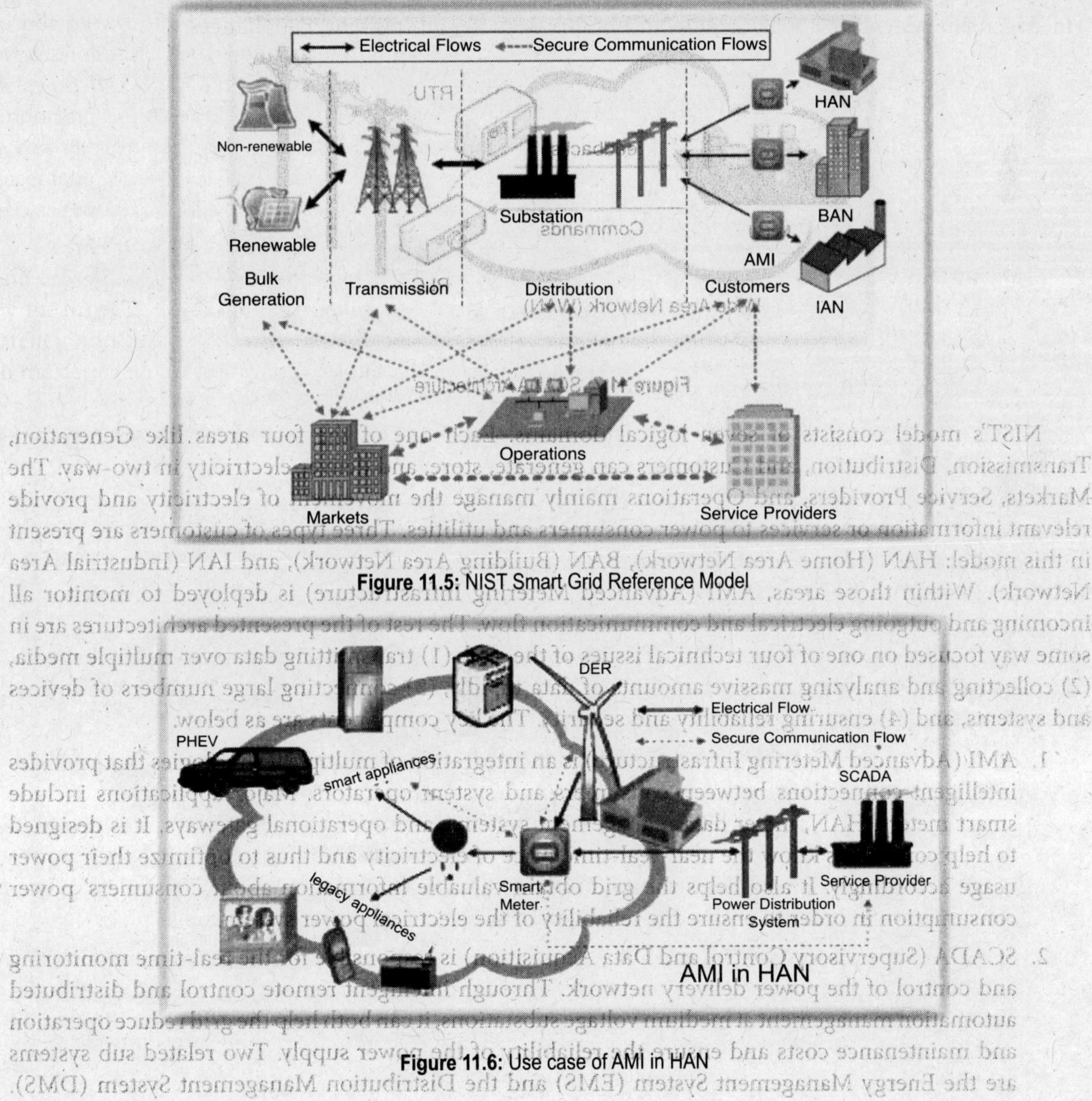

Figure 11.5: NIST Smart Grid Reference Model

Figure 11.6: Use case of AMI in HAN

measurements from field devices. (2) Volt-Ampere Reactive (VAR) compensation controls reactive power injection or absorption to improve the performance of transmission. The Distribution control signals consist of two branches. (1) Load Shedding helps in preventing a system collapse during emergency operating conditions. (2) Advanced Metering Infrastructure (AMI) is responsible for collecting, measuring, and analyzing electric energy consumption data, as well as transmitting this data to a central collection facility. In a smart grid, the electricity usage of consumers is measured by a smart meter that can transmit its measurement data to the operators through a network connection.

Although there are various designs for the grid architecture, almost every case follows the common reference model proposed by the U.S. National Institute of Standards and Technology (NIST).

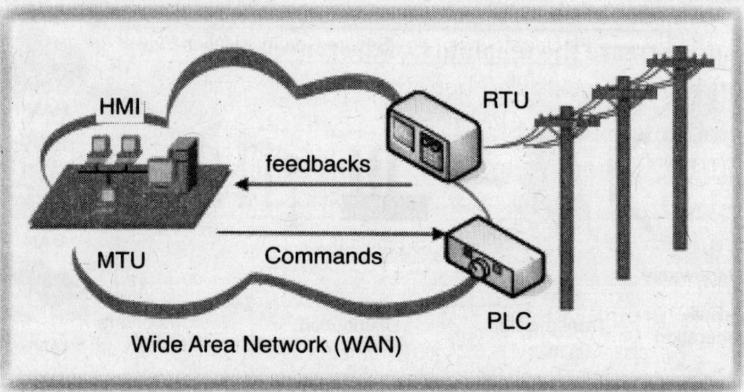

Figure 11.7: SCADA Architecture

NIST's model consists of seven logical domains. Each one of the four areas like Generation, Transmission, Distribution, and Customers can generate, store, and deliver electricity in two-way. The Markets, Service Providers, and Operations mainly manage the movement of electricity and provide relevant information or services to power consumers and utilities. Three types of customers are present in this model: HAN (Home Area Network), BAN (Building Area Network), and IAN (Industrial Area Network). Within those areas, AMI (Advanced Metering Infrastructure) is deployed to monitor all incoming and outgoing electrical and communication flow. The rest of the presented architectures are in some way focused on one of four technical issues of the grid. (1) transmitting data over multiple media, (2) collecting and analyzing massive amounts of data rapidly, (3) connecting large numbers of devices and systems, and (4) ensuring reliability and security. The key components are as below.

1. AMI (Advanced Metering Infrastructure) is an integration of multiple technologies that provides intelligent connections between consumers and system operators. Major applications include smart meters, HAN, meter data management systems, and operational gateways. It is designed to help consumers know the near-real-time price of electricity and thus to optimize their power usage accordingly. It also helps the grid obtain valuable information about consumers' power consumption in order to ensure the reliability of the electrical power system.
2. SCADA (Supervisory Control and Data Acquisition) is responsible for the real-time monitoring and control of the power delivery network. Through intelligent remote control and distributed automation management at medium voltage substations, it can both help the grid reduce operation and maintenance costs and ensure the reliability of the power supply. Two related sub systems are the Energy Management System (EMS) and the Distribution Management System (DMS).

Basically, SCADA systems consist of four parts 1) field data interface devices such as Remote Terminal Units (RTUs) and Programmable Logic Controllers (PLCs) 2) a communication system (e.g., telephone, radio, cable, satellite, etc.) 3) a central Master Terminal Unit (MTU), and 4) Human Machine Interface (HMI) software or systems. By using RTUs and PLCs, most control actions can be performed automatically and remotely. The current SCADA system has lots of vulnerabilities. To secure a SCADA network, a variety of technologies are involved, including user and device authentication, firewalls, IPSec (Internet Protocol Security), VPN, IDS, etc.

3. PHEV (Plug-in Hybrid Electric Vehicle) in addition to reducing carbon emissions and reliance on fossil fuels, could also provide a means to support Distributed Energy Resources (DER) in the smart grid. Since most PHEV batteries are designed to speed up rapidly for fast discharge, parked PHEVs can supply electric power to the grid. This vehicle-to-grid concept may improve the efficiency and increase the reliability of the power grid. However, it is still under development and the tradeoff between costs and benefits is still uncertain.
4. Communication Protocols and Standards: The communication standards for the power industry were developed by leading organizations such as IEEE, IEC (International Electro-technical Commission), DNP3 (Distributed Network Protocol) Users Group etc. The most prevalent protocols for SCADA communication systems are IEC 60870-5 and DNP3. The IEC protocol is typically used in Europe for communication between MTU and RTUs in SCADA systems. The DNP3, which is derived from IEC 60870-5 and recognized by the IEEE 1379 standard, is widely used in Asia and North America. IEC 61850 has now been released to support more enhanced capabilities including a peer-to-peer communication mode for field devices. It can be regarded as a successor to the DNP3. IEC 62351 is a standard that specifies security constraints and concerns of the above communication protocols and standards. It consists of few parts. The first two parts present an introduction to its background and a glossary of terms. Part-3 specifies the security requirements for TCP/IP profiles in IEC 60870 and IEC 61850. In particular, it describes the TLS (Transport Level Security) configuration for secure interactions. Part-4 addresses MMS (Manufacturing Message Specification, ISO 9506) protocol security in the IEC 61850 standard. Specifically, the MMS will work with the TLS to secure communications. Not all components are required to adopt this secure mechanism. Part-5 focuses on the security of serial communication in IEC 60870 and DNP3. It suggests that the TLS (Transport Layer Security) encryption mechanism can be utilized for serial communication to enable confidentiality and integrity. As for the authentication, the serial version can only address replay, spoofing, modification, and some DoS attacks. It cannot prevent eavesdropping, traffic analysis, or repudiation due to its limited computing capability. However, it could be protected by alternate technologies, such as VPNs or "bump-in-the-wire" which is a scheme that use an IPSec device as a firewall to filter unwanted packages from the internet, depending upon the capabilities of the devices and communications involved.

One of the goals of the smart grid is to improve the reliability and security of the power grid. However, by widely incorporating information technology and networks, the power grids will become exposed to computer vulnerabilities and a growing number of attackers. The smart devices deployed in the smart grid are primarily based on commodity hardware and software and will be vulnerable to the security vulnerabilities of other networked devices. A worm that spreads between smart meters, meter bots, distributed denial-of-service attacks, usage loggers, smart meter rootkits, meter-based viruses, and other malware are also expected to appear. In addition to these vulnerabilities, the large-scale deployment of smart devices will increase the number of entry points that can be exploited by attackers. The similarity of many devices means that a vulnerability found in one can be exploited in many, allowing attackers to remotely launch wide-ranging attacks. Before the introduction of smart meters, one had to attack a single meter using low-tech mechanical devices. Old attacks include, inversion attacks that turns the meter around and makes them run backwards, high intensity magnets that lowered the rate recorded by the meter, and simple physical destruction of smart meters etc. The effects of these attacks were on a single customer. Moreover, the attacks were easily detectable by the person who read the meter. The new smart meters are low-cost commodity devices that are installed in physically insecure locations. Attackers like house owners can compromise a meter and carefully tailor the changes to manipulate the energy costs without being detected. AMI systems have introduced new threats to power metering by allowing these attacks to be launched remotely, in larger scale, and with lower probability of detection as AMI removes the need for regular reading of the meter-reader employees. The ability to simultaneously affect multiple assets from a distance is critical for the reliability of the power grid. The reliability of the bulk power systems today is based on the assumption of localized failure and attacks. With the new infrastructure, this assumption does not hold anymore and new reliability risk models must be developed to incorporate the potential for simultaneous loss of multiple assets and largescale failure of devices. Devices with new functionalities such as remote relays in distribution automation, or smart meters with remote disconnect options are an attractive target for organizations and groups with the aim of disrupting normal power grid operations and causing blackout. Consequences of these attacks will be different than traditional attacks. Attacks to the smart grid can have a devastating effect on other infrastructures in physical world. There have been already a number of reported incidents involving power grids. We can identify three broad classes of computer related incidents such as targeted attacks, nontargeted attacks, and accidents. The computer-based accidents may cause the same damage as an intentional attack. The non-targeted attacks to power systems are similar to those against any computer connected to the Internet. It includes using compromised computers for botnet activities, worm infections, spam relays, and the like. The targeted attacks comprise the class of attacks where the miscreants know that they are targeting power systems, and therefore, they tailor their attack strategy with the knowledge of the physical system under control. Targeted attacks against power systems are not new. Physical attacks for reasons such as extortion and terrorism, are a reality in some countries. Cyber-attacks can be seen as the natural progression of physical attacks. They are cheaper, less risky for the attacker, are not constrained by distance, and are easier to replicate and coordinate.

An example of a targeted attack occurred in 2007 when a system administrator at the California Independent Systems Operator Corporation (CAL-ISO) shutdown the computers that were used to communicate with the electricity market. The resulting disruption prevented CAL-ISO from communicating with the electricity market for two hours, leaving the electrical power grid vulnerable to shortages. Another attack was in 2008, when a senior analyst for the CIA mentioned that there was an evidence of computer intrusions into some European power utilities, followed by extortion demands.

The threat that power systems face has been best demonstrated by the Stuxnet worm. In June 2010, the malicious software Stuxnet was detected. This piece of malware has the properties of a worm since it exploits several vulnerabilities in order to infect other systems and at the same time it is considered an ICS rootkit since it inadvertently modifies the way in which PLCs behave. This worm was conceived as a cyber weapon for sabotage. It focuses on Siemens specific software and hardware, modifying the logics of Siemens S7 PLC microcontrollers and hiding this from the supervisory software application/operators. Stuxnet is a very advanced piece of software: it exploits several zero-day vulnerabilities, it makes use of valid (stolen) digital certificates, and it masters Siemens WinCC SCADA application. Public press reported that security experts consider that only governmental services may have the capacity and resources to produce and release such a sophisticated attack tool. There is no official confirmation but security experts think that Stuxnet's target was the Iranian Natanz nuclear facility which is considered by many to be a key part of Iran's nuclear weapons program. Moreover, it was confirmed that since Stuxnet they have suffered numerous faults with no straightforward explanation. Stuxnet has made clear that there are groups with motivations and skills to mount sophisticated computer-based attacks to critical infrastructures, and that these attacks are not just speculations but they do happen and deserve in-depth studies. Although the target of Stuxnet worm has not been established with certainty, evidence suggests that the target is the controllers that are used in nuclear reactors.

Stuxnet is a worm that spreads by infecting windows computers. Stuxnet uses multiple methods and zero-day exploits to spread itself through LANs or USB sticks. It is likely that propagation by LAN has been used first, and propagation through removable drives was used to reach PCs that are not directly connected to networks, hence allowing attack on networks that were isolated from the Internet. Stuxnet intercepts requests to read, write, and locate blocks on a PLC. By intercepting these requests, Stuxnet is able to modify the data sent to, and returned from, the PLC, without the knowledge of the PLC operator. Once Stuxnet infects a computer, it installs its own driver into windows computers. Because these drivers have to be signed, Stuxnet uses two stolen certificates. Stuxnet also installs a rootkit to hide itself. The goal of the worm in a windows computer is to search for WinCC/Step 7, a type of software used to program and monitor PLCs. If Stuxnet does not find this software in the infected windows machine, it does nothing. If it finds the software, it infects the PLC with another zero-day exploit, and then reprograms it. Stuxnet also attempts to hide the PLC changes with a PLC rootkit. The reprogramming is done by changing only special parts of the code and so it is impossible to predict the effects of this change without knowing exactly how the PLC is originally programmed and what it is connected to. The malware sits quietly on the system doing reconnaissance for about two weeks, and then launches its attack quietly, increasing the frequency of the converters for 15 minutes, before restoring them to the normal frequency. The frequency remains at this level for 27 days, before Stuxnet kicks in again and drop the frequency down for 50 minutes. Stuxnet uses four zero-day exploits, a windows rootkit, the first known PLC rootkit, antivirus evasion techniques, peer-to-peer updates, and stolen certificates from trusted certifying agencies. There is evidence that Stuxnet kept evolving since its initial deployment. The malware was upgraded with encryption and exploits, apparently adapting it to conditions that were found on the way to the target. The command-and-control architecture used two servers if the infected machines were able to access the Internet, and a peer-to-peer messaging system for machines that were note isolated from the network. In addition, the attackers had a good level of intelligence about their target: they knew all the details of the control system configuration and its programs. The sophistication of this attack has lead many to believe that Stuxnet is the creation of a state level sponsored attack. Since Iran has an unusually high percentage of reported infections of the worms in the world, there has been some speculation that the attack targeted the frequency converters used by Uranium enrichment centrifuges in Iran, thus targeting the Iranian nuclear program. Stuxnet is very difficult to detect. Most of the traditional security best practices cannot prevent or cannot guarantee the detection of Stuxnet. Because Stuxnet used four zero-day vulnerabilities, having an up to date and fully patched system could not provide defense against Stuxnet. Antivirus software could not have prevented the attack because they have difficulties dealing with low-volume threats. The first antivirus signatures were issued after the worm had been in circulation for more than six months. In addition, victims attempting to detect modifications to their embedded controllers would not see any rogue code as Stuxnet hid its modifications with sophisticated PLC rootkits and validated its drivers with trusted certificates. In addition to technical security concerns, there are many organizational concerns including human factors and regulation problems, which can affect the security of new smart grid deployments.

New technologies used in smart grids rely on a wide collection of user data including power usage, which can reveal personal information. Smart grid technologies can be used to infer the location and behavior of users including if they are at home, the amount of energy that they consume, and the type of devices they own. By increasing the amount of collected consumer information, new forms of attack will become possible. Without a well-thought regulatory framework for consumer protection, the electricity consumption data that is collected by smart grid devices could severely jeopardize consumers' privacy. A court in the Netherlands found a smart meter law to be contrary to the European Convention on Human Rights. Within the current regulatory and judicial environment, it is possible to repurpose the household consumption data gathered by AMI projects to reveal and exploit personally identifying information. By monitoring high granularity energy consumption, detailed information about electricity users' lives can be inferred. This includes the time they eat, when they watch TV, when they take a shower, whether individuals tend to use a microwave for cooking, or use a stove etc. Such information is highly valuable to advertising companies. Governments and law enforcement also have interest in obtaining fine grained power consumption data for profiling users, sometimes exceeding their constitutional right to do so. For example, the Austin city police used power consumption data provided without warrant by a local utility for locating customers who were growing marijuana. In the United States the fourth amendment protects citizens against unwarranted search and seizure, and in Europe, section 8 of the European Convention on Human Rights provides citizens with the right for the privacy of their family life. Today, many cases of smart grid applications are evolving so it is difficult to design a regulatory framework and the supporting technologies that can protect consumers' privacy. The low level of public awareness about smart grid technologies and associated privacy risks, further complicates this situation. An important related issue is the question of data ownership. Historically, utilities in the United States are mandated to protect the privacy of consumers by safekeeping their electricity consumption profiles. However, new market models and tools to measure and manage electricity for consumers will challenge this situation. Consumers are beginning to share their authentication credentials with their utilities with companies that manage their electricity consumption, which means that it will become unknown what data will be shared with whom.

In March 2008 the Edwin I nuclear power plant in USA, was forced to make an emergency shutdown for 48 hours due to a software update. This software update was applied to the computer system in charge of monitoring chemical and diagnosis data of one of the plant's primary control systems. After applying the update, the computer was rebooted and this lead to a lack of monitoring information. Safety systems misinterpreted this and signaled that the water level in the cooling systems for the nuclear fuel rods had dropped, which caused an automatic shutdown. There was no danger to the public, but the power company lost huge revenue and had to incur the substantial expense of getting the plant back on-line. In terms of the distribution and transmission domain, one of the most relevant incidents could be the attack suffered by the US electrical grid in 2009. Officials recognized that cyber spies had hacked into the electricity grid and hidden software that could be used to disrupt power supplies. It was confirmed that attackers could use this software backdoors to cut electricity at will.

Concerning AMI, at the US Black Hat conference of 2009, a security consultant, proved the weaknesses of the whole metering architecture and in particular of smart meters that were being deployed on those days. By means of a proof of concept he demonstrated that a cyber-attack could be used to get remote control of about 15,000 out of 22,000 homes in a 24-hour time. To show that his team created a simulator as well as a real piece of malicious software capable of self-replicating and self-distributing across an area where all houses are equipped with the same brand of meter. In 2009 an electric utility in Puerto Rico asked them to help investigate widespread incidents of power thefts that it believed were related to its smart meter deployment. They discovered that former employees of the meter manufacturer and employees of the utility were altering the meters in exchange for cash. Presumably, they hacked into the meters using an optical serial port that allowed them to connect their computers locally and change the settings for recording power consumption. They just needed a software program that could be directly downloaded from the Internet.

Night Dragon was a targeted attack in United States. Their main objective was to compromise the industrial control system of several energy companies including oil, gas and petrochemical. These attacks relied on a combination of several techniques, tools and vulnerabilities such as spear-phishing, social engineering, windows bugs and remote administration tools – RATs. Although the attacks were not very sophisticated and did not exploit any zero-day vulnerability, the information obtained by attackers was very valuable for competitors. That information included financial documents, related to oil and gas field exploration and big negotiations, as well as operational details of production supervisory control and data acquisition systems.

Duqu is a computer worm that was discovered in September 2011 and which is believed to have been created by the same authors of Stuxnet. Its purpose was totally different to that of Stuxnet. Duqu main objective was to collect information such as keystrokes and system information to prepare future attacks against industrial control systems such as smart grid. Duqu's executables have been found in a limited number of organizations, including those involved in the manufacturing of industrial control systems. Experts are still analyzing the code but they consider that Duqu may be used to enable a future Stuxnet-like attack or might already have been used as a basis for the Stuxnet attack.

Cyber security vulnerabilities are conditions present in any cyber asset or organizational process at different levels, including its design, implementation, configuration, operation or management. Smart grids make heavy use of ICT and therefore attackers could exploit these vulnerabilities for a number of different purposes. It can penetrate corporate network; gain access to control software either in substations or central systems; manipulate smart meters to commit fraud, introduce malware to gain remote control, etc. Smart grids offer cybercriminals with more entry points than present grid. A two-way communication infrastructure will connect every house and building to the central network which will widen the attack surface. On the other hand, smart grids can be considered as a large system of systems. They span the whole electricity value chain, from generation to consumption. Many smart grid applications and features depend on each other and many times these applications and features are not under the control of the same actor. This is the case of Advanced Distribution Automation, which heavily depends on substation automation but also needs AMI data and Distributed Energy Resources information to perform correctly. Therefore, smart grids can be seen as a system of heterogeneous interconnected systems such as virtual power plants, transmission grid, distribution grids, etc. Each one has its own set of communication equipment and technologies, intelligent devices, automated control elements and algorithms, processing applications, connection points, specific procedures, different organizational approaches, etc. This heterogeneity, diversity and complexity make highly difficult its protection and at the same time introduce new and complex and likely vulnerable interrelationships and dependencies which were not present in traditional power systems.

11.6 CASE STUDY – SMART VEHICLE SECURITY & PRIVACY

The annual costs estimate associated with traffic accidents such as hospital bills and property damage total nearly three percent of the world's gross domestic product (GDP). Further compounding this, the number of vehicles is increasing faster than the number of roads, leading to frequent traffic jams. Additional issues include pollution and scarce parking spaces. In response to these problems, governments and manufacturers have launched several initiatives such as mandatory safety-belt laws, airbags, and anti-blocking brake systems (ABS), which have improved the situation to some extent. Upcoming traffic safety initiatives rely heavily on information technology, which means that vehicles must be able to authenticate themselves and be traceable whenever necessary, be it for law enforcement like detection of speeding vehicles, crash reconstruction, or toll collection. Presently the tracking operations that rely on reading license plates has become obsolete. Reading number plates has been replaced with authentication over a radio link requesting an onboard device to transmit a cryptographic identity. This is popular at toll roads and bridges. There is tremendous encouragement to adopt generalized wireless authentication, especially in advanced safety mechanisms, however, this has deep implications for privacy, even greater than it does for cellular networks. A mobile phone can be switched off at any time, but a vehicle identity cannot be done.

An important evolution for the automotive industry is the one toward context awareness, meaning that a vehicle is aware of its neighborhood including the presence and location of other vehicles. Modern cars now possess a network of processors connected to a central computing platform that provides Ethernet, USB, Bluetooth, and IEEE 802.11 interfaces. Newer cars also have such features as an Event Data Recorder (EDR), like the "black boxes" found on airplanes. The EDRs record all major data from the vehicle for crash reconstruction. It has a GPS receiver, the accuracy of which can be improved by knowledge of road topology and front-end radar often used for adaptive cruise control for detecting obstacles at distances as far as 200 meters and short-distance radar or an ultrasound system, typically used for parking. Inter-vehicle communication supports many important features, particularly in the area of crash prevention by informing vehicles about traffic congestion. A set of communicating vehicles is an example of a mobile ad hoc network. The computing platform supervises protocol execution, including those related to security. The communication facility supports wireless data exchange with other vehicles or fixed stations.

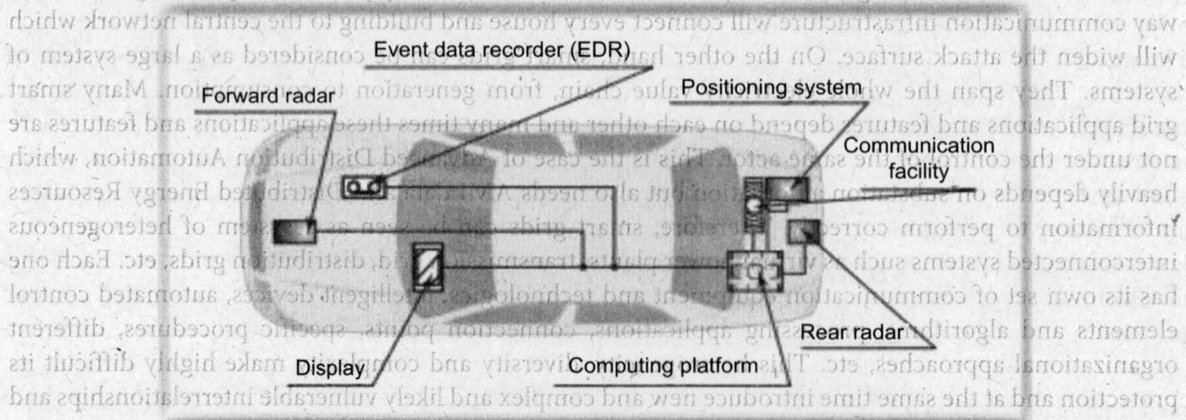

Figure 11.8: Smart Vehicle's Onboard Instrumentation

Roads can be made smart, too. Fixed communication devices installed along a road can inform passing vehicles about the road's precise topology. It requires an enormous financial investment, which, at first, would benefit a small minority of drivers. The observation of what happens on roads is called traffic monitoring, which has a primary purpose of detecting anomalous situations, such as those generated by an accident or difficult driving conditions. If an accident occurs, rescue teams will have immediate access to relevant information. With smart cars and roads, traffic monitoring itself will improve because it relies on much more accurate data. Ideally, traffic monitoring will eventually provide personalized advice to each driver through a personal navigation system. Smart vehicle's benefits will range from simplifying the payment process for the driver in tolls, parking, and fuel to helping the driver find an available parking place, to assisting authorities in fighting crime and terrorism. Terrorist activities often involve car bombs, automatic identification can help stop suspicious vehicles before they can access sensitive areas. With more smart vehicles and roads, we can expect many changes. First, the number and severity of accidents should decrease. By integrating information about position and mutual distance with other vehicles, a given vehicle will be able to permanently assess the level of danger and trigger a warning to the driver, if necessary. In future, it could even override the driver and activate the brakes or take control of the steering.

Most people overlook the security and privacy questions that vehicular technology's evolution raises. Currently, registration authorities have made substantial progress toward electronically identifying vehicles and similar progress is being made toward machine-readable driving licenses. To allow the wireless authentication of vehicles, these authorities must provide each vehicle with a private/public key pair, along with a shared symmetric key, and a digital certificate of its identity and public key. Such authorities will most likely be cross certified, making it possible for any vehicle to check any other vehicle's certificates. To guard against misuse, the overall organization for such a system's security architecture must be very carefully designed, especially if it's deployed worldwide an because of the information it will protect, so registration authorities must devise an appropriate Public Key Infrastructure (PKI). In magnitude, this challenge is equivalent to securing credit cards or mobile phones, but it also includes

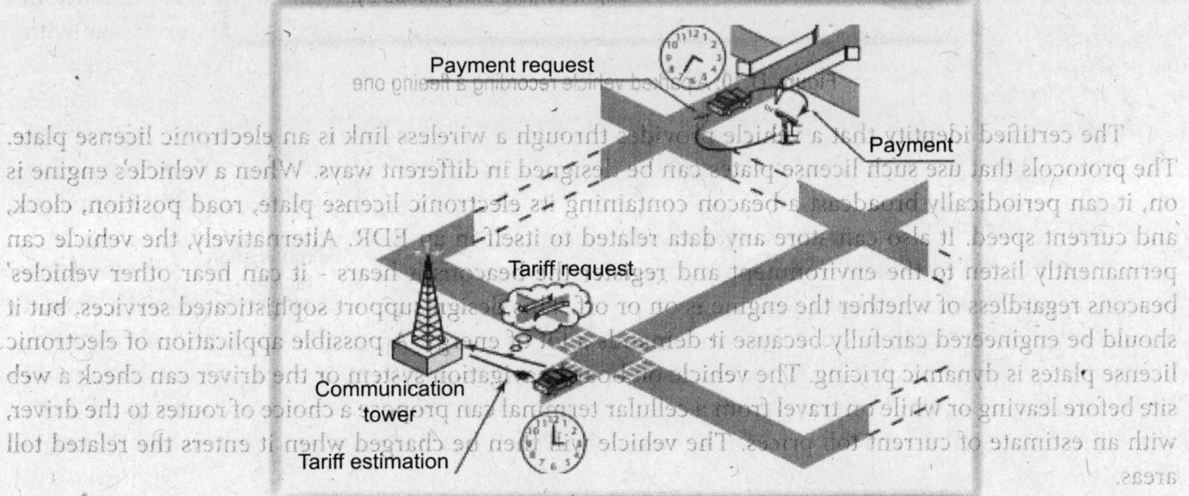

Figure 11.9: Dynamic pricing

newer, more difficult problems: it must embed security features in stringent real-time protocols such as those used to prevent accidents, secure physical location and distance, and support communication within highly sporadic groups of participants. The public's acceptance of electronic tracking might be fuelled by the prospect of improved safety and optimized traffic for travelers and potential revenues for manufacturers. After all, privacy concerns haven't prevented the widespread acceptance of the Internet, cellular networks, or electronic payment systems. Therefore, the right question is not whether it should happen, but how to make it happen in the most desirable way. An important task is to devise appropriate privacy preserving protocols, which are typically based on anonymity schemes, relying on temporary pseudonyms. Fortunately, anonymity can be quantified, meaning that we can compare different proposals.

In figure 11.9, the driver assisted by a navigation system decides on a route. The payment of any tolls automatically occurs when entering the toll road or bridge.

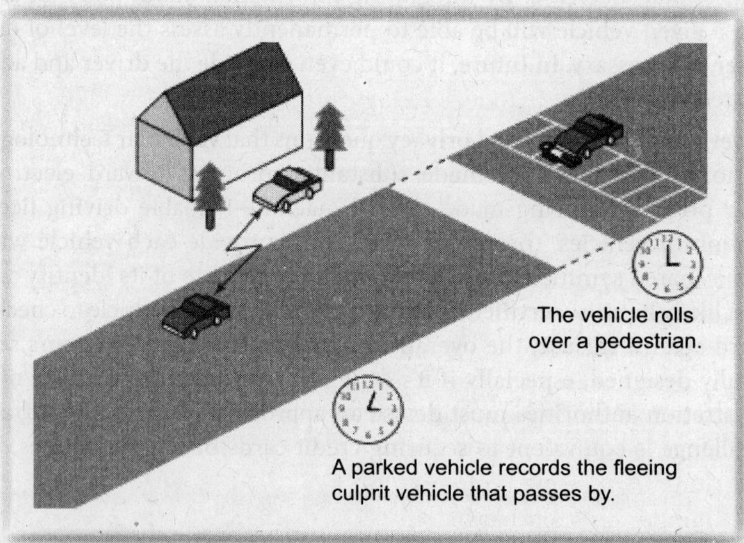

Figure 11.10: A parked vehicle recording a fleeing one

The certified identity that a vehicle provides through a wireless link is an electronic license plate. The protocols that use such license plates can be designed in different ways. When a vehicle's engine is on, it can periodically broadcast a beacon containing its electronic license plate, road position, clock, and current speed. It also can store any data related to itself in an EDR. Alternatively, the vehicle can permanently listen to the environment and register the beacons it hears - it can hear other vehicles' beacons regardless of whether the engine is on or off. This design support sophisticated services, but it should be engineered carefully because it demands a lot of energy. A possible application of electronic license plates is dynamic pricing. The vehicle on board navigation system or the driver can check a web site before leaving or while on travel from a cellular terminal can propose a choice of routes to the driver, with an estimate of current toll prices. The vehicle will then be charged when it enters the related toll areas.

Another way to use electronic license plates is to find drivers who flee the scene of an accident. Even if no vehicle is in the radio power range, the culprit's vehicle likely will soon pass a parked car that can record its identity. The recorded data can help the police identify the culprit. By interrogating the EDRs of nearby parked cars, police can retrieve the identities of all vehicles that have passed a specific spot at a given time. Although powerful, electronic license plates are vulnerable to attack. A first, obvious threat is the attempt by the smart vehicle's owner or thief to disable its communication and storage capabilities in particular, the EDR. Prevention is easier to automate for electronic license plates than it is for physical ones. We can try to protect the EDR physically, or trigger an alarm or alert law enforcement. A second threat is the impersonation attack. A vehicle owner deliberately stealing another vehicle's identity and attributing it to his or her own car, or vice versa. We can prevent this type of attack by storing the vehicle's identity in tamper-resistant hardware, having it properly certified, and using modern authentication protocols. Electronic license plates are much more resistant to this sort of attack than physical ones. A more dangerous attack is denial of service. An attacker systematically or selectively jamming the signals that vehicles exchange. There is no purely technical solution to such attacks, which is one of the reasons why we won't see a car overriding its driver in the near future. To make the use of radio-transmitted information to track a given car's location and its driver socially acceptable, it should protect driver privacy, at least as long as no collisions occur. For this reason, the broadcasted certified identity must be not real that changes over time. Only the regional or national authorities should be able to determine the relationship between a not real one and its real identity as the car's public key is broadcasted as well, it must also change periodically. In this way, any personal information the electronic license plate transmits would be negligible when compared to that provided by its physical counterpart.

Any vehicle's location can be determined by using GPS or with the help of on-road infrastructure inter vehicle communication. Existing positioning and distance estimation techniques assume that vehicles cooperate in determining or reporting their locations or distances, but some might try to report false distances or locations. Let's look at two solutions for verifying vehicle location Each vehicle should have a tamper-proof GPS receiver that registers its location at all times and provides this data to fixed stations or other vehicles in an authentic manner. Fortunately, this doesn't require any additional infrastructure and can be implemented independently in each vehicle. However, one drawback is its availability in urban environments: buildings, bridges, or tunnels often block GPS signals. Another disadvantage is that this option relies on tamper resistant hardware, which has well-known weaknesses. The most serious problem with this approach is that GPS-based systems are vulnerable to several different kinds of attack, including blocking, jamming, spoofing, and physical attacks. Moreover, relatively unsophisticated adversaries can successfully execute them. The most dangerous attack involves fooling the GPS receiver with a GPS satellite simulator, which produces fake satellite radio signals that are stronger than legitimate ones.

Another solution for verifying vehicle location is based on roadside infrastructure and uses distance bounding and multilateration. It is a localization technique based on measuring the difference of the distances between the vehicle and landmarks. Multilateration also termed hyperbolic positioning is a technique for determining a 'vehicle's' position based on measurement of the times of arrival (ToA) of energy waves (radio, acoustic, seismic, etc.) having a known waveform and speed when propagating either from navigation or to surveillance multiple system stations. ToA is the absolute time instant when a radio signal emanating from a transmitter reaches a remote receiver. These stations are at known locations and have synchronized 'clocks'. Prior to computing a solution, the time of transmission (ToT) of the waves is unknown to the receiver on the 'vehicle' (navigation) or the receivers at the stations (surveillance). Consequently, also unknown is the wave time of flight (ToF). Time of flight is the measurement of the time taken by an object, particle or wave to travel a distance through a medium. This approach removes the need for tamper-proof hardware, but requires the installation of a set of base stations controlled by a central authority. The infrastructure covers an area of Interest, such as specific roads or city blocks, and can verify vehicle locations. In verifiable multilateration, four verifying base stations with known locations perform distance bounding to the vehicle, the results of which give them four upper bounds on distance from the vehicle. If the verifiers can uniquely compute the vehicle's location using these distance bounds, and if this location falls into the triangular pyramid formed between the verifiers, then they conclude that the vehicle's location is correct.

Figure 11.11 shows an example of verifiable multilateration. The intuition behind the technique is that a vehicle might try to cheat about its location. As we mentioned earlier, the vehicle can only pretend that it is further from the verifier than it really is because of the distance bounding property. However, if it increases the measured distance to one of the verifiers, it would need to prove that at least one of these distances is shorter than it actually is, to keep its claimed location consistent with the increased distance. This property holds only if the claimed location is within the triangular pyramid formed by the verifiers: if an object is located within the pyramid and it moves to a different location within the pyramid, it will certainly reduce its distance to at least one of the pyramid vertices. The same holds in two dimensions. In a real deployment, the number of base stations would of course be much larger than what we see in Figure; as a result, a vehicle would always be within the geometric shape that three or four stations form. Verifiable multilateration also detects distance enlargement attacks from outside attackers: If an attacker tries to jam the signal that the vehicle sends to the verifiers and delay its response, the verifiers detect this attack in the same way as if the vehicle itself performed the distance enlargement. The distance measurements' precision is very important. Today's technology based on time of flight and ultra-wide band can achieve a precision of 15 cm for distances up to 2 km.

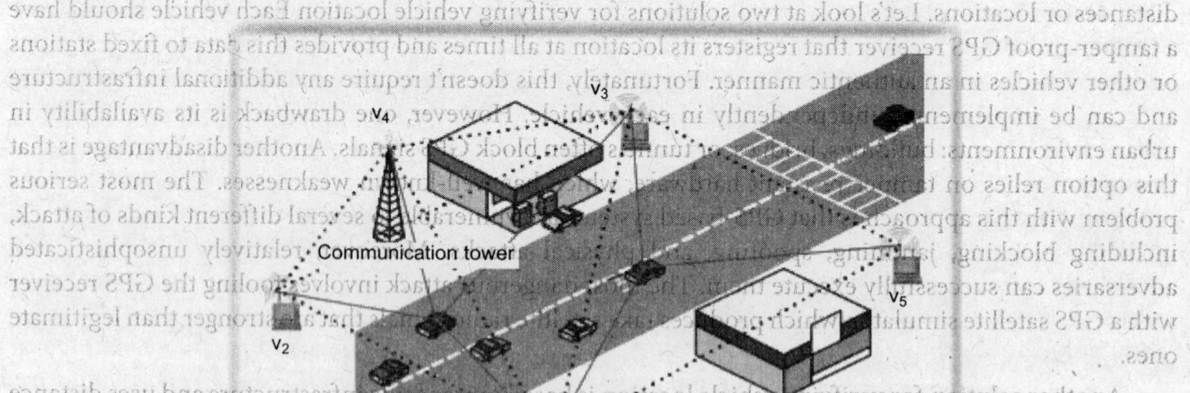

Figure 11.11: Verifiable Multilateration

In figure 11.11, base stations v1, v2, v3, and v4 can verify a vehicle's location in three dimensions if the vehicle is located in the triangular pyramid that v1, v2, v3, and v4 forms. Base stations v1, v3, and v5 can verify a vehicle's location in two dimensions if the vehicle is located in the triangle formed by v1, v3, and v5.

Once we verify a vehicle's identity by its electronic license plate and location, we can implement several new functions, including cooperative driving. Vehicles that pass through critical points such as highway entrances and crossings those without traffic light control must coordinate to avoid collisions. With the Inter Vehicle Communication (IVC) support, this coordination can be at least partially automated. Coordination functions that share resources among a group of nodes are usually achieved by group communication primitives such as mutual exclusion in computer networks, but the problem we face here is more challenging: human lives are concerned, the nodes are mobile, the groups are highly transient, and the communications are wireless. A potential solution to this challenge is a light weight group communication system managed by a token. Every vehicle within the transmission range sees the wireless link with one of its neighbors as outgoing; the neighbors see this link as incoming. As a result, a Directed Acyclic Graph (DAG) forms to link the members of a contention group. This is the group of vehicles contending for a common point together. A directed acyclic graph is a directed graph that has no cycles. DAG is used to represent the structure of basic blocks, to visualize the flow of values between basic blocks, and to provide optimization techniques in the basic block. The sink is a node without an outgoing link. The sink of the DAG is elected among the nodes closest to the critical point. This node then initiates a token which is a small message that grants the right to access a resource and goes across the point. The token then passes to one of the nodes that have outgoing links to the token holder, which lets that node move forward. We can apply different policies to control the behavior of token passing; for example, the token can switch from vehicles on one road to those on the other one at a highway's entrance which merges the two flows of vehicles. In any case, a policy would use each vehicle's verified position and identity to fine-tune the token's circulation and provide each driver with appropriate information.

In the figure 11.12, the dark color car holds the token that lets it access the resource at a blind crossing (a) and at a highway entrance (b).

Figure 11.12: Cooperative driving

A related problem is that when vehicles arrive at a given spot such as at a crossroad or travel together for a while such as on a highway, they might need to exchange many messages and therefore may have to establish a shared symmetric key based on their certified public keys. Many people have proposed solutions for this recurring issue, usually based on so-called multiparty Diffie-Hellman agreement protocols. Most of these protocols rely on an underlying group communication system to achieve fault tolerance, but in our case, the protocols must cope with stringent real-time constraints and the fact that human involvement is not possible. Obviously, such protocols still must be designed. Because many safety features require some level of cooperation between vehicles, bootstrapping the adoption of the necessary hardware is a major business challenge. Of course, this push requires a substantial effort from the standardization bodies before it can materialize. The security and privacy challenges related to this area have been overlooked, but the two solutions we've sketched in this article are a good place to start. In particular, electronic license plates have the potential benefit of allowing a much more accurate definition and control of what data law-enforcement agencies can access; this is likely to be one of the most relevant challenges in the area of wireless security. Location verification is the cornerstone of cooperative safety mechanisms, and the smarter vehicles become, the more their safety features will need to be secured.

11.7 CASE STUDY 2 - WEARABLE COMPUTING SECURITY AND PRIVACY

Wearable Technology (WT), is a computing technology device that can be worn on the human body, either a computer that are incorporated as an accessory or as part of material used in clothing. These devices come in many different forms such as watches, glasses, wristbands or as jewelry items. Wearable devices are defined by six main characteristics which are un monopolizing, unrestrictive, observable, controllable, attentive and communicative. The development of the applications that can work with WT cover a broad field from those focused-on healthcare, fitness, industrial applications, entertainment and arts. WT offers new opportunities to monitor human activity continuously with the miniature wearable sensors embedded. It improves efficiency, productivity, service and engagement across industries. However, there are few challenges faced on WT which are power consumption, communication capacity, design constraints, and security issue. Due to limited bandwidth and processing power, wearables provide less security compared to other computing devices. The possibilities for the security vulnerabilities increases to an array of possible attacks which will put users' safety and privacy at risk. Wearable computing brings new challenges and opportunities for user authentication.

One main challenge in adopting a good approach to a secure authentication in wearable is due to the nature of its operations in which wearable devices are not standalone devices as they will require to pair with other gadget such as smartphone to perform most functions. This complexity of communication creates security vulnerabilities such as man-in-the-middle attack. Imagine a user who uses his smartwatch to control his smart home. The need for a communication between the smartwatch and the application which is stored within the smartphone is prone to information leakage leading to other security attacks through the art of manipulation of data. The other challenge is the lack of a keyboard and sometimes even a touchscreen causes difficulty in providing authentication mechanism.

The work aims to present a brief review on security and privacy attacks that occur in wearable technology to understand its security and privacy loophole that exists in wearable technology and present a security analysis on various wearable technology devices. A security analysis is done by evaluating three main wearable devices such as Google Glass, Fitbit and Smartwatch.

Wearable Technology is the latest technology in the electronic devices field. It has been designed in many different forms that can be worn on the human body from head to toe such as glasses, shirt, wristband, watches and other forms. It not only can perform the basic task like what smartphones do, but the embedded, wearable sensors also recognize and provide wearer's actionable information in a real time context. Wearable device has the following characteristics.

Table 11.2: Characteristics of Wearable Devices

Feature	Operation	Description
Hands-free	Unrestrictive	Users can do other things when using the wearables
Always on	Controllable	It is a responsive system and users can grab control of it at any time
Environment-aware	Attentive	Wearables are environmentally aware, multimodal and multisensory
Attention-getting	Observable	It can keep users continuous attention when users want it to such as receiving alerts, messages or reminders
Connected	Communicative	Wearables are connected to a wireless network so that information exchange can be happened in the real-time situation
Un monopolizing	Ubiquitous	Which mean it does not cut users off from the outside world

Wearable sensors are often combined with the other sensors to detect human activities of daily living such as walking, running, sitting and eating. Different sensors are deployed on wearable devices depending on what kind of activity monitoring information to be collected. Accelerometer is used to measure linear acceleration. The accelerometer embedded inside wearable can determine whether the device is horizontal or vertical, and whether it's moving or not. The basic function of an accelerometer in wearable is to count steps on people's activities such as walking. Gyroscope determines the orientation by using earth's gravity based on principle of rotation. Both accelerometer and gyroscope are inertial measurement unit sensors that are commonly used in wearables. Both of them can determine orientation, but the gyroscope provides greater precision and it gives measurements for angular velocity. Global Positioning System (GPS) is a location sensor that is widely used for navigation. Most wearables now include an integrated GPS tracking system to locate a person's location. It detects the location using either GPS, triangulation of cell towers or Wi-Fi networks with a database of known location. A microphone is defined as acoustic sensor that converts sound into an electrical signal. Most wearables are embedded with this sensor for voice activity detection. Next an analysis on various wearable devices such as Google Glass, Fitbit devices and Samsung smartwatch in term of their security aspect is given.

The wearable computing model has evolved around factors such as minimization of computer size, increasing the computational power, increased mobility of people, and increasing personalization of devices. Wearable mobile computing can empower professionals to higher levels of productivity by providing more seamless and effective forms of access to knowledge at the point of work, collaboration and communication. The new technology of wearable mobile computing will meet the need of many individual professionals for acting more flexibly, effectively and efficiently in the increasingly complicated and challenging work environment. It can be used to enhance jobs in industry and services to make them both more rewarding and effective and re-elevate the role of the professional at work.

An example where wearable computing could enable process innovation is at hospitals where presently a lot of work is paper-based, which require a lot of work to be repeated, with the outcome of higher costs, less time with patients for doctors and nurses, risk for errors when typing new notes into patient files or typing out orders for medication from handwritten papers. There is also a need to store all the paperwork and it is also quite inefficient sending paperwork around inside a hospital or between hospitals. At the ward round in hospitals, doctors and nurses may want to do things that might require personal login to a variety of applications due to reasons of traceability, accountability etc. which makes it hard to use only a group laptop used by ward round members not directly in contact with patients.

If all the doctors and nurses that do the ward rounds could be online using wearable computers, it would add another dimension of usability and possible context awareness. This would require other ways than ordinary, to operate the computer and input information. Sensors on for instance arms, legs and feet as well as voice may be used to operate the computer without a keyboard as well as delegating the authority to input information to a doctor or nurse close by. Regarding security, wearables usually have limited processing power, memory, local storage facilities and possibilities to add devices which make it harder to set up a security baseline for needed security services which might be required by the users' organizational information security policy. The challenges in wearable computing are explained below.

Authentication - As the user of wearables might not be able to type in a password etc. on a keyboard, the need for stable and mature biometric authentication solutions that are integrated into clothing is required to make the wearable easier to use and operate.

Unsecure networks and hostile environments - Using wearables and laptops outside of controlled wireless networks, requires higher communications security regarding encryption, information integrity and maybe also non-repudiation. If using ad-hoc networks or unreliable access points, there are a number of well-known security problems and attacks regarding both the information sent as well as availability of the network access. Unfortunately, for instance encryption and integrity checks require some processing power, which might put limitations on the strength of encryption algorithms and encryption key lengths used for wearables.

Body area network security - A new challenge for wearables is the body area network which comprises of the wearable computer, all attached devices and sensors, opens up for a number of security threats. Sensitive information stored on the wearable device is at risk, privacy and safety issues might arise if the wearer is identified and the electronic identity is stolen.

New ways of using computers will appear as wearables are introduced to substitute paper-based work or laptops and PDAs. That introduces a need for novel and more advanced authorization mechanisms such as authorization by proximity where the surrounding context also needs to be taken into account.

An example is the ward round scenario in a hospital where a doctor visiting a patient wants to order an x-ray for the patient, and the doctor asks a nurse participating in the ward round to order it on his behalf using her or his personal wearable computer.

Another example scenario is related to airplane maintenance. A specialized worker making some maintenance inside a wing may replace some mechanical parts and may delegate one of his co-workers to digitally track the part number of the mechanical parts being replaced using the wearable. This is often referred to as authorization by proximity, which is a mechanism that allows the controlled transfer of authorization privileges from an authorizing party to the party who is normally unauthorized to perform that task. For authorization by proximity to be useful, it needs to be combined with the traditional user authorization within applications. Each application should also declare a list of tasks where authorization by proximity can be used, and a list of parties allowed to transfer and receive authorization by proximity. Context awareness will provide the application with the information needed to detect at run-time if and how authorization by proximity is possible. Such information should comprise information on task and surrounding parties. It should be possible to maintain the traceability and accountability of tasks or actions where authorization by proximity is used, by logging information on both the user who transferred authorization and the user who received it. If any actions or tasks need a digital signature to be completed, it must be done with the authorized person's personal encryption key preferably at the wearable, or perhaps in a smart card if used, where the personal key resides.

To better illustrate authorization by proximity where dynamic context information is used to connect the authorizing party with the conducting party, let us consider the situation of lead doctor needs to set up a ward round context at the start of the ward round either using all participants RFID tags, perhaps also pre-selecting an initial person who is authorized to order x-rays or medicines etc. It is also assumed that the patients are identified with an RFID tag and that the medical staff when logging in to their personal wearable, using for instance biometric authentication, also opens up their smart card or similar where among other things their personal digital encryption keys are stored. As the ward team may need to access encrypted information, group keys for wards could be used to protect the patient file information. The group keys need to be distributed to the users. One option is to use static groups of users, typically those often involved in specific ward rounds, and securely store the needed group keys in their credential stores. Another option is to distribute the group keys when needed in a context. The first option using static groups of users is not as dynamic as the second option, where dynamic groups of users are set up by the context at run-time. The following are possible context types to be used for linking the ward round context to the doctors/nurses and the patients, as well as the patient to the doctor.

Context	Description
Ward round	Ward name; date, start, stop; patient RFID, lead doctor RFID, list of doctors, list of nurses, 'person authorized by lead doctor' RFID, etc.
Personal	Name, RFID, type of profession (doctor, nurse etc), level of authentication, etc.
Patient	Name, patient RFID, sign in date, name of doctor, doctor RFID,etc

After having created the initial ward round context, the context may change depending on which patient is in focus and the lead doctor may change to be the one identified by the patient context. The person authorized by the lead doctor may of course also change during the course of the ward round depending on skill set or if someone has to leave the ward round. Thus, the contexts are dynamic and may change during the course of the ward round.

The level of authentication in the personal context could give single sign-on to the hospital's applications where all orders for treatment, medicaments etc can be processed. The patient's electronic file could directly be updated during the ward round eliminating today's paper-based systems where the electronic patient file needs to be processed by a nurse after the ward round ends. For traceability reasons, changes in the ward round context could be logged automatically, as well as that all tasks conducted are logged in the applications as described earlier (for accountability reasons if authorization by proximity is used). If anything needs to be signed, like the electronic patient file, the lead doctor may do it in his or her personal wearable and thus a hash etc. of the patient file needs to be sent to the doctor's wearable or smart card to be signed with the personal key and then the resulting signature needs to be returned and stored in the application database. If any user interaction is needed from the lead doctor when signing, it could be displayed on the bedside screen and handled by either using gestures or by using the voice to keep the hands clean and free.

Typically, a user is tied into work-processes with other users, like a doctor with his nurse or a group of workers doing maintenance. In a wearable scenario this entails the coupling of wearable devices as well, which raises the need for a security policy that treats working groups and their devices as a kind of a pool of services where all must trust each other in order to be shared. The world surrounding the user today unfortunately requires the users of wearables and common computers to protect themselves from hackers, viruses, malicious code, and spy ware etc. This is usually managed by having a minimum requirement level of security software. However, the baseline might differ depending on what context and where a computer is used. Having an advanced dynamic IT-security policy that is context dependent and dynamically changes the level of the baseline depending on the surrounding environment, would be suitable for almost all computers but in particular wearables due to the limited system resources. To realize such dynamics, a more intelligent policy management is needed for optimized security related load on wearables system resources. However, a similar result may be achieved by using a number of predefined security zones or static contexts which are set either when initiating the computer, when recognizing which network is used, or manually set. Security analysis on real examples of few wearable devices are discussed below.

Google Glass can be considered as the first wearable device that kick start the growth of wearable technology. This is an eyewear device that has built-in computer in the frame of a pair of glasses. It provides numerous innovative features that make people life more fun. However, many concerns have been raised from various sources regarding to some issues that could be threatened wearer's security and privacy. There are few research findings that point out some vulnerability in term of security and privacy aspect on Google Glass. For example, Glass does not have a secure enough PIN system or authentication in place currently. Besides authentication issues, found that the privacy of user' appears at risk as well by the eye tracking technology supported in Glass. In addition, pictures and videos can be recorded without user's consent which violate people privacy policy. More importantly, there are several real cases regarding security vulnerability associated with Google Glass were reported at the time of its release. For example, engineers at the security firm Lookout Mobile revealed a serious security vulnerability on how Google Glass interpret Quick Response (QR) codes while it snaps a photo back in May 2013. They found that Glass would scan a malicious QR code that forced it to be connected to a hostile Wi-Fi access point and someone could remotely gain root access to a Google Glass device and take control of it without the wearer's knowledge. Fortunately, the bug has been reported to Google and a patch was released to fix the problem in a timely manner. However, a few months later, Symantec reported that Google Glass is still vulnerable to Wi-Fi Hijacking despite QR photo bombing. This happened because someone can set up a Wi-Fi access point using the same Wi-Fi name as the one that people previously use to connect before using a device called Wi-Fi Pineapple. It can impersonate any network that a device searches for by borrowing the network Service Set Identifier (SSID). For example, when Glass checks to see if that prior network is available the attacker's Wi-Fi Pineapple will simply answer the request and pretend to be that specific network. It causes Glass to be at risk with the same sort of attacks that can arise when connecting to a hostile network such as sniffing traffic or redirection to malicious sites. Lastly, wearable technology raises the issues of privacy as described in, ninety percent of the survey target feel uncomfortable if someone recording a video of them using Google Glass. The feature and functionality of any wearable device allow user to capture images or record video using their wearable device without the notice of their target. Some entertainment place like cinema and casino have even banned the usage of such devices in their business area due to the privacy problem. In this case, we may conclude that the level of acceptance of people with certain wearable devices is low due to the fact that such device affects people's perception of their privacy.

Fitbit is known for its products which is a smart fitness band that can be worn on the wrist. It provides human activity measurement such as number of steps walked; sleep quality and other personal health metrics like heart-rate and body temperature. However, one of the major security vulnerabilities found in Fitbit is lack of authentication. Potential attacker can easily get the data without the knowledge of users. For instance, FitBite is a tool developed to launch several attacks on Fitbit devices such as data injection attack, DoS and battery drain hacks to prove the statement. The result showed that the vulnerable Fitbit device could allow malicious hackers to hijack Fitbit users' account, access or even manipulate their personal health data. Fitbit Flex is vulnerable due to leaky Bluetooth Low Energy (BLE) technology. This is because it did not change the privacy address or MAC address remains the same and it can be easily tracked based on the Fitbit's Bluetooth advertisement. In consequences, it could lead to privacy breach as third parties can track activities for specific users. Insurance companies may also take this advantage to create a "gray market" for getting users' health information data. Besides that, Fitbit devices could potentially threaten users' privacy risk. For example, it allows malicious people to track user's location or places visited to make phishing attack such as send fake email that offer deals with the link that actually linked to spyware or a virus.

Samsung Smartwatch is another wearable device that offers significant innovative functionalities that makes the enhancement of people's daily life. In fact, the biggest selling point is the notification features in Android Wear Smartwatch. It has enabled to synchronize data to the phone and all the important alert and notifications will get pushed directly on the wrist. In a HP recent study on top ten popular Smartwatches in the market, found that 100 percent of the tested Smartwatches contain significant vulnerabilities, including poor authentication, lack of encryption and privacy issues. 70% of watch firmware is without encryption. 30% watches were vulnerable to account harvesting, which is an attack that gain access to the device and data by looking for weak passwords. Only 50% of tested devices offered the ability to implement a screen lock either by PIN or pattern. Researchers from Romania-based Bitdefender had created proof of concept hack to access a Samsung Gear Live Smartwatch, paired with a Google Nexus 4. The result showed that the six-digit PIN code and Bluetooth communication between the two paired devices could be decrypted easily using the brute force attack by using any open-source sniffing tool. And thus, the users' security and privacy are in risks without a strong authentication scheme in place. Besides that, user does not need to unlock the Smartwatch and thus data can be accessed from a computer without authentication. For instance, revealed that information data such as messages, emails and contacts can be pulled out easily from Samsung Gear 2 as Samsung did not do encryption properly as it needed for the Smartwatch devices. The security vulnerabilities and security attacks on selected devices are summarized in the table.

Table 11.3: Security Vulnerabilities and Attacks found in Various Wearables

Wearable Devices	Security Vulnerabilities	Attacks
Google Glass	Unsecure PIN system or authentication in place	The gesture based authentication scheme can be recorded easily by people nearby.
	Privacy: Pictures and videos can be recorded without user's consent and unauthorized eye movement tracking	Eaves dropping and spyware
	It relies on QR codes for Wi-Fi setup	QR photo bombing malware
	Unsecure network and hostile environment	Wi-Fi hijacking, man-in-the-middle attacks such as session hijacking or sniffing

Fitbit Devices	Lack of Authentication	Data injection attack, Denial of Service, and battery drain hacks.
	Leaky Blue Tooth Low Energy Technology	It can be easily tracked
	Privacy - User's location and places visited can be tracked	Phishing
Samsung Watch	Authentication mechanism not secure enough	Brute force attack

From Table 11.3, it showed that there is a common security vulnerability exists between the selected wearable devices that have been chosen to be analyzed which is lack of authentication. From the table, we can observe that without proper security authentication implemented, wearable devices can be exploited to some several attacks such as eavesdropping, DoS, and brute force attacks. For instance, Samsung Smartwatch analysis showed that it can be decrypted using brute force attack and easily gain control access to the device.

There are a few key challenges in WT which are power consumption, communication capacity, design constraints, and security and privacy issues. The security vulnerabilities in WT can be exploited by an array of possible security and privacy attacks. When the security vulnerability is exploited, there will be a loss. The loss can be loss in term of Confidentiality, Integrity, Availability or Authenticity. Privacy attacks are categorized by user identity, data integrity, time and location-based attacks. The security solutions can mainly be discussed using two different terms which are authentication and encryption. Below are the common challenges identified in the wearable technology that will need to be addressed by further researchers in order to improve it.

- **Power consumption:** One of the major challenges is the high-power consumption of wearable devices. The battery power of wearable devices can only last for one to two days since most devices use wireless networks, GPS, and other technologies that consume a lot of power. Hence, short battery life and high-power consumption of wearable devices will cause people reducing the usage and adoption.
- **Communication capacity:** The communication range is limited, which mean that the covered area range of wireless transmissions is usually limited because of both technological and energy-savings considerations.
- **Design constraints:** Some wearables are designed in bulky size and it does not really make users feel comfortable.
- **Security issues:** The wearable devices contain a lot of user's data which are putting users' security and privacy on the risk. It also may consist of sensitive information data such as address, credit card number, and health-related data. Therefore, security issues will be the key challenges for WT to be adopted widely in the market.

Security and privacy issues could be the major reasons for wearable technology security vulnerabilities. It can lead to the serious breach and loss, if the security vulnerability is not handled properly. The loss could be either static assets such as files, documents or dynamic asset like credit card number. At the end, it will cause data and financial loss or even safety issues. Furthermore, user's trustworthiness towards wearable will decrease and discourage people to get their own wearable. Security issues are the major concerns that potentially reduce user acceptance and trustworthiness towards devices. Therefore, it is important to investigate on the security vulnerability on the devices for user protection.

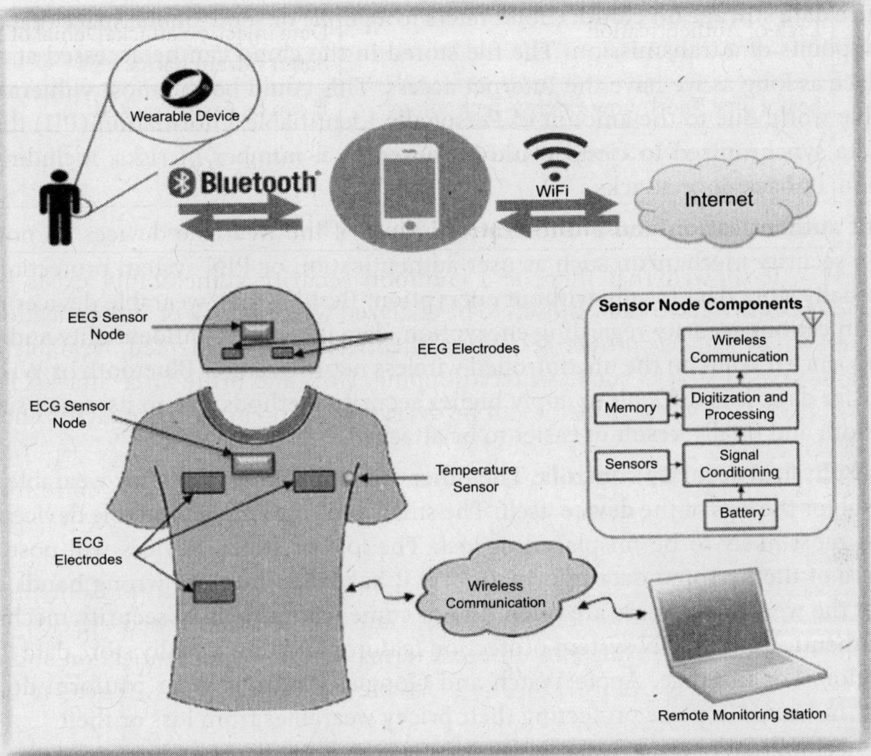

Figure 11.13: Data Acquisition Architecture in Wearable Technology

The most common security vulnerabilities that can be found in wearable devices are shown in Figure 11.13. The factors that contribute to the security attacks are discussed below.

(i) **Unsecure transmission of data through Bluetooth for local device storage:** Wearable devices rely on Bluetooth to do transmission of data collected from embedded wearable sensors to integration devices such as smartphone as currently it cannot communicate directly to the Internet. As a result, attacker can exploit the bug in the device to extract data stored locally, such as health-related records by using wearable as an access point. For example, an attacker can simply make use of sniffers to steal unauthorized data by detecting the broadcast signals while a wearable device is communicated over Bluetooth. As a consequence, there will be a loss on either in term of monetary, the safety or even life of the people.

(ii) **Software communication to the cloud via a cellular or Wi-Fi network:** More personal sensitive data can be stolen as data is transmitted from the local storage in the smartphone to the Cloud application, as it is typically combined with personally identifiable data such as name, email, telephone number, and location to ensure that the data is being sent to a proper account. The attacks that can take place by exploiting this security vulnerability include man-in-the-middle and redirection attacks, which could cause data to be sent to the wrong server. Hence, the potential loss of private data is high and privacy and safety issues might arise as well if the wearer is identified.

(iii) **Insecure data storage on cloud:** Cloud refers to a public or semi-public space that exists between the endpoints of a transmission. The file stored in the cloud can be accessed at any time from any place as long as we have the Internet access. This could be the most vulnerable area in the wearable world due to the amount of Personally Identifiable Information (PII) that is available. The data synchronized to cloud could be posed by a number of risks, including DDoS, SQL injection, or back door attacks.

(iv) **Lack of authentication and authorization:** Most of the wearable devices do not come with a built-in security mechanism such as user authentication or PIN system protection features and they usually store data locally without encryption. Besides that, wearable devices require higher communications security regarding encryption, data integrity, confidentiality and other security services since it relies on the uncontrolled wireless network either Bluetooth or Wi-Fi connection to transfer data. It is difficult to apply higher security methods due to its' small size and limited bandwidth and finally, result in easier to be attacked.

(v) **Lack of physical security controls:** The other security vulnerability for wearable devices is the potential for the loss of the device itself. The small and tiny size of wearable device such as fitness band is most likely to be misplaced or lost. The lost or stolen devices will pose a risk on the exposure of the personal data information, if it has fallen into the wrong hands. Furthermore, most of the wearable devices are often do not come with a built-in security mechanism such as user authentication or PIN system protection features and they usually store data locally without encryption. For instance, Apple Watch and Google's Android Wear platform do not have any security measures in place protecting their pricey wearables from loss or theft.

Wearable technology privacy issue is one of the major challenges yet to be solved in wearable computing. Not only because wearable can sense, capture and store sensitive information about the users, and surrounding but it is able to do it continuously and discreetly. The privacy attacks that pose in WT can be categorized into user-based privacy, data-based privacy, time-based privacy and location-based privacy.

(i) **User Identity and Data Privacy:** Embedded sensors such as cameras and microphones, capture data about the individual and also the surroundings, often without their consent. These data often are personal, confidential and sensitive, which invade users' privacy. For example, Glass can be easily hacked as it has no strong authentication implementation. The attacker can take full control the Glass and monitor everything the owner doing with the camera and microphone. Besides that, security researcher from Stanford University and Israel's defense research group Rafael found that gyroscope, a sensor that used to measure angular velocity can even eavesdrop on the conversation. They found that the MEMS (Micro Electro Mechanical Systems) gyroscope is sensitive enough to recognize the sound and can pick up some sound waves and turn them into crude microphones. Therefore, it proved that the conversation could easily eavesdrop without user consent since iOS and Android do not require special permissions from users to access gyroscope.

(ii) **Time and location-based privacy:** GPS embedded inside wearable is able to track a person's location at a specific time. It brings greater benefits for people to do navigation, but it also poses greater risks as well. It raises serious issues on the user's privacy, if the location of the people can be tracked. For instance, Symantec revealed that wearable can also do location tracking, although there is no GPS sensor built in. This happened because the data exchange process between phone and fitness band could potentially broadcast the location information. They performed an experiment to illustrate that by using a portable scanner, a unique hardware address that each fitness tracker emits when syncing to the user's phone via Bluetooth could be picked up. In addition, some collected data that are shared consist some information that an individual did not intend to share. For example, Inertial Measurement Unit (IMU) is a collection of measurement tools. When installed in a device, these tools can capture data about the device's movement. IMUs contain sensors such as accelerometers, gyroscopes, and magnetometers shared with caregivers may reveal some sensitive medical conditions, such as seizures, that one may wish to keep private.

It is supposed that wearable devices should be protected with secure authentication mechanism as it contains a huge amount of sensitive information. On the other hand, due to its' small device size, their processing power and bandwidth are further limited and this makes it difficult to apply with higher security measurements. In addition, the danger of wearable devices at this point is that developers are not prioritizing security and privacy. As wearables making more and more use of user personal data - from fitness status to health records, security should be put into a high priority. Unlike mobile devices, wearable devices are potentially always-on and always gathering data. In this way, it not only brings the uniqueness on the WT with the added dimension, but at the same time it is also open to more threats to user sensitive information and activities at any time anywhere without user's consent. Security measures are not only important for protecting personal data, but are critical as smartwatch are introduced to the workplace and connected to corporate networks as well. Therefore, it is very important to pay extra attention for maintaining confidentiality, integrity and availability (CIA triad) for wearable displays. Serious security breaches could happen if the wearable device that has poor user authentication are being attacked. For example, a smartwatch can be used to make online transactions. If in the case that the smartwatch was stolen or lost, someone with bad intention could likely access all of the personal data or even modify transaction content or insert additional transactions with the credit card information. In the consequences, it not only causes loss of security, but it violates the confidentiality and integrity policy and results in loss of money as well. As a result, the users' security and privacy are in risks without a strong authentication scheme in place. It is important to pay more attention on wearable authentication in order to protect users' data from malicious, unauthorized access since a massive quantity of private data can be collected from the wearables. Therefore, authentication issue must be tackled definitely to ensure the security of wearable is preserved thoroughly.

As the IoT market advances, WT is growing in popularity for their convenience and capabilities. WT offers better functionalities by providing real time data communication, but also poses a greater security and privacy risks. People are concerned about the security of the wearable as the data collected might consist sensitive information about themselves and their surroundings such as identity, health-related information, credit card number, and the location. Although this advance technology does benefit people but there are still some security loophole and privacy issues that required extra attention and effort of designer in designing wearable technology model.

11.8 CASE STUDY 3 - MOBILE HEALTH

Internet of Medical Things (IOMT) means connecting different things to different people within a healthcare organization or across the healthcare ecosystem to acquire aggregate and analyze data in order to get actionable insights. The more common use cases in healthcare involve connecting people, consumers, clinicians and caregivers. Healthcare organizations have piloted many connected health projects mainly aiming at consumer engagement. The ability to connect consumers and patients and affect their behavior will encourage them to make healthier decisions, which in turn will lead to better outcomes and lower healthcare costs. Monitoring to consumers vital signs and activity and thus holding them accountable for healthcare decisions will help further drive compliance. Across the globe, there is an evolving focus on improving the health of the population to control healthcare costs.

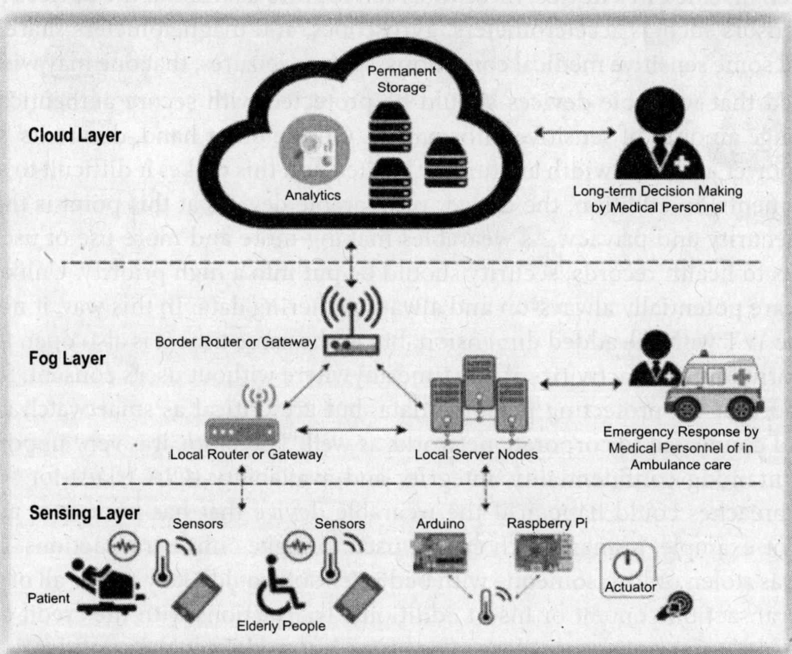

Figure 11.14: Internet of Medical Things Architecture

The three challenges for medical device manufacturers are security, compliance and cost of product development. Medical devices like pacemakers, insulin pumps, and the signal between the pacemaker-defibrillator and the programmer are vulnerable. These vulnerabilities can be life threatening. People rely on pacemakers to keep their heart running but there can be vulnerabilities in pacemakers. In August 2011 on "Black Hat Technical Security conference", a person successfully hacked into an insulin pump that was attached to his abdomen and completely disabled it. He was a diabetic and this pump was part of an insulin delivery system that was intended to keep him alive by monitoring and stabilizing his blood glucose levels. This onstage demonstration has opened the debate on the safety of wearable medical devices and whether the manufactures of such medical devices are taking necessary steps to avoid such attacks. In May 2017, a ransomware called WannaCry shutdown 65 hospitals in the United Kingdom. This cyber-attack not only affected computers in the hospitals but also affected the storage refrigerators and MRI machines. Most of the health monitoring wearable devices have login in clear text and the passwords of these devices are recorded in logfiles as plaintext. The data transmitted between different domains is sent as plain text and no security measures are used like encryption while transmitting the data. Most of the data in apps are stored in cloud or the application storage database. The security and privacy of the patient data is highly at risk stored in the medical health applications. Public should be made aware of issues and government agencies; research institutes and manufacturers need to overcome these obstacles to have a smooth implementation.

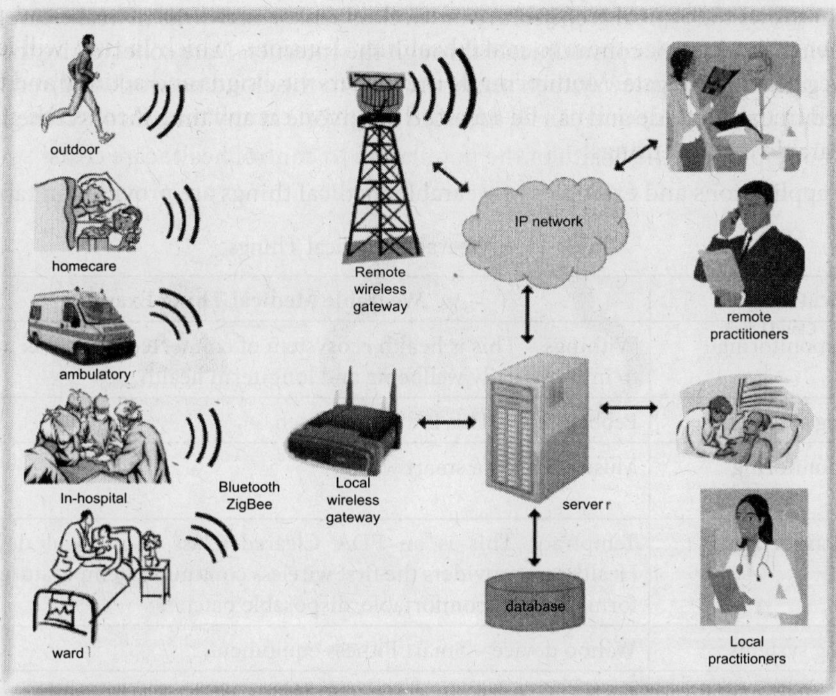

Figure 11.15: Wireless Sensor Networks Architecture in Healthcare

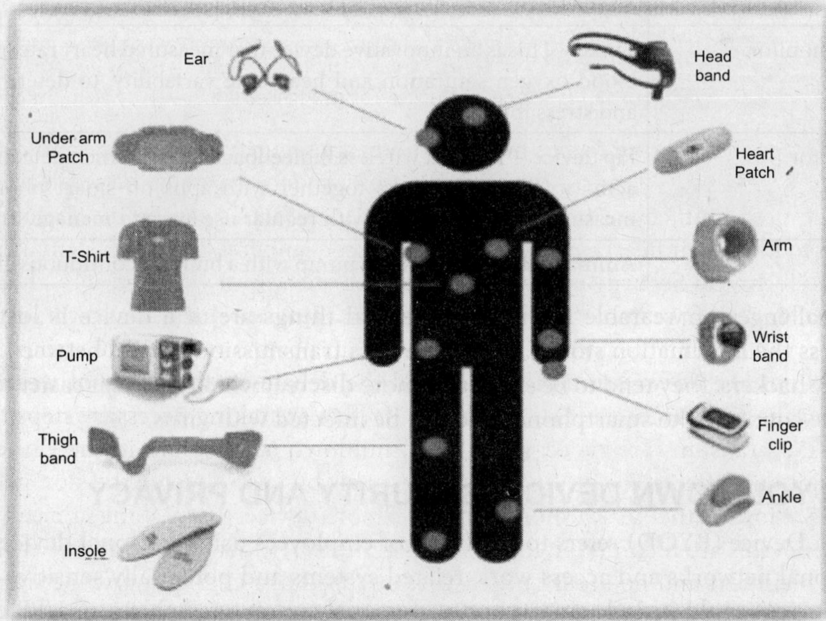

Figure 11.16: Wearable Medical Things

Figure 11.15 shows the typical architecture of wireless sensor networks in healthcare applications. It shows how the wireless network communicate through the Internet. Date collected by the sensors is sent wirelessly to the gateway. The gateway then sends the data to the cloud network or directly to the server. The data is stored in the database and can be accessed be anyone at any time through the Internet. Figure 11.16 shows wearable medical things.

Few of the applications and examples of wearable medical things are provided in table 11.4

Table 11.4: Wearable Medical Things

Application	Wearable Medical Thing Example
Blood pressure monitoring systems	Withings – This is health ecosystem of connected devices & apps is designed to improve daily wellbeing and long-term health.
Sleep monitoring systems	Pebble time – This is a smart watch.
Brain activity monitoring systems	Muse – This is a smart watch.
Temperature monitoring systems	Temptraq- This is an FDA Cleared Class II medical device that gives Healthcare providers the first wireless continuous temperature monitor in the form of a soft, comfortable, disposable patch.
Pulse monitoring systems	Wahoo device – Smart Fitness equipment.
Daily physical activities monitor	Fitbit – This is a range of fitness bands, smart watches and accessories to track your steps, exercise, heart rate, weight, and more.
Heart electrical monitor	ECG (EKG). ECG is in English (Electro Cardio Gram) and the EKG is based on the German spelling (Elektro Kardio Gramm).
Cardiac fitness monitor	Tinke – This is an innovative device that measured heart rate, respiratory rate, blood oxygen saturation and heart rate variability, to determine key fitness and stress indices.
Stress level monitor	Pip device – This is a wireless biofeedback device which detects electrodermal activity (EDA). It works together with apps on smart phone to help you measure, understand and with regular use learn to manage stress.
Insulin Pump	Animas Vibe - is an insulin pump with a built for continuous glucose monitor.

The few challenges of wearable Internet of medical things are, if a device is lost or misplaced, anyone can access the information stored locally, wireless transmission of data between the parties can be intercepted by hackers, they tend to be small and more discreet which makes it easier to steal sensitive data and they are connected to smartphones and can be infected with virus.

11.9 BRING YOUR OWN DEVICE SECURITY AND PRIVACY

Bring Your Own Device (BYOD) refers to the trend of employees using personal devices to connect to their organizational networks and access work-related systems and potentially sensitive or confidential data. Personal devices could include smartphones, personal computers, tablets, or USB drives. As more and more organizations support employees working from home, maintaining a flexible schedule, or connecting while on work travel or commutes, BYOD solutions have become more prevalent. Some companies may sanction BYOD, while others may not.

The rapid advancement in information technology systems brought about the emergence of mobile computing, and later BYOD. Organizations chose to embrace BYOD, because the organization benefits from lower corporate cost, less technical training for employees, and increased productivity. The drive behind BYOD can be traced back to the 1980s when many organizations identified the ideal employee as one with creativity, initiative and determination, who could get things done by any means across geographical borders. This recognition by organizations caused employees to harness new and quicker ways of working, in order to prove competence to their employers. Presently, BYOD is common in corporate environments, and is re-organising ownership and control of organizational information systems and resources.

At corporate levels, information security concerns the protection of valuable assets of organisations. These assets are information that is either processed, recorded or stored, and owned by the organisation. Information security concerns in BYOD are mainly centered on the confidentiality of data, since it is the organisational asset at risk. Other security concerns revolve around the risk introduced by mixing of personal and work data, and applications. Unlike organization owned devices that only have IT approved software on them, BYOD devices may have different applications downloaded and installed. There is also a chance for data exfiltration from one app to another on BYOD devices. Another matter of concern is the lack of adequate safeguards implemented on devices, retainment of confidential organisational data on devices by employees, and stolen, lost or hacked devices. These all could easily introduce malware and viruses that can infect devices and potentially lead to compromise and exposure of confidential data.

Mobile malware is a well known threat to mobile devices and is rapidly growing as a result of BYOD adoption. The aim of malware is to break-in to a mobile device to spy or steal users' information, and damage the device. Mobile users are often deceived by attackers to install malicious software applications on their device. In some cases the hackers wait for opportunities when the mobile device is vulnerable to remotely access the device. Malware threats can consist of viruses, worms, Trojans, and botnets. Malware deployed on mobile devices, has the ability to communicate non-stop with remote "command and control" sites, avoiding many corporate security measures.

Phishing, social engineering attacks are well thought-out methods of deception that a hacker uses to collect or force mobile device users to send confidential information about themselves. This can be used to trick BYOD users to download malware onto their mobile device. Other planned methods of deception can be email messages sent from persons recognized by the recipients asking them to reply with confidential information. Invitation to register personal details on a website, or persuading individuals to install malware or to download an attachment which runs a hidden key-logger program to their BYOD device, is also another method used by hackers.

Hackers can use their intellectual skills to identify and analyze a particular mobile device system, and then launch direct attacks against it. The aim of the attack is typically to access, destroy, rewrite/modify, and extract confidential information or to popularize the hackers for their exceptional talents. Direct attack with the intent of stealing, destroying or modifying confidential data can have huge effects on organizations, particularly those providing services to customers through the Internet.

Data communication interception or spoofing can be major threats to wireless networks used by BYOD devices. If a mobile user sends information over the Internet and it is intercepted, this becomes a serious concern, because of the risk that the data can be accessed, modified, or even destroyed. At the same time if a mobile device can be spoofed through a wireless network and deceived into sending information to a wrong recipient or receiving any kind of malicious data, this can result into an even greater security concern. Even if the network is encrypted, there is still the risk of access point owners or malicious insiders having something physically attached to the network that could attempt to exploit a VPN tunnel. The continuous interception and spoofing of wireless data streams, and the use of deceptive ways to attract mobile device users to fraudulent wireless access points, have become a major threat to mobile technology itself, and a big security challenge to BYOD organizations.

Mobile devices loss and theft is an increasing concern, as they are more likely to occur with mobile devices than traditional computers. While mobile devices have brought increased flexibility, they can be easily lost or stolen. When mobile devices are lost or stolen, valuable information can easily fall into the wrong hands, and may be used for fraudulent and other illegal purposes. In the majority of cases, the cost of the device to the owners or the organizations is nowhere as important as the value of the information stored on the device.

Government and other large business organizations have long been reporting how malicious insiders have exposed confidential data. Malicious insiders are one of the most challenging and problematic security issues to handle. Insiders have direct access to organizational information resources and networks; hence it is easier for them to steal, modify or destroy data. With BYOD, malicious insider threats are easier to realize, since mobile device users have access to organizational systems and resources anytime anywhere. BYOD employees who are malicious insiders have the possibility of executing malware attacks, phishing, data interception and spoofing, and easy theft of mobile devices can occur without notice in the organizations.

A user policy violation is one of the easiest ways to expose a BYOD device to vulnerabilities. BYOD users do not require any malicious intent. Ignorance and carelessness, such as accessing and downloading untrusted web content that might contain malware, and disabling antivirus and firewall applications to increase speed and performance, can expose BYOD devices to vulnerabilities and threats. The Citigroup financial company experienced a breach that exposed the data of over 5000 of their customers, due to one of their employee's using a peer-to-peer (P2P) filesharing application from a BYOD laptop device on their network. Organizations are constantly faced with challenges of ensuring their employees comply with user policies. BYOD does not only reduce organizational control of systems that employees conduct business on, but the mobile nature of devices makes it difficult for organizations to enforce policies and restrictions on employees working with BYOD devices. Moreover, contemporary studies by mobile security researchers indicate that attackers will continue to exploit vulnerabilities and issue threats to mobile devices to modify or destroy organizational data, particularly using malicious software. Traditional security methods and processes, such as host-based firewalls and content filtering, are becoming outdated against the emerging threats in mobile devices, mostly because they take up system resources. Hence, organizations need to make security and privacy of BYOD devices as top priority. Technological advancements, like mobile computing devices and the boosted increase in computing power, have made it easier and cheaper for personal information to be compromised. At an organizational level, information privacy is a critical for businesses, and is a problem by the introduction of BYOD. Organizational information privacy is the behavior or attitude of firms towards protecting their information resources and their customers' personally identifiable information. There is a growing concern of how individual's personal information is exposed by organizations either intentionally or as a result of their information systems being hacked due to usage of mobile devices by employees. In BYOD, information breaches are a key issue that the majority of organizations are facing worldwide. As a result, organizations are implementing control measures that allow them to remotely wipe personal data on BYOD devices, force install apps, and monitor device usages. Such measures can lead to private data retention, and privacy exposure. Also, from BYOD organization employees' standpoint, the fact that they own their devices does not exempt the devices from forensic reviews in cases of litigation. This will require all personal information such as browsing history, pictures, movies/songs played and downloaded, personal contacts, calls, emails, text messages, and other social networking activities stored on the devices to be accessible. Employers who use mobile device management tools also have the ability to deliberately track and monitor employees' online activities and the real time location of their devices. As many organizations around the world continue to shift towards BYOD based environments, a considerable attention should be given to information privacy and security.

11.10 SUMMARY

In this chapter, security and privacy case studies related to smart home, smart power grid, smart vehicle, wearable computing, mobile health care and BYOD are discussed.

11.11 OBJECTIVE QUESTIONS

The answer of the multiple-choice questions is marked in **bold**.

1. .... is safe guarding user identity.
   (a) **Privacy** (b) Security
   (c) All of these (d) None of these

2. In electric power smart grid, two way electricity flow happens at ....
   (a) Generation (b) Transmission (c) Distribution (d) **Customers**

3. .... is not an o-board instrumentation in smart vehicle.
   (a) **ABS** (b) EDR (c) Radar (d) None of these

11.12 REVIEW QUESTIONS

1. Explain IoT security.

2. Explain IoT privacy.

3. Compare various aspects of security and privacy in IoT.

11.13 ABBREVIATIONS AND SYMBOLS

Abbreviations	Full Form	Description
ABS	Anti-blocking Brake System	ABS, is a system which is designed to prevent from "locking" up brakes, or applying so much pressure to brakes that the axle and wheels themselves stop turning completely.
AGC	Automatic Generation Control	AGC is a system for adjusting the power output of multiple generators at different power plants, in response to changes in the load.
AMI	Advanced Metering Infrastructure	AMI is an integrated system of equipment, communications, and information management systems for utilities to remotely collect customer water usage data in real time.

Abbreviations	Full Form	Description
BAN	Building Area Network	BAN is a local area network (LAN) that covers an entire building. It may be a collection of smaller local area networks.
CoAP	Constrained Application Protocol	CoAP is a specialized Internet application protocol for constrained devices, as defined in RFC 7252. It enables those constrained devices called "nodes" to communicate with the wider internet using similar protocols.
DAG	Directed Acyclic Graph	DAG is a conceptual representation of a series of activities.
DDoS	Distributed Denial of Service	DDoS is a method where cybercriminals flood a network with so much malicious traffic that it cannot operate or communicate as it normally would.
DER	Distributed Energy Resources	DER refers to often smaller generation units that are located very near on the consumer's side.
DMS	Distribution Management System	DMS is a collection of applications designed to monitor & control the entire distribution network efficiently and reliably.
DoS	Denial-of-Service	DoS is a cyber-attack in which the perpetrator seeks to make a machine or network resource unavailable to its intended users by temporarily or indefinitely disrupting services of a host connected to a network.
EDR	Event Data Systems Recorder	EDR is a device installed in automobiles to record information related to traffic collisions.
EMS	Energy Management System	An energy management system is a system of computer-aided tools used by operators of electric utility grids to monitor, control, and optimize the performance of the generation or transmission system.
GDP	Gross Domestic Product	Gross domestic product is a monetary measure of the market value of all the final goods and services produced in a specific time period.
GPS	Global Positioning System	GPS is a satellite navigation system used to determine the ground position of an object. GPS receiver combines the broadcasts from multiple satellites to calculate its exact position using a process called triangulation.
HAN	Home Area Network	HAN is a network contained within a customer's home or business that connects a customer's qualified energy monitoring device to a smart meter.

Abbreviations	Full Form	Description
HMI	Human Machine Interface	HMI refers to a dashboard or screen used to control machinery.
HTTP	Hypertext Transfer Protocol	HTTP is an application layer protocol in the Internet Protocol suite model for distributed, collaborative, hypermedia information systems.
IAN	Industrial Area Network	IAN covers an entire industrial environment and connects its machines to control and monitoring systems.
JSON	JavaScript Object Notation	JSON is an open standard file format and data interchange format that uses human-readable text to store and transmit data objects consisting of attribute–value pairs and arrays.
MQTT	MQ Telemetry Transport	MQTT is a lightweight, publish-subscribe network protocol that transports messages between devices.
MTU	Master Terminal Unit	MTU in SCADA system is a device that issues the commands to the Remote Terminal Unit (RTU) which are located at remote places from the control, gathers the required data, stores the information, and process the information and display the information in the form of pictures, curves and tables.
NFC	Near Field Communication	NFC is a set of communication protocols for communication between two electronic devices over a distance of 4 cm or less.
NIST	National Institute of Standards & Technology	NIST is a physical sciences laboratory and non-regulatory agency of the United States Department of Commerce. Its mission is to promote American innovation and industrial competitiveness.
PHEV	Plug-in Hybrid Electric Vehicle	PHEV is a hybrid electric vehicle whose battery pack can be recharged by plugging to an external electric power source, in addition to its on-board internal combustion engine-powered generator.
PKI	Public Key Infrastructure	PKI is a set of roles, policies, hardware, software and procedures needed to create, manage, distribute, use, store and revoke digital certificates and manage public-key encryption.
PLC	Programmable Logic Controller	A programmable logic controller is a type of tiny computer that can receive data through its inputs and send operating instructions through its outputs. Fundamentally, a PLC's job is to control a system's functions using the internal logic programmed into it.
RFID	Radio Frequency IDentification	RFID is a form of wireless communication that uses radio waves to identify and find objects.

Abbreviations	Full Form	Description
RTU	Remote Terminal Unit	RTU is a microprocessor-controlled electronic device that interfaces objects in the physical world to a distributed control system or SCADA system by transmitting telemetry data to a master system, and by using messages from the master supervisory.
SCADA	Supervisory Control And Data Acquisition	SCADA is a control system architecture comprising computers, networked data communications and graphical user interfaces for high-level supervision of machines and processes.
VAR	Volt Ampere Reactive	VAR is the measuring unit for reactive power, which is created by energizing transformers and powering motors, pumps, air conditioners, and other similar devices.

11.14 LIST OF FIGURES AND TABLES

The details of figures and tables used in this chapter is as below.

CHAPTER 12

Software Defined Networking

CONTENTS

12.1 SOFTWARE DEFINED NETWORKS

Software-Defined Networking (SDN) is an approach to networking that uses software-based controllers or Application Programming Interfaces (APIs) to communicate with underlying hardware infrastructure and direct traffic on a network. It is an architecture that gives networks more programmability and flexibility by separating the control plane from the data plane. The role of software defined networks in cloud computing lets users respond quickly to changes. SDN management makes network configuration more efficient and improves network performance and monitoring. SDN enables directly programmable network control for applications and network services. Software defined network architecture decouples network control and forwarding functions from physical hardware such as routers and switches to create a more manageable and dynamic network infrastructure.

Software defined networking is for restructuring the current network infrastructure. SDN is an umbrella term encompassing several kinds of network technology aimed at making the network as agile and flexible as the virtualized server and storage infrastructure of the modern data center. The goal of SDN is to allow network engineers and administrators to respond quickly to changing business requirements. In an SDN, a network administrator can shape traffic from a centralized control console without having to touch individual switches, and can deliver services to wherever they are needed in the network, without regard to what specific devices a server or other hardware components are connected to. The key technologies for SDN implementation are functional separation, network virtualization and automation through programmability. Software-defined networking improves network connectivity for sales, customer service, internal communications, and document sharing. SDN allows organizations to use software and hardware from multiple vendors to have customized network services and infrastructure.

12.2 LIMITATIONS OF CURRENT NETWORK

The architecture of traditional network is shown in the figure 12.1.

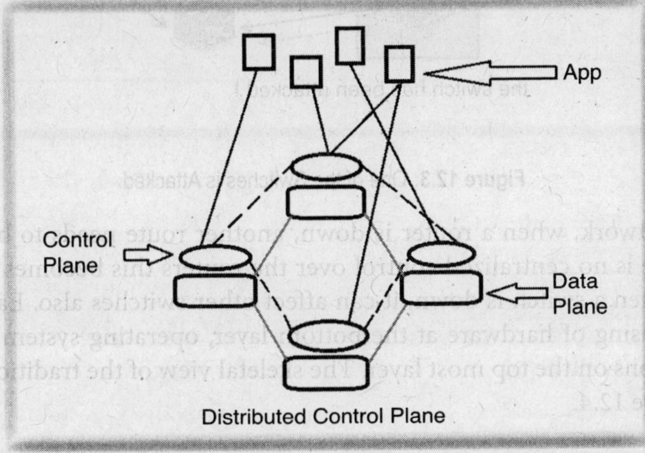

Figure 12.1: Traditional Network Architecture

Consider the scenario of traditional networks. For this we are taking the example of a wired network with Layer3 (L3) switches. These switches act both as switch and router. Figure 12.2 shows the network topology of current network.

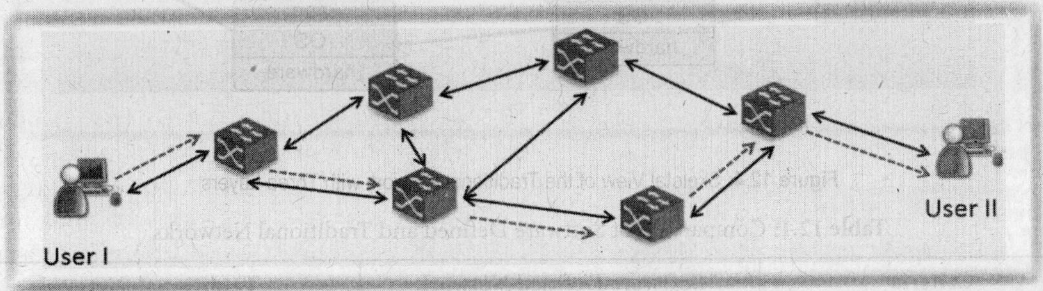

Figure 12.2: Network Topology of Current Network

The data needs to be send from user 1 to user 2 and vice versa as shown in Figure 12.2. The data can be sent through several routes. The packet traverses through multiple L3 switches before it reaches its destination. The protocol used for switching is the Open Shortest Path First (OSPF) protocol. OSPF is a routing protocol for Internet Protocol (IP) networks. Each router knows to which router the packet needs to be sent based on the routing table it has. Each router doesn't have a global view of the network as a whole.

Consider the situation where one of the routers or switches has been attacked as shown in Figure 12.3. The attacked switch will be down for one reason or another.

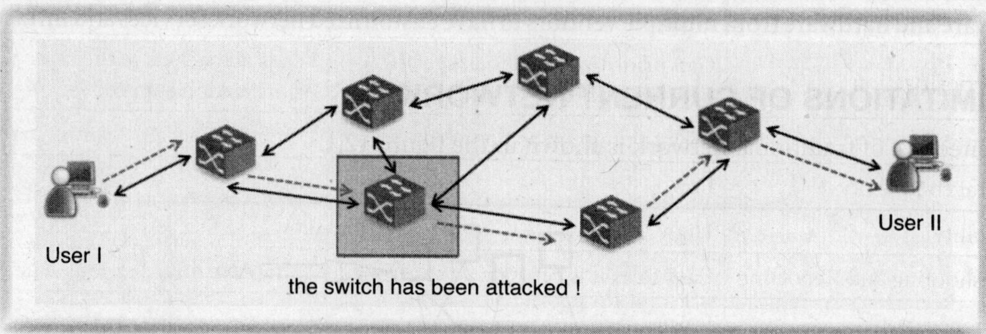

Figure 12.3: One of the Switches is Attacked

In a traditional network, when a router is down, another route needs to be identified to transfer the packets. Since there is no centralized control over the routers this becomes a difficult task. So in a traditional network, when a switch is down, it can affect other switches also. Each router in a network has three layers comprising of hardware at the bottom layer, operating system running on top of the hardware and applications on the top most layer. The skeletal view of the traditional network with these layers is shown in Figure 12.4.

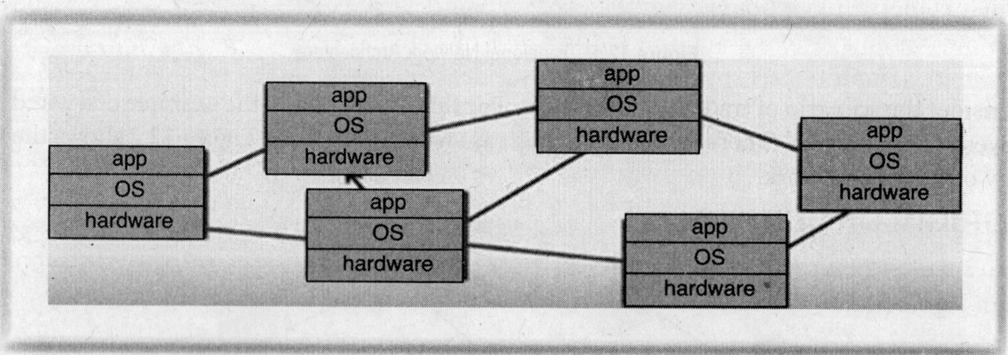

Figure 12.4: Skeletal View of the Traditional Network with Three Layers

Table 12.1: Comparison of Software Defined and Traditional Networks

Criteria	Software Defined Network	Traditional Network
Approach	Virtual networking	Conventional networking.
Control	Centralized Control	Distributed Control
Flexibility	Programmable	Non programmable
Interface	Open Interface	Closed Interface
Plane	Data plane and control plane are decoupled by software	Data plane and control plane are mounted on same plane

Criteria	Software Defined Network	Traditional Network
Configuration	Automatic.	Static/Manual
Speed	High	Low
Packet Prioritization	Can prioritize and block specific network packets	Leads all packets in the same way no prioritization support
Programmability	Easy to program as per need	Difficult program again as per use
Structural complexity	Low	High
Extensibility	High	Low
Troubleshooting and Reporting	Easy to as it is centralized controlled	Difficult as it is distributed controlled
Maintenance cost	Low	High

There are several limitations in current network which are as below.

- Centralized control of the network is not feasible in traditional networks.
- Vendor-specific architecture of switches limits dynamic configuration according to application-specific requirements.
- Each switch may have different operating system. Switches are required to configure according to the installed operating system.

In a traditional network, each router or switch will be running thousands of lines of code. Each router may comprise of millions of logic gates contributing to 10 GB RAM approximately, cost expensive and running various kinds of application programs such as routing, mobility management etc. Each of the routers in traditional network has specialized packet forwarding hardware, different operating system and different applications for routing, mobility management etc. The goal of the software defined networking is to overcome the limitations or challenges of traditional network.

12.3 ORIGIN OF SDN

The concept of SDN is to separate the hardware from the operating system and application programs as shown in Figure 12.5.

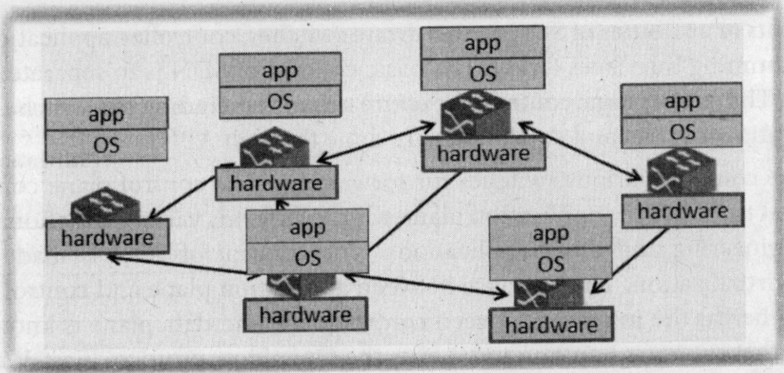

Figure 12.5: Concept of SDN

The history of SDN principles can be traced back to the separation of the control and data plane first used in the public switched telephone network as a way to simplify provisioning and management well before this architecture began to be used in data networks. The Internet Engineering Task Force (IETF) began considering various ways to decouple the control and forwarding functions in a proposed interface standard published in 2004 appropriately named "Forwarding and Control Element Separation" (ForCES). The ForCES working group also proposed a companion SoftRouter architecture. Additional early standards from the IETF that pursued separating control from data include the Linux Netlink as an IP Services Protocol and a Path Computation Element (PCE) based architecture.

These early attempts failed to gain traction for two reasons. One is that many in the Internet community viewed separating control from data to be risky, especially owing to the potential for a failure in the control plane. The second is that vendors were concerned that creating standard application programming interfaces (APIs) between the control and data planes would result in increased competition. The use of open source software in split control/data plane architectures traces its roots to the Ethane project at Stanford's computer sciences department. Ethane's simple switch design led to the creation of OpenFlow. An API for OpenFlow was first created in 2008. That same year witnessed the creation of NOX which is an operating system for networks. Work on OpenFlow continued at Stanford, including with the creation of testbeds evaluating use of the protocol in a single campus network, as well as across the WAN as a backbone for connecting multiple campuses. Beyond academia, the first deployments were by Nicira in 2010. The Open Networking Foundation was founded in 2011 to promote SDN and OpenFlow.

12.4 SDN ARCHITECTURE

Software Defined networking (SDN) is an approach to using open protocols, such as OpenFlow, to apply globally aware software control at the edges of the network to access network switches and routers that typically would use closed and proprietary firmware. SDN is meant to address the fact that the static architecture of traditional networks is decentralized and complex while current networks require more flexibility and easy troubleshooting. SDN suggests centralizing network intelligence in one network component by disassociating the forwarding process of network packets (Data Plane) from the routing process (Control plane). The control plane consists of one or more controllers which are considered as the brain of SDN network where the whole intelligence is incorporated. Figure 12.6 shows the architecture of SDN.

The components or attributes of SDN are hardware switches, controller, applications, flow-rules and Application Programming Interfaces (API). The basic concept of SDN is to separate control logic from hardware switches. The control logic controls the entire network including the switches. Communication between the application, control and data planes are done through APIs.

The data plane contains various switches for forwarding. The control plane contains the network operating system. At the top is the application plane which performs various functionalities like security, routing, traffic engineering and other applications. The concept of SDN is made possible through network function virtualization. The interface between application plane and control plane is known as Northbound API whereas the interface between control plane and data plane is known as Southbound API. The protocol that supports Southbound API is the OpenFlow protocol. East-Westbound APIs are used to communicate among multiple controllers in the control layer.

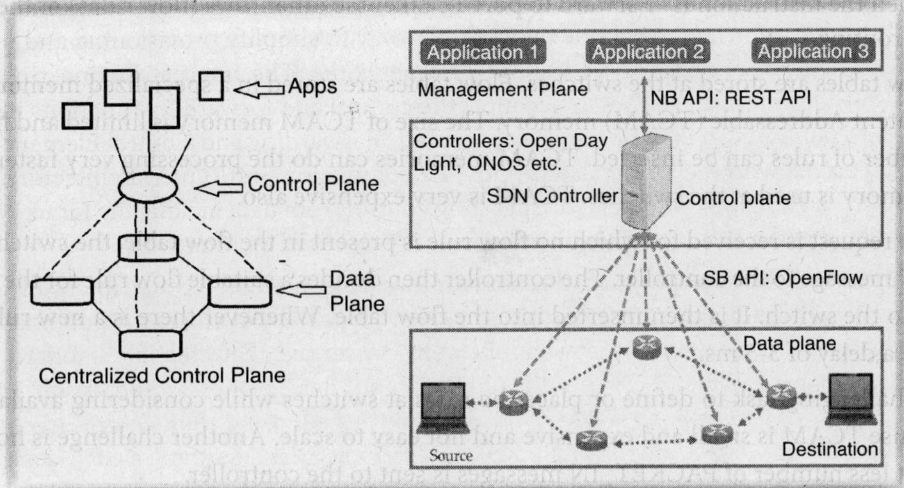

Figure 12.6: Architecture of Software Defined Network

The current status of SDN shows that companies such as Google have started to implement SDN at their data center networks. The current networks could be replaced with SDN in a phased manner. With SDN, operational cost and delay caused due to link failure can be significantly minimized. The two main challenges in the implementation of SDN are rule placement and controller placement.

12.5 RULE PLACEMENT

Switches forward traffic based on a rule called "Flow Rule". This is defined by the centralized controller. In the traditional network, there will be a routing table at every switch or router. Here in SDN, a flow table is maintained at every switch. Each entry in the flow table is the flow rule. Each rule has a specific format, which is defined by a protocol. In SDN, it is OpenFlow protocol. Table 12.2 shows an example for flow rules based on OpenFlow protocol.

Table 12.2: Example for Flow Rules based on OpenFlow Protocol

Match SDN applications first and use normal for unmatched packets (Hybrid default forwarding)										
Priority	**Ingress Port**	**MAC Source Address**	**MAC Destination**	**Protocol**	**Van ID**	**IP Source Address**	**IP Destination**	**Source Port**	**Destination Port**	**Instructions**
10000	"	"	"	TCP	"	"	10.1.1.20/32	"	60	Forward to Port 1
5000	"	"	"	"	"	"	10.1.1.0.24	"	"	Forward to Port 2
300	"	"	"	"	2600	"	"	"	"	Send to Controller
0	"	"	"	"	"	"	"	"	"	OF Normal

Consider the first row of the flow table. When a packet arrives at a router, it will check for the priority. If the priority matches, the values for Ingress port, MAC source address, MAC destination can be anything because it is a wildcard. If the protocol is TCP, IP destination is 10.1.1.20/32 and destination port is 60, then the instruction is "Forward to port 1". Likewise other rows (flow rules) of the flow tables are used for routing.

The flow tables are stored at the switches. Flow tables are stored in a specialized memory known as Ternary Content Addressable (TCAM) memory. The size of TCAM memory is limited and hence only a limited number of rules can be inserted. TCAM memories can do the processing very faster and that is why this memory is used at the switches. TCAM is very expensive also.

When a request is received for which no flow rule is present in the flow table, the switch will send a PACKET-IN message to the controller. The controller then decides a suitable flow rule for the request and sends back to the switch. It is then inserted into the flow table. Whenever there is a new rule insertion, there will be a delay of 3-5 ms.

It is a challenging task to define or place the rules at switches while considering available TCAM. This is because TCAM is small and expensive and not easy to scale. Another challenge is how to define rules, so that less number of PACKET_IN messages is sent to the controller.

12.6 OPENFLOW PROTOCOL

OpenFlow protocol is the only one protocol that is available for rule placement. It has different versions like 1.0, 1.1, 1.2, 1.3 etc. to have different number of match fields. Different match fields include source IP, destination IP, source port, priority etc. One of the issues with OpenFlow protocol is how long a flow rule is to be kept at the switch. For addressing this issue, two strategies are used. The first one is the hard timeout and the other one is the soft timeout. In hard timeout, all the flow rules are deleted from the switch. This can be used to reset the switch. In a soft timeout, if no flow is received associated with a rule, then the rule is deleted. This is used to empty the rule space by deleting an unused rule.

SDN and OpenFlow is not the same. SDN is a technology or concept while OpenFlow is a protocol used to communicate between data plane and control plane. There are various softwares associated with OpenFlow implementation. Some of them are given below.

Indigo: This is an open source project aimed at enabling support for OpenFlow on physical and hypervisor switches.

LINC: This is a pure OpenFlow software switch. It gives a lot of flexibility and allows quick development and testing of new OpenFlow features. It supports OpenFlow protocol 1.2, OpenFlow protocol 1.3 and OpenFlow protocol 1.4. It has a modular architecture which is easily extensible.

Pantou: This turns a commercial wireless router or access point to an OpenFlow-enabled switch. OpenFlow is implemented as an application on top of OpenWrt. Pantou is based on the BackFire OpenWrt release (Linux 2.6.32).

Of13softswitch: This is an OpenFlow 1.3 compatible user-space software switch implementation. The code is based on the Ericsson TrafficLab 1.1 softswitch implementation, with changes in the forwarding plane to support OpenFlow 1.3.

Open vSwitch: This is an open source software which is the most popular one which is present today for SDN implementation.

12.7 CONTROLLER PLACEMENT

Controllers define flow rules according to the application specific requirements. Control logic is taken care by the control plane. The controller knows what has to be done with a particular flow. The controllers must be able to handle all the incoming requests from the switches. Rules should be placed without incurring much delay. Typically, a controller can handle 200 requests in a second through a single thread. Currently multi-threaded applications are also possible in controllers.

The controllers are logically connected to the switches in one-hop distance. The switch thinks that controller is just a hop away from it. Physically, they are connected to the switches in multi-hop distance. If we have a very small number of controllers for a large network, the network might be congested with control packets i.e. PACKET-IN messages. Various architectures for controller placement are flat architecture, hierarchical (tree) architecture, ring architecture and mesh architecture. Figure 12.7 shows a flat architecture for controller placement.

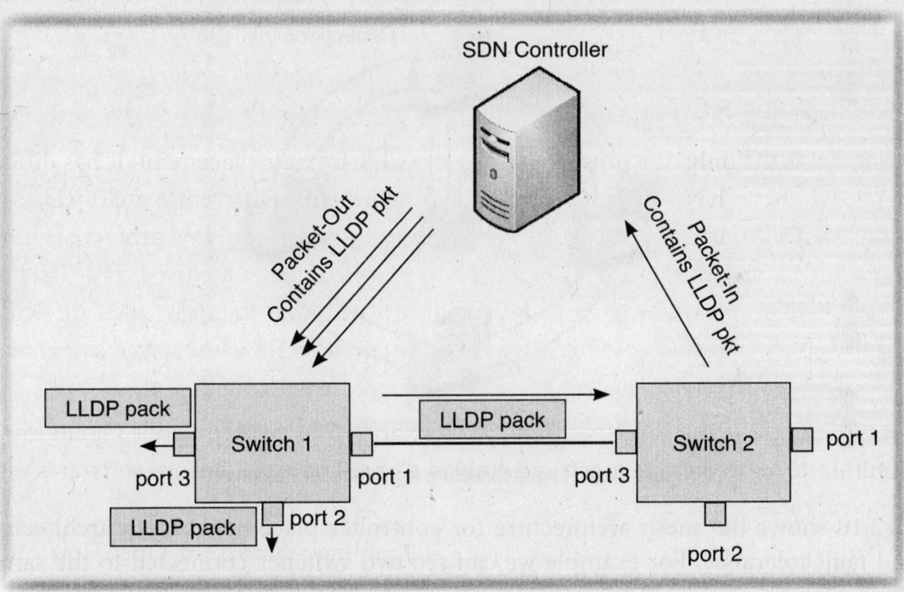

Figure 12.7: Flat Architecture for Controller Placement

In flat architecture, the controller is logically one hop away from the switch. The switch sends the PACKET-IN message to the controller, if the flow rule for the particular flow that it has received is not in the flow table. The controller sends back the new flow rule to the switch. The Link Layer Discovery Protocol (LLDP) is a vendor-neutral link layer protocol used by network devices for advertising their identity, capabilities, and neighbors on a local area network based on IEEE 802 technology. Figure 12.8 shows the hierarchical (tree) architecture for controller placement.

In a hierarchical architecture, the controllers and switches are arranged like a tree structure. Figure 12.9 shows the ring architecture for controller placement. In a ring architecture, multiple controllers are arranged in a ring fashion. But a particular switch is connected to only one controller. A PACKET-IN message will be sent to a single controller only and the controller sends back the flow rule to that particular switch.

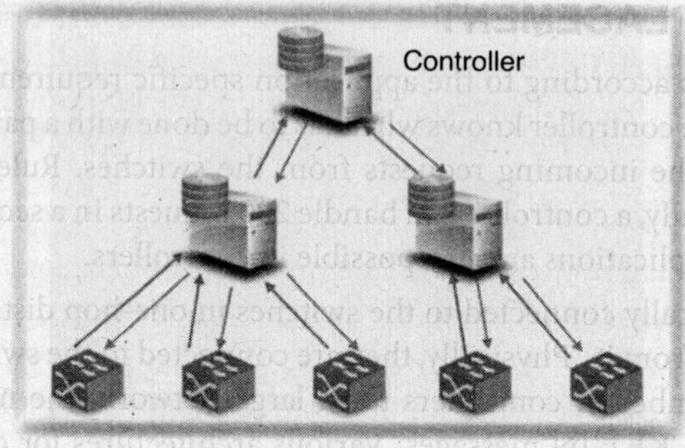

Figure 12.8: Hierarchical (Tree) Architecture for Controller Placement

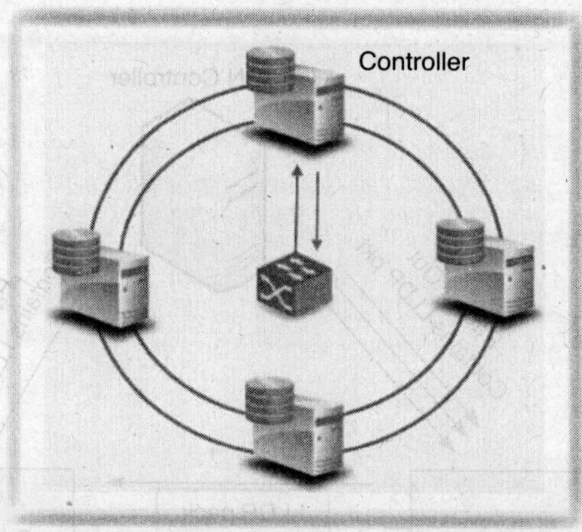

Figure 12.9: Ring Architecture for Controller Placement

Figure 12.10 shows the mesh architecture for controller placement. Mesh architecture increases reliability and fault-tolerance. For example we can see two switches connected to the same controller. Even if a switch goes down, the other switch can take care of it.

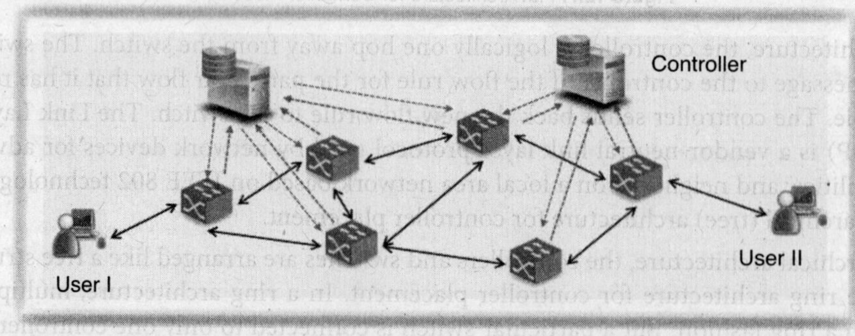

Figure 12.10: Mesh Architecture for Controller Placement

The control mechanisms can be either distributed or centralized. In a distributed control mechanism, the control decisions can be taken in a distributed manner. For example, each sub-network is controlled by a different controller. In a centralized control mechanism, the control decisions are taken in a centralized manner.

For experimenting with SDN, we need simulators or emulators. The emulators can be connected to the real network and can analyze the data. Simulators on the other hand, simulate the entire network including nodes and packet flows. The simulator or emulator takes care of infrastructure deployment and controller placement. Both must be supported with open flow protocol. In controller placement, the controllers can be either remote or local. In a remote controller, the controller can be situated in a remote place and communicated using IP address and port number.

For switch deployment, mininet software based on python language can be used. This software can be used to create a virtual network with open flow enabled switches. It supports both remote and local controllers. Various softwares are available for controller configuration like Pox, Nox, FloodLight, OpenDayLight and ONOS.

Performance of SDN depends on rule placement and controller placement in the network. Control message overhead may be increased due to additional number of packets (PACKET-IN) messages. Unified network management is possible using SDN, while leveraging the global view of the network.

12.8 SECURITY IN SDN

There is enhanced security while using SDN. The security is implemented using firewall, proxy, HTTP and Intrusion Detection System (IDS). Figure 12.11 shows a topology to implement security in SDN.

1. When an HTTP request comes, it is first forwarded to Firewall 1 (FW1).
2. From the Firewall 1, it is sent to Intrusion Detection System 1 (IDS1).
3. From (IDS1), it is sent to Proxy 1
4. Finally, it is sent from Proxy1 to the outside network.

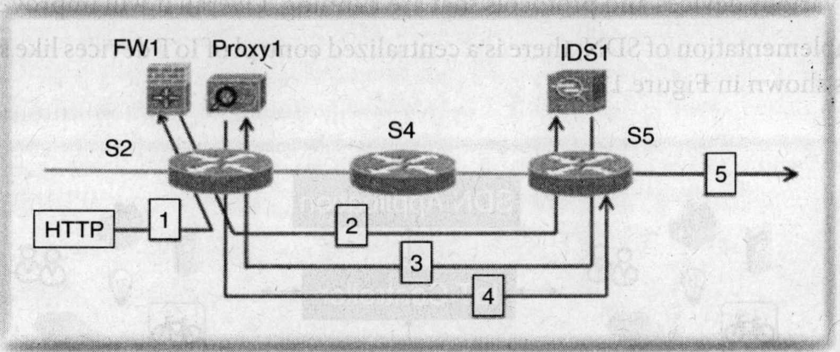

Figure 12.11: Topology to Implement Security in SDN

12.9 INTEGRATING SDN IN IOT

In this section we will see how SDN can be used with IoT. There are several benefits of integrating SDN with IoT.

1. With SDN, intelligent routing decisions can be deployed.
2. Simplification of information collection, analysis and decision making.
3. Visibility of network resources which includes network management simplification based on user, device and application specific requirements.
4. Intelligent traffic pattern analysis and coordinated decisions.

Consider the use of SDN for IoT as shown in Figure 12.12. In this there are several IoT devices in different sub-networks. The data from these devices through mobile access channels or fixed access channels are collected and transmitted to the data aggregator. The data aggregation from various IoT

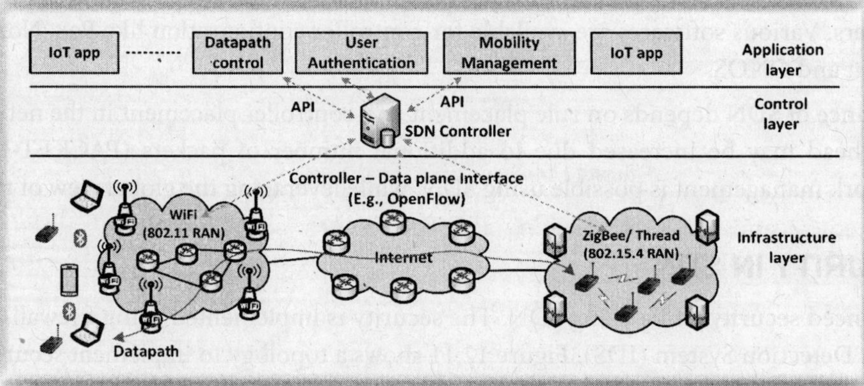

Figure 12.12: SDN for IoT

devices takes place at the data aggregator and then it passes through a transport network. From there it goes to different gateways and the packet segregation is done at the packet gateways. When we integrate SDN with IoT, we are going to integrate SDN controller with various devices, performs better orchestration of various devices and protocols that are running. Overall it will improve the service logic.

With the implementation of SDN, there is a centralized control of IoT devices like sensors, actuators, RFID tags etc. as shown in Figure 12.13.

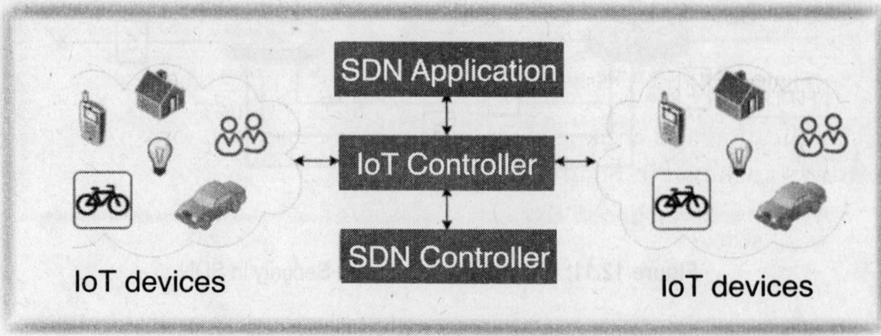

Figure 12.13: Centralized Control of IoT Devices

The rule-placement at access devices, while considering mobility and heterogeneity of end-users can be taken care by the fixed access channels, mobile access channels and intelligent aggregation as shown in Figure 12.14.

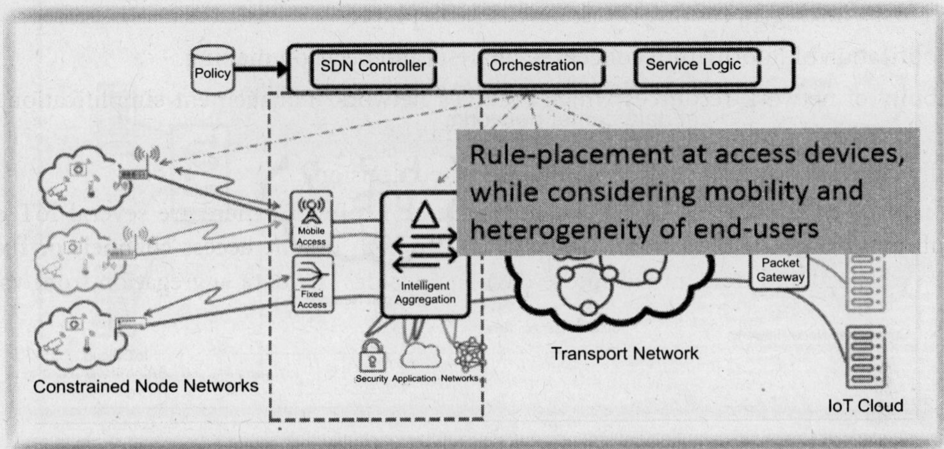

Figure 12.14: Rule Placement at Access Devices

Rule placement and traffic engineering at backbone networks is implemented by the transport network as shown in Figure 12.15.

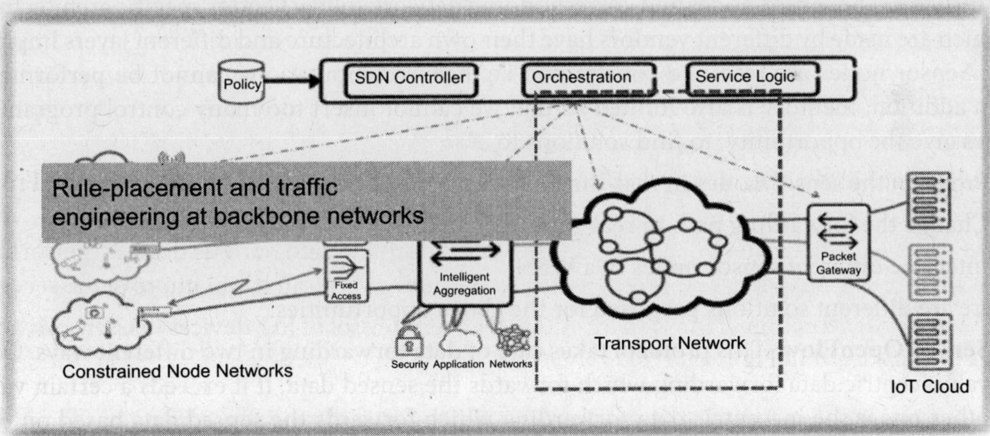

Figure 12.15: Rule Placement and Traffic Engineering at Backbone Networks

Finally flow classification and enhanced security at data center networks is done at packet gateways or data center networks as shown in Figure 12.16.

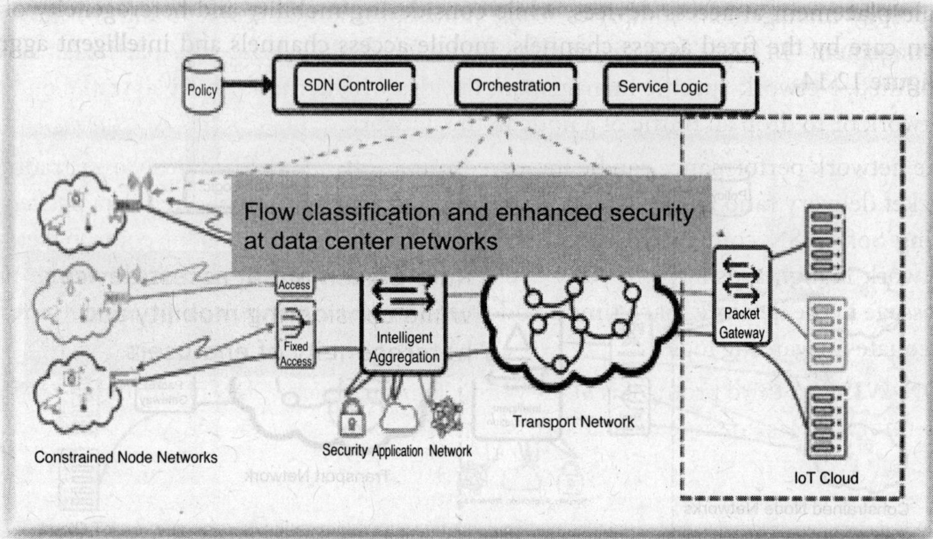

Figure 12.16: Flow Classification and Enhanced Security at Packet Gateways

12.10 SOFTWARE DEFINED WIRELESS SENSOR NETWORKS

There are several challenges in Wireless Sensor Network (WSN). Real-time programming of sensor nodes is difficult. The sensor nodes and corresponding network follow vendor specific architecture. Each nodes which are made by different vendors have their own architecture and different layers implemented in them. Sensor nodes are resource-constrained i.e. heavy computations cannot be performed at the nodes. In addition, memory is also limited so that we cannot insert too many control programs. These challenges give the opportunity to find solutions to

- Program the sensor nodes in real-time
- Change the forwarding path in real-time
- Integrate different sensor nodes in a WSN

There are different solutions proposed for the above opportunities.

- **Sensor OpenFlow:** This protocol takes care of data forwarding in two different ways. One is the value-centric data forwarding which forwards the sensed data, if it exceeds a certain value. The other one is the in-centric data forwarding which forwards the sensed data based on the ID of the source node. Real life implementation of such a method is not available. It still exists in its infant stage.
- **Soft-WSN:** Soft-WSN is another protocol for sensor device management and topology management. The sensor device management comprises of (a) sensor management (b) delay management and (c) active-sleep management. In sensor management, multiple sensors can be implemented in a single board and sensors can be used depending on application-specific requirements. In delay management, delay for sensing can be changed dynamically in real-time. In active-sleep management, the status of active and sleep mode can be changed dynamically.

Topology management comprises of (a) node-specific management and (b) network-specific management. In node-specific management, forwarding logic of a particular sensor can be modified. Network-specific management decides whether to forward all traffic of a node in the network or to drop all traffic of a node in the network.

The network performance can be improved using software defined WSN over traditional WSN. Packet delivery ratio in the network increases and number of replicated data packets is reduced using Soft-WSN compared to the traditional WSN. The number of control messages in the network is higher using Soft-WSN over the traditional WSN. This is due to the PACKET-IN message in the network. Each time a node receives a new packet, it asks the Controller for getting adequate forwarding logic.

- **SDN-WISE:** A third protocol is SDN-WISE. This proposes a SDN platform for WSN. Flow table for the rule placement is available at sensor nodes. Any programming language can be used through API to program the nodes in real-time. In SDN-WISE, the sensor node includes IEEE 802.15.4 protocol, Micro Control Unit (MCU) and IEEE 802.15.4 stack over which the SDN-WISE really functions.

12.11 SDN FOR MOBILE NETWORKING

Meeting current market requirements is virtually impossible with traditional mobile network architectures. Faced with flat or reduced budgets, enterprise IT departments are trying to squeeze the most from their networks using device-level management tools and manual processes. Carriers face similar challenges as demand for mobility and bandwidth explodes. Profits are being reduced by escalating capital equipment costs and flat or declining revenue.

Existing network architectures were not designed to meet the requirements of today's users, enterprises, and carriers. Network designers are constrained by the limitations of current networks, which include the following.

(a) **Complexity:** Networking technology to date has consisted largely of discrete sets of protocols designed to connect hosts reliably over arbitrary distances, link speeds and topologies. To meet business and technical needs over the last few decades, the industry has evolved networking protocols to deliver higher performance and reliability, broader connectivity and more stringent security. Protocols tend to be defined in isolation, with each solving a specific problem and without the benefit of any fundamental abstractions. This has resulted in today's networks complexity. For example, to add or move any device, IT must touch multiple switches, routers, firewalls, Web authentication portals, etc. and update Access Control Lists (ACLs), Virtual LANs (VLANs), Quality of Services (QoS) and other protocol-based mechanisms using device-level management tools. In addition, network topology, vendor switch model and software version all must be taken into account. Due to this complexity, today's networks are relatively static as information technology seeks to minimize the risk of service disruption. The static nature of networks is in contrast to the dynamic nature of today's server environment, where server virtualization has greatly increased the number of hosts requiring network connectivity and fundamentally altered assumptions about the physical location of hosts.

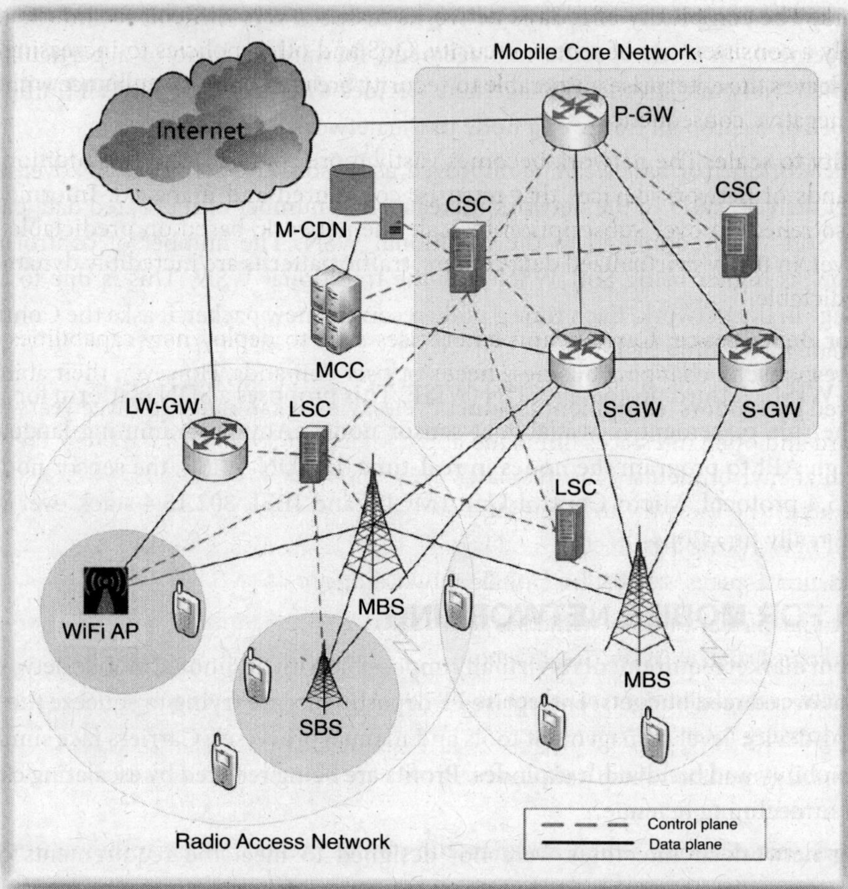

Figure 12.17: A Software Defined Mobile Network

Prior to virtualization, applications resided on a single server and primarily exchanged traffic with select clients. Today, applications are distributed across multiple virtual machines (VMs), which exchange traffic flows with each other. VMs migrate to optimize and rebalance server workloads, causing the physical end points of existing flows to change (sometimes rapidly) over time. VM migration challenges many aspects of traditional networking, from addressing schemes and namespaces to the basic notion of a segmented, routing-based design. In addition to adopting virtualization technologies, many enterprises today operate an IP converged network for voice, data and video traffic. While existing networks can provide differentiated QoS levels for different applications, the provisioning of those resources is highly manual. Information technology must configure each vendor's equipment separately and adjust parameters such as network bandwidth and QoS on a per-session, per-application basis. Because of its static nature, the network cannot dynamically adapt to changing traffic, application and user demands.

(b) **Inconsistent policies:** To implement a network-wide policy, IT may have to configure thousands of devices and mechanisms. For example, every time a new virtual machine is brought up, it can take hours, in some cases days, for information technology to reconfigure ACLs across the entire network. The complexity of today's networks makes it very difficult for information technology to apply a consistent set of access, security, QoS and other policies to increasingly mobile users, which leaves the enterprise vulnerable to security breaches, non-compliance with regulations and other negative consequences.

(c) **Inability to scale:** The network becomes vastly more complex with the addition of hundreds or thousands of network devices that must be configured and managed. Information technology has also relied on over subscription to scale the network, based on predictable traffic patterns. However, in today's virtualized data centers, traffic patterns are incredibly dynamic and therefore unpredictable.

(d) **Vendor dependence:** Carriers and enterprises seek to deploy new capabilities and services in rapid response to changing business needs or user demands. However, their ability to respond is hindered by vendors' equipment product cycles, which can range to three years or more. Lack of standard and open interfaces limits the ability of network operators to tailor the network to their individual environments. This mismatch between market requirements and network capabilities has brought the industry to a tipping point. In response, the industry has created the software defined networking architecture and is developing associated standards.

The important aspects of SDN for mobile networking are

- Flow table model of SDN which is well suited for end-to-end communication over multiple technologies such as WiFi, 3G, 4G etc.
- Logically centralized control which is particularly useful for efficient base station coordination for addressing inter-cell reference.
- Path management in which data can be routed based on service requirements without depending on core routing policies.
- Network virtualization which abstracts the physical resources from the network services. This helps in providing seamless connectivity and service differentiation among users.

Figure 12.18 shows the diagram for interference management in Software Defined Wireless Mobile Network (SDWMN).

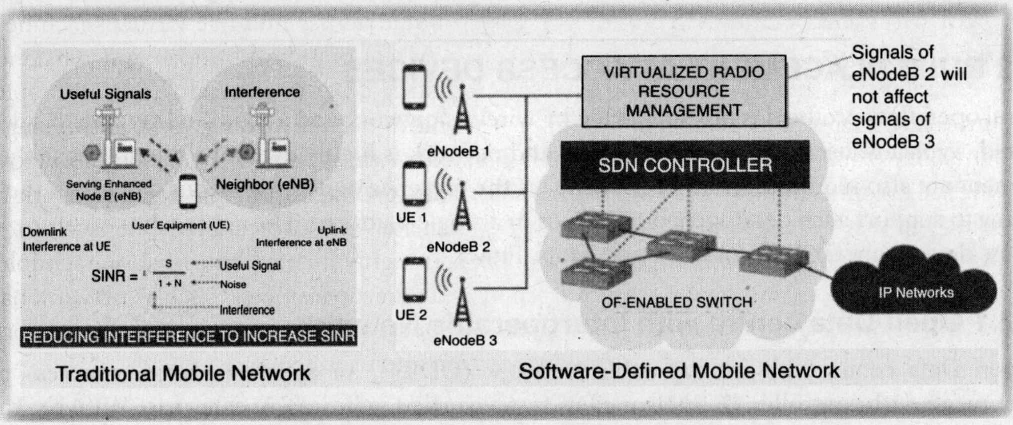

Figure 12.18: Interference Management in SDWMN

Consider a traditional mobile network. When mobile equipment operates, it connects with a base station or access point for sending data back and forth. At the same time, the equipment may get affected by another access point which is known as interference. SDWMN tries to address the problem of interference with the help of SDN. In the Figure 12.18, we can see an SDN controller and Virtualized Radio Resource Management Unit which takes care of interference. The signals from eNodeB2 will not affect the signals eNodeB3.

Mobile traffic management in Software Defined Wireless Mobile Network (SDWMN) is shown in Figure 12.19. The Access Network Discovery and Service Function (ANDSF) takes care of the mobile traffic management in SDWMN. When a user moves, he can be first connected to WiFi and then to the cellular network 3G, 4G and so on. The SDN enabled wireless networks takes care of the traffic management and connectivity.

The key benefits of SDN in mobile networks are centralized control of devices manufactured by multiple vendors, higher rate of integration of new services and abstract network control and management which includes networks abstracted from the user.

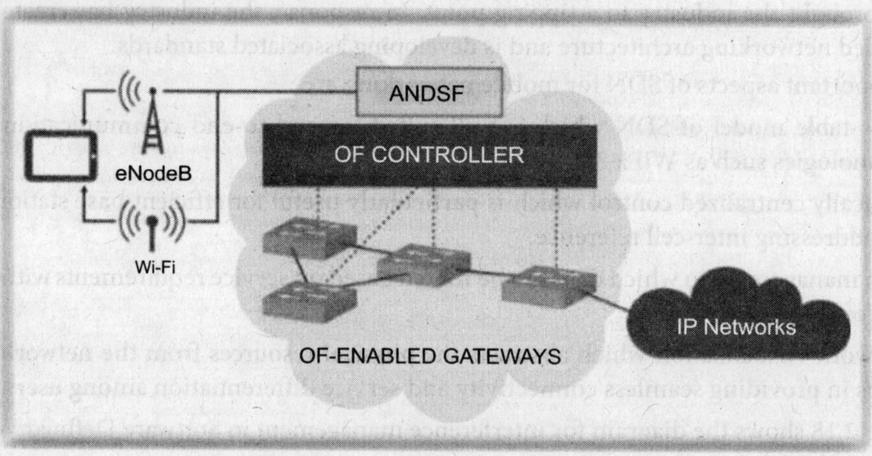

Figure 12.19: Mobile Traffic Management in SDWMN

12.12 RULE PLACEMENT AT ACCESS DEVICES

General open flow protocol is not supported by wireless network and a modified version of open flow is required. Typically, users are mobile in nature and network is highly dynamic. Frequent changes in rule placement are also required. Another challenge is the presence of heterogeneous devices in the network and how to support such heterogeneous devices in a single platform. The approaches for rule placement at access devices are ODIN, Ubi-Flow and Mobi-Flow.

12.12.1 Open Data centre with Interoperable Network

In Open Data center with Interoperable Network (ODIN), an agent is placed at access points to communicate with controller. ODIN is an SDN framework programmable enterprise WLANs. It provides a platform for developing typical enterprise WLAN services such as mobility managers, and load balancers as "network applications". Two components are present – an ODIN agent and ODIN master.

ODIN agent is placed with the physical devices and ODIN master is placed at the controller end. Figure 12.20 shows the architecture of ODIN.

ODIN's architecture comprises of a single master and a set of agents that run on the Access Points (APs). The master is implemented as an OpenFlow application on top of the controller. The agents are implemented and run on the APs. The APs run Open vSwitch so that OpenFlow rules can be installed at each AP as well. Every Light Virtual Access Point (LVAP) has a set of OpenFlow rules attached to it, which enable faster mobility and can potentially be used to do access control as well.

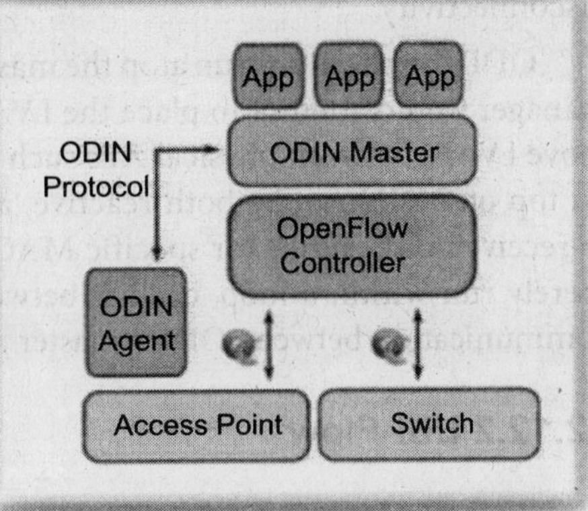

Figure 12.20: Architecture of ODIN

An LVAP is basically a per-client, virtual AP. Every time a client performs a probe scan, a central controller spawns an LVAP on a physical AP close to the client. The LVAP is what responds to the client's probe scan with a probe response. The client can then continue the regular 802.11 association handshake with the LVAP. Once this is done, an association is formed between a client device capable of mobility and an LVAP. At this point, the client is only concerned with getting ACKs for the data frames it generates and receiving beacons from its LVAP in a timely fashion.

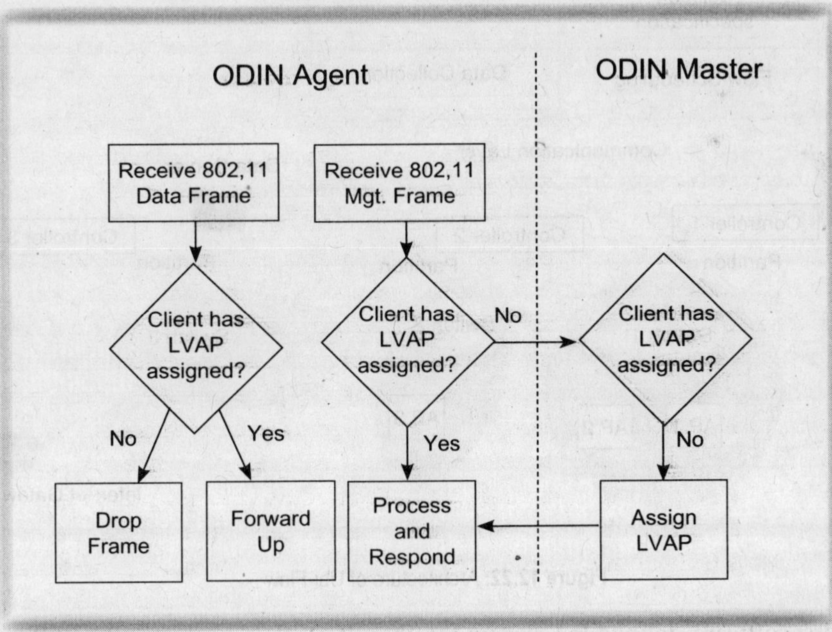

Figure 12.21: Flow Diagram for Communication between ODIN Master and ODIN Agent

Just like virtual machines in a data center can be migrated to a different physical server, an LVAP can be migrated to another physical AP. If an LVAP is migrated to another physical AP fast enough such that it retains all the necessary state to maintain its associations and the client continues to receive ACKs and beacon frames, then the client can continue transmitting data frames without having to perform a re-association. Thus, an LVAP migration gives the effect of a handoff, without actually inducing a state machine change at the client and if this is done fast enough, the client won't even notice any period of disconnectivity.

ODIN applications run atop the master, and control the placement of LVAPs. For instance, a mobility manager would attempt to place the LVAPs as close to the client as possible, and a load balancer would move LVAPs between physical APs such that the APs have an even processing load. Applications written on top of ODIN can be both reactive, and proactive. Reactive applications use a pub-sub mechanism to receive notifications for specific MAC layer events that they can subscribe to. Proactive applications merely run within a loop, cycling between sleeping and doing some work. The flow diagram for the communication between ODIN master and ODIN agent is shown in Figure 12.21.

12.12.2 Ubi-Flow

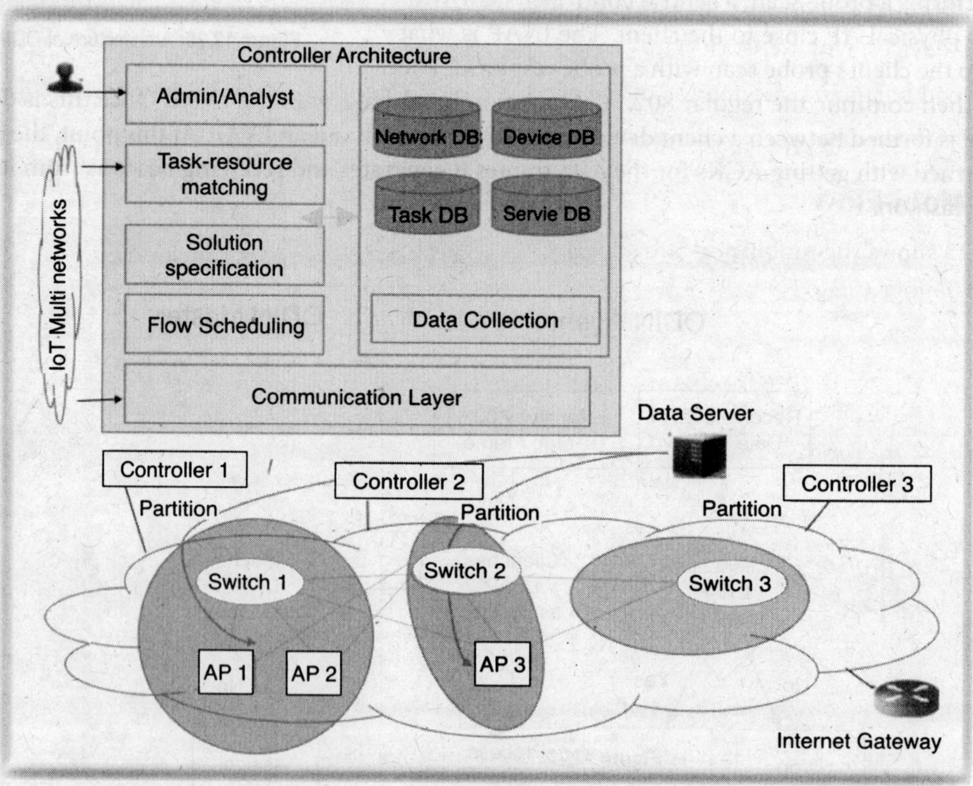

Figure 12.22: Architecture of Ubi-Flow

Ubi-Flow is the first software-defined IoT system for ubiquitous flow control and mobility management in urban heterogeneous networks. To achieve light-weight processing in IoT devices, in UbiFlow all jobs related to mobility management, handover optimization, access point selection and flow scheduling are executed by the coordination of distributed controllers. Specifically, UbiFlow adopts multiple controllers to divide an urban-scale SDN into different geographic partitions to achieve distributed control of IoT flows. A distributed hashing based overlay structure is proposed to maintain network scalability and consistency. Based on this UbiFlow overlay structure, relevant issues in mobility management such as scalable control, fault tolerance and load balancing have been carefully taken care of. The UbiFlow controller differentiates flow scheduling based on per-device requirements as well as whole-partition capabilities. Flow scheduling comprises of network partition, network matching and load balancing. Therefore, it can present a network status view for the optimized selection of access points in multi networks to satisfy flow requests, while guaranteeing the network performance in each partition. Figure 12.22 shows the architecture of Ubi-Flow.

The key contributions of Ubi-Flow are:

- A novel overlay structure to achieve mobility management and fault tolerance in software-defined IoT.
- An optimal assignment algorithm for the controller to match the best available access points to IoT devices, with network status analysis and flow requests as inputs.
- A load balancing scheme for distributed controllers by analyzing the variations in flow traffic characteristics.

12.12.3 Mobi-Flow

Figure 12.23 shows the mobility aware adoptive flow-rule placement (Mobi-Flow) in Software Defined Internet of Things (SDIoT).

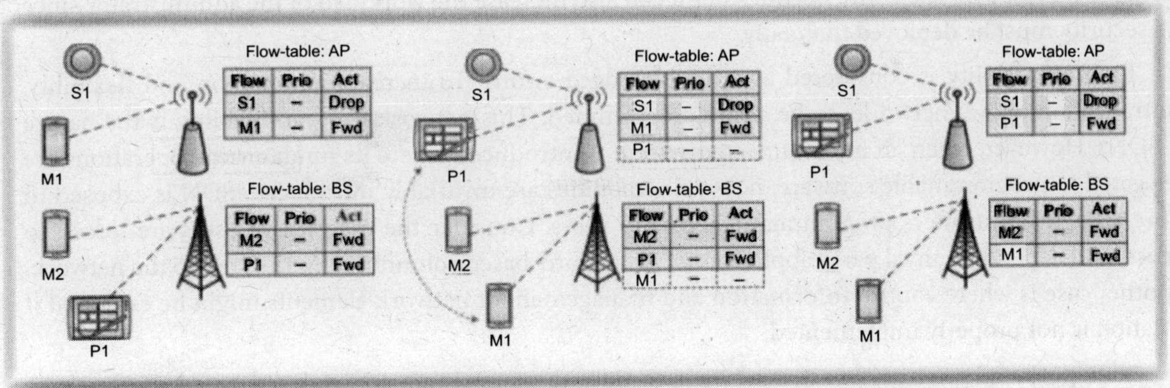

Figure 12.23: Mobi-Flow Architecture

There are devices S1 and M1 connected to one Access Point (AP) and another two devices P1 and M2 connected to another Base Station (BS). The corresponding flow tables are also available. Imagine that the device P1 and M1 has interchanged its position. So a new flow rules need to be added in the respective flow tables. But the memory of flow tables is restricted. In Mobi-Flow, a proactive rule placement takes place depending on user's movement in the network. The approach is to predict the location of end users at (t+1) time, while the users are at (t) time. Mobi-Flow place flow rules at the Access Points (APs) which can be associated to the users based on their predicted locations.

For location prediction, it uses Order-K Markov predictor which takes K^{th} location instances to predict the next location. For flow rule Placement, linear programming is used to select optimal Access Point (AP). Control message overhead and energy consumption can be minimized significantly using Mobi-Flow compared to the conventional Flow Rule placement schemes.

Anomalies can be monitored through OpenFlow. This can be done by monitoring each flow in the network. It is also possible to collect the port statistics of the switches. If there is any anomaly, it may generate large number of packets in the network which leads to network congestion.

12.13 ATTACK ON SDN

Software defined network attacks are a reality at present, so let's see how they try to breach into the network. Many things have been said about the ability of SDNs to solve security problems. However, this technology is still unfamiliar to many network engineers, the history of attacks is unknown and thousands of undiscovered vulnerabilities are out there.

The centralized controller can be a main target to an intruder. New network technologies can introduce threats that didn't existed before or it can even make things worse. Besides the existing attack vectors on traditional networks, the controllers and the connections to the control plane bring new security challenges that are unique to the SDN. A single vulnerability could cause a lot of damage, so security should be a basic component built into SDN. By compromising the SDN controller, a hacker could have total control of the network. Hackers go for a high-value target, so leaving the controller as a single point of failure is not such a good idea. By centralizing the control plane, the SDN can provide excellent control over the entire network but it can also increase the workload of the administrator since the security must be deployed manually.

Programmability is considered as a double-edged sword. To increase automation and flexibility, centralization allows networks to be easily programmed. This network programmability is the nature of SDNs. However, when an interconnected system is introduced where its fundamental operations are delegated to programmable software, new vulnerabilities are invariably introduced. SDN is exposed to more risks when it offers programmatic access to users. Consider the case where users are forced to "trust" and depend on third party applications or standard-based solutions with the keys to the network. Another case is where control information and management of network elements might be exploited if isolation is not properly implemented.

Nine potential security threats and their counter-measurements are analyzed based on the three planes of the SDN architecture such as data, control and application.

The evolution of networks is creating new types of attacks which are identified and unidentified risks as well as zero-day exploits. Zero-day exploit is an unknown exploit in the wild that exposes a vulnerability in software or hardware and can create complicated problems well before anyone realizes something is wrong. There may not have history of past SDN real-case attacks so it is challenging to define existing vulnerabilities and build security from that. A classification of potential attacks is listed in order to be used as a reference and lay the ground for security.

- **Network Manipulation:** A critical attack that occurs on the control plane. An attacker compromises the SDN controller, produces false network data and initiates other attacks on the entire network. To mitigate this attack, the SDN controller should have a redundant entity and the communication channels should be protected using strong encryption.

- **Traffic Diversion:** This attack occurs to the network elements at the data plane. The attack compromises a network element to redirect traffic flows and allow eavesdropping. The network can be protected from this type of attack by securing network elements and its communication channels with strong encryption.

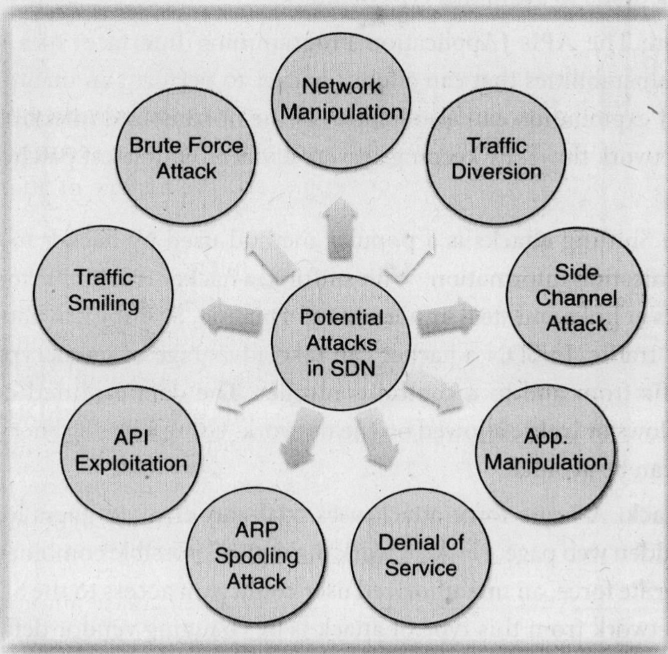

Figure 12.24: Security Attacks in SDN

- **Side Channel Attack:** The network elements at the data plane can be the target of this attack. Timing information, such as how long a new network connection takes to establish, can inform an attacker if a flow rule exists or not. Securing network elements with strong an encryption algorithm will protect from side channel attack.
- **App Manipulation:** This attack takes place in the application plane. An exploit of application vulnerability could cause malfunction, disruption of service, or eavesdrop of data. An attacker could gain access with high privilege to an SDN application and perform illegal operations. By keeping servers updated with latest patches, the network can be protected from App manipulation attacks.
- **Denial of Service:** Denial of Service (DoS) is one of the most common attacks and can affect all parts of the SDN. By applying a DoS, an attacker could cause reduction or complete disruption of SDN services. Using rate limiting and packet dropping techniques at the controller plane, the DoS attack can be avoided.

- **ARP Spoofing Attack:** ARP spoofing is a type of attack in which a malicious actor sends falsified ARP (Address Resolution Protocol) messages over a local area network. A hacker can use an ARP spoofing to infiltrate the network, sniff traffic, modify it and even stop it. This type of attack corrupts the network topology information and the topology-aware SDN applications. Poisoning can also happen through other protocols such as Link Layer Discovery Protocol (LLDP) or Internet Group Management Protocol (IGMP). It is recommended to use strong authentication methods to avoid this type of attack.
- **API Exploitation:** The APIs (Application Programming Interface) of a software component might contain vulnerabilities that can allow a hacker to perform an unauthorized disclosure of information. API exploitation can also happen at the northbound interface and can lead to the destruction of network flows. By keeping servers updated with latest patches will avoid this type of attack.
- **Traffic Sniffing:** Sniffing attacks is a popular method used by hacker to capture and analyze network communication information. With sniffing, a hacker is also able to eavesdrop data from network elements or links and steal important information. Sniffing can happen anywhere where there is constant traffic. In SDN a hacker can take advantage of unencrypted communications to intercept traffic from and to a central controller. The data captured could include critical information on flows or traffic allowed on the network. Using a strong encryption method, these types of attacks can be avoided.
- **Brute Force Attack:** A brute force attack uses trial-and-error to guess login info, encryption keys, or find a hidden web page. Hackers work through all possible combinations hoping to guess correctly. With brute force, an unauthorized user could gain access to the SDN. The methods for protecting the network from this type of attack is by changing vendor default passwords, using strong passwords and by frequently updating them.

12.14 SUMMARY

This Chapter explains software defined networking in detail. Limitations of current network, origin of SDN, its architecture, rule placement, OpenFlow protocol and controller placement are well explained. Integrating SDN in IoT, Software Defined WSN and SDN for mobile networking is described. Finally rule placement approaches at access devices including ODIN, Ubi-Flow and Mobi-Flow are illustrated. The chapter concludes with discussion on security in software defined networks.

12.15 OBJECTIVE QUESTIONS

The answer of the multiple-choice questions is marked in **bold**.

1. Which is a limitation of traditional network?
   (a) Centralized control not possible (b) Vendor specific architecture
   (c) Switches with different operating system (d) **All of these**

2. Which is high in software defined network?
   (a) **Speed** (b) Cost
   (c) Structural complexity (d) All of these
3. Which is a software associated with Open Flow implementation.
   (a) Indigo (b) LINC
   (c) Pantou (d) **All of these**
4. Which is the software using for controller configuration?
   (a) Pox (b) Nox
   (c) ONOS (d) **All of these**
5. Which is a protocol in mobile SDN?
   (a) ODIN (b) Ubi-Flow
   (c) Mobi-Flow (d) **All of these**
6. .... is a potential SDN attack.
   (a) DoS (b) Brute Force
   (c) Side Channel (d) **All of these**

12.16 REVIEW QUESTIONS

1. Discuss the requirement of software defined network.
2. Explain the architecture of software defined network.
3. Explain rule placement in software defined network.
4. Discuss Open Flow protocol.
5. Discuss controller placement in software defined network.
6. Discuss security in software defined network.
7. Explain integration of SDN in IoT.
8. Explain software defined wireless sensor networks.
9. Discuss the application of SDN for mobile networking.
10. Explain interference management in software defined wireless mobile network.
11. Discuss on open data centre with interoperable network.
12. Explain Ubi-Flow.
13. Explain Mobi-Flow.
14. Discuss attacks on SDN.

12.17 ABBREVIATIONS AND SYMBOLS

Abbreviations	Full Form	Description
MCU	Micro Control Unit	A control unit whose binary control variables are stored in memory is called MCU.
ACL	Access Control List	ACL contains rules that grant or deny access to certain digital environments.
ANDSF	Access Discovery and Service Function	ANDSF is an element of the 3GPP standard that is designed to assist mobile devices in discovering offload destinations, including Wi-Fi, WiMAX, and CDMA2000 networks. The feature was designed to provide mobile devices with information about available alternative wireless networks and to enforce policies for selecting and using those networks.
API	Application Programming Interface	API is a set of defined rules that explain how computers or applications communicate with one another. APIs sit between an application and the web server, acting as an intermediary layer that processes data transfer between systems.
ARP	Address Resolution Protocol	ARP is a communication protocol used for discovering the link layer address, such as a MAC address, associated with a given internet layer address, typically an IPv4 address.
CSC	Core SDN Controller	SDN controller is the application that acts as a strategic control point in a software-defined network. Essentially, it is the "brains" of the network.
GB	Gigabyte	GB is equal to 1,000,000,000 bytes (8 bits).
IGMP	Internet Group Management Protocol	IGMP is a communication protocol used by hosts and adjacent routers for multicasting communication with IP networks and uses the resources efficiently to transmit the message/data packets.
NPP	Network Packet Processing	NPP describes how data can be switched, routed, buffered, processed, scanned, and filtered over networks using field-programmable gate.
LLDP	Link Layer Discovery Protocol	LLDP is a layer 2 neighbor discovery protocol that allows devices to advertise device information to their directly connected peers/neighbors.
LLPD	Link Layer Discovery Protocol	The Link Layer Discovery Protocol is a vendor-neutral link layer protocol used by network devices for advertising their identity, capabilities, and neighbors on a local area network based on IEEE 802 technology, principally wired Ethernet.

Abbreviations	Full Form	Description
LSC	Local SDN Controller	Local SDN controller can either be the backup controller when connection to the global SDN controller is lost or the primary SDN controller when wireless communication to a global controller is not practical.
LVAP	Light Virtual Access Point	LVAP is dynamically assigned to a physical access point near the current location of the terminal. In IEEE 802.11 (Wi-Fi) terminology, a station (STA) is a device that has the capability to use the 802.11 protocol. As long as the STA only "sees" a single access point, it will not make any roaming decision, thus enabling the network to run a coordinated management of clients. This is achieved without any modification in the STA which runs standard IEEE 802.11.
M-CDN	Multi Content Delivery Network	M-CDN is the combination of multiple Content Delivery Networks (CDN) from different providers into a single network. CDN refers to a geographically distributed group of servers that work together to provide fast delivery of Internet content.
MP	Management Plane	The management plane of a networking device is the element of a system that configures, monitors, and provides management, monitoring and configuration services to, all layers of the network stack and other parts of the system.
NB API	North bound Application Programming Interface	North bound APIs are the link between the applications and the SDN controller. The applications can tell the network what they need (data, storage, bandwidth, and so on) and the network can deliver those resources, or communicate what it has. These APIs support a wide variety of applications.
ODIN	Open Data centre with Interoperable Network	An open data center is an IT facility that employs a clearly defined and standardized set of hardware and software products designed to make the data center interoperable with other IT facilities. An interoperable network is a computer network that uses open protocols so that many different types of networks and facilities can be transparently linked together, and allows multiple services to be provided to different users over the same network.
OSPF	Open Shortest Path First	OSPF is a link-state routing protocol that was developed for IP networks and is based on the shortest path first algorithm.
P-GW	Packet Data Network Gateway	P-GW is a critical network function for the 4G mobile core network, known as the evolved packet core (EPC). The PGW acts as the interface between the LTE network and other packet data networks, such as the Internet or SIP-based IMS networks.

Abbreviations	Full Form	Description
RAM	Random Access Memory	Random-access memory is a form of computer memory that can be read and changed in any order, typically used to store working data and machine code.
RAN	Radio Access Network	RAN is part of a mobile telecommunication system. It implements a radio access technology. Conceptually, it resides between a device such as a mobile phone, a computer, or any remotely controlled machine and provides connection with its core network.
REST API	Representational State Transfer	A REST API (also known as RESTful API) is an application programming interface that conforms to the constraints of REST architectural style and allows for interaction with RESTful web services.
SB API	Southbound Application Programming Interface	Southbound application program interfaces are used to communicate between the SDN Controller and the switches and routers of the network.
SD IoT	Software Defined Internet of Things	IoT created by using SDN is called SD IoT.
SDN	Software Defined Network	SDN is an approach to networking that uses software-based controllers or application programming interfaces to communicate with underlying hardware infrastructure and direct traffic on a network.
SDWMN	Software Defined Wireless Mobile Network	SDWMN uses SDN concepts in wireless networks.
TCAM	Ternary Content Addressable Memory	TCAM is a specialized type of high-speed memory that searches its entire contents in a single clock cycle.
VM	Virtual Machine	VM is a computer file, typically called an image, that behaves like an actual computer.
WSN	Wireless Sensor Network	WSN can be defined as a self-configured and infrastructure-less wireless networks to monitor physical or environmental conditions, such as temperature, sound, vibration, pressure, motion or pollutants and to cooperatively pass their data through the network to a main location or sink.

12.18 LIST OF FIGURES AND TABLES

The details of figures and tables used in this chapter is as below.

Figure / Table	Description
Figure 12.1	Traditional Network Architecture

CHAPTER

13 Cyber-Physical Systems

CONTENTS

13.1 INTRODUCTION

In this chapter, we will discuss the relationship between Internet of Things and Cyber Physical Systems. The cyber physical systems applications, architecture, components, security and deployment are explained.

13.2 IOT AND CYBER PHYSICAL SYSTEMS

Internet of Things (IoT) is about connecting "Things" (Objects and Machines) to the Internet and eventually to each other. Cyber-Physical Systems (CPS) are integrations of computation, networking, and physical processes. Embedded computers as well as networks monitor and control the physical processes, with feedback loops where physical processes affect computations and vice versa. A CPS is composed of highly-integrated computation, communication, control, and physical elements. "Cyber" is a prefix used to describe a person, thing or idea as part of the computer and information age. The figure 13.1 shows evolution from embedded systems to IoT.

An embedded system is a microprocessor-based computer hardware system with software that is designed to perform a dedicated function, either as an independent system or as a part of a large system. Some examples of embedded systems are MP3 players, mobile phones, video game consoles, digital cameras, DVD players, etc. Household appliances, such as microwave ovens, washing machines, dishwashers etc have embedded systems to provide flexibility and efficiency.

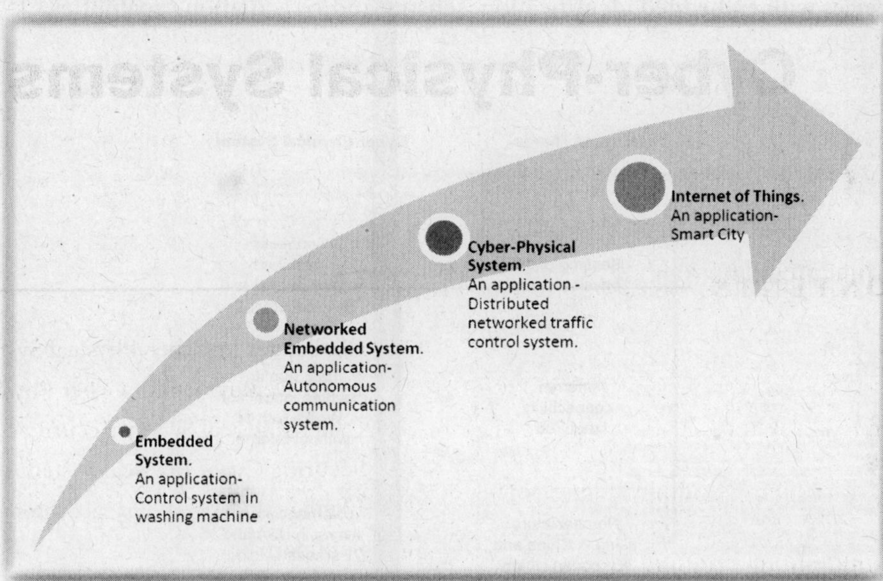

Figure 13.1: Evolution of CPS and IoT

Networked embedded systems are connected to a network to provide output to other systems. Examples of networked embedded systems are home security systems and Point Of Sale (POS) systems.

The cyber physical system consists of cyber components and physical components, so we call it as cyber physical system. This is based on an information processing computer system, which is embedded into a product, like a car, plane or similar devices. These computer systems are used to perform specific tasks. For Example, in a car an embedded system would be the Anti-lock Braking System (ABS) to control break force. These embedded systems are no longer stand alone. This system interacts with the physical environment by means of sensors and actuators. They share their data through internal communication networks and sometimes by the Internet. Cloud computing can also be utilized where data from many embedded systems can be collected and processed. This will be creating a system of systems. Connected embedded systems can be controlled and decentralized by a computational unit. The collected data can be processed automatically or by Human Machine Interface (HMI).

IoT is a technology, in which devices are connected through the Internet and enables the remote collection of real time information which can them be processed or shared with other devices.

Both IoT and CPS concepts emerged from different communities. CPS primarily emerged from a system engineering and control perspective. A cyber-physical system is a system of collaborating computational elements controlling physical entities. It is when the mechanical and electrical systems are networked using software components. They use shared knowledge and information from processes to independently control logistics and production systems.

In contrast, the IoT concept emerged primarily from a networking and information technology perspective, which envisioned integrating the digital region into the physical world. The term "Internet-of-Things" is used as an umbrella keyword for covering various aspects related to the extension of the Internet and the web into the physical region, by means of the widespread deployment of spatially distributed devices with embedded identification, sensing and/or actuation capabilities.

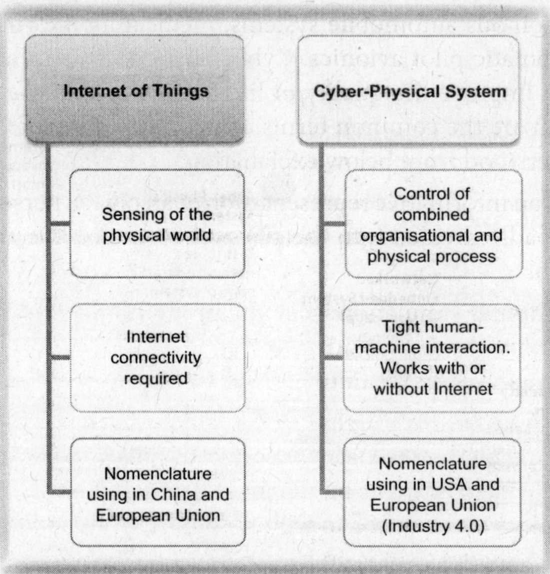

Figure 13.2: Differences between IoT and CPS

IoT and CPS does not have a clear distinction. We can say that all Internet of Things devices are Cyber-Physical Systems. CPS are not necessarily connected to the Internet and the devices in it need not be IoT devices. The cyber physical system can be the network of any type of cyber components and physical components. CPS is based on an information processing computer system, which is embedded into a product, like a car, plane or other device. These computer systems are used to perform specific tasks.

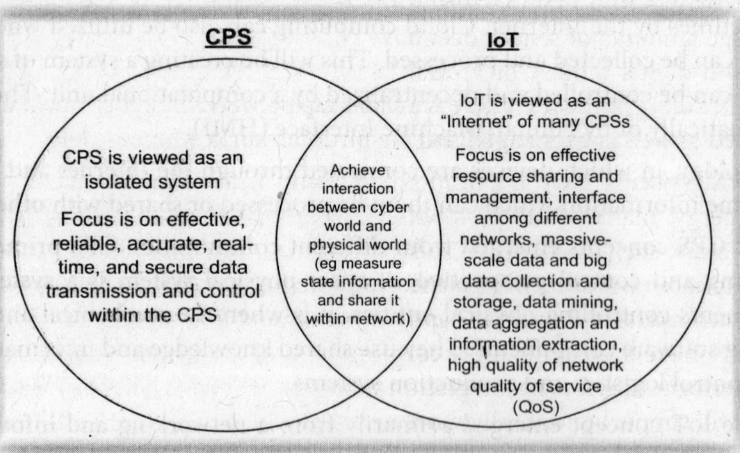

Figure 13.3: Cyber Physical System and Internet of Things

A simple example of cyber physical system is a smartphone, because it combines on one side the connection to the real world via embedded sensors such as geolocalisation sensors or other kind of sensors, and on the other side the connection to a "virtual world" through the information technology network or Internet which can be wired or wireless. Examples of cyber-physical systems include smart electric power grid, autonomous automobile systems, medical monitoring, industrial control systems, robotics systems, and automatic pilot avionics. Cyber-physical systems are key infrastructures for our modern society. They can improve the quality of life of citizens and the competitiveness. The model, simulation and digital twin are the common terms using in the study of CPSs and IoT. The differences between them can be understood from below explanation.

- **Model:** A model is an informative representation of an object, person or system. Representational models can be broadly divided into the physical form and the abstract which is expressed in mathematical form.
- **Simulation:** A computer simulation is an attempt to model a real-life or hypothetical situation on a computer so that it can be studied to see how the system works. A good example of the usefulness of using computers to simulate can be found in the field of network traffic simulation.
- **Digital Twin:** A digital twin is a digital representation of a physical object, process or service. A digital twin can be a digital replica of an object in the physical world, such as a jet engine or wind farms, or even larger items such as buildings or even whole cities. As well as physical assets, the digital twin technology can be used to replicate processes in order to collect data to predict how they will perform. A digital twin is, in essence, a computer program that uses real world data to create simulations that can predict how a product or process will perform.

13.3 CYBER-PHYSICAL SYSTEMS APPLICATIONS

Like the Internet has transformed the way people interact with information, cyber physical systems technologies are transforming the way people interact with engineered systems. CPS are becoming data-rich enabling higher degrees of automation and autonomy. The integration of artificial intelligence and machine learning with CPS for real-time operation creates new opportunities with major societal implications. One of the main driving forces in the era of cyber-physical systems is the introduction of massive sensor networks into manufacturing processes, connected cars, precision agriculture and so on. Therefore, large amounts of sensor data have to be ingested at the server side in order to generate and make the "twin digital model" or virtual factory of the existing physical processes for predictive simulation and scheduling purposes. There is a small gap between the cyber world where the information is processed, altered as well as exchanged and the physical world where we live.

Cyber physical systems have applications in many fields like consumer, health care, military, transportation, energy, manufacturing, robotics, infrastructure etc. The applications are coming up across multiple sectors, such as adaptive cruise control and anti-theft devices in vehicles, flight control and electrochromic cabin windows in airplanes, location services in cell phones, entertainment, gaming, flight control, pacemakers in humans, haptic systems and robotic vacuum devices at homes. The applications of CPS make human life more comfortable and the advances in CPS can make applications faster as well as perform distributed integration of largescale systems like automated road and airspace traffic control. It will support temporally more and spatially precise activity like telerobotic surgery and will demonstrate high efficiency in zero-net energy buildings. The autonomous search and rescue or disaster recovery application in hostile or not reachable environments will enhance quality of life.

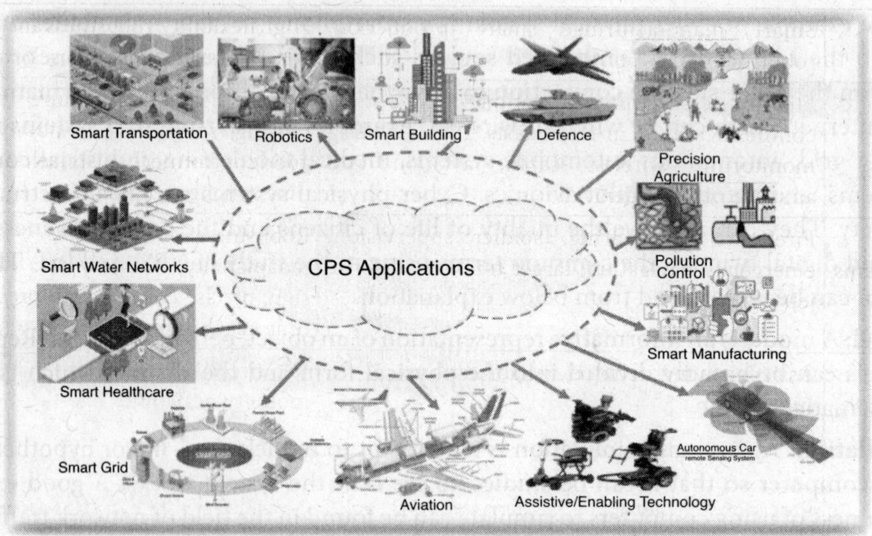

Figure 13.4: Cyber Physical System Application

The table 13.1 illustrates details of few important cyber physical system applications.

Table 13.1: Applications of Cyber-Physical System

Application	Domain Key Areas of Applications	Requirements
Transportation	Autonomous vehicle, smart transportation, railroad systems, vehicular networks and smart highways, accident signaling, collision avoidance, traffic jam information, optimal traffic management.	CPS for the automotive industry demand high computing power due to complex traffic control algorithms. Also, robustness, mobility, and self-adaptation are some other requirements.
Water sector	Leakage detection and monitoring, leak control, pressure management, water quality monitoring, water network monitoring, water flow and pressure control, water resource management.	Robustness, self-adaptation, flexibility, and time synchronization.
Healthcare sector	Smart healthcare, patient's drug administration, robotic microsurgery, health management networks, and epilepsy seizure detection.	Robustness, self-adaptation and flexibility, high precision sensing, data confidentiality, mobility, and quality of service.
Environment	Wastewater monitoring, industrial waste control and monitoring, weather monitoring, pollution monitoring, air quality monitoring.	Robustness and self-adaptation, long operation without intervention with little energy consumption.
Infrastructure	Smart building, green building, asset management, structural health monitoring.	CPSs for infrastructure application demand a precise and reliable control mechanism, robustness, and flexibility.
Energy	Smart grid, smart energy metering, real-time cooperative control of protection devices, power generation and distribution, energy conservation.	Robustness, self-adaptation, and flexibility

Industry	Smart manufacturing, smart production, robotics, process control.	High flexibility, robustness and security, good control mechanism, and self-adaptation.
Aeronautics/ Aviation	Flight test instrumentation, pilot–crew communications, in-flight tests, flight landing monitoring, wireless cabin, aviation and airspace management.	CPSs for aviation require high precision sensing, robustness, flexibility, precise and good control mechanism, self-adaptation, and time synchronization.
Defense/ Military Systems	Firefighter monitoring, soldier supervision, emergency navigation, target tracking, defense jets, etc.	Robustness, flexibility, self-adaptation (adaptability), military data integrity provision, precise control, high precision sensing, time synchronization, and good coverage.
Enabling Environment or Assistive Technology	Assistive living, robotics, rehabilitation supervision.	Requires high precision sensing, robustness, mobility, scalability, and flexibility
Agriculture	Precision agriculture, smart irrigation, green house cultivation, disease prediction, and animal localization.	The main requirements of CPSs in the agriculture domain are flexibility, robustness, and scalability.

13.4 CYBER-PHYSICAL SYSTEM ARCHITECTURE

The cyber physical system architecture consists of three main layers which is derived from the high-level requirements is described below. It is important to mention that the layers are relaxed for the purpose of building a flexible architecture.

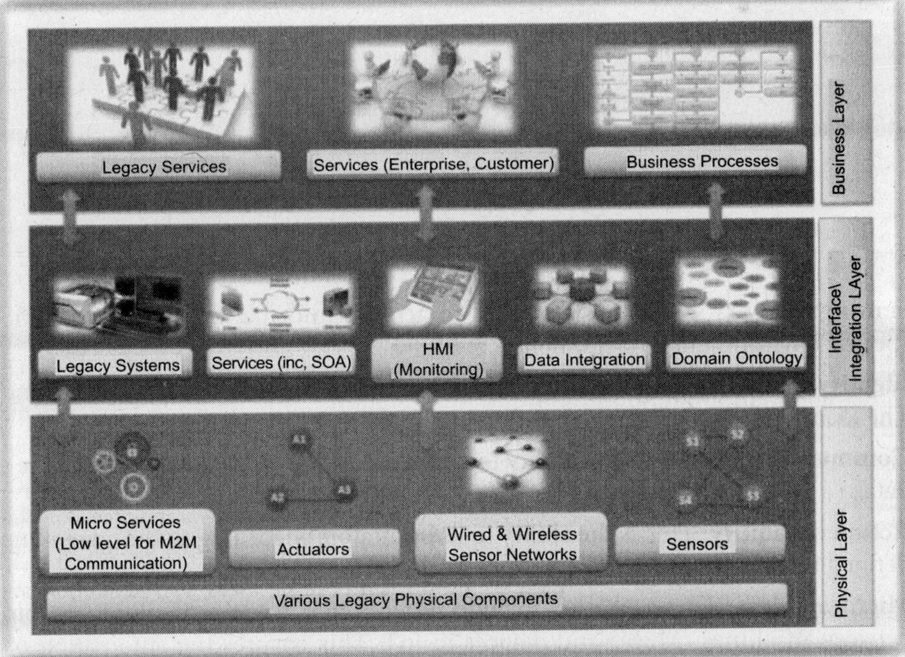

Figure 13.5: Cyber Physical System Layers

The architecture of CPS systems consists of different layers and components, which rely on different communication protocols and technologies to communicate among each other across the different layers. The CPS architecture consists of three main layers, the physical layer, network layer, and application layer, which are presented and described in figure 13.6.

- **Physical Layer:** It is also known as recognition, sensing or perception layer. It includes equipment such as sensors, actuators, aggregators, Radio-Frequency IDentification (RFID) tags, Global Positioning Systems (GPS) along with various other devices. These devices collect real-time data in order to monitor, track and interpret the physical world. It includes all the entities that collect data from the physical environment (using sensors), interact with the physical environment using actuators, and relay the data to the upper level using wired, Ad-hoc, wireless networking components. Below are the capabilities of physical layer.

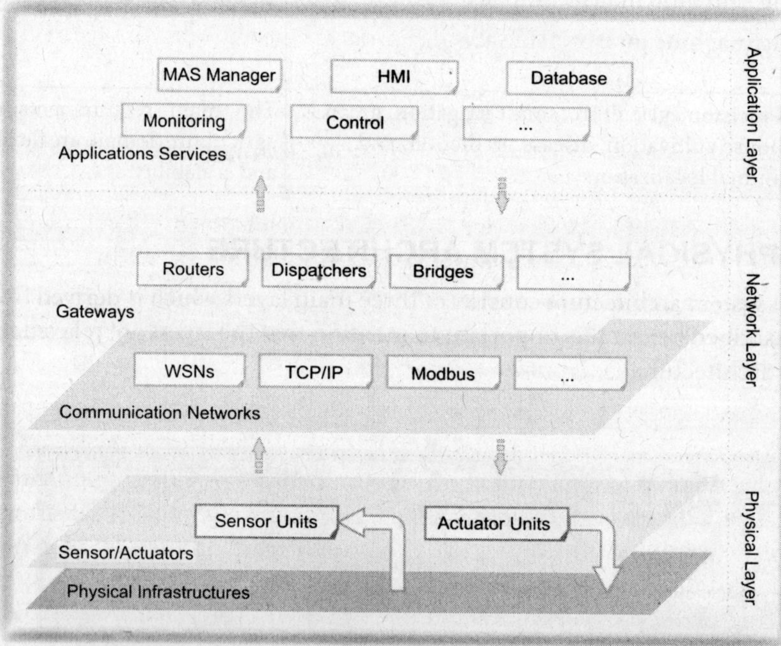

Figure 13.6: Three-layer Architecture of Cyber Physical Systems

- **Sensing:** Sensors in this layer is used to acquire information about a specific entity or a specific environmental phenomenon.
- **Identity:** This layer has the ability to identify oneself to the rest of the entities and the system. The identity will be unique that differentiates it from other entities.
- **Communication:** This is the ability to connect to a network and communicate the acquired data.
- **Action capability:** This is the ability to use actuators according to the current needs or well-defined rules.
- **Micro-Services:** This capability include services that act as a medium for communication between machines (M2M) and devices in IoT. This ensures the automation of tasks using machines located in same or different sites.

- **Network Layer:** It is also known as the transport layer or transmission layer. This layer interchanges and processes data between the physical and application layers. Data transmission and interaction is achieved through the Internet using LANs and communication protocols which includes Bluetooth, 4G, 5G, IR, ZigBee, Wi-Fi, LTE and other technologies. For this purpose, various protocols are used to address the increase in the number of Internet-connected devices, such as IPv6. This layer also ensures data routing and transmission using cloud computing platforms, routing devices, switching and Internet gateways, firewalls and intrusion detection systems or intrusion prevention systems. This layer is also known as interface or integration layer. It has the role of connecting and integrating data from the upper and lower levels of the system. It may also include a human machine interface. It provides the foundation for the computational units. Computational units include capabilities such as
  - Handling semantic interfaces to access both virtual and physical resources.
  - Handling machine interpretable abstraction of the system's domain expressed in an ontology form.
  - Managing system components subscription to semantic events handling such as subscribe a system component C to events generated by the temperature sensors from area A with a specific event generation rule.
  - Service components like Service Oriented Architecture (SOA), Service Component Architecture (SCA), Service-Oriented Business Applications (SOBA)
  - Legacy systems are the implementation in hardware and possibly software components such as embedded operating systems and related embedded software components of the legacy services from the upper layer
- **Application Layer:** It is the third and most interactive layer. It processes the received information from the data transmission layer and issues commands, which are to be executed by the physical units. This is done by implementing complex decision-making algorithms based on the aggregated data. Moreover, this layer receives and processes information from the perception layer before determining the rightly invoked automated actions. In fact, cloud computing, middleware, and data mining algorithms are used to manage the data at this layer. Protecting and preserving privacy requires protecting private data from being leaked. The most known protective approaches include anonymization, data masking (camouflage), privacy-preserving, and secret sharing. Moreover, this layer also requires a strong multi-factor authentication process to prevent unauthorized access and escalation of privilege. Due to the increase in the number of Internet-connected devices, the size of the generated data has become a significant issue. Therefore, securing big data calls for efficient protection techniques to process huge amounts of data in a timely and efficient manner. This layer is also known as business layer. It includes similar aspects necessary to the developments of traditional enterprise systems like core business processes, rules execution engines, business workflows, components, and entities, legacy services, enterprise and customer services, domain specific business applications like ERP. The enterprise services as well as customer services implement the underlined enterprise business processes. Legacy services may include relevant procedures and terminology for the current business. However, these legacy services may not be directly integrated with the new services but are still needed.

13.4.1 Five Layer Architecture of Cyber-Physical Systems

The industrial requirements and structure are highly complex. To meet the requirements, a five-level architecture, popularly known as 5C is the proposed model. The 5Cs are connection, conversion, cyber, cognition and configure.

The autonomous intelligent manufacturing subsystems and the relationships between them are too complicated to manage by human in real time. The solution is to control production process using an

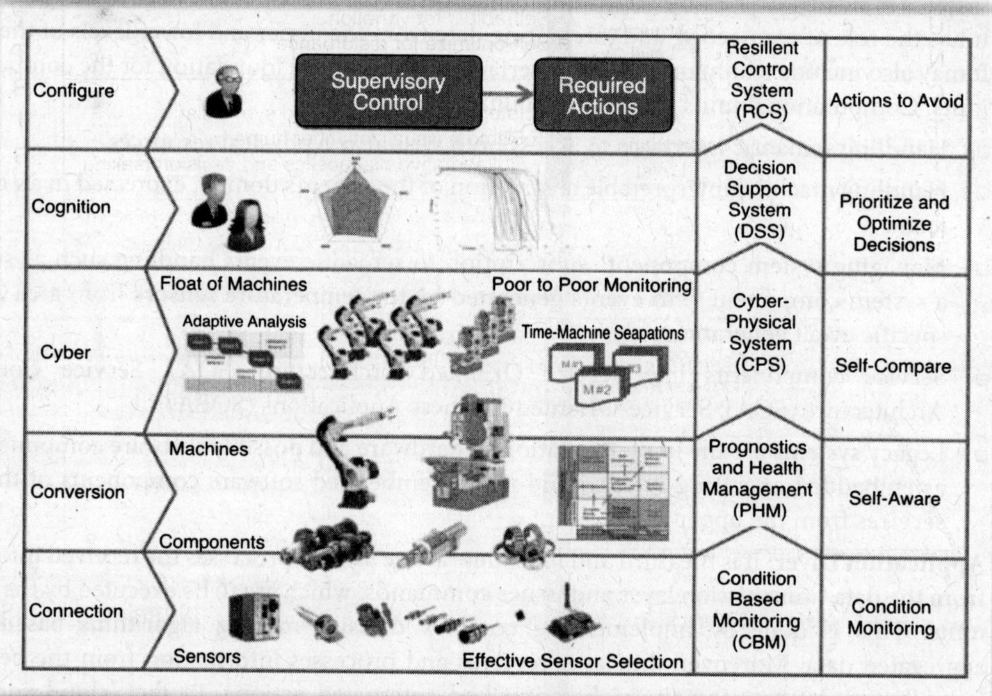

Figure 13.7: Basic parts of CPS Five Layer Architecture

intelligent software with artificial intelligence using neural networks technology. Decisions relevant to management in modern factories will be obtained through a real-time simulation that includes all the states, processes and components of the real world. The technology of digital twins, virtualization and simulation of processes in a virtual environment is an important aspect in the management of production systems. By using digital twins, it is possible to predict the machine settings and parameters in a simulation environment in the virtual world. By this, switching to a different product or any change in the production process allows the devices to be set up to configuration based on simulations in the virtual world. This approach significantly reduces machine setup times, improves quality and prevents malfunctions. In the pyramid model of figure 13.8, it is assumed that architecture of the manufacturing enterprises realized in accordance with the industry 4.0 concept represented by layers. The lower level consists of intelligent sensors and regulators interconnected by IoT technology. The process of obtaining accurate and reliable data from devices and their components is the first step in the implementation of cyber-physical system. Data can be directly measured by sensors in the production process or can be obtained from management or enterprise production systems like ERP or MES.

The ever-increasing use of sensors and machines in the network, results in continuous generation of large data volume (Big Data). For processing of such amount of data, special techniques and technologies are to be used. Proper processing and evaluation of these data is very important for softness and quality simulation model in twin digital production process.

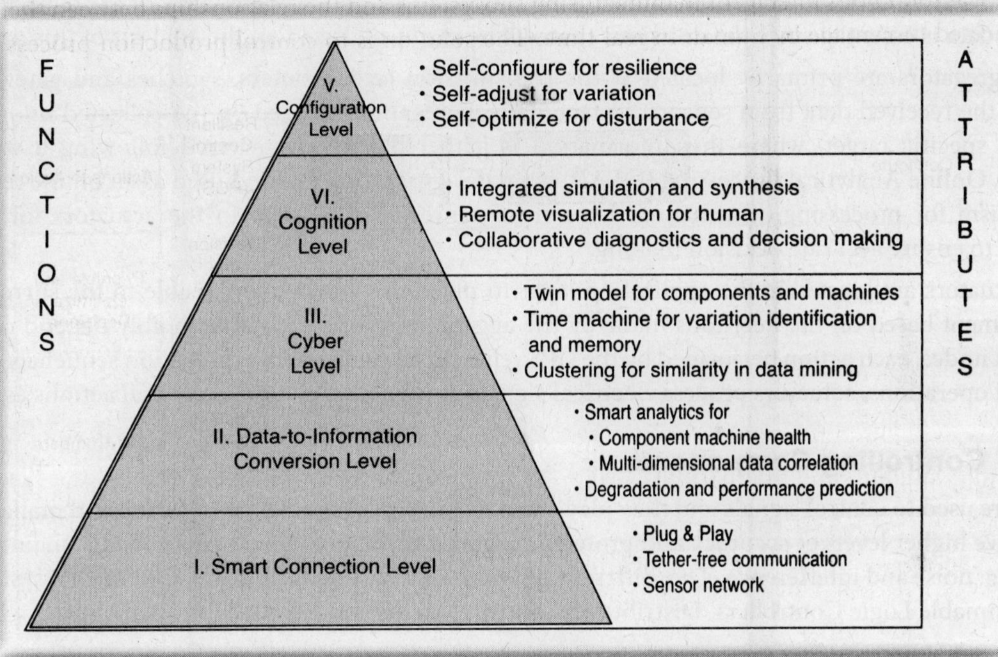

Figure 13.8: Cyber Physical System Five Layer Architecture

13.5 CYBER-PHYSICAL SYSTEM COMPONENTS

Cyber-physical systems components are used for sensing information, or for controlling signals. In this regard, CPS components are classified into two main categories. They are sensing components which sense and collect information, and the controlling components that monitor and control signals. Concerning the relation between components and architectural layers, it can be seen that sensing components are mainly deployed at the perception and transmission layers, while the controlling components are deployed at the application layer.

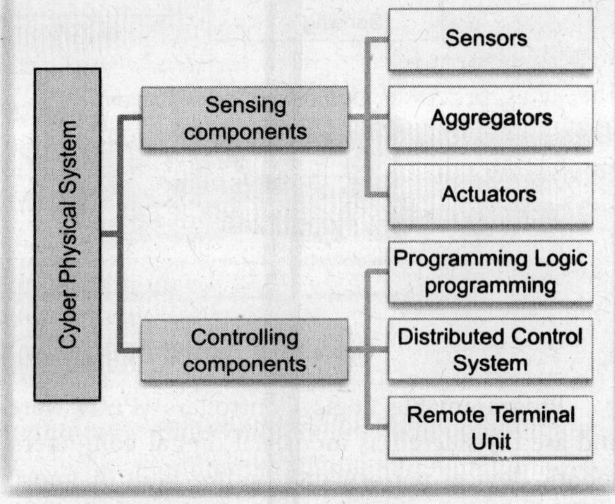

Figure 13.9: Cyber Physical System Components

13.5.1 Sensing Components

These are primarily located at the perception layer. The sensing components consist of sensors, aggregators and actuators.

Sensors will collect data and forward them to aggregators. They collect and record real-world data followed by correlation process named "calibration", to assess the correctness of the collected data. Sensing data is essential since the decisions that will be made are based on the analysis of this data.

Aggregators are primarily located at the transmission layer (routers, switches and gateways) to process the received data from sensors. In fact, data aggregation is based on the collected information about a specific target, where this information is gathered and summarized following a statistical analysis. Online Analytical Processing (OLAP) is a data aggregation method used as an online reporting mechanism for processing information. Data from aggregators are sent to the actuators for further analysis to ensure accurate decision making.

Actuators are located at the application layer to make the information visible to the surrounding environment based on the decisions made by the aggregators. Since actuators highly depend on other network nodes, each action performed by the CPS relies on an earlier data aggregation sequence. Also, in terms of operations, actuators process electrical signals as input and generate physical actions as output.

13.5.2 Controlling Components

These are used to control signals and they play a key role in signal control, monitoring and management to achieve higher levels of accuracy and protection against malicious attacks or accidents, mainly signal jamming, noise and interference. The different types of control systems that are used in CPS systems are Programmable Logic Controllers, Distributed Control Systems and Remote Terminal Units.

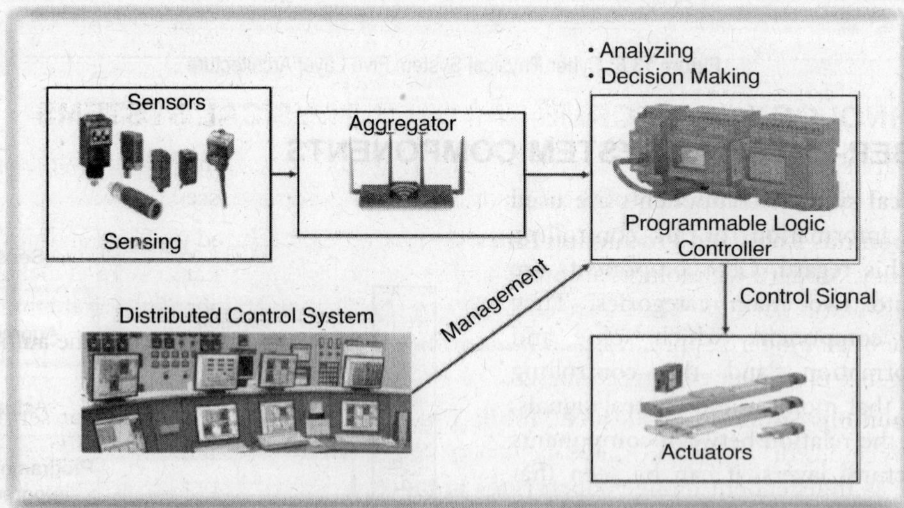

Figure 13.10: Sensing and Controlling Components of Cyber Physical System

Programmable Logic Controllers (PLC) were initially developed to replace hard-wired relays, and are considered as industrial digital computers that control the manufacturing processes such as robotic devices performance and/or fault diagnosis processing; hence achieving better flexibility and resiliency.

Distributed Control Systems (DCS) are computerized control systems that allow the autonomous controllers' distribution throughout the system using a central operator supervisory control. In some cases, DCS can be similar to Supervisory Control and Data Acquisition (SCADA) systems.

Remote Terminal Units (RTU) or Remote Telemetry Units are electronic devices controlled by a microprocessor such as the Master Terminal Unit (MTU). Unlike the PLC, they do not support any control loop nor control algorithm. Thus, making them more suitable for wireless communications over wider geographical telemetry areas. RTU's main task is to interface SCADA to the physical objects using a supervisory messaging system that controls these objects through the system's transmission of telemetry data.

Both RTUs and PLCs use a small computerized "artificial brain" to process inputs from sensing devices and use Intelligent Electronic Devices (IED) to transmit data flow or trigger an alarm in case of any intrusion. Table shows a comparison between PLCs and RTUs.

Table 13.2: Comparison between PLC and RTU

Criteria	PLC	RTU
Design	Digital computers designed for output arrangements and multiple inputs.	Electronic device controlled by a microprocessor.
Application	Automates electro-mechanical processes	Interfaces SCADA physical objects
Control loops and algorithms	Support	Does not support
Immunity to electrical noise and vibration	Immune	Low to null
Suitable for	Local geographical areas	Wider geographical areas
Communication	Wired	Wired /Wireless

13.6 TECHNOLOGY PLATFORMS IN CYBER-PHYSICAL SYSTEMS

We can summarize the technologies necessary for the implementation of a modern enterprise to various cyber physical system platforms. Few of these platform concepts are discussed below.

- **Autonomous Robitized Production Lines:** Autonomous robotized production lines maximize efficiency. Modern technology, accuracy and speed of production are essential elements in the implementation of CPS. The future of flexible production and cyber-physical manufacturing is the use of all modern approaches, communication between all components, the autonomy and intelligence of all elements in production.
- **Autonomous Supervisory/Service Mobile Units:** Autonomous supervisory or service mobile units includes drones with camera system or handlers to carry light objects. Drones are easy to use as independent mobile supervisory units equipped with a camera or as highly mobile transport units with the appropriate equipment for the transfer of objects.
- **3D Printing:** Technology of 3-dimensional printing is able to provide a high degree of efficiency and variability in the production of a wide range of products. By creating 3D objects based on data from materials such as plastic or metal, it is possible to create complex, easily customizable products whose design is impossible to carry out with classic production techniques. The 3D printing is also called additive manufacturing.

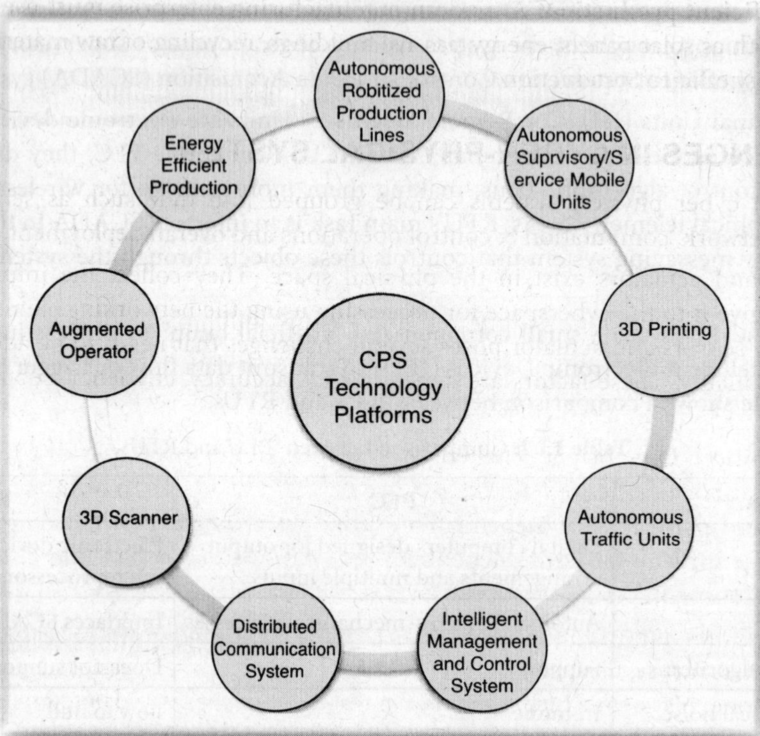

Figure 13.11: Various CPS Technology Platforms

- **Autonomous Traffic Units:** Autonomous traffic units are autonomous carts and manipulators for ground handlers and vehicles for transporting heavy loads are forming a connection between the individual modules of CPS.
- **Intelligent management and control system:** Intelligent management and control system of all production processes and units must be implemented in such a way to eliminate the possible errors in the management of complex and time-dependent production processes. This presupposes the exclusion of classical control centers with human service. Manufacturing processes should be managed by an appropriate intelligence management system with an ERP and CRM connection management interface.
- **Distributed Communication Systems:** Distributed communication systems in the production process have to communicate with the control system wirelessly. Together with the sensor system, they create an information data network. Based on these data, the central management system is able to analyze production procedures and processes and optimize them to achieve even greater production efficiency.
- **3D scanner intelligent control system:** 3D scanner intelligent control system accurately identifies the parameters of complex elements and products through a set of cameras and 3D scanner.
- **Augmented operator:** In the case of excessively complicated manufacturing processes, the physical capabilities of human staff need to be improved using an additional technical solution which is known as augmented operator.

- **Energy efficient production:** A modern manufacturing enterprise must use renewable energy sources such as solar panels, energy passive buildings, recycling of raw materials and the like to form energy efficient production.

13.7 CHALLENGES IN CYBER-PHYSICAL SYSTEM

The challenges in cyber physical systems can be grouped into four such as sensors & actuators, communication network, computation & control operations and overall deployment.

The sensors and actuators exist in the physical space. They collect the information from the surrounding and give it to the cyberspace for processing using the networking elements. The practical deployment of the sensors and actuator poses several challenges that needs to be addressed to achieve the desired functionality. These factors are dependability, accuracy, efficiency, robustness, availability and cost.

- **Dependability:** One of the challenges is dependability which is the characteristic of a system to carry out desired functionalities during its operation without degradation in its outcome and performance. Dependability indicates the degree of reliability put in the entire system. It is difficult to assure dependability before actual system operation. An example of this is the timing uncertainties of sensor readings and deterioration of actuation which affects dependability.
- **Accuracy:** Accuracy means the degree of match between a system's measured values to its calculated one. A system which is highly accurate should give actual outcome as close as possible. Maximum accuracy is required for the applications of CPS where even small imprecision will lead to system break downs. For example, If an object tracking system uses imperfect sensor, based on incorrect object position, estimation may take for untimely control action, which will cause the system failure.
- **Efficiency:** Efficiency means the amount of usage of resources such as energy, cost, time etc. that are required by the system to perform required functionalities. A system which is highly efficient should operate correctly and use optimum amount of system resources. Usually, the sensors and actuators use power to perform their operations. In CPS applications efficiency is mainly needed for energy management. CPS applications can be developed in such a way that it consumes minimal energy by keeping the sensors in a sleep mode based on the criticality of the application. The sensors and actuators which are placed in the outside world can have the feature to use renewable energy resources like solar energy.
- **Robustness:** Robustness is the ability to with stand different environmental conditions. Usually, the sensors will be placed in the physical world which leads to challenge of facing different environmental conditions. So, the sensors and actuators should be manufactured in a way that they can work under any kind of environmental conditions without any inaccuracy in the expected out comes.
- **Availability:** Availability gives the ratio of total time that a system or a component is functional during a specified period and the length of the period. The availability of the sensors and actuators is very important. In case of any failure these should be a mechanism to notify the occurrence of failure and also to with stand at least till the notification is sent to the concerned. In any situation, the system should be designed in such a way that in case of

critical applications the availability should be made as hundred percent by keeping redundant systems.

- **Cost:** Cost of the sensors and actuators is an important concern to develop an application of CPS. Even though the networking hardware is available at affordable prices, the cost of sensors and actuators is still high. Advances in research of developing affordable hardware with accurate sensibility should be done to make CPS applications more available to all classes of people.

The communication network acts as intermediate connection between the physical world and the cyber world. The cyber and physical worlds can be integrated using wireless or wired networks each of which has its own challenges. Some of the challenges related to the communication network are discussed below.

- **Wiring:** It is difficult to implement CPS applications using wired network. The cost of wiring is an important factor which effects the deployment of application. Maintenance of wiring is also a tedious task. But in wired network, loss of data will be less and reliability as well as security will be high. Presently most of the CPS applications uses wireless networks.
- **Power and Energy:** The network elements used for CPS applications consume power and energy to transmit the data to cyber space. A mobile device is small in size, and the ability to deliver the power by its power source may not be as much as like a fixed device. When a device is allowed to move freely, it is generally hard to receive a continuous supply of power. A mobile device should be able to operate in an efficient and effective manner to conserve energy. It should be able to transmit and receive in an intelligent manner so as to minimize the number of transmissions and receptions for certain communication operations.
- **Mobility:** CPS applications such as smart cities may require the networking elements to be mobile. Unlike wired networks, all devices are free to move in a wireless network. To support mobility, as a user moves around, an ongoing connection should be kept alive. In any network, when a mobile host moves from the coverage of a base station or access point to that of another one a handoff occurs. Therefore, we need a protocol to ensure seamless transition during a handoff. This involves many issues like deciding how data is routed during the handoff process and when a handoff should occur. Sometimes, packets are lost during a handoff. In an adhoc network, when a mobile host moves the topology changes. To cater for the topological changes of an ongoing data communication, the transmission route may need to be recomputed. As an adhoc network may consist of many mobile hosts, the design of an effective and efficient routing protocol is challenging.
- **Data Rate:** A CPS application requires increasing the current data rates to support future high-speed applications. If application requires large amount of data transfer like live video streaming, then high data rates is required. Data rate is a function of various factors such as the data compression algorithm, power control, data transfer protocol, and the interference mitigation through error-resilient coding. Therefore, the design should be well thought out by the manufacturer that considers these factors in order to achieve higher data rates. Improving the existing data compression algorithms to produce high quality audio and video is important. Unfortunately, highly compressed multimedia data is more sensitive to interference and network errors and it is necessary to use the algorithms to protect sensitive data from being spoiled. We should explore efficient error control algorithms with low overhead. Other solution to improve

the data rates would be to employ intelligent data transfer protocols that adapt to the traffic characteristics and time-varying network.

- **Security:** CPS applications require more security which is a big concern in wireless networking. Mobility of devices increases the security concerns in a wireless network. An application like smart work places in large enterprises deploys IP network level security solution to ensure that the corporate network and proprietary data are safe. To make access to fixed access networks reliable Virtual Private Network (VPN) is an option.
- **Signal Fading:** Compared with wired media, wireless transmission of may lead to distortion of signal or weakened signal. It is transmitted over an unprotected, open, and ever-changing medium with unclear boundary. In addition to that, before it arrives at the receiver the same signal may disperse and travel on different paths due to diffraction, reflection, and scattering due to the obstacles. To reach the destination, the dispersed signals on different paths may take different times. Thus, the resultant signal after summing up all dispersed signals may have been significantly attenuated and distorted when compared with the actual transmitted signal. The receiver may not recognize the signal and hence the transmitted data cannot be received. The unreliability of the wireless networks causes a substantial number of packet losses.

Different applications of CPS require different type of computations and control operations. If application is just to trigger an action if some event occurs then the computing system does not require high storage but response time should be low. If application is in such a way that it stores data and perform some analytics and deliver such information to the users, then the system requires huge storage and processing capabilities. Usually, the computations and control operations are done by the servers. So based on application there are different challenges are in computation and control operations. Some of them are

- **Processing Speed:** CPS applications have to find and analyze the relevant data quickly. Visualization helps applications perform analyses and make decisions much faster, but the challenge is high volume data processing speed. As the degree of granularity increases, the challenge grows. Some vendors are using powerful parallel processing and increased memory to crunch large volumes of data quickly. Another method is putting data in-memory but using a grid computing approach, which involves many machines to solve a problem. Both approaches allow the applications to explore huge data.
- **Understanding Data:** If the application of CPS requires data analysis, then it takes a lot of understanding to get data in the right shape so that we can use visualization. Visualization tools are likely to be of less value to the user, without some sort of context. The solution to this challenge is to have the proper domain expertise in place. The people analyzing the data should have a deep understanding of what audience will be consuming the data, where the data comes from and how that audience will interpret the information.
- **Accuracy and Timeliness:** These are very important factors in CPS applications. Even if an application can find and analyze data quickly and keep it in the proper context for the audience that will be consuming the information, the value of data for decision-making purposes will be reduced if the data is not accurate or timely. This challenge is there in any data analysis, but when considering the volumes of information involved in CPS applications with big data, it becomes further more pronounced. To solve this problem, applications need to have an information management process or data governance in place to ensure that the data is clean.

- **Storage:** Some applications of CPS that involves data analytics may need to store large volumes of data. Conventional WAN-based transport methods cannot move terabytes of data at the speed required for applications. It uses a portion of available bandwidth and do transfer at speeds that are unsuitable for such huge volumes, introducing unacceptable delays in storing retrieving and processing data.
- **Control:** CPS applications involve lot many devices that capture the data from the physical world and also the devices that transfer the data from physical to cyber world. So this poses a challenge for the node that control all these devices. Identifying the exact device and controlling it is a difficult task.

13.7.1 Deployment of Cyber Physical Systems

To deploy the cyber physical systems applications, we need some elements which will fall under categories such as sensors and actuators, communication network and computing nodes. The sensors and actuators collect the data from physical world. The collected data will be transmitted over the network to the computing nodes where the data will be processed and result will be generated and displayed in a format that is required by the end users. Each area has several challenges that need to be addressed when actual deployment is done in the real world. The challenges in the overall deployment of CPS are discussed below.

- **Maintainability:** Maintainability is the ability of a system to be repaired in case any failure occurs. A system which is highly maintainable should be repaired in a simple and quick manner with minimum expenses of supporting resources, and it should not cause additional problems during the maintenance process. If there is a close interaction among the system components like sensors, actuators, networking components, and physical components constituting CPS infrastructure, we can propose autonomous predictive /corrective diagnostic mechanisms. Using such mechanisms continuous monitoring and testing of the infrastructure can be performed. The result of monitoring and testing facilities help finding which units need to be repaired. Some elements, which causes frequent failures, can be designed again or disposed and replaced with better quality elements.
- **Availability:** Availability is the characteristic of a system to be available for accessing even when errors occur. A system is said to be highly available if it isolates malfunctioning portion from itself and resume the operation even in the absence of it. Harmful cyber-attacks question the availability of the system services significantly. For example, in medical applications of cyber-physical systems, necessary actions will be taken in a timely manner to save a patient's life based on medical data. Cyber-attacks or failure of systems or components may lead to the loss of medical data causing risk to the patient's life.
- **Safety:** Safety is the quality of a system not to cause any danger, harm or risk anywhere around it while it is in operation. A system which provides high safety should be in accordance with all kinds of safety regulations to a maximum extent and should implement guaranteed safety mechanisms if anything goes wrong. For Example, Safety of manufacturing industries can be guaranteed using embedded control systems with an automated process control and sensors and actuators that collect the data across the manufacturing industry. Sensors connected to a smart network could detect operational failures and help in prevention of dangerous incidents due to those failures.

- **Resilience:** Resilience is the property of a system to continue in its operation and provision of services in an acceptable quality even though the system is exposed to any kind of errors. A system with high resiliency should be able to detect any kind of failures as early as possible and should be able to self-heal and also should be able to recover faster to continue to meet the demands for services. If an application is critical then high resilience comes into play (e.g. automated brake control in vehicular cyber-physical systems). While designing a highly resilient CPS we need to have a complete understanding of important failures and errors, the resilience properties of the required application, and evolution of system due to the dynamically varying nature of the operational environment.
- **Adaptability:** Adaptability is the ability of a system to survive by adjusting its own configuration in accordance with different circumstances in the environment. A system with high adaptability should be quickly adjust to changing needs. Adaptability is one of the important features in the next generation air transportation systems. The capability of the next generation should enhance performance of air space using its computerized air transportation network which allows air vehicles immediately to accommodate themselves to changing environment such as weather conditions, routing of air vehicle, air traffic congestion, and other issues related to security. Sustainability is the ability of a system to last long without compromising requirements of the system, while continuing to use the system's resources efficiently.
- **Sustainability:** A system that is highly sustainable must be durable, adaptable and resilient. The crucial part of energy provision and management policies is to achieve sustainability from energy perspective. For example, the smart grid allows energy distribution, management, and customization from the customer's perspective by utilizing green sources of energy extracted from the physical environment. However, obstructions like irregular energy supply and unknown load characterization damages the efforts to maintain long-term operation of the smart grid. To maintain sustainability, the applications of CPS like smart grid requires use of real-time performance measurements, dynamic optimization techniques for usage of energy, environment-aware duty cycling of computing units, planning and operation under uncertainties, and devising self-contained energy distribution facilities.

13.8 CYBER-PHYSICAL SYSTEM SECURITY

Cyber physical systems are prone to various cyber and physical security threats, attacks and challenges. This is due to their heterogeneous nature, their dependence on private as well as sensitive data and their large-scale deployment. Intentional or accidental exposures of these systems can result into catastrophic effects, which makes it critical to implement robust security measures. The various probable attack methods in cyber physical systems are explained below.

The various attack methods are wireless exploitation, GPS exploitation, information gathering, password cracking, malicious third party, water hole attack and side channel attack

- **Wireless Exploitation:** This is commonly known as wireless network attacks. Penetration and intrusion acts that target wireless networks pose serious threats. Wireless network attacks aim to capture the information sent across the network and/or intrude with the traffic of information. It requires knowledge of the system's structure and thus, exploiting its wireless capabilities to gain remote access or control over a system or possibly disrupt the system's operations. This causes collision and/or loss of system control.

- **GPS Exploitation:** Hackers can track a device or a vehicle by exploiting GPS navigation systems, resulting in a location privacy violation.
- **Information Gathering:** This is the act of gathering different kinds of information against the targeted victim or system. There are various tools, techniques, and websites for this. An example of this is WHOIS which is a query and response protocol that is widely used for querying databases that store the registered users or assignees of an Internet resource, such as a domain name, an IP address block or an autonomous system. nslookup can help hackers to gather information. nslookup is a network administration command-line tool for querying the Domain Name System (DNS) to obtain the mapping between domain name and IP address, or other DNS records. Software manufacturers gather files and audit logs stored on any given device in order to sell this huge personal information for marketing and commercial purposes in an illegal manner.
- **Password Cracking:** Password cracking means recovering passwords from a computer or from data that a computer transmits using various methods.

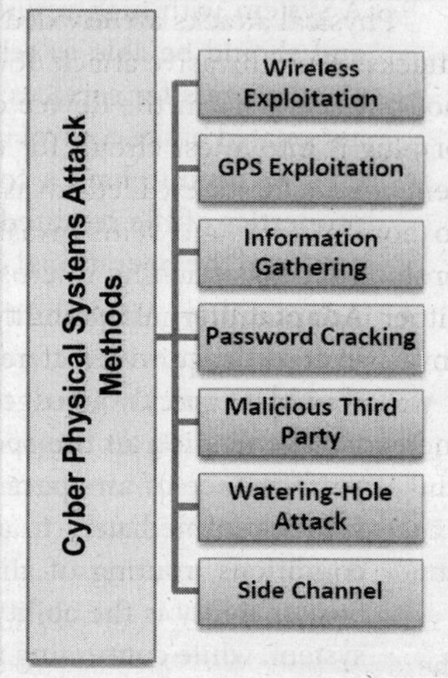

Figure 13.15: Cyber Physical Systems Attack Methods

- **Malicious Third Party:** This includes software that secretly exploit data aggregation network and compromises them, mainly using botnets, trojans or worms to infiltrate information through a CPS encrypted channel from an internal system like PLC, ICS or RTU through the dependence on trusted third party in disguise, to a botnet command-and-control server.
- **Watering-Hole Attack:** In a watering hole attack, the attacker compromises a site likely to be visited by a particular target group, rather than attacking the target group directly. The attacker scans for any cyber-physical security weakness. Once a weakness is identified, the chosen CPS website will be manipulated by a "watering hole" where a malware will be delivered mainly through backdoor, rootkits or zero-day exploit.
- **Side-Channel:** This is based on the information gained from the implemented CPS system such as timing information, power consumption and electromagnetic leaks that can be exploited.

13.8.1 Types of CPS attacks

The main cyber-attack types in cyber physical system can be zero day attack, evil maid attack or resonance attack. A zero day attack is an attack that exploits a system on the same day that the vulnerability is identified. Hence the number of days are zero between the time of the vulnerability is discovered and the first attack. An evil-maid attack is a security exploit that targets a computing device that has been left unattended. Here the evil maid can be an internal staff attacker who boot the system with a boot loader or USB drive, installs a key logger to capture encryption keys and then uses it when the victims is off.

In resonance attack, the attacker compromises some sensors or controllers that forces the physical system to oscillate at its resonant frequency. For instances, the attacker compromises the real time of the health systems and make it provide wrong information. The actuators will not able to pick up the correct signals from the sensors.

Physical attacks are divided into three categories such as noninvasive, semi-invasive, and invasive attacks. A noninvasive attack does not require any initial preparations of the device under test, and will not physically harm the device during the attack. The attacker can either tap the wires to the device, or plug it into a test circuit for the analysis. Hardware attacks that require physical manipulations on semiconductors are called invasive. Invasive attacks are most powerful and expensive in comparison to non-invasive and semi-invasive attacks. One well-known invasive attack is micro probing. Micro probing means attaching microscopic needles onto the internal wiring of a chip. This can be used to either read out internal secrets that are not intended to leave the chip, or it can be used for fault attacks. Invasive attacks require direct access to the internal components of the device, which normally requires a well-equipped and knowledgeable attacker to succeed. As chip sizes shrink and device complexity increases, invasive attacks are becoming demanding and expensive. There is a gap between noninvasive and invasive attacks. Many attacks fall into this gap, called semi-invasive attacks. They are not very expensive as invasive attacks, but are easily repeatable as noninvasive attacks. The various types of cyber-attacks are discussed in chapter" Cyber Security".

In most of the cyber physical systems, security services were not incorporated by design, leaving the door open for various vulnerabilities and threats by attackers. One of the reasons for this is the heterogeneous nature of CPS devices meaning they operate in different IoT domains and communicate using different technologies and protocols. Table 13.3 shows the possible attacks in each of the three-layer architecture of CPS and the proposed security measures.

Cyber physical systems have been integrated into critical infrastructures like smart electric power grid, industry, supply chain, healthcare, military, agriculture, etc., which makes them an attractive target for security attacks for various purposes including economical, criminal, military, political and terrorism as well. Thus, any CPS vulnerability can be targeted to conduct dangerous attacks against such systems. Different security aspects can be targeted including confidentiality, integrity, and availability. In order to enable the wide adoption and deployment of cyber physical systems and to leverage their benefits, it is essential to secure these systems from any possible attack, internal or/and external, passive or active. Cyber physical system security vulnerabilities can be classified into three main categories such as based on network, platform and management.

Table 13.3: CPS Attacks and Security Measures

Layer	Objective	Threat/Attack	Target	Security measure
Perception	Data and information collection	• Eves dropping • Port scan • Passive replay	• Confidentiality • Privacy • Authentication	• Trust management • Source authentication • Secure data/systems • Data protection
Transmission	Data and information transmission	• Man-in-the-Middle • Repudiation • Replay	• Confidentiality • Authentication • Integrity • Availability	• Strong password policy • Strong authentication • Light weight dynamic symmetric encryption • Secure tunnelling

Layer	Objective	Threat/Attack	Target	Security measure
Application	Data and information analysis and decision making	• Code injection • Malware • Control Hijacking	• Authentication • Privacy • Security • Safety	• IDS/IPS • Firewalls • Strong authentication • Strong authorisation • Trust management

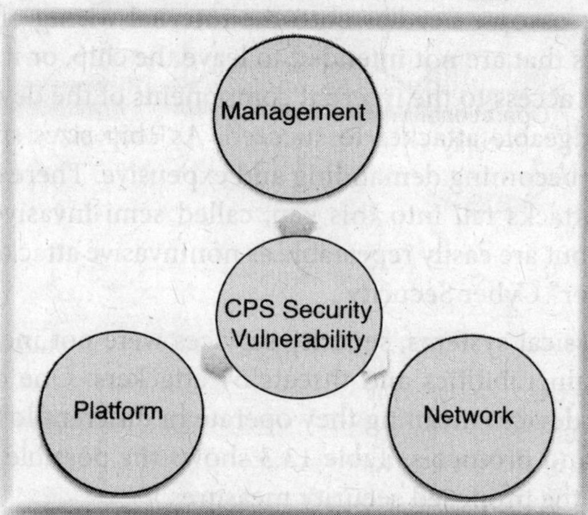

Figure 13.12: Cyber Physical Systems Security Vulnerability

Network vulnerabilities include weaknesses of the protective security measures. Platform vulnerabilities includes hardware, software, configuration, and database vulnerabilities. Management vulnerabilities includes lack of security guidelines, procedures and policies.

CPS security threats can be either cyber or physical threats. If these are combined, it can result to cyber-physical threats. The main cyber physical system security requirements are defined and discussed below.

- **Privacy:** In cyber physical system, a huge data collection process is constantly taking place. A person has the right to access his own data, along with the right to know what type of data is being collected about them by data collectors, and to whom these data is being given or sold to.
- **Dependability:** Intelligent physical world ensures that the CPS adaptive behavior is achieved to bring a higher dependability and ensure the right Quality of Service (QoS) through the adoption of fault-tolerance mechanisms in a timely manner. Dependability includes two other qualities, such as safety and reliability. Safety is often an objective defined in terms of the organization's goals. This is due to the negative impact of cyber-security risks, where vulnerabilities can be compromised and exploited by a hacker, or due to cyber physical system failure. Reliability is based on the ability to adapt to changing conditions to overcome and recover from any possible disruption either based on cyber or/and physical attacks led, in addition to natural disasters.

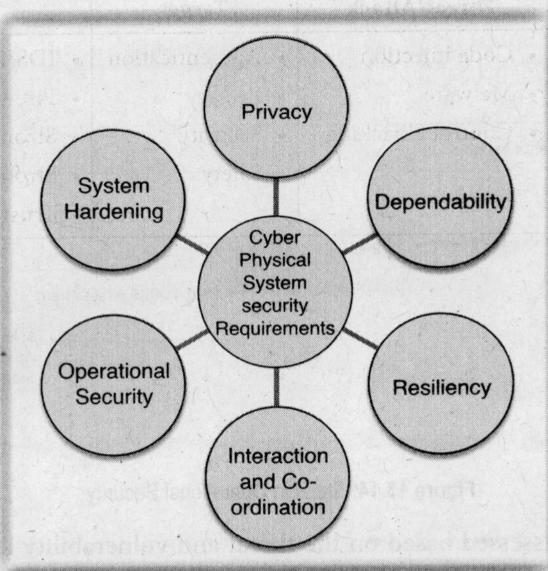

Figure 13.13: Cyber Physical Systems Security Requirements

- **Resiliency:** Resilience is the ability to withstand adversity and bounce back from difficult life events. Cyber physical systems must be resilient to overcome accidents and malicious attacks. Resiliency is achieved by each CPS component in a base architecture, where each communication and physical connection path between elements is granted access by the base architecture's connectors. This requires the base architecture system to know and identify every possible path, while overcoming any connection disruption.
- **Interaction and Co-ordination:** These are essential to maintain an all-time operational CPS security. CPS interaction and coordination between cyber and physical system elements are a key aspect. The main physical world characteristics are based on the constant system change over time whereas the cyber world characteristics are based on sequence series with no temporal semantics.
- **Operational Security:** Operational security ensures physical security, information security, and personnel security through careful planning, risk assessment and risk management. Its primary task is to ensure operational effectiveness by denying any adversary access to public or private information. To achieve this task, operational security involves five main steps.

Step 1: Identification of information that can effectively degrade a CPS's operational effectiveness or place organization's success at risk and develop an initial plan to protect it.

Step 2: Determines potential threat of capabilities to gather, process, analyze and use the needed information.

Step 3: Studying the weaknesses of a given cyber-physical system and the strengths of an attacker. Thus, building a possible view over how a potential attacker might exploit this security gap to perform a security breach.

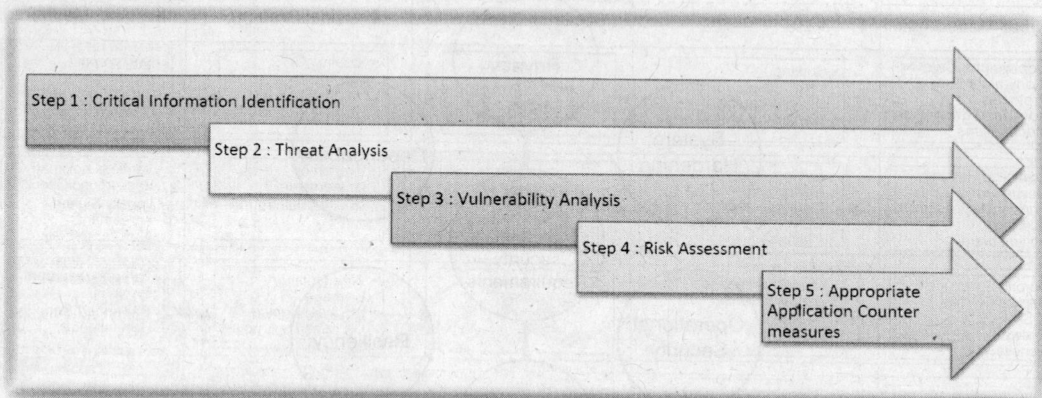

Figure 13.14: Steps in Operational Security

Step 4: Here risks are assessed based on the threat and vulnerability levels combined, depending on how high or how low these levels are. Risk assessment levels include evaluating the cost of implementing the right security measures by ensuring a trade-off between the effective cost and benefit balance.

Step 5: Once the trade-off is achieved in the earlier phase, the appropriate countermeasures are then developed to offer the best protection of CPS against these ongoing threats in terms of feasibility, cost, and effectiveness.

- **System Hardening:** System hardening, also called Operating System (OS) hardening, is the process of securing a system by reducing its surface of vulnerability. System hardening can be used to defend a wider range of threats. To boost security, it is highly recommended to isolate critical applications that lack the proper security measures, from any operating system that is not trusted. Trusted Platform Module (TPM), Trusted Execution Environments (TEE), Secure Elements (SE), and Encrypted Execution Environment (E3) increases the operating system's integrity. It is essential to set the right privileges which is task-based, role-based, rule-based, etc. Strong password policies will enhance the security. Get rid of old unused accounts and unused ports to reduce the exposure to remote wireless attacks.

13.9 SECURING CYBER PHYSICAL SYSTEM

Securing cyber physical system is not a straightforward task. For this reason, various existing solutions are mentioned and discussed in this section. All of these schemes are presented to protect cyber physical system domains against attacks that target the confidentiality, integrity, availability, authentication and privacy of both data and systems.

CPS systems relying on safety, security, privacy, consistency, dependability, resiliency, reliability, interaction and coordination, all of which are combined to form a well-designed and trustworthy system. If this condition is satisfied, a perfect CPS mechanism is achieved. As a result, several CPS testing tools were used to evaluate the security of industrial control devices upon their development. Few of these tools are mentioned in below table.

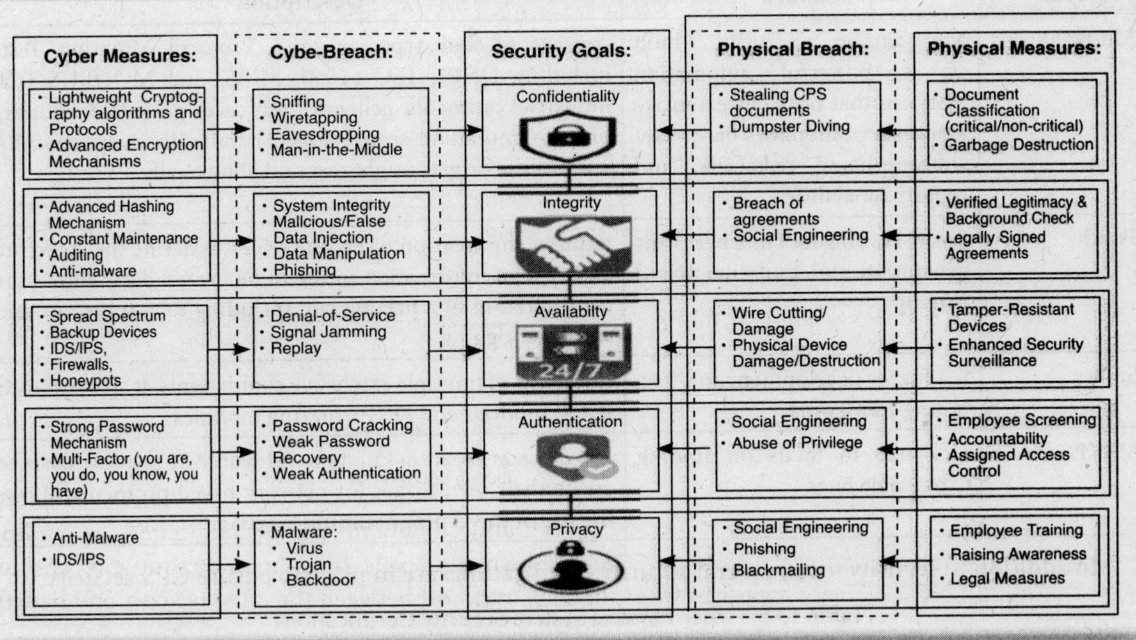

Figure 13.17: Targeting CPS Security Goals

Table 13.4: Cyber Physical Systems Testing Tools

Tools	Nature	Description
Achilles	Uniquely designed for embedded and industrial control devices	uses Wurldtech proprietary fuzzing algorithms to generate tests of known and unknown vulnerabilities, provides the analysis of the attack impact, monitors the whole system
BreakingPoint	Designed as the industry's first cyber tomography machine	a 4 RU rack-mountable, modular system that accurately recreates a live network environment and identifies network devices "Breaking-Points". It measures and hardens the resiliency of CI component against crippling attacks
beSTORM	Automated tool	programmed to make an excessive search of all possible input combinations, tests any product for potential weaknesses
Codenomicon Defensics	A specialized fuzzing tool which supports the security of industrial protocols	sends to the system invalid or unexpected inputs that expose software defects and vulnerabilities, ensures a broader test coverage, can be used to test digital media, wireless infrastructures and network protocols. Easy integration. Proactive testing. Integrated online documentation

Tools	Nature	Description
Mu-8000	Mu Studio Security, built on a powerful automation platform that provides extensive automation, monitors hardware/ software-based restarters, and reports capabilities	consists of four types of tests, Protocol Mutation Tests including DNP3, IEC 61850, MMS, and MODBUS/TCP industrial protocols, generates test cases packets containing protocol mutations secure targets handles them successfully, non-secure targets might respond abnormally
Peach	Smart Fuzzing tool that performs generation and mutation based fuzzing	requires the creation of PeachPit files to define the structure and type of information in the to be fuzzed data, allows the configuration of a fuzzing run including data transport and interface logging
Sully	is a fuzzer development and fuzz testing framework	It consists of multiple extensible components, it also supports ICCP, modbus and DNP3 fuzzing modules
SPIKE	Designed to focus on finding exploitable bugs	It is a fuzzer creation kit, it provides an API to allow users to create their own fuzzer for network based protocols, allows the use of the C programming language

In addition to security tools, several security certifications are in place to ensure CPS security.

Table 13.5: Cyber Physical System Security Certifications

Certification name	Levels	Description
WST Achilles Certification	1	includes basic testing Layer 2–4 Industrial Protocols
	2	includes in-depth testing Layer 2–4 Industrial Protocols
Exida Certification	N/A	includes three main types which are functional safety, functional integrity, and cyber security
ISASecure EDSA Certification	N/A	consists of Functional security assessment (FSA), Software development security assessment (SDSA), and Communication robustness testing (CRT)
MuDynamics MUSIC Certification	Foundation	includes various protocols such as ARP, IPv4, TCP, UDP, and IEEE 802.lp/Q
	Advanced	includes various protocols such as DNP3, FTP, HTTP, MODBUS/TCP, and Telnet

Cyber physical systems can be divided into four main types based on the aspect of their criticality.

- **Safety Critical:** In such a CPS type, an attack can led to loss of life or to chronic deadly diseases, with significant damage to the environment such as fire, floods, radioactivity.e.g. Chernobyl in 1986 and Fukushima in 2011 incidents.
- **Mission Critical:** For this type of CPS, an attack can result into a fatal/non-fatal, total/partial failure of a CPS to achieve its objectives.
- **Business Critical:** In such a CPS type, an attack can result into huge financial and economic losses, damaged reputation and loss of CPS contractors and clients.
- **Security Critical:** For this type of CPS, an attack can result into a security breach of the cyber-physical system (security gap, exploitable vulnerability, rootkits, backdoors, etc.).

Maintaining a secure cyber physical systems environment is not an easy task due to the constant increase of challenges, integration issues and limitation of the existing solutions including the lack of security, privacy and accuracy. This can be mitigated through different means including cryptographic and non-cryptographic solutions

Cryptographic measures are mainly employed to secure the communication channel from active/ passive attacks, along any unauthorized access and interception, especially in SCADA systems. In fact, traditional cryptography approaches based on utilizing ciphers and hash functions are not easily applied to CPS. As a result, the main focus should not be limited to data security alone, instead it should maintain and ensure the efficiency of the overall system process along. Therefore, various solutions were presented. These solutions are classified in terms of them fulfilling one of the security goals such as confidentiality, integrity, availability, authentication and privacy preserving.

Many non-cryptographic solutions are used to mitigate and eliminate any possible cyber-attack or malicious event. This is done by implementing Intrusion Detection Systems (IDS), firewalls and honeypots.

13.10 INTELLIGENT CYBER-PHYSICAL SYSTEMS

Cyber-physical systems are orchestrations of computers, machines, and people working together to achieve goals using computation, communications, and control (CCC) technologies. Although the term CPS was coined only in 2006 by Helen Gill of the National Science Foundation (NSF), the CCC core technologies of CPS have had a rich and long history. Major milestones for CPS include control theory in 1868, wireless telegraphy in 1903, cybernetics feedback in 1948, embedded systems in 1961, software engineering in 1968, and ubiquitous computing in 1988. CPSs have risen from the field of embedded systems to the region of digital ecosystems and are becoming increasingly intelligent as a result of analytics and machine-learning capabilities being readily available in the cloud and accessible over networks.

Over the past two decades, the number of cyber components has grown gradually to the point where CPSs are now software-intensive systems with more and more integrated computing hardware and computational algorithms. In today's CPS, software dominates all aspects of connecting the physical and cyber worlds by orchestrating the CCC technologies. Consequently, the engineering of high-confidence CPSs has also evolved. The resulting process is neither an extension of traditional engineering nor a straightforward application of software engineering but a new system engineering science. Granting agencies around the world have recognized this problem and initiated large research programs to investigate CPS foundations. A key goal of the NSF CPS research program is to develop the core systems science needed to engineer complex CPSs. The idea is to abstract from specific systems and application domains to reveal fundamental CPS engineering principles.

Over the years, engineers have been highly successful in developing models for specific control system applications. Integrating discrete, continuous, and adaptive control as well as deterministic and nondeterministic models are fundamental challenges in dealing with uncertainty in modern CPSs. Developing models and modeling frameworks for CPS has become a mature research field. The software engineering community has made tremendous strides in designing and operating highly dynamical software systems by developing methods and techniques to standardize and distribute CPS components and services effectively through autonomic computing (for example, the Monitor-Analyze-Plan-Execute loop operating on a shared Knowledge [MAPE-K] base), to control feedback in computing systems, to deal with inherent uncertainty in CPS through models at runtime, and to adapt and then validate CPS at runtime. Several research communities have emerged to deal with software engineering aspects of CPS, including CPS conferences and workshops (such as CPS Week), software engineering for adaptive and self-managing systems (SEAMS),7Models@run.time, as well as runtime validation, verification, and certification techniques.

The primary reason for CPS revolution now is the recent confluence of technologies, including adaptive systems and runtime models, an increasingly instrumented world due to pervasive sensing and actuating capabilities, advanced real-time and networked control, analytical and cognitive capabilities, and compute and storage clouds. With the advent of cognitive intelligent assistants readily available on personal devices, human-in-the-loop CPSs are proliferating in our lives. In other words, CPS is at the center of a perfect technology storm. Countries around the world are investing heavily in CPS research programs, seeking a technological and economic edge.

CPS is at the center of a perfect technology storm.

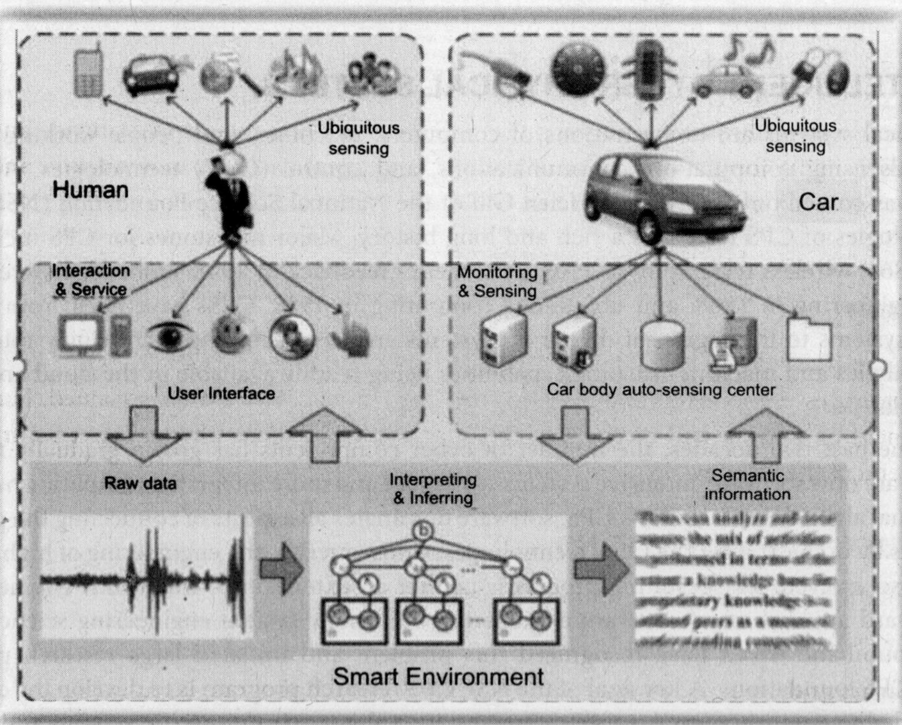

Figure 13.18: Architecture of Intelligent Cyber-Physical System

There are several terms and fields closely related and competing with the notion of CPS, including embedded systems, the Internet of Things (IoT), Internet of Everything (IoE), machine-to-machine (M2M), Industry 4.0, Smarter Planet, cyber-physical-human systems (CPHS), smart and intelligent systems, and adaptive systems.

There are many challenges that must be addressed to be able to harvest CPS's rich economic opportunities.

First and foremost is the creating and maintaining a skilled workforce to support the design, engineering, deployment, and operation of future CPS is a significant challenge for industry, academia, and governments. CPS engineers, scientists, and developers need not only strong backgrounds in CCC, but also significant knowledge in relevant application domains. Existing engineering and computer science programs are challenged in teaching the comprehensive skills required for a successful career in the CPS area. Urgently, computer science and software engineering programs need to require control engineering courses, and traditional engineering programs need to include advanced software engineering courses.

CPS technologies are becoming the key enablers for building smarter infrastructures for industrial applications. Growing human populations consume enormous natural resources and require increasingly instrumented and optimized food supply chains. Flourishing cities require renewable energy systems and instrumented transportation infrastructure. Connected and autonomous vehicles combine situational awareness in vehicles with the networked infrastructure of the modern city. Rising costs put pressure on healthcare and elder care, requiring outcome prediction based on improved diagnostics using smart medical devices. Assistive healthcare systems including wearable sensors, implantable devices, and home monitoring systems are being developed to improve outcomes and quality of life. Thus, the technologies and applications emerging from combining the cyber and physical worlds will provide an innovation and incubation engine for a broad range of industries—creating entirely new markets and platforms for years to come. Our modern societies and economies increasingly depend on integrated, software-intensive CPS.

13.11 SUMMARY

In this chapter, we have discussed on the development and comparison of CPS and IoT. The applications, various architectures, components and platforms of cyber physical systems are explained. The challenges and deployment of CPS as well as the security and intelligent cyber physical systems are discussed towards the end of the chapter.

13.12 OBJECTIVE QUESTIONS

The answer of the multiple-choice questions is marked in **bold**.

1. .... is an application of CPS.

(a) Smart grid (b) Robotics

(c) Smart Transportation (d) **All of these**

2. Which is not a level in five level CPS architecture?

(a) **Network** (b) Connection

(c) Conversion (d) Cognition

3. Which is the top level of 5C architecture of CPS?

(a) **Configuration** (b) Cognition

(c) Cyber (d) Connection

4. .... is a controlling component of CPS.
   (a) Sensor (b) **PLC** (c) Actuator (d) Aggregator
5. .... is a eves dropping attack.
   (a) **Traffic Sniffing** (b) IP Spoofing
   (c) Worms (d) Buffer overflow

13.13 REVIEW QUESTIONS

1. Differentiate IoT and CPS.
2. Differetiate between a model, a simulation and a digital twin.
3. Discuss the applications of cyber physical systems.
4. Explain three-layer architecture of cyber physical systems
5. Explain five-layer architecture of cyber physical systems.
6. Discuss on components of cyber physical systems.
7. Discuss various technology platforms in cyber physical systems.
8. Discuss the challenges in cyber physical systems.
9. Discuss on security requirements of cyber physical systems.
10. Explain various steps in cyber physical system operational security.
11. Discuss various methods of CPS attacks.
12. Discuss various types of CPS attacks.

13.14 ABBREVIATIONS AND SYMBOLS

Abbreviations	Full Form	Description
PLC	Programmable Logic Controller	PLC is an industrial computer control system that continuously monitors the state of input devices and makes decisions based upon a custom program to control the state of output devices.
CD	Compact Disk	CD is a molded plastic disc containing digital data that is scanned by a laser beam for the reproduction of recorded sound and other information.
C-FLAT	Control-Flow Attestation for Embedded Systems Software	C-FLAT enables remote attestation of an application's control-flow path, without requiring the source code.
CRM	Customer Relationship Management	CRM is a technology for managing all your company's relationships and interactions with customers and potential customers.
DCS	Distributed Control System	DCS is a system of sensors, controllers, and associated computers that are distributed throughout a plant.
DNP3	Distributed Network Protocol 3	DNP3 is a set of communications protocols used between components in process automation systems.

Abbreviations	Full Form	Description
DSS	Decision Support System	DSS is a computerized program used to support determinations, judgments, and courses of action in an organization or a business.
E3	Encrypted Execution Environment	E3 is an execution environment in which the executed application software is encrypted; its goal is to enable application execution without revealing the instructions that comprise the application.
ERP	Enterprise Resource Planning	ERP is a process used by companies to manage and integrate the important parts of their businesses.
GPS	Global Positioning System	GPS is a space-based radio-navigation system consisting of a constellation of satellites broadcasting navigation signals and a network of ground stations and satellite control stations used for monitoring and control.
HMI	Human Machine Interface	HMI is a user interface or dashboard that connects a person to a machine, system, or device.
ICS	Industrial Control System	Industrial control system is a general term that encompasses several types of control systems and associated instrumentation used for industrial process control.
IED	Intelligent Electronic Devices	IEDs are devices that can be connected to a LAN and communicate with other devices over the LAN and have processing capabilities.
MTU	Master Terminal Unit	MTU in SCADA system is a device that issues the commands to the Remote Terminal Unit (RTUs) which are located at remote places from the control, gathers the required data, stores the information, and process the information and display the information in the form of pictures, curves and tables.
OLAP	Online Analytical Processing	OLAP is a category of software that allows users to analyze information from multiple database systems at the same time.
RCS	Resilient Control System	A system is resilient, if it provides required capabilities despite excessive stresses that can cause disruptions.
RFID	Radio Frequency Identification	RFID refers to a wireless system comprised of two components such as tags and readers.
RTU	Remote Terminal/ Telemetry Unit	RTU is a microprocessor-based device that monitors and controls field devices, that then connects to plant control or SCADA
SCA	Service Component Architecture	Service Component Architecture is a software technology designed to provide a model for applications that follow service-oriented architecture principles.
SCADA	Supervisory Control and Data Acquisition	SCADA is a system that aims to monitor and control field devices at your remote sites.

Abbreviations	Full Form	Description
SE	Secure Elements	SE is a chip that is by design protected from unauthorized access and used to run a limited set of applications, as well as store confidential and cryptographic data.
SOA	Service Oriented Architecture	SOA is an architectural style for building software applications that use services available in a network such as the web. It promotes loose coupling between software components so that they can be reused.
SOBA	Service Oriented Business Applications	SOBAs are business apps that perform in a service-oriented setting to deliver discrete units of business-level performance by means of well-defined service contracts.
TEE	Trusted Execution Environment	TEE is a secure area of a main processor. It guarantees code and data loaded inside to be protected with respect to confidentiality and integrity.
TPM	Trusted Platform Module	TPM is a microcontroller that can securely store artifacts used to authenticate the computer.
USB	Universal Serial Bus	USB is an industry standard that establishes specifications for cables and connectors and protocols for connection, communication and power supply between computers, peripherals and other computers.
VPN	Virtual Private Network	VPN is an encrypted connection over the Internet from a device to a network.

13.15 LIST OF FIGURES AND TABLES

The details of figures and tables used in this chapter is as below.

Figure / Table	Description
Figure 13.11	Various CPS Technology Platforms
Figure 13.12	Cyber Physical Systems Security Vulnerability
Figure 13.13	Cyber Physical Systems Security Requirements
Figure 13.14	Steps in Operational Security
Figure 13.15	Cyber Physical Systems Attack Methods
Figure 13.16	Cyber Attack Types in Cyber-Physical Systems
Figure 13.17	Targeting CPS Security Goals
Figure 13.18	Architecture of Intelligent Cyber-Physical System
Table 13.1	Applications of Cyber-Physical System
Table 13.2	Comparison between PLC and RTU
Table 13.3	CPS Attacks and Security Measures
Table 13.4	Cyber Physical Systems Testing Tools
Table 13.5	Cyber Physical System Security Certifications